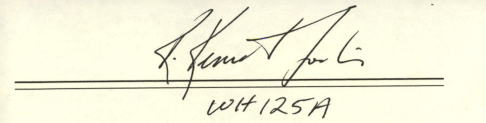
The Politics
of Interests

TRANSFORMING AMERICAN POLITICS
Lawrence C. Dodd, Series Editor

Dramatic changes in political institutions and behavior over the past two decades have underscored the dynamic nature of American politics, confronting political scientists with a new and pressing intellectual agenda. The pioneering work of early postwar scholars, while laying a firm empirical foundation for contemporary scholarship, failed to consider how American politics might change or to recognize the forces that would make fundamental change inevitable. In reassessing the static interpretations fostered by these classic studies, political scientists are now examining the underlying dynamics that generate transformational change.

Transforming American Politics will bring together texts and monographs that address four closely related aspects of change. A first concern is documenting and explaining recent changes in American politics—in institutions, processes, behavior, and policymaking. A second is reinterpreting classic studies and theories to provide a more accurate perspective on postwar politics. The series will look at historical change to identify recurring patterns of political transformation within and across the distinctive eras of American politics. Last and perhaps most importantly, the series will present new theories and interpretations that explain the dynamic processes at work and thus clarify the direction of contemporary politics. All of the books will focus on the central theme of transformation—transformation in both the conduct of American politics and in the way we study and understand its many aspects.

TITLES IN THIS SERIES

The Politics of Interests: Interest Groups Transformed, edited by
Mark P. Petracca

*The Supreme Court and Partisan Realignment: A Macro- and
Microlevel Perspective*, John B. Gates

*The Transformation of the Supreme Court's Agenda: From the
New Deal to the Reagan Administration*, Richard L. Pacelle, Jr.

Public Opinion in America: Moods, Cycles, and Swings,
James A. Stimson

The Parties Respond: Changes in the American Party System, edited by
L. Sandy Maisel

*The Electoral Origins of Divided Government: Competition in U.S. House
Elections, 1946–1988*, Gary C. Jacobson

Congress, the President, and Public Policy, Michael L. Mezey

*Issues and Elections: Presidential Voting in Contemporary America—A
Revisionist View*, Euel W. Elliott

Remaking American Politics, edited by Richard A. Harris and
Sidney M. Milkis

Democracies in Crisis: Public Policy Responses to the Great Depression,
Kim Quaile Hill

*Managing the Presidency: The Eisenhower Legacy—From Kennedy to
Reagan*, Phillip G. Henderson

FORTHCOMING

Creative Campaigning: PACs and the Presidential Selection Process,
Anthony Corrado

Congress and the Administrative State, Second Edition,
Lawrence C. Dodd and Richard L. Schott

The Congressional Experience: A View from the Hill, David E. Price

The Politics of Interests

INTEREST GROUPS TRANSFORMED

EDITED BY

Mark P. Petracca

University of California–Irvine

Westview Press

BOULDER • SAN FRANCISCO • OXFORD

Transforming American Politics

Copyright © 1992 by Westview Press, Inc.

Published in 1992 in the United States of America by Westview Press, Inc., 5500 Central Avenue, Boulder, Colorado 80301-2847, and in the United Kingdom by Westview Press, 36 Lonsdale Road, Summertown, Oxford OX2 7EW

Library of Congress Cataloging-in-Publication Data
The Politics of interests : interest groups transformed / edited by
    Mark P. Petracca.
        p.   cm. — (Transforming American politics)
    Includes bibliographical references and index.
    ISBN 0-8133-1000-8 — ISBN 0-8133-1001-6 (pbk.)
    1. Pressure groups—United States.   I. Petracca, Mark P.
II. Series.   III. Series: Transforming American politics series.
JK1118.P65   1992
322.4′3′0973—dc20   91-34437
                                                                              CIP

Printed and bound in the United States of America

The paper used in this publication meets the requirements of the American National Standard for Permanence of Paper for Printed Library Materials Z39.48-1984.

10   9   8   7   6   5   4   3   2   1

For Gina Francesca

Contents

Preface   xiii
Acknowledgments   xv
Introduction   xvii

PART ONE
APPROACHES TO INTEREST GROUPS

1 The Rediscovery of Interest Group Politics   3
     Mark P. Petracca

2 A Deliberative Theory of Interest Representation   32
     Jane J. Mansbridge

3 Interest Groups and the Policymaking Process:
   Sources of Countervailing Power in America   58
     Andrew S. McFarland

4 American Interest Groups in Comparative Perspective   80
     Graham K. Wilson

PART TWO
THE ORGANIZATION OF INTERESTS

5 Interest Group Membership and Organization:
   Multiple Theories   99
     Paul A. Sabatier

6   Triangles, Networks, and Hollow Cores:
     The Complex Geometry of Washington
     Interest Representation   130
          Robert H. Salisbury
          John P. Heinz
          Robert L. Nelson
          Edward O. Laumann

7   Changing Patterns of Interest Group Activity:
     A Regional Perspective   150
          Clive S. Thomas
          Ronald J. Hrebenar

8   The Political Mobilization of Business   175
          David Plotke

PART THREE
POLITICAL INSTITUTIONS AND INTEREST GROUPS

9   Organized Interests and the Nation's Capitol   201
          John T. Tierney

10   Interest Mobilization and the Presidency   221
          Mark A. Peterson

11   Representing the Public Interest:
     Consumer Groups and the Presidency   242
          Joan Lucco

12   Conservative Interest Group Litigation
     in the Reagan Era and Beyond   263
          Karen O'Connor
          Bryant Scott McFall

PART FOUR
INTEREST GROUP ACTIVITY AND INFLUENCE

13   Social Movements as Interest Groups:
     The Case of the Women's Movement   285
          Anne N. Costain

14 Money, Technology, and Political Interests:
    The Direct Marketing of Politics   308
        R. Kenneth Godwin

15 The Rise and Fall of Special Interest Politics   326
        Paul E. Peterson

PART FIVE
LOOKING AHEAD

16 The Future of an Interest Group Society   345
        Mark P. Petracca

Appendix: The Changing State of Interest Group Research   363
References   373
About the Book and Editor   403
About the Contributors   405
Index   409

Preface

The initial idea for an edited volume on the transformation of interest group politics grew out of a panel on interest groups and the presidency that I arranged for the Midwest Political Science Association and a chance meeting with Jennifer Knerr, political science editor at Westview Press. For some time I had been studying the representation of organized interests on federal advisory committees and was beginning to think and write about the changes that had taken place in the advisory committee system courtesy of the Reagan administration (see Petracca 1986, 1988). Little is known about the ways in which advisory committees connect organized interests to the administrative state or about the influence these interests have as a result on national policymaking. Scholars of European politics are familiar with advisory committees as part of societal corporatism; Americanists are rarely familiar with them, if at all. Having previously coauthored a text on the American presidency with Benjamin I. Page, I was also aware of just how little the discipline seemed to know about the general relationship between interest groups and the presidency (see Page and Petracca 1983). With the panel I organized, I hoped to bring together a few scholars working on the various ways in which interest groups are connected to the presidency.

My original intent was to edit a volume focused narrowly on the changes that had taken place in the relationship between interest groups and the presidency during the Reagan era. *The Politics of Interests* is a far more ambitious undertaking, in large measure because of the intellectual stimulation and encouragement of Jennifer Knerr, the vision of Larry Dodd, and the sound advice of the anonymous reviewers for Westview Press. This is how *The Politics of Interests* came to join *Remaking American Politics*, edited by Richard A. Harris and Sidney M. Milkis, and *The Parties Respond*, edited by L. Sandy Maisel, in the Westview series Transforming American Politics, under the general editorship of Lawrence C. Dodd.

As I was convinced by my own research (Petracca 1988) and a growing body of literature that President Reagan had changed the relationship between interest groups and the White House (see Peterson and Walker 1986; Ginsberg and Shefter 1988; and Peterson and Rom 1988), I was also predisposed, if not determined, to edit a volume hailing the transformation of the U.S. interest group system. Indeed, once I saw the title of Maisel's excellent volume, *The Parties Respond*, which was reminiscent of a Star Wars movie, I was gearing up to title my own volume *Interest Groups Strike Back*. As it turned out, my intended companion to Maisel's volume on political parties had to be filed in the "books-to-be-written" box. Although there have been very important changes in the interest group system and changes in the way scholars study interest group politics, there hasn't been anything near the definitive transformation necessary to merit such a snappy title.

Many of the changes that originally stimulated my interest are carefully explored below, but *The Politics of Interests* is now a far more ambitious exploration of interest group politics than I had initially envisioned. This aptly reflects my intellectual transformation during the writing and editing of this volume as well as the variety and scope of changes that characterize the past twenty years of interest group politics in the United States.

Mark P. Petracca
Irvine, California

Acknowledgments

It has been my privilege to incur a great many intellectual debts to a number of individuals who have motivated, guided, trained, and sustained my interest in American politics. Theodore J. Lowi, Martin Shefter, Ira Katznelson, Kenneth Prewitt, Theodore Marmor, Lloyd Rudolph, Philippe C. Schmitter, Paul E. Peterson, and the late J. David Greenstone have all contributed indirectly to this volume. I am also grateful to Jack Peltason, who even as chancellor of a growing university has never been too busy to give generously of his time and good counsel. Benjamin I. Page and David Easton, teachers, colleagues, and friends, have been a constant source of support and guidance throughout my professional development. I have knowingly not always followed their advice but am deeply appreciative of their sincere interest in my work and well-being.

The preparation of this manuscript was aided by the careful editorial attention of Michelle Head and the word-processing skills of Ziggy Bates and most recently Roz Holler. Research assistance and substantive commentary from beginning to end was provided by Catheryn Kidd Markline.

My most enduring debts are to the supportive, professional, and responsive contributors to this volume; to the much-appreciated guidance and understanding of Larry Dodd, editor of this series; the skillful copyediting of Alice A. Colwell; the production assistance of Jane Raese; and, most of all, to Westview's Jennifer Knerr. Without Jennifer Knerr, there would never have been a *Politics of Interests*. Her vision, encouragement, and confidence made this project possible from beginning to end. "Thank you" is insufficient to capture her contribution to this volume and to my involvement with it, but it will have to do. Our reward, I hope, is contained in the pages that follow.

M.P.P.

Introduction

The Politics of Interests identifies and analyzes the continuities and changes that have taken place in the American interest group system and in scholarly research on interest groups during the past two decades.

The challenge of discovering, documenting, and analyzing political change is a mainstay of contemporary political science. A disciplinary inclination to focus on the subject of political change is evident in the titles of many popular and influential books about American politics. *The End of Liberalism* by Theodore J. Lowi (1969); *The Changing American Voter* by Norman H. Nie, Sidney Verba, and John R. Petrocik (1976); *Building a New American State* by Stephen Skowronek (1982); and *Politics by Other Means* by Benjamin Ginsberg and Martin Shefter (1990) (to name but a few of my favorites) beckon the reader to explore the changes detailed within. These books join a plethora of works that have in their titles the words *decline, renewal, development, decay, rise, transformation, resurgence,* or *collapse*—all pronouncements of change—modifying the standard array of American political processes and institutions, such as Congress, the presidency, the bureaucracy, parties, the law, and the courts, to identify some of the usual suspects.

Edited volumes are probably even more prone to trumpet the arrival of political change as a means to intellectual distinctiveness and market promotion. In the first edition of *The New American Political System,* Anthony King (1978) considered "the profound changes" in the American political system that had taken place since the inauguration of President John F. Kennedy in 1961. A dozen years later, King edited a "genuinely new" second edition of *The New American Political System* that contrasted the "new" system of the 1970s with the developments that had taken place in the ensuing decade. The "transformation of American politics" by the Reagan administration was the subject of *The New Direction in American Politics,* edited by John E. Chubb and Paul E. Peterson (1985b). *Remaking American Politics,* edited by Richard A. Harris and Sidney M. Milkis (1989), focused on "the massive and profoundly important institutional developments of the past two decades" in order to understand the "major realignment" of the U.S. political system that occurred during the 1970s.

There are many reasons political scientists are drawn to the discovery and explanation of political change. Professional reputations are more easily built by discovering and explaining political change than they are by tiresome proclamations of similarity. Because political scientists have "an impetus to do good," as Samuel P. Huntington (1988:4) put it, they frequently become advocates of political reform, which by definition necessitates change. Additionally, the intellectual roots of Western political science, as represented by the writings of Aristotle, Plato, Cicero, Hobbes, Locke, Madison, Mill, Marx, Durkheim, and Weber, commend broad historical or system comparisons through which scholars strive to explain political developments or differences. In any case, the analysis of change is always a necessary part of the research agenda. Finally, in political life, as Machiavelli realized, *"fortuna,* the bitch goddess of unpredictability, has never been dethroned" (MacIntyre 1973:228). Unlike physicists and chemists, political scientists are privileged (or condemned, depending upon how you look at it) to study a subject that transforms individuals and the communities within which they live. As a result, the study of political change is a staple on the research menu of political science.

During the past decade, political scientists had rediscovered interest groups as a suitable subject for study resulting in an avalanche of new empirical data on various aspects of the interest group system. A number of studies conducted during the 1980s transformed what we know about the origin and maintenance, activities and techniques, organization, structure of interaction, and influence of interest groups in the United States. Surely now that we knew so much more about the American interest group system and at a level of precision and detail unprecedented in the analysis of interest groups, charting the transformation of that system would be a relatively easy task. At least this is what I thought. I was mistaken.

Unlike political parties, interest groups are too diffuse and numerous to respond, as Sandy Maisel has characterized changes in the American party system. Indeed, what would interest groups respond to? Neither have interest groups experienced the morbidity afflicting political parties during the past three decades, permitting (or necessitating) a response even if one were possible. To the contrary, as I argue in Chapter 1, American interest groups are quite robust and healthy, Ronald Reagan's efforts notwithstanding. After laboriously reviewing the historical and contemporary literature on interest groups and pondering the splendid contributions made to this volume, I've concluded that the American interest group system of the 1990s is characterized by about equal parts of consistency and change compared to the system of the late 1960s and 1970s.

This conclusion may strike some as cowardly, resembling a buffet at which the host offers a little bit of this and a little bit of that and everyone usually goes home happy. Nevertheless, it makes the most sense to me given the available evidence. To be sure, it is not necessarily a conclusion all the contributors to this volume share, neither will it be the one every reader reaches.

The extent to which the interest group system has changed is largely a function of the baseline date used for such an assessment. There have been significant, possibly even profound, changes in the interest group system during the past twenty years, as detailed in Chapter 1 and throughout the volume. Many of these changes are the direct or indirect result of larger institutional and behavioral developments taking place during the same period in American politics. The transformation of interest group politics in the United States, to the extent that it's accurate to describe it as such, did not occur in isolation. The processes of political transformation identified in *Remaking American Politics* are at work in the interest group system as well.

> Harris & Mikis

When I take a broader look at the interest group system, however, I am less inclined to view the past two decades as a uniquely transformative period for the interest group system. To begin with, a number of the most notable changes have important historical analogues, as occasionally noted in Chapter 1. Political scientists and pundits of yesteryear observed, described, and lamented in their times many of the same changes attributed to the period under study in this volume. Second, the essential structure of the interest group system is much as it was at the beginning of the "modern" system of interest representation back in 1946 (see Salisbury 1986:148–149). In addition, the kinds of groups mobilized and their activities have also remained the same. In their influential study of organized interests, Kay Lehman Schlozman and John T. Tierney (1986:389) conclude that "in terms of both the kinds of interests represented and the kinds of techniques of influence mobilized, what we have found is more of the same." Of course the sheer quantitative impact of "more of the same" may have a significant qualitative effect on the character of contemporary politics. Such consistency deserves careful description precisely because it occurred in the face of so many compelling institutional changes during the 1970s and the Reagan-Bush 1980s.

Americans have always had mixed feelings about interest groups, variously referred to as factions, vested interests, pressure groups, the lobby, the "snake doctors of politics," the third chamber, the "despair of patriots," special interests, and by many other terms of disapproval. On the one hand, Americans have long accepted the inevitability of interest groups and on most occasions have celebrated the positive functions they serve in a representative democracy. On the other hand, since the nation's founding (if not before), Americans have been wary of the dangers that interest groups pose to the fairness and governability of the political system. This triple tension among the inevitability, indispensability, and dangers of interest groups tends to further confuse our assessments of change and continuity in the interest group system.

Thus after we finish documenting and explaining the changes that have taken place and the continuities that have endured, we are still left to ponder if what we have is good or bad for the polity. Perhaps it is obvious, but even when there is agreement about a change in the interest group system, there is considerable disagreement about its political consequences. Two distinguished social scientists, David Knoke (1990) and Peter Drucker (1989), for example, agree that the so-called advocacy explosion of the past two decades has led to a "new pluralism" of interest group competition in the United States. Knoke (1990:231) praises this "cacophony of voices" as "our best hope for fate control in a society whose state is increasingly dominated by powerful institutions that are unaccountable to the citizenry." Conversely, Drucker (1989:102–103) views the new pluralism that dominates politics as parasitic and paralyzing. Such normative disagreements further diminish the certainty and clarity of our evaluations of the interest group system.

In the face of similar findings, in *Remaking American Politics* Hugh Heclo (1989:293) offered this rather comforting observation: "We should be open to the idea that trends in our political life appear contradictory and confused because they really are contradictory and confused." Thus in my bookend contributions to this volume—the first and last chapters—I am obliged to sort out change from consistency but feel less of an obligation to square all of this with some as yet unknown unified theory of interest group politics.

My introductory chapter focuses on the changes and continuities that have occurred in the interest group system and in Americans' attitudes toward it during the past two decades. The concluding chapter discusses the role that interest groups play in the American political system, assesses interest group influence, summarizes the changes and continuities in the interest group system that are revealed in the other fifteen chapters, identifies a set of paradoxes that spring forth from the contemporary politics of interests, and offers a few predictions about the future of interest group politics. A separate appendix gives a background essay on the changing state of interest group research.

Between my two chapters rests an array of distinctive and distinguished scholarship reflecting some of the most creative empirical, theoretical, and normative research on interest groups in the discipline. In the first part of the volume, three different approaches to the study of interest groups are advanced. What role do and should interest groups play in the processes of democratic governance? Jane J. Mansbridge argues that in addition to exerting pressure or adding a new force to the search for equilibrium among interests, interest groups make an important contribution to deliberative processes—competitive, collaborative, and corporatist—by bringing to bear additional information and new perspectives and thus changing the preferences of individuals involved in political governance. Mansbridge devotes a healthy portion of Chapter 2 to a consideration of reform proposals designed to maximize the deliberative benefits of interest groups while minimizing their rent-seeking costs.

Is political power in the United States divided among competing interest groups, as the pluralism of David Truman and Robert A. Dahl forcefully maintained? Or is the policymaking process captured by organized interests, as Theodore J. Lowi, Mancur Olson, and other plural elitists contend? In Chapter 3 Andrew S. McFarland responds to this classic debate over the distribution of political power by arguing that new sources of countervailing power have emerged in the interest group system that help resist the decline to interest group stasis predicted by prominent critics of pluralism.

How do American interest groups stack up against interest groups in other representative democracies? American political scientists have a tendency either to dismiss comparisons to other polities, given claims of American exceptionalism, or to ignore as uninstructive such comparisons. In Chapter 4 Graham K. Wilson shows that there is much to learn by comparing American interest groups with their counterparts in Western Europe. Wilson finds that economic groups in the United States are less powerful than those in Western Europe, whereas noneconomic interests, such as the women's movement, are more successful than those in Western Europe. Wilson links the cause of these differences to the weakness of class and ideological variation as forces in American politics.

Part 2 focuses attention on the organization of interests. Why do people join and organize interest groups in the first place? In Chapter 5 Paul A. Sabatier compares the effectiveness of five different theories at explaining why people join interest groups in light of new data from one economic and one noneconomic interest group involved in a regional land-use controversy of national significance. Rejecting a number of these theories as flawed as complete explanations, Sabatier concludes that the best interpretation comes from an expanded exchange theory that relies on a variety of incentives for joining and organizing groups but views political beliefs and information costs as more important than traditionally thought.

How are groups organized in relationship to one another in various policy domains? Conventional wisdom describes such relationships in terms of spatial metaphors, such as the classic "iron triangle" or the now popular "issue network." Drawing on data generated from one of the largest studies ever completed of Washington-based interest groups, Robert H. Salisbury, John P. Heinz, Robert L. Nelson, and Edward O. Laumann explore the differences that exist in the policy domains of labor, agriculture, energy, and health when it comes to interest representatives and government officials who participate, the effects of partisanship, the degree of specialization, and the specific tasks of interest group activists. The data they present in Chapter 6 reveals that the overall pattern of American politics and public policy is characterized by "concatenations" of groups and officials "too large, too heterogeneous, and too unstable" to resemble either issue networks or iron triangles.

One major change in the interest group system during the last twenty years points to the growing significance of states as new locations for interest group activity. Why has this happened? Do states vary in the extent of interest group activity? With what consequences for political governance? Based on an exhaustive study of interest groups in all fifty states, Chapter 7 contains responses to many of the questions raised by the heightened importance of state-level interest group activity. Clive S. Thomas and Ronald J. Hrebenar make a strong case for the significance of interest group activity at the state level, explain the explosion of interest group activity that has taken place there, and discover important regional differences in the organization and influence of interest groups at the state and regional levels.

Although the political mobilization of business during the 1970s and 1980s is a widely acknowledged change in the interest group system, less is known about why the mobilization took place. Finding rationalistic accounts of business mobilization inadequate, David Plotke develops an innovative explanation centered on the discursive development of a new growth model for business by business elites. In Chapter 8 Plotke shows that "political processes among business elites," as opposed to "given business interests," "were crucial to overcome collective action problems and provide a concrete definition of interests to guide strategic choices" during the decade.

The third part of this volume offers four assessments of interest group activity in three national political institutions: the presidency, Congress, and the courts. Chapter 9 is an analysis of the relationship between organized interests and the U.S. Congress, one of the traditional focal points for research on interest group politics. Drawing on the voluminous survey and interview work he completed with Kay Lehman Schlozman, John T. Tierney outlines the various techniques utilized by organized interests to influence congressional decisionmaking, assesses the differences in these techniques over time, and identifies the essential conditions under which interest groups are likely to exercise the most influence in the Capitol.

Political scientists have recently discovered the methods available to interest groups intent on influencing the presidency, but we are just beginning to fully comprehend the strategies presidents utilize in their policymaking struggles with Congress. Mark A. Peterson's study of interest mobilization systematically evaluates "three group-directed strategies presidents have pursued to advance their political and programmatic interests." Peterson concludes Chapter 10 with the provocative observation that connections between the presidency and interest groups do not pose the threat to the rejuvenation of political parties other analysts frequently assume. The threat to governability in the United States, as Peterson would have it, is not the proliferation of interest groups but rather the increasing role of presidentially led mass politics.

In Chapter 11 Joan Lucco also treats the presidency as a venue for interaction with interest groups, evaluating the struggle and success of consumer groups in gaining access to the presidency as a means of achieving the goals of the consumer movement. Lucco examines the tenuous and often troubled relationship between consumer groups and the presidency from Kennedy through the first years of the Bush administration. Except during the Carter presidency, Lucco discovers, consumer groups were not very effective at gaining the advantages of access to the White House. The value of a president as a champion of group causes, it seems, turns on a president's general effectiveness—a conclusion relevant to the entire universe of citizen and public interest groups clamoring for attention from the Oval Office.

During the Reagan era it was widely supposed that conservative public interest groups would gain greater and greater political clout by using the liberal litigation strategy to further their political agenda. In the final chapter in Part 3 Karen O'Connor and Bryant Scott McFall dispute this contention by examining sponsored litigation and the submission of amicus briefs by conservative and liberal public interest groups from 1981 to 1987. In their analysis, supplemented by extensive personal interviews with key participants in the conservative public interest movement, O'Connor and McFall conclude that there was simply not as much conservative litigation during the Reagan era as previously thought, and what did occur was not always successful. After explaining why expected litigation did not take place, O'Connor and McFall predict that the Reagan era may yet be a boon for conservative legal talent and the long-term success of conservative litigation.

The fourth part of this volume brings together examinations of recent changes in the activities and influence of contemporary interest groups. How do we explain the success of the women's movement? Basing her ideas on a new study of legislation addressing women as a group and the degree of agitation on behalf of women's rights in the United States, Anne N. Costain compares two theories—the traditional resource mobilization theory and the political process theory—to answer this question. In Chapter 13 Costain argues that movement success is a function of the opportunities and inducements provided by the government more than the mobilization of resources or traditional assertions of interest group power.

There is little question that the development of direct-marketing techniques has significantly enhanced the ability of organized groups to raise funds in pursuit of political goals. Much less is known about the effects of direct marketing on group membership and group influence. R. Kenneth Godwin investigates both of these issues in Chapter 14. His study of direct marketing shows that it brings more, but not significantly different, participants into interest group politics, solidifying the socioeconomic bias of the interest group system. Direct marketing also increases public attention on social and moral issues and radically changes the lobbying and electoral behavior of elites who depend on direct marketing for resources.

To what extent are interest groups influential in the determination of national public policy? Frequently based on collections of anecdotal evidence, speculative responses to this key question abound among political scientists and journalists alike. Paul E. Peterson's examination of special interest influence on government programs during the past twenty years moves beyond the speculative by examining the extent to which special interests have influenced government spending in residual categories of the federal budget. Peterson shows in Chapter 15 that after a decade of considerable success, the influence of special interests declined precipitously during the Reagan years. Noting that a complete reversal of this trend is unlikely in the near future, Peterson finds that special interests have influence on government programs only if fiscal opportunities are available and the structures of government decisionmaking are conducive to their goals.

At the risk of overstating the impact of Peterson's analysis, we might conclude that more interest groups are engaging in more activity and yet are receiving less of the government's largesse than ever before. I discuss this and other paradoxes and predictions pertinent to the American interest group system in Chapter 16.

This volume has been organized and written to appeal to undergraduates and, by necessity, their teachers; we also intend it to be valuable to research scholars and others interested in the politics of interests. This is not, to be sure, an edited textbook, although it fits well with many of the themes raised by available texts in the field. I willingly concede that as a presentation of original research along with a good deal of creative and exciting thinking, this volume is not comprehensive. It was not intended to be a wide-ranging compendium of articles on interest groups, nor do I think there are many good intellectual reasons for pursuing a subject matter in such a fashion.

As a consequence, certain important topics are not treated at length or, in a few cases, at all in this volume. Political action committees (PACs), for example, are discussed in a number of places but have not earned treatment in a separate chapter. The literature on PACs is so voluminous that it should be relatively easy to locate the latest word about them from the research community by consulting the references in Chapter 1. There are other subjects, such as the impact of interest groups on local politics and the growing significance of transnational lobbies, about which much more needs to be said and discovered. That may be the purpose of a second edition. It's certainly one of the intentions of this volume to further research about the interest group system, to stimulate exploration at the boundaries of our current knowledge. Once we've accomplished this, it will be easier to bring you an update of *The Politics of Interests* a few years hence. Let us and the good people at Westview Press know how we're doing!

PART I

Approaches to Interest Groups

1

The Rediscovery of
Interest Group Politics

MARK P. PETRACCA

American politics is the politics of interests. Throughout American history, a seamless web of commentary variously accepts, elevates, or bemoans the centrality of interests in political life. Thomas Paine, the first international revolutionary, denounced factions and parties for their tendency to subvert government by using it to further their own particular interests at the expense of the public good.[1] In the *Federalist* 10, James Madison acknowledged the inevitability of the faction, warned of its potential for majority tyranny, and defended the capacity of a representative republic to check and balance its mischief. Alexis de Tocqueville praised the propensity of Americans to join associations as an essential ingredient of democracy. The radical Democrat William Leggett (1836) recommended the "principle of combination" as the "only effectual mode" of opposing "a common enemy."[2] The protection of interests was central to John C. Calhoun's (1853) theory of the "concurrent majority" that "tends to unite the most opposite and conflicting interests and to blend the whole in one common attachment to the country."[3] Just past midcentury, the eminent political scientist Francis Lieber (1859) argued that "the American spirit of self-government" was dependent upon the nation's "all-pervading associative spirit." During the latter half of the century, attention turned to the rise of the lobby—"an institution peculiar to America," in the words of Arthur G. Sedgwick (1878). That peculiar institution figured prominently in the young Woodrow Wilson's (1885) critique of congressional government.

The politics of interests has shaped American politics, how we view ourselves as a nation, and how others view us as well. It also shapes the way we study political life and therefore what we can confidently know about American politics. As the first in a volume of original articles about the politics of interests, this chapter sets the stage for subsequent analysis and prediction. I begin by revisiting the group approach to political inquiry and consider the continuity of American attitudes toward interest groups in American democracy. The bulk of this opening chapter is dedicated to the identification and analysis of changes that have taken place in the American group system during the past two decades.[4]

GROUPS AND POLITICS

In the postwar era, American political science has been dominated, indeed defined, by the study of groups.[5] Conventional wisdom credits David B. Truman (1951) with bringing Arthur Bentley's 1908 work on groups into the mainstream of behavioral political science. Among Bentley's influential phrases is one on the explanatory power of group analysis: "When the groups are adequately stated, everything is stated. When I say everything I mean everything" (1967:208).[6] The group basis or theory of politics "transformed, if it did not wholly replace, traditional modes of political analysis and became the basis for a modernized theory of political pluralism" (Odegard 1967:xxvi). Once the undisputed sine qua non of American democracy, pluralism continues to serve as a model of American politics and as a foil for contemporary political analysis.

Truman alerted a new generation of scholars to the empirical and normative importance of groups in American politics. However, both the use of groups as a *unit* of political analysis and studies *of* interest groups preceded the impact of *The Governmental Process*. By the mid-1930s, the dean of modern political science, Charles E. Merriam (1964:31–39), had already recognized the role of groups in the birth of power and the process of governance. The prewar pluralists, led by British political scientists, reconceptualized the state as nothing more than a federation of groups and in so doing made groups an essential component of political analysis.[7]

Indeed, prewar studies of interest or pressure groups (as they were often called) represent some of the analytical gems of prebehavioral political science. Studies of the economic basis of politics, the Anti-Saloon League, group representation before Congress, and "new" lobbying were in the first wave of post-Bentley interest group research.[8] During the following decade, distinguished studies on tariff policy, public administration, pressure groups in New York, and "the pressure boys" in the nation's capital were capped by V. O. Key, Jr.'s, classic text of 1942, *Politics, Parties, and Pressure Groups*, which remained in publication for more than two decades.[9]

As statements about interest group politics and examples of political science methodology, these works remain a useful baseline against which to assess contemporary changes and continuities in the interest group system and the scholarly analysis of interest groups. For that purpose, and to enrich our understanding of contemporary interest groups with relevant historical insight, references to these and other prewar studies of interest groups are made throughout this volume.

The pluralist tradition that emerged from the writings of Truman (1951), Latham (1952a), Lindblom (1963), and Dahl (1961) became both the empirical account and normative vision of American politics.[10] Politics, for the pluralists, was defined as the resolution of group conflict. Citizens ought not to participate directly in the processes of agenda-building, policy formulation, or policy resolution, except insofar as they voted in competitive elections. Instead, citizens were to participate indirectly through membership in interest groups or by identifying with groups supporting their goals.

Political power for the pluralists was dispersed among political institutions and interest groups. The essence of the pluralist finding regarding the distribution of political power within a community was that different people have different kinds of power in different issue arenas. Political resources were distributed unequally in the polity to be sure, but those inequalities were dispersed and noncumulative. Given the fragmented and decentralized nature of the American political system, there were numerous multiple access points for group influence and representation in government. Taking as his point of departure a particular reading of Madison's *Federalist* 10, Robert Dahl (1956, 1961) argued that a balance among groups, actual and latent, would both assure political stability and achieve the public good.[11] Pluralism has been criticized as an apology for the pursuit of private interests by public means (see Kesselman 1982) and, as Andrew McFarland suggests in Chapter 3, for its tendency to produce political stasis. Yet despite extensive criticism, pluralism remains the standard by which most accounts of American politics are compared and evaluated.

What is an interest group? Interest groups go by many names—special interests, vested interests, pressure groups, organized interests, political groups, the lobby, and public interest groups. This varied terminology yields a diverse collection of operational definitions.

Definitions have varied over time: Some offer a normative appraisal; others reflect the analytical goals of the scholar using the terminology. Where it was once standard practice to use the term *pressure group*, this phrase has given way to the apparently more neutral *interest group* and *organized interest* in contemporary scholarship.[12] *Pressure group* was widely used because it clarified that the activities of organized groups were designed to influence governmental policy. The term does, however, have a normative ring to it, implying lurid images of what might be used to impose or induce pressure (see Salisbury 1975:176–177). Of course the images conjured up by *pressure group* are nowhere near as vivid as those invoked by references to interest groups as "the snake doctors of politics" or the "despair of patriots."[13]

Contemporary scholars are more likely to use terms that have meanings specific to their research. In order to include "hidden lobbies" in their analysis (lobbying entities not required to register under the laws of various states), Clive Thomas and Ronald J. Hrebenar (Chapter 7) adopt a rather broad definition of an interest group: "any association of individuals, whether formally organized or not, that attempts to influence public policy." Paul E. Peterson (Chapter 15) develops a very specific definition of special interests in order to identify expenditures in the federal budget as potential targets of their influence: "An interest is special if it consists of or is represented by a fairly small number of intense supporters who cannot expect that their cause will receive strong support from the general public except under unusual circumstances."

As the chapters in this volume illustrate, there are different terms and even different meanings for the same term currently in common use by scholars. Functional definitions try to distinguish interest groups from other associations of politically interested persons, such as political parties. For example, V. O. Key, Jr., (1958:23) distinguished between the two by arguing that pressure groups "promote their interests by attempting to influence government rather than by nominating candidates and seeking responsibility for the management of government." There are also definitions that emphasize the representational aspects of the interest group, such as Graham Wilson's (1981:4): "It is an organization which seeks or claims to represent people or organizations which share one or more common interests or ideals."

Some definitions stress what an interest group does, such as the widely used standard of Robert H. Salisbury (1975:175): "An interest group is an organized association which engages in activity relative to governmental decisions."[14] Other definitions simply suggest why the group formed in the first place. R. M. MacIver (1937:144) defined interests and the groups united to pursue them as "a number of men" united "for the defense, maintenance or enhancement of any more or less enduring position or advantage which they possess alike or in common." And there are definitions that recognize that not all groups trying to influence government policy have members. Kay Lehman Schlozman and John T. Tierney (1986:10) reserve the terms *interest groups* and *pressure groups* for membership associations and employ the term *organized interests* to include associations with individuals or organizations as members along with politically active organizations that do not have members in the ordinary sense.

In this chapter I use the term *interest group* in the same way that Schlozman and Tierney generally use the term *organized interest*—with apologies to their reasons for differentiating between them. *Interest group* is the most frequently employed term in this volume and throughout much of the contemporary literature. Indeed, it has become a generic term used to refer to membership- or nonmembership-based organizations or institutions that engage in activities to seek specific policy or political goals from the state.[15] This is the general meaning of the term as used throughout the volume unless given a more precise or differentiated meaning by the author or authors of a particular chapter.

AMERICAN ATTITUDES TOWARD INTEREST GROUPS

The study of groups is central to an understanding of American politics, not only for the influence of Madison and Tocqueville or Bentley and Truman but because Americans have a constitutional right to form associations and petition the government for redress of grievances, a propensity to form and join associations, and an abiding awareness of how the politics of interests complicates representation and governance in a democratic republic.

How do Americans feel about interest groups and the politics of interests? This is a very difficult question to answer in a systematic, empirical fashion. Absent reliable public opinion data on this topic, we are left to speculate about American attitudes from the behavior of ordinary citizens and from the commentary of various opinion leaders and scholars.

We know that Americans increasingly identify with various social groups as opposed to political parties. National Election Survey data from 1972 to 1984, for instance, show "a rise in identification with social groups is a major trend in American public opinion, encompassing greater psychological ties to religious, class, occupational, racial, gender, and age groups" (Wattenberg 1990:157–158). We also know that many Americans are members of, active in, and contribute to many different associations and organized groups.[16] The terms *special interest* or *vested interest* typically imply that only a very small number of Americans are members of such organizations. However, a Gallup Poll (1981:45–55) conducted in 1981 showed that as many as 20 million Americans are members of special interest associations and another 20 million gave money to such groups in 1980. Indeed, roughly 26 percent of Americans either joined or contributed to special interest groups in 1980.

Widespread identification with various groups and even membership in special interest groups does not necessarily mean that Americans support the role that interest groups play in politics. Beginning with Madison, Americans have recognized that interest groups are inevitable in a free society. They are produced by the "diversity in the faculties" of human beings and "the instinct of self-preservation" (Hamilton et al. 1961:78; Root 1907:11). Interest groups are neither anomalous nor pathological.

"Lobbying is as ancient as governing . . . it is also as legitimate and necessary" (Parton 1869:361). In fact, "all politiking [sic] is done by 'interested' persons and the term 'interest group' involves a truism, not a pathological condition" (DeGrazia 1958:113). The causes of faction cannot be cured without a tremendous loss of liberty—a "remedy worse than the disease," as Madison wisely put it. As a consequence, the United States has largely surrendered to the existence of interest groups, but not without considerable consternation and anxiety.

Throughout the early part of the twentieth century, the distinguished historian Daniel T. Rodgers (1987:182) observes, "the Interests, were by definition, alien and predatory: sores on the body politic." That's a scholarly account of how Progressive reformers felt about interest groups. Yet writing during that time period, political scientist E. Pendleton Herring (1929b:492) noticed "popular support [for the lobby] . . . a wide spread faith in its efficacy . . . [and] belief in its indispensableness." "Good or bad, honest or corrupt," Herring noted, the lobbies "are in the capital because thousands of citizens want them there."

How might these two conflicting observations be reconciled? It's possible that public attitudes shifted dramatically between the Progressive era and the late 1920s when Herring made his observation. An attitudinal shift did occur, but, according to Rodgers, not until the late 1930s. By then, at least in the political science community, laments about interest groups had given way to the hope that they could somehow be resisted and controlled. Rodgers (1987:211) concludes: "The Interests were no longer alien to the body politic. The roiling, inconclusive contest of interested groups *was* politics." A decade later the pluralism of contemporary political science had started to blossom.

A second possibility is that Rodgers and Herring have observed two different strains or currents running through American attitudes about interest groups.[17] One current is wary and fearful of the influence that interest groups wield in the political system; the other current values the role that interest groups play in the process of political representation. The first current is concerned with the mischiefs of faction whereas the second views interest groups as indispensable to democratic government. These currents may exist simultaneously, with one or the other occasionally dominating public discourse in response to changes in the interest group system.

Andrew S. McFarland's (1991) theory of "interest groups and political time" offers a useful way to think about the systematic relationship that may exist between these two currents and changes in the interest group system. Changes in the interest group system occur in a cycle alternating between periods of public and private action (not necessarily of equal duration). During periods of public action (e.g., in the decades of the

1900s, 1930s, and 1960s), purposive and noneconomic groups interested in political reform proliferate. During periods of private action (e.g., in the decades of the 1890s, 1920s, 1950s, and 1980s), there is a resurgence of economic interest groups concerned with the well-being of business. Other periods in the cycle (e.g., the 1910s, 1940s, and 1970s) are transitional.

The cycle of public and private action precipitates a reaction on the part of the public. Most likely, this reaction, emphasizing one current or the other, will lag behind the precipitating change. Thus, although the two currents may be present in public attitudes at any given period, one current may be more prominent in response to such cyclical changes in the interest group system.

This theory has yet to be fully developed, and it is not my intention to take on that challenge here. Rather, as amended, this theory offers a partial explanation for why a period of significant growth in the interest group system of one sort might soon be followed by demands for change in an entirely different direction.

The literature on interest groups during the twentieth century suggests a pattern, if not precisely a cycle, of condemnation following periods of "private action" and calls for new forms of interest representation following periods of "public action." Put more simply, business mobilization (McFarland's private action) results in cries against interest group influence and demands for mobilization by reform groups; public interest mobilization (what McFarland calls public action) leads to charges about the negative effects of more government and calls for greater mobilization by economic interest groups. A few examples help to illustrate how the interest group cycle precipitates the dominance of one of the two currents.

Progressive reforms—the mobilization of professional and public interest groups—resulted in calls for "a new order of representation" (Logan 1929:291), characterized by functional economic representation to supplement territorial representation (Herring 1929b, 1930a). "Representative government has failed," proclaimed Mary Follett (1965:5), "because it was not a method by which men could govern themselves. . . . Group organization is to be the new method in politics, the basis of our future industrial system, the foundation of international order." Functional representation, even a form of quasi corporatism, was employed on various war boards during the first and second world wars and was a prominent feature of the National Recovery Administration (NRA) (see Brand 1988). This experience was, however, short-lived.

The resurgence of business interests in the 1950s after the unprecedented growth of government during the New Deal and World War II led E. E. Schattschneider (1960) to denounce the bias of the interest group system and Hans Morgenthau (1960:266) to condemn it as a "new feudalism." By the end of the turbulent 1960s, private action had given way to "lobbying for the people" (see Berry 1977).

The public interest movement of the late 1960s and early 1970s resulted in a dramatic increase in government legislation and regulation. By the end of the 1970s, business leaders were calling on their troops to wage an aggressive defense of their interests (McGrath 1979).[18] As David Plotke shows in Chapter 8, the mobilization of business was successful. Yet by mid-decade, a veritable symphony of outrage about the "special interest Congress," the "special interest state," "the best Congress money can buy," and "the new power game" was reaching a crescendo.[19] Scholarly and journalistic concerns notwithstanding, the changes in the interest group system during the 1970s and early 1980s also created a public outcry against the troublesome influence of interest groups. Jeffrey Berry (1989a:16) offers this poignant assessment of popular attitudes toward interest groups: "Currently, a pervasive, popular perception is of an unprecedented and dangerous growth in the number of interest groups and that this growth continues unabated. . . . the popular perception is that interest groups are a cancer, spreading unchecked throughout the body politic, making it gradually weaker, until they eventually kill it."

Fear and fascination, trepidation and trust, despair and delight go hand in hand when it comes to American attitudes about interest groups. These attitudes vary in their emphasis over time as a function of changes in the interest group system. Yet these two currents can and do coexist in the body politic, even if somewhat uncomfortably. Americans recognize that "interest groups are indispensable for the functioning of a modern democracy," yet they "distrust" interest groups for they "might abuse the power derived from the exercise of legitimate functions" (Ehrmann 1968:490). "Distrust" encapsulates a number of very specific concerns about interest groups that speak directly to fundamental issues of democratic theory and political governance, such as representation, fairness, accountability, the distribution of political power, and governability. Some of these concerns are posed below as a set of simple questions:

1. Do all individuals have the ability to join interest groups to represent their interests? Put another way, can all "interests" mobilize for political action?
2. How are decisions made within interest groups?
3. Do interest groups have equal access to government?
4. Assuming that everyone can join a group and that every group has equal access to government, do they have equal resources to bring to bear on the policymaking and electoral processes?
5. How do interest groups influence electoral politics and policymaking in the United States?

6. How does the interest group system affect the capacity of the government to govern?
7. Do we want a political system defined and determined by the "politics of interests"?

These questions take on added relevance when there are perceived or actual changes in the interest group system—stimulating attention, anxiety, challenge, and often new research. It is to the systematic identification and explanation of the most recent round of changes in the American interest group system that I now turn.

CHANGES IN THE INTEREST GROUP SYSTEM

How has the American interest group system changed during the past twenty years? Because change is an inevitable and inherent part of politics, we should not be too surprised to find some in the interest group system. The real question, therefore, is whether any of the developments have been significant. The answer to this question is, "Yes, but. . . ." Significant changes during this period have been heralded by a number of scholars. David Knoke (1986:15) describes these changes as an "advocacy explosion"; Jeffrey Berry (1989b:239) prefers the phrase "lobbying explosion." Mark A. Peterson (1990b:115) found "a dramatic transformation of the structure of interest representation" in his study of executive-legislative relations. The growth of interest representation in Washington, says Salisbury (1990:204), has brought about "a transformation in the way much public policy is made."

Yet there are also important caveats to the certainty of these assessments.[20] The absence of reliable baseline data about interest groups, from which comparisons can be made over time, makes the identification of significant change difficult and necessarily speculative. If the current trend in empirical research on interest groups continues, then this problem may be solved for future analysts. But it is a limitation on the certainty of judgments that we must still confront in the present. Thus the judgments we arrive at below about the magnitude and significance of changes in the landscape, activities, and influence of interest groups must rely upon contemporary observations and assessments and comparisons with trustworthy historical accounts.

This leads to a final caveat. Interestingly, previous declarations of change in this century by skilled observers and analysts do not differ all that much from one era to another.[21] Consider the following assessments of interest group mobilization, activity, and influence. When was each observation made? (Try not to peek at the endnotes!)

A. "Single-cause pressure groups modeled on the Temperance movement have since come to dominate politics, especially in the United States."[22]

B. "The lobby army—small enough to be overlooked in normal times but big enough to fight a Central American boundary war—still is busy in Washington burning the bridges between the voter and what he voted for."[23]

C. "There has been an increase in the amount, tempo, and intensity of pressure group activity in recent decades. . . . The multiplication and differentiation of pressure groups have been matched by a refinement of various techniques and greater use thereof to maximize political effectiveness."[24]

D. "The explosion of interest-group activity has brought a large number of new participants who aggressively seek to influence legislators and agency officials."[25]

E. "A large number of voluntary associations have sprung up during the past twenty years, devoted to the propagation of special economic interests or special political and social ideas."[26]

F. "In the last decade, there has been an amazing development of the practice of employing legislative agents to represent special interests during the sessions of legislative bodies. This practice is, of course, not particularly new, but never before have legislative bodies been subjected to such a continuous and powerful bombardment from private interests as at present."[27]

G. "During the past few decades the number of pressure groups has rapidly multiplied, the scope of their activities has vastly expanded, and their methods and tactics have become more professionalized and subtle. Today, the more highly organized groups have lobbyists in Washington and in many state capitals, well-staffed bureaus of press agents and research personnel, and active membership groups across the nation."[28]

H. "During the past two decades, the coherence of the American state has also been undermined by the growing involvement of interest groups in administrative decision-making. Having no commitment to executive prerogatives, Congress increasingly has authorized interest groups to participate directly in administrative rule making. Groups that enjoy access to Congress, can, in effect, write their own priorities into law."[29]

It's very difficult to tell when these observations were made. They identify changes in the extent of interest mobilization, location of group activity, degree of organization, types of activities pursued, techniques of influence utilized, and impact on policymaking and politics. With some modernization of the language, they might all be accurate descriptions of the period under study here, 1970–1990. Yet only three of the assessments—A, D, and H, by Peter Drucker, Jeffrey Berry, and Benjamin Ginsberg and Martin Shefter, respectively—were made during the past twenty years. The remainder span seventy-five years of commentary about American interest groups.

The resemblances among these assessments should add caution to any conclusions we reach about the developments of the past two decades and soften any alarm attendant to the recent advocacy, lobbying, and interest group activity "explosions."

The Interest Group Landscape

A significantly larger number of groups of greater diversity, located throughout the political system and interacting in new configurations with each other and with the government, fairly characterizes recent changes in the landscape of American interest groups.

"Explosion" is a completely accurate way to describe the massive number of interest groups that have descended upon Washington, D.C., since the 1960s. Not long after the Civil War, J. Parton (1870) wrote about the fifty lobbyists who "winter in Washington pushing for objects" obviously "beyond the constitutional power of Congress." Since then, sporadic counts of interest groups and their representatives located in Washington during the twentieth century indicate just how much the presence of interest groups in the capital has grown. In 1929 Herring (1929b:492) estimated 500 organizations "whose purpose it is to keep in contact with the government and present their views to Congress"; Oliver McKee, Jr., (1929:350) placed the number at 300 "effective lobbies." During the high point of the New Deal, Crawford (1939:3) counted 6,000 active lobbyists "more or less" and 5,000 attorneys in Washington. During the 1940s the Temporary National Economic Committee (cited in Chase 1945:22) and Herman Finer (1949:459) counted 400 lobbies in the nation's capital, and Wilfred Binkley and Malcolm Moos (1958:156) estimated there to be 12,000 lobbyists in Washington during World War II. Key (1958:143) said that "perhaps around 500 organizations have a continuing interest in national policy and legislation . . . but hundreds of others have an occasional interest in legislation." Donald Blaisdell (1957:59) placed the number of lobbyists during the 1950s at 1,180, a figure close to Daniel Berman's (1964:97) count of 1,100 registered lobbyists in the early 1960s. Lester Milbrath (1968:443) suggested that there were from 800 to 1,000 registered lobbyists in Washington during the 1960s. By 1981, Hedrick Smith (1989:236) says, there were 5,662 registered lobbyists, a number that jumped to 23,011 by 1987.

The best systematic data we have on the number of interest groups and interest representatives comes from *Washington Representatives* (see Close

1977–1991), a directory of "persons working to influence politics and actions to advance their own or their client's interest" that has been published annually since 1977. Figure 1.1 shows the remarkable increase in the number of interest representatives located in Washington; going from 4,000 in 1977 to more than 14,500 in 1991. In just over a dozen years, the number of individuals listed in this directory has tripled, and even the editors concede that this may underestimate the true number of Washington-based interest representatives.[30] In fact, there are so many lobbyists in Washington that the lobbyists now have lobbies—the American Society of Association Executives, the American League of Lobbyists, and the National Association of Business Political Action Committees serve a growing clientele of member interest groups, interest representatives, lobbying firms, association executives, and PACs (see Jackson 1988:322). Much of this growth is attributable to a rise in representatives from institutions, not from traditional membership-based organizations: "Institutions have come to dominate the processes of interest representation in American national politics" (Salisbury 1984:64). For example, only 18 percent (or 2,200) of the individual representatives listed in *Washington Representatives 1990* are advocates of special cause groups that might arguably be membership-based. Of the remaining 10,300 representatives, 3,750 were representatives of trade and professional associations, 1,700 were from individual corporations, 2,000 were lawyers registered as lobbyists or foreign agents, 2,000 were consultants and professional managers from client associations and interest groups, and 100 were from policy think tanks.[31]

The advocacy explosion in Washington is very diverse, including not only lawyers and law firms, nonprofit associations, and corporations but also citizen groups, governmental entities, and foreign interests. Only 45 out-of-town law firms had offices in Washington in 1965, yet by 1983 that number had risen to 247. In the ten years from 1973 to 1983, membership in the District of Columbia Bar more than tripled, from 10,925 to over 37,000 attorneys (Laumann et al. 1985:467; see also Nelson et al. 1987).

Washington has also become a headquarters for national nonprofit associations. In 1971, for instance, only 19 percent had headquarters in the District of Columbia; ten years later that number was 29 percent. By one estimate there are as many as 80,000 association employees in Washington, and more than 4,000 corporations retained representatives there as well (Laumann et al. 1985:467). In 1971 only 175 business firms had registered lobbyists in Washington; by 1979, 650 had them (Vogel 1989:197). Indeed, of the 7,000 organizations that maintain a continuing presence in Washington either by keeping an office or hiring counsel to represent them, nearly half are corporations (Schlozman and Tierney 1986). By 1980 the renewed presence of business in Washington was staggering. According to David Vogel (1989:197–198):

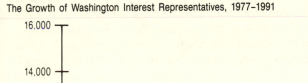

FIGURE 1.1
The Growth of Washington Interest Representatives, 1977–1991

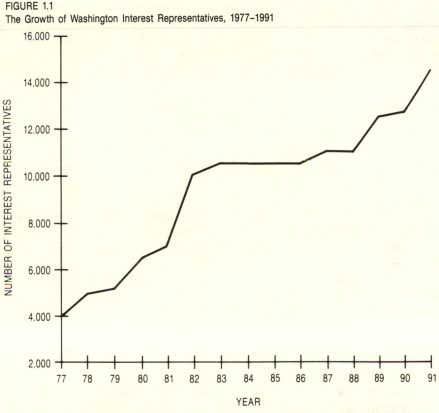

YEAR

Source: Data compiled from Arthur C. Close, ed., *Washington Representatives, 1977–1991* (Washington, D.C.: Columbia Books, 1977–1991).

All told, as of 1980 there were in Washington 12,000 lawyers representing business before federal regulatory agencies and the federal courts, 9,000 business lobbyists, 50,000 trade association personnel, 8,000 public relations specialists, 1,300 public affairs consultants, and 12,000 specialized journalists reporting to particular industries on government developments affecting them. The number of individuals employed by the "private service industry" exceeded the number of federal employees in the Washington metropolitan area for the first time since before the New Deal.[32]

The mobilization of business was all the more significant because of the thirty-year decline of labor in the United States (see Goldfield 1987). By some measures the political activity of unions has been increasing (see Masters and Delaney 1985), but in general the broadly representative power of labor has been on the wane (see Edsall 1984:141).

Most significant for the "public interest," Washington also experienced a dramatic increase in citizen groups ranging from the Citizens Clearinghouse for Hazardous Wastes and the Sierra Club to the American Association of Retired Persons (AARP) and the Consumer Federation of America. Although lawyers, associations, and corporations have long been able to support some kind of presence in Washington, the arrival of citizen groups was truly a new phenomenon. Some 76 percent of citizen groups and 79 percent of welfare groups located in Washington had come into existence since 1960 (see Schlozman and Tierney 1986:76; Walker 1983; Gais et al. 1984). Yet by 1980 citizen groups made up more than one-fifth of all political interest groups in Washington, and 30 percent of these groups had been founded just since 1975 (see Walker 1983; Peterson and Walker 1986).

Related to the growth of citizen groups was the rise of single-issue groups during the late 1970s. These "passionate blocs" of voters, as George Will (1978) described them, "say they will vote against any legislator who votes the 'wrong' way on a particular issue." It is difficult to accept the premise implied by the label that any of the groups so designated are really "single-issue" or "single-cause" groups. However, their rise to prominence in electoral politics prompted wide-ranging debate about the danger they posed to political parties and governability (see Broder 1979; Phillips 1978; Longman 1983). Conversely, issue politics was defended as a way of transforming American politics in a fashion more compatible with authentic democracy (see Tesh 1984).

Since the mid-1960s, intergovernmental lobby activity surged in response to the growing size and complexity of federal domestic programs and direct encouragement from the federal government. Large peak associations, such as the U.S. Conference of Mayors, the National Governors' Association, and the National League of Cities, along with a growing number of states and major cities, set up permanent lobbying offices in Washington. By the early 1980s, twenty-five states maintained such offices, and, of those, fifteen states had additional lobby offices for specific line agencies (see Cingranelli 1983). Although their budgets and staffs had grown significantly during the 1970s, President Reagan changed all of this. Reagan's success at "defunding" state and local advocacy groups increased the level of conflict among these groups and changed the political battlefield from expansion to survival (see Levine and Thurber 1986).

Foreign interests also account for the rise in Washington-based interest representatives. A growing number of American interest representatives are now also registered as foreign agents for various interests in South Korea, France, Mexico, Saudi Arabia, and Canada, to name a few. Even Third World insurgency groups such as the Islamic Unity of Afghanistan Mujahideen, the Khmer People's National Liberation Front, and the National Union for the Total Independence of Angola have also hired lobby-ists in Washington (see Cooper 1986). Japan is in a category by itself, with 122 organizations listed as having registered foreign agents in the United States. This list includes obvious and well-known high-tech firms such as Hitachi, Mitsubishi, and Toshiba, but it also includes the Japan Whaling Association, Japanese Tanner Crab Association, and the Tokyo Electric Company (see Choate 1990). It's worth noting that many of these foreign agents are assigned lobbying tasks at the state and local levels as well (see Levy 1987).

The rise of foreign lobbying has given a real boost to the employment prospects of former government officials. A 1986 study by the Government Accounting Office showed that seventy-six former federal officials had become registered foreign agents, representing 166 foreign clients from fifty-two nations and two international organizations. One-third of these former federal officials went to work for Japanese organizations (see Choate 1990:18).[33]

Washington has not been the only site of an advocacy explosion. Re-sponding to the "new federalism" and the decentralization of the Reagan administration, interest groups took on state capitals as an essential "sec-ond front."[34] In California the number of groups and firms employing paid persuaders tripled from 1975 to 1985, so that some 1,700 organizations employing 838 registered lobbyists are represented in Sacramento. In 1975 roughly $20 million was spent per year on lobbying; by 1985 that amount had exceeded $70 million (Zeiger 1989).

The escalation of state interest group activity was also evident in New York, where the number of interest groups grew from 1,294 in 1979 to 1,488 in 1983, and the number of clients went from 580 to 625. Even less populous states were not immune. Montana, Wyoming, and New Hamp-shire, for example, saw increases in the number of lobbyists from the mid-1970s to the early 1980s of roughly 100 percent, 30 percent, and 47 percent, respectively (Bell 1986:14–15). There is also evidence that interstate lob-bying organizations are beginning to develop. A number of lobbying and consulting firms now have branch offices in neighboring states, and some, such as A-K Associates of California, are in most other large states throughout the nation (Bell 1986).[35]

The landscape of the interest group system was also changed by the emergence of relationships between groups and government (or, more aptly put, the state). The metaphor of subgovernments or iron triangles has long been used to describe the symbiotic relationship that exists among interest groups, legislators, and agency bureaucrats, especially in the policy domains of agriculture, public works, and defense.[36] McFarland (Chapter 3) and Salisbury, Heinz, Nelson, and Laumann (Chapter 6) show that policymaking in iron triangles has given way to issue networks of those knowledgeable about policy in some policy area (see Heclo 1978) or "larger concatenations of groups and officials, most of which are too large, too heterogeneous, and too unstable in their linkages to qualify even as real networks, and certainly not as old-fashioned triangles" (see Chapter 6).

In the mid-1970s the number of subgovernments was "proliferating" as the power of some twenty congressional committees was dispersed to well over 100 subcommittees (Fiorina 1977:62). Yet within a decade, the policymaking process had been transformed. In the regulatory arena, James Q. Wilson (1980a:391) and his students found no evidence of iron triangles, concluding that the linkages they did see "appear to be of a metal far more malleable than iron." What happened? The proliferation of interest groups, especially citizens' groups, the explosion of lobbying activity, the professionalization of interest group activity, the continued congressional decentralization, the movement of congressional power from the committee to the floor, and increased control of the bureaucracy by the Reagan White House all contributed to the demise of subgovernment policymaking.[37]

Of course, no one is suggesting that issue subgovernments have vanished as have marginal seats in the House of Representatives. For example, the policymaking system of consultation and collaboration characteristic of the new social regulation led Richard Harris (1989b) to conclude that neocorporatism is the new collective noun for the old system of subgovernments. Likewise, in the arena of energy policy, John E. Chubb (1983:251) discovered that bureaucratic subsystems continue to bias national energy policy, referring to the subsystem as "quasi-corporatist." Nevertheless, most scholars seem to agree that even in policy arenas traditionally defined by iron triangles, such as agriculture (see Browne 1985, 1990), the exclusivity, reciprocity, and privacy that once tempered the iron triangle have gradually disappeared.

Interest Group Activity

What do interest groups do to influence government policy, and have these activities changed during the past twenty years? We know from the chapters in this volume that interest groups lobby Congress and participate in election campaigns (Chapter 9); litigate (Chapter 12); raise a great deal of money and mobilize grassroots support for candidates and political issues (Chapter 14); lobby the White House (Chapters 10 and 11); form coalitions with other organizations (Chapter 3); interact with other interest representatives and the bureaucracy (Chapter 6); and mobilize mass publics (Chapter 13). Are any of these activities unique to the past two decades? Of course not. Not only are examples of each or a similar activity readily available throughout much of the postwar era, but for many activities examples can also be located in prewar studies of interest groups.[38]

What is new about interest group activity is its breadth and magnitude, enhanced by new communications technologies.[39] "All groups, even previously active ones, are doing more. The effect is therefore multiplicative; with more organizations each doing more, the product is an explosion in the amount of organized interest activity in Washington" (Scholzman and Tierney 1986:169).

The conventional wisdom about interest group activity during the 1950s and 1960s was largely influenced by Bauer, Pool, and Dexter's monumental study of reciprocal trade policy and Milbrath's landmark study of Washington lobbyists.

> The tactical basis of pressure-group activities seemed to be to assist men already on their side to do the job of persuading fellow legislators. Direct persuasion of uncommitted or opposed congressmen or senators was a minor activity of the lobbies. (Bauer, Pool, and Dexter 1963:442)

> Most lobbying effort, then, is aimed not at conversion, but at actuating the favorable member or at least ensuring that he remains committed and votes correctly! (Milbrath 1970a:411)

These two studies showed that interest group activity was mostly about preserving and mobilizing legislators known to support the group's position. Activities such as presenting research results, testifying at hearings, working with staff, and using intermediaries (see Milbrath 1970b:390–391) represent the heart of what Hedrick Smith (1989:216) calls the "old inside game of lobbying." Old-fashioned lobbying is a game played on the inside of the political process *with* insiders, which is why so many "old-breed" lobbyists are former members of the legislative and executive branches. As Smith (1989:230) explains, "Their game thrives on the clubbiness of the old-boy network. It turns on the camaraderie of personal friendships, on expertise born of experience. It taps old loyalties and well-practiced access. It draws on the common bond of old battles and the certain knowledge that you may lose on this year's tax bill, but you'll be back to revise it next year, and that yesterday's foe may be tomorrow's ally. It depends on relationships for the long haul." Clark Clifford, Robert Strauss, Charls Walker, Howard Baker, Robert Gray, Lyn Nofziger, and Michael Deaver are prominent examples of "old-breed" superlobbyists—each of whom translated an insider's knowledge of the White House or Capitol Hill into a lucrative career as a lobbyist-for-hire.

Old-fashioned, extensive, private lobbying continues unabated in the nation's capital—and in an ever growing number of state capitals as well.[40] What's different about interest group activity today is that a new, outside lobbying game has grown up alongside it during the past two decades. "The new-breed game," as Hedrick Smith (1989:235) refers to it, "reflects the organic changes in American politics and the institutional changes in Congress. Its medium is mass marketing; its style is packaging issues; its hallmark is wholesale lobbying."[41]

Interest groups are now actively involved in the electoral politics armed with new direct-marketing technologies for mobilizing voters and raising campaign funds. In a study of the role that party played in congressional campaigns in the 1980s, Paul Herrnson (1988:87–105) discovered that interest groups exercised considerable influence in mass-market advertising, fund-raising, and recruitment of volunteer campaign workers; they were somewhat less influential in candidate recruitment. Groups have developed an aggressive presence in national elections by becoming prominent sources of campaign financing (Manes 1990) and as influential players in the presidential selection process (Rapoport et al. 1991). Beyond elections for public office, interest groups have become active participants in ballot initiatives and referenda in state and local politics. Indeed, these forms of direct democracy would be almost unthinkable in populous, industrial states without the participation of organized interests (see Cronin 1989).

Raising and spending money is an extremely important—some might say the dominant—interest group activity. The ability of political action committees to raise and aggregate money "endows interest groups with two new and important powers: First, it permits them to magnify their group's political influence without relationship to the numbers of their members or the merits of their arguments. Second, it allows the group to impose huge costs on the rest of the population" (Stern 1988:9). The sheer growth in the number of PACs and their expenditures is truly staggering. In 1976 there were 1,146 PACs, by 1982 the number had leaped to 3,722, and by 1988 it approached 5,000. In 1976, PACs contributed nearly $23 million to all candidates for the House and Senate, in 1982 they contributed $84 million, and in the 1987–1988 election cycle they contributed a whopping $160 million. Total PAC spending—including all contributions and independent expenditures—was $103 million in 1982. By 1988 that amount had skyrocketed to $364 million.[42]

A great deal of controversy surrounds the effect of PACs on election outcomes and legislative decisionmaking. The commonsense view that expenditures of this magnitude must influence congressional voting decisions is not borne out by empirical research (see Nugent and Johannes 1990; Grenzke 1990; Magleby and Nelson 1990). This is not to suggest that money and PACs are without influence; only that expenditure patterns do not correlate very well with voting behavior, all other things being equal. However, other empirical studies show that PAC contributions are associated with shifts in congressional support on particular policies (see Ginsberg and Green 1986) and influence the intensity with which group positions are promoted by the recipients of such funds in the legislature (see Hall and Wayman 1990). Money may not buy votes, as is frequently alleged by those who believe that PAC contributions are just another form of "honest graft" (see Jackson 1988). Instead, the effects of interest group expenditures "are more likely to appear in committee than on the floor" and "the behavior most likely affected is members' legislative involvement, not their votes" (Hall and Wayman 1990:797, 814). As a result, money matters most at the stage in the legislative process—the committee stage—that matters most for having a direct bearing on policy outcomes.

With such great sums of money raised and the skills of professional lobbying and consulting firms to spend it on, interest groups across the political spectrum now pursue grassroots lobbying with a vengeance. What was once the technique of choice by underfunded, liberal reform groups is now a primary activity of Washington's corporate and trade association lobbying community when "old-breed" lobbying fails. The new, professional lobbyists can turn any issue—natural gas deregulation, the Chrysler bailout, or funding for the B-1 bomber or the MX missile system—into a political campaign, complete with national and targeted advertising designed to shape public opinion and stimulate an appropriate outpouring of public support for the advocated position. Whereas old-fashioned pork-barrel lobbying seeks to mobilize the "folks back home" for a specific benefit relevant to their congressional district, the new grassroots lobbying "is an attempt to seek to influence congressional votes on legislation of national importance, legislation that is seen or thought to transcend parochial boundaries" (Edsall 1984:109–110).

Most analysts credit grassroots lobbying by the banking industry in 1983 for defeating an amendment to the 1982 tax law that required banks to withhold 10 percent of their customers' income from interest and dividends. The Leo Burnett Company of Chicago, hired by the American Bankers Association, launched a massive national grassroots campaign to stimulate anxiety about the proposed change in the tax law and induce a response. The campaign worked, causing 22 million pieces of mail to be sent to Congress. Over the objections of President Reagan and Senate Majority Leader Robert Dole (R–Kans.), both of whom supported the amendment, the Senate reversed its earlier decision, voting 86–4 against tax withholding, killing the amendment and eventually the law (see H. Smith 1989:242–244).[43]

Another aspect to the new outside game of interest group politics is the widespread use of group coalitions. Coalition-building has long been characteristic of American politics. Noteworthy about contemporary coalition-building by interest groups is "how numerous are the coalitions designated . . . and also how many counterpart coalitions, generally called caucuses, have been formed in Congress" (Salisbury 1990:218). These coalitions are quite fluid, joining various interests together to lobby for a specific policy, making at times for some very strange political bedfellows. When Chrysler was looking for a government bailout program in 1978, it brought a Democratic law firm (Patton, Boggs, and Blow) together with a big Republican lobbying firm (Timmons and Company). Conversely, in a polity characterized by "shifting coalitions" (see King 1978), it is not unusual for lobbying partners to wind up on opposite sides of political campaigns. For example, in 1986 the firm of Wexler, Reynolds, Harrison, and Schule ran fund-raisers for rival candidates in Senate races from Florida and Maryland. Professional consulting firms in particular are not averse to working both sides of the aisle (see Petracca 1989). Aside from lobbying activities, these coalitions also play a special role in gathering and sharing information.

Indeed, the search for information instead of influence is one of the most profound changes in interest group activity. Information is of central importance in the policy process: It is both a resource to influence others and essential for the determination of sensible and appropriate political behavior. A study of how interest representatives spend their time in the policy domains of agriculture, energy, health, and labor found that "information exchanges claim a higher priority than position taking, and intraorganizational efforts along with monitoring of the political environment are of central importance" (see Salisbury 1990:227). The point is not just that information matters; it's that in Washington's complicated policymaking environment, interest groups find themselves dependent upon government to obtain the information they so desperately need to effectively pursue their goals. As Salisbury (1990:227) surmises, interest representatives "need access to officials not so much to apply pressure or even to advocate policy as to be told when something important to them is about to happen."

As we'll see throughout this volume, interest groups can and do influence government policy in a wide variety of ways, even though, as I argue in Chapter 16, interest group influence is less significant than commonly supposed. Interest groups pursue old- and new-breed activities to influence the outcome of elections, the government's agenda, and governmental decisions. More groups are doing more in more ways than ever before. But along with the obvious connection between activity and influence, we must also take Salisbury's (1990:229) observation seriously in any assessment of what groups do and why they've come to Washington to do it: "These groups have come to Washington out of need and dependence rather than because they have influence." Thus, even in its dependence on government for essential information, interest group activity has changed from the conventional wisdom.

Explanations

Interest group politics have changed, but why? How do we explain the transformations that have occurred in the landscape and activities of the interest group system? Single explanations for all the changes identified would be economical and might have the greatest appeal to the reader. The decline of political parties might explain the proliferation of interest groups and the expansive breadth of their activities. When parties are weak, interest groups are strong (see Dahl 1982). Conversely, multiple explanations for single changes would probably be more accurate though much more cumbersome. The rise of citizen groups is probably best explained by a combination of factors: the growth of the middle class in the 1960s, a revolution in communications technology, and the emergence of interest group patrons (see Gais, Peterson, and Walker 1984). Unfortunately, single explanations miss a number of the essential details whereas multiple explanations for single changes may be overburdened by detail. We should therefore search for middle ground where the economy of explanation meets the imperative of necessary detail.

Changes in the interest group system are not sui generis; they are neither unique nor divorced from the other changes characteristic of American politics during the 1970s and 1980s. Rather, the changes that characterize interest group politics are products of developments in the larger political system, such as changes in the role and structure of government, in the conditions necessary for the organization of groups, and in communications technology, political parties, and electoral mobilization.

When we ask why the interest group system has changed, we are really asking what aspects of American politics changed to transform the interest group system. I recognize the danger inherent in identifying changes to explain change, especially the possibility of getting trapped in an infinite regression of queries. But absent a general theory to explain why interest groups emerge and why they do what they do applicable across time and to other representative democracies, there are few alternatives.[44]

Political entrepreneurs both in and out of government helped to stimulate the formation of groups. In addition, patrons became an important source of financial and political support for organizations struggling to overcome the quintessential problems of mobilizing for collective action. Although political entrepreneurs are necessary to initiate the process of group mobilization, they are not sufficient for successful group maintenance. For that to occur, as Jack Walker (1990b:185) discovered, institutions must be identified that "will serve as sponsors or patrons for their efforts."

Government also stimulated the emergence of groups, often indirectly and on occasion through direct action. The very size, reach, and influence of the federal government has been both a magnet and an invitation to interest group activity since the 1960s (see Silbey 1990). As government increased its penetration into the lives of Americans, it created a wide-spread "interest," so to speak, in public policy encouraging group formation. This not only explains why there is a relationship between the expansion of the federal government and the expansion of interest groups, but it also helps to explain why so many groups have set up permanent residence in the nation's capital. Quite simply, Washington is where the action is.

The 1960s and 1970s were periods of enormous growth in legislation, regulation, and government expenditures (see Vatter and Walker 1990). Interest groups came to Washington to be a part of that process—to promote their interests. Ironically, the budgetary constraints imposed by the Reagan years—political constraints that became economic constraints because of the enormity of the federal deficit—have given these groups a reason to stay in Washington, as promotion has turned into a life-and-death struggle for protection. Competition among the groups is also keen for the few remaining morsels of the federal budget not restricted by prior statutory commitments. In addition, budgetary constraints coupled with the new federalism and decentralization of federal programs elevated the importance of state capitals in the policymaking process, precipitating the sharp increase in interest group activity across the nation, as I noted earlier in this chapter and as Thomas and Hrebenar observe in Chapter 7.

More specific governmental actions, such as legislation, also encourage the formation of interest groups. For example, some 50 percent of the groups representing the elderly were formed after 1965, the year Medicare and the Older Americans Act were passed (Walker 1983). In other cases, as Anne Costain (Chapter 13) argues in the case of the women's movement, groups are facilitated and enabled by the favorable attitudes and policies of government officials.

In still other cases the government steps in, mobilizes groups, and orchestrates support for its policies directly. Mark A. Peterson (Chapter 10) illustrates the various group strategies available to a president to help achieve his political and programmatic objectives. As many scholars have noted, Reagan was particularly skilled in transforming the political identities of established groups, dividing the identities of others, and creating new groups to support Republican party policy aims. "One of the outstanding successes of the public liaison operation [in the Reagan White House] was the orchestration of favorable interest groups and party activists in mobilizing support in 1981 for the president's budget cuts in the Democratic-controlled House" (Rockman 1988:18). Beyond this specific case, as Ginsberg and Shefter (1988:321) showed, "the Reaganites united Catholic and Protestant religious conservatives; they forged linkages among business owners, managers and upper-income professionals, essentially restoring the political unity of the bourgeoisie; and they politically reunified American business and attached it to the Republican party."[45]

The evolving structure of the federal government, especially the Congress, also played a major role in stimulating the advocacy explosion. Interest group activity has always been linked to the fragmentation of political power in the United States, the "literally uncountable points" in the policymaking process that facilitate access and influence for individuals and groups (see Grodzins 1966:14–15). Changes in the structure of Congress during the 1970s contributed to the further dispersion of political power and hence to an expansion of interest group activity.[46] Full committees and their chairs steadily lost power to a proliferation of subcommittees; resources for individual members of Congress, such as staff support and travel allowances, expanded. With much larger numbers of staff came their increasing professionalization, the seniority system was diminished in importance, new "sunshine law" requirements opened up meetings, and voting and amendment activity on the floor increased. These changes multiplied "the number of actors in Congress to whom an organized interest might usefully seek access" and increased "the number of points in the law making process at which interests may try to exert influence." As a result, "organized interests bent on influencing officials" were left with "little choice but to escalate the range and volume of their activities" (Schlozman and Tierney 1986:302).

Ironically and, some would argue, tragically, the dispersion of power in Congress not only enhanced opportunities for interest group influence but increased congressional dependency upon interest groups for information, expertise, and political support in light of congressional decentralization. Along with the post-Watergate reforms, which gave rise to the rapid development of PACs overflowing with funds to influence the political process, Congress is responsible for creating at least some of the conditions that encouraged the advocacy explosion and its own dependence on special interest groups (see Sheppard 1985).

There are also extragovernmental explanations for changes in the interest group system. The revolution in communications technology—the development of satellites, cable, videocassette recorders, and computers—has transformed the way interest groups organize and mobilize members, raise money, and influence government policy.[47] By making it easier for groups to organize and raise funds, this new technology has enabled the expansion of interest groups and to a large extent escalated the impact that interest groups can have on policymaking and elections. Numerous citizen action groups and political action committees, for example, could not exist without the computer-enabled technique of direct marketing.

As R. Kenneth Godwin shows in Chapter 14, interest group membership, leadership, and tactics have all been changed by the direct-marketing technology. The new media is most effective when used to put pressure on political leaders by arousing the public. Although grassroots mobilization has long been a staple of American politics, "the generic properties of the new media—their speed, reach, targeting capacity, and two-way channels of communications—are allowing lobbyists to mobilize their reserve troops as never before" (Abramson et al. 1988:128). Lobbying and consulting firms have sprung up around the Washington beltway selling their skills at using phone banks, computer-aided targeting strategies, and direct-mail techniques to manufacture and channel public support when needed by a client interest group (see Cooper 1985:2036). Almost on demand, these firms can generate thousands of mailgrams from interested citizens to a member of the House or Senate or to the president, supporting or opposing nearly any policy issue.[48]

The new communications media has also been used to influence legislators directly through video distribution techniques and to gather and distribute political intelligence to subscribers through on-line data services such as Legi-Slate, owned by the *Washington Post*, and Washington Alert Service, owned by the *Congressional Quarterly* (see Abramson et al. 1988:127). The new communications technologies have facilitated the presence of interest groups in the policymaking process by making group formation and maintenance easier and by providing effective new ways of promoting their political and programmatic goals.

As I mentioned at the beginning of this section, the decline of political parties is a frequently cited explanation for the rise of special interest groups. Historians attribute the growth of interest group politics in the 1920s to the success of antiparty Progressive reforms (Silbey 1990; Rodgers 1987). Similarly, studies of state interest groups show an inverse relationship between the strength of the party system and the strength of the interest group system (see Thomas and Hrebenar, Chapter 7). California, a state with a notoriously weak party system, also has one of the strongest interest group systems in the nation.

Many scholars view parties and interest groups as organizations in competition for the attention and resources of citizens.[49] "Where political parties are strong, interest groups are likely to be weak. As parties decline in strength, interest groups are likely to become more powerful" (James Q. Wilson, quoted in Etzioni 1984:271).[50] There is no need to belabor the well-documented decline of American political parties.[51] As parties have become less relevant to Americans since the 1960s, they have lost their ability to mobilize citizens. Although parties as organizations may be on the rebound, there is little evidence to suggest that parties in the electorate are gaining in strength. As the salience of political parties in the electorate has declined, "group identifications have become increasingly important to voters as alternative political reference points" (Wattenberg 1990:156).

Indeed "a 1983 Gallup poll found that nearly half the population (45 percent) saw interest groups as best representing the respondent's political needs, compared to only about a third (34 percent) who believed that either of the parties did so" (Sabato 1988:177). As long as "candidate-centered" campaigns and politics in America keep the parties in the electorate weak, interest groups in the capital will likely remain strong.[52]

Organization may also be its own cause, or, to put it another way, mobilization begets countermobilization.[53] Perhaps this is a truism with little authentic explanatory power, especially because there has not been a steady linear growth of interest groups either during the past twenty years or during the previous seventy-five. Growth comes in spurts, some larger than others. When it comes to explaining why business mobilized during the late 1970s and early 1980s, however, this proposition has considerable explanatory power. Business leaders advocated the political mobilization of business not only as a response to the growth of government regulations but also as a reaction to the rise of public interest and citizen groups. Murray Weidenbaum's (1981:329) explanation for the mobilization of business reads like a call to action:

> The rising impact of government regulatory activities on business decision making is resulting in renewed interest by business executives in participating directly in the political process. The substantial political role of other interest groups, such as labor and agriculture, and the antibusiness orientation of many political activists working under the banner of the public interest, continue to encourage business people to enter the political arena more actively.

This account is also consistent with the idea that interest group politics moves in a cycle, with the success of one cycle ensuring the arrival of the next in response.

Finally, the growing frustration and alienation of the American public seems certain to be related to the changes in the interest group system. The electoral demobilization of the American public has not meant the demobilization of interests. Rather, it means that in this postelectoral era Americans are much less likely to pursue or express their interests through the election of political representatives.[54] Instead, they turn to the interest group system to provide representation and satisfaction for their interests. The continuing failure of the American electoral system to incorporate and mobilize citizens may turn into a permanent boon for the appeal of interest groups across the entire political spectrum.

CONCLUSION

Interest groups are an essential part of the American political landscape and have dominated political scientists' analysis of political life in the

United States for decades. Since 1970 change and continuity have fairly characterized the American interest group system. Americans remain suspicious and optimistic about the role of interest groups in American democracy, torn between fear of factional mischief and faith in their indispensability. There are many more interest groups today than there were twenty years ago, but this is not the first time that such a precipitous surge in their presence has occurred. Membership groups and institutional representatives are now abundant in Washington and throughout many state capitals. They are a diverse lot in terms of the interests they represent—traditional interests such as business, labor, and agriculture along with new constellations of citizen, intergovernmental, single-issue, and foreign interest groups and representatives.

They are also diverse in terms of how they accomplish their representational tasks. The expanded breadth of interest group activity has been impressive, ranging from the refinement of traditional approaches to inside lobbying, to new outside strategies of political mobilization designed to protect, promote, and enhance their political and policy aims. In the current array of interest group pursuits, grassroots lobbying to influence legislative elections and decisionmaking has joined conventional interest group efforts to provide information and expertise to government officials: Interest groups now spend at least as much time keeping informed about the world of public policy as they once did trying to influence it.

There are many reasons for these changes, many related to the development of American politics generally during the past twenty years: new resources for the mobilization and maintenance of groups, governmental stimuli to group mobilization and activity, changes in the structure of Congress, the development of new communications technologies, the continued decline of political parties, and the demobilization of the American electorate.

Changes in the interest group system helped to stimulate the scholarly rediscovery of interest group research. After a fifteen-year hiatus, a surge of new empirical studies of interest groups has transformed our knowledge of the system. Laments about the state of interest group research have been ameliorated by studies focusing on a wide variety of questions: Who joins, who is represented, how groups are formed and maintained, what groups do, who has power among Washington interest representatives, who works with whom, and when groups are most (and least) influential are just some of the questions this new research addresses.

The chapters that follow continue to document, test, investigate, and critique these and other issues. They contribute to a more detailed, rigorous, and empirical understanding of a feature central to the heart of American politics: the politics of interests.

NOTES

1. I admit that I risk the scorn of other scholars by opening a volume on interest groups with Paine instead of Madison. In my defense, Paine was a major influence on the American Revolution. But more important for students of interests and interest groups, Paine understood that a republic could not flourish unless its "citizens are sufficiently virtuous and public-spirited to sacrifice their own interests for the good of the community" (Philp 1989:37–38). For similar expressions among contemporary analysts, see Mansbridge 1990, Bellah et al. 1985, and Macedo 1990.

2. William Leggett, "Associated Effort," *Plaindealer*, December 10, 1836, reprinted in Blau (1954:82).

3. In John C. Calhoun, *A Disquisition on Government and Selections from the Discourse,* edited by C. Gordon Post (New York: Liberal Arts Press, 1953), 37.

4. Throughout this chapter I employ the phrase *interest group system* in a way compatible with Harry Eckstein's (1960:151) definition of the "pressure group system" as "an ordered pattern of relations" within a larger system, such as the political or social system, in which the elements of that system impinge upon the activities of interest groups and the activities of interest groups upon the elements of the larger (in this case) political system.

5. See Greenstone 1975; Garson 1978. Additional background on the state of interest group research can be found in my Appendix to this volume.

6. Despite contemporary usage, Bentley's "group" is a term far broader than the rather narrow connotation of an interest or pressure group.

7. See Laski 1921.

8. See Beard 1947, Odegard 1928, Herring 1929a, and Logan 1929.

9. See Schattschneider 1935, Herring 1936, Zeller 1937, Crawford 1939, and Dillon 1942.

10. One might even go so far as to suggest that for a generation or two of American political scientists it became ideology. The pluralist tradition has been well documented in Greenstone 1975, Polsby 1980, Ricci 1984, and Dahl 1989.

11. A different reading of Madison, with very different implications for the theory of interest groups in the United States, is provided in Sunstein 1985.

12. The last book I have been able to find with the term *pressure group* in the title was published in 1967 (see Mahood 1967). Although the phrase is frequently used in discussions of historical research, it is seldom used in contemporary scholarship.

13. The former is a quote from Senator T. R. Caraway (D–Ark.) cited in McKee 1929:350 and the latter is from Chase 1945.

14. An older version of this definitional approach with more detail is provided by Mary E. Dillion (1942:472): "A pressure group is a non-partisan organization of a segment of the people formed to exert influence upon the legislature, the executive, or other governmental agency through public opinion for the enactment or the rejection of certain legislation, or for the adoption, modification, or discontinuance of a public policy."

15. The term *state* is used instead of *government* to account for a broader range of potential interest group targets. For intellectual and professional definitions of the state, see Skinner 1989 and Rodgers 1987, respectively.

16. See Milbrath 1965; Verba and Nie 1972.

17. It's also possible that either Rodgers or Herring is mistaken.

18. On the calls for business mobilization, see Plotke's Chapter 8 as well as writing from the period: Ehrbar 1978; Gray 1978a and 1978b; Guzzardi 1978 and 1980; Kroger 1978a and 1978b; Levitt 1980; *Nation's Business* 1978; Pearson 1979; Schwartz 1981; Seligman 1979 and 1980; and Weidenbaum 1981.

19. See Sheppard 1985, Etzioni 1984, Stern 1988, and H. Smith 1989.

20. These and other academic authorities are certainly most aware of such limitations.

21. This is not to suggest that there are no differences, only that general assessments of the American interest group system from one era to the other are remarkably similar.

22. Drucker 1989:102.

23. Crawford 1939:3.

24. Mahood 1967:295–296.

25. Berry 1989b:244.

26. Croly 1915:317.

27. Pollock 1927:336.

28. Turner 1958:63.

29. Ginsberg and Shefter 1990:177-178.

30. The recent explosion of interest group advocacy has not been limited to the United States. In Great Britain (Doig 1986; Grant 1983; Jordan 1985), Canada (Duchesne and Ducasse 1984-1985; Jacek 1986), and France (Keeler 1985), among other nations, interest group activity is on the rise, as are expected concerns about its effects on representation and governability (see Black and Burke 1983; Wilson 1990b).

31. Institutional representation "intensifies the fragmenting, disaggregating tendencies in public policy," "may be expected to be far more durable and persistent in policymaking circles than most purposive groups or even membership groups," is more pragmatic than purposive groups, and is far more responsible for the oft-noted conservative bias of the interest group system than are membership interest groups (see Salisbury 1984:75).

32. The mobilization of business in the United States may still be far less than that in many Western European countries. See Wilson 1985a.

33. A list of these former federal employees, their new foreign clients, and fees is available as appendix A in Choate 1990.

34. The importance of lobbying at the state level for the insurance industry is explained in "Why the Democratic Process Cannot Function without Lobbying," *Journal of American Insurance*, no. 3, 1984:1–4.

35. There is almost no systematic data on the proliferation of interest groups at the local level. However, some studies point to a growing relevance of interest groups on local decisionmaking and their impact on city councils (see Abney and Lauth 1985 and Galaskiewicz 1981).

36. The literature on iron triangles and subgovernments is a staple of American political science. For excellent overviews of this area, see Dodd and Schott 1979, Jordan 1981, Adams 1982, Hamm 1983, McCool 1989, and Berry 1989b.

37. These explanations are derived from King 1978, Gais et al. 1984, Berry 1989b, Fiorina 1989, Peterson 1990b, and Heinz et al. 1990.

38. Bryce (1910) discusses the professionalization of interest groups; Turner (1958) the use of "new" media technology by groups; Odegard (1930) the importance of grassroots lobbying; Childs (1938) the increasing attention given to the executive branch by interest groups; and Lowell (1913), McKee (1929), and Kent (1938) the growing presence of groups active in the electoral process. For general overviews of interest group activity, see Logan 1929, Childs 1938, Finer 1949, Penniman 1952, and Key 1958.

39. In the section on "Explanations" in this chapter, I discuss new communications technologies as a factor in the advocacy explosion; see also Godwin, Chapter 14.

40. See Schlozman and Tierney 1986 and Chapter 7.

41. The distinction between inside and outside lobbying is also made in Salisbury 1990.

42. This data was gathered from Sorauf 1988, Magleby and Nelson 1990, and Alexander 1990, which are also among the best treatments of the role of money in American politics and political action committees.

43. Other examples can be found in Edsall 1984, Green and Buchsbaum 1980, Galvin 1987, and Keller 1981.

44. The development of such theories—with historical and cross-national applications—constitutes one of the most important challenges to the future of interest group studies. With many changes taking place in the interest group systems of other representative democracies, the time is ripe to expand such cross-national studies. See note 30 above.

45. Congress is also often in the business of funding new interest groups. See Bennett and DiLorenzo 1987.

46. Thorough and informative accounts of these changes are provided by Dodd and Oppenheimer 1981; Schlozman and Tierney 1986; Sheppard 1985; and Shepsle 1989.

47. The best account of these changes and their impact on American politics is Abramson et al. 1988, from which my account draws heavily.

48. Numerous examples are provided in Godwin 1988a.

49. Also consider Price 1968 and Dahl 1982 and compare to Lane 1949, who views the lobby and party as "sister agents of representation." Likewise, Mark A. Peterson (1990b and Chapter 10) argues that the threat to parties from interest groups is exaggerated.

50. Compare with Polsby (1981-1982:560), who argues that interest groups are at once the cause and consequence of party decline.

51. This literature is well reviewed in Maisel 1990.

52. The phrase "candidate-centered" campaigns and politics originates with Sorauf (1964:108) and has been used frequently during the last two decades to describe the movement of candidate campaigns away from the control of political parties. See Orren and Mayer 1990 and Herrnson 1990.

53. See Key 1958. A similar argument about the escalation of lobbying activities is in Logan 1929 and Milbrath 1963.

54. The pattern of "post-electoral politics" is detailed in Ginsberg and Shefter 1990.

2

A Deliberative Theory
of Interest Representation

JANE J. MANSBRIDGE

Interest groups function both to pressure and to persuade. Yet most Americans, including political scientists and members of the public alike, see politics largely if not exclusively as the exercise of power, ignoring the way politics can also change people's preferences and help them create new options. Having conceived politics to mean power, we also tend to see interest groups only as seeking benefits for their members, in a zero-sum or fixed-pie world in which a benefit for one must harm another. This view ignores the long tradition of research on how interest groups generate information of value to legislators, as well as more recent research on how interest groups provide forums for deliberation that shape their members' preferences.

In this chapter I argue that interest groups contribute to deliberative processes by bringing to bear additional information and new perspectives—thus by changing preferences rather than simply by exerting pressure or adding a new force to the search for an equilibrium among interests. I look first at how the deliberative function of interest groups fits into a normative theory of democracy, then at three ways empirical political scientists have recently described that deliberative function, and, finally, at suggestions for reform of the system by which we represent interests. I argue that these suggestions follow the implicit maxim "Maximize deliberative benefits; minimize rent-seeking costs."

INTEREST GROUPS IN NORMATIVE DEMOCRATIC THEORY

The Theory of Adversary Democracy

Modern Western democracy, based on decisions according to the equation of one person/one vote and the assumption of conflicting interests, differs in its essential conception from earlier or non-Western democracies based on the search for a common good. In ancient Greece, where majority rule emerged, and in the Middle Ages, when the practice was preserved in church councils, majority rule was apparently considered no more than a time-saving substitute for reaching a consensus on the public good, on the grounds that when people disagreed, the larger number was more likely than the smaller number to be right. Mid-seventeenth-century England saw the beginning of a significant change in the understanding of majority rule, as it evolved from a rough measure of the common good to a procedure for settling disputes authoritatively when citizens had fundamentally conflicting interests. In the twenty years from 1640 to 1660, the English Parliament rapidly began to forgo its traditional search for consensus and make more (by 1646 more than half) of its decisions by majority rule. In the same few years, deputies to Parliament began to compete regularly in contested elections rather than being chosen by "selection." The word *party* began to lose its negative connotations of faction—a process that would take two more centuries to complete. In this critical period in seventeenth-century England, leading thinkers argued that prosperity and civil peace depended on accepting as inevitable conflicting economic interests and conflicting religious convictions.

Modern majority rule was thus born in an era that was slowly giving up the ideal of one right answer—the one just price, the one true God, or the one best course for the ship of state—and settling for permanent but peaceful conflict over prices, religion, and public policy. The legitimacy of one-person/one-vote solutions rests in part on abdicating substantive political ideals for the procedural ideal that when politics is no more than a matter of conflicting wills and interests, each individual should count for one and none for more than one. The legitimacy of such solutions also rests on accepting as legitimate the coercive power of some over others.

Almost all practicing democracies since the seventeenth century have been *mixed democracies.* They have combined the substantive search for a solution best for the public as a whole with the procedural recourse to counting individual wills. The mix they have chosen has depended on two factors: the degree of congruence of underlying interests on a given issue (or an expected collection of issues) and the extent to which political actors believe that deliberation can help them understand their conflicts rightly or transform those conflicts to create a public good. In the United States after World War II, both descriptive and normative democratic theory began to deviate from the everyday practice of democracy and focus on the counting of individual preferences, deemphasizing the role of deliberation in promoting the common good. The new theory of *adversary democracy* derived both from a growing skepticism among political scientists about the possibility of any public interest in the nation as a whole[1] and from the increasing legitimacy of self-interest in politics.

I have argued elsewhere that adversary democracy, which accepts fundamental conflict as inevitable, derives a central part of its normative legitimacy from the mandate to give to each citizen as close as possible to equal power over the outcome (Mansbridge [1980]1983). If votes are weighed equally, the result is legitimate. Conversely, unequal votes, or unequal power, can be legitimated only by common interest. The strongest democratic arguments for unequal power focus on the need for leadership. From Plato's guardians to Lenin's vanguard, from the captain of the ship of state through the doctor with his patient, unequal power relationships have been sanctioned by appeals to common interest. If you and I both need to get to Boston, I can fall asleep in the back seat and let you drive, giving you all the power, because our interests are the same. I need not pay the price in inefficiency of equalizing our power because I know with reasonable certainty that you will not turn around and drive to Chattanooga. When interests conflict, adversary democracy—the unspoken normative theory behind many descriptive analyses of democratic pluralism—has a hidden radical edge: It is normatively satisfied only if the democratic process represents each citizen equally.[2]

Normative Justifications for Interest Groups

If there is no public interest, it is not easy to make a normative case for interest groups within the framework of a democracy that legitimates decisions by weighting each citizen's preference equally. The presumed purpose of interest groups, after all, is to apply unequal pressure.

What are the normative arguments for interest groups? Inequalities of power exerted through interest groups reflect, in part, differences in intensity of feeling. The normative mandate of utilitarianism, to produce the greatest pleasure for the greatest number, assumes that individuals who feel intensely experience more pleasure in having their preferences prevail than those who feel less intensely and suggests as a consequence that those who feel more intensely should have more power. Thus even when interest groups lead to inequalities in power, these inequalities could be justified if interest groups were devices for measuring intensity of feeling. Yet even granting the persuasiveness of the claim that greater intensity legitimates greater power, small corrections for differences in individual intensity could not plausibly legitimate the large inequalities in political power that interest groups presently produce in American politics.[3]

Defenders of American interest groups therefore use two other arguments to legitimate such groups. Their most common line of reasoning, which has great resonance in a polity heavily committed to liberty, implies that interest groups are a product of the "right" of free association and must therefore be protected from interference, or possibly even regulation. Many writers in this tradition cite Madison's comment in the *Federalist* 10 that restricting liberty in order to control faction creates a remedy worse than the disease. Defenders of interest groups also portray these groups primarily as bottom-up, citizen-initiated phenomena, part of the voluntary process of people's coming together to govern themselves.

In this chapter I do not focus on defenses of interest groups that base their case on liberty. The argument for *pure* laissez-faire works no better in the modern polity than in the modern economy. A laissez-faire economy inevitably creates monopolies and oligopolies, whose immense power must be regulated to limit intolerable distortions of the market. Similarly, in today's polity, the most powerful organized interests often look no more like the textbook citizen-initiated voluntary associations than General Motors looks like a ma-and-pa store. I believe a strong case can be made that the oligopolistic power of certain interest groups must be regulated to prevent distortions of the legislative process. But I only begin to develop that case here.

Instead, I focus on the other, second most common justification for interest groups, namely, that they provide lawmakers with important information otherwise not available. This justification, made in almost every major, American government introductory textbook from 1970 to 1990, highlights the importance of deliberation. It points to a process in which decisionmakers, including citizens and their representatives, use the information and insights that interest groups feed into the deliberative process to decide what is best for them individually and narrowly, what is best for the larger groups of which they are a part, what is best for the nation as a whole, and, on the basis of all these considerations, how they want the polity to act.

The Meaning *of* Deliberation

The process of deliberation may be summarized as a "probing of volitions" (Lindblom 1990). Inquiring into what one wants, individually and as part of a larger whole, requires both factual and emotional information, both surveying (within limits) the information and perspectives available and probing one's own "reactions of love, hate, revulsion, sympathy, admiration or horror" (Lindblom 1990:32; also Barber 1984:174). Citizens and representatives engage in both emotional and rational processes as they watch ads on television, see and hear dramatic evocations of their own and others' lives, read direct mail, and talk with friends and colleagues, forming and reforming their conceptions of their own good, the good of groups to which they belong, and the good of the larger polity.

Advertising and other forms of one-way persuasion figure in deliberation conceived as a broad and ongoing process of probing volitions.

Deliberation should illuminate both conflict and commonality. When interests conflict in important ways, deliberation can and should lead those affected by a decision to recognize and understand the character of their conflicts. At this stage, remaining within the framework of conflicting interests and coercion, the interest bargaining that takes over from deliberation can range between two endpoints. At one end, in a purely laissez-faire coercive setting, each group marshals the resources available to it and tries either to subdue the other entirely or to achieve a compromise based on comparative potential coercion. In this compromise the amount that each party concedes to the other depends on its ability to inflict harm on the other parties by withdrawing from the bargaining session (market power). At the other end of the spectrum, in a democratically coercive setting, adversary democracy mandates settling conflicts on the basis of one-person/one-vote procedures.[4] When the state becomes involved in coercive bargaining of this sort, it usually tries to dilute market power by introducing procedures that come closer to resolving conflict on the basis of one person/one vote.

But interests do not always conflict. When interests coincide or can be made to coincide, deliberation should lead individuals to recognize the interests they have in common, the ways they can make the interests of others their own, and the circumstances in which they should give moral priority to what is good for others or for the polity as a whole. Deliberation involves changing preferences. It may even involve changing character. After absorbing new insights and information and after experiencing new ways of feeling, citizens and representatives may be expected to change their minds about what ought to be done. They may decide that what they previously thought were common interests masked conflicts or that commonality can be created where earlier it had seemed impossible. A process of deliberation can also, over time, shape the character of those who engage in it, teaching them the habits of recognizing conflicts of interest or of creating commonality.

Deliberation can involve self-interest and altruism. Altruism in turn derives from both empathy and commitment to principle.[5] The deliberative process is not neutral between self-interest and altruism. The presence of others encourages "we" rather than "I" thinking, although the "we" may be a subgroup whose interests conflict with those of others in the larger polity. When a society seeks to discourage individual self-interest and encourage altruism, deliberation in public will often serve that end. When, as is often the case, the more powerful groups in a society dominate public discourse, individuals and groups whose interests and identities are subordinated need to form oppositional deliberative enclaves to work out their own conceptions of their interests.

Although deliberation should help people understand commonality and conflict, in practice polities develop cultures that make one or another outcome more likely. In general, polities whose members expect interests to conflict on most issues do not invest much time or effort in deliberation, preferring to shorten their investment in talk and thought by proceeding directly to a vote that produces an authoritative decision. Such polities develop a culture that sees preferences as fixed and politics as a matter of conflict and power. In contrast, polities whose members expect common interests on many issues are likely to invest time in deliberation, believing that their talk and thought will usually produce a better decision for all. Such polities develop a culture that sees preferences as open to change and politics as a matter of potential commonality, persuasion, and deliberation on the merits. Put into practice, these differences in culture tend to mean that the expectation of generating solutions better for all is associated with an emphasis on deliberation, whereas the expectation of conflict is associated with strategies for amassing and exercising power.

Much of American political science has been written from within an adversary political culture. Interest groups, consequently, have been conceived primarily as vehicles for pursuing conflict and power. This reasonable conception captures the primary goal of many interest groups, which are deliberately organized to act as rent-seekers. By *rent-seeking* I mean that they use the unequal power they derive from their organizations and funding to wrest from the public treasury, or with the public police power, benefits (or rent) for their officers, staff, and members.[6] In these instances the interest groups use what one might call power (threats of sanction or force that are not in someone else's interests) instead of what one might call influence (persuasion that is in someone else's interests).[7]

Such rent-seeking involves transfers of resources in a zero-sum world: Whatever I get must be taken from someone else. But the world is not always zero-sum. Interest groups can also be economically and socially productive, making politics a positive-sum game. By changing preferences, deliberation often makes possible solutions that were impossible before the process began. For democrats interested in holding interest groups to a normative democratic standard, the problem is how to get as many deliberative gains as possible with as few rent-seeking costs.

THREE EMPIRICAL MODELS
OF INTEREST GROUP DELIBERATION

Deliberation is a dynamic process, often requiring a change in preferences. Yet most textbook descriptions of interest groups assume fixed preferences. A useful taxonomy of the ways interest groups contribute to public deliberation must consider both situations in which preferences are fixed and those in which they change in various ways. The common American model, which I will call the *competitive* model, usually involves fixed preferences among interest group members. What I will call the *collaborative* model involves preference changes among interest group elites. What has usually been called the *corporatist* model institutionalizes preference change among elites. This model has a democratic variant, promoted by Claus Offe and others (see Offe and Wiesenthal 1980; Offe and Preuss 1991), addressing processes that change preferences among the rank and file. But none of these models pays sufficient attention to the processes of preference change. Attention to these processes would require describing, and incorporating into the model, preference change among the public and their elected representatives prompted by the information and insight that interest groups generate, preference change among interest group elites in the course of their deliberations and negotiations with one another, preference change among the interest group members, and, finally, reciprocal preference change, incorporating the ways interest group representatives and those they represent exchange the information and perceptions necessary to change their minds on policy that affects them.

Competitive Deliberation

In *On Liberty*, J. S. Mill proposed what others have called the "adversary theory of truth." This theory sees the world as a deliberative stage on which opinions of every sort compete for support. Although obfuscation or falsehood often reigns,[8] truth is most likely to prevail when opinions are free to gain adherents through competition.

The standard interpretation of interest groups' information function follows this model. Interest groups on both sides of an issue collect facts and present their most persuasive arguments; the arguments of one side spur the other to find new evidence and refine its persuasive position. Citizens and their representatives use the information so generated to decide on public policy. Just as lawyers compete before a jury in the Anglo-American system of justice, so interest groups compete before the public and its representatives. Both cases implicitly assume the existence of a truth (or a good public policy), the system being designed to elicit the best result through a competition constrained by rules of fair play.

Although information is most likely to get a hearing when it confirms what policymakers already "know," new facts and new perspectives can change both elite and public debate. For example, in the midst of a wave of public concern for the effect of crime on the elderly, a national victimization survey discovered that the elderly were among the least likely to suffer from crime. This new fact led congressional committees on the aging to stop promoting programs directed specifically to crime against the elderly (Cook and Skogan 1990). Similarly, in congressional deliberation on deregulation, studies showing that deregulated airlines had not on the average reduced their service to small airports answered one of the major objections of congressional skeptics and reduced their opposition to the measure (Derthick and Quirk 1985:125–130). When Citizens for Tax Justice, a group supported by organized labor, demonstrated that 73 percent of the largest 250 corporations paid no taxes at all in at least one of the years between 1981 and 1983, this evidence helped build political support for subsequent corporate tax increases (Berry 1989a:106).

The competitive model, in which interest groups marshal evidence and persuasive arguments for the external public and policymakers, does not require internal preference change among the interest group members. Nor need the groups involved in persuasion be "public interest" groups. As in the economic market, purely self-interested motivation provides sufficient incentive for each interest to invest in collecting and disseminating the information that best makes its case. The competitive model of deliberative democracy does, however, implicitly require some public-spirited motivation among at least some policymakers and public. Some group must act as the "jury," using the information and arguments that the interest groups provide to weigh the costs and benefits of a policy to the public as a whole. The model requires what is in fact the case, namely, that both citizens and their representatives can be influenced by arguments about what is in the public interest.[9]

Collaborative Deliberation

In the last several years, political scientists have begun to notice the effects within the interest group structure of what Hugh Heclo (1978:87–124) called "issue networks." An issue network is "a shared-knowledge group having to do with some aspect (or, as defined by the network, some problem) of public policy." In these issue networks the members, who often disagree with one another on policy matters, usually affect one another through what I have called influence rather than power. As Heclo describes the members of these networks,

Any direct material interest is often secondary to intellectual or emotional commitment. . . . The price of buying into one or another issue network is watching, reading, talking about, and trying to act on particular policy problems. . . . the true experts in the networks are those who are issue-skilled (that is, well informed about the ins and outs of a particular policy debate) regardless of formal professional training. . . . instead of power commensurate with responsibility, issue networks seek influence commensurate with their understanding of the various, complex social choices being made. . . . Increasingly, it is through networks of people who regard each other as knowledgeable, or at least as needing to be answered, that public policy issues tend to be refined, evidence debated, and alternative opinions. worked out—though rarely in any controlled, well-organized way. (1978:102–104)

Some members of these elite issue networks are members of administrative agencies; some are staff to members of Congress or a congressional committee; some work for foundations; some are academics with a policy specialty. Some work for interest groups. Many influential members of the various issue networks are staff or officers of public interest groups. But even within "private interest" groups, the staff and officers may worry about the public interest as well. The social worker who directs legislative affairs for the Illinois Association of Social Workers knows that her job is mostly to increase benefits for social workers. But because cutbacks in government spending directly affect social workers and because she personally is committed to helping the disadvantaged, her motivations are mixed. One such legislative affairs specialist told me that in her estimate all the people with whom she had worked in "anti-Reaganomics" coalitions in the state had some personal commitment beyond their jobs, to a larger progressive politics: "Some are professional activists, and they can't just do volunteer work all their lives, so they get into these jobs" as staff for public or private interest groups whose views they share.[10]

Heclo (1978:107) points out that issue networks share information about people as well as policy problems. A network member's reputation depends on the assessment of the other members, who often have different jobs with nominally different interests. Members of these networks thus often behave as if they were accountable not only to the external interests they represent but to one another, giving other members the power to reward and punish their behavior (Meidinger 1987).

The large literature on coalitions among interest groups emphasizes elites, not only within groups that specifically represent the public interest but also within more narrowly self-interested groups. Interaction with other elite members of the issue network can change these members' preferences for themselves as well as their conceptions of what is best for the public. As these elites interact, they come to speak among themselves a language of the public interest. They often believe, or can come to believe, that they are acting in the public interest, even when an outside observer might see their beliefs as rationalizations for their own self-interest or the self-interest of the groups they represent. Although great harm can be done in any negotiation or democratic process by the parties not recognizing their own self-interest in a policy, that interest group elites often think in terms of the public interest also has obvious benefits.

Many researchers have explored the differences between elite and membership preferences in interest organizations,[11] sometimes beginning to parse the effects of these differences on internal and external deliberation. In the next section I turn to ways that institutionalizing the relations between interest groups and the state draws attention to preference change among elites, among members, and in the interaction between elites and members.

Corporatist Deliberation

Besides using arguments based on liberty and information, writers on American government sometimes justify interest groups with arguments based on representation. As long ago as 1929, E. Pendleton Herring wrote that because representation based on territory is inadequate, citizens want and need interest groups to provide a "rudimentary form of functional representation" (1929b:493). I use the word *corporatist* to describe this understanding of interest groups, which values them as institutional mechanisms for representing interests that are not well represented in territorial elections. I focus on the corporatist idea that such interest groups can, by negotiating and deliberating, achieve outcomes superior to those achievable in a laissez-faire market or a majoritarian democratic process.

Traditional corporatist arrangements link interest groups directly with state lawmaking and law-enforcing processes. By giving some groups privileged access to decisionmaking, they exclude others more or less permanently and rigidify the system of interest representation. To deal with this problem, Philippe Schmitter (1988:38–50) has proposed allowing all sorts of interest groups to take on semipublic status. These semipublic groups would be publicly financed, with each citizen dividing a fixed amount of money among the interest organizations of his or her choice. In return, these interest associations would agree to a charter guaranteeing democratic rights for their members. Public policy affecting the interests that a group represented would then be made in consultation with that group. The voucher system would allow each citizen to distribute his or her money to as many or as few associations as desired.

Congress is unlikely to adopt a scheme with so few roots in the traditional way of doing things in the United States. Yet Schmitter's proposal has heuristic value in demonstrating that corporatist arrangements need not entail the rigid privileging of some groups above others. Much recent corporatist thinking is, indeed, a reaction against existing inequalities in the processes of negotiation and deliberation within and between groups. Such thinking seeks state intervention partly to make the parties in those deliberations more equal.

A corporatist system can be nothing more than a series of conduits through which representatives bring into the policy arena their constituents' previously existing preferences and negotiate compromises with groups that have conflicting interests.[12] But in more recent deliberative models of corporatist representation, "negotiation" includes changing preferences as well as aggregating them (Offe and Wiesenthal 1980; Schmitter 1988; Cohen and Rogers 1989). As I use the word, *negotiation* denotes a mix of power and influence. It stands between pure conflict, based only on power (the threat of sanction or force), and pure persuasion, based only on influence.[13] In negotiation, the parties involved not only maneuver for advantageous positions, as they do in conflict; they also try to understand what the other really wants, in order, for example, to offer what may be a cheaper satisfaction of that want than what the other is demanding. The quest for understanding requires asking and listening, correctly interpreting the other's language and putting oneself in the other's place. It requires making suggestions that the other may not have thought of, and learning from both acceptance and refusal. When negotiators engage in this quest for understanding, they can use the understanding so gained to change the other's preferences. They can help others discover what they really want, creating new preferences that better reflect the others' needs or values. They can even help others develop new values. Successful negotiations in the real world rarely rely on mere jockeying for advantage in the conflict. Successful negotiators often find ways of meeting one another's real needs at less cost than seemed originally required.[14]

A full understanding of deliberation must include negotiation both among and within interest groups. Traditional corporatist models focus on external negotiation, in which the leaders of interest groups established to represent their members' interests negotiate with one another to reach agreements that are then adopted by the state as law. More recent democratic corporatist models add internal negotiation, in which leaders also negotiate with members of their interest groups to reach agreements the members can accept as binding.

Negotiation Among Groups in the United States: Elements of Traditional Corporatism. In the executive branch of the U.S. government, administrative agencies have for a long time consulted affected interests regularly. Many observers believe this process results in private interest groups' "capturing" the relevant agency (e.g., Stigler 1971). In the 1970s, however, Congress and the federal courts began to require federal agencies to admit conflicting interests into the deliberative process. The new requirements permitted the inclusion of interest groups that had traditionally been ignored, either because they were small or because their interests were diffuse. Such incremental developments, which often came as decisions handed down by judges, led Richard Stewart in 1975 to conclude that American administrative law was undergoing a "fundamental transformation" into "a model of interest representation" (Stewart 1975:1669,

1723). The new model, which included material and occasionally ideological interests, required "participation rights" and "adequate consideration" for the interested parties through the formal participation of interest groups in decisions by agencies in the executive branch (Stewart 1975:1748, 1756). As the courts began to call for such arrangements, it became less necessary for them to invoke the constitutional prohibition on delegating legislative authority established in the 1930s.[15] Although many of these requirements were underenforced or even repealed in the Reagan era,[16] their introduction suggests a growing concern with deliberative inequalities in interest representation.

Congress also occasionally relies on agreements negotiated among opposing interest groups. For more than two decades, for example, Congress worked on the copyright law of 1978 but could not resolve several important issues, including photocopying. The Association of American Publishers and the Authors League of America lobbied Congress to institute strict provisions against photocopying, while the Ad Hoc Committee of Educational Institutions and Organizations on Copyright Law Revision had lobbied equally vehemently on the other side. Finally, with the blessing of Congress, the major opposing interest groups and their lawyers independently worked out their own compromise, embodied in a formal "Agreement on Guidelines," signed by representatives of the three groups. Passing the copyright law, Congress took no official position on what would constitute the legally prescribed "fair use" in copying but commented through the relevant committee report, "This committee believes the Guidelines are a reasonable interpretation of the minimum standards for fair use."[17]

Short of such explicit arrangements for "lobby-made" law, interest groups often act through ad hoc coalitions, ongoing alliances, and peak associations to negotiate proposals that can then be presented to Congress as common demands. Pointing out that "most of the workload of Congress consists of legislation in which conflict is minimal," Costain and Costain (1981:258) argue "that prior resolution of conflict is occurring" through extensive external negotiations among interest groups.

The Democratic Corporatist Model: Negotiation Within Groups. Scholars who study the internal deliberations of interest groups in the United States generally describe them as "aggregating" existing preferences. This language downplays the potential for preference change. Although Costain and Costain (1981), for example, explicitly reject a view of interest groups as simply "interest articulators," their own "broader view" turns out to involve only recognizing "efforts by groups to reduce the range of alternatives on the legislative agenda and to mobilize support for preferred political positions" (251). Although they make a good empirical case for studying activity within interest groups in the United States, they repeatedly describe that activity simply as "reducing" the number and range of demands on the political system (255), "submerging disagreement" (257), "winnowing out options" (259), "screening out policies that divide" (260), and "reducing intergroup conflicts" (271).

Other scholars describe the internal activity of interest groups as distilling and ordering existing preferences both by encouraging their members to think about, talk about, and bring to conscious decision considerations on various sides of an issue, and through internal democratic processes, as constituents choose the policies that most attract them, either by voting on policies or leadership or, more informally, by joining or sending money to the organization that most appeals to them out of a range of competing groups. This process of distillation and ordering makes negotiation, and consequently legislation, more fruitful, as the interest group takes on the burden of letting the other parties in the negotiation know what its constituency, in its present state of consciousness, wants most.

Richard Freeman and James Medoff demonstrate that even American unions, hardly models of a developed deliberative ideal, provide a forum in which collective "voice" can instruct employers on workers' needs more efficiently than can worker "exit," a traditional market mechanism (Freeman and Medoff 1984, using the language of Hirschman 1970). Exit is often more costly for both worker and employer than collective voice. Moreover, voice can often produce more complete information and negotiation more creative solutions than can autonomous management decisionmaking. Union firms usually settle on a compensation package that weighs wages less heavily and working conditions or fringe benefits more heavily than nonunion firms do, in part because of the greater flow of information about worker desires in unionized firms. Concluding from their quantitative research that in the United States "unions are associated with greater efficiency in most settings," Freeman and Medoff attribute that result primarily to deliberative efficiencies.[18] Yet they summarize these productive internal activities with the static and aggregative formula: "Unions collect information about the preferences of all workers" (Freeman and Medoff 1984:13, table 1-1).

In 1963 Raymond Bauer, Ithiel de Sola Pool, and Lewis Anthony Dexter produced what has become a classic study of the interest groups involved in foreign trade. In their 1972 preface to the second edition, they criticized pluralists, antipluralists, and rational choice theorists for failing to see that "individual and group interests get grossly redefined by the operation of the social institutions through which they must work." "The heart of political analysis," they wrote, "is the discovery of [these] transformative processes" (1972:ix). They then, however, focused on what they called the "structural parameters" that "determined" how people saw their interests rather than on more interactive and open-ended deliberative processes.[19]

In 1969 Dexter described the interest representative in Washington as "the man in the middle," who must teach clients to "live with" the government and the society, help those clients balance and determine priorities among the opportunities and problems the government presents, and somehow handle working on occasion for the clients' "interests" rather than their "desires." Dexter thus pointed directly to the importance of deliberative processes within interest groups, without, however, elaborating on those processes.

More recently, Kay Schlozman and John Tierney (1986:134ff.) have documented the great amount of time most interest group elites spend on communicating with their members—warning them of upcoming developments, generating letters and other expressions of support, trying to convince them that some matters are more worthy of their attention than others, and, most importantly, "assisting members in understanding the complexities of Washington politics that render necessary accommodation and compromise in the face of competing demands made by public officials and other private interests" (145). They review the relatively widespread internal democracy within unions and note the extensive deliberative processes of the League of Women Voters.[20] They mention that the American Hospital Association has institutionalized mechanisms for articulating the interests of subgroups, pointing out that such mechanisms are rare. Their brief overview does not, however, examine how any existing internal deliberative processes actually work.

European corporatists have access, through the philosophical contributions of Jürgen Habermas (1975:107–108, 1979:186) and others, to a language of deliberation and changing preferences. Wolfgang Streck and Philippe Schmitter (1985:16) therefore write of "organizations as transforming agents of individual interests." They argue that existing organizational theory fails to adopt "a political concept of interest," which would reveal interest groups as "much more than passive recipients of preferences put forward by their constituents and clients": "Organized group interests are not given but emerge as a result of a multi-faceted interaction between social and organizational structure. . . . This interactive relationship is only partly described as one of organizational goal formation; at the same time it is one of collective identity formation . . . [in an] institutional context within which group interests and identities are defined and continuously revised" (Streck and Schmitter 1985:19). Given this nuanced description of the processes of identity change that can accompany group deliberation, it is puzzling that the empirical work Streck and Schmitter collect in their volume does not address either the presence or absence of these processes. And when Streck and Schmitter themselves describe the internal functions of interest groups, they do so narrowly, as "controlling the behavior of their members" and "offering . . . to deliver the compliance of their members." External negotiations, they conclude, must be kept "informal and secretive in an effort to insulate them as much as possible from . . . dissidents within the associational ranks."[21]

Offe and his colleagues (Offe and Wiesenthal 1980; Offe and Preuss 1991), however, develop a more democratic corporatist agenda, encouraging researchers to investigate what they call the "dialogical" processes within interest groups. Indeed, like other European theorists, Offe may be drawn to the study of internal deliberation precisely because tying interest groups to the state has had the effect, in Europe, of diminishing internal participation. Streck (1982:71) argues, in fact, that "a low degree of political participation by members is functional for unions participating in a liberal-corporatist system of interest intermediation." These organizations "have to be independent enough of their membership to be responsive not only to them but also to the demands of the community-at-large; to be in a position to recognize 'economic realities' and to view the interests they represent in a long-term rather than in a short-term perspective; and to be able to enforce whatever 'reasonable compromise' they arrive at against 'irresponsible' groups within their own ranks." Streck attributes to these functional necessities the observed professionalization, centralization, formalization, and elimination of decisionmaking on systemwide issues at the lowest level that has arisen or increased with greater interest group–state ties.

In short, although existing interest groups may not have developed many internal deliberative processes, normative democratic theory suggests that such processes are desirable. We need empirical research describing the processes of mutual consultation and deliberation within interest groups where they exist and reporting their absence elsewhere. Such research would indicate how representatives of interests influence one another outside the group, how (if at all) the rank and file influence one another within the group, and how (if at all) members and representatives engage in mutual influence.[22] It would ask how new patterns of interest fragmentation, interest coalition, and the growing importance of policy institutes and citizens' groups affect both external and internal deliberative processes. Robert Salisbury (1990), who documents these new patterns in the United States, suggests that in "today's world of complex, interdependent interests and policies, it is often quite unclear what the 'true interests' of a group or an institution may be. The policy that will be maximally advantageous to an association often cannot even be framed without prolonged and searching analysis involving extensive discussion."[23] These new conditions, he concludes, force lobbyists "to shift much of their energy away from lobbying, that is, away from advocating policies and influencing government officials. Before they can advocate a policy, they must determine what position they wish to embrace" (Salisbury 1990:225). Policy interests are thus "continuously constructed," in Laumann and Knoke's (1987) phrase.

It is not clear whether, as Salisbury implies, the deliberative function of interest groups has been growing over time. Nonetheless, attitudes toward the deliberative process in the discipline of political science are changing. Political scientists have long recognized the generation of information as a productive process. The transformation of preferences, perhaps toward a more inclusive or public-interested view, is now increasingly recognized as productive, too. Because these are the two main collective benefits of any system for representing interests, efforts at reforming that system should try to maximize the functions of informing and persuading while minimizing the costs of the system in "rents" paid to private groups.

MAXIMIZING DELIBERATION AND MINIMIZING RENT-SEEKING

In the United States today, interest groups represent the different interests in society unequally and often act as unproductive rent-seekers for their constituents. These defects are not immune to correction. Either Congress, the executive, or the courts could act to diminish inequalities and restrict rent-seeking, thus helping to facilitate productive deliberation among interest groups while minimizing the costs of this activity. I argue, indeed, that the mandate "Maximize deliberative benefits; minimize rent-seeking costs" lies behind, or should lie behind, all present suggestions for reforming the interest system in the United States.

Inequalities

When the deliberative process is heavily influenced by a laissez-faire market in interest representation, different interests have very unequal chances of having their voices heard. In the United States, huge disparities in political contributions mean that the interests of the rich are better articulated than those of the poor. Groups whose interests are intense and concentrated, like the potential beneficiaries of tariff protection on a particular product, are far more likely to be heard in the deliberative arena than groups whose interests are dispersed, like the consumers of that product. Because the members of groups with concentrated interests get a greater individual payoff from organization, they are more likely to pay the costs of organizing. Large groups, and groups whose members' needs are not easily quantifiable and negotiable, are much harder to organize.[24]

In the normative theory of adversary democracy, legitimate decisions can derive from summing conflicting preferences under the mandate that each citizen counts for one and none for more than one. Deliberative theory also provides two normative reasons for making the power of interests more nearly equal, but in this case the norm aims at equality among groups rather than among individuals.

First, effective deliberation requires that those with information the public should know have the minimum resources necessary to make their evidence and views heard. Depending on the context and the audience, that minimum may be high. In some contexts, how one's resources compare to those of the opposition determines whether one will be heard at all. When the public or its representatives have only a limited interest or time for a subject, relative resources may be what matter most. Those with many resources crowd out everyone else. When having any access at all depends on relative position, improving deliberation is likely to require some device for ensuring that conflicting perspectives get more nearly equal time.

Second, deliberative theorists may want to equalize power among groups in order to remove power per se from the deliberative arena. When opposing groups with equal power neutralize one another, they effectively create a situation in which neither side gets the other to do anything through threat of sanction or force. In an ideal situation of equal "power," only "influence" can prevail. Some such rationale probably lies behind the common American idea that in negotiating situations power ought to be divided fifty-fifty between business and labor. The individualist perspective of adversary democracy would require that labor, with its greater numbers, ought to have proportionately greater power. The perspective of the marketplace would let each side have as much power as its money, organizational resources, and structural position could command. But when each of two opposing sides has half the power, power per se is met by power, and the outcome is stalemate. In those circumstances, each side will be forced to put forth considerations designed to persuade the other. If all affected parties, including diffuse interests, are represented with equal power, the result of their deliberation, ideally, will be a policy that reflects the public interest.

Deliberative norms build in contest over the definition of relevant groups. The argument from discussion based on a variety of information suggests a cutoff in public support to groups who fall below some contested minimum. It also suggests a standard, "groups with relevant information the public should know," that is itself contested—but has not been impossible to enforce in applications of the fairness doctrine in broadcasting. The argument from discussion based on persuasion suggests another standard, "groups with important affected interests," whose content is again far from self-evident. Each deliberative reason for moving toward equality in group power defines a ground of contest.

Several recent suggestions for reforming the interest system in the United States focus on deliberative inequalities. Joshua Cohen and Joel Rogers's (1989) defense of contemporary corporatist thinking, for example, stresses the importance of including in negotiations the interests of unorganized groups and the public at large. They suggest that rather than ignoring the many formal ties that already exist in the United States between interest groups and all levels of government, thus ignoring the inequalities in representation built into those ties,[25] we should borrow from corporatist theory and practice to make moves toward equalizing power among competing interests a conscious goal of public policy.[26] Schmitter's (1988) voucher scheme, designed to be both open to new interests and responsive to a variety of citizen preferences, has the same aim.

Both the adversary reasons for equalizing individual power and the deliberative reasons for equalizing group power lie implicitly behind these corporatist thoughts and behind the many contemporary suggestions for restricting or eliminating political action committees, limiting political advertising, and providing public funding for electoral campaigns (e.g., Farber and Frickey 1987:912, 925). Such suggestions all assume that the state must involve itself in some way in associative arrangements—through the courts, executive administrative agencies, or Congress—to even out some of the inequalities that otherwise dominate the interest group market.

Rent-Seeking

Both judicial and corporatist scholars have suggested ways of limiting the tendency of interest groups to use the public treasury and public police power to benefit themselves at the expense of others. Cass Sunstein (1985) argues that in the system of checks and balances set up by the Constitution, the federal courts should check the excesses of private interest and "naked preference" that can tempt the legislative branch. If the courts were consciously to accept such a role, which in a traditional and unrecognized form they already play, they could develop existing "rationality review" and administrative law to serve as partial guarantors of the public interest.

Sunstein harks back to a civic republican tradition that animated both the Anti-Federalists and many writings of the Federalists. In that tradition,

The role of politics was above all deliberative. Dialogue and discussion among the citizenry were critical features in the governmental processes. . . . [This] conception carries with it a particular view of human nature; it assumes that through discussion people can, in their capacities as citizens, escape private interests and engage in pursuit of the public good. In this respect, political ordering is distinct from market ordering. Moreover, this conception reflects a belief that debate and discussion help to reveal that some values are superior to others. (1985:31–32; see also Sunstein 1991)

Sunstein argues that the "core demand" of the equal protection, due process, contract, and eminent domain clauses in the Constitution is that "measures taken by legislatures or administrators must be 'rational'" (49), that is, rationally related to a legitimate public purpose and not simply the result of pressure from competing interests.[27] He therefore suggests that to combat rent-seeking the federal courts enforce more stringently the rationality requirement of these clauses, not simply assuming public-interested legislative purposes without specific evidence that those purposes played a part in the legislature's action. The courts should also require that laws have more than a merely plausible connection to the public purpose the legislators claim the laws were intended to serve.

In administrative law, Sunstein argues that the federal courts should develop further the recently evolved "hard-look doctrine" for judicial review of the work of administrative agencies, which at present requires that agencies give detailed explanations for their decisions, justify departures from past practices, allow a wide range of affected groups to participate in the regulatory process, and consider reasonable alternatives, explaining why those alternatives were rejected.[28]

Jonathan Macey (1986) also advises using the judicial system to reduce interest group rent-seeking. He argues that the courts should use legislative history more extensively, should consciously stress a public purpose, should give less weight to administrative agencies' interpretations to avoid possible capture, and should narrowly construe remedial statutes.[29]

Corporate theorists believe that in addition to balancing interest groups against one another to produce an environment less permeated by power, bringing political actors who represent opposing interests together regularly would shift their incentives and motivations so that they would begin to weigh the public good more heavily in their own mix of desires.[30] The authors of the *Federalist Papers* once hoped the institutions they framed would call forth public spirit in the nation's representatives. Today, even theorists such as Anthony Downs and James Buchanan, who once suggested that properly designed democratic institutions could rely on the motive of self-interest, have begun to ask how constitutional arrangements can foster public spirit among these representatives.[31] Corporatist arrangements may well foster public spirit in the representatives of interest associations by bringing those representatives together in circumstances designed, by balancing power against power, to elicit arguments and ways of thinking that have as their goal the larger public good. Corporatist thinking thus formalizes and extends the process of encouraging public spirit that may already be partially at work among networks of policy elites.

Yet elite deliberation must be supplemented with deliberation among the rank and file. Only citizens themselves can know, through deliberation, what outcomes they want. Elites can easily develop distorted understandings of the interests, including the public-regarding interests, of those they represent. The movement to incorporate the Equal Rights Amendment into the U.S. Constitution, for example, involved primarily public-spirited motivation. Yet even in this highly democratic movement, incomplete internal deliberation produced decisions that may not have reflected the considered volitions of its members. The elites of the movement, the feminist constitutional lawyers and Washington-based heads of the national ERA groups, never had the opportunity to see what its grassroots activists might have formulated as good public policy, based on their experience with state legislatures, if elites and activists had been able to pool their perspectives (Mansbridge 1986).

When processes of accountability are functioning, a narrowly self-interested citizenry will eventually throw out its public-spirited representatives. Yet ordinary citizens can commit themselves to public-spirited rather than self-interested action and build structures of cooperation based on conscience and group feeling.[32] Offe and others have pointed out that effective social cooperation cannot proceed without social identification, mutual trust, and obligation. Deliberative processes within interest groups could help participants affirm or alter their identifications, place limits on their own and others' options through agreed procedures, and work out or reinforce obligations to neighbors, colleagues, opponents, and other participants in the political process (Schmitter 1988:10, 17–18, citing Offe). With appropriate participatory institutions, lessons learned making hard decisions in internal deliberation might generalize to a larger citizenship.

Obstacles to Reform

The chief obstacles to any reform of a governmental system are those who benefit from and control the present system. As a consequence, reformers usually either advance their proposals primarily as a spur to thought (e.g., Schmitter 1988) or fall back on institutions like the courts that are relatively immune to such benefits (e.g., Sunstein 1985). At the moment, however, the Supreme Court itself stands in the way of certain reforms designed to promote more effective deliberation among interest groups in the United States.

In *Buckley v. Valeo*, 424 U.S. 1 (1976), and subsequent decisions, the Supreme Court has begun to define the expenditure of money as a form of speech, subject to First Amendment protections. In *Buckley*, the Court distinguished between limitations on contributions to an individual politician, which it allowed under the First Amendment, and limitations on contributions to a political cause, which it disallowed. This distinction rests in part on the potential in the case of individual politicians for contributions to involve a quid pro quo in which monetary power buys public power. In the case of contributions to a larger political cause, where the potential for an individual and personal quid pro quo is not usually present, the Court ruled that legislation limiting contributions to a political cause contravenes First Amendment guarantees of free speech. Indeed, the court has taken an explicit position against the governmental interest in "equalizing the relative ability of individuals [to] influence the outcome of elections," saying repeatedly that "the concept that government may restrict the speech of some . . . in order to enhance the relative voice of others is wholly foreign to the First Amendment" (*Buckley v. Valeo* and *First National Bank of Boston v. Bellotti*, 435 U.S. 765 [1978]).

Following the same logic, the Federal Communications Commission (FCC) has repealed most of the "fairness doctrine," which had required that "each side" of the discussion of public issues be given "fair coverage" (*Red Lion Broadcasting Co. v. FCC*, 395 U.S. 367 [1969]). The FCC grounded its repeal partly on the conclusion that "the fairness doctrine, on its face, violated the First Amendment," which the commission interpreted as guaranteeing a laissez-faire "marketplace of ideas" (FCC 1987:5043, 5044, 5056, 5057; see also Entman 1989:102ff.).

The First Amendment, however, was intended neither to promote political deliberation actively nor to defend pure laissez-faire among interest groups. Given that the framers intended and the wording mandates neither result, our own generation must decide which course better fits the spirit of the First Amendment in the context of the political system the United States has developed. When the post–New Deal Supreme Court decided that the guarantees of "life, liberty and property" in the Fifth, and by extension the Fourteenth, Amendment did not include a pure liberty of contract or the marketplace, it left open the question of how to distinguish the now diminished rights (like the right to contract) from other rights (like the rights to speech, press, and association) to which it wanted to give priority. In a frequently quoted footnote to the *Carolene Products* decision, Justice Stone suggested that "legislation which restricts those political processes which can ordinarily be expected to bring about repeal of undesirable legislation" should perhaps be subjected to more exacting judicial scrutiny than most other types of legislation (*U.S. v. Carolene Products Co.*, 304 U.S. 144 [1938]). The Court did not consider that issue in *Carolene Products* and has not since committed itself to that reasoning. Since the New Deal, however, the Court has elevated to almost sacred status the First Amendment rights of speech, association, and the press.

In another arena, it has created a new right, the right to an equal vote, from the bare constitutional statement that members of the House of Representatives are to be chosen "by the People" (*Wesberry v. Saunders*, 376 U.S. 1 [1964]). This parallel evolution, seemingly congruent with evolving public opinion, may stem implicitly from a recognition that the Court's position outside the electoral system fits it to watch over the democratic process. If one major goal of First Amendment preeminence is to protect the democratic process, the amendment should not be used to undermine that process. Although the First Amendment, which is worded negatively ("Congress shall make no law . . ."), would not itself seem to mandate legislation making the power of interest groups more equal in the political process, the First Amendment should at least not be used to rule such legislation unconstitutional.

CONCLUSION

Present models of representation, whether normative or descriptive, rarely incorporate interest groups formally into the larger system of representation. When they do, both their descriptive and normative apparatus is thin.

In this chapter I contend that interest groups play a central role in deliberative political processes. They provide much of the information and insight that changes the preferences of the public and their elected representatives. They also provide the institutions through which another set of representatives, the interest group elites, deliberates and decides upon the best interests of their constituents and of the polity as a whole. To a lesser degree they also provide institutions through which members of the interest group can deliberate with one another and with their representatives.

The most familiar contemporary model of interest group deliberation, competitive deliberation, simply pits one group's information and insight against that of another, assuming fixed and relatively self-interested preferences among the members of the interest groups. The model implicitly postulates a citizenry and elected legislature to act as final judges of the public interest, but it neither dwells on the judging function nor suggests how citizens and representatives whom the model expects to act in a primarily self-interested fashion can be transformed for this function into public-spirited judges.

The collaborative model moves in descriptive accuracy beyond the model of simple competition. It points out how policymaking elites come to speak the same language, respect one another for their policy expertise, and may occasionally adopt roughly similar ideas on policy issues. It begins to analyze how the process of deliberation within the interest group structure in the United States actually works. Some who describe these operations approve normatively the way conceptions of the public interest tend to infiltrate and even dominate the conscious thinking of many such elites. Yet the constraints of their structural positions ensure that the conception of the public interest these elites develop will not always incorporate the understandings of the people they represent.

Corporatist descriptions of interest group representation make it easier to understand the deliberative functions of interest groups and the agreements now made in conjunction with formal lawmaking processes. Corporatist theories also bring to the fore the critical normative issues of inequality and rent-seeking. Yet the goals of curbing both inequality and rent-seeking are not sufficiently furthered by corporatist suggestions of the traditional sort, which concentrate on deliberation among elites. Empirical research on the deliberative aspects of interest representation should begin to describe and model existing mechanisms both for deliberation among rank-and-file members and for interchange between members and their formal and informal representatives. Normative theory should explore the ways different forms of deliberation might illuminate or obscure the political process of probing volitions.

NOTES

For their comments on an earlier draft, I am grateful to Christopher Jencks, Ken Kollman, Benjamin Page, Mark Petracca, Cass Sunstein, and participants in the Conference on the Political Economy of the Good Society at Yale University and the Conference on Competing Theories of Post-Liberal Democracy at the University of Texas at Austin. I am particularly grateful to Kay Schlozman, whose timely reading of a late draft saved me from some important inaccuracies. The Center for Urban Affairs and Policy Research at Northwestsern University provided time to write and a hospitable intellectual environment.

1. For political scientists' views on the impossibility of a public interest, see Mansbridge [1980] 1983:340, n. 31. But for a definition of the public interest as "those interests which people have in common *qua* member of the public," see Barry 1965:90. For other definitions, see Flathman 1966.

2. For a fuller presentation of the ideas in these four paragraphs, see Mansbridge [1980] 1983 and 1990. Many political theorists define democracy as equal power (for references see Mansbridge [1980] 1983:334, n. 1). Dahl (1956:37, 84; 1961:3; 1970:12) has often made "equality of power" central to his definition of democracy; Downs (1957:24) defines democracy as based on one person, one vote.

One can think of allowable inequalities in a democracy as reflecting no more than principal-agent relationships, as long as such relations can include the natural coincidence of interest as well as the congruence of interests constructed through means of control.

I do not intend the ideas in these paragraphs to define democracy inclusively. A complete survey of the cluster of norms we associate with "democracy" would include minority rights and liberty, both justified independently from either equal power or the common good, and sometimes in conflict with them.

3. Scholars disagree on how much power interest groups exert in the United States. This controversy derives in part from the difficulty of attributing cause both generally (Hume [1739-40] 1978) and specifically in politics, power being a form of cause (Nagel 1975). Hall and Wayman (1990) summarize the literature failing to tie specific monetary contributions to specific votes but argue that "political money alters members' patterns of legislative involvement" in ways that affect legislative outcomes. See also Jacobson 1980, Schlozman and Tierney 1986, and Ferguson and Rogers 1986.

4. The adversary mandate for equal power can be fulfilled using either majority rule or some procedure, like taking turns, that results in proportional outcomes (to which Europeans give the name *consociationalism*). Consociational systems work better than majority rule in polarized polities with few crosscutting cleavages (Mansbridge [1980] 1983:267–268).

5. From Hume's time to the present, philosophers and social scientists have distinguished between "love" and "duty" (empathy and conscience, "we-feeling" and principle) as the two primary forms of altruism (see authors cited in Mansbridge 1990).

6. For a review of the literature on rent-seeking, see Bhagwati 1982. Some economists define public policies like minority set-asides as rent-seeking. This appellation is justified, in my view, only insofar as the policy does not have a public purpose, such as producing justice, repairing past wrongs, or creating a community that reflects the larger national diversity. Because much rent-seeking behavior pretends to have a public purpose, citizens and policymakers must always ask both whether they think the purpose is a genuinely public one, that is, whether it might be thought to benefit the polity as a whole in reasonable proportion to its costs, and also whether the policy in question is likely to further that public purpose (see Mansbridge forthcoming).

7. The distinctions among the threat of sanction, force, and persuasion derive from Bachrach and Baratz 1963. The distinction between actions in another's interest and against another's interest derives from Lukes 1974, which in turn was heavily influenced by Bachrach and Baratz.

8. "Wherever there is an ascendant class, a large portion of the morality of the country emanates from its class interests and its feelings of class superiority" (Mill [1859] 1974:65).

9. The literature on legislatures is summarized in essays by Paul J. Quirk and Steven Kelman, and on citizens in essays by David O. Sears and Carolyn L. Funk and Tom R. Tyler, all contained in Mansbridge 1990. As Berry (1989a:81–84) puts it, the first two "rules" of "effective lobbying" are "credibility comes first" (stretching the truth will undermine your effectiveness) and "only the facts count." He concludes, "The optimal role for a lobbyist to play is that of a trusted source of information whom policymakers can call on when they need hard-to-find data." See also Berry 1989a:143–144 and Mansbridge 1988.

10. Kalt and Zupan (1984) call "ideological shirking" legislators' acting for ideological reasons (e.g., for the public interest) against their constituents' preferences. The staff and officers of some private interest groups may also engage in "ideological shirking."

11. E.g., McConnell 1966; McFarland 1976; Mansbridge 1986; Hayes 1986. Others have documented the distortions arising when state elites assume that their own motivation to pursue the public interest guarantees such an outcome (e.g., Konrad and Szelenyi 1979, Moynihan [1969] 1970).

12. For a critique of the "conduit" or, as she calls it, the "transmission-belt" model, see Schwartz 1988.

13. There is no commonly accepted terminology in the field. For *power* and *influence*, see note 10 above. My distinction between *negotiation* and *deliberation* borrows from Bessette 1979. Schelling (1960), however, defines a "bargaining" situation to require the condition of non-zero-sum conflict.

14. Pruitt (1982) suggests that when negotiation can achieve joint gains, the forms of agreement possible, in order of increasing difficulty, are: (1) compromise, where the factions

make comparable, moderate concessions on each issue in dispute; (2) trade-off, where they exchange large or even complete concessions on different issues; (3) compensation, where one faction concedes the original issues and the other makes up for it on unrelated matters; and (4) reorientation, where both factions abandon their initial positions to adopt a fundamentally new alternative (summarized in Quirk 1989). I would suggest that a measure of reorientation is required in many negotiations.

15. The cases of *A.L.A. Schecter Poultry Corp. v. U.S.*, 295 U.S. 495 (1935), and *Panama Refining Co. v. Ryan*, 293 U.S. 388 (1935), are "the only ones in our history where the Supreme Court has struck down an entire statutory delegation as invalid" (Stewart 1975:1694, n. 121). See also citations pro and con in Sunstein 1985:60; 1989).

16. E.g., requirements for intervenor financing. I am grateful to Kay Schlozman for pointing out the relapses of the 1980s.

17. House Committee on the Judiciary, *Copyright Law Revision*, report no. 94-176, 94th Cong., 2nd sess., September 3, 1976, 72, referring to the "Agreement on Guidelines for Classroom Copying in Not-for-Profit Educational Institutions" (Mansbridge 1988:74–75). Costain and Costain (1981) review the literature on "agreed bills" since Gilbert Steiner's *Legislation by Collective Bargaining* (Urbana: University of Illinois Press, 1951).

18. Freeman and Medoff (1984:19). The authors point out that "in a non-union setting, where exit-and-entry is the predominant form of adjustment, the signals and incentives to firms depend on the preferences of the 'marginal' worker, the one who might leave because of (or be attracted by) small changes in the conditions of employment" (9). This worker is generally young and mobile. "In a unionized setting, by contrast, . . . the desires of [older] workers who are unlikely to leave are also represented" (10), thus resulting in a compensation package more tilted toward deferred benefits, such as pensions and life, accident, and health insurance, which older workers favor and which are, "on balance, to be viewed as a social plus" (20).

19. See also "crucial parameters—those that *determine* how people define their interests and thus how they frame the issues in terms of which they may then act rationally" (Bauer, Pool, and Dexter [1968] 1972:ix). The authors then provide a thoughtful list of several ways perspectives might change in the course of deliberation: long-run/short-run time perspective; locus of desired benefit, as for self, firm, community, party, constituency, nation, or some combination of these; definition of the good to be maximized, as earnings, security, political influence, or some combination of these; definition of costs, as money, time, friendship, and others; and, finally, considerations of political feasibility: "What is in the interest of each are policies that he perceives as likely to be perceived as sufficiently in the interest of many others so that these others will act to make them realities, provided they too see them in the same way" (xi–xii).

20. They also point out that the league's decentralized and consensual deliberative processes keep it from acting quickly and dilute its impact by publicizing internal disagreements.

21. Streck and Schmitter (1985:11, 12, 13). Schmitter's (1988:26) voucher scheme is explicitly nonparticipatory (see 15, 26–29, 52–53, but also suggestions on 10, 18, and 45 that his scheme may make the public more public). Although in their 1985 essay Streck and Schmitter are concerned with organizations that are "limited and fixed" (10) and defined by a "collective self-regarding interest" (17), Schmitter (1988) later drops these requirements.

22. The present literature on negotiators' relations with their constituencies (e.g., Wall 1975, Klimoski and Breaugh 1977) only begins to model the actual and potential reciprocal relationships.

23. Salisbury 1990:225. Salisbury's language, however, suggests that he recognizes the importance of deliberation only on matters involving the direct self-interest of members of the association ("maximally advantageous") and only among elites ("those who are knowl-

edgeable about both the technical substance of the issue and the feasibilities of the relevant political situation").

24. Mancur Olson (1965) provided the classic formulation of the "free-rider" problem: When a good, once made available, will be available to all regardless of contribution, each individual has an incentive to use the good once available without contributing to producing it. Russell Hardin (1982) pointed out that the free-rider problem is one form of a prisoner's dilemma, in which the rational pursuit of individual benefit generates collective harm. Moe (1980) and Frohlich, Oppenheimer, and Young (1971), among others, have applied this logic to interest groups and social movements (see Cohen and Rogers, 1989, for summary). Jack Walker (1983) points out that foundation and government support makes it easier for new interest groups to start and maintain themselves, thus helping overcome collective action problems.

25. Petracca (1986), for example, points out that advisory committees set up by the executive and legislative branches usually include members from the most directly affected interest groups, but with little concern for balance between potentially conflicting interests.

26. Cohen and Rogers, arguing for more equality among interest groups, contend that European corporatist arrangements have produced noticeable "gains in productivity, productive equity, efficiency of state administration, and general social peace" (1989:3). They examine in detail the objections of Lowi (1969, 1979) and others to quasi-corporatist arrangements.

27. Sunstein explains in a footnote: "Thus, for example, when a state enacts a statute banning the sale of milk in paperboard milk cartons, the government must show that the prohibition serves some public interest and is not merely the product of a successful imposition of pressure by the plastics industry. See Minnesota v. Clover Leaf Creamery Co., 449 U.S. 456 (1981). Or when a state prevents opticians, but not ophthalmologists, from selling certain services, it must justify its action by showing that the measure is a means of protecting consumers and not simply a reflection of pressures imposed by ophthalmologists. See Williamson v. Lee Optical, Inc., 348 U.S. 483 (1955)" (1985:49, n. 82). See also Sunstein 1984:1689 and 1982:127.

28. Sunstein 1985:61. Sunstein also argues (1985:62–63) that the recent judicial prohibition of "ex parte contacts," or off-the-record communications between government officials and the private parties who might be affected by their decisions, stems from an implicit attempt to favor a more deliberative role on the part of administrators, as against response to constituent pressures. See also Sunstein 1983:177.

29. Sunstein (1989), broadly in agreement with many of these proposals, warns against a stress on legislative history, on the grounds that interest groups often design legislative history to serve their rent-seeking purposes. He proposes instead that when statutory language is unclear, the courts should adopt presumptions first in favor of decisions by politically accountable actors, second in favor of processes that promote political deliberation, and then against the delegation of legislative authority and against narrow interest group transfers.

30. Schmitter (1988:26) says that "public-regardingness will be maximized if the leadership and staff of associations can be ensured some degree of autonomy from the immediate preferences of their members" (see note 22 above). Quirk (1989) also argues on these grounds for insulating elites from the public.

31. Buchanan 1986; Downs 1989. In her introductory essay, Mansbridge 1990 documents the evolution within the public choice field from an exclusive focus on self-interest to the incorporation of altruistic motivation (Mansbridge 1990).

32. For examples of successful social-dilemma interactions based on "we-feeling" and conscience rather than coercion, see Dawes, van de Kragt, and Orbell in Mansbridge 1990.

3

Interest Groups and the Policymaking Process: Sources of Countervailing Power in America

ANDREW S. McFARLAND

Countervailing power is a term now out of favor with political scientists. To many it brings to mind the most uncritical assumptions of group theory from the 1950s, subsequently absorbed into the pluralism of the 1960s. Countervailing power seems to be an intellectual shortcut, simplifying the questions of power structure and group analysis by a misleading assumption that power begets counterpower. When citizens have circled their wagons against the onslaught of some power elite, hearken, the bugles of countervailing power sound the imminent rescue. Even if true to life, the picture is boring.

Yet the term remains descriptive of routine political bargaining, as one might say "the pork producers' lobby provides countervailing power against the feed-corn growers' lobby." The term can be comfortably extended to the Left in referring to the activities of blacks, women, and environmentalists, for instance, to organize countervailing power against the Reagan administration. And in international relations, the analogous term *balance of power* is seen as useful for both normative and descriptive purposes.

Perhaps *countervailing power* need not be banned from our lexicon if we remember not to confuse it with the idea of "sufficient" countervailing power. One picture associated with the term is the scales of justice; if a weight is dropped on one side of the scales, a countervailing weight may be applied to the other side. This can be deemed a countervailing force, or "power," but it may not be sufficient to strike a balance.

This metaphor provides a useful shorthand. The pluralists seemed to imply that the weights on the scales of the policymaking process are in balance. Theodore J. Lowi (1969), Mancur Olson (1965), and similar critics of the pluralists leave the impression that the scales are totally unbalanced. Still later students of interest groups, such as Jack Walker and associates (see Gais, Peterson, and Walker 1984; Walker 1983) and James Q. Wilson (1980a, 1980b), find countervailing weights but avoid the claim that a balance is normal. Each of these three views or schools posits separate scales for many separate "issue-areas." Power-elite theorists, in contrast, believe there is only one set of scales that matters. Marxists argue that the metaphor of scales, forces, and balancing misses the fundamental point of power structures that are universally rigged.

The terminology of countervailing power is useful for introductory or general discussions of the political process and will likely be in use for a long time. Further, the perspective of time and the logic of discussion indicate that the prevalent view will be the one advocated by Walker and Wilson, if one accepts the parameters of the countervailing power concept. The power-elite concept of C. Wright Mills (1956) is infrequently used by political scientists except to discuss situations in which critical national security issues are involved. Although Olson successfully dispatched the pluralists' balance-of-forces argument, many case studies continue to show the existence of significant, if not entirely equal, countervailing power in contrast to the outlook of the "plural elitists."

The emergent argument is that some countervailing power exists in most issue-areas. This point is incorporated into the concept of "triadic power" (see McFarland 1987), reflecting the frequent appearance of inter-acting forces by economic producers, autonomous government agencies, and countervailing power lobbies within particular policy areas. Albeit useful, this conception needs to be extended and refined.

As a metaphor, countervailing power captures a major generalization about interest group research during the last twenty years, herein por-trayed as a division between theorists of interest group stasis and theorists of countervailing power. Olson (1965 and 1982) and Lowi (1969) have been the most influential theorists of stasis, and for a few years in the late 1970s, their outlook attained wide acceptance by political scientists. Olson argued that there is a normal tendency for the special interests of a few to be more readily organized into interest groups than the general interests of the many. A society of highly organized, special interest economic groups emerges, and with the passage of two or three generations, the special interest economic groups eliminate economic growth by success-fully persuading government to underwrite or grant loans and subsidies, set artificially high prices, support oligopolistic markets, set barriers to eliminate new competition domestically and internationally, or restrict products. With time, the growing influence of special interest lobbies destroys markets, competition, and economic development, leading to a condition termed here interest group stasis, at best a static, if not declining, economy.

capture?

Lowi made an argument similar to Olson's, though the variables were somewhat different. Lowi saw a tendency for American legislators to refuse to enact laws with clear standards that could be enforced fairly and effectively. Indeed, in Lowi's view, legislators increasingly preferred vague legislation that delegated the interpretation of the law to administrators. Unfortunately, for reasons Olson described, such administrators are likely to interpret vague laws in the interests of well-organized groups. Thus American government is becoming a giant pork barrel in which benefits are parceled out to hundreds of organized interests.

Interest group stasis, then, refers to the theory that numerous well-organized special interests get control over government policies on a piecemeal basis, each group controlling policies in its own area of activity. In time this results in economic standstill. It also results in political standstill, as it becomes impossible for government to initiate policies in the general interest. What is the cause of this condition? Not a single power elite. The problem is many elites or *plural* elites.

This notion is compelling, but it is now opposed by theorists of countervailing power. The theory of interest group stasis is based on the observation that those with the greatest economic stakes become the best organized and thus tend to control government policy in some area. But around 1980, research by James Q. Wilson, Jack L. Walker, and others renewed the observation that the pattern of interest group organization is often complex, with many groups effectively organized to influence policy in some area of government activity. The complex pattern of group organization means that other groups are exercising countervailing power to the special interest group that might otherwise dominate an area of policy. Consequently, there is a division among writers about interest groups. Olson, Lowi, and the plural elitists emphasize those tendencies that eventually result in political and economic stasis. Wilson, Walker, and others emphasize findings of countervailing power in group organization that oppose the social processes of interest group stasis.

INTEREST GROUP STASIS:
THE THEORY OF PLURAL ELITES

The theory of plural elites generally replaced the pluralist theory of the 1960s, which stressed (among other characteristics) widespread organization of interest groups, countervailing power among groups, and dispersal of political power among decentralized political institutions as important factors in promoting democracy (see McFarland 1987). The pluralist outlook,[1] associated with the work of David B. Truman (1953), Robert A. Dahl (1961), and Charles E. Lindblom (1963), was widely replaced by "plural elitism," which admitted the absence of a single power elite but viewed public policy as fragmented into hundreds of separate political arenas, many of them under the control of particular elites such as iron triangles. These particularistic elites would normally prevent the implementation of policies as set by decisionmakers representing widespread constituencies, as when Congress or the president acts in this capacity.

The propositions presented below indicate the convergence among various plural elitists.[2] Probably no single writer would agree with every proposition. Certainly, the writers disagree among themselves about the proper prescription for rule by special interests, for example, responsible political parties (Schattschneider 1960) versus juridical democracy (Lowi 1969) versus strengthening the presidency (McConnell 1966), and so forth. Nevertheless, among the plural elitists there is considerable agreement when it comes to the diagnosis of special interest rule.

Proposition 1. Organizational Costs. Presuming economic, cost-benefit reasoning, widely shared interests will not be organized because it is not to the benefit of any individual to incur the time and money costs of organizing the group (Olson 1965).

Proposition 2. The Free-Rider Problem. When an interest group produces public goods (collective benefits), members lose the incentive to contribute to the maintenance of the interest group because they will receive the benefit anyway. This is particularly true of large groups. Because of this free-rider problem, an interest group will lose influence and may cease to exist (Olson 1965).

Proposition 3. The Few Defeat the Many. The interests of a few are less prone to high organizational costs and to the free-rider problem. The organization of very widespread interests, on the other hand, is very susceptible to these problems. Therefore, within a particular policy system, the few tend to be better organized (Olson 1965).

Proposition 4. Symbols in Politics: The Few Defeat the Many. Very widespread but unorganized publics are prone to irrational perceptions of political reality. Such publics confuse symbol with substance—that is, elites manipulate public opinion by creating political forms that give the impression that some problem is being solved or some policy is being followed when this is not the case. In contrast, political groups consisting of a few corporations do not usually confuse symbol with substance. Such small groups, following rational political strategies, will frequently defeat the interests of very large publics confused by political symbols and following irrational political strategies (Edelman 1964).

Proposition 5. Restricting the Scope of Conflict. Manipulation of the scope of conflict is a basic political strategy. Therefore, well-organized special interests will manipulate the context of political conflict to prevent "public interests" from manifesting themselves in the conflict (Schattschneider 1960).

Proposition 6. The Structure of American Political Institutions. The decentralized and fragmented nature of American political institutions frequently helps the few defeat the many. On the one hand, public interests are best represented by the presidency, the Supreme Court, and within general conflictual policy debates in Washington. On the other hand, special interests tend to be more powerful in state and local politics and within fragmented administrative policy systems, which are not subject to public control by the president or by the federal courts. Americans share an ideology of the virtue of political decentralization, but this ideology in fact helps special interests defeat public interests (McConnell 1966).

Proposition 7. Congress Creates Unneeded Bureaucracy. During the 1970s, members of Congress learned to increase their probability of reelection by legislating new federal bureaucracy, which created a myriad of new regulations. Members of Congress then helped their constituents with problems resulting from such regulations, which increased the popularity of incumbent members. The result is a special interest coalition: the Washington establishment (Fiorina 1977).

Proposition 8. Ambiguous Statutes. In enacting general-interest legislation, American legislators write ambiguous statutes. Vaguely written laws provide opportunities for special interests to redirect the implementation of such laws to their own benefit (Lowi 1969, 1979).

Proposition 9. Power Structure Varies by Issue-Area. Although some policy areas are characterized by pluralism, other areas are characterized by elite dominance—an area-specific elite controls policy without effective political competition. In addition, class conflict may ensue if the existing distribution of property is at issue (Lowi 1964a).

Proposition 10. Subgovernments. In American public administration, the few defeat the many through the mechanism of the subgovernment. This is a coalition of interest groups, public administrators, and members of Congress serving on the relevant committees that controls the administration of public policy for the benefit of those within the subgovernment. Such policies usually benefit established economic interests. A subgovernment will try to destroy executive agencies operating within the same policy-area but outside of the subgovernmental coalition. These agencies, which compete with subgovernments, include a disproportionate number representing general interests or the poor. The political patterns described in the other propositions are manifest in the politics of subgovernments (McConnell 1953, 1966; Lowi 1969; and Cater 1964).

Proposition 11. Reform Cycles. American politics is subject to reform cycles in specific areas of policy. At times general-interest coalitions defeat the subgovernmental coalitions and enact reform legislation in specific areas of public policy, but subgovernments reestablish their control (Lowi 1964b; McConnell 1966; Edelman 1964; and Bernstein 1955).

Proposition 12. Interest Group Liberalism. Since the New Deal, an ideology of "interest group liberalism" has prevailed among political scientists, moderate and liberal politicians and civil servants, and intellectuals. This ideology is the phenomenological equivalent of the academic theory of pluralism. Interest group liberalism implies that people know their own interests, are able to express these interests in political organizations, and are then able to gain access to policymakers. The resultant policy outcomes are seen as fair because interest groups balance one another. It is believed that significant social change can be achieved within the present structure of group organization. However, this ideology distorts the perception of American political reality, which is primarily characterized by a lessening of the degree of democracy (Lowi 1969, 1979).

It is noteworthy that these propositions can be added together to form a general argument concerning interest group politics. The gist of this argument is that (1) many widely shared interests cannot be effectively organized within the political process; (2) politics tends to be fragmented into decisionmaking in various specific policy areas, which are normally controlled by special interest coalitions; (3) there are a variety of specific processes whereby plural elitist rule is maintained; and (4) a widespread ideology conceals this truth about American politics.

A few more propositions taken from this school illustrate the basic generalization that the polity and economy eventually decay because of inefficient policies introduced by congeries of subgovernmental coalitions. Perhaps the most general statements are by Olson and Lowi.

Proposition 13. The Decline of Pluralistic Democracies. Within pluralistic societies, interest groups are free to organize without significant governmental restriction. But because of the logic of collective action, groups with specific economic interests will defeat groups representing the general public. Over time, this leads to inefficient governmental regulation, subsidies, and oligarchic economic organization, which eventually eliminate economic growth (Olson 1965, 1982).

Proposition 14. Government Subsidies Lead to Political Stasis. Beginning in the 1960s, the federal government instituted vast programs of subsidies (especially through subsidized loans) for established interest groups. This tends to freeze the political system in the status quo, retard policy innovation, and lessen the influence of newly emerging interests (Lowi 1979).

The two authors make parallel statements. Both agree that in pluralist democracy, economic innovation is increasingly difficult to introduce. Lowi adds that the pervasive politics of the distribution of benefits renders unattainable other policy goals such as regulation or the redistribution of wealth.

George Stigler makes a point similar to that of Olson, but he is more specifically concerned with the effects of lobbying and regulation on public policy.

Proposition 15. Government Regulation Benefits Special Interests. It is a normal process in industrial society for particularistic business or professional lobbies to mobilize political resources to gain legislation or regulations that principally benefit that business or profession. Such regulations typically limit entry into a business or profession, retard the rate of growth of new firms, eliminate substitute products or services, establish protective tariffs, fix prices, and gain subsidies from public funds (Stigler 1975).

The special interest politics of government expenditures can lead to a continual increase of spending, which in the long run is economically inefficient, according to such writers as Aaron Wildavsky (1980) and William A. Niskanen (1971). Some view this as the most important instrument of the economic decline Mancur Olson foresaw.

Proposition 16. Iron Triangles Continually Increase Government Expenditures. If political cultural norms restricting governmental spending break down, collusion among interest groups, governmental agencies, and legislators will produce spending increases in numerous particular arenas of governmental action. The size of governmental bureaucracies will continually expand as each government agency collaborates with its allies to increase its budget (Wildavsky 1980; Niskanen 1971).

Other writers state that even if new policy-oriented bureaucracies are formed, they must compromise major goals to fend off powerful subgovernments, as Philip Selznick (1953) observed about the Tennessee Valley Authority (TVA). The more pessimistic Grant McConnell (1953, 1966) seemed to conclude that any policy-oriented bureaucracy in the agricultural or natural resources domains would be destroyed or captured by powerful subgovernments. Such observations leave little room for effective policy implementation.

Proposition 17. Co-optation. Government programs in agriculture, natural resources, and other areas will be co-opted by locally oriented subgovernments and their goals diverted to the distribution of benefits to local elites (Selznick 1953; McConnell 1953, 1966).

The general conclusion of plural elitism can be summarized in the phrase *interest group stasis.* Both political and economic innovation is unstable and quickly dissipates into the relatively simple organization of political-economic oligopoly. The main thrust of politics becomes negotiations among the various policy-area elites in a massive system of logrolling. These elites trade political support to maintain one another's subsidies:

California defense contractors and their representatives might agree to support subsidies for public housing construction in the Northeast, and vice versa. Dairy farmers trade support for pro-industry trucking regulation in return for votes for ever higher milk price support, and so forth. A minority of citizens aided by well-organized lobbies gain in the short run, but everyone loses in the long run. Government spends more and more; budget deficits increase as special interest lobbies gain exceptions in the tax code. The economy deteriorates.[3]

In the real world of political behavior, the "citizens" victimized by interest group stasis would presumably overthrow it, substituting some form of political-economic organization with greater promise for fulfillment of the public interest. One powerful stimulus to such an overthrow would be the maintenance of national political and economic sovereignty in an environment of heightening international economic competition. Indeed, in the real world of American politics, one would expect antistasis politics to appear before the whole system came close to economic collapse. This is the politics of countervailing power.

NEOPLURALISM

Objections to plural elitist theory began to consolidate by the end of the 1970s. The first criticism is not surprising. Scholars of lobbying and policymaking discovered that groups other than subgovernmental elites had significant effects on public policy. In the area of air pollution, for instance, studies by Bruce A. Ackerman and William T. Hassler (1981), Norman Ornstein and Shirley Elder (1978), Charles O. Jones (1974), and Lettie M. Wenner (1982) all found that environmentalist groups have significant effects on public policy. These findings are typical of many other policy-areas, including the political mobilization of business David Plotke describes in Chapter 8.

In different ways, other scholars found more countervailing group power than one would expect from the theory of plural elitism. Jeffrey M. Berry (1977), Andrew S. McFarland (1976, 1984), Robert C. Mitchell (1984), Mark V. Nadel (1971), and David Vogel (1980–1981), among others, chronicled the significant strength of public interest lobbies. Jo Freeman (1975), Anne N. Costain and W. Douglas Costain (1983), Ethel Klein (1984), and Joyce Gelb and Marian Lief Palley (1982), among others, found women's lobbies to be important. John D. McCarthy and Mayer N. Zald (1977) generalized from such observations to develop the resource mobilization theory of social movements, which implies that movements frequently create lobbying organizations. Samuel Beer (1976), Donald Haider (1974), and others described the phenomenon of governments lobbying other governments— associations of cities, counties, and so forth lobbying in Washington and elsewhere. Walker (1983) and his collaborators (Gais, Peterson, and Walker 1984) found a great increase in lobbying by associations of nonprofit organizations (e.g., churches, hospitals, and colleges); professions, especially including groups of government employees; and ideological cause groups. Kay Lehman Schlozman and John T. Tierney (1986) found a great increase in the number of Washington lobbies since 1960, although they argue that this has not substantially decreased business domination of other lobbies.

The second major criticism of plural elitism is that government agencies in the United States often influence policy independent of group pressures. Of course, this is not an entirely new argument, as indicated by Dahl's (1961) treatment of politicians reshaping their political environment in his study of community power in New Haven. One recalls Herbert Kaufman's (1960) classic study of the role played by professional values in shaping policy, *The Forest Ranger*, or perhaps Francis Rourke's (1984) insistence that state agencies often shaped events by founding and maintaining interest groups to support the agency. Mark A. Peterson makes a similar point in Chapter 10, in which he discusses how presidents use group-directed strategies to advance their own political agenda.

Additionally, some writers form a school sometimes called "statism." In his work *On the Autonomy of the Democratic State*, Eric Nordlinger (1981) makes the title's argument against the plural elitists. In *Defending the National Interest*, Stephen Krasner (1978) says that the U.S. State Department often does autonomously defend the national interest without closely reflecting interest group pressures. In *Building a New American State*, Stephen Skowronek (1982) argues that from 1877 to 1920, professionalized army officers, civil servants, and regulatory commissioners escaped the control of the politics of pressure and patronage. By the mid-1980s, few political scientists rejected the proposition that government agencies sometimes have an autonomous effect on public policy. The argument became, instead, whether the new school of statism actually presented a novel approach at all (see Almond 1988).

In summary, political scientists are defining a new view on interest groups and public policy. This perspective emphasizes the frequent appearance in the same decisionmaking situation of organized economic producer interests, countervailing power lobbies (such as environmentalists), and autonomously acting government officials. Elsewhere I have referred to these three units as "the power triad," which can serve as a focal point for the analysis of influence in many public policy decisions (see McFarland 1987). Other important elements—the president, legislatures seen as a whole, courts, and groups of experts—can be analyzed in relationship to the three units of the triad.

In *The Politics of Regulation* (1980b) and other works, James Q. Wilson and his students found that environmentalists and other interests have organized countervailing lobbies that reduce the influence of dominant economic producers in some sectors of policy (see also Derthick and Quirk 1985; Katzmann 1980; and Kelman 1981). Wilson subscribes to the idea that individual political leaders, styled "political entrepreneurs," find it to their advantage to organize widely diffused interests into countervailing lobbies. The clash between the producers and the countervailing lobbies enhances the tendency toward agency autonomy, although this conflict is not a necessary condition for agency autonomy. Countervailing power can also occur when two economic producer groups, such as the lumber industry and the recreation industry, oppose one another.

Wilson (1980b) and others show that agency autonomy occurs to a significant extent and that the professional value systems of government decisionmakers have major effects on policy. Although it may have been co-opted by interest groups in the 1950s, the Federal Trade Commission (FTC) during the 1970s had considerable autonomy, for example. Many of its policies were best understood as a product of the clash between economists, who preferred the initiation of antitrust actions based on priorities set by economic theory, and agency lawyers, who set priorities based on the range of legal consequences and the strength of the legal case (see Katzmann 1980).

As we did for plural elitism, we can identify a number of propositions that summarize portions of the neopluralist outlook.

Proposition 1. Power Triads Occur Frequently. Power triads may be found just as frequently in the American administrative process as the classic "iron triangle" or subgovernment. This should not be confused with the assertion that all interests are equally or somehow justly represented. The triad may exist, but some interests may not be organized (Wilson 1980).

Proposition 2. Countervailing Power Enhances Agency Autonomy. Countervailing power limits producers, enhancing agency autonomy. The claim is not made that countervailing power is a necessary condition of agency autonomy, although this may be the case. Further, some instances of countervailing power occur when two economic interests oppose one another (Wilson 1980b).

Proposition 3. Variety in Countervailing Coalitions. Certain business groups may join public interest groups, professional associations, local property-holders, and so on to form countervailing coalitions to producer interests on specific policy issues. Varied coalitions including some business interests are a major source of countervailing power (Berry 1985; Nadel 1971; Vogel 1989; Nadel and Vogel 1977).

For instance, representatives of bakeries and soft-drink bottlers might join with consumer lobbyists to oppose federally mandated minimum prices for sugar, earnestly sought by producers of cane and beet sugar.

Proposition 4. Professionalism in Agencies. Professional value systems substantially affect agency policy. If there is countervailing power, then there is agency autonomy. In some instances, especially in local administration, no interest groups are organized, thereby enhancing agency autonomy and the effects of professionalism (Wilson 1980a, 1980b; Peterson, Rabe, and Wong 1986).

Proposition 5. Legality in Administration. The impartial enforcement of general standards is enhanced if there is countervailing power, leading to agency autonomy and professionalism (Wilson 1980a, 1980b).

Although this parallels Wilson's point about professionalism, it contradicts Lowi, who argues that the normal situation is plural elitism, which undermines legality.[4]

Added to these five propositions are five more that emphasize the idea of "high politics" versus "routine politics" and subsystem cycles.

Proposition 6. Routine Versus High Politics. Routine politics is defined as normal, day-to-day decisionmaking and administration in a policy area. High politics is defined as the politics of making general decisions that would have a major impact on changing policies or the structure of participation in a policy area. Congressional committee or subcommittee members are frequent participants in routine decisions and are then added to the structure of the triad. High politics involves one or more of these participants: presidential policymakers, major sectors of Congress in addition to routine participants, federal appeals courts, or the Supreme Court (Redford 1969; Selznick 1957; and Ripley and Franklin 1984).

Proposition 7. High Politics Coalitions. During high politics, presidential policymakers most commonly, but also Congress or the courts, may significantly reduce agency autonomy. Presidential policymakers may side with either producers or countervailing power holders. During high politics, then, the president in coalition with either producers or countervailing power holders will attempt to restructure policy and participation.

Wilson (1980a:389–390) argued that the president ordinarily is not part of the politics of regulation. This accurately described the 1970s but doesn't describe President Reagan's effective intervention into the policymaking of the FTC, the Environmental Protection Agency (EPA), the Occupational Safety and Health Administration (OSHA), and the Equal Employment Opportunity Commission (EEOC). One hallmark of the Reagan administration was the conversion of routine regulation and administration into high politics. Congress may be the initiator of high politics within some particular policy-area when it takes the initiative to pass legislation, as was frequently the case in the early 1970s. The federal courts also have the capacity to initiate high politics in a policy-area, for example, by abolishing agencies for unconstitutional abridgement of separation of powers and limiting affirmative action policies in the civil rights area.

> *Proposition 8. Split High Politics Coalitions.* Split coalitions may form, for example, when Congress, with countervailing power groups, opposes the president and producers.

This sometimes happened during Reagan's first term.

> *Proposition 9. Triad to Subgovernment Cycles.* A space may be defined between triadic and subgovernmental power. The position of policy-areas in this space changes with time. As countervailing power or agency autonomy or both diminish, the policy-area approaches the subgovernmental model; as they increase, policy approaches the triadic model. High politics may intervene to move policy through the definitional space.

For instance, A. Lee Fritschler's (1983) account of smoking and politics in America shows some movement in this policy-area away from agency co-optation and toward triadic power. As the Reagan administration attacked the autonomy of such agencies as EPA, OSHA, and the Civil Rights Commission, there was movement away from triadic power toward the model of co-optation by business. Paul J. Culhane (1981) found movement away from the co-optation model in Bureau of Land Management policy in the 1970s, but this doesn't preclude movement back toward the co-optation model in the 1980s (see Clarke and McCool 1985:107–122; Miller 1985; and Davis and Davis 1986). Policy need not be described as fully co-opted or fully triadic; there are obviously gradations. Similarly, it is a mistake to assume that policy always remains at the same point; high politics may intervene to restructure any given policy-area.

> *Proposition 10. Reform Cycles.* The reform cycle of plural elitist theory can be described as the movement of a policy area from subgovernment to triad and then back to subgovernment. Reform cycles are frequent but not absolute; usually agency autonomy and countervailing power remain present to a lesser degree as the policy area moves back to subgovernment relationships (McFarland 1991).

Reform frequently moves at the rate of three steps forward, two steps backward. The professionalization and institutionalization of government agencies fluctuates but on average increases in the long run (see Skowronek 1982).

The countervailing political processes of neopluralism oppose the interest group stasis of plural elitism. Such processes are in truth dependent on the appearance of countervailing power, or countervailing lobbies, to provide some balance to the skewed political world of plural elitism. As Wilson (1980a) points out, once there is something of a balance of power among groups, then we can expect the appearance of agency autonomy within some policy-area. It seems that countervailing group power still plays a central role in the concepts of revised interest group theory; it continues to be a focal point for analysis.

What are the sources of countervailing power in contemporary American politics? We now examine four ideas from recent interest group theory about the sources of countervailing power in order to relate these to the idea of interest group stasis.

THE SOURCES OF COUNTERVAILING POWER

Issue Networks

The concept of issue networks has become a basic component of public policy research in the 1980s. Following Hugh Heclo (1978), we may define an issue network as a communications network of those knowledgeable about policy in some area, including government authorities, legislators, businesspeople, lobbyists, and even academicians and journalists. A lively issue network constantly communicates criticisms of policy and generates ideas for new policy initiatives. An issue network is obviously not the same as an iron triangle or subgovernment. However, Heclo admits that sometimes iron triangles do exist, making it difficult for the criticisms and initiatives circulating in an issue network to influence subgovernmental decisionmakers.

Issue networks are seen as counteracting subgovernments. In an often-cited quotation from Heclo, the unfashionable term *countervailing power* is not used, but the language amounts to much the same thing:

> It would be foolish to suggest that the clouds of issue networks that have accompanied expanding national policies are set to replace the more familiar politics of *subgovernments* in Washington. What they are doing is to overlay the once stable political reference points with *new forces* that complicate calculations, decrease predictability, and impose considerable strains on those charged with government leadership. (Heclo 1978:105, emphasis added)

Thus, issue networks generate new forces that create strains and change previous behavior of subgovernments and other governmental structures. It might be argued that this is a form of countervailing power.

Through a series of examples, Heclo indicates how issue networks provide countervailing power:

The overlay of networks and issue politics not only confronts but also seeps down into the formerly well-established politics of particular policies and programs. Social security, which for a generation had been quietly managed by a small circle of insiders, becomes controversial and politicized. The Army Corps of Engineers, once the picture book example of control by subgovernments, is dragged into the brawl on environmental politics. (Heclo 1978:105)

Further examples indicate that developing issue networks that include many technical experts frequently circulate information contradicting the outlook of the various plural elites. This is an important instance of countervailing power, for a basic strategy of a policy-area elite is to restrict public information about that policy. If the decisionmakers of high politics do not know what is going on, they will have little incentive to challenge the control of a policy elite, thereby letting routine politics run its course.

Heclo mentions, but does not develop, a second aspect of countervailing power: "Knowledge does not necessarily produce agreement. Issue networks may or may not, therefore, be mobilized into . . . a conventional interest organization" (Heclo 1978:104). Heclo neglects an obvious implication here, namely, that portions of issue networks may be mobilized into interest groups if appropriately stimulated. One may hypothesize that government agencies or independent political entrepreneurs will organize interest groups from the newer issue networks. Or previously existing groups will tend to expand into issue networks upon contacting sympathetic persons. Because an issue network by definition implies the existence of a communications network, the costs of organizing an interest group are lowered by getting preexisting information about who in the network cares about what. An issue network performs the same function for group organizing as does a mailing list and, in the case of some technical policy journals, amounts to much the same thing.

Proposition 11. Issue Networks. An active and diverse issue network tends to undermine subgovernmental control but is not a sufficient condition for doing so. Such an issue network tends to maintain triadic power in the reform cycle because critical and innovative ideas are communicated to countervailing power and agency autonomy. A portion of an issue network may be readily mobilized into a conventional interest group because of the relatively low costs of organization (Heclo 1978; Berry 1989b).

The issue network is not a panacea for the problems of plural elitism. Issue networks are diverse. They contain persons critical of a policy, such as laissez-faire conservatives or personnel of regulated businesses. Some people in an issue network are supportive of emergent subgovernments. Further, top policymakers may ignore issue networks, either out of principle or ideology, depending on one's point of view. During the Reagan administration, for instance, most members of issue networks in arms control, acid rain, and toxic waste disposal were ignored.

Interest Group Patrons

Jack Walker's concept of interest group patrons indicates another possible source of countervailing power. This refers to the active role of wealthy individuals, government agencies, and foundations in financing the organization and maintenance of interest groups in the United States (Walker 1983). This type of idea is conventionally viewed against the background of the group theory of the 1950s. Writers such as Bentley (1967), Truman (1953), and Latham (1952a) apparently conceived of interest groups as coalescing from the attitudes or interests of individuals, and then moving to wield influence over public policy, with policy the result of the push and pull of the various organized groups. In this model, the role of the government was secondary, perhaps as that of a particular type of "official" group.

But since the 1960s, no widely cited political scientist has argued in print that groups affect government but government does not affect groups. Even most writers regarded as "pluralists" did not believe this; indeed, one goal of *Who Governs?* was to show that government leaders organize groups, just as Mayor Richard Lee organized the Citizen Action Commission to further his urban renewal policy (Dahl 1961:5–6, 15–17). However, the idea that some believe in one-way causation of groups' affecting government serves as a useful rhetorical device and therefore persists in discussions of bureaucratic power and state autonomy (see Almond 1988).

It remained for Walker to gather data on 564 voluntary associations, several dozen of which received financial support from the government in their initial organizing stage and about 200 of which received such support at one time or another. Walker expanded the familiar concept of government aid to groups to the idea of "patrons," to include wealthy individuals and foundations. He found 189 groups aided by foundations and 257 aided by wealthy individuals. Overall, Walker presents convincing evidence that such patrons are a major factor in overcoming the logic of collective action to form some degree of countervailing power (Walker 1983:392, 399).

Extending Walker's analysis a bit, we can see that patrons and issue networks acting together facilitate group organization. The meetings, journals, and mailing lists of issue networks cut the costs of organizing. The patron is likely to finance one or more political entrepreneurs arising out of an issue network to organize the group. Such entrepreneurs are likely to have acquired years of experience with the personalities and opinions of those within some issue network.

Most of those in an issue network are in this position because of jobs financed by business, government, academic institutions, nonprofit organizations, and newspapers. The network facilitates group organization, and other institutions finance the network. In addition, patrons finance the entrepreneurs who organize portions of the network into an interest group.

The role of the state as group patron is a matter of law, as is its direct financing of interest group organization. Walker makes this point at the conclusion of his pathbreaking article:

> The success of efforts to create and maintain political interest groups also depends upon such legal and institutional factors as the provisions of the tax code governing the ability of business firms to claim deductions for the expenses of lobbying, subsidies in the form of reduced postal rates for not-for-profit groups heavily dependent upon direct mail solicitation, the availability of financial support from regulatory agencies for groups that wish to testify at administrative hearings. (1983:404)

Laws affecting the organizing and maintenance of interest groups cut both ways: They can help or hinder producers and countervailing power. But the role of patrons in financing groups seems particularly beneficial to countervailing power, which tends to have a more difficult job than do producers in gaining contributions because of Olson's logic of collective action. The existence of patrons seems important in the maintenance of at least some countervailing groups to provide some competition to subgovernments. Thus we can add the following propositions to our inventory.

Proposition 12. Reciprocity of Organization. Government subsidizes producers and countervailing power in some circumstances. General rules posit a number of subsidies to lobbying organizations. Subgovernments can be expected to find ways of aiding producer trade associations. Agency autonomy may aid countervailing power groups through regulations establishing associations of clients, subsidizing programs of countervailing power groups, providing funding for policy research, and so forth (Walker 1983).

Proposition 13. Patrons. Foundations and wealthy individuals, as well as state agencies, fulfill the role of patron in helping to finance the organization and maintenance of interest groups. Patrons fulfill multiple roles and are ordinarily distinct from political entrepreneurs, who specialize in organizing a single group (Walker 1983, 1990b).

Social Movements

Social movements are an important source of countervailing group power (see McFarland 1983), a point treated at length in Chapter 13 by Anne N. Costain. This is especially true when the movement espouses goals that attract large segments of the middle class, as do environmentalism, government reform, and women's rights. The civil rights movement successfully appealed to the white middle class in the 1960s but has not since met with similar success in its economic appeals. Social movements that seek benefits for the poor have an especially difficult task (see Piven and Cloward 1977).

In the academic division of labor, the formation and activity of social movements has traditionally resided in the province of sociology. When social movements formed lobbies, engaged in litigation, and had goals implemented through public policy, this was seen as appropriate subject matter for political science. Those who concentrated on resource mobilization and social conflict sought to break down this division as they broke with the prevalent value-strain interpretation advanced by Parsonian sociology (see McCarthy and Zald 1977; Oberschall 1973; Pinard 1975; Freeman 1975; Smelser 1963).

The resource mobilization school emphasizes the formation of new interest groups, although, of course, this is not seen as the totality of the movement. This interpretation is influenced by Olson, and these discussions of group formation are similar to those of political scientists in their concern for the role of the political entrepreneur, selective benefits to group members, and all the other variables associated with overcoming the problems of collective action. Resource mobilization theory embodies the idea of patrons, and from this theory it is clear that foundations, wealthy individuals, and government are active in the formation and maintenance of groups. Writing in this tradition, Jo Freeman (1975:51–56) places some emphasis on the formation of the President's Commission on the Status of Women, established in 1961, and on the inclusion of sex discrimination in the 1964 Civil Rights Act as ways in which government fostered the women's movement.

The McCarthy-Zald interpretation apparently does not focus on the existence of communications networks as a cause of social movements. But this interpretation implies some focus on the appearance and possible policy success of rather limited movements, such as the recent campaign against drunk driving. In such cases, the movements may achieve policy success and establish their own issue networks, which provides continuing employment for movement entrepreneurs. The new issue network provides a continuing employment resource for organizing new interest groups to press for goals similar to those of the original movement.

Pinard, Oberschall, Freeman, and other writers in the social conflict perspective on movements have made an important addition to interest group theory. They stress that by serving as communications networks, existing group organizations spread social movements. For instance, black churches served as forums for the civil rights movement, and established women's groups such as the American Association of University Women and the Business and Professional Women's Club communicated the new ideas of the women's movement of the 1960s (see Marx 1969; Freeman 1975). These new movements in turn establish new interest groups. They may achieve policy success and establish new issue networks, which eventually generate new groups. This mechanism of social change does not often rely on the plural elitist groups of producers' associations.

Through the dissemination of social movements, apolitical groups create more groups, including those with countervailing power. Sometimes this means that groups encourage movements, which establish issue networks, leading to the organization of different groups in the future. At any rate, we understand why the existence of numerous intermediary groups does not necessarily quash radical social change. This suggests the following proposition.

Proposition 14. Social Movements and Interest Groups. Social movements are an important source of countervailing power. Resource mobilization by political entrepreneurs or by patrons is a source of movements and new interest groups. Existing groups provide communications networks to spread the ideas of new social movements. Policy success by movements leads to the appearance of new issue networks, which, in turn, lower the costs of group organization (McCarthy and Zald 1977; Oberschall 1973; Pinard 1975; Freeman 1975).

Social movements can be a source of social renewal and can counteract interest group stasis. But movements like McCarthyism sometimes have such negative overall effects as to wipe out this positive effect. Movements certainly are not immune to plural elitist tendencies, as in the case of movement participants in local antipoverty agencies colluding with consulting firms and shielded by friendly politicians.

The Limits of Collective Action

Olson's *Logic of Collective Action* (1965) is the definitive critique of countervailing group power. As such, some scrutiny of Olson is likely to be useful. A lengthy discussion of this work and the impressive body of research in its wake is beyond the appropriate scope of this chapter. Nevertheless, there is an observation to help fit the logic of collective action into the foregoing discussion.

Olson's work poses an insistent question: Why do so many interest groups exist that logically should not exist? Olson's answer—selective benefits—is treated as an important idea but one subject to great problems of tautological formulation (see Olson 1965; Barry 1970:33–37). If a group is found to exist, anyone clever enough to earn a Ph.D. can invent one or more plausible selective benefits to account for its existence. The Catholic church might be said to convince millions that it controls the selective incentive of "the stairway to heaven," for instance.

Moving beyond selective benefits, scholars have indicated a variety of answers to the question why interest groups exist. Such theories have included cooperation over time, the evolution of cooperation, federally structured groups, Kantian motivations, minimal regret, and various types of political entrepreneurs.[5] These and others come equipped with convincing formal models, experiments, or data from the world of groups. The research situation is doubly confusing: After reading Olson we don't know why groups exist, yet we now have a surfeit of plausible explanations as to why they do.

The post-Olson study of interest groups might learn something from the study of leadership in small groups, which flourished in the 1940s and 1950s. Social psychologists conducted many hundreds of experiments in this field, and it seems plausible that more than a thousand journal articles were published. As is widely remembered, these researchers initially attempted to find "leadership traits" but concluded this was a misleading concept. The general conclusion was of a limited relativism: Leadership varied with the nature of followers and the nature of the situation. It then seemed useful to classify variables by these factors (leadership, followers, situation) and to find recurring patterns in the variables. For instance, democratic leaders might achieve more success with democratic followers than authoritarian followers under certain conditions of group size, communication, reward structure, and so forth (see Verba 1961; Gibb 1954).

This research outcome is similar to what academics have learned about teaching ability—that there are few readily generalizable good teaching traits and that different professors perform well in different circumstances in relation to different students. The dramatic professor does best in large introductory classes with students who have previously not studied the subject, whereas the methodological, Socratic, but undramatic professor will doubtlessly do better in a graduate seminar.

The main conclusion from leadership and small group studies can be applied to post-Olson interest group studies. The work can be divided into those emphasizing structural factors, leadership, or followership (Bavelas 1960:491–498). Structural factors include Hardin's (1982) iteration of games, provision of public goods by a few acting in their own interest, and Schelling's prominent solutions cutting group organizing costs. Or they might include the evolution of cooperation or the federal structure of groups (see Axelrod 1984; Bendor and Mookherjee 1987). Salisbury (1969) and Frohlich, Oppenheimer, and Young (1971), among others, have emphasized the utility structure of leaders or political entrepreneurs. Finally, some scholars hypothesize that a number of followers' traits, ranging from ignorance to the categorical imperative, are the key to Olson's dilemma (see Moe 1980; Hardin 1982).

Consequently, the mysteries of collective action may be illuminated as the mysteries of leadership or of teaching. A number of patterns—clusters of structural, leadership, and followership variables—emerge as useful to understanding interest groups in the United States. Thinking in these terms, several packages of factors might eventually be found to be favorable to organizing and maintaining countervailing power. Extending the preceding analysis, we see that an important structural factor is a preexisting issue network. This cuts organizational costs, as a communications network is financed by salaries from various institutions. A second structural factor is the extent of possible patron activation. The leader or entrepreneur is likely to appear from the network and may activate patron financing. But the difficulty of organizing and maintaining the group also varies with followers' motivations in combination with another structural factor—the extent of possible selective benefits. This type of situation seems common in reference to the organizing of so many professions and subprofessions, as well as associations of nonprofit organizations in the last decade. Walker's data described a capital in which one finds lobbies of fire chiefs and state attorneys general; or political scientists, psychologists, economists, and almost every academic discipline; or different types of colleges, hospitals, and other nonprofit organizations (Walker 1983; Gais, Peterson, and Walker 1984).

Groups within issue networks have a much easier time when it comes to organization and maintenance than do national voluntary groups funded by contributions from strangers unconnected to a network. And yet in the last generation there has been a remarkable increase in the number of citizens' groups lobbying in Washington, many of which were not organized in the context of issue networks. One structural factor that helps explain the emergence of citizens' groups may be the opinion changes induced by social movements. These changes can then be tapped by entrepreneurs to organize such groups, sometimes assisted by patrons, as described by resource mobilization theory (see McFarland 1984).

CONCLUSION

The plural elitists have stated an impressive theory of interest group stasis in the American political system. Countervailing power, then, might be considered to be the collection of processes opposed to interest group stasis. Some insight into these processes is gained by considering the operations of issue networks, patrons, and social movements. Theories discussing the logic of collective action offer other ideas.

Many political scientists have already accepted an argument analogous to the one I advance in this chapter. E. E. Schattschneider (1935 and 1960), for example, reacted against the plural elitist debacle of the Hawley-Smoot

Tariff Act described in his first book to argue the necessity of stronger national political parties to represent the views of majorities against minority power. This argument has been adopted by many political scientists, who thus regard strong national political parties as "countervailing power" in the sense I use. Other political scientists offer different prescriptions for special interest power, such as Lowi's (1979) juridical democracy or Wildavsky's (1988) advocacy of a constitutional amendment to restrict spending by the federal government.

The national Republican party acted together in strong and unified fashion in 1981, and congressional voting patterns, national direct-mail fund-raising, and some local organizational efforts indicate that the decline of national political parties may have been arrested (Maisel 1990). But we are still a long way from having strong national parties capable of counteracting subgovernments and reducing budget deficits. Similarly, the failure of the Gramm-Rudman-Hollings Act of 1985 to reduce the federal deficit illustrates the difficulties of controlling spending by constitutional and other legal means. Lowi's (1979) juridical democracy is dependent upon major changes in the behavior of presidents, Congress, and the Supreme Court.

But I take a different approach to the problem of plural elitism. I argue that a new group theory demonstrates how newly understood processes of group behavior counteract the problems of minority control. This theory is based on numerous case studies of how groups affect public-policy making, and this could serve as an important empirical basis for advocacy of politically feasible reforms that have effects desired by the reformers.

It might be argued that the idea of interest group stasis applies to all large, complex political systems. Olson has already observed that collusive cliques adversely affect the economic performance of a variety of nondemocratic systems (Olson 1982). Reform leaders of the USSR must combat special interest coalitions of regional party personnel, industrial production managers, and local government officials to protect the organizational status quo. Indeed, as Philippe Schmitter (1974) pointed out, a centuries-old tradition of political theory known as corporatism stressed the organized nature of politics and society and criticized group pursuit of self-interest.

Most Americans rejected this corporatist tradition as authoritarian, identifying it with the political practice of Mussolini and Franco. But as Schmitter indicated and Peter Katzenstein (1985) demonstrated, varieties of democratic corporatism exist in contemporary Scandinavia, Belgium, the Netherlands, Austria, Switzerland, and Germany. Such countries make important economic policies through state-initiated mechanisms for the coordination of interest groups. Corporatist countries aim to preserve national economic and political sovereignty through coordinated economic policymaking, limiting the power of particular interest groups. The idea of corporatism has become an essential part of the vocabulary of American political scientists.

Virtually all political scientists now agree that the United States is not a corporatist system, as Graham Wilson suggests in Chapter 4 (see Salisbury 1979; Wilson 1982; cf. Petracca 1986). Because of our traditions of liberal individualism, American business and labor reject the idea of organizing themselves into national federations that would follow the orders of a central council on such matters as prices or wages. In addition, Americans reject policies of overt state-directed and planned capitalism, such as those conducted by France or Japan.

Although the United States lacks national corporatism or statism, our system nevertheless resists the decline into interest group stasis that Olson and Lowi described. The processes that prevent this decline, termed countervailing power, are subtle, complex, but a vital part of interest group politics and policymaking.

NOTES

A grant from the Humanities Institute of the University of Illinois at Chicago provided time for doing background research for this chapter.

1. An earlier view of pluralism is Bentley (1967). My extended views on pluralism are found in McFarland 1969.

2. Many of these propositions are derived from McFarland 1987.

3. In Chapter 15 Paul Peterson gives an empirical evaluation of the influence of special interests on the federal budget during the past two decades.

4. Herbert Kaufman (1960:226) described a rule-oriented, legalistic administrative unit, but he admitted that the character of the Forest Service was related to a balance of power between "conservationists" and economic producer interests.

5. See Hardin 1980, 1982; Axelrod 1984; Bendor and Mookherjee 1987; Ferejohn and Fiorina 1974, 1975; Salisbury 1969; and Frohlich, Oppenheimer, and Young 1971. The most effective way to gain entrée to this literature is to inspect the bibliographies of articles about collective action in the *American Political Science Review* or *Public Choice* over the past few years.

4

American Interest Groups in Comparative Perspective

GRAHAM K. WILSON

Political scientists do not completely agree on a definition of the term *interest group*.[1] Some use the term to refer to broad sectors of the population such as women, the young, or the old. Most, however, use the term to refer to organizations whose formal membership requirements (e.g., paying subscriptions) differentiate them from society as a whole, including their potential supporters. Not everyone who shares the values expressed by an interest group or who benefits from its activities belongs to the organization proper. Interest groups are also distinguishable from government and political parties, even though cooperation with government departments or political parties is often extremely close.

The term *interest group* is applied to a wide variety of organizations ranging from desperately poor environmental interest groups to lavishly financed corporations. All such organizations attempt to influence public policy without accepting (as do political parties) public responsibility for running government. Yet certain generalizations about some of these organizations do not apply to others. One way to categorize interest groups is in terms of their membership: Some have a mass membership; others are either offshoots of organizations or do not have a mass membership in the ordinary sense of the phrase. Business corporations, for example, support *trade associations* to represent the collective interests of their industry and also operate as interest groups themselves, as when they lobby executive branch agencies or Congress. Another way to categorize interest groups is in terms of their aims: Some pursue goals that are clearly in the self-interest of their members (such as subsidies for farmers); others are concerned with diffuse interests (such as the Common Cause goal of promoting "good government").

In practice, the value of various schema for classifying interest groups depends on the reason for studying them. Writers concerned primarily with why or how interest groups come into existence will find classifications based on mass membership particularly important. Writers concerned with the impact of interest groups on government will find such a categorization less useful. For reasons that will become apparent, the distinction I draw in this chapter is between *economic* interest groups that represent economic forces such as corporations, farmers, and workers—the means by which people obtain their incomes—and interest groups not based on economic sectors of society, such as women's groups, the National Rifle Association (NRA), or Common Cause. If we ask how the American interest group system compares with those of other countries, the answer we obtain will depend very much on which of these categories of interest groups we are considering.

THE ASSESSMENT OF INTEREST GROUPS

How can we assess the strength or success of various interest groups? The most obvious test of an interest group's effectiveness is whether policymakers accept its policies. In practice, however, this test has only limited utility. It is very rarely the case that we can isolate the effect of an interest group from the effects of other political forces such as electoral competition, the prevailing values of a society, or the independent (some would say autonomous) wishes of policymakers or "state managers." Political scientists therefore tend to look to a number of different measures of the strength of interest groups. One measure is the *density* of membership that an interest group achieves, density being the proportion of the potential membership recruited into an interest group. Another measure is the *standing* of the interest group with policymakers: Is the interest group seen as the authoritative voice of people in society who share an interest or attitude? Is the interest group consulted frequently by policymakers, and do the policymakers strive to secure the endorsement of the interest group's leaders for their proposed course of action?

Other indicators of potential interest group strength include the *resources* available to them. In a democracy, the most obvious interest group resource is a large membership prepared to vote for the interest group's friends and against its enemies. In the United States an interest group is also able to reward friends and punish enemies by making campaign contributions via political action committees the interest group operates. But interest groups possess many other resources that are of value to policymakers. Two that are particularly important are the ability to give *technical advice* and the ability to assist in *policy implementation*. Policymakers rarely understand or have information on all the complexities of the issues they decide; advice from interest groups helps. Many types of policy can be implemented more easily, cheaply, and effectively if the relevant interest groups cooperate. The NRA and the American Farm Bureau Federation (AFBF) were given government assistance early in their histories partly because they helped the government achieve its own goals. The NRA increased the number of people already trained in shooting who could be recruited into the army in time of war, and the AFBF encouraged farmers to adopt more efficient farming practices. Finally, interest groups have media contacts that they can use either to make trouble or spread sympathy for policymakers.

I now look at how the two different types of interest groups—economic and representational—in the United States compare with their counterparts in other countries.

ECONOMIC INTEREST GROUPS

Until the late 1960s, most political scientists who studied interest groups focused on economic interest groups. Those great political scientists V. O. Key, Jr., (1964) and David Truman (1951) naturally concentrated on farmers, unions, and business and professional organizations such as the American Medical Association. Indeed, in his highly influential study, *The Logic of Collective Action,* Olson (1965) explained why freestanding, mass membership organizations would find it difficult to recruit people. In brief, individuals would not join mass membership organizations because they would generally receive the benefit the organization campaigned for whether or not they belonged and because they could not be sure that even if they were to become members other people would follow their example. Thus no rational person would join an environmental group because that person would receive the benefits the group pursued, such as clean air, irrespective of whether or not he or she joined it. Anyone asked to join an environmental group who was told that "if everyone behaves selfishly like you, nothing will get done" could reply, "But even if I join, I have no reason to believe that everyone else will." Unions could overcome the problem of the free-rider who took the higher wages negotiated by the union without joining it by imposing a closed shop (i.e., all workers in a plant must join the union). Other interest groups could offer "selective incentives" (e.g., discounts on hotels or car rentals) available only to individual members. However, as Claus Offe and H. Wisenthal (1985) noted, the mass membership interest group is at a disadvantage when it comes to organizing. It would always be much more costly and difficult for environmentalists to form and maintain an interest group than for chemical companies to oppose them.

Surprisingly, however, American economic interests seemed poorly organized compared to their counterparts in most other democracies. On all the dimensions of interest group strength described above, economic interest groups in the United States fared poorly.[2]

Most economic interest groups in the United States achieved a comparatively low density of membership. This is most obviously and clearly true of unions. In West Germany in the late 1980s, about 38 percent of the work force was unionized, in Britain about 47 percent, and in Sweden over 80 percent; the comparable figure for the United States was about 17 percent (Wilson 1990b:7). A much higher proportion of British than of American farmers belong to agricultural interest groups (see Wilson 1990b). Moreover, American economic interests were typically organized by numerous competing groups. American farmers, for example, were recruited by the AFBF, the National Farmers' Union (NFU), the National Farmers' Organization and, in the 1980s, the American Agriculture Movement. In addition, dozens of interest groups represented individual commodities such as wheat, cotton, or dairy goods. Businesses were offered the choice of belonging to the U.S. Chamber of Commerce, the National Association of Manufacturers, and, depending on their size, the National Federation of Independent Business or the Business Roundtable. For most of the period since World War II, unions have been disunited, with the Teamsters, the United Auto Workers (UAW), and the United Mine Workers outside the American Federation of Labor–Congress of Industrial Organizations at different times. The AFL-CIO's cumbersome title demonstrated how little unity labor achieved even after the merger of the AFL and CIO in 1955 (see Salisbury 1970; Wilson 1981).

The low membership density and fragmentation of American economic interests contrasted vividly with the situation in many other democracies. In most Western democracies, a single organization has been accepted as the authoritative voice for its sector of society. Confindustria in Italy, the Federation of German Industries (BDI), the Patronat in France, the Keidanren in Japan, the Swedish Employers' Confederation (SAF), and the Confederation of British Industry (CBI) all achieved government recognition as the authoritative voice of business. No single group in the United States has been able to achieve such a status.

Low density rates and fragmentation had other predictable consequences. First, American economic interest groups generally lacked the resources to make informed, technical contributions to policy debates. Bauer, Pool, and Dexter (1963) found that the average trade association representing employers in a single industry lacked money, staff, and expertise and therefore also lacked the respect of policymakers. The influence of economic groups was further diminished by the probability that the competing interest groups would make conflicting demands on policymakers. This danger was seen at its most extreme in agriculture. The AFBF, the largest farm group, argued for returning agriculture to a free market in which government would play a minimal role; the National Farmers' Union, supported by many of the other farm organizations, argued for *greater* government action to raise farm incomes by manipulating the market more. The squabbling among farm organizations naturally diminished the respect politicians had for any of them (Wilson 1977b).

The fragmentation of interest groups in the United States also made it more difficult for government to devolve policy implementation to interest groups. The British government was able to ask the CBI and the union federation, the Trade Union Congress (TUC), to take over responsibility for making detailed regulations on health and safety at work in part because there were just two organizations that represented employers and workers; no two bodies with comparable prestige to whom such policy could be entrusted exist in the United States.[3] Thus the fragmentation of economic interest groups reduced their influence on both the formulation and implementation of policy.

What of the more obviously political forms of interest group power? Most economic interest groups had little hope of influencing many votes. Unions probably had the best chance of developing a block vote that they controlled, and they made great efforts to build up effective organizations to mobilize labor voters. It speedily became apparent, however, that workers were no more likely to follow union leaders' wishes at the ballot box than to follow the wishes of the chief executive officer of their union. Eisenhower, Nixon, and Reagan all received a much larger proportion of the blue-collar vote than most union leaders would have wished. Unions became a major source of campaign funds by the 1950s. Corporations were theoretically barred from making direct contributions to campaigns by the Tillman Act of 1907 and subsequent legislation until the 1970s. In the absence of adequate enforcement, however, corporations managed to sidestep these prohibitions. The Smith-Connally and Taft-Hartley acts of the 1940s extended the ban on campaign contributions to labor unions and also barred corporate and union contributions from primary elections and nominating conventions (Sabato 1984:5–6). The revelation that corporations had legally and illegally contributed up to $30 million to Nixon's 1972 reelection campaign resulted in campaign finance reform. Thereafter, federal legislation allowed corporations to contribute up to $5,000 per candidate per campaign. In practice, however, the ability to make campaign contributions brought economic interest groups less reward than they had hoped. Labor unions gave nearly all their money to Democrats— usually liberal Democrats—who regarded unions as a constituency they could take for granted while they courted more marginal, less dependable constituencies such as professional-class environmentalists. Business distributed its contributions widely in part because incumbent legislators came to require contributions from lobbyists who sought access to them, turning contributions into an unofficial tax on interest groups. In general, business campaign contributions flowed to politicians with power rather than to those whose policies were most appealing to corporations. Moreover, as most contributions are made by individual unions or corporations and not by business organizations or the AFL-CIO, the current system of campaign finance reinforces the fragmentation of American interest groups.

Finally, American economic interest groups also suffer from limited legitimacy. Warnings that economic interests are taking over the government have recurred throughout U.S. history. The Jacksonian attacks on the Bank of the United States and the writings of authors such as C. Wright Mills (1956) in more modern times reflect a deep suspicion in American culture of collusion between business and government. Economic interests are often attacked as "special interests" that corrupt democracy. Only in exceptional circumstances such as war or depression is a partnership between government and economic interest acceptable, and then only temporarily. In contrast, in many other democracies a partnership between economic interests and government has been regarded as highly desirable. France and Japan achieved high rates of economic growth through a partnership between government and selected economic interests, especially business. In the so-called neocorporatist countries (such as Sweden, Austria, Norway, and possibly the Netherlands and Switzerland), government has shared responsibility for the management of the economy and society with interest groups representing business and labor. The sharing of sovereignty between government and economic interests that is taken for granted in Sweden or Austria would seem undemocratic to many Americans. Another small example is telling. In France and Japan, it is customary for high-ranking government officials to move out into jobs running major corporations, the practice known as *pantouflage* in France and *amakudari* (literally, descent from heaven) in Japan. Such moves are seen as producing a desirable integration of the goals and assumptions of government and industry. In the United States such career shifts are seen as a revolving door that corrupts government. In American political culture, economic interests and government should not be too close.

Finally, economic interest groups in the United States are not the only representatives of economic interests. Unlike many democracies, the United States not only elects legislators from territorial units rather than from a national party list but also has such decentralized politics that the political fate of an individual legislator is relatively unconnected to the fate of the legislator's party. Individual legislators take very good care to know, independently of the activities of interest groups, what the farmers, businesses, or workers of their constituencies want. Legislators build their own local coalitions of support to supply the organization, votes, and campaign contributions that their electoral survival requires, and they build such coalitions in part by serving local interests. The tradition of requiring legislators to promote the economic interests of their state or district in order to assure reelection makes American legislators as active as interest groups in promoting many "special" interests.

To summarize, economic interest groups in the United States have been severely handicapped in their attempts to influence government. Low membership densities, fragmentation, limited legitimacy in the political culture, limited technical skills and resources with which to supply policy advice, and competition in representing interests from other parts of the political system have taken their toll. Later I try to suggest deeper reasons for the comparative weakness of American economic interest groups. But first, after a short digression, I point up the contrast between the comparative status of economic and noneconomic groups.

TWO DECADES OF CHANGE

A number of political scientists have emphasized the growth in activity by economic interest groups that has taken place since 1970 (see Berry 1984; Vogel 1989; Wilson 1981). Has this growth made the picture of the comparative weakness of American economic interest groups outdated?

There is no doubt that nearly all economic interest groups are increasingly devoting resources to politics. Corporations in particular maintain more lobbyists in Washington and contribute more to political campaigns than ever before. In a survey of Washington interest groups, Kay Schlozman and John Tierney (1986) found that trade associations were much better funded than when Bauer, Pool, and Dexter conducted their research in the 1950s. Although some corporations and industries—especially the oil industry—were obliged to reduce their Washington staffs in the 1980s because of poor economic performance, there is little doubt that American business is much better represented in Washington today than in the recent past.

For a number of reasons, this does not mean, however, that economic interest groups in the United States have made up all the gap between their standing and the standing of economic interest groups in other countries. In the first place, not every economic interest has gained as much politically as business. The 1980s were a decade of almost unrelieved gloom for labor unions; the proportion of the work force they organized and their influence in Washington shrank dramatically. Second, much of the increase in business political activity was intended not to increase the general influence of business in Washington but to win federal contracts or trade protection for individual corporations. Third, the fundamental weaknesses of American interest groups remained and may have grown worse. The fragmentation of economic interest groups may have been compounded by the tendency for individual corporations as well as trade associations or business umbrella groups to employ lobbyists in Washington. The vast majority of campaign contributions are made by individual unions or corporations, not by umbrella organizations representing unions or corporations in general. The UAW and Teamsters have rejoined the AFL-CIO, but only because of the startling and possibly terminal decline in the power of organized labor. Farm organizations are as fragmented as ever.

Economic interest groups in the United States are certainly no closer to being taken into that partnership with government found in neocorporatist countries, France, and Japan. Indeed, more stringent procedural rules on how government officials may interact with interest groups, combined with competition for influence from noneconomic interest groups, may even have further weakened links between government departments and economic interest groups. Unlike their foreign counterparts, who are often partners of government, American economic interest groups are outsiders trying to force policymakers to pay attention. Whereas the typical employee of an economic interest group in Germany, Japan, or Sweden would be a technocrat or economist used to working in partnership with a government official, the typical employee of an American economic interest group is a lobbyist who tries to persuade politicians or bureaucrats. American economic interest groups are much more active than in the past, but this increase in activity has not changed their status fundamentally; instead, as Schlozman and Tierney (1986:389) commented, the changes amount to "more of the same."

REPRESENTATIONAL GROUPS

It is common in writing on interest groups in the United States to suggest that Americans have a peculiar propensity for forming interest groups. In the nineteenth century, Tocqueville elegantly argued that an important reason for the success of democracy in America was that Americans were unusually likely to participate in voluntary associations or interest groups. Interest groups could guard against the tyranny of the majority by both empowering minorities and training citizens in democratic procedures. Modern social scientists have argued somewhat less elegantly than Tocqueville that Americans are more likely to join interest groups than are citizens of other democracies (see Almond and Verba 1963; Verba and Nie 1972). The survey evidence on which social scientists base such claims must be treated with some skepticism. Undoubtedly, some people merely claim to participate politically because they want to give the socially acceptable response. It is noticeable that survey evidence on political participation suggests far higher levels of participation in elections than actually occurs. Similarly, the great value set on participation in voluntary organizations in American culture may lead many people to say they are active in interest groups when they are not.

In the case of economic interest groups, it is demonstrably incorrect to suggest that Americans join interest groups more often than citizens of other democracies. As we have noted, economic interest groups in the United States typically achieve low membership densities. When we turn to noneconomic interest groups, however, it is indeed the case that Americans have been mobilized by interest groups on a scale unmatched in any other democracy. Of course there are interest groups in democracies such as Britain that work to protect the environment, civil liberties, and the rights of women. Indeed, it has been said that one British interest group that could scarcely be classified as an economic interest group, the Royal Society for the Protection of Birds (RSPB), has more members than any British political party. On issues that are of great importance in British culture, such as the protection of animals and the countryside, voluntary groups have some significant standing. In addition to the RSPB, the Royal Society for the Prevention of Cruelty to Animals (RSPCA) has great standing with policymakers; the Council for the Preservation of Rural England and the National Trust have been able to do much to preserve the British countryside. Yet in general, as officers of most British noneconomic interest groups would be the first to say, the British groups have fewer members, fewer resources, and lower status with policymakers than their American counterparts. Common Cause, one of the United States' premier good-government groups, is a major presence in Washington. Although there are analogous organizations in London working on issues such as freedom of information, none has the strength or status of Common Cause.

A particularly striking example of the unusual strength of noneconomic interest groups in the United States is the women's movement (see Randall 1987). Obviously, there are feminists and probably feminist groups in all democracies and probably all countries. Women demanded full citizenship rights in countries such as Britain no later than American women. Yet, whereas in Washington today the National Organization for Women (NOW) is an established part of the interest group system, women's groups in London remain on the margins. NOW is part of networks of interest groups including such economic groups as the AFL-CIO working to secure passage of liberal legislation, it is consulted on the confirmation of federal judges (and, if the Democrats control the White House, on their nomination), and it is highly visible at party conventions (particularly the Democratic convention). There are, of course, numerous other women's organizations that pursue different strategies. However, the main point for my purposes is that NOW has a status inside the established interest group system of the United States that is unequalled by any women's group in Britain.

Despite these differences, we should be cautious for a number of reasons. First, to say that noneconomic interest groups are unusually strong in the United States is not to say that they achieve a particularly high density of membership. The proportion of women who belong to NOW, citizens who belong to Common Cause, and the breathers of air or drinkers of water who belong to environmental groups is very low in the United States. Those who join noneconomic interest groups are a small and at least sociologically unrepresentative minority in the United States. One might even argue that it is better to say that noneconomic interest groups fare less badly in the United States than in other democracies than to say they are successful. Second, as Walker and his associates (see Walker 1983; Gais, Peterson, and Walker 1984; also Salisbury 1984) showed, many noneconomic interest groups depend not on the contributions of millions of Americans for their resources but on the support of a few millionaires or a single foundation. Indeed, many noneconomic groups do not have a membership as such and are run by political entrepreneurs who raise funds for their activities from foundations or even government in return for fulfilling certain specified tasks. Third, whatever the fund-raising successes of noneconomic interest groups, inequalities between interest groups remain. It is much easier in the United States and elsewhere for chemical manufacturers to find resources to fight stricter government regulation than for environmentalists to find resources to push for it. Anyone who visits the Washington offices of most noneconomic interest groups will be struck by the obvious shortage of money to employ staff, buy equipment, or rent space.

Nonetheless, noneconomic groups in the United States have had an impact on policy and politics. In spite of the epidemic of murders in American cities, few politicians wish to confront the NRA by supporting laws to regulate guns. (Nevertheless, in 1991 both houses of Congress overcame extensive NRA lobbying to pass the Brady Bill, which provides for a mandatory waiting period before an individual may purchase a gun.) In spite of the advantages that we might suppose business enjoys in mobilizing political resources, environmental groups have obtained important environmental legislation and successfully defended it against attacks from the Reagan administration. Economic interest groups in the United States have indeed enjoyed significant advantages, as Olson would have predicted, compared with mass membership groups. The inexorable logic of collective action does make it difficult and expensive to create and maintain mass membership organizations representing diffuse constituencies. Yet noneconomic interest groups in the United States have been more successful in challenging economic interest groups than their counterparts in other countries. The United States has produced both weak economic interest groups and strong noneconomic groups. Why is there this contrast?

EXPLAINING THE CONTRAST

The character of interest groups is the product of the interaction of social forces, political culture, and political institutions. In many respects the traits of American interest groups reflect the wishes of the framers of the Constitution as well as the unique American political culture and society.

The comparatively unimpressive nature of American economic institutions is explained in part by the more restricted role that government has played in American society than in other advanced democracies. In countries where a single economic interest group speaks for its sector of society (e.g., workers, employers, farmers), that monopoly has been created or strongly encouraged by the state. The Confederation of British Industry was created at the behest of a Labour government that wanted to work more closely with manufacturing employers (Grant 1987); during the Fifth Republic, the French government prompted and assisted in the modernization and improvement of the Patronat and the farmers' group FNSEA (Fédération Nationale des Syndicats d'Exploitants Agricoles) so as to better adapt the two organizations to the planning process (Keeler 1987). Groups such as the Keidanren in Japan maintain their authority in part because government makes it clear that it will regard the organization as the sole legitimate representative of that sector of society (Johnson 1982).

In general, governments that have reinforced the monopoly of certain interest groups (as in the examples above) have done so because they need the cooperation of strong interest groups to further particular types of policy. Two kinds of policy have generally required government to build up a strong interest group. First, *economic planning* or *government-led growth*, in which the state and business are partners in planning growth, has called for the development of strong organizations to work with government in formulating and implementing the plans. The Patronat and Keidanren are obvious cases. However, British government strengthened the National Farmers' Union to work with government in modernizing and expanding farming in Britain and encouraged the creation of the CBI during the apogee of interest in indicative planning in Britain. The second type of policy is *incomes policy*. Neocorporatist countries such as Sweden have relied heavily on employers' organizations and union federations to restrain the inflationary potential of their commitment to full employment by agreeing with government on limits on the rate of wage increases.

It is striking that U.S. administrations have been little interested in either of these two types of policy. Proposals for an industrial policy in which the federal government would stimulate economic growth and industrial renewal were made during the 1980s as the U.S. economy began to lag behind those of Japan and West Germany. For a variety of reasons, however, such proposals have thus far been rejected. Not only would government "interference," through economic planning, be seen as illegitimate, but their strong localism makes American political institutions particularly ill suited to directive industrial policy (see Wilson 1990b:60). Incomes policy was tried briefly in the early 1970s as part of Nixon's "New Economic Policy," taking the form of wage and price controls. Although the management and administrative difficulties of implementing a wage and price control policy may have led Nixon to abandon the program, it was also argued that these policies actually increased inflation in some sectors of the economy and may have worsened subsequent inflationary episodes. As a consequence, U.S. administrations have lacked the incentive to build up the strong, monopolistic interest groups characteristic of governments intent upon economic planning or incomes policies.

Even if American administrations had felt the need to build up strong monopolistic interest groups to speak for economic sectors, they would have encountered almost invincible problems in so doing. A characteristic of parliamentary regimes (including, for this purpose, France, which has a blend of presidential and parliamentary institutions) is that as long as the government is able to command a majority in the legislature, political power is centralized in the hands of the executive branch; the leaders of the majority party (or, if there is a stable coalition, parties) that form the government control both the legislative and executive branches. Courts are nowhere else as important as they are in the United States. In other systems it is possible to control the *access* that interest groups have to policymaking. Interest groups granted a monopoly by government can be sure that no rival organization will have much opportunity to influence government. The assistance such interest groups give their governments in policy formation and implementation is predicated on the assumption that their monopoly position is secure.

In the United States, in contrast, no interest group can be assured of a dominant, let alone monopoly, position in policymaking. Even if the administration promised to talk only to the AFBF, for example, there would be no guarantee that the House or Senate agriculture committees would not choose to pay more attention to the NFU. When the AFL-CIO lined up against the Republican administration of President Reagan in 1984, the president strengthened his links to the Teamsters, who endorsed him in the 1984 election campaign. By relaxing the requirements for standing to sue in the 1960s and 1970s, moreover, U.S. courts made it far easier for a wide variety of interest groups to challenge policies in the courts, a particularly important development in the politics of regulation. In contrast to the centralization of parliamentary regimes, the institutional fragmentation of American government precludes its building up powerful economic interest groups.

Finally, American political culture has usually discouraged the development of strong economic interest groups, often in contradictory ways. On the one hand, as noted above, the political culture has been antagonistic to close ties between government and economic interests. On the other hand, American political culture, by its almost monolithic commitment to capitalism, has usually precluded serious challenges to the major economic interests in society. At times—for example, during the Progressive era, the New Deal, or the wave of regulation to protect the environment and consumers in the late 1960s to mid-1970s—business felt that its collective interest was threatened. Business has responded (for instance, in the late 1970s) by strengthening its political defenses. However, such threats have generally passed quickly. By the 1980s, political support for capitalism in the United States was stronger than for many decades, so that corporations were able to use political resources to seek individual advantage (government contracts, protection from foreign trading rivals, etc.) rather than to defend the collective rights of business as such.

The individualistic political culture also discouraged the development of strong unions; in other countries the strength of the challenge from organized labor has historically encouraged the growth of business organizations. The weakness of business and union organizations in the United States has in turn decreased the likelihood that other economic groups in society (e.g., farmers) will feel the same need to develop a strong cohesive organization as did their British counterparts. Many of the strongest economic interest groups are found in countries where class conflict has been institutionalized, routinized, and finally tamed within the interest group system. Sweden is a case in point. Class conflict has never been a strong factor in American society. In the absence of a strong challenge from organized labor or an anticapitalist political movement, corporations and industries have been free to focus on the issues that divide them.

James Madison would have been pleased by the fragmentation of economic interest groups. Despite how they are usually interpreted, the *Federalist Papers* justifying the new Constitution were not enthusiastic about interest groups. Madison believed that interest groups were inevitable in free societies but that they needed constraining. The solution proffered in the *Federalist Papers* (particularly in number 10) was to have a multiplicity of interest groups, so that competition among them would restrain their power. The fragmentation of economic interest groups is in keeping with this outlook. The success of Madison's vision, however, has not been without its costs. American government has rarely been able to obtain the same degree of help in policy formulation or implementation that governments in other systems have enjoyed. Moreover, rivalry among economic interest groups has often encouraged policy irresponsibility in order to attract members. For example, business groups competed with each other in the 1970s in part by exaggerating threats to businesses from federal regulatory agencies such as OSHA in order to scare business executives into joining. A diplomatic acceptance of the desirability of many of OSHA's rules would not have been as effective in attracting new members.

A number of the factors that explain the weakness of economic groups explain the strength of noneconomic groups. The weakness of class and ideological differences as forces in American politics have created more space in which noneconomic interest groups can operate. Again, the women's movement provides a good example. British feminism has been handicapped by the difficulty of persuading anyone interested in any form of social change to operate outside the framework of the Labour party. Yet within the Labour party, feminists are a small voice compared to the barons who are the leaders of labor unions affiliated to the party and who cast the vast majority of votes at its annual conference. Feminists also have to contend with competition from Labour party members for whom feminism is not the major concern. Such problems for the women's movement are by no means unique to Britain. Wherever a strong left-of-center party (such as the Swedish Social Democratic party) exists, reform-minded interest groups such as feminists are under heavy pressure to work through it. The highly fragmented, all-inclusive nature of the U.S. Democratic party presents no similar barrier to feminist organizations' autonomous pursuit of their own objectives in the United States, as Costain illustrates in Chapter 13.

The weakness of the institutionalized links between government and economic interest groups presents noneconomic groups with enlarged opportunities. When economic interest groups help in the tasks of governance, they are naturally accorded a privileged position in advising on policy formulation. Noneconomic groups tend to be squeezed out. In Britain, for example, the Ministry of Agriculture, Fisheries, and Food (MAFF) developed close partnerships with the National Farmers' Union and the food manufacturers because both these groups could aid MAFF in its own objectives. The NFU could help achieve a more efficient and productive sector by organizing farmers to cooperate with MAFF in modernization, and the food manufacturers, by voluntary "self-regulation," could ease the demands on MAFF to secure a hygienic and healthy food supply through its own inspection efforts. In contrast, public interest groups concerned with food safety, accuracy in labeling, and dangers inherent in modern farming techniques had little practical help to offer the ministry and in consequence were accorded second-class status. The enthusiasm of MAFF for irradiating Britain's food supply in the early 1990s clearly shows the bias toward food manufacturers that their practical usefulness to the ministry produced. The stronger the relationship between government and economic interests, the more likely it is that public interest groups will be squeezed out. American public interest groups are beneficiaries of the comparative weakness of the institutionalization of links between government and economic interests in the United States.

The fragmentation of government in the United States has also helped the noneconomic interest groups. The division of American government into three equal branches, which are in turn fragmented, provides multiple points of access. Indeed, U.S. politics can be pictured as a marketplace in which competing politicians in competing institutions are vying for the public's—or at least the media's—attention, apropos McFarland's discussion of countervailing power. The political traders are always anxious to find a new product, that is, a new policy idea or concern that will help them in this competition. Noneconomic interest groups are an important potential source of ideas for political entrepreneurs in Congress, the executive branch, or even the courts who wish to draw a crowd to their stall. Whereas centralized systems of democracy (such as that in Britain) favor interest groups that can help in the tasks of governance, the fragmented American system provides opportunities for any group that has an idea that attracts attention. This characteristic of the American system was less obvious when power in Congress was more centralized. Since the early 1970s, however, the power of committees and committee chairs has been attenuated, and in the age of television politics, individual legislators have been less willing to accept norms of specialization. Both of these developments have disrupted the "iron triangles" that used to be an important feature of American interest group politics, allegedly tying legislators, agencies, and interest groups together.[4]

Iron triangles have also been disrupted by the explosion in the number and range of interest groups in the United States since the mid-1960s. As Heclo (1978) notes, farm groups (which rarely agree with each other anyway) now have to contend with environmental and consumer groups for control over agricultural policy. What explains this upsurge in interest group activity? Three characteristics of American political culture and society stand out. First, although participation in politics has long been honored in American political culture (though not always, as the abysmally low voter turnout rate shows, in American political practice), political parties have always had a dubious standing. Political independence has a higher standing in American political culture than in most others. When people were politically mobilized by the events of the 1960s (Vietnam, civil rights, and race problems), energy went into interest groups, not political parties. Second, computer-based technology and cheap telephone service spread more rapidly in the United States than elsewhere. Computerized mailings and WATS lines for soliciting memberships were available in the United States sooner than in France, for example. Finally, although *money* wages in the United States lag behind those in half a dozen other countries, the *real living standard* of Americans remains among the highest in the world. Affluence has two consequences. First, it allows citizens to take for granted basic economic needs and worry instead about issues such as the environment that are promoted by noneconomic groups. Second, affluence makes it more likely that citizens—particularly upper-middle-class citizens—will be willing to contribute to interest groups.

CONCLUSION

Thus the American interest group system presents a remarkable contrast in comparative perspective. The economic interest groups seem fragmented and often weak compared to foreign equivalents, the noneconomic interest groups strong. Economic interest groups, as we have noted above, frequently make a useful contribution to the tasks of governance. Noneconomic groups are less equipped to do so. In its interest group system, the United States reflects a balance that might be said to be true of its political system more broadly: Emphasis is placed more on representation and less on effective governance. No interest group system exceeds the capacity of the American one to represent effectively a wide diversity of views. Of course, many sectors of society (such as the poor) are badly represented, but diffuse interests (such as the protection of the environment or the rights of women) are represented better in the American interest group system than in most others. In contrast, the opportunities for producing better governance or improved growth through the sort of partnership between government and economic interests found in Japan or Sweden are absent in the United States.[5]

NOTES

1. For an interesting discussion of the problems of terminology, see Schlozman and Tierney 1986.
2. For a classic study of the weakness of business organizations, see Bauer, Pool, and Dexter 1963.
3. Wilson 1985b. For an interestingly similar contrast between the United States and Sweden, see Lundquist 1980 and Kelman 1981. For a more general comparison of the American and British modes of regulation, see Vogel 1986.
4. Heclo 1978. For an earlier argument that iron triangles were not as common as usually suggested, see Wilson 1977a.
5. For additional perspectives on the comparative study of interest groups, see Alderman 1984; Berger 1981; Jordan and Richardson 1987; Miller 1987; Scholten 1987; Streek and Schmitter 1985; Willetts 1982; F. Wilson 1987; G. Wilson 1990b; and Zeigler 1988.

PART II

The Organization of Interests

5

Interest Group Membership and Organization: Multiple Theories

PAUL A. SABATIER

Prior to the mid-1960s, the formation and internal organization of interest groups in the United States aroused relatively little serious research among American political scientists. Most scholars seemed to take the impressive array of business, labor, farm, ethnic, religious, and professional groups for granted. It seemed that people who shared a set of beliefs were, in most instances, able to organize in their defense, particularly when threatened (Truman 1951) or when assisted by government (McConnell 1966). This portrait was reinforced by a five-nation study showing that interest group membership was more widespread in the United States than in Great Britain, West Germany, Italy, or Mexico (Almond and Verba 1963).

The major concern raised was that, in the words of Schattschneider (1960:35), "the chorus [in the pluralist heaven] sings with a strong upper-class accent." The relative disorganization of the poor was widely recognized, and one of the strategies of the war on poverty was to correct this imbalance through a major—albeit unsuccessful—effort to organize them with governmental assistance (Moynihan 1970; Piven and Cloward 1977). In addition, scholars of regulatory policy generally perceived consumer and environmental interests to be less effectively organized than industrial, labor, and farm groups (Bernstein 1955; McConnell 1966; Nadel 1971). Finally, the extent to which interest group leaders reflected the policy views of their members was of some concern, particularly in labor unions (Michels 1958; Lipset et al. 1956).

Almost all of these scholars accepted Truman's (1951) view of interest groups as people with shared views or interests who united in order to have an impact on other groups in society; if they used governmental institutions to do so, they were political interest groups.[1]

Then in 1965 an economist, Mancur Olson, published *The Logic of Collective Action*; it revolutionized the study of interest groups. Assuming

99

that individuals are self-interested, rational actors, Olson (1965) argued that it would be irrational (and thus uncommon) for people sharing a set of policy beliefs to join a group in pursuit of collective goods, such as government benefits, accruing to both members and nonmembers. Instead, he hypothesized that members join either in exchange for selective material benefits (such as low-cost insurance) or because they are forced to do so (e.g., in a union shop). In such cases, the collective political goods pursued by interest groups are simply a "by-product" of members' real concerns with nonpolitical selective benefits. The basic implication of Olson's work was that primarily political interest groups are very difficult to organize and maintain.

Olson's classic has generated a great deal of empirical and theoretical research on previously neglected topics:

1. How do political interest groups get organized? Who bears the organization costs and why?
2. Why do people join an interest group that espouses political concerns?
3. What percentage of people who share a political belief actually join an interest group that seeks to promote that belief?
4. How important are the group's political positions to its leaders and members?
5. What implications does this have for the extent of belief congruence between members and leaders within interest groups?

As one might expect, diverse answers to these questions have been proposed. In this chapter I first describe the various responses generated over the last forty years:

1. Truman's view of groups as ordering social relations
2. Olson's "by-product" theory as a fundamental challenge to Truman
3. Salisbury's (1969) version of "exchange theory," which views interest group entrepreneurs as critical but follows Olson in viewing material self-interest as the key force motivating their behavior
4. A broader version of exchange theory espoused by most contemporary scholars, which relies upon a variety of incentives for joining and organizing interest groups but views political beliefs and information costs as being more important than did Olson or Salisbury
5. A final view that assumes commitment to the collective political goals of the group is critical to understanding both decisions to join and group internal dynamics.

I then test these theories on two interest groups—one environmental, the other economic—involved in a regional land-use controversy of national significance.

THEORIES OF INTEREST GROUP ORGANIZATION

Truman's Social Order and Disturbance Theory

In 1951, David Truman published *The Governmental Process*, a book that strongly influenced political scientists' conception of interest groups for the next twenty years.

Truman (1951:ch. 2) follows Aristotle in viewing man as a social animal. Individuals are naturally part of a variety of neighborhood, work, ethnic, religious, and other groups, each composed of people with shared skills or attitudes who interact on a regular basis. Formal interest groups emerge largely as a means of ordering internal relations among group members or their relations with other groups. Once a group of people with shared attitudes reaches a certain size, procedures need to be developed for deciding activities, resolving disagreements, and so on. In addition, organization is strongly encouraged by threats to the group's welfare, arising either from other groups or from changes in the socioeconomic environment.[2]

For example, most labor unions in this country emerged when workers who shared a particular craft (carpentry, plumbing, printsetting) interacted regularly and formed unions to stabilize relations among themselves and to bargain with employers. Similarly, most trade associations, professional groups, and farm organizations emerged as a result of normal interaction among people with shared concerns, efforts at mutual assistance, and responses to social disruptions, often in the business cycle (Truman 1951:ch. 4). Almost all these groups increasingly turned to government over time to arbitrate disputes with other groups and to dampen socioeconomic disruptions. Because Truman viewed the formation of interest groups as a natural outgrowth of social interaction, he didn't consider it problematic and thus gave very little attention to groups of people with shared interests who were *not* effectively organized (the poor, consumers, environmentalists).

With respect to internal cohesion within an interest group, Truman's emphasis on shared attitudes as a defining characteristic of a group did not, however, lead to assumptions of homogeneity. Because he perceived most individuals to be members of several groups, he saw multiple and conflicting memberships creating dissensus within any single group (Truman 1951:chs. 6–7). For example, although some members of a steelworkers' union oppose the imposition of unproductive pollution controls on their employers as endangering their firms' competitive position and thus their jobs, other members who enjoy fishing or whose families suffer from respiratory diseases might support such controls. Truman viewed cohesion as especially problematic in large federated groups such as the AFL-CIO, the U.S. Chamber of Commerce, or the American Medical Association. He did not, however, foresee any systematic cleavages between group leaders and members. In fact, one of the principal roles of leaders is to reduce dissensus through internal propaganda and by emphasizing external threats.

Olson's By-Product Theory of Political Interest Groups

Truman assumed that man is a social animal naturally drawn to interact with people of similar views, whereas Olson began with the premise that individuals are autonomous and seek to maximize their own material well-being. Not surprisingly, these two authors came to very different conclusions concerning interest group formation and membership.

Before discussing Olson, one needs to distinguish three types of benefits that can accrue to an individual by belonging to an interest group. The following categories, first developed by Peter B. Clark and James Q. Wilson (1961), have subsequently been used by virtually all interest group scholars:

- material—tangible rewards that can usually be translated into monetary terms
- solidary—social rewards that derive from associating in group activities
- purposive—rewards associated with ideological or issue-oriented goals that offer no significant tangible benefits to members

Olson (1965) added a crucial distinction between selective and collective benefits (or incentives): *Selective* benefits accrue only to members of the organization; *collective* benefits accrue to both members and nonmembers. As illustrated in Table 5.1, the two typologies are crosscutting: Material and solidary benefits can be either selective or collective, although purposive benefits are necessarily collective.

Olson developed by-product theory to explain the behavior of large economic groups, but he felt his analysis should apply to all large groups.[3] Assuming that individuals operate with perfect information to maximize their self-interest, Olson argued that rational people perform benefit-cost calculations in deciding whether to participate in an interest group. Because the provision of *collective* benefits from a group's lobbying activities is very seldom contingent upon any single individual's decision to join a group and, when provided, accrue (by definition) to nonmembers as well as members, rational individuals will "free-ride" rather than join. That is, they will let others pay for the organization and its lobbying while they reap their share of the benefits of that lobbying. This is true even when their share of the collective benefits exceeds the costs to them of joining.

TABLE 5.1
Typology of Benefits for Interest Group Members

	Scope of Beneficiaries	
Type of Benefit	Selective (only to group members)	Collective (wider than group members)
Material (tangible, usually monetary, rewards)	Discounts on insurance, member publications	Seeking change in law to lower taxes for everyone
Solidary (rewards from social interaction)	Member-only dances, participation in group decisionmaking	Public dances or BBQs
Purposive (psychic/moral satisfaction from pursuing official goals related to public welfare)		Working for changes in law to benefit underprivileged

Source: Adapted from Clark and Wilson 1961, Olson 1965, and Wilson 1973:ch. 3.

In such instances, individuals seeking to maximize their own welfare will increase income by not paying fees at the same time they continue to receive their share of the collective benefits. Interest groups must either resort to coercion or entice potential members to join through some type of *selective* material or solidary incentive that only group members receive (Olson 1965:16). According to this view, the political activities of an interest group—insofar as they seek to produce legal or financial benefits available to classes of people broader than the group's membership—are a by-product of the provision for selective incentives.

If Olson is correct, the formation of any interest group is very problematic. Organization is most likely in situations in which an individual concludes that the collective good will not be provided if he or she does not organize the group *and* the individual share of collective benefits exceeds the share of the organization costs. It may also happen in situations in which an individual's—or a small subset of individuals'—contribution is sufficiently large to be noticeable to other members *and* in which members have some means of monitoring tendencies toward free-riding and of convincing free-riders to contribute (Olson 1965:34, 44). Organization will definitely *not* happen when any potential organizer's share of the benefits is relatively small. As a result, groups are most likely to get organized in situations in which the number of beneficiaries is small (and hence an individual's share of the benefits quite large and the costs of monitoring free-riding quite low) *and* where organization costs are low relative to an individual's share of the collective benefits (Olson 1965:46–48). Once groups are organized, new members can be added both by providing selective benefits and by coercion.

Olson's analysis suggests that most groups should be local—at least in the initial stages—because beneficiaries are relatively few and organization costs relatively low. He maintained that national trade associations exist because most industries are oligopolistic—hence, they have large per share benefits and can easily monitor free-riding (Olson 1965:143). Olson could clearly explain the relatively unorganized status of groups with large numbers of small per share beneficiaries and high organization costs—consumers, environmentalists, and the poor. Yet these interests are not completely unorganized: Where did the Sierra Club, Audubon Society, Consumers' Union, and NAACP come from? For that matter, where did the plethora of labor unions and professional associations come from?[4] Once organized, they gain members through coercion (union shops) and selective incentives (Olson 1965:132–141), but Olson had difficulty explaining how they got organized in the first place.

One temptation for Olson was to expand the range of benefits to include the psychic rewards to the individual from providing a collective good. According to this "explanation," John Muir was willing to bear the enormous costs of organizing the Sierra Club through years of struggle over damming the Hetch Hetchy Valley because it made him "feel good." Although Olson toyed with this idea, he ultimately rejected it (1965:61, n.)—to his credit. Expanding self-interest to include the personal satisfaction from altruistic acts renders the entire enterprise nonfalsifiable: *Any* behavior becomes "self-interested," and *any* benefit can be reclassified as "selective," that is, accruing only to the individual who participated (Barry 1970:33; White 1976:271; Hardin 1982; Margolis 1982:106). Although nonfalsifiable assumptions may sometimes be justified as premises from which falsifiable deductions are drawn, to introduce them as a major element of the topic under investigation is to violate one of the basic principles of the scientific method (Popper 1959). Thus the preferred strategy is to limit Olson's concept of selective incentives to material and solidary benefits and see how much this clear, parsimonious model can explain.

With respect to membership in existing interest groups, at least two falsifiable hypotheses can reasonably be deduced from Olson's argument: (1) Only a very small percentage of the potential beneficiaries of a group's lobbying activities will voluntarily join a group (or remain in it). As such activities usually provide collective benefits, rational individuals will freeride;[5] (2) Because almost all members join a group for its selective benefits, they should so respond when asked. The evidence accumulated since 1965 regarding these hypotheses is mixed. Consistent with the former hypothesis, several studies show that only a small minority of people who share a collective interest are actually members of interest groups that ostensibly seek to further that interest (Mitchell 1979; Olson 1979). But the extent to which free-riding is the major reason for not joining is, to my knowledge, an unexplored topic. With respect to the second hypothesis, surveys of members of both economic and purposive groups sometimes provide clear support for the sort of selective material and solidary benefits Olson envisaged (Browne 1976) but usually indicate that collective benefits are more important inducements to membership (Marsh 1976; Tillock and Morrison 1979; Moe 1981:540–541; Godwin and Mitchell 1982; Cigler and Hansen 1983; Cook 1984; Rothenberg 1989).

By-product theorists, however, are very skeptical of such evidence for the importance of collective incentives. Respondents may simply be providing the socially acceptable response (Olson 1979:149; Shackleton 1978:376). A convincing case requires a comparison of the views of *members* and *potential members* and evidence that members are more ideological (i.e., more concerned with collective/purposive goods) than potential members who share the same interests but do not join. Olson would expect no difference between members and potential members on public policy topics of interest to the group because support for collective goods is, in his view, irrelevant to the decision to join and thus should be uncorrelated with that decision.[6] Later in this chapter, I make precisely that sort of comparison between members and potential members for two interest groups.

Finally, Olson never said much about congruence between group *leaders* and *members* concerning policy attitudes relevant to the group's goals. But a reasonable inference (borrowed from Moe 1980) is that congruence should *not* be expected as members are drawn to the organization by selective material and solidary benefits rather than the collective political benefits.

Salisbury's Exchange Theory:
Group Entrepreneurs as Small-Business People

In an important paper, Salisbury (1969) developed an early version of exchange theory that was consistent with Olson's basic argument but expanded it in several important respects. First, like Olson, he explicitly rejected Truman's (1951) contention that interest groups naturally arise out of the interaction of people with common interests responding to societal disruptions. For both Salisbury and Olson, the formation of an interest group was exceedingly problematic: It requires somebody to emerge who is willing to bear the substantial costs of organizing a group by locating potential members, organizing meetings, and convincing them to contribute time and money to the new group. Although Salisbury did not emphasize free-riding as much as did Olson, he, too, began with the premise that most individuals are preoccupied with their material self-interest and thus would be unwilling to contribute much to the provision of a collective good.

Salisbury's solution to group formation was to point to individual entrepreneurs willing to bear the initial organization costs in return not for a share of the collective benefits but instead for a staff job with the new organization. This enabled him to account for the formation of a variety of consumer, farm, labor, and environmental groups with which Olson had difficulty. Acknowledging that the organizers of some purposive groups might be skilled at articulating a common group interest, Salisbury nevertheless argued that group organizers were essentially small-business people offering benefits for the price of membership in order to finance their jobs (1969:11–13, 17–18, 25).

Second, he argued explicitly "that most group activity has little to do with efforts to affect public policy decisions but is concerned rather with the internal exchange of benefits by which the group is organized and sustained" (Salisbury 1969:20). These benefits can be selective material, solidary, or expressive, with the first predominating in most viable organizations. For Salisbury, as for James Q. Wilson (1973), group leaders were preoccupied with organizational maintenance—with providing whatever was necessary to keep the dues coming.

Finally, Salisbury spent very little time on leader-member belief congruence, arguing that it was irrelevant as long as the benefits offered were sufficient to maintain membership. He did suggest, however, that congruence would probably be high in organizations where collective policy benefits provided important inducements to membership (1969:27–28).

Salisbury's emphasis on the importance of interest group entrepreneurs is a major contribution to the field. In a study of the origins of eighty-three national public interest groups, for example, Jeffrey Berry (1977:24; 1978) found that only twenty-four could be explained by Truman's disturbance theory whereas fifty-five could be traced to the efforts of a specific "entrepreneur."

Yet most of the examples Berry discussed—such as Ralph Nader, John Gardner of Common Cause, Cleveland Amory of the Fund for Animals—hardly fit Salisbury's portrait of a salesperson looking for a staff job. Instead, they seemed to be people deeply committed to the cause they were espousing who organized a group to assist them in that effort. Salisbury's entrepreneur may, however, be more important in organizing economic interest groups. But like Olson's, his view of individuals as exceedingly self-interested—and of group leaders as preoccupied with keeping their business operating—seemed to miss something critical in a wide variety of consumer, environmental, civil rights, and other groups.

An Expanded Version of Exchange Theory: Dominant but Less Parsimonious

In the more than twenty years since the publication of Salisbury's essay, exchange theory has become the dominant paradigm among students of interest group organization. Most of the major texts give a prominent role to exchange relationships between leaders and members, to the importance of various incentives, and to problems of organizing and maintaining such groups (Berry 1984; Schlozman and Tierney 1986; Hrebenar and Scott 1990). But the modern version has expanded and modified Salisbury's original proposal in several important respects.

First, and perhaps most importantly, several studies have shown that members of most groups—economic as well as purposive—view contributing to collective political benefits as a more important inducement to membership than the sort of selective material and solidary benefits Salisbury and Olson emphasized (Marsh 1976; Moe 1980, 1981; Godwin and Mitchell 1982; Cigler and Hansen 1983; Cook 1984; Rothenberg 1989). As noted previously, however, these results from member surveys should be taken with a grain of salt pending evidence that members are, in fact, more committed to the organization's policy goals than are nonmembers.

Second, Salisbury's notion of the entrepreneur has been expanded considerably. Rather than being viewed primarily as small-business people trying to make a living selling memberships, the organizers of many groups are perceived as being genuinely motivated by policy goals (Berry 1977; McFarland 1976, 1984). In addition, the critical role of government agencies and foundations in organizing and funding many groups has been repeatedly documented (Sabatier 1975; Walker 1983; Hansen 1985).

Third, leader-member exchange relationships in many groups are not as critical as Salisbury envisaged. For example, Berry (1977:28) found that 30 percent of national public interest organizations in the early 1970s had *no* members; they were supported almost entirely by foundation and government grants. Jack Walker's (1983) survey of national interest groups found that citizen and nonprofit organizations received an average of 43 percent and 24 percent of their revenues, respectively, from nonmember sources, primarily government, foundations, and individual gifts. Organizational maintenance is still critical, but many groups are less dependent upon member dues than was once thought.

Finally, with respect to leader-member belief congruence, scholars working within the exchange tradition have conflicting views. Some contend that interest group staff are preoccupied with maintenance needs and thus very solicitous of members' policy preferences, whereas others argue that they are often given considerable freedom to pursue their own policy agendas as compensation for substandard salaries (Wilson 1973; Hayes 1986).

In analyzing congruence, Terry Moe (1980, 1981) distinguishes between organizations in which selective material incentives are important inducements to membership versus groups in which purposive or collective policy benefits predominate. In the former, there is no reason to expect leader-member policy congruence, as the organization's policy positions are irrelevant to group maintenance. In the latter—comprising most business and farm organizations, as well as virtually all noneconomic groups (Moe 1981:54)—congruence should be substantial as leaders will be solicitous of members' views and will go to considerable lengths to influence them. He also notes, however, that information costs probably preclude most members from having accurate perceptions of their leaders' beliefs and actions (Moe 1980).

The expanded version of exchange theory can clearly account for a higher percentage of the organizational features of interest groups than the theories previously proposed by Truman, Olson, and Salisbury. Truman completely missed the importance of selective incentives and the problems of turning potential groups into viable organizations. Olson and Salisbury offered clear and parsimonious explanations of those phenomena, but their view of the individual as exceedingly egoistic and materialistic has great difficulty accounting for the presence of hundreds of viable consumer, environmental, civil rights, and other groups. In fact, there is increasing evidence that many citizens are willing to bear what they perceive to be their "fair share" of providing collective goods, rather than simply maximizing their own material well-being (Sears et al. 1980; Marwell and Ames 1981; Margolis 1982; Tyler 1990).

The broader version of exchange theory is becoming so inclusive, however, that it risks losing its coherence and parsimony. Stating the "first principles" of the expanded version is becoming more difficult. A theory that appears to account for everything—after the fact—may be incapable of predicting anything. The proponents of this view might consider concentrating their efforts on developing a clearer set of theoretical premises and falsifiable hypotheses.

Commitment Theory

Whereas Olson and, to a lesser extent, Salisbury started from the assumption that most people are egoistic materialists, commitment theory received its initial impetus from empirical research demonstrating that political party activists are more ideologically extreme than ordinary party members (McCloskey et al. 1960; Miller and Jennings 1987). From this came its basic premise: The high degree of time, energy, and resources needed to be involved in group activities stems from "beliefs about good policy" (Sabatier and McLaughlin 1990). Expected *collective* benefits arising from a group's political activities thus are critical to political participation.

These benefits may be material—for example, financial benefits arising from changes in law—or they may be more ideological/purposive. In many cases, they will be a mixture of the two. Self-interested behavior typically becomes intertwined with congruent conceptions of improving social welfare, either out of self-respect or concerns of political efficacy (Tesser 1978; Margolis 1982:100). Although material self-interest may create an incentive to join an interest group, typically only those individuals for whom the perceived benefits are quite large or who have buttressed self-interest with ideological incentives will be sufficiently committed to join and, then, to become leaders. Thus commitment theory expects to find increasing degrees of commitment to collective benefits as one moves from the potential members of a group to its members and then to its leaders (Sabatier and McCubbin 1990).

Commitment theory would expect a group to be organized by potential members or by entrepreneurs strongly committed to its collective political goals. Their motivation could be significant material self-interest (e.g., adjacent landowners organizing a group to save a scenic area) or it could be ideological (e.g., Ralph Nader) (McCarry 1972).

Members would come from the subset of particularly committed people within its "potential" group (i.e., people who professed allegiance to the interest group's purposes or who would share in its collective benefits). These committed people, however, make up only a small percentage of potential beneficiaries. Commitment theory, then, agrees with by-product theory in hypothesizing that only a small percentage of the beneficiaries of a group's political activities will be members, but it does so for radically different reasons. Olson argued that rational individuals will free-ride unless the group offers selective incentives greater than the cost of membership. I contend, instead (Sabatier and McCubbin 1990), that most potential members will lack the material or ideological commitment to take the time and expense to join; most people are simply not very interested in, or informed about, policy issues (Verba and Nie 1972; Lau and Sears 1986).

As for belief congruence between members and leaders, commitment theory clearly predicts that leaders will be more committed to the group's collective purposes—more ideologically extreme—than its members because it is that commitment that makes them willing to bear the costs of going to meetings, writing letters, and all of the other mundane tasks necessary to keep the group going (Sabatier and McLaughlin 1990).

Commitment theory might seem to apply better to purposive groups than to traditional economic interest groups. We'll see.

Summary Comparison of Theories

The arguments of each of the five theories on various topics related to group formation, membership, and belief congruence between leaders and members are summarized in Table 5.2.

BACKGROUND AND DATA BASES

It is now time to apply these theories to two interest groups involved in land-use and environmental policy in the Lake Tahoe Basin. Although primarily a regional issue involving the states of California and Nevada, Tahoe is also of national significance. It has been the subject of three national statutes—the Tahoe compacts of 1969 and 1980, as well as the 1980 Burton-Santini Act—and the federal government has spent approximately $200 million since 1965 on water quality and land acquisition in the area.[7] Although caution should certainly be exercised in generalizing Tahoe results to other groups, most interest groups are, in fact, local or regional. And we probably have more detailed comparative information on the views of potential members, actual members, and leaders at Tahoe than anywhere else.

TABLE 5.2
Expectations Regarding Group Formation, Membership, and Leader-Member Belief Congruence

	Theoretical Approach				
Topic	Truman's Order and Disturbance Theory	Olson's By-Product Theory	Salisbury's Exchange Theory	Broader View of Exchange Theory	Commitment Theory
FORMATION How do groups get organized?	Result of natural interaction and societal disturbances	Very problematic. Only situations of few beneficiaries and low organizational costs	Result of entrepreneurs seeking livelihood	Many ways, usually by purposive entrepreneurs, governmental organizations, or foundations	Result of purposive individuals or organizations
MEMBERSHIP Why do people join?	Natural interaction of people with similar beliefs and interests	Selective benefits or coercion	Primarily selective benefits	Selective and purposive benefits	Collective material and purposive benefits
PERCENTAGE JOINING What percentage of people who share a belief join a group? If they don't join, why not?	Relatively high	Very low because of free-riding	?	?	Low because policy beliefs not salient for people
BELIEF CONGRUENCE Do group leaders mirror the policy views of members?	Leaders try to reduce member dissensus arising from conflicting membership	Probably low because of selective incentives	Depends on benefits: *Low* for selective, *High* for collective	Depends on benefits: *Low* for selective, *High* for collective except for info costs	No; group leaders more extreme than members
IMPORTANCE OF POLITICS How important are groups' political positions to leaders and members?	Increasing over time	Low	Generally low	Depends on benefits, but generally high	High

Interest Groups at Tahoe

Lake Tahoe is a large, extremely beautiful lake in the Sierra Nevada Mountains on the California-Nevada border, about 200 miles east of San Francisco. Over the past twenty-five years, the Tahoe Basin has become one of the premier recreation areas in the United States. Although this trend has been viewed with favor by most local government officials and businesspeople, it has also created rather serious problems of sewage disposal, soil erosion, the gradual urbanization of a scenic mountain setting, and a significant reduction in the lake's exceptional clarity (Goldman 1981). The desirability of land-use controls and their effects on environmental quality, the viability of the basin's economy, and property rights have been the subject of intense debate over the last thirty years—resulting in the formation of the bistate Tahoe Regional Planning Agency (TRPA) in 1970, a major revision to the TRPA compact in 1980, and numerous interventions by water-quality control agencies (Strong 1984; Ingram and Sabatier 1987). Among the principal interest groups involved in this conflict have been the League to Save Lake Tahoe and the basin's chambers of commerce.

Since its formation in 1965 by second-home owners concerned about the development of highways and casinos in the basin, the League to Save Lake Tahoe has been the major interest group concerned with protecting environmental quality in the area.[8] It initially grew very rapidly, attaining a peak of 7,000 members in 1972, but membership declined to about 2,500 at the time of our research team's 1984 survey. In 1984 approximately 58 percent of league members owned second homes in the basin, 11 percent had a principal residence or some other form of property there, and 31 percent owned no basin property at all.

The league is primarily a political and educational organization, relying heavily upon litigation and lobbying by its staff and board to achieve its aims of protecting the scenic and environmental qualities of the Tahoe Basin. Its 1984 budget of $225,000 supported two full-time staff and a substantial lawsuit. Dues of $25 per year accounted for about 30 percent of revenues, with the remainder coming from a variety of fund-raising events and special contributions. Selective incentives included a newsletter appearing several times a year and whatever solidary benefits could be gleaned from participating in the league's annual meeting and two or three social fund-raisers annually.

There are four chambers of commerce in the Tahoe Basin, two in each state. Our analysis focused on the North Tahoe Chamber of Commerce, formed in 1953, with jurisdiction over the north and west shores on the California side.[9] Its 1984 membership included approximately 250 businesses, most of them in the service sector and many tourist related. In

1984 it had a staff of two and a budget of $70,000. About $25,000 came from member dues ($35 for individuals, $120 for businesses), the remainder from the county ($19,000 for running a tourist information bureau) and special fund-raising events. The chamber lobbied for business interests before various governmental bodies and engaged in a wide range of community activities from business promotions (e.g., an Oktoberfest) to educational programs and beautification efforts. In addition to these activities, which provided collective benefits to the North Tahoe business community, the chamber also offered its members a variety of selective benefits, including customer referral services and discounts on health insurance and bulk mail.

Data Bases

The data used in this chapter come from a set of interviews with leaders of the various organizations, from documents in their files, and from several mail surveys administered in fall 1984.

To ascertain members' views, we sent similar questionnaires to random *samples* of the membership of the League to Save Lake Tahoe and the North Tahoe Chamber of Commerce. As I explain in greater detail below, the potential members of the two interest groups were identified as second-home owners in the basin (for the league) and businesspeople on the California north shore (for the North Tahoe Chamber). Their attitudes were taken from a shorter questionnaire mailed to a random *sample* of all basin property owners. Finally, the *entire* leadership (staff and board members) of the two organizations were surveyed as part of a general survey of policy elites in the Tahoe Basin (see Sabatier and McLaughlin 1988, 1990 for details).[10]

RESULTS

Group Formation

As indicated previously, the League to Save Lake Tahoe was organized by about a half dozen second-home owners who felt the natural beauty of the area was being threatened by development. Some of the organizers were fighting projects (e.g., the Roundhill Casino) near their homes. Most were lawyers and businesspeople from the San Francisco Bay Area who were also personal acquaintances. They began writing letters, appearing at hearings, lobbying governmental officials, and so on. The organization grew quite rapidly and after about a year was able to hire its first staffperson.[11]

The formation of the league is probably most consistent with commitment theory: The focus was clearly on collective purposive and material benefits, and the initial leaders were very committed. It is also consistent with Truman: The formation was in reaction to disturbances (proposed construction projects) and was facilitated by previous interaction patterns. It clearly was *not* consistent with Salisbury: None of the original organizers ever had a staff position with the organization. Olson does not provide much help: The league was organized by a small group of people, but the relatively minor benefits to most and the enormous number of potential beneficiaries would not really fit his oligopolistic scenario. Finally, the results are consistent with the expanded version of exchange theory—but, then, virtually any formation scenario would be.

Less is known about the formation of the North Tahoe Chamber of Commerce in 1953. The available evidence indicates that it was organized by a few prominent local businesspeople in order to promote the area's tourist economy.[12] This would clearly be compatible with commitment theory and even with Olson (i.e., a few large beneficiaries bearing the costs to provide a collective good that would not otherwise be provided). In fact, it would be consistent with all of the theories except Salisbury's, as none of the organizers of the chamber apparently ever held a staff position with the organization.

Percentage of Potential Members Who Join

This requires that the potential members for each organization first be identified. Potential members of the North Tahoe Chamber are the owners and managers of all businesses on the California north shore. In 1984 its executive director estimated 800 to 900 such businesses, of which 250—or about 30 percent—were members of the chamber.

Identifying the set of potential members for the league is more difficult. As already mentioned, it has two principal types of members: people with second homes in the basin (58 percent) and those with no property in the basin (31 percent). Operationalizing a potential constituency for the latter group is impossible, as it includes anyone living outside the basin who is concerned about protecting environmental quality at Lake Tahoe. On the other hand, the potential constituency for the former group is all second-home owners in the basin—easily operationalized from our property-owners survey—and that is the subset of league members used in our analysis. This assumes that all second-home owners have a collective incentive to protect the basin's environmental quality (presumably one of the reasons they decided to purchase a vacation home in the basin rather than elsewhere). The best estimate is that about 6 percent of second-home owners in 1984 were members of the league.[13]

Reasons for Joining

The membership surveys for the league and the chamber each contained a set of items developed by the organization's leadership dealing with topics of concern to them. Many of these items can be conceptualized in terms of selective and collective incentives.[14]

Table 5.3 reports league members' ratings of the importance of eleven activities, with the activities subsequently categorized as yielding collective or selective benefits. The results clearly point to collective benefits as more important. Of the nine activities yielding collective benefits, four were rated as "very important" by at least 60 percent of the membership and an additional two were rated as "important" by at least 80 percent. Three of the top four involved classic lobbying for governmental programs, whereas the fourth involved public information. In contrast, none of the four activities involving selective benefits generated anything like this level of support. Only the newsletter was deemed important (or utilized) by even a bare majority of the respondents. Although these items dealt with members' priorities for the league rather than their reasons for joining, another question that dealt specifically with that topic produced similar results.[15] Finally, Table 5.3 indicates that the priorities for league second-home members were very similar to those for all league members.

We turn now to the North Tahoe Chamber. The data in Table 5.4 are based on questions soliciting members' views on the proper roles for the chamber (from a list of seven developed by chamber leaders) and the most important role for the chamber. The data again indicate the importance of collective benefits. The two roles identified as "the most important" were providing a tourist information center (40 percent of respondents) and serving as a community organizer (30 percent). Both help the North Tahoe (business) community as a whole, not just chamber members. In fact, 91 percent of the activities considered "most important" for the chamber by its members could be classified as providing collective benefits. The only selective benefit deemed important by respondents was the chamber's customer referral service. In fairness to Olson, it should be mentioned that the bulk-mail service and insurance available through the chamber were omitted from the questionnaire, as was the possible utility of membership in developing business contacts. Even if these selective material and solidary incentives *may* have been important in members' decisions to join the chamber, they apparently were not viewed as sufficiently important by chamber leaders to include in the survey instrument.[16]

Members of both the league and the North Tahoe Chamber thus profess to view collective benefits as more important than selective ones. This would seem to support the broadened version of exchange theory, as well as commitment theory and Truman. It would argue against by-product

TABLE 5.3
Activities Members of the League to Save Lake Tahoe Feel the League Should Pursue: Selective vs. Collective Benefits

	All League Members (n = 302)			League Members with Second Homes (n = 165)		
	% Very Important[a]	% Important[a]	Mean	% Very Important[a]	% Important[a]	Mean
Activities with Collective Benefits						
Inform public of environmental issues	81	18	3.80	76	22	3.75
Lobby state and federal government	80	18	3.78	77	22	3.76
Lobby government in the basin	67	27	3.61	66	30	3.61
Increase funds for erosion control and land buyout	60	37	3.57	51	46	3.47
Sponsor research in Tahoe problems	32	57	3.20	25	62	3.11
Become involved in outside environmental issues that affect the basin	20	62	2.96	17	64	2.91
Protect property values at the lake	14	35	2.49	17	37	2.58
Increase public recreation at the lake	5	22	2.05	5	20	2.00
Become involved in national environmental issues	4	19	1.96	2	22	1.92
Activities with Selective Benefits						
Better inform members through more newsletters	7	45	2.53	6	48	2.52
Organize activities and outings	1	21	2.02	1	16	1.92
Attend educational lectures on Tahoe issues, e.g., erosion control[b]	11	—	—	10	—	—
Attend league-sponsored recreation, e.g., a square dance[b]	4	—	—	3	—	—

[a] These are ranked on a 4-point scale, where 4 = very important, 3 = important, 2 = of little importance, and 1 = no importance. Only the percentages for the first two categories—plus the overall mean—are given here.
[b] These are ranked on a 3-point scale, where 3 = frequent, 2 = infrequent, and 1 = never. Only the percentage for the first category is reported here.

TABLE 5.4

Members' Views of the Proper Roles and Most Important Role for the North Tahoe Chamber of Commerce: Selective vs. Collective Benefits (n = 90)

	Proper Roles[a]		*Most Important Role*	
	Frequency	*% Total*	*Frequency*	*% Total*
Activities with Collective Benefits				
Tourist Information Center	86	96	30	40
Community Organizer	80	89	23	30
Representative to Government Agencies	54	60	10	13
Political Advocacy Group	26	29	4	5
Educator/Seminars[b]	39	43	2	3
Subtotal			69	90
Activities with Selective Benefits				
Customer Referral	56	62	6	8
Prestige Symbol	15	17	1	1
Subtotal			7	9

[a]A respondent could list several different roles as "proper."
[b]This is really a mixed collective/selective benefit. The seminars, e.g., on telephone marketing, were open to all residents of the area, and 30 to 40 percent of those attending were not chamber members.

theory. Olson (1979:149) would reply, however, that such statements should be viewed with great skepticism, particularly because some possibly important selective benefits were omitted from the chamber questionnaire. In his view, a convincing case for collective benefits would require evidence that such benefits are more important to members than to potential members; if not, collective benefits may be important to everyone but irrelevant to joining an interest group. It is to this topic that we now turn.

Comparing Members' Views with Those of Potential Members and Leaders

Potential groups are people who share a certain interest, such as environmental protection or public health. Both Olson and commitment theory agree that only a small percentage of any potential group will take the time and expense to join an interest group seeking to promote that value through governmental activity. But they disagree radically on the motives for joining. Olson views selective incentives as the key. Thus there should be no significant difference in policy views (related to the group's interest) between members and potential members, as policy views are irrelevant to the decision to join. In contrast, commitment theory argues that members should be *more* committed to those policy views than potential members, as commitment to the collective interest is the core reason for bearing the costs of membership (Sabatier and McCubbin 1990).

By the same reasoning, commitment theory hypothesizes that people who take the time and effort to become leaders of an interest group should be even more committed to its collective benefits than ordinary members (Sabatier and McLaughlin 1990). In contrast, broadened exchange theory would contend that groups for whom collective incentives are important inducements to membership should have substantial congruence in views between leaders and members because leaders are preoccupied with group maintenance and thus will be careful not to offend members (Moe 1981). This would not necessarily be the case for groups dependent upon selective incentive, collective benefits being irrelevant to the membership decisions. As collective benefits are apparently important inducements for both the league and the chamber, however, broadened exchange theory would expect to find substantial leader-member congruence.

To test these hypotheses, this section compares the policy views of members of the league and the chamber with their (1) potential members and (2) leaders (boards and staff). Following the advice of Gormley et al. (1983), comparisons will be made on several different levels of attitudes related to the group's collective benefits, including general ideological scales, a set of specific policy proposals, and evaluations of the performance of various institutions.[17]

Table 5.5 compares the views of members of the League to Save Lake Tahoe with those of potential members (people with second homes in the basin) and those of organizational leaders. Also provided are the views of the overall league membership in order to demonstrate that members with second homes are not noticeably different from the total.

The data in Table 5.5 provide striking confirmation for commitment theory, which predicts increasingly pro-environmental, antidevelopment views as one moves from potential member to member to leader. A difference-of-means test[18] suggests that the views of league members with second homes differed significantly from those of all second-home property owners (the potential membership) on all three general attitudinal scales, on thirteen of the fourteen specific policy proposals, and on all ten of the organizational performance evaluations. Leaders were more extreme than members on two of three general attitudinal scales, eleven of fourteen policy proposals, and five of ten organizational performance evaluations.

Moreover, in virtually every case, the difference was in the predicted direction. As participation increased from potential member to member to leader, people perceived greater environmental degradation; they were more in favor of environmental regulation; they were less politically conservative; they were more supportive of public transit and less supportive of highway expansion; they were more opposed to growth-inducing measures such as expanded airplane service and sewage-treatment plants; they were more in favor of concentrating development and prohibiting it on steep, erodible slopes; and they evaluated the performance of land developers, casinos, property rights groups, and local governments more negatively and the environmental agencies (the California TRPA and Lahontan Water Board) and the League to Save more positively. There were a few exceptions, particularly the policy proposal to increase public shoreline and beaches, but the overall trend was clear.

Conversely, Olson's by-product theory comes out quite poorly. The consistent differences between members and potential members suggest that members' professed commitment to collective benefits was not simply the socially correct response. Members were, in fact, more committed to collective benefits than people in a similar situation—owners of a second home—who did not join. By the same token, expanded exchange theory certainly would not have predicted that leaders were more extreme than members about half the time in a purposive organization. Moe and others could, though, take refuge in the lack of significant differences about half the time and the possibility that information costs kept members from knowing how extreme their leaders really were.

A quite different story, however, emerges with respect to the North Tahoe Chamber of Commerce. Commitment theory would predict increasingly pro-development, conservative views as participation increased from potential member to member to leader. By-product theory would predict no significant differences in policy views between members and potential members, whereas expanded exchange theory would expect few differences between members and leaders (given the apparent importance of collective benefits to the membership, as shown in Table 5.4). The results are found in Table 5.6.

In general, the data reveal few significant differences between North Tahoe Chamber members and potential members in the north shore business community (or the entire basin, for that matter). The differences were statistically significant ($p < .05$) on only one of the three general scales, three of fourteen policy proposals, and three of ten performance evaluations. On virtually all items where major differences existed, they were in the direction *opposite* from that predicted by commitment theory. Chamber members were less conservative than potential members, more supportive of concentrating development, more in favor of increasing public access to the shoreline, and more favorably disposed toward the TRPA. Although these results reflect poorly on commitment theory, the general absence of significant differences between members and potential members is consistent with by-product theory.

The differences in Table 5.6 between chamber members and their *board*, however, tended to be larger and in the direction expected by commitment

TABLE 5.5
Comparing the Attitudes of the Board, Members, and Potential Members of the League to Save Lake Tahoe

		Members		Potential Members
	Board of Directors (n = 32)	All (n = 302)	with Second Homes (n = 165)	Property Owners with Second Homes (n = 432)
Attitudinal scales				
Perceived environmental problems scale (from 0 to 100)	77.0	77.0	75.2[a]	60.9
Pro-environmental and antilocal scale (from 1 to 7)	6.7[d]	6.2	6.2[a]	5.3
Political conservatism scale	3.4[d]	4.0	4.1[a]	4.8
Policy proposals (from 1 to 7)				
Limit auto use and improve transit	5.3[f]	4.9	4.6[c]	4.2
Expand highways in basin	1.6[f]	2.0	2.1[a]	3.4
Road toll for visitors	6.1[d]	4.6	4.5[a]	3.0
Tax for public transport	6.2[d]	5.3	5.2[a]	4.4
Expand air service	2.5[f]	3.2	3.4[b]	4.0
Prohibit more gaming casinos	6.8[f]	6.4	6.3[b]	5.8
Expand sewage capacity to accommodate development	2.2[f]	2.9	2.9[a]	3.8
Concentrate development/ prohibit sprawl	5.7[f]	5.3	5.4[a]	4.6
More development on flat lands	1.8[d]	2.4	2.4[a]	3.2
No housing on steep slopes	6.9[d]	6.3	6.2*	5.9
Public buyout of down-zoned property	6.6[d]	5.8	5.7[b]	5.2
Remove ugly buildings and redevelop	5.6	5.3	5.2[a]	4.6

(continues)

TABLE 5.5 (continued)

| | Board of Directors (n = 32) | Members | | Potential Members |
		All (n = 302)	with Second Homes (n = 165)	Property Owners with Second Homes (n = 432)
Increase public shoreline	4.1	4.2	3.8c	4.4
Create national recreation area in basin	5.5g	5.3	4.8b	4.2
Performance evaluations (from 0 to 100)				
Land developers	22.7	17.6	16.0a	30.6
Gaming industry	11.0	11.7	9.8	31.6
Business groups, e.g.,				
Chamber of Commerce	20.0f	28.5	30.0a	44.3
Property rights groups	20.1e	33.0	36.3a	50.7
Local governments	22.0f	30.2	31.3a	40.5
TRPA	46.8	50.1	51.2c	45.8
U.S. Forest Service	64.1	54.3	57.2a	64.8
CTRPA	63.0f	51.0	52.3a	43.7
Lahontan Water Board	63.4	55.4	57.9b	50.2
League to Save	82.3f	76.9	75.5a	55.0

[a,b,c] = Probability (.005, .01, .05, respectively) of making an error in asserting that the mean value of the beliefs of second-home members differs from that of potential members (i.e., Basin property owners with second homes); * = $p < .05$ on one-tailed test.

[d,e,f,g] = Probability (.005, .01, .05, .10) of making an error in asserting significant differences between the board and members with second homes; two-tailed test.

Note: All the policy proposals and the latter two attitudinal scales have values ranging from 1 (not at all in favor) to 7 (very much in favor). All the performance evaluations range from 0 (extremely poor job) to 100 (extremely good job), and the first attitudinal scale goes from 0 (not at all a problem) to 100 (extremely serious problem).

TABLE 5.6
Comparing the Attitudes of the Board, Members, and Potential Members of the North Tahoe Chamber of Commerce

	Board of Directors (n = 20)	Members (n = 90)	Potential Members	
			Northshore Business People (n = 54)	All Tahoe Business People (n = 127)
Attitudinal scales				
Perceived environment problems scale (from 0 to 100)	37.8	46.8	48.0	47.3
Pro-environmental and antilocal scale (from 1 to 7)	3.5[d]	4.6	4.1	4.0
Political conservatism scale	5.3	4.9	5.3	5.3
Policy proposals (from 1 to 7)				
Limit auto use and improve transit	4.1	4.4	4.1	3.9
Expand highways in basin	4.2	3.4	3.4	4.3
Road toll for visitors	3.2	3.6	3.1	3.0
Tax for public transport	3.2[e]	4.7[b]	3.4	3.5
Expand air service	5.5	4.6	5.0	5.2
Prohibit more gaming casinos	5.3	5.2	4.5	5.0
Expand sewage capacity to accommodate development	5.3[f]	4.2	4.4	4.5
Concentrate development prohibit sprawl	3.7	4.4[c]	3.6	3.9
More development on flatlands	4.6	3.8	4.1	4.3
No housing on steep slopes	3.7[f]	4.9	4.8	5.0
Public buyout of down-zoned property	5.8	5.7	6.0	5.9
Remove ugly buildings and redevelop	5.3	4.9	4.4	4.6
Increase public shoreline	3.7[g]	4.6[c]	3.8	4.0
Create national recreation area in basin	2.4[e]	4.1	3.3	3.3

(continues)

TABLE 5.6 (continued)

| | Board of Directors (n = 20) | Members (n = 90) | Potential Members | |
			Northshore Business People (n = 54)	All Tahoe Business People (n = 127)
Performance evaluations (from 0 to 100)				
Land developers	48.7	41.8	43.0	39.2
Gaming industry	53.5[f]	35.1[c]	47.5	51.6
Business groups, e.g., Chamber of Commerce	48.5	42.5	51.5	53.8
Property rights groups	47.4	48.0	42.0	40.0
Local governments	62.2[d]	43.7	47.5	49.9
TRPA	38.3	41.0[c]	31.8	27.3
U.S. Forest Service	47.4	47.6[c]	59.7	58.8
CTRPA	19.8	35.2	26.9	21.7
Lahontan Water Board	35.2[f]	47.2	40.3	38.0
League to Save	28.4	44.6	36.7	32.4

[a,b,c] = Probability (.005, .01, .05, respectively) of making an error in asserting that the mean value of the beliefs of chamber members differs from that of potential members among Northshore businesspeople; two-tailed test.

[d,e,f,g] = Probability (.005, .01, .05, .10, respectively) of making an error in asserting significant differences between the board and members; two-tailed test.

Note: All the policy proposals and the latter two attitudinal scales have values ranging from 1 (not at all in favor) to 7 (very much in favor). All the performance evaluations range from 0 (extremely poor job) to 100 (extremely good job), and the first attitudinal scale goes from 0 (not at all a problem) to 100 (extremely serious problem).

theory. Significant differences ($p < .05$) existed in eleven of the twenty-seven items, with one more being significant at the .10 level (see also Sabatier and McLaughlin 1990). The board was more conservative, more in favor of development, and less supportive of environmental regulation than the membership. Even if these differences might be a little more than expanded exchange theory would predict, that assessment would change if chamber members were, in fact, more concerned with selective incentives than they indicated in Table 5.4 (as Olson could reasonably contend).

CONCLUSION

What does one conclude from all this—beyond the obvious, that the results, as usual, are mixed? If one accepts Popper's (1959) premise that the proper strategy for science is to focus on rejecting proposed theories, the one that probably comes out poorest—at least in this case—is Salisbury's. He was completely wrong about the league: It was not founded by an entrepreneur interested in a staff position; members are not primarily interested in selective benefits; belief differences between leaders and members are much greater than he would expect; and there is no evidence that members and leaders are preoccupied with internal exchange relationships. He does better with the chamber but is apparently wrong on his critical assumption concerning its formation: None of the organizers ever had a staff position with the organization.

Olson does slightly better. With respect to the league, he was correct that only a small percentage of potential members join but apparently wrong about the founding of the organization and the reasons people join. And he would not have predicted the systematically more extreme views of leaders than members. He does better on the chamber. The apparent formation of the organization by a few large beneficiaries is perfectly consistent with his theory. And though the data in Table 5.4 on the apparent importance of collective incentives to the membership is inconsistent with his expectation, the data in Table 5.6 support his skepticism concerning such responses.

This brings us to a fundamental limitation Salisbury and Olson have in common. Both do better on the chamber than on the league. This can probably be traced to their assumptions that people are egoistic and materialistic. That's probably true much of the time, but there is growing evidence that many people some of the time are also genuinely concerned with making a "fair-share" contribution to the provision of collective goods—with making some contribution, particularly if others do so as well (Marwell and Ames 1979, 1980, 1981; Sears et al. 1980; Margolis 1982; Rhoads 1985; Mueller 1986; Tyler 1990; Tyler et al. 1986). These people are particularly attracted to purposive groups like the league but also appear to play important roles in many economic groups as well (Moe 1981).

In fact, Olson's assumption that potential members who fail to join an organization are necessarily free-riding is *much* too simple. Commitment theory offers another explanation: Most people aren't interested enough in public policy to do much of anything, let alone join an interest group. Truman offers another: People who are potential members of conflicting groups may join neither. Additional plausible reasons include (1) ignorance about the organization's existence (or how to join), (2) family budgets that allow people to join only a small percentage of the organizations whose goals they support, and (3) disagreement with some of the organization's policies. In short, the reasons people fail to join an interest group are desperately in need of research. Free-riding may turn out to be an important reason, but let's be careful about following Olson in *assuming* it is *the* reason.

It's difficult to decide what to do with Truman. Despite the immense temptation to dismiss anyone who views group formation as unproblematic, he comes closer to explaining the formation of the league and the chamber than does Salisbury. And joining the chamber may be explained as a "natural" result of social interaction among businesspeople threatened by regulatory agencies. But there is no comparable explanation why people join the league—given that most of its members do not interact socially. And Truman's view of group leaders as seeking to moderate among the multiple and conflicting loyalties of its members simply does not fit the data in Table 5.5 showing league leaders to be consistently more extreme than members.

Commitment theory does a great job on the league. It accounts for the league's formation, the low percentage of potential members who join, the importance of collective goods in membership decisions, and the increasingly extreme environmental views as one moves from potential member to member to leader. On the chamber, the theory can account for its formation, the more conservative views of leaders vis-à-vis members, and the apparent importance (in Table 5.4) of collective incentives to the membership. But it fails miserably in explaining why people join the chamber, and that, in turn, casts doubt on the validity of the data in Table 5.4. This case would suggest that commitment theory does a better job on purposive than on economic groups.

Expanded exchange theory may do the best job. It's broad enough to account for the formation of the two organizations, for the variety of incentives important to the membership, and for the apparently greater importance of collective incentives in a purposive group like the league than in an economic group like the chamber. Yet it clearly would not have predicted the extent of leader-member differences in the league during a period of high conflict (Sabatier and McLaughlin 1990)—unless one takes into account that members may well be unaware of the extent of incongruence. But that again raises the disturbing possibility that the theory may have become so broad as to be nonfalsifiable.

Obviously, one should be extremely cautious about generalizing from our findings on the League to Save Lake Tahoe and the North Tahoe Chamber of Commerce to all interest groups. We have sought to integrate these findings with those from other studies conducted over the past twenty years. In the future, research should seek to test several of the theories discussed in this chapter and to focus on the reasons people do *not* join an interest group pursuing policy objectives they profess to support. That's clearly one of the more serious voids in our understanding of interest group dynamics. Olson's assumption of free-riding is probably part of the explanation, but is it really the dominant one?

NOTES

The research reported in this chapter was funded by the National Science Foundation (NSF SES 84–11032), the Dean of the College of Agricultural and Environmental Sciences, University of California at Davis, and the Institute of Governmental Affairs, University of California at Davis. I would also like to thank Susan McLaughlin, Don McCubbin, and Neil Pelkey for helping with the data analysis. All errors and interpretations remain, however, the responsibility of Ken Meier.

1. Truman (1953:33, 37) defined an interest group as "any group that, on the basis of one or more shared attitudes, makes certain claims on other groups in the society" (if that group is a government, the interest group would be a political interest group). Although it was, and still is, common to acknowledge that many fraternal and religious groups have very little concern in governmental policy, it was assumed that governmental interest groups had a major, if not dominant, goal of influencing public policy (Hrebenar and Scott 1990:7–8; also Baumgartner and Walker 1988:921).

2. Truman (1953:31, 36, 56, 61). The clearest formulation of his argument occurs with respect to trade associations: People with similar skills that produce similar interests may at any time become an active group. Their interaction is increased . . . as a consequence of . . . disturbances: changes in techniques, shifts in economic status. . . . Development of organized associations follows in order to regularize such interaction and to facilitate stabilization of the group's internal and external relations. In the process of attempting to establish and protect an equilibrium of this sort, the association usually . . . resorts to the institutions of government. . . . (97).

3. What constitutes a "large" versus a "small" group for Olson is not always clear. At times, he distinguishes "small primary groups" from "large associations" (Olson 1965:20). But his dominant argument seems to be that a group is "small" when a potential member's free-riding would "bring about noticeable differences in the welfare of some, or all, of the others in the group" (Olson 1965:43; see also 22–36). By either of these definitions, the two interest groups in this chapter would be classified as "large."

4. In discussing trade unions, Olson (1965:ch. 3) argues that most began as rather small, local organizations. That's true, but his theory would still not explain their formation because

the per share collective benefits to almost all initial members had to be smaller than their per share costs. If their members had been rational egoists, unions would never have formed.

5. The exception would occur when a group was able to provide selective benefits deemed important by almost all potential members at a lower cost than they could find elsewhere.

6. Olson never explicitly made this argument in *The Logic of Collective Action*, but it is certainly a logical extension of his theory. To Olson, a person's support for a group's policy positions was as irrelevant to joining that group as the individual's eye color. Both should thus be randomly distributed with respect to the decision to join.

7. This is a rough approximation. The 1979 federal assessment (Western Federal Regional Council 1979) estimated federal capital expenditures of $60 in the 1970–1979 period, exclusive of land acquisition. We'll assume an average price of $1,000 per acre for the 35,000 acres purchased by the Forest Service between 1965 and 1979. Since 1980, expenditures have included $10.5 million to purchase the Jennings Casino site and approximately $11.5 million per year in Burton-Santini funds for land acquisition and erosion control.

8. This material on the league was gathered from league documents, the 1984 survey, and interviews in 1983–1986 with about twenty of its leaders since its inception.

9. The material in this paragraph is based primarily upon conversations with Beverly Bedard, executive director of the North Tahoe Chamber since 1980. Only the North Tahoe was surveyed in 1984 because we were replicating a set of 1972 surveys conducted by Constantini and Hanf (1973).

10. The number of respondents and the response rates for each of the groups are as follows:

Group	N	Percentage Response
Membership surveys		
League membership: total	302	61
Second-home owners in basin	165	–
North Tahoe Chamber membership	90	35
Potential members		
All respondents to property-owners survey	961	48
Second-home owners (for league)	432	–
Businesspeople (for chamber)		
Northshore only	54	–
Entire basin	127	–
Leaders (from elite survey)		
League board	32	86
Chamber board	20	69

The rather low response rate for the North Tahoe Chamber membership arouses some concern. Although we used the same three-wave strategy for all surveys, chamber members did not respond as well. (Even the chamber was able to obtain only a 23 percent response rate to its own survey in 1990.) A comparison of early and late respondents—on the assumption that the latter would more resemble nonrespondents—revealed no statistically significant differences between the two groups of chamber members on any of the twenty-seven items used in Table 5.6. Thus we feel reasonably confident about the representativeness of our chamber sample.

11. The league quickly became the most vocal opponent of development and, as such, basically absorbed the members of several homeowners' groups, including the Tahoe Im-

provement and Conservation Association (TICA). This material is based on interviews with most of the original organizers, as well as Jim McClatchy (TICA president).

12. The evidence comes primarily from a recent interview with Betty Layton, executive director of the chamber starting in 1962. Her perception is that the chamber was organized by several local businesspeople, including Carlton Konarske of the Nevada Lodge (a casino), Fred Schultz (a local realtor), and an official of the local utility. Her perceptions were generally confirmed by Konarske. Similarly, the South Tahoe Chamber was organized by the owner of a prominent casino and the owner of a local resort (interviews with John Wynn and others). None of the organizers ever held a staff position with either chamber.

13. A 1984 league membership of 2,500, of whom 58 percent had second homes in the basin, would equal 1,450 league members in that category. The property-owners survey indicated 42 percent of the 60,000 parcels in the basin had second homes, for a total of 25,200. The league total of 1,450 divided by 25,200 equals 6 percent.

14. As a quid pro quo for allowing us to survey their members, we encouraged the leaders of each organization to add a page or two to the survey. The data reported here represent our interpretation of those results. Although we made some effort to tailor their questions to concerns in the interest group literature, our principal goals were to examine change over time and belief congruence between various elites and constituencies (Sabatier and Mc-Laughlin 1988, 1990). In retrospect, we should have been more careful to include a full list of selective incentives, particularly for the chamber.

15. Another question asking respondents for their "most important reason for joining the league" produced comparable results: (1) a general concern for the environmental fate of the basin: 76 percent; (2) a concern for the recreational and aesthetic qualities of the basin (of interest to short-term users as well as property owners): 13 percent; (3) a general concern for environmental problems of the nation and the world: 6 percent; (4) a concern for the possible impact of environmental problems on property and investments in the basin: 5 percent. We feel these are less useful for our purposes, in part because they don't fall so neatly into collective versus selective benefits.

16. In recent conversations, the chamber's executive director (Beverly Bedard) has reiterated her doubt that selective material incentives (such as bulk mail and health insurance) are important inducements to join. And the chamber's executive director in the 1960s, Betty Layton, said the organization offered no such discounts during the 1960s. Instead, it started as a tourist promotion organization and then broadened into community betterment (e.g., architectural controls). Developing business contacts, however, may be an important incentive. A 1990 survey developed by the North Tahoe Chamber and administered to its members produced 69 responses out of 300 distributed (a 23 percent response rate). Included was a set of items specifically dealing with members' reasons for joining:

Reason	Percentage Who Disagree	Percentage Who Agree
To gain additional contacts and visibility for my business	11	60
To improve the quality of life in the North Tahoe area	9	56
Being a member helps my business	27	40

The second is a purely collective benefit; the first and third are probably a mixture of selective and collective.

17. The policy proposals were all measured on a seven-point Likert scale from 1 ("not at all in favor of proposal") to 7 ("very much in favor"). The organizational evaluations were

measured on a thermometer scale, where 0 = "extremely poor job" and 100 = "extremely good job" in recent years with respect to what respondents wanted to see.

The attitudinal scales were developed via a factor analysis of relevant questions in the survey; the items in the dominant factor were then checked for internal coherence via a reliability test. This resulted in three separate scales:

1. Perceived Environmental Problems Scale, consisting of six items dealing with water pollution, loss of open space, air pollution, and so on. Each item had a factor loading r > .60 and the Cronbach's a = .86.
2. Pro-Conservatism Scale, consisting of seven items praising small government, market solutions, local government, individual initiative, and so on. Each item loaded r > .50 and the scale a = .80.
3. Tahoe Environmental Protection Scale, made up of five items arguing that environmental protection at Tahoe requires rigorous enforcement of regulations, regionwide planning, and less concern for economic growth. Each item loaded r > .52 and the scale a = .83.

An appendix on scale construction is available from the author; it was omitted here because of space constraints.

18. A difference-of-means test is a statistical test designed to ascertain the probability that difference in two samples is also true of their population(s). Because the two samples used here came from different populations rather than the same population, we had to use a test with separate variance estimates.

6

IG. ≠ Policy Process: Δ's or Networks?? [handwritten annotation]

Triangles, Networks, and Hollow Cores: The Complex Geometry of Washington Interest Representation

ROBERT H. SALISBURY
JOHN P. HEINZ
ROBERT L. NELSON
EDWARD O. LAUMANN

In recent years a voluminous literature has appeared attempting to characterize the patterns of relationships between the Washington representatives of private interests—lobbyists in the broadest sense of that term—and the government officials with whom they interact in their pursuit of favorable public policy. Much of this literature is in the form of case studies of particular interest groups, governmental agencies, or specific policy decisions. Some of it rests on a broader sampling of observations from one or more of these three sources. Whatever the research foundation may have been, both normative and empirical judgments about this relationship abound in textbooks and other summary treatments.

The most concise statements of group-government relationship have usually been expressed in some kind of spatial metaphor. Ernest Griffith (1939) used the term "whirlpool," Douglas Cater (1964) brought "triangle" into common usage, and Charles Jones (1979) added "sloppy hexagon." Hugh Heclo (1978) contended that the triangle metaphor was "disastrously incomplete" and urged instead the more complex but still spatially located concept of "issue networks." Cater, J. Lieper Freeman (1965), and many others, on the one hand, have applied terms like *subgovernment* or *subsystem* to the same observables, implying that there was some stable pattern of power involved in the relationship but choosing not to give it a particular spatial form. John Heinz et al. (1990) and Edward Laumann and David Knoke (1987), on the other hand, discuss interest group–government agency interactions in terms of definite spatial forms—

often some sort of sphere or doughnut shape—but are less clear about whether and to what extent some participants have meaningful power, either over other participants or over policy outcomes.

What we might call the "textbook triangle" theory—the theory that "everyone knows" to be true in its essentials—goes more or less this way: Interest groups, congressional committees and subcommittees, and executive agencies are tied symbiotically together, controlling specific segments of public policy to the effective exclusion of other groups or government authorities. This control is exercised so that the groups benefit from the policies, the Congresspeople involved benefit from electoral support by the groups, and the agencies benefit from jurisdictional and appropriations support by Congress. The mechanisms of support include campaign contributions by the groups to the key members of Congress and are enhanced by keeping debate over the substantive issues at stake relatively quiet and confined to a specialized set of concerned actors, both inside and outside of government. When low salience is combined with disaggregated benefits that can be widely distributed among subsystem participants, as in the classic pork barrel of rivers and harbors appropriations (Ferejohn 1974) or, in the view of some (Jones 1961; Cater 1964; Lowi 1969), agricultural price supports, the triangular symbiosis is likely to be especially close.

In some versions (Green 1975, e.g.) the triangle legs are said to be strengthened by exchanges of personnel. Most often noted has been the tendency for former regulatory officials and congressional staffers to capitalize on their experience and contacts by moving to the private sector and going to work as lobbyists. The "revolving door" usually works in both directions, however, and so an administration may fill key policy positions from among the pool of interest group representatives likely to be sympathetic to its purposes (see Mackenzie 1987).

Heclo, in criticizing the triangular view, contended that the policy domains, once dominated by such tripartite arrangements, had experienced significant and somewhat contradictory changes that largely destabilized the established patterns. Even within the subsystem, policy specialization increased. The more specialized the issues and interests became, the less successful the old triangles were at maintaining control. Authority devolved from the committee chairs to the subcommittee and beyond. Additionally, peak associations were displaced by more specialized trade associations and individual producers. At the same time, Heclo (1978:99) noted the great increase in the number of "highly knowledgeable policy-watchers," which include the greatly expanded roster of interest groups present in each policy domain; the much-enlarged staffs available to members of Congress, which enable the latter to broaden their policy attention span; and the proliferation of specialized newsletters and other communications media that permit a larger network audience to keep up with what is happening.

Most, if not all, of the elements contained in these interpretations of the structure of U.S. policymaking processes are amenable to systematic empirical investigation, but until recently there had not been a sufficiently broad-gauged effort to gather the necessary data to test most of them. Happily, this has begun to change. The work of Berry (1977), Walker (1983, inter alia), Schlozman and Tierney (1986), and our own group (Nelson et al. 1987; Heinz et al. forthcoming, inter alia), has provided us with substantial information about the interest group leg of the postulated triangles, and from that data we can make some reasonable inferences about the *appropriateness* of the traditional geometric patterns.

The project from which our data will be taken has been described in detail elsewhere (Nelson et al. 1987), so we provide only the briefest summary here. Selecting four domains of public policy—agriculture, energy, health, and labor—we determined which private interest organizations had actively sought to influence federal government decisions during the period from 1977 through 1981. In due course we interviewed a sample of 311 such organizations, distributed across the four policy domains, and asked who represented their interests in Washington. From those nominated we interviewed a sample of 776 (to which we added thirty "notable" interest representatives filling out a roster recommended to us by informants). In the course of lengthy interviews with these representatives (during 1983–1984), we asked which government officials they interact with most often, and from those names interviewed 297, divided almost evenly between people located in the congressional milieu and people in the executive branch. As a result, we have a set of respondents who may all be assumed to have been active participants in the shaping of federal policy within their respective domains during the period immediately prior to our interviews. We do not have a sample of all government officials, of course, nor have we represented the full range of policy issues or domains. The data are substantial in amount, however, quite rich in content, and suitable to the task at hand.

In the analysis that follows we utilize these data to examine the personal backgrounds of interest representatives and officials to determine whether the people in one policy domain differ from those with other policy concerns. We go on to examine the extent to which partisanship is a significant factor in differentiating interest group representatives from government officials or distinguishing one policy domain from another. We assess the degree to which these policy activists specialize in a single domain or spread their energies across several areas. This in turn leads us to look more closely at the specific work tasks in which these activists engage. At the end of this review of the research findings, we reach some judgments regarding the shape of policy domain relationships and the validity of the notions of triangle and network.

POLICY ACTIVISTS: AN INTERCHANGEABLE ELITE?

An inference might plausibly be drawn from the triangle tradition that all three legs are occupied by essentially the same kinds of people. One version of this argument would base it upon a more general elitist theory in which a small minority of individuals with highly select social background characteristics, common life experiences and career paths, and shared values wield effective power in and through the governmental institutions of the United States. A second version, and one more in keeping with the subgovernment argument, would predict that within each policy domain the policy activists would share important personal characteristics regardless of their organizational position, whether inside the government or out and in either the legislative or the executive branch.

What do we find when we examine the data? As Table 6.1 indicates, there is no doubt whatever that the policy activists are disproportionately well educated, predominantly male, and almost exclusively white. Having said this, however, we must immediately note the significant differences that distinguish one policy domain from another and one institutional cohort from another. Thus in both branches there are considerably more women in the health policy domain than in any other and more Jews in labor, but there are more women and Catholics in the legislative branch and twice as many Jews and Protestants of high socioeconomic status on the executive side. In their personal background characteristics, the private interest representatives are grouped between the two institutionally defined sets of officials, but they display very similar differences among the four policy domains.

Several points may be made about these background factors. First, the substantive differences among policy domains have a significant effect on the recruitment of people who are actively involved in shaping policy in each. The bulk of the activities and organizational interests involved in agriculture and energy are located in the South and West; hence substantially more of the people active in those fields come from those regions, either through self-selection or client determination. The reverse is true, even more strikingly, regarding the health and labor dependence on people who grew up in the northeastern quadrant of the nation. These regional effects are also felt in the religious affiliations—more Jews and Catholics are in labor and health, for instance. But even more impressive is the large difference in religious composition of executive officials and legislative officials. One is tempted to conclude that the greater electoral sensitivity of the legislative branch makes it more inclined to recruit members of large

TABLE 6.1
Selected Personal Characteristics by Institution and Policy Domain (in percent)

| | Washington Representatives (n = 776) | | | | | Government Officials (n = 297) | | | | | |
	All	Agriculture	Energy	Health	Labor	Legislative Branch	Executive Branch	Agriculture	Energy	Health	Labor
Women	12	7	10	19	12	12	7	12	5	18	4
Jewish	10	4	7	12	18	8	15	7	10	14	16
Catholic	19	12	20	21	23	23	13	10	18	23	21
Type I Protestant	23	31	26	22	16	12	26	17	15	21	23
N.E. origin	35	19	29	49	42			25	38	60	55
S.W. origin	34	44	42	23	28			39	41	23	27
Law degree	34	28	37	30	42			23	38	16	54
Other advanced degree	46	38	45	62	35			45	38	53	26

Source: Data compiled from a study by the authors.

minorities, such as Catholics, but because others, such as African Americans, are largely absent, the argument may not take us very far. Both the substance of public policy and institutional location are somehow implicated in producing these effects, however, and we must probe further to develop adequate explanations.

Next let us examine the extent of embeddedness in the Washington community. We want to know if these policy activists are old hands in the nation's capital or if they are more recent arrivals. Is there a more or less permanent Washington establishment of which they are core elements, or was there a noticeable infusion of fresh faces to implement the Reagan revolution? The signals are somewhat mixed. Only about two-thirds of our sample of interest representatives reside in the Washington area. The remainder visit the capital from elsewhere, and this group includes substantial fractions of the labor union lobbyists and the chief executives of business firms and nonprofit institutions (see Birnbaum 1990). Those who are Washington residents, however, tend to be longtime residents (the mean is sixteen years). This is somewhat longer on average than for the government officials, but the latter display considerable variation. Thus career bureaucrats, senators, and House staff average at least fifteen years in residence, whereas top-level department personnel and Senate staff (recall that the Senate had come under Republican control in 1981, resulting in substantial staff turnover) have considerably briefer experience. Similar differences are found regarding the length of time people have been with their current organizational employer. Group representatives reported an average of twelve years, which is nearly identical to the mean experience of officials in the federal government. The latter, however, move around a good deal among different positions, so, except for the elected members of Congress, the average time in each job is quite brief. Nevertheless, the total Washington experience is substantial for nearly all those in our sample, whether they were working in the private sector or for the government. If the Reagan tide brought new talent to Washington, it does not seem to have had much impact on the connections linking interest groups and public officials. These folks are largely veterans of the policy wars.

Another perspective on the degree to which policy activists are embedded in "the system" is provided by examining the so-called revolving door. To what extent have interest representatives and public officials, respectively, been employed on "the other side," dealing with public policy issues from the other end of the group-government relationship? Nearly half (45 percent) of the group representatives have had federal government experience, and somewhat more (56 percent) of the officials had previously served in some capacity representing private interests. The proportion among career bureaucrats was obviously much lower, but it was generally quite high among those officials whose actual tenure in government was relatively brief. Thus even when policy activists are comparatively new to their present positions, they tend to be experienced players in the policy games.

There are few policy-domain differences of interest, either among interest representatives or officials, in the extent of their embeddedness. There is some variation among different types of interest groups. Citizens' groups, for example, tend to be represented by somewhat younger, less experienced (and less well paid!) people. Independent lawyers and consultants, in contrast, are deeply embedded in the Washington community, as they may well need to be to cultivate both contacts and clients. For the most part, however, despite these differences there is not much in our data thus far to contradict the view that policy activists constitute a Washington establishment.

THE IMPORTANCE OF PARTY

There is a strong interpretive tradition among political commentators to the effect that interest groups generally try to avoid partisan commitments, rewarding friends and opposing enemies among public officials regardless of party affiliation. The assumption is that for a group to become closely tied to one party or the other would place its influence in jeopardy at each election. This assumption of bipartisanship has been challenged by the strong ties connecting organized labor, civil rights and minority groups, and many of the post-1960 wave of citizens' groups to the Democratic party and by the warm support given to Republicans by much of the business community. The tendency of business PACs since 1982 to support incumbent Congresspeople, however, has moved back toward bipartisan pragmatism, so this traditional view may again be persuasive.

Our data reveal sharp partisan divisions among both the representatives of private interests and the government officials with whom those representatives most actively work. Half the outside interest representatives are *strong* party identifiers. One-fourth are independents, but only 8 percent decline to lean toward one party or the other. Democrats outnumber Republicans in the aggregate, but there are clear differences among both policy domains and types of organizations. For example, the energy domain is dominated by business corporations and trade associations and is predominantly Republican. In both health and labor there are twice as many Democrats as Republicans, reflecting the prominence in those policy areas of labor unions, citizens' groups, and the more scientifically oriented professional associations. Independent lawyers and consultants are also predominantly Democratic by about two to one.

TABLE 6.2
The Partisanship of Policy Activists (in percent)

	Republican	Independent	Democrat	N
Washington Representatives				
Agriculture	39	23	36	192
Energy	41	27	29	184
Health	24	25	49	206
Labor	24	23	51	194
Outside lawyers	25	26	47	108
Consultants	23	23	46	35
Government Officials				
Agriculture	51	18	31	69
Energy	59	20	21	67
Health	31	30	38	65
Labor	41	15	44	63
Senators	53	0	47	15
Senate member staff	54	13	33	21
House members	33	0	67	28
House member staff	20	20	62	20
Senate Committee staff	34	33	33	12
House Committee staff	10	17	73	27
White House/Executive Office	69	25	6	15
Top department	73	19	6	27
Mid-department	37	33	29	73
Independent agencies	54	15	32	26

Source: Data compiled from a study by the authors.

Government officials are also generally partisan, too, of course. Given the political balance at the time of our interviews, it is not surprising that the proportion of Republicans is somewhat higher and that party strength varies sharply among different positional cohorts. In the top levels of the executive branch, there are only one or two stray Democrats, whereas the House members and staff with whom groups interact are primarily Democratic. Officials in the four policy domains differ along essentially the same lines as the group representatives: Energy is Republican; labor and health have more Democratic strength; agriculture is in-between. Among the officials, however, there are significant numbers of strong Republicans in all four domains, so that, for example, when union leaders approach the government, especially the executive branch, they will have little choice but to talk to Republicans. Of course, precisely this kind of situation has persuaded most commentators to conclude that interest groups must mute their partisanship. But do they?

We can gain additional perspective on this question by examining other aspects of partisanship among the group representatives. Nearly half of

they give $$ to PACs

the group representatives give money to PACs, and one-third are active in other forms of political fund-raising. Over 40 percent have been significantly involved in political campaigns, and one-fourth have held office in political organizations. There are only minor differences among the policy domains on these items, but in some kinds of organizations—professional associations, for instance—the representatives are distinctly less political, whereas in others—labor unions, business firms, and trade associations stand out—the Washington representatives tend to be actively involved partisans.

Within this picture of a relatively partisan set of interest representatives interacting with an even more partisan array of government officials,[1] we find a curious feature. Fifty-two percent of the interest representatives say that party affiliation never affects their work. Moreover, although just over 10 percent said that party affiliation had become more important since the Reagan administration had taken office, nearly as many said it was less significant, and the responses bore no relationship to any of the several facets of political involvement. The question therefore remains: Does partisanship make a difference to the interest group–government relationship, and, if it does, how and when does it influence decisionmaking?

There appear to be at least two aspects to the answer. First, the more deeply involved in political party affairs, the more likely a group representative is to think partisanship makes a difference. This is particularly true for those whose political involvement antedates their tenure as interest representatives. For instance, those whose careers include government service prior to becoming government affairs officers are likely to regard their political past as having continuing relevance. If, on the other hand, they have come up through the organizational ranks and participated politically—through PACs, for example—on a more or less ex officio basis, they may well view that participation as less important.

A second way in which partisanship reveals itself is in certain patterns of group-government contacts. For example, active Republicans work more with the Republican congressional leadership, and active Democrats are closer to the Democratic leaders. Partisan involvement also affects the frequency with which groups are able to contact the White House and the Office of Management and Budget (OMB). Interaction with congressional committees and executive departments, however, displays a rather different pattern. Involvement with party organizations and campaigns is unrelated to these contacts in three of the four policy domains. Energy is the exception. In that domain partisan activity makes a difference. To put the same point differently, energy, a policy area in flux and turmoil in the early 1980s, seems to be the most "political" in the way in which interests are represented. On the other hand, interest representatives' involvement in political fund-raising and distribution is positively associated with committee and agency contacting *except* in the health policy domain. That would appear to be the least "political" domain, in the sense of being affected by active partisanship. Thus there are differences not only among policy domains but also in the kind of political activity that matters. Among the government officials there is also a discernibly partisan component to their interactions with one another, but few would have thought otherwise. Republicans contact Republicans more often, but they do not ignore relevant Democrats, and the same, in reverse, may be said of the Democrats.

There is one other type of structured interaction in which interest group representatives are embedded that has a significant partisan character. This is the personal network of colleagues and acquaintances. We asked respondents to identify three people with whom they were likely to discuss the policy issues of the domain for which they were sampled. Representatives tended to select people in their own organization or one like it but were even more strongly (approximately two-thirds at the time) inclined to select people they knew to be of the same partisan affiliation, especially if they were located in Washington with a full menu of political choices. A second view of this question is provided by the patterns of acquaintance with notable interest representatives in Washington. Again, the active connections reveal a strongly partisan or ideological structure or both. Republican interest representatives knew the prominent Republicans, and Democrats knew Democrats. This also reflected the very considerable bias in organizational selection. That is, business interest representatives knew the leading spokespeople of business interests but generally only knew *of* the union leaders or the citizens' group lobbyists (see Heinz et al. 1990).

All this leads us to conclude that in the representation of interests and the making of public policy affecting those interests, party affiliation matters. It contributes to the structuring of individual-level values and is reflected in the hiring preferences of both interest organizations and government officials. It is an active dimension affecting the patterns of interaction among groups, among officials, and between those two sets of actors. But though party is always present, it rarely provides a sufficient explanation of who does or gets what, when, and how, and even though our ambition in this chapter is far more modest than that, we must go on to examine some other factors.

POLICY SPECIALIZATION

The triangle metaphor clearly implies that policy advocates, including both government officials and private groups, will tend to concentrate their efforts on a relatively small fraction of the total range of public policy issues. In part, this understanding grows out of the conclusion of both scholars and practitioners of the 1950s and early 1960s that a principal way to secure power and influence within Congress was to specialize (Matthews 1960). Mastery of policy detail would eventually gain the attention and respect of colleagues, and through a normative structure of reciprocal deference among experts the system would get its business accomplished with reasonable efficiency. The corollary to this wisdom held that interest groups likewise gained legitimacy by concentrating their efforts on those issues that were most salient to them, husbanding their inevitably scarce resources to focus on the items that really mattered to them (Dahl 1961; Bauer, Pool, and Dexter 1963).

During the past two decades or so, however, what might be thought of as the Sam Rayburn norms would seem to have lost much of their effect.[2] Changes in the rules, the incentive structure, and the electoral connection of Congress are partially responsible. So, we surmise, are certain structural changes in the policy agenda of the nation. In particular, the creation of the budget process, with its focus on a bottom-line deficit and the trade-offs among policy domains that focus mandates, has challenged hitherto cozy networks of mutual support and forced more players to become involved in a broader array of issues. Moreover, the expansion of congressional staff (Malbin 1980), on the one hand, and of the permanent interest group presence in Washington (Walker 1983; Salisbury 1986), on the other, have enabled participants to undertake larger agendas of action.

A further element in this development is the emergence of the so-called externality groups (Hadwiger 1982), including the many public interest advocates, assertive environmental organizations, and a wide range of others. What these groups have in common is a concern with the externality, or third-party, effects of public policies, present and prospective. Do farm policies encourage the use of pesticides that pollute the streams? Do jobs in the coal mines carry a price tag called acid rain? There has been a broad intellectual awakening to and heightened awareness of the side effects of what government does. In turn, this development has meant a considerable expansion of the numbers and changes in the shape of the interest group universe. Specific to our focus here is the point that the rise of externality groups inevitably means some breakdown in policy specialization. As more and more issues are seen to be interdependent, participation in each will no longer be left to the cozy few.

The present research cannot make any comparisons across time, and no one previously has attempted to measure the degree of policy specialization as we have done. Consequently, although we can make some inferences about how things may have changed, most of what we have to present are observations from 1983–1984. In deriving these estimates, however, we have had to grapple with the problems of how to define specialization. What operational meaning should we give to the concept?

As we suggested previously, we offer in what follows a series of test borings, as it were, that we believe address this problem. As we review these data, we should keep in mind that for a group or an individual to be "interested" in a policy issue does not necessarily imply any intention to try to influence its outcome. The breadth of an issue agenda reflects the scope of *concern*, and the dimensions of concern about policy results may be rather different from those we associate with more conventional lobbying.

First of all, we may ask how much of their total work time these policy activists actually devote to matters of federal policy. In most of these roles there may well be other tasks to perform. It should not be a complete surprise, therefore, to discover that interest group representatives devote somewhat less than half of their time on average to policy concerns, whereas one-third of their effort is spent on matters involving the maintenance and management of their respective organizations. These proportions differ somewhat depending on the type of organization—union representatives are more heavily involved in the affairs of their unions—and organizational position—government affairs officers spend substantially more time on policy issues than do the CEOs of the organizations. In general, however, we would stress that lobbyists are by no means completely caught up in the policymaking process.

To a significant extent this is true as well of government officials. They do spend somewhat more of their time (approximately 15 percent) on policy concerns, but routine contacts both inside and outside of government—interagency communication by bureaucrats or constituency relations by congressional personnel, for example—and internal administration take up substantial portions of their time. Again, there are differences among organizational positions: Congressional officials spend more time on policy and less on administration than do those in the executive, and this is increasingly the case, as we would expect, as we move down in the bureaucratic hierarchy. There are modest, but also interesting, differences among policy domains. Officials in labor are rather heavily involved in policy issues but those in agriculture somewhat less so. We suspect this reflects the high level of issue conflict in the labor domain, much of it heavily partisan, and the comparative quiescence at that particular time in agriculture. This suspicion draws further support from other data showing that these two domains tend to be perceived by participants as high and low, respectively, regarding both conflict and partisanship.

We have determined that policy activists do a good deal besides working on the shaping of policy. Next we assess the degree to which they concentrate on one particular domain of policy or spread their efforts more broadly. In view of the great complexity of most modern policy controversies, we might expect to find considerable specialization. As we observed earlier, substantive specialization is implied by the iron triangle hypothesis, and it was certainly one of the informal norms by which the Rayburn-Johnson Congress of the 1950s was governed. On the other hand, as we also noted, a good case can be made for increased interdependence among previously separate policy areas—consider the environmental or foreign policy effects of agricultural policies, and vice versa—which has been reinforced by the emergence of citizens' groups with broad agendas of concern. The increased use of multiple referrals in Congress whereby bills are sent to more than one committee points in the same direction. What do we find?

First, nearly half of our "subsystem inhabitants" spend half or more of their policy-centered time on matters within the domain for which they were sampled. Officials focus their efforts somewhat more than private interest representatives, and executive branch officials are more specialized than people on Capitol Hill. Among the latter, the staff are considerably more narrowly focused than the elected members, as of course we would expect. Similarly, the officials in the Executive Office of the White House are more broadly engaged than the other executive branch officials whose positions are substantially defined in terms of domain-specific policy jurisdiction.

One other difference on this dimension warrants particular attention. Among both officials and interest representatives, those in the labor domain are significantly less focused on issues within that domain than is true of the other three policy areas. In part, this may reflect that, at least among the officials, there was a somewhat narrower range of interest in the particular policy controversies of that domain. Lower-level executive officials were generally indifferent on most of the issues arising in the labor field. In a larger part, however, it would seem to result from the tendency of labor union leaders, many of the lobbyists for such peak business organizations as the U.S. Chamber of Commerce or the National Association of Manufacturers, and members of Congress active on labor issues to pursue a broad range of policy objectives. The catalog of federal policy concerns published biennially by the AFL-CIO regularly lists some ninety or more issues that attract its commitment, and its rival business organizations are also engaged across a broad spectrum. Labor concerns have been a touchstone signifying engagement in much broader struggles over economic and social issues, often providing the basis for ideological framing and articulation of those issues. Our having selected the labor domain for attention, therefore, guaranteed that we would find less domain specialization than if we had looked only at fields like energy or health. But then we would have failed fully to appreciate the very important point that there is considerable variation among policy areas in the degree to which those most active in shaping its policies specialize in that particular domain.

We can turn the question of policy specialization around and ask in how many broad policy areas (from a list of twenty) does each respondent spend more than 5 percent of the policy-related working time. The answers, not surprisingly, follow lines that generally resemble those we just reviewed, but there are some additional features requiring comment. In general, policy activists devote a nontrivial amount of attention and effort to several fields. To be sure, these may often be quite closely related: Health issues overlap broader questions of both welfare and taxation, for example; labor policy impinges upon civil rights concerns; and environmental issues are raised in the policy domains of both agriculture and energy. Policy-domain interdependence, of course, is antithetical to the assumptions of iron triangle insulation, so to find such widespread incidence of multidomain participation is to cast grave doubt on the triangle interpretation of "normal" policymaking.

The next point to stress is the very sharp difference in domain specialization between the pool of congressional officials and the rest of the activists. In all four policy areas, the number of fields that attract significant investment of time from the Hill is about double that of executive officials and nearly as much greater also than the interest group representatives. Moreover, it is not just the elected officials who display this tendency, though, as expected, they report a serious interest in the largest number of policy domains. Even the committee staff, though narrower than elected officials or their staff, are more broadly involved than most executive officials or lobbyists. In the much more populous House milieu, there is greater specialization than on the Senate side, but those differences are smaller than between the Hill as a whole and the rest of the "establishment."

Among the four policy domains, the most striking finding is that, except in Congress, the health domain is significantly more specialized. This is particularly true of professional associations concerned with health issues and their counterparts in government, the health policy bureaucrats in the National Institutes of Health (NIH) and other such specialized agencies. In our study the health domain draws a relatively large fraction of its activist officials from the career bureaucracy, and because our sample of officials reflected the choices made by the group representatives, we conclude that this tilt toward a narrow policy focus results primarily from the limited needs of the interest groups active in the health domain. It is interesting that these representatives also perceive their domain as the least conflict-ridden, and by and large they are the least likely to identify particular organizations as hostile to their policy goals (Salisbury et al. 1987). It would seem fully compatible with the iron triangle view of the policy process to find low levels of conflict associated with a high degree of specialization in a particular policy domain. We find this largely to be true in health, but even then we must note that a specialized domain focus does not characterize health policy activists in Congress.

A final test of substantive specialization can be made by examining the patterns of interpersonal interaction among the policy activists in each issue area. The more specialized the policy focus, the more we would expect that contacts with relevant others would be restricted to targets within the institutional core that dominates that policy domain. Thus we might find lobbying efforts concentrated on the congressional committees or executive agencies with primary jurisdiction over a domain, and, to the extent that contacting occurred across a broader array of institutional targets, triangle-like specialization would be less likely. Our data show, first of all, that when presented with a list of fifty-odd possible targets relevant to their field of endeavor, official respondents identify a substantial number with which they are "regularly" in touch. (There is an overall mean of 8.0 for officials compared to 4.5 for group representatives.) There are interesting variations in frequencies: For both officials and representatives, the number of contacts is high in the energy field and low in labor; House personnel cultivate more targets than do people from the Senate; committee staff in each branch exceed member staff who, in turn, cast broader nets than elected members; top department executives have more than twice as many regular targets as lower-ranking bureaucrats. Although there are some indications of tendencies toward substantive domain specialization, then, they are not very strong. There appear to be too many institutional targets relevant to each policy area to permit the kinds of symbioses described in the classic triangle literature to survive intact.

Let us look at this question from a slightly different angle and ask how often particular institutional targets are chosen for regular contact. The data in Table 6.3 present two striking findings. First, there is a remarkable parallelism between the patterns of official contact with other officials on the one hand and interest representative–official contact on the other. Officials engage in more contacting activity, but the two sets of actors distribute their efforts in very similar ways. The second point is that in each domain the principal congressional committees attract more than twice as much attention from lobbyists and officials as the congressional party leadership. The primary executive departments vary in their "pulling power," presumably because they exercise quite different degrees of policy leadership. The secretary of labor, for example, has considerably less impact on labor policy than does the secretary of agriculture over matters in that department's jurisdiction and so receives fewer contacts. Lobbyists report comparatively infrequent contact with the White House or OMB, but this is surely not because those targets are irrelevant for the

TABLE 6.3
Frequency of Representatives Contacting Officials by Policy Domain[a] (in percent)

Target	Agriculture	Energy	Health	Labor
Senate				
Democratic leadership	13.8	13.4	11.6	16.5
Republican leadership	15.9	15.5	13.4	11.5
Lead committee	41.0[b]	34.8[c]	25.9[d]	30.0[d]
Significant second committee	—	18.2[e]	20.4[f]	18.0[f]
Budget committee	3.6	6.4	9.7	7.0
House				
Democratic leadership	20.5	12.3	15.3	18.8
Republican leadership	14.4	14.4	11.6	10.0
Lead committee	39.0[b]	30.5[g]	20.8[g]	25.5[h]
Significant second committee	—	15.0[i]	19.4	
Budget committee	4.6	4.8	7.9	7.0
White House	6.2	11.8	3.7	10.0
OMB	6.2	7.5	5.6	8.0
Office of secretary, lead department	25.6	19.8	13.9	13.0

[a]Percentages are those who say they *regularly* contacted the office or agency during the past year.
[b]Agriculture.
[c]Energy and Natural Resources.
[d]Labor and Human Resources.
[e]Environment and Public Works.
[f]Finance.
[g]Energy and Commerce.
[h]Education and Labor.
[i]Interior and Insular Affairs.

Source: Data compiled from a study by the authors.

policy-shaping purpose. Rather, they are less accessible to "outsiders," whereas congressional leaders and congressional committees are quite freely available to all comers.

There are some interesting differences in contacting frequencies between officials and lobbyists. The officials reach a larger number of regular targets, and, as Table 6.4 shows, a considerable part of that increment in frequency involves contacts with the Executive Office, which government officials reach twice as often as the group representatives, and the Office of Secretary in the primary executive department, which officials do not disdain as, to some extent, lobbyists do. As noted earlier in this discussion, the pattern of contact is significantly affected by partisan attachment. Republican lobbyists more often contact Republican congressional leaders and administration officials, and Republicans in government office are even more partisan in their selection of contacts. Democrats likewise give

TABLE 6.4
Contact with Officials by Party and Branch

| Target | Washington Representatives | | | Government Officials | | | | | |
| | | | | Legislative | | | Executive | | |
	Rep	Dem	Ind	Rep	Dem	Ind	Rep	Dem	Ind
Republican congressional leaders	2.7	1.9	1.9	3.0	1.2	1.1	2.8	.6	.9
Democratic congressional leaders	2.3	2.5	2.0	1.2	2.6	.4	1.7	.5	.8
Lead Senate Committee	1.8	1.6	1.6	2.0	1.7	2.0	1.6	1.0	1.3
Lead House Committee	1.4	1.4	1.2	1.6	2.0	2.4	1.3	.6	.6
Executive Office of the President	1.8	1.3	1.5	2.3	1.4	2.3	2.5	1.0	1.6
Office of secretary, lead department	1.4	1.1	1.3	1.6	1.3	1.7	1.6	1.1	1.7
N	243	318	186	44	86	14	79	34	32

Numbers = the mean frequency of contact with officials (0 = never in past year; 3 = regularly).

N = the number of individuals under each heading.

Source: Data compiled from a study by the authors.

much greater attention to other Democrats. It is interesting to note that the "residual" Democrats in the administration do not in fact do much regular contacting at all, whereas among the group representatives, although there are partisan differences in target selection, the differences are quite small. It would appear that lobbyists cannot afford to indulge fully their partisan preferences.

The conclusion we reach regarding specialization is, in a sense, ambivalent. There is clear evidence of specialized attention to particular policy domains and their institutional components on the part of both officials and group representatives, more in health and less in labor, more in the bureaucracy and less in Congress. As William Browne (1988) has shown, the quest for a protected policy "niche" continues among both interest groups and policymakers. At the same time, however, it is also clear that in the processes of interest representation and policy formation it is necessary for activists to explore multiple paths, to seek out sources of information and help wherever they can be found, and to cultivate a relatively broad range of contacts and connections. In part, this necessity is a result of the differential accessibility of governmental agencies. Congress is far more permeable than OMB, for example. In part, it mirrors the overlapping and interdependence among interests, governmental programs, and the organizations, public and private, that represent those interests and create and administer the programs. The specific mix of specialized interests, politically insulated against "outside" intrusion, and more complex structures of interaction varies with the substantive domain, so that one courts analytic disaster by ignoring either the continuing examples of "niche" politics or the larger and less specialized networks of relationships that have emerged in recent years.

CONCLUSION

The conventional use of the iron triangle metaphor rested on the assumption that at bottom the objective of the interest groups involved was to influence the policy decisions of public officials. It constitutes a fundamental challenge to this perspective, therefore, to be able to show that much of what both interest group representatives and government officials actually do has little direct connection with efforts to influence policy decisions as such. We presented our respondents with an inventory of tasks (cf. Schlozman and Tierney 1986); the frequencies with which each of those tasks was undertaken are presented in Table 6.5. There are a few differences in these aggregate figures: Officials give more attention to drafting legislation and providing information to other officials, whereas lobbyists are much more active in arranging political contributions and mobilizing grassroots support. In general, however, the task structures of representatives and officials are quite similar. This becomes more apparent when the eighteen-item inventory is subjected to a factor analysis and through this statistical procedure reduced to four groups of related items. For both sets of respondents, the first group of items were those that involved monitoring and providing information. Policy advocacy formed a separate and distinct group for all respondents. That is, the tasks of keeping track of what is happening in government and among the interest groups and alerting one's principal concerning anything of relevance to the interests of the client or employing organization are of major importance to both sides of the group-government connection. These monitoring tasks tend to be given to different individuals than are the efforts to cultivate contacts, present policy recommendations, mobilize political support, engage in litigation, or, for officials, supervise policy implementation.

The prominence of the monitoring function is of considerable theoretical significance. For one thing, it is the logical result of the great expansion of governmental activity during the past several decades and the impingement of that activity upon more and more groups and institutions. Increasing population densities and assorted functional interdependencies have forced us all to pay closer attention to what our neighbors were doing and how it might affect us. New interest groups have been formed, and both old and new groups have increasingly sought representation in Washington. Some of this presence is motivated, to be sure, by the hope of affecting the choices of public officials. Much of it, however, reflects the growing

TABLE 6.5
Frequency of Task Engagement[a]

Task	Interest Representatives	Government Officials
Alerting client regarding issues	4.3	4.4
Developing policy and strategy	4.3	4.5
Preparing testimony or official comments	3.4	3.6
Testifying	2.7	2.5
Drafting legislation or regulation	2.7	3.3
Providing information to officials	3.5	3.9
Contacting officials informally	3.7	4.2
Monitoring proposed changes in rules and laws	3.7	3.7
Monitoring interest groups	2.8	3.1
Litigation	2.1	1.9
Arranging for political contributions	2.0	1.3
Commentary for press, public speaking	3.2	3.5
Mobilizing grassroots support	3.0	2.4
Maintaining good government relations	3.8	
Contacting allies	2.5	
Contacting opposition	2.6	
Resolving internal organizational disputes	2.5	
Working on amicus briefs	1.6	
Making informal contact with interest representatives		4.1
Providing technical information to officials		4.1
Attempting to persuade officials on policy		3.6
Attempting to persuade extragovernment organizations		2.9
Supervising policy implementation		3.5

[a]1 = never, 5 = regularly.

Source: Data compiled from a study by the authors.

need of private organizations of all kinds to be aware of current developments in the policymaking world so that they can make timely adaptations. Monitoring is necessary in order to learn whether one's interests are affected by developments in the Department of Housing and Urban Development (HUD) or NIH, what adjustments may be needed to meet new contract requirements of the Department of Defense (DOD), and a great deal of other information. It is certainly true that monitoring will sometimes identify the need or opportunity to try to affect policy decisions, when the more traditionally understood repertoire of lobbying tasks will be brought into play. But much of what the growing ranks of government affairs officers do remains primarily a matter of scanning the crowded informational circuits for whatever bits of material they can use to enable the client organization to operate more effectively in its own milieu (see Salisbury 1990).

What does this shift in functional emphasis mean for the geometric metaphors so often employed in interpreting the interest group universe in the United States? First, as we have noted, there are surviving triangles, most of them with rather modest jurisdictional niches but able to hang on to turf and budget with considerable success. Second, however, and of greater significance to the overall patterns of American politics and public policy are larger concatenations of groups and officials, most of which are too large, too heterogeneous, and too unstable in their linkages to qualify even as real networks, and certainly not as old-fashioned triangles. The labor policy domain is distinctive, for there two reasonably coherent alliances incorporating both officials and interest groups, with clearly articulated structures of connection and interaction, face one another without a mediator. Indeed, we have found that in other policy domains as well the cores are hollow, no interest groups, individual free-lance lawyers or lobbyists, or government officials providing much connective tissue across the domain (Heinz et al. 1990).

We would not wish to leave the impression that the new patterns of policy activism are simply crowds, lacking any semblances of structure or continuities of interaction. Substantively sensible interpretations can be constructed as more or less bounded systems of connected policy activity are identified and examined. Our own search for appropriate metaphors to characterize these systems, however, has tended to take us away from geometry and its elegant simplicity. We need more complex images to catch the protean richness and complexity of the emerging systems of interest representation and policymaking.

NOTES

The research that undergirds this essay was supported by the American Bar Foundation and the National Science Foundation. The authors are grateful for the generous backing of these organizations and for comments on an earlier draft presented at the American Political Science Association annual meeting, Washington, D.C., 1988.

1. Although we will not burden the reader with the data, it should be noted that the partisanship we are examining is strongly correlated with opinions on economic and social questions. Strong Republicans are also conservatives, and their opposite numbers, the strong Democrats, are liberals. There are occasional exceptions, to be sure, but in this highly articulate and self-conscious fragment of the political world, the anomalous combination of party and ideology is rare.

2. Sam Rayburn (D–Tex.) was speaker of the House from 1940 until his death in 1961 (except for two brief periods when Republicans controlled the House). The main facets of the Rayburn style included "personal friendship and loyalty, permissiveness, restrained partisanship and conflict reduction, informality, and risk avoidance." See Joseph Cooper and David W. Brady, "Institutional Context and Leadership Style," in Glenn Parker, ed., *Studies of Congress* (Washington, D.C.: Congressional Quarterly Press, 1985), pp. 334–336.

7

Changing Patterns of
Interest Group Activity:
A Regional Perspective

CLIVE S. THOMAS
RONALD J. HREBENAR

Since the first major research by Arthur Bentley in 1908 and David Truman in the late 1940s, the study of interest groups and their impact on public policy in the United States has focused predominantly on national organizations and their activities in Washington, D.C. Much less attention has been paid to interest groups in the fifty state capitals, in the regions, and in the thousands of cities, towns, and county seats across the nation.

Yet understanding something about group activity at the subnational level can provide a more complete picture of the role of interest groups in American politics and policymaking. It can also tell us much about the diversity of American politics from state to state and from region to region. Historically, interest groups have exerted even more influence in the states than in the nation's capital. Developments as of the early 1970s have increased group activity and impact and have forged closer links between national groups and their state and local affiliates. This growth and integration will continue as the federal government increasingly divests itself of responsibility for social programs, regulation, and funding in general, and interest groups turn to the states and localities to fill these voids.

With fifty states and thousands of local governments, subnational interest group activity has always exhibited considerable diversity. Even though the nationalizing tendencies since the beginning of the 1970s have reduced this diversity, it is still significant, reflecting differences in political development, such as the strength of political parties, the power of governors and legislatures, and diversity in political culture. Such differences can be conveniently categorized by region—the Northeast, the South, the Midwest, and the West. Variations in political development have always made regionalism an important aspect of American politics. Because past studies have shown that these differences include the activities of interest groups, a study of subnational groups focusing on the regions can tell us much about variations in U.S. politics.

With all this in mind, we see this chapter as having two purposes. The first is to show the value of subnational interest group studies in the study of American interest groups. The second and major objective is to identify changing patterns of interest group activity in the states and regions.

THE VALUE OF SUBNATIONAL
INTEREST GROUP STUDIES

Interest group studies in the United States have concentrated predominantly on national groups and the nation's capital because of three major factors. First, Washington, D.C., appears to be the place where the most significant public policy decisions in the nation are made. Consequently, political scientists have viewed interest group activity at the national level as much more significant than that in state capitals. Second is the relative ease of collecting data. Information on group activity can be gleaned from a few fairly complete sets of records, such as those kept by the Congress or the Federal Election Commission. In contrast, in the states and localities there are no common data sources. The data and the participants are spread across fifty states, and the extent of information available varies considerably among states.[1] Third is what might be termed the "cumulative effect." As more and more research is gathered on national groups, a body of information is created that provides a basis for other studies. And as most political scientists conducting research on group activity and supervising graduate students are oriented primarily toward national groups, this focus is passed on from one generation of scholars to the next.

There are, however, good reasons for studying group activity at the subnational level—reasons that have become increasingly compelling since 1970. As noted, state-level interest groups have always been significant, often dominant, influences on policymaking. Whereas the large number of interests operating at the national level has produced a pluralism that has prevented any one interest from dominating national politics, this has not historically been true in the states. One or a handful of interests—mining and railroads in the West, agriculture in the South and Midwest, for example—have been able to dominate state policymaking for long periods. Consequently, a very good case can be made that, over the years, interest groups have had a more visible and much greater impact on public policy in the states than in Washington, D.C. Evidence also strongly suggests that group impact in the states has increased even more. This has occurred as interests fill the power void left by declining political parties, as groups take on an increasing role in funding campaigns in the states, develop more sophisticated techniques of access and influence, and exert increased pressure on state governments to take over the responsibilities and fill the funding gaps left by the reduced role of the federal government.

Another major reason for studying subnational interest groups is the increasing importance of the relationship between these and national groups. This link has four aspects to it. First there is the formal link between many national groups and state and local affiliates, such as the National Education Association (NEA) and its state chapters—the Kansas NEA and the Rhode Island NEA, for example. Second is the process of cross-fertilization of ideas and techniques: An increasing exchange of information concerning group organization and strategy is disseminated among levels of group operation. And this flow is not always from the top down. Groups in states like California, New York, and Florida have developed techniques that have been used by national groups and by groups in other states. Third, because of the increasing role of government since the 1960s and the increase in intergovernmental relations in the formulation and implementation of policies such as agriculture, education, environmental protection, and business regulations, groups are often forced to develop strategies that include more than one level of government. Finally, and a related point, national, state, and local groups have been forced into more concerted action as the agencies and units of the various levels of government have become increasingly active as "lobbying" forces themselves. Although most government agencies are not required to register as formal lobbying organizations, governments lobby for their budgets and for programs and against policies and issues that would adversely affect them.[2] An increasing amount of this lobbying is conducted between levels of government, often with the aid of private groups that either have a direct interest in the issue or are simply building up political capital for the future.

The mounting importance of these four facets of the link between national and subnational groups has worked to integrate the interest group systems at all levels of American government. These systems are becoming more and more interdependent. If we add to this the longtime significance of interest groups in state policymaking and their increased importance since the 1970s, then it becomes clear why it is helpful to understand the activities of subnational groups. To study only national groups and their activities in Washington, D.C., provides a very narrow perspective of the role and significance of interest groups in the American political and governmental system. Such a perspective is likely to become even narrower in the immediate future, as more and more policy and funding decisions are shifted to state capitals.

A NEW STUDY: DATA AND DEFINITIONS

The information used in this chapter is drawn from two major sources. The review of past patterns of regional group activity is based on secondary sources, though, as we shall see, there are only a few such studies available. The primary and by far the bulk of the information is taken from the Hrebenar-Thomas project we organized, which involved seventy-eight political scientists.

Ours was the first study of interest groups in all fifty states. Its primary purpose was to provide a comprehensive understanding of interest group activity in the states that would facilitate comparative analysis. Unlike most previous researchers, to develop the most complete understanding of group activity in each state, we focused on interest group activity in state capi*tals* and not just state capi*tols*, that is, not just state legislatures. The subjects researched in each state included the development of groups; the range of groups operating today; the extent and enforcement of lobby laws; the types and styles of lobbyists; group tactics, including groups' roles in elections and in dealings with the three branches of government; and an assessment of group power, both of individual groups and of the group system as a whole.[3]

In our attempt to make this study as comprehensive as possible, we also used a broad definition of the term *interest group*. Most researchers use the legal definition of an interest group to include *only* those groups required to register by federal, state, and, in the few places where they exist, local laws. Such a narrow definition excludes many lobbying entities, most notably the so-called hidden lobbies (those not required to register by law), particularly the myriad of governments and their agencies at all levels of the political system. As we explained in the last section, governmental lobbies are becoming increasingly important. To embrace these hidden lobbies, we defined an interest group as *any association of individuals, whether formally organized or not, that attempts to influence public policy*.[4]

By combining the information on the states within each region, we were able to identify regional patterns. The regional divisions that we use in this chapter are set out in Figure 7.1.

PREVIOUS REGIONAL PATTERNS

No previous study of subnational groups has focused on the regions. So to piece together past patterns of regional group activity, we had to glean the rather meager information from studies of groups in the states. Nevertheless, these studies provided an important source of information and formulated the first theories on state interest group activity. Of partic-

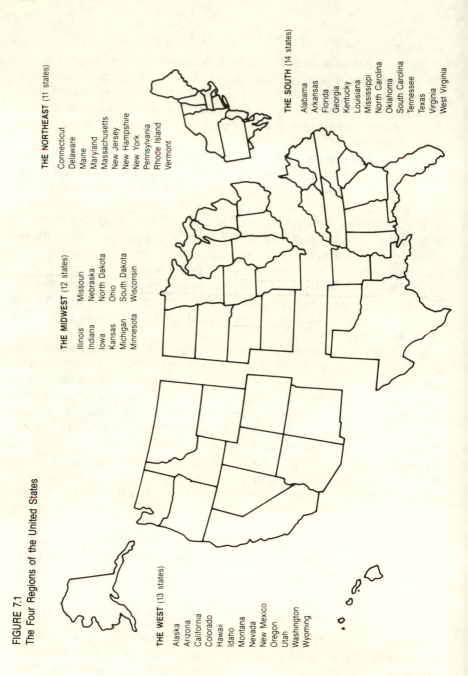

FIGURE 7.1
The Four Regions of the United States

THE NORTHEAST (11 states)

Connecticut
Delaware
Maine
Maryland
Massachusetts
New Jersey
New Hampshire
New York
Pennsylvania
Rhode Island
Vermont

THE MIDWEST (12 states)

Illinois   Missouri
Indiana   Nebraska
Iowa   North Dakota
Kansas   Ohio
Michigan   South Dakota
Minnesota   Wisconsin

THE SOUTH (14 states)

Alabama
Arkansas
Florida
Georgia
Kentucky
Louisiana
Mississippi
North Carolina
Oklahoma
South Carolina
Tennessee
Texas
Virginia
West Virginia

THE WEST (13 states)

Alaska
Arizona
California
Colorado
Hawaii
Idaho
Montana
Nevada
New Mexico
Oregon
Utah
Washington
Wyoming

ular importance is work by Belle Zeller, Sarah McCally Morehouse, and Harmon Zeigler.[5]

To provide a consistency of comparison between this and the following sections, we divide our consideration of past and present patterns of regional group activity into five categories: the number and types of groups active, lobby registration laws, lobbyists, group tactics, and group power. Taken together, these five categories of information enable us to piece together a picture of both past and present activities and impact of interest groups on public policy in the regions.

The Number and Types of Groups Active

In her consideration of state legislatures, Zeller (1954:214) noted: "Lobbies and pressure groups representing almost every conceivable aspect of human endeavor are extremely active at the state level." Yet more than twenty years later and on the basis of more extensive research, Zeigler (1983:99) concluded that a rather narrow range of interests operated in the states. He grouped these into five categories referred to as the traditional interests in the states, narrowed during the 1960s to business, labor, farmers, education, and local government groups. If we assume that the more extensive research by Zeigler was more accurate, each region had a far less diverse range of groups operating than is the case today, and their numbers were also relatively small.[6]

Although no detailed account of the regional variations in the specific types of groups was produced, if we extrapolate from available research, we find that these variations were very much influenced by differences in state and regional economies. Thus manufacturing and labor groups were much more prominent in the Northeast than in the South or West. And agricultural groups and resource-extraction interests—mining, lumber, oil, and gas—were especially prominent in the West and in parts of the Midwest and the South.

Lobby Registration Laws

Lobby registration laws constitute one of three types of public disclosure provisions. The other types are campaign finance disclosure (including financial contributions made by political action committees) and conflict-of-interest regulations. Together, these three aspects of public disclosure can provide information about who is lobbying whom, how much groups are spending, which interests supported which candidates at election time, and which public officials have financial or other connections with which groups and interests.

Evidence suggests that the existence of public disclosure laws affects the way an interest group will operate in trying to access and influence a public official. It also affects the way public officials are willing to deal with these groups. Though the relationship is far from simple, the more public disclosure of lobbying that exists in a state and the more stringently these laws are enforced, the more open is the process of group attempts to influence public policy. Accordingly, there are two criteria for evaluating lobby laws: their inclusiveness and the stringency with which they are enforced. It is the latter that will largely determine the impact of lobby laws, as opposed to their mere existence.

No information on the stringency of enforcement of these laws in the states and regions is available prior to the 1980s. But work by Zeller (1954:217–225) does enable us to assess the extent to which lobbies were regulated in the early 1950s. She reported that in 1953 thirty-eight states plus the territory of Alaska had provisions for the regulation of lobbying. These regulations, however, varied widely, as did the definition of exactly what constituted lobbying. Only twenty-nine states plus Alaska required lobbyists to register, though most states excluded state and local government employees when they were performing their official functions. Only nineteen states required the reporting of lobbying expenditures.

Categorizing this information regionally, the West had the least extensive laws. Four of the eleven western states—Nevada, New Mexico, Washington, and Wyoming—had no lobby laws at all. Another four—Arizona, Montana, Oregon, and Utah—had no registration or reporting requirements. The Northeast, with the exception of the three mid-Atlantic states of Delaware, New Jersey, and Pennsylvania, had the most extensive laws, which by today's standards were not very comprehensive. The Midwest and the South fell in between these two regions, with a slight edge to the Midwest in terms of inclusiveness.

Lobbyists

Lobbyists are often referred to in the press and by the public as if they were identical in all respects, forming some monolithic group. Yet there are five different categories of lobbyists. Distinguishing among them is necessary in order to understand the development of interest group activity in the states and regions and, more importantly, to understand their political power base and thus their methods of operating.

Contract lobbyists are those who work on contract for an interest group. These are the so-called hired guns of the lobbying business and the ones who get the most attention from the news media. Contract lobbyists often represent more than one client and in a few instances as many as twenty-five clients. *In-house lobbyists* are those who, as part or all of their job, represent their employer to government. Executive directors of school teachers' associations, farmers' organizations, and hospital associations are examples. The third group are *government legislative liaisons*, who represent their government or government agency to the legislature and executive branches of government. Then there are *citizen or volunteer lobbyists*. These are usually unpaid and represent citizen and community groups. Finally, *private individual or self-styled lobbyists* simply represent themselves.

To piece together a picture of the state lobbying community in the past, we have to extrapolate from various popular and academic sources, especially the four-state study by Zeigler and Baer (1969), and draw on the historical background from our own study. Generally, the number of lobbyists in state capitals in all the regions was much smaller than today. It appears that in-house and not contract lobbyists have always made up the largest segment of the lobbying community in the states. The rise of the contract lobbyist is a post-1930s phenomenon. Also, because state government tended to be small and largely unprofessionalized, the demand for expertise and technical information from lobbyists was minimal. This is partly responsible for the apparent predominance of the "wheeler-dealer" or "good ol' boy" lobbyist in all regions, who was aided by the lack of enforcement of public disclosure laws, especially in the South and West. Because the role of government was much less through the 1960s than it is today, the number of legislative liaisons and volunteer lobbyists was probably also small, though as no data at all exists on these, we have no accurate way of confirming this assumption. Piecing together information, we also conclude that women formed a very small proportion of lobbyists—perhaps less than 5 percent—in any region.

Group Tactics

A similar problem resulting from lack of data confronts us when we try to make comparisons between regions regarding group tactics. As today, it does appear that the major (and probably often the only) tactical device was the use of one or more lobbyists. With a much smaller role for government then, a narrow range of groups operating, and with only minimal public awareness of lobbying activity, there was little need for other lobbying tactics such as are common today. In this atmosphere one or a few lobbyists often exerted great influence in state politics. Arthur Samish did so in California, working for twenty years, up to the early 1950s, from his office in the Senator Hotel, across the street from the capitol in Sacramento (Syer 1987:34). And in the 1920s Alexander McKenzie was the key player in North Dakota politics. He controlled the Republican party machine, championing the interests of the railroads and the milling, banking, and elevator companies that dominated the state (Wilkins 1981:3–39).

Group Power

It is in the area of group power that the best data exist for comparing past interest group activity between states and regions. In the study of subnational interest groups, the concept of group power has two meanings. It can refer to the power of individual groups and interests within a state, such as doctors, truckers, public employees, and senior citizens. Or it can mean the overall impact of the interest group system on the public-policy-making process in relation to other parts of the political system, such as political parties or legislative or executive institutions.

The only assessment of the most effective individual groups in all fifty states made prior to our study is that compiled by Morehouse (1981:108–112).[7] The Morehouse assessment reveals the predominance of the power of the five traditional interests that we identified above, particularly business interests. As we noted earlier, until the 1960s many states and some regions were dominated by one or a few interests.

As to the overall power of group systems, past patterns reveal some major regional variations. Figures 7.2 and 7.3 illustrate the changing strength of these regional patterns between the early 1950s and the early 1970s. In both periods the interest group systems in the South were overwhelmingly strong, whereas the Northeast exhibited the least powerful systems. The West and Midwest, which exhibited a tendency toward strong interest group systems in the early 1950s, had more moderately powerful systems twenty years later.[8] This shows that, with the exception of the South, there was a general decline in the power of interest group systems in the two decades between the surveys. Fewer and fewer states were being dominated or "run" by interest groups.

EXPLAINING THE VARIATIONS
IN INTEREST GROUP ACTIVITY

How do we account for the previous differences between regions? Do these explanations help us understand contemporary differences and perhaps future variations among the West, the Midwest, the South, and the Northeast? Previous research explained diversity in state and regional group systems primarily through three variables: socioeconomic factors, political party strength, and the level of integration of the policymaking process. Although these variables were and remain important, our research shows that they are not the only significant factors in understanding variations in group activity. Furthermore, the effects and long-term consequences of these three factors appear to be more complex than originally believed.

The types of groups active were explained primarily as a function of the economy. The more diversified the economy, the wider the range of

FIGURE 7.2
Overall Impact of State Interest Group Systems by Region in the Early 1950s: The Zeller Assessment

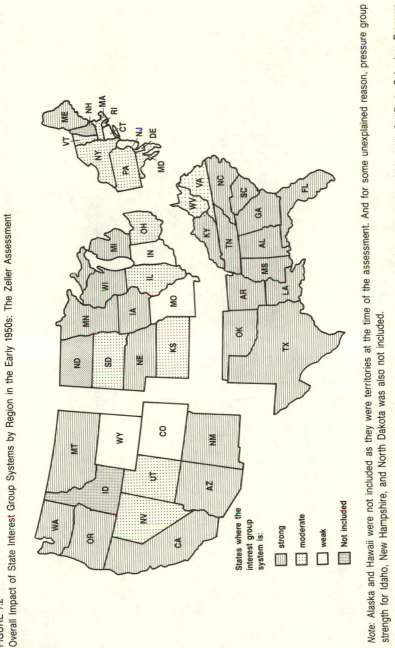

States where the interest group system is:

☐ strong

☐ moderate

☐ weak

☐ Not included

Note: Alaska and Hawaii were not included as they were territories at the time of the assessment. And for some unexplained reason, pressure group strength for Idaho, New Hampshire, and North Dakota was also not included.

Source: Developed from Belle Zeller, *American State Legislatures,* 2nd ed. (New York: Thomas Y. Crowell, 1954), table 9, "Party Cohesion, Pressure Politics, Local and National Issues in State Legislatures," 190–191. Printed with permission.

FIGURE 7.3
Overall Impact of State Interest Group Systems by Region in the Early 1970s: The Morehouse Assessment

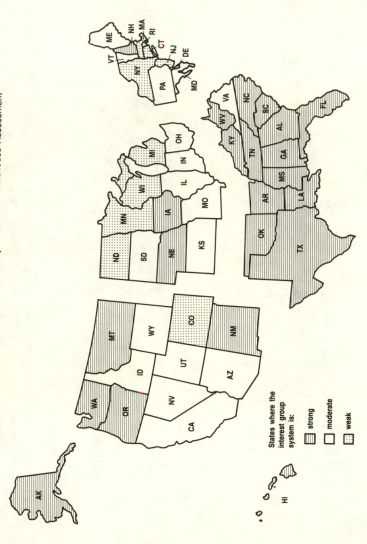
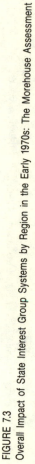

States where the
interest group
system is:

strong

moderate

weak

Source: Developed from Sarah McCally Morehouse, *State Politics, Parties and Policy* (New York: Holt, Rinehart and Winston, 1981), table 3.2, "Listing of the Significant Pressure Groups by State," 108–112. Printed with permission.

groups. In addition, the larger the percentage of middle- and upper-middle-class people in the population, the more diversified and larger the number of groups. This is because the middle classes are more politically active and more likely to join groups than the working class, the less educated, and the poorer members of society (see Zeigler 1983:111–117; and Morehouse 1981:107–117).

The strength of a group system was seen to be largely a function of party strength and whether or not the policymaking process was integrated through strong parties and other factors such as a strong governor and a minimum number of independent boards and commissions. It was argued that an inverse relationship existed between party strength and the overall impact of interest groups on the making of public policy (Zeller 1954:190–193; Morehouse 1981:116–118, 127). Where parties were strong, as in the Northeast and parts of the Midwest, the overall impact of groups was weak. This was because the organizational and policy control of parties enabled them to fetter the activities and flexibility of interest groups. In contrast, in the South and much of the West, where parties were relatively weak and other centralizing policy influences (strong governors, for example) were less, interest group systems were strong. Between these two categories was a midpoint where both parties and interest group systems were moderately strong.

Taken together, these theories predicted certain developments in state and regional interest group systems. As state and regional economies and social structures became more diverse, this would tend to increase the number of groups operating, which in turn would increase competition. This would have the dual effect of reducing the power of individual dominant interests and at the same time gradually move all group systems toward the weak category. Morehouse (1981:131) also attempted to explain the extent of lobby regulation in terms of the power of interest group systems. The more powerful the system, the less comprehensive the regulations.

In our study we found that there were other important elements that affect interest group activity at the subnational level and help to explain state and regional variations. In all we identified eight major elements, which are combined into a conceptual framework set out in Table 7.1. In practice the eight elements are interrelated. Consequently, a change in one will likely impact the others. For example, increased social and economic diversity (factor 6) will likely increase professionalism in government (factor 5), as well as bring pressure for increased state services (factor 1). The combination of these developments will likely increase the number and range of groups operating, the level of professionalism and techniques of lobbyists, and may well affect the power of certain groups. When

TABLE 7.1
Eight Major Factors Influencing the Makeup, Operating
Techniques, and Impact on Public Policy of Interest Group
Systems in the States and Regions

1. State Policy Domain: Constitutional/legal authority of a state affects which groups will be politically active. Policies actually exercised by a state affects which groups will be most active. The policy priorities of a state will affect which groups are most influential.

2. Centralization/Decentralization of Spending: This refers to the amount of money spent by state governments versus that spent by local governments. The higher the percentage of state spending on individual programs and overall on services, the more intense will be lobbying in the state capital.

3. Political Attitudes: Especially political culture, and political ideology viewed in terms of conservative/liberal attitudes. Affects the type and extent of policies performed; the level of integration/fragmentation and professionalization of the policymaking process; acceptable lobbying techniques; and the comprehensiveness and stringency of enforcement of public disclosure laws, including lobby laws.

4. Level of Integration/Fragmentation of the Policy Process: Strength of political parties; power of the governor; number of directly elected cabinet members; number of independent boards and commissions; initiative, referendum, and recall. Influences the number of options available to groups: Greater integration decreases the options whereas more fragmentation increases them.

5. Level of Professionalization of State Government: State legislators, support services, bureaucracy, including the governor's staff. Impacts the extent to which public officials need group resources and information. Also affects the level of professionalization of the lobbying system.

6. Level of Socioeconomic Development: Increased socioeconomic diversity will tend to produce a more diverse and competitive group system; a decline in the dominance of one or an oligarchy of groups; new and more sophisticated techniques of lobbying, such as an increase in contact lobbyists, lawyer-lobbyists, multiclient/multiservice lobbying firms, grassroots campaigns, and public relations techniques; and a general rise in the professionalization of lobbyists and lobbying.

7. Extensiveness and Enforcement of Public Disclosure Laws: Including lobby laws, campaign finance laws, PAC regulations, and conflict of interest provisions. Increased public access to information about lobbying activities influences lobbying methods, affecting the power of certain groups and lobbyists.

8. Level of Campaign Costs and Sources of Support: As the proportion of group funding increases, especially that from PACs, group access and power increases.

Sources: Adapted from figure 4.1 in Clive S. Thomas and Ronald J. Hrebenar, "Interest Groups in the States," chapter 4 in Virginia Gray, Herbert Jacob, and Robert Albritton, eds., *Politics in the American States: A Comparative Analysis,* 5th ed. (Glenview, Ill.: Scott, Foresman/Little, Brown, 1990), 137.

significant changes take place in most or all of the eight elements, then a major transformation will take place in the interest group system.

Here, then, is a conceptual framework that can help explain and predict development in interest group systems as socioeconomic, legal, and political circumstances change. Although this framework has its limitations, we can put it to immediate use to explain recent changes in the five aspects of interest group activity upon which we are focusing in this chapter—the number and types of groups operating, lobby laws, lobbyists, group tactics, and group power.

TRANSFORMATIONS IN STATE INTEREST GROUP ACTIVITY

Since the 1970s, major developments have occurred in interest group activity in the states and regions. In this section we summarize these changes for the fifty states as a whole. Then in the next section we consider how these changes exhibit similarities and differences among regions.

The Number and Types of Groups Active

Changes in the number and types of groups active in the states parallel changes at the national level, in large part because of the increasing interdependence of state and national group activity. One development is that the number of registered groups has expanded in the states, partly as a factor of the increased stringency of lobby registration requirements. Perhaps more important is that many traditional interests like local governments and business have fragmented, individual cities, special districts (especially school districts), and businesses now lobbying for themselves as well as using the lobbying representation of their umbrella organization—a municipal league or a trade association, for example. Group numbers have also been augmented in state capitals by the appearance of new groups such as social issue groups, and so-called single-issue groups like anti-abortion and pro-choice organizations.

This increase in numbers has been accompanied by a broadening of the range of interests. This is so much the case that we can no longer talk of a narrow range of interests operating in state capitals. The range of groups has also been expanded by a marked increase in the activities of hidden lobbies, especially government at the local and state levels. A third development is that groups are lobbying more intensely as a result of increased competition and an increased role of government (Thomas and Hrebenar 1990:129–131).

Lobby Registration Laws

The Watergate affair of 1973–1974 provided a major impetus for states to tighten their public disclosure laws, including lobby registration requirements, and for states that lacked some or all of these regulations to enact such laws. As a consequence, all fifty states now have some kind of public disclosure laws including lobby laws and laws affecting the operation and reporting of contributions by PACs (Council on Governmental Ethics Laws 1988:79–115, 157–168).

Because of the First Amendment clause on the "right to petition government" and similar provisions in many state constitutions, laws cannot restrict or limit lobbying. What they can do is limit certain activities in connection with representation to government, such as making gifts to public officials and entertaining them. But probably the major value of lobby laws is in providing public information on who is lobbying whom. This increases public and particularly press scrutiny of lobbying. We concluded from our study that the more extensive these laws, the greater the impact on lobbying practices in terms of professionalizing interest group activity. But even today, as we will see, lobby laws vary from region to region in their inclusiveness and in the degree of stringency of enforcement.

Lobbyists

Three major developments regarding lobbyists have occurred in the states since the early 1970s. Once again, these parallel those taking place in the nation's capital. First, the number of lobbyists has expanded as a greater number of groups join the political fray. This includes many government legislative liaisons as well as volunteer lobbyists. Because most of these are not required to register, it is hard to estimate their numbers. However, looking at samples from several states, we conclude that as many as one-third of the lobbyists in state capitals on any one day during the legislative session represent some form of government unit or agency.

Second, lobbyists as a group are becoming increasingly professionalized. That is to say, although political contacts and working the system are still of major significance, technical knowledge on issues is of increasing importance. This rising professionalism has been the product of the greater number and complexity of issues dealt with by state government, which has affected the level of professionalism of all those involved in the governmental process. What it has meant for the lobbying community is that though the old wheeler-dealer survives, if under a more sophisticated guise, there is a new breed of lobbyists who are the technical experts much sought after by policymakers.

Third, as far as contract lobbying is concerned, the lone lobbyist is still a significant part of the scene, but more and more law firms are taking on lobbying. This is partly a product of the growing complexity of government and the increasing importance of legal issues. Also, more and more contract lobbying is being performed by multiservice lobbying firms. These provide not only lobbying services but lobby campaign organizational services to help improve a group's political clout.

Group Tactics

One of the reasons for the rise of these multiservice lobbying organizations is that lobbying tactics have become much more sophisticated in the states, as at the national level, since the 1960s. Although the use of lobbyists is still the core of any group's lobbying effort, many groups, particularly those well financed and well organized, now supplement this by other techniques. These new techniques include public relations campaigns to win support for a group and ultimately to influence public officials; networking, the development of sophisticated group-member contact systems to orchestrate members' bringing pressure to bear on decisionmakers; and the use of PACs. We find that the rise of the use of PACs in the states has been as significant as that at the national level.

This increased sophistication has largely been the result of stiffer competition between groups, which has resulted as more and more groups fight for state funds and to affect policy and try to meet public officials' demands for information. The refinement of tactics has been made possible, in part, by advances in technology, especially in computers, as also noted by Godwin in Chapter 14. However, we should not let these developments obscure that the rudiments of lobbying remain unchanged. These rudiments involve a two-stage process: first, gaining access to policymakers and, second, influencing their decision. The new techniques and tactics are all geared to these two basic ends. The phenomenal rise in the use of PACs, for example, is testimony to their helping enhance group success in this two-stage process.

Group Power

What have all these changes meant for group power, both for individual groups and interests, and for the group system in each state? As to the power of individual groups and interests, this appears to have changed surprisingly little. Just because there are now more groups active in state capitals does not necessarily mean that the new groups are politically powerful. As Paul Peterson suggests in Chapter 15, more interest groups does not necessarily mean more influence. This is evidenced by comparing the range of groups operating in state capitals with those considered to be influential by policymakers and political observers. It is certainly true that increased competition among groups has forced the longtime powerful interests such as business to share power. But business interests are still significant political forces in almost all states, as are professional groups, especially doctors and lawyers. Blue-collar unions have lost some influence, but the white-collar sector of labor, especially schoolteachers and state and local employees, has gained considerable influence. Agriculture, in contrast, has seen a gradual diminution of its power, even in traditional farm states. And despite their proliferation in recent years, single-issue, social-issue, and good-government groups are rarely among the most influential in the states. Senior citizen, environmentalist, and women's and minority groups have enjoyed limited success.[9]

Since the Morehouse assessment of the 1970s, there have been some significant changes in the power of group systems in individual states. It appears that interest group systems are not moving toward the weak category, as previous research predicted, but more toward the moderate category. This means that recent socioeconomic and political developments have not worked to significantly reduce the power of interest group systems in the states. Rather, these group systems are consolidating their influence on a par with other political institutions.

TRANSFORMATIONS IN THE REGIONS

This general description of developments in group activity in the states masks some significant variations among regions. These variations both reflect differences in political developments and in turn influence that political development. As our review of past patterns in the regions showed in an earlier section, the variations are more important in some areas of interest group activity than in others.

With the exception of Florida, which has very comprehensive registration requirements, the least inclusive and the least stringently enforced lobby laws are in the South. Until 1988, when the voters passed a ballot proposition that included lobby registration and reporting, Arkansas had the weakest lobby laws of any state. The other three regions manifest a mixed pattern. The most inclusive laws are found in the upper midwestern states like Michigan, Wisconsin, and Minnesota, which are also the states that tend to be more strict in enforcement. In the West, California, Oregon, and particularly Washington and Arizona have very inclusive requirements and, with the possible exception of Arizona, fairly rigid enforcement. Next to the upper Midwest, the Northeast has the most inclusive and the most stringently enforced laws.

Ironically, the states and regions that have traditionally had the most powerful groups and have suffered the most abuses from these interests (and thus need lobby regulation the most) tend to have the least inclusive and stringently enforced laws. This, not surprisingly, is because proposals for such measures can be defeated by these powerful interests supported by a very conservative or individualistic political culture. The South is a case in point. In contrast, states that have experienced the least abuses tend to have the most inclusive and stringent laws. Our research suggests that much of the reason for this is explained in varying political attitudes among regions and varying levels of socioeconomic development (factors 3 and 6 in Table 7.1).

Variations in lobbyists center on three characteristics: gender, the professionalization of contract lobbyists, and the number and range of volunteer lobbyists. The South, with some exceptions such as North Carolina and Virginia, appears to have the smallest percentage of women lobbyists—by our estimates only about 12 to 15 percent compared with 20 to 25 percent for the Northeast and West. The South also appears to be less advanced along the path of professionalization of contract lobbyists. The wheeler-dealer still appears to be prominent in the region, and the development of multiservice lobbying firms has been slower than elsewhere. Because social-issue and grassroots organizations tend to be less numerous in the South than in the Northeast and West, the South also appears to have fewer of these in its state-capital lobbying communities. This also partly accounts for the smaller number of women in the southern lobbying community, as many legislative liaison lobbyists and most volunteer lobbyists are women.

In this area of group activity, it is difficult to identify any major differences from region to region. In general, the variations that do exist tend to follow patterns similar to those in the above three categories. For example, overall, the use of PACs appears to be more extensive in the Northeast than in most of the South, Midwest, and West. And with relatively less competition between groups in many southern and midwestern states, lobbying strategies appear to be less sophisticated there than in the Northeast.

Table 7.2 sets out a comparison of the forty most effective interests in the four regions in relation to the fifty states as a whole. Clearly, the dominant interest overall is schoolteachers' groups. Besides this, however, there are sometimes wide variations. For example, traditional labor ranks third in the Midwest but tenth in the South. In contrast, state employees rank as low as twentieth in the Midwest but eleventh in the South. General farm organizations rank sixth in the Midwest but only twenty-sixth in the Northeast. Insurance groups rank third in the Northeast but twenty-second in the South.

The major explanation for these variations in power appears to be the significance to the regional economy of the particular interest concerned

TABLE 7.2
Ranking of the Forty Most Effective Interests in the
Regions Compared with the Fifty States Overall

Interest and Overall Rank in the Fifty States	Overall Rank			
	West	Midwest	South	Northeast
1. Schoolteachers' organizations (predominantly NEA)	1	1	1	2
2. General business organizations (chambers of commerce, etc.)	3	4	3	1
3. Bankers' associations (includes savings and loan associations)	7	2	2	10
4. Manufacturers (companies and associations)	8[a]	9[a]	4	5[a]
5. Traditional labor associations (predominantly the AFL-CIO)	8[a]	3	10	4
6. Utility companies and associations (electric, gas, telephone, water)	2	11	7	9
7. Individual banks and financial institutions	6	13	9	7
8. Lawyers (predominantly state bar associations and trial lawyers)	15	5	5	12
9. General local government organizations (municipal leagues, county organizations, etc.)	4	17[a]	12	5[a]
10. General farm organizations (mainly state farm bureaus)	11	6	8	26
11. Doctors	16	7	6	17[a]
12. State and local government employees (other than teachers)	5	20	11	8
13. Insurance (companies and associations)	17	15	22[a]	3
14. Realtors' associations	22	14	20[a]	11
15. Individual traditional labor unions (Teamsters, UAW, etc.)	23[a]	8	27	13
16. K–12 education interests (other than teachers)	19	16	16	23[a]
17. Health care groups (other than doctors)	31	12	28[a]	15
18. Agricultural commodity organizations (stockgrowers, grain growers, etc.)	8[a]	23[a]	20[a]	NM[b]
19. Universities and colleges (institutions and personnel)	18	17[a]	22[a]	23[a]
20. Oil and gas (companies and associations)	13[a]	23[a]	19	30[a]

(*continues*)

TABLE 7.2 (*continued*)

Interest and Overall Rank in the Fifty States	Overall Rank			
	West	Midwest	South	Northeast
21. Retailers (companies and trade associations)	NM[b]	9[a]	17[a]	21
22. Contractors/builders/developers	20	33[a]	13[a]	16
23. Environmentalists	25[a]	26[a]	25[a]	14
24. Individual cities and towns	13[a]	23[a]	34[a]	20
25. Liquor, wine, and beer interests	25[a]	21	17[a]	30[a]
26. Mining companies and associations	12	22	28[a]	NM[b]
27. Truckers and private transport interests (excluding railroads)	29[a]	28[a]	13[a]	27[a]
28. Public interest/good-government groups	35	NM[b]	25[a]	17[a]
29. State agencies	NM[b]	28[a]	13[a]	35[a]
30. Forest product companies	23[a]	NM[b]	28[a]	27[a]
31. Senior citizens	28	31[a]	34[a]	17[a]
32. Railroads	33[a]	31[a]	22[a]	NM[b]
33. Women and minorities	21	NM[b]	32[a]	35[a]
34. Religious interests	27	NM[b]	34[a]	23[a]
35. Hunting and fishing (includes anti-gun-control groups)	NM[b]	28[a]	34[a]	22
36. Gaming interests (racetracks, casinos, lotteries)	32	33[a]	32[a]	30[a]
37. Anti-abortionists[a]	NM[b]	19	NM[b]	NM[b]
Tourist industry groups[a]	29[a]	33[a]	NM[b]	27[a]
38. Newspapers/media interests[a]	NM[b]	33[a]	31	35[a]
Taxpayers' groups[a]	33[a]	26[a]	NM[b]	35[a]
39. Tobacco lobby	NM[b]	NM[b]	NM[b]	30[a]
40. Miscellaneous (all other groups mentioned)	NOM[c]	NOM[c]	34[ad]	30[ae]

[a]Tied ranking.

[b]NM = not mentioned as an effective interest in any state in the region.

[c]NOM = no other groups mentioned as effective in the region.

[d]The only other group mentioned in the entire region was legislative caucuses in Louisiana.

[e]The only two other groups mentioned in the region were certified accounts in Rhode Island and a group for the mentally ill in Vermont.

Source: Rankings for the fifty states and for the regions are based on appendix 1, "The Most Effective Interests in the Fifty States," and table 4.2, "Ranking of the Forty Most Effective Interests in the Fifty States," in Clive S. Thomas and Ronald J. Hrebenar, "Interest Groups in the States," chapter 4 in Virginia Gray, Herbert Jacob, and Robert Albritton, eds., *Politics in the American States: A Comparative Analysis,* 5th ed. (Glenview, Ill.: Scott, Foresman/Little, Brown, 1990).

and the level of diversity of the economy (Table 7.1, factor 6). Thus insurance is much more important to the Northeast than it is to the South, whereas government employment is relatively more important to the West than to the Midwest. Such major economic interests also usually have the resources to organize and lobby at a high level of political sophistication. Taken together, these factors translate into political power. State policymakers cannot ignore these interests if they want a stable and healthy economy and if they want to remain in power.

There are, however, other variables that contribute to individual group power. These include party strength and the level of integration and fragmentation of the policy process, the level of professionalization of government, the strength of public disclosure laws, and the source of campaign funds (factors 4, 5, 7, and 8).

The overall impact of groups in the four regions is set out in Figure 7.4. To represent variations in group power, we use a terminology and classification system different from that used by previous researchers. The old classification system—strong, moderate, and weak—can lead to some misleading impressions. For example, it is unlikely that interest groups have ever been weak—of minor importance in public-policy making—in any state. A more accurate statement would be that interest groups have been subordinate to other aspects of the political system in the policymaking process. To avoid such misimpressions and more accurately reflect the situation in the various states and regions, we developed a five-part classification.

States classified as *dominant* (roughly corresponding to the "strong" classification of Zeller and Morehouse) are those in which groups as a whole are the overwhelming influence on policymaking. The *complementary* category (corresponding to the old "moderate" grouping) includes those states where groups are forced to work in conjunction with or are constrained by other aspects of the political system. The *subordinate* category (approximating the former "weak" grouping) represents a situation in which the group system is consistently subordinated to other aspects of the policymaking process. The absence of any states in this category indicates that interest groups are not consistently subordinate in any state. The *dominant/complementary* category includes those states whose group systems alternate between the two situations or are in the process of moving from one to the other. Likewise with the *complementary/subordinate* classification.

Figure 7.4 shows that the South still retains the most influential group systems, followed by the West. The Midwest and the Northeast have the least powerful systems. In fact, four of the five states in the complementary/subordinate category—Connecticut, Delaware, Rhode Island, and Vermont—are in the Northeast, and the other, Minnesota, is located in the

FIGURE 7.4

Overall Impact of State Interest Group Systems by Region in the Late 1980s: The Hrebenar-Thomas Assessment

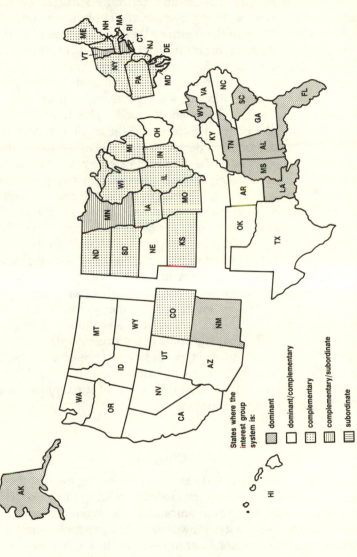

Source: Adapted from table 4.3, "Classification of the Fifty States According to the Overall Impact of Interest Groups," in Clive S. Thomas and Ronald J. Hrebenar, "Interest Groups in the States," chapter 4 in Virginia Gray, Herbert Jacob, and Robert Albritton, eds., *Politics in the American States: A Comparative Analysis*, 5th ed. (Glenview, Ill.: Scott, Foresman/Little, Brown, 1990).

Midwest. A partial explanation for these variations is also provided by reference to the conceptual framework in Table 7.1. Of particular importance is the level of integration/fragmentation of the policy process (factor 4). With stronger political parties and generally stronger governmental institutions in the Northeast, the overall impact of group systems in this region is much less than in the South or West, where the policy process is more fragmented. Also important in determining group system strength are political attitudes (factor 3), particularly political culture, which (as noted earlier) influence the extensiveness of public disclosure provisions; the level of professionalization of state government (factor 5); and the extent of socioeconomic development (factor 6). The more liberal and the less individualistic the political culture, and the more advanced is professionalism and socioeconomic development, the more likely the group system is to move away from the dominant category.

However, as noted earlier, though the trend in the power of group systems is away from the dominant (or strong) category, it is not, as previously predicted, toward the subordinate (or weak) category. Furthermore, there may be no simple explanation as to the course these developments may take. The actual course appears to depend on the importance to each region of the individual factors in Table 7.1. For example, although the general movement of the power of group systems is toward the complementary (middle) category, the reasons for this trend may be different in different regions. In the South, a longtime dominant interest group region, increased party competition, as well as economic diversity and the breakdown of the traditionalistic political culture, may have played a part in this shift. In the West, however, parties and a changing political culture appear to have had very little to do with the drift toward the middle category. Here, increasing professionalization of government and social pluralism appear to be the major factors.

CONCLUSION

Two forces are simultaneously at work in affecting interest group activities in the states and regions. First is a nationalizing influence. This force, engendered by improved communication, the increased role of government, and heightened political awareness, has produced similarities between developments in interest group activity in the nation's capital and those in the fifty state capitals. At the same time, local variations survive for a variety of factors, including economic and social circumstances, political institutional structure, and political attitudes. Furthermore, some of the similar developments in the regions may not be the result of equal impact by the same forces or indeed of the same forces at all.

In the future, although variations in the states and regions are likely to diminish even further, these local circumstances will probably prevent a complete homogenization of the American interest group system. Yet exactly what path such integration and diversity will take is the subject of some speculation. This is because we conclude that there are many more variables involved in the development of state and regional interest group systems than previously realized.

The conceptual framework set out in Table 7.1, however, can help elucidate the changes and developments in interest group systems. It can do much to throw light on the major expansion in group activity that has taken place in the regions, the increase in public disclosure provisions, and the rising professionalism of lobbyists. The framework also clarifies the changes in the power of individual groups and lobbies and of group systems in particular states.

Although many unanswered questions remain, one contribution of our study is to provide a more complete understanding of state and regional politics. Interest group studies certainly have value in themselves. But groups are just one part of the various political systems operating in the United States, and, as we have seen, groups affect and are affected by other aspects of these systems, such as electoral processes, political parties, and legislative and executive institutions. The real value of interest group studies lies in their ability to enhance an understanding of the interaction of groups with these other aspects of the political system and thus provide a more complete understanding of the policy process at the various levels of government.

NOTES

1. Besides the problems of geography and inconsistency of source material, two other formidable barriers to subnational interest group research are money and organization. The cost of a fifty-state investigation by a small team of researchers would far exceed that of a study on Washington, D.C., and a comprehensive study of urban and local interest groups would be even more costly. In recent years national granting agencies have not been disposed to fund research on state and local government. The fifty-state study on which this chapter is based was, in fact, undertaken with no research grants. The only feasible way to conduct unfunded subnational studies is to use experts from the states and localities.

2. For a brief consideration of these government interests and their activities see, Deil S. Wright, *Understanding Intergovernmental Relations*, 3d ed. (Pacific Grove, Calif.: Brooks/Cole, 1988).

3. The results of the Hrebenar-Thomas project are being published in a series of four books: Ronald J. Hrebenar and Clive S. Thomas, eds., *Interest Group Politics in the American West; Interest Group Politics in the Southern States; Interest Group Politics in the Midwestern States;* and *Interest Group Politics in the Northeastern States.* An overview of the findings in all fifty states is presented in Clive S. Thomas and Ronald J. Hrebenar, "Interest Groups in the States," ch. 4 in Virginia Gray, Herbert Jacob, and Robert Albritton, eds., *Politics in the*

American States: A Comparative Analysis, 5th ed. (Glenview, Ill.: Scott, Foresman/Little, Brown, 1990).

4. In our study we also distinguished between an interest group, an interest, and a lobby. An *interest group* is a specific organization like the Missouri Bus and Truck Association, which is an association of bus and trucking companies, but the members of this organization are also part of the broader *interest* category of transportation. This includes, for example, air carriers, railroads, and petroleum suppliers. Bus and truck operators are also part of the even broader category of the Missouri business *lobby,* which includes all those groups and organizations—such as manufacturing companies, bankers, retailers, liquor dealers, and a host of others—interested in promoting conditions favorable to business operations. Although it is often difficult to draw hard and fast lines between the terms *interest group, interest,* and *lobby,* the distinction is useful for understanding the various aspects of group activity presented here.

5. The major works on state interest groups are Zeller 1954:190–191 and ch. 13, "Pressure Group Influence and Their Control"; Morehouse 1981, especially ch. 3, "Pressure Groups Versus Political Parties"; Zeigler 1983; Zeigler and van Dalen 1976; and Zeigler and Baer 1969. Related academic works are John C. Wahlke, Heinz Eulau, William Buchanan, and Leroy C. Ferguson, *The Legislative System* (New York: John Wiley and Sons, 1962); and Wayne L. Francis, *Legislative Issues in the Fifty States: A Comparative Analysis* (Chicago: Rand McNally, 1967).

Historical perspectives on interest groups in the states can be supplemented by popular works such as John Gunther, *Inside U.S.A.* (New York: Harper and Brothers, 1951); and the series of books by Neal R. Peirce on the various subregions of the United States, plus Neal R. Peirce and Jerry Hagstrom, *The Book of America: Inside Fifty States Today* (New York: W. W. Norton, 1983). In the absence of formal academic studies, many political scientists have turned to these and other popular studies for information on state interest groups.

6. However, the only numbers on group registrations available on a comparative basis are those presented by Zeller in 1954. By her account, the number of registrations range from 490 in Kansas in 1953, to 422 in California in 1951–1952, to 94 in Indiana in 1953, to none in Georgia in the same year (Zeller 1954:223–224).

7. The Morehouse assessment was based on thirteen books and one journal article on state politics. She relied heavily on Peirce's series of books on the subregions of the country. An updated version of the Morehouse table was produced by Michael Engel, *State and Local Politics: Fundamentals and Perspectives* (New York: St. Martin's Press, 1985), 241–242. Most of Engel's updating, however, appears to be based on Peirce and Hagstrom, *The Book of America,* cited in n. 5 above.

8. Two other studies have attempted to assess aspects of overall group power in the fifty states: Francis, *Legislative Issues,* cited in n. 5 above; and Glen Abney and Thomas P. Lauth, "Interest Group Influence in the States: A View of Subsystem Politics," paper delivered at the 1986 annual meeting of the American Political Science Association, Washington, D.C. However, both based their assessments on studies of only one aspect of the process. Francis concentrated on the legislature, whereas Abney and Lauth based their listing on a survey of administrators.

9. For a listing of the most powerful interests in the fifty states, see appendix 1 in Gray, Jacob, and Albritton, *Politics in the American States,* cited in n. 3 above.

8

The Political Mobilization of Business

DAVID PLOTKE

The prominent role of business in politics during the Reagan-Bush era did not emerge out of a vacuum. In the 1970s, a major political mobilization of business occurred in the United States that was important in shaping politics over the next decade and beyond. Political organizations and discourses concerned with the overall state of the American political economy were central pieces in this process. Contrary to prevailing views, political efforts by business cannot be explained solely in terms of strategic calculation aimed at realizing economic interests. Rather, such political efforts are conceived and pursued when economic phenomena are interpreted in the light of normative political and cultural commitments. This process, which entails shaping political identities, is discursive: It involves a sequence of claims and descriptions whose connections are established with reference to shared meanings and symbols.

Most accounts of business in politics recognize that by the mid-1970s a decline in economic performance affected wide sections of American business. Business elites also felt threatened by the antibusiness sentiment of the late 1960s and early 1970s. Growing government regulation was regarded as both a major immediate problem and a dangerous symptom of antibusiness attitudes that promised further difficulties. In response to these challenges, business elites formed organizations and took initiatives aimed at restricting government regulation and improving economic conditions.

Business made a strong and well-funded case against many of the Democratic social welfare policies of the 1960s and the social and economic regulation that persisted into the next decade. In new business associations and political action committees, business elites slowed the growth of regulation and helped prepare the way for the pro-business public policies of the 1980s (Edsall 1984; Ferguson and Rogers 1986; Krieger 1986; Vogel 1989).

This view of business political action properly calls attention to the political power of business and continues to shape much of the research on business and politics. Emphasizing the size and strength of business groups in national interest group politics might seem such an obvious point as to be tedious. Yet a number of valuable studies in this area seem not even to consider it worthy of mention. This inattention cannot be justified—unless one believes that it is possible to separate the organizational side of interest groups from the social and political forces that are being organized (a reasonable analytical claim) *and* offer the organizational account as a sufficient explanation of how actual groups form and interact, as exemplified by Salisbury and associates in Chapter 6 (Salisbury 1984: 64–76; Salisbury et al. 1987:1217–1234; and Laumann and Knoke 1987).

Gauged by the number and scale of lobbying efforts and political action committees generated in the 1970s, business was preeminent in its capacity to mobilize resources in politics. By 1980, corporations and trade associations together operated 50 percent of all lobbying offices in Washington and contributed roughly 60 percent of all PAC funds that went to House and Senate candidates.[1] When conflicts between business and other groups occurred, two efforts by "nonbusiness" groups—labor's political mobilization (including its PACs) and public interest groups' attempts to expand and reform economic and social regulation—were outmatched. Both initiatives in the 1970s met a massive business response, one that continues through the present.

To explain the preceding narrative of business mobilization, two accounts can be given. For the first, business political mobilization expressed a straightforward effort to achieve already given business interests. In this case, mobilization is a function of the capacity of business groups to solve collective action problems; outcomes are explained by the ability of business groups to use their resources to advance their interests. In the second, political processes among business elites were crucial to overcome collective action problems and provide a concrete definition of interests to guide strategic choices.

In the remainder of this chapter, I compare the two views. I first discuss efforts to explain business mobilization mainly in terms of the direct effects of economic shifts, notably changes in profits. After criticizing major elements of this view, I present a political account of business mobilization and argue that it can better explain the most important aspects of business political efforts that took place in the 1970s and still take place in the 1990s.

FALLING PROFITS AND BUSINESS MOBILIZATION

Business is always in politics. Economic decisions about investment, employment, and prices have major effects on the political fortunes of governments and oppositions. Should this form of influence on politics be conceived in terms of a "blind" logic of economic relations, or partly in terms of political choices by business elites? Do firms make important economic decisions in part to achieve short- and medium-term political objectives? I do not address these questions here, nor do I enter the debates about electoral cycles in which economists and political scientists explain what public officials do in terms of the expected political results of their economic choices (Nordhaus 1975:42, 169–190; Tufte 1978; Hibbs 1987:255–279).

Links between business and political-administrative elites also provide regular channels of communication and influence. Both modes of business influence have occasioned great debate (Alt and Chrystal 1983; Block 1977). In this chapter I examine a third mode of business involvement in politics: explicit efforts by business groups and associations to shape the course of politics. In the subsequent examination of business mobilization between 1974 and 1980, I treat business as an organized interest group and quasi movement.[2]

The following features of political intervention by business in the United States during the 1970s are widely recognized:

- Profits were lower in the 1970s than in the 1960s.
- The interest organizations of business were weak.
- Public distrust of business had reached unprecedented levels.
- Major new social and economic regulations had been put in place or proposed, and further regulatory measures seemed possible (Edsall 1984; Pertschuk 1982; Vogel 1989).

These features of the subsequent business mobilization are also recognized:

- Business organizations were revitalized to engage in more extensive lobbying activities vis-à-vis federal agencies, Congress, and the states.
- New business organizations took shape, notably, in 1973–1974, the Business Roundtable, whose economically powerful members approached Congress and agencies directly.
- Corporate PACs proliferated; by 1980 the number of business PACs was more than ten times larger than in 1974.
- New forms of business political intervention appeared, such as advertising that offered a general defense of free enterprise or efforts to influence school curricula.
- Pro-business intellectual efforts were well funded, as in new public policy institutes (Bradshaw and Vogel 1981:33–47; Alexander 1984; Saloma 1984; Schlozman and Tierney 1986; Useem 1984).

TABLE 8.1
Business in Politics in the 1970s, Rationalistic View

A. Declining profits led to:

B. Business opposition to government regulation, taxes, and unions.

C. This opposition appeared politically in new business organizations that aimed to reduce regulation and taxes.

D. Business arguments for these policies were broadened in arguments for a new pro-business course.

E. Business power encouraged the Carter administration to curtail its reformist impulses.

F. (D) and (E) prepared the way for the ardently pro-business policies that followed the election of Reagan.

What results followed?

- Pro-business Republicans received increased funding, both as incumbents and challengers.
- Pro-business Democrats also benefitted; all Democrats were encouraged to sympathize with articulated business preferences.
- The growth of regulation slowed as pro-labor and redistributive tendencies in the Carter administration declined.
- Strongly pro-business Republicans were elected president by large majorities three times in the 1980s and carried out policies broadly similar to those advocated by leading forces in the political mobilization of business in the 1970s and early 1980s.
- Public views of business became significantly more positive (Burnham 1982; Ferguson and Rogers 1986; Vogel 1978:45–78).

By any reasonable standard, business political mobilization in the 1970s was successful. It helped produce administrations responsive to business and opposed to new government regulation. The reality of business mobilization is not in question; the problem is how to explain it. The following sequence, presented in Table 8.1, offers one view of the sources and elements of business political action. Here mobilization refers to a double process: growing business political action and a strong anti-Democratic shift in its aims.

Abstracted from a number of accounts that include its main themes, this sequence is stated sharply in order to clarify the analytical issues.[3] It provides a starkly rationalistic explanation of business political action as driven by the strategic pursuit of immediate economic interests. Indeed, this model starts where such a view of business collective action needs to start, with profits. Does Table 8.1 give an adequate account of business political action during this period?

The Pattern of Business Mobilization

An account of business political mobilization as a response to declining profits should be able both to demonstrate that a decline occurred and to show clear, strong connections between that decline and political processes. Business mobilization should take place after a decline in profitability, and it should be initiated or at least most strongly supported by the industries and sectors most affected by declining profits.

Data on profits suggest a positive relation between falling profits in the first half of the 1970s and the business mobilization, but they do not warrant depicting profits as a sufficient or even primary determinant of business collective action.[4] The decline occurred mainly in 1970 and 1974, with a drop of about 2 percent in each year; thus it was not fully evident until well into the decade.

If profits were the determinant of business mobilization, one would expect the latter to lag declining profits by a period corresponding to the requirements of overcoming collective action problems.[5] Yet business mobilization was clearly under way by the mid-1970s and did not rise and fall directly with profit levels. Additionally, it did not decline immediately as profits rose into the 1980s.

Did different sectors of the business community mobilize in response to sector-specific declines in profit? The answer also appears to be no. To the extent any substantial claims have been made about relations between sectoral experiences and business mobilization, they do not entail a direct correlation between decreasing profits and increased political activity.[6] We cannot claim that the sectors most damaged by a decline in profits were politically most active. The best predictor of whether or not a corporation became active in politics in the 1970s was its size.[7]

In sum, both the timing and shape of business mobilization suggest that profit problems in the early to mid-1970s were a major part of a group of elements that business interpreted as requiring a political response, but by no means were they a sufficient cause of business political action.

A second problem with the explanation outlined in Table 8.1 above concerns its conception of relations between falling profits and opposition to government regulation, taxes, and unions. Those who led the business mobilization criticized federal regulatory efforts (Vogel 1989:172; Harris in Harris and Milkis 1989:260–286). Business may have believed regulation was a key problem and acted to block it. Any belief that regulation was the central economic problem, however, could not have been generated automatically by economic trends. Even the broadest reasonable interpretation of the effects of new social and economic regulation stops short of such a claim (Lilley and Miller 1977:49–61).[8]

Beyond regulation and labor costs, other worthy targets for economic blame existed that did not yield central themes of the business mobilization: military spending, declining human capital investments, faulty firm-level decisionmaking regarding investments, inefficient management in organizing production, and international competition (Bowles and Gintis 1982:51–93; Scott and Lodge 1985:13–70).

The point is not that business complaints about regulation, wages, and taxes had no basis; rather, none of these factors (nor all in combination) can be accorded a determining role with regard either to the short-term drop in profits or broader emerging economic problems. Even if one accepts that declining profits in the early to mid-1970s caused the business mobilization, profit problems could have been attributed to a number of domestic and international factors. Focusing on regulation (or even regulation plus "taxes") required political interpretation.[9] It meant grouping together virtually every public activity that impinged on economic life, to call them all "regulation" in strongly negative terms. That grouping was effective and was linked to an apolitical view of social and economic relations as natural and autonomous, counterposed against government activity as unnatural and intrusive. Such images of the economy are as wrong as the idea that a purely economic logic could select regulation as the key problem.[10]

Business Organization and Politics

Further problems arise with the explanation of business mobilization presented in Table 8.1, as this view offers no persuasive account of how free-rider problems could be overcome within the terms of a rationalistic account of business action. Why would firms with profit problems combine for political action at all?

One might claim that they didn't combine but merely acted as autonomous agents setting up separate lobbying efforts and political action committees. Any overall political consequences resulted from the interaction of disparate firm-level efforts. Although plausible, this explanation faces severe empirical problems, because extensive business cooperation rebuilt old interest organizations and established new ones, in addition to building new policy and research institutes and aiding candidates.[11]

Consider the case of the Business Roundtable. By all accounts it was a key organization in the new mobilization. It contributed significantly as part of a leadership dispersed across several institutions and informal alliances and provided an important forum for political-economic discussion among business elites. The Business Roundtable is best viewed as a major coordinating body. Yet if its target membership was composed of firms driven purely by concern for short-term profits, its very formation would seem unlikely. The proposed membership of roughly 200 was large enough to preclude small group effects. It could not force firms to join. And its initial supply of selective incentives was limited. One might count potential future influence as a selective incentive, and the possible gain from participating in the Business Roundtable does seem to have been attractive. But unless one stretches the notion of a selective incentive to include almost any positive motivation, it is more accurate to regard this aim as an indication that free-rider problems were bypassed by reasoned judgments about political prospects at the national level, judgments made within political networks and discourses.[12]

There does not seem to be a defensible "natural" explanation for the mobilization of business. Rather, to explain the sequence of concerns about profitability, antiregulation, and defense of the market requires reference to discursive processes that join these themes, linking firms' opposition to particular regulations with a wide critique of government policy. Firm-level concerns cannot dictate a general business approach to political-economic problems if several political-economic arrangements at the macro level are responsive to immediate firm problems. The selection among those arrangements has to be explained both with reference to economic tendencies and with respect to major efforts at political argument and organizing. When the latter efforts are treated as determined by a natural logic (of profit-seeking), the result is a strong tendency to accept uncritically the diagnoses of economic problems offered by politically active business elites. Business claims about the need for certain measures in order to sustain profits are taken as accurate expressions of an underlying reality rather than as political interpretations of economic problems.

The final steps in Table 8.1 claim that the new business political mobilization checked reformist tendencies in the Carter administration and helped produce Reagan's victories. These are reasonable descriptions of major events. Yet without the prior arguments, they have little explanatory power of the type intended by the profit-based account.

BUSINESS MOBILIZATION AS A POLITICAL PROJECT

A rationalistic account of collective action by business cannot explain its powerful, effective emergence in recent American politics. A better account, presented in Table 8.2, focuses on the political process of interpreting economic problems and defining responses. It differs from the first schema at most points. At the outset, the recognition of problems by business elites is not conceived as a natural expression of profit problems but as an active interpretation of the overall prospects for business. Busi-

TABLE 8.2
Business in Politics in the 1970s, Political View

A.	A deteriorating business climate (unsettled labor relations, international economic uncertainty, low public esteem for business, growing regulation, declining profits) led to:
B.	Political debate among business elites regarding the inadequacies of national policies.
C.	Through political and economic argument and conflict, a new model of growth based on reducing social and economic regulation, weakening the power of unions, limiting social spending, and reforming "Fordist" production techniques gained wide business support (Boyer 1988; Gordon, Edwards, and Reich 1982).
D.	This orientation generated specific proposals about public policies.
E.	The limits of existing business associations led business elites to create new political forms and reshape older ones.
F.	Through these forms, business political mobilization attempted to persuade political elites and popular opinion of the merit of the proposed political-economic model and of specific policies.
G.	This mobilization also contributed importantly to a series of electoral outcomes that ratified business proposals.

ness interests are not pregiven but are defined (steps C and D) as a new model of growth takes shape and gains support. These interests then help specify public policy preferences and generate pressure for them (steps E, F, and G).

This sequence shares significant elements with the previous account. But it conceives those elements as discursively linked in such a way that nondiscursive elements cannot be accorded a primary causal role. Rather than driven by a natural economic logic, this sequence is organized around a growth model, that is, an account of the political and socioeconomic conditions necessary for sustained economic growth. Such models designate ways of organizing production and markets and show the political and social relations deemed essential for them.

Explaining business mobilization still involves identifying problems faced by business elites. But much of the explanation concerns the formation of political interests—thus the following questions: How did business elites come to define the business climate as bad? Why did business attach such importance to the issue of regulation? On what basis was a new growth model proposed, and why did it defeat alternatives? How could business create effective new organizations to advance its perspectives and influence national politics?

The Substance of Business Concerns

If the profit-driven account were adequate, business discourse should express significant concern about that issue at a relatively early point in the process of mobilization. Concern about profits would then generate specific policy initiatives. The business critique of public policies by 1972–1973 addressed a wide range of problems, including regulation, labor relations, and tax and social-spending policies. Given the constraints of public political discourse, the infrequent focus on profits is not decisive evidence of anything. But the timing is significant, insofar as business complaints about the overall political-economic situation were widespread before a large part of the decline in profit rates occurred (in 1974). When business elites asked what to do about a deteriorating business climate, they considered an interrelated set of problems that required general political-economic debate.

The context for this ferment was the prior collapse of a political order with which business had made a conditional and always reluctant agreement, evidenced in the tense relations with the Kennedy administration and a warmer relationship with the Johnson administration through the mid-1960s. After 1966 the Democratic order was in disarray and seemed to foster dangerously antibusiness currents. The reformist Keynesianism that Democrats had articulated through the first half of the decade came under suspicion as a source of wage pressure, excessive government spending, and intrusive regulation.[13]

By the mid-1970s, new business political efforts were under way in most settings, from political action committees to lobbying efforts to research institutes. Stances on particular questions were proposed in terms of how they would enhance business performance in general.[14] Debate among business groups had a political character that allowed it to escape from collective action problems that might have been crippling if firms had only articulated their most immediate needs. Thus broad issues about political-economic relations were present from the start.

Widespread concern with regulation was a political interpretation of economic problems. New regulatory requirements were expensive for some firms and sectors; regulation was a serious enough problem that it was reasonable for the issue to be raised in debates about the business climate. Many business leaders viewed regulation as ominous regarding greater future costs. And the enduring antistatism of much of the American business meant a predisposition toward emphasizing the negative aspects of regulation.[15]

The focus on regulation may also have been partly strategic. The evidence is not clear (and reliable accounts of conversations and meetings among business leaders are hard to find). But it would have been reasonable to think that opposing social and economic regulation would have greater appeal than conventional anti-union complaints or efforts to reduce corporate taxes (Freeman and Medoff 1984).

The Shape of Business Mobilization

A profit-based explanation would predict business political mobilization to proceed from the bottom upward in 1974–1980. It would start with immediate concerns about profits and gradually expand depending on the outcome of those conflicts. Local fights would widen when frustrated firms sought larger arenas in which to achieve their aims. New business organizations might then emerge. Local conflicts certainly contributed to the new political mobilization, which is hard to imagine without them. Some business elites considered broader political involvement partly out of frustration with local and state politics. The analytical problem is to specify the meaning and relative importance of these conflicts.

Business initiatives early in the mobilization sought to redefine the national political agenda regarding business and economic development. The Business Roundtable appeared as an active and important new force by 1973–1974, not the end of the decade. Business PACs with national aims appeared widely in 1974–1975 and grew rapidly. Efforts to revitalize traditional business associations took place before the end of the decade (Edsall 1984:123–128; Levitan and Cooper 1984:12–26).[16]

The timing of the business mobilization, as noted above, suggests that political efforts to reshape the national situation were present very early. They cannot be depicted as the sum of an earlier, purely local group of conflicts but instead as crucial and distinct attempts to address national problems. Such political efforts drew strength and credibility from their capacity to explain and represent frustrating local experiences, but in this interaction the broader efforts also played a role in defining the very meaning of local conflicts. From the early to mid-1970s, responses to a deteriorating business climate included both diagnoses of the problems and positive proposals. In this process, a perceived decline in profits was an important element of the political-economic context evaluated by business leaders when they proposed political action.

Selecting a Model of Growth

Between the rationalistic and political accounts of business mobilization is an interest group explanation. Business groups would aggregate all the complaints of their members and seek to remedy them politically. Any common program would result from adding up the demands of firms and sectors.

Interest group activity was extensive, as it has continued to be. As documented in Chapter 1 and throughout the volume, there was a proliferation of trade associations and industry lobbies and of Washington offices maintained by large companies for political purposes (Schlozman and Tierney 1986; Alpin and Hegarty 1980:23, 438–450; Epstein in Malbin 1980:107–151). Yet the political mobilization of business is not reducible to such efforts; if it were, we would rapidly return to economic critiques of interest group conceptions of political activity. And reasonably so, as the logic of interest-seeking by individual firms would seem to block most interfirm cooperation. The ability to overcome collective action problems in mobilizing business derived mainly from a widespread acceptance of the need for a political approach to the questions at hand. Business elites regarded national political-economic decisions as salient and important. Collective action problems were reduced, even bypassed, in a discursive framework within which political action was reasonable and potentially effective. Business leaders were political as well as economic agents. Sabatier (Chapter 5) also shows the limits of collective action explanations for why individuals join groups.

Business political action began with a critique of previous Democratic policies, which were accused of producing a bad business climate. To transform the situation, business proposed an alternative view of political-economic relations focused on a new growth model.[17] This level of discourse would have been superfluous if in the 1970s only one growth model had been feasible. If there had been only one way to respond effectively to economic problems, it could be argued that this route functioned as a sort of magnet, as a deep economic logic shaping the interest-seeking efforts of firms. Arguments over broad political-economic formulations could then be treated as only expressing the powerful forces leading toward the selection of that single growth model.

One can specify several models of growth that might reasonably have served as a referent for business interest formation. Although the model proposed by the Business Roundtable became ascendant in business circles and came to shape much of public policy, it was not the only reasonable course. Other alternatives could be defended on economic grounds as recently successful at the subnational level in the United States or in other nations, or as plausibly related to emergent economic tendencies. Prospective models of growth included

1. Radical antistatism: an anti-union, low-wage, labor-intensive growth effort (Goldwater Republicans)
2. Moderate antistatism: cutting back social and economic regulation while maintaining countercyclical economic efforts, opposing union

growth, and advocating free trade and a "neo-Fordist" design of industrial relations (the Business Roundtable)

3. Liberal Keynesianism: restoring the mid-1960s political-economic approach, with Keynesian economic policies, high wages sustained in older areas and economic sectors (and where possible in new zones), and a renewed emphasis on industrial mass production (large parts of the Democratic party and the AFL-CIO)

4. Business corporatism: explicit business-government cooperation (including labor in a subordinate role) to spur growth yet contain inflation (elements among Democratic business elites)

5. Liberal corporatism: expanded state social and economic intervention, with growth and redistributive aims, and a formal inclusion of labor in national cooperative efforts (the Left of the AFL-CIO and sections of the Democratic Left)

These growth models combined macroeconomic policies, social policies (regarding both social welfare and regulation), and conceptions of how to organize production. All these approaches were economically feasible in that real-world referents could be found to provide at least minimal evidence of their viability, and they could be framed as coherent responses to widely acknowledged problems.[18]

Was the perspective advanced by the Business Roundtable the best proposal for business? Was it the best proposal for overall economic performance? Perhaps positive judgments would result from a thorough analysis of economic conditions from the mid-1970s to the present. There are reasons to doubt that unqualified positive judgments would result.[19] Nevertheless, among business elites the moderate antistatism of the Business Roundtable predominated. Although not the sole leading agent, the Roundtable was the single most important business organization in leading a bloc of business-linked political forces to conceive and fight for a new growth model. This is a strong claim about its importance, given a setting where the power of individual firms, the density of interfirm networks, and the variety of business political organizations prevented any single agent from determining business policies.[20]

There was nothing secretive or conspiratorial about the development and articulation of this perspective, which was advanced in public documents and testimony before legislative committees from the mid-1970s. Measured on the political spectrum in the 1960s, this view was well to the right of center. Measured in terms of the prior spectrum of business opinion, it was also to the right, although not as much of a shift as the radically antistatist currents influential within business and Reagan's political coalition would have preferred. The Business Roundtable perspective marked a significant shift to the right by business and encouraged the broader public political shift to the right that occurred in the 1970s and early in the next decade.

The Business Roundtable view was consistent with long-standing political inclinations in the business community. Yet if antistatist impulses were already widespread, significant innovation did occur in how they were expressed. Exceptions to the general principles of government nonintervention and reliance on market forces were acknowledged, and few calls for the root-and-branch eradication of state activities were made from business leadership groups such as the Business Roundtable, even when such calls were rising from several sections of the Reagan coalition in the late 1970s and early 1980s.

Moreover, the grounds given for business policy preferences were much broader and more political than conventional pleas for favorable treatment based on sectoral or firm needs. Business elites argued that their political-economic proposals would facilitate overall social and political development. This argument entailed a deeper shift away from defending business positions simply on the basis of property rights and business entitlements. Instead, the case was made that deregulation, for example, would yield productivity increases and growth that would permit a quasi-automatic attainment of the explicit objectives regulators had proposed, but more rapidly and at less cost (e.g., growth reduces hours of work per person, which decreases individual chances of being seriously injured on the job).

This powerful move provided good grounds for combating populist and left-liberal critiques of business as selfish in practice and fundamentalist in principle, critiques that often influenced political arguments for modes of public action business sought to avoid. Yet the longer-term meaning of this shift is uncertain for business as well as other groups. If business practices are to be justified in republican terms, then barriers to public intervention are likely to be constrained by mainly practical considerations rather than by a principled refusal to interfere with liberties regarding market choices.[21]

Despite lively conflicts among proponents of diverse models of growth, the Business Roundtable perspective emerged as dominant among business elites. If not attributable to an objective economic logic, then what caused its acceptance? First, it was credible economically; it was among the feasible approaches to the problems of the 1970s.[22] Second, it was compatible with the preexisting political inclinations of diverse groups among business elites, whose antistatism had endured even through recent episodes of practical cooperation with Democratic administrations. Third, after the Democratic defeats of the late 1960s and early 1970s, this course was politically viable to a much greater extent than a decade earlier and had far greater political potential than the radical antistatist approach. Fourth, its proposals were attractive to business elites insofar as they occasioned less disruption within firms and sectors than most alternatives. Finally, influential and persuasive protagonists of this perspective could expend great resources on its behalf.

The moderate antistatist view was widely disseminated among business elites and the public through business organizations, research and public policy institutes, and direct public appeals in advertising and political action. As a commonsense framework, it supplied a means both for defining immediate business interests and evaluating efforts to achieve them. Certainly by 1975–1976 a causal force could be attributed to this model of growth, whereby a proposal consistent with the moderate antistatist approach was advocated and eventually implemented because business elites perceived it as in their interest and expended substantial resources to attain it.

A Growth Model as a Frame for Policy Choices

The conflicts over a growth model solidified business interests. Although immediate experiences influenced the formulation of overall business perspectives, business elites, especially at the top of large corporations and in organizations such as the Business Roundtable, were participants in a debate about the best political-economic course to a much greater extent than purely profit-based accounts begin to acknowledge.

Major policy proposals from business elites in the 1970s and early 1980s derived from general business perspectives rather than from the aggregation of immediate business experiences. Within broad limits, the meaning of particular experiences was open to interpretation in terms of overall judgments of desirable political-economic tendencies.

To take a relatively hard case for this view, most firms doubtless experienced regulations mainly as a cost. But it was known that competitors were forced to pay similar costs, and there were cases when short-term benefits might result. Even if the short-term assessment of regulation was largely negative, reasonable arguments could be made for its positive medium- or long-term consequences. Business opposition to new social and economic regulation thus cannot be depicted as the simple sum of immediate firm experiences whose meaning was always clear. Instead, the opposition to regulation that came to be a major and durable business interest expressed the view that a good national business climate required reducing regulation. That belief signals a choice among growth models, as several were less hostile to regulation.[23]

Thus even where firm-level experiences can be predicted to yield mostly negative judgments of a policy, the complexities of those experiences indicate that general political opposition to regulation could not derive purely from firm-level concern about profits. When unified business positions emerge on questions that seem divisive at the firm and sectoral levels, the implication is that such a position called for broad political debate and did not arise from a uniformity of local responses to a given issue.[24]

The development of the Business Roundtable provides indirect evidence about the role of a growth model in shaping views on particular policies. The noisy departure of Lee Iacocca from the organization when it refused to support government assistance to rescue Chrysler is a significant episode (Green and Buchsbaum 1983:205–213). It suggests that the Business Roundtable was taken seriously by its members—they were willing to maintain an important position even when it meant the departure of a major participant.

Since the mid-1970s few conflicts in the organization have been sharp enough to produce lasting antagonisms or major resignations. If no one cared what the Business Roundtable did, the lack of disagreement would also be unimportant. But the Business Roundtable has played a major political role, and business elites have regarded it as worth their attention. Thus the existence of a broadly shared political commitment can be inferred from the stability of the organization over time. It is easy to identify major sources of intense antagonism if we consider issues narrowly in terms of firm-level concerns or take them one at a time: Absent a general framework as a basis for agreement, there is every reason to think the Business Roundtable would have exploded through conflicts of immediate interest.

Mobilizing Business Through New Organizations

In the 1970s, new organizations appeared in the political mobilization of business. How could this occur? Business groups had become politically weak over the course of the Democratic order throughout the 1960s, allowing new efforts to emerge outside the control of existing groups. The expansion of business institutions required the resolution of collective action problems. A profit-based account of business political action provides little basis for explaining how sustained mobilization could result from cooperation among strategically minded firms. An increase in lobbying by firms would arguably have occurred, though firm-based economic calculation would probably have yielded much less new activity than took place. Political action committees, politically active trade associations, public policy centers, and especially businesswide organizations would at least have been much less well supported, in some cases nonexistent.

I argued above that collective action problems were bypassed partly because the firms that supported business political activity were not purely economic agents but political actors as well. This claim refers both to general relations between large firms and political-economic issues, and to more specific developments in the 1960s and 1970s that facilitated political action. There are two important presuppositions for cooperation among business elites: Relations between firms cannot be purely antagonistic, and economic and social ties should exist among business leaders across firms.

Changes in interfirm relations made political cooperation more feasible among business elites. Strong and dense networks across especially large firms opened more space for intrabusiness debate and improved the chances that such discussion would focus on the overall business climate. The point is not that competition and intrabusiness conflicts were eliminated but that growing networks among firms created a setting in which those responsible for major firms were apt to perceive their environment in cooperative as well as competitive terms. Thus social and economic changes facilitated political institution building within the business community (Useem 1984; Burt 1983; Mintz and Schwartz 1985; Sabel et al. 1989; Zukin and DiMaggio 1990).[25]

The deteriorating business climate of the 1970s also contributed to business mobilization. Although profits were not the only basis for business judgments about economic prospects, by the middle years of the decade their decline brought attention. At the same time an evidently serious group of problems in political-economic relations also commanded attention. Because business responded politically to the overall context, the sharp decline in perceived conditions prompted a general consideration of prospects and alternatives, in effect weighing the advantages of different growth models. Thus a crisis in the previous organization of the political economy compelled business elites to reconsider commitments.

In addition, the expansion of regulation in 1965–1975 had the mainly unintended effect of opening new fronts for business political intervention in response to government action. As some defenders of the business political mobilization have argued, the growing political role of business arose partly as a response to public policy initiatives perceived as placing new and unwarranted constraints on firm behavior.

These contextual changes—in organization and relations among firms, in the overall business climate, in government regulatory intervention—encouraged a more explicitly political discourse among business elites. As these elites took on a newly active and creative political role, their question became, What should we do politically, and how? This differed from the question whether political participation made any sense at all. The institutional side of this process was the creation of the Business Roundtable, a renovated chamber-of-commerce network, and research and policy institutes, all of which required a political process among business elites.

Once formed, these new groups, as well as business PACs and trade associations, contributed to shaping a broad perspective that defined concrete interests. If the growth model that arose from this process was not highly original, the circumstances of its formulation were novel in the degree of business involvement in political-economic debate and the creative advocacy of business positions among political elites and the public.

CONCLUSION

Did business succeed? The rationalistic account of business mobilization discussed earlier and the alternative political account agree that business efforts played a significant role in restricting reformist initiatives during the Carter administration.[26] Business political efforts also made a major contribution to the three Republican presidential victories of the 1980s. Nonetheless, there are important differences between the two accounts. Arguments about business political action based on rationalistic conceptions of firms depict the main (and sometimes only) significant contribution of business to national political outcomes as economic. Business subsidized candidates it preferred, warred on some it feared, and sponsored PACs and other new organizations. Less directly, business threatened the national (Carter) administration and local (mainly Democratic) administrations with reduced investment if the desired public policy choices were not made.

Business involvement in elections and policymaking continued throughout the 1980s. For example, the number of corporate PACs, to say nothing of those representing trade associations, grew from 433 in 1976 to 1,557 by 1982, and over 2,000 by 1988. Contributions to all congressional campaigns by corporate PACs grew from $27.3 million in 1980 to $50.4 million (in constant 1989 dollars) (Magleby and Nelson 1990:74, 84). Of greater significance for the future of business activity in both arenas is the considerable room that business has for further mobilization: "Nearly half of the Fortune 500 companies have yet to establish a PAC and more than half of the nation's thousand largest firms do not have a Washington office. Nearly two-thirds of the nation's six thousand trade associations are still not headquartered in Washington, D.C., and nearly three-quarters of the nation's small businesses are not affiliated with a business or trade association" (Vogel 1989:297).

These things certainly happened and show that business is more than one among many potentially powerful interest groups. However, business political mobilization was successful partly because it could supply more than threats and money: It provided a growth model that was politically attractive for much of business and for substantial elements of other political and social groups.

An exclusive focus on economic resources diverts attention from the substance of political shifts at both the mass and elite level. The business mobilization of the 1970s was political. It proposed an overall view of what was wrong with the political economy and what to do about it, shaping broad policy choices and specific programs. Without this model or vision and resulting credible proposals, it would have been hard for business to utilize vast resources effectively.

The business political mobilization of the 1970s was a successful political effort on its own terms. We should not presume, however, that business success meant economic success, because business preferences cannot be accorded a privileged economic status. We know that business got much of what it wanted, but that does not mean it achieved optimal economic results (or even good ones), either from the perspective of business itself or from other standpoints. Profit levels stopped declining significantly after the mid-1970s, and along many dimensions economic conditions improved early in the next decade. These results certainly count for something in gauging the business mobilization, but not for nearly as much as they might if we imagined that a natural economic logic drove the entire process. It remains open to debate whether the policies business proposed were responsible for the upturn and whether different policies might have generated a greater improvement. It also remains to be seen if the growth model will continue to mobilize business and define the boundaries of political interaction between business and government during the 1990s.

Rationalistic accounts, whether neoclassical or Neo-Marxist, present themselves as tough-minded in focusing on the pursuit of interests. But such accounts are misleading when applied to business collective action in American politics, as explaining such action requires the recognition of major political elements, such as the specification of choices among models of growth and the strategies for realizing them. At the global level, political organization and discourse are central to reducing and even bypassing the strategic problems that would probably cripple efforts to mount and sustain collective action by firms acting purely as short-term economic maximizers. At the local level, models of growth provide crucial referents as business groups develop rather than intrinsically possess interests.

This line of argument has significant political implications in a contemporary American setting in which business claims about the requirements of economic development have a high degree of credibility. The point is that such claims need not be accepted as expressing an essential economic logic. Instead, business claims deserve political-economic evaluation, including rigorous comparisons with other proposals about how desirable economic conditions should be achieved and sustained.

Both neoclassical and Neo-Marxist theories tend to impute a false necessity to the political-economic choices made by business, depicting business elites as driven by an unambiguous economic rationality.[27] Both approaches treat interest formation as instrumental and virtually nondiscursive. Yet the actual formation of interests proceeds through politics in and beyond firms. Formulating and pursuing a general interest for business elites is an active, creative process—it entails defining a conception of economic and social order and development. A new growth model establishes a framework in which interests gain a general normative character.

Thus the mobilization of business can rarely be explained as expressing only the logic of essential and necessary economic interests. Instead, business mobilization depends on political judgments about economic choices, judgments made on the basis of debate and discussion among business groups (and others). Correct or not, these assessments provide a framework for defining broad political-economic projects and for gauging the merit of specific policies. These judgments are open to question within the business community and by other political and social actors. The point is not that all judgments are equally right (or wrong or arbitrary) but that no group begins the political argument about economic choices with a privileged claim to knowledge of the best alternative. As a result, a complete explanation for the mobilization of business in the United States— and probably the mobilization of interests generally—must account for the formation of this discursive framework and the political dynamics it creates.

NOTES

For valuable comments on a prior draft, thanks to Fred Block, Cathie Jo Martin, Sylvia Maxfield, Anne Norton, Adolph Reed, and Eve Weinbaum (who also provided research assistance).

1. These figures understate the role of business, as a number of professional associations are also business associations, such as groups of executives. Unions, citizens' groups, civil rights groups, social welfare lobbies, and women's groups maintained roughly 17 percent of the offices and made about 27 percent of PAC expenditures (of which 21 percent were made by unions) (Schlozman and Tierney 1986:67, 249).

2. Another big question that receives little attention here: how to understand relations among these three modes of business political influence. It is tempting to propose that direct political intervention by business is most likely when the other two modes are disrupted and insufficient for achieving objectives. This suggests that business might intervene more when economic conditions deteriorate or when a government is perceived as thoroughly hostile. Pressures toward direct political intervention do arise when economic difficulties seem to have political sources and when economic threats and quasi-public negotiation with governing elites do not promise relief. The plausible basis of this view is that democratic politics is a difficult endeavor for business anywhere universal suffrage exists. But this hydraulic conception of relations among modes of business influence likely overstates the dangers and understates the importance to business of public political action. For definite conclusions about these relations, it would be necessary to have a fuller map of business political activity than now exists. The universe of business organizations whose activities are significantly political includes trade and industry associations of all types, some professional associations,

federated organizations such as the U.S. Chamber of Commerce and National Association of Manufacturers, national organizations including the Committee for Economic Development (CED) and the Business Roundtable, and business-linked research institutes. It also includes Washington lobbying offices of major firms. If this map were filled out to a greater extent than has been accomplished so far, it would be easier to gauge the merit of claims about the importance of various forms of business political action. It would also be desirable to analyze business political action from within—to start from inside large firms and examine all aspects of their political intervention. Very few studies of political activities by business take the internal processes of firms as their focal point (Levitan and Cooper 1984; Coleman 1988).

3. The extent to which the business mobilization had significant direct effects on popular opinion rather than mainly influencing the actions of political elites has been debated, as some have minimized the degree of genuine popular support for Reaganism (Ferguson and Rogers 1986).

4. By one calculation, the annual rate of return on nonfinancial corporate capital fell from 10.2 percent in 1969 to 6.9 percent in 1974. One issue is whether this decline was part of a gradual downward trend over a long period rather than a mainly cyclical fluctuation. If we take 1974 as an end point and compare the previous four- or five-year periods, the average rate of return on nonfinancial corporate capital is as follows:

1950–1954	11.8%
1955–1959	10.4%
1960–1964	11.1%
1965–1969	12.2%
1970–1974	8.1%

The decline of the early 1970s was not the continuation of a long prior decline, but that decline was greater than during any previous postwar phase (Feldstein and Summers 1977:211–228).

After 1974, data on profits are even less supportive of a profit-based rationalistic account. Census data treat profit as a post-tax percentage of stockholders' equity, and there is a shift after 1973 to a new series, whose methods of calculation seem to produce a result from 1 to 2 percent higher than the old series. The figures on manufacturing corporations should be surprising for efforts to center an account of business political action on profits: From 1975 to 1979, the average rate of profit was 14.3 percent; in 1980 to 1984 and 1985 to 1989, the figures were 12 percent and 12.6 percent. If we subtract 2 percent from these figures to make the two series roughly equivalent, the 1970–1974 period indeed seems to be a steep short-term drop, after which profits return to postwar levels, though not to the peak level of the late 1960s (Bureau of the Census 1990).

5. The length of time required for assembling autonomous economic actors into a political force would vary according to the severity of collective action problems and resources for overcoming them. But it is hard to imagine grounds for claiming that such actors could make an immediate and direct political response to economic difficulties (Olson 1965).

6. No such claims are made, for example in Edsall 1984:107–140; Ferguson and Rogers 1986:78–113.

7. In 1978, 40 percent of *Fortune's* top 500 industrials and 41 percent of leading 300 nonindustrials had PACs. Within the top 500 industrials, the rate varied from 70 percent of the top 100 to 15 percent of the fifth hundred. In the next 500 industrials, the overall rate fell to 8 percent. At the national level, 45 percent of all PACs were linked to these 1,300 corporations; the other 55 percent were scattered among all other corporations in the United States. Industry figures indicate few strong connections between the type of firm and its likelihood of having a PAC. One unsurprising association exists: Industries already subject

to extensive government regulation or about which major legislative proposals are on the agenda are more likely to have a high rate of PAC formation (Epstein 1980b:355–372; Budde in Malbin 1980:11).

8. When business complained about regulation, it often targeted what was called the new "social regulation" of the late 1960s and 1970s, although many studies also aimed at showing the inadequacies of older forms of economic regulation. In the late 1970s, the figure of $100 billion a year was circulated in the business press as the cost of "regulation," based on studies by Murray Weidenbaum and associates. This unreasonable figure amounted to about half of yearly corporate profits in the period. Common sense should have sufficed to dispose of it; given the recent imposition of much of the regulation, if it had been as large a negative force as claimed, it should have been easy to find a huge prior sum of profits now being turned over to the state or simply dissipated.

Such estimates were inflated, as were the complaints of individual corporations, by some or all of the following practices: (1) making worst-case assumptions about the short-term effects of regulation; (2) projecting those assumptions into the future, with little or no effort to consider adaptive responses by firms that would reduce the effects of regulation; (3) not treating regulatory costs as marginal costs with respect to already existing internal administrative procedures but as entirely new costs for which new administrative systems had to be created; and (4) not considering the savings that might arise in industries and the economy as a whole from new regulations (Weidenbaum 1978, 1980, 1988:225–247; Pertschuk 1982; Schwartz 1983; Noble 1986; Derthick and Quirk 1985; Wilson 1980b).

9. Perhaps business targeted regulation for strategic reasons, because it believed that more could be won there than elsewhere in the short term. So far, no one has provided convincing evidence of such decisions; it seems most likely that strategic elements played a marginal role in the focus on regulation, and most of that choice came about because of wrong judgments about its importance.

10. An expansive definition of regulation and a conception of economic relations as prepolitical derive from and strengthen suspicion of political processes. Noll considers regulatory activities to include those that "control aspects of transactions such as the price or the quality of the good transacted, that mandate certain features of the production process such as emissions-control methods and worker-safety requirements, or that control entry, as by licensing. . . . It may well be the case that the theory of regulation is very close to the general theory of government policy" (Noll 1985:10).

In another context, Noll and Owen express a conception of the economy that appears in much of the literature on regulation: "Regulations that have any effect at all—good or bad—cause the structure of the economy to depart from its unregulated state" (Noll and Owen 1983:34). If regulation is defined as broadly as Noll does above, there is no such thing as an unregulated state of the economy.

11. The key distinction is between trade associations on the one hand and research institutes and business organizations on the other. It is possible to explain the formation of trade associations in terms of the operation of small-group effects, if the boundaries of a group are tautly defined. As Olson noted, defining an industry or trade group narrowly provides boundaries in which to organize a small group. Research institutes whose product is generally available and business organizations whose political efforts are public goods for business require a different explanation (Olson 1965:141–148; Steinfels 1979).

12. The problem of starting such an organization is different from the question of its economic effects. At its most ambitious, the Business Roundtable had features of an encompassing organization; its restriction to "only" the nation's largest firms prevented it from achieving that status. Nor did it ever gain the degree of power as an organization that would have enabled it to engage in corporatist negotiations with other national organizations. What cannot be claimed in a strategic account is that the economic efficiency of encompassing

organizations *causes* them to emerge; this would posit firms as directly seeking public goods (Olson 1982:47–53).

13. The political disaffection of business from the Democratic order thus began prior to the downturn of profits in the 1970s. At the political level, it was registered in declining business support for Hubert Humphrey as against Lyndon Johnson, and then a collapse in business support for George McGovern. Business leaders were not wholly committed to the Republican party, much less Nixon personally, so much as they came to reject the overall Democratic trajectory from the mid-1960s on.

14. Within the business mobilization, the Business Roundtable was built in the early 1970s out of several discussion groups among business elites. Here is how the organization recently described its formation: "The Business Roundtable was established in 1972 through the merger of three existing organizations. One was the March Group, made up of chief executive officers, which had been meeting informally to consider public policy issues. John Harper, then chief executive of Alcoa, and Fred Borch, the chief executive of General Electric, were notable among the leaders. Another of the founding groups was the Construction Users Anti-Inflation Roundtable, an organization devoted to containing construction costs, which was headed by Roger Blough, former chief executive of U.S. Steel. The third was the Labor Law Study Committee, made up largely of labor relations executives of major companies.

They founded The Business Roundtable in the belief that the business sector in a pluralistic society should have an active and effective role in the formation of public policy." The organization addressed major political-economic questions of the day rather than focusing on narrow demands about the immediate problems facing member companies. The quote is from the organization's 1989 statement, "What the Roundtable Is, Why It Was Founded, How It Works." In 1975 Business Roundtable statements included: "Antitrust Civil Process Act Amendments," "Background Material Concerning the Proposed Agency for Consumer Protection," "A Survey of Business Roundtable Members on Business Conduct Guidelines," and "Wage/Price Controls Are Not the Answer to Inflation" (Business Roundtable 1990).

The broader features of business discourse get little attention in most accounts that stress business power in shaping public policy. In the major business press—*Fortune, Business Week, Wall Street Journal*—arguments are made for particular policies in terms of their likely overall effects on the political economy. When arguments are made for strengthening specific sectors, the case involves showing how that sector's welfare is of general interest.

15. American business leaders have usually opposed forms of state intervention that enhance public power. This inclination can be linked to specific policy debates, such as those about environmental regulation or occupational safety and health. Even if the economic impacts of "social" regulation were neither as large nor as negative as business elites and academic critics of regulation claimed, it was doubtless politically threatening in raising the possibility of wider government intervention. Whether that prospect is deemed economically difficult but acceptable, troubling and undesirable, or disastrous and deserving of unqualified opposition is not a purely economic matter, however, but a question of the overall political-economic orientation of business elites. It is subject to considerable variance across time and place (Kelman 1981; Noble 1986). Insufficient attention to the political inclinations of American business can lead to underestimating the complexities of regulatory reform in the United States. To take a major example, the emphasis on legal enforcement measures derives not only from political and administrative misjudgments by those designing the procedures but from the weakness of shared norms and the strength of business resistance to intervention.

16. The National Association of Manufacturers registered as a lobbying organization in 1975 and expanded its political and organizational initiatives shortly thereafter. The United States Chamber of Commerce began to expand rapidly by 1976 and continued to grow into the next decade, especially in 1981–1982 (Edsall 1984:123–128; Levitan and Cooper 1984:12–26).

17. What does *business* mean here? The organizational and political development of the 1970s makes this term suitable as a way to describe the complex of institutions including the Business Roundtable, U.S. Chamber of Commerce, and closely related research institutes such as the American Enterprise Institute. The point is not that a prior secret elite network was activated but that new networks were created and through them a general political-economic perspective was disseminated. There was a process of unification and politicization, not the natural expression of a prior unity.

18. One might add a sixth growth model—postindustrial growth, with decentralization, expanded human capital investments, and flexible production systems. It was economically conceivable but was not clearly formulated, nor did its fragmentary expressions have substantial political support (Block 1990; Hirschhorn 1984; Piore and Sabel 1984).

19. Elements of business corporatism or liberal corporatism (models 4 and 5), as well as of emergent postindustrial proposals, might have been usefully incorporated into the predominant political-economic course. Aspects of these models might have helped address problems of infrastructural development, human capital investment, and productivity. Even if a full analysis concluded that the moderate antistatist model was economically superior to the others, its proposals were open to reasonable debate; if it was the best alternative, that is not because leading business groups came to prefer it or because it was implemented (Bowles et al. 1983; Boyer 1988; Freeman 1989; Scott and Lodge 1985).

20. Almost all accounts accord the Business Roundtable substantial influence and characterize its political efforts as relatively effective. Its power could be diminished by comparing it with peak employers' associations in European corporatist political economies—but this was not the relevant alternative (Guzzardi 1980).

21. This moderate antistatist view was articulated against several of the alternatives noted above, in debates within and outside business elites in the 1970s and early 1980s. First, and most emphatically, business elites criticized Democratic policies of the 1960s and their successors in the next decade. Against that liberal Keynesian approach, this view stressed the need to cut back government spending and regulation, the desirability of limiting unions, and the feasibility of renewing growth without relying on deficit spending.

Second the Business Roundtable and those who shared its perspectives fought skirmishes with antistatist business groups who proposed a much sharper reduction in government activity and an energetic anti-union offensive. The latter groups flirted with abandoning New Deal social welfare policies and even with refusing to intervene to modify the force of the business cycle. This radical antistatism, when formulated in populist terms, had popular appeal. When it appeared as a serious political force—as in initiatives to curtail state spending—business elites who favored a more moderate antistatism were not supportive (Sears and Citrin 1985). Third, these elites and like-minded intellectuals vigorously opposed the initiatives toward renewed government economic intervention proposed as "industrial policy" in the late 1970s, on grounds that the market can better select winners and losers than can any political procedure.

22. The economic problems of the 1970s were not as convulsive as those of the 1930s and did not dramatically discredit business leadership groups socially and politically. In *Fluctuating Fortunes*, Vogel (1989) argues that business political power varies inversely with economic conditions, a claim that his own narrative only partly sustains for the 1970s and 1980s. Whether the direct exercise of political power by business is more or less effective in declining economic conditions seems to depend on the severity of the decline and public perceptions of its causes.

23. Firm-level benefits might arise in several ways. Regulations might spur product improvements that individual firms would otherwise have been reluctant to undertake. Or they might reduce the future costs of externalities that would eventually have jeopardized significant firm activities. The lack of serious consideration of these possibilities in the routine

denunciations of business organizations or the academic antiregulation literature suggests the role of political commitments in shaping responses to complex policy issues (Sunstein 1990).

24. Because critiques of rationalistic and naturalistic views of economic action are so often taken to be claims that outcomes are indeterminate or arbitrary, it is worth restating a point made earlier. In selecting a new growth model, the set of feasible choices was limited, not infinite; within that set a combination of normative and strategic criteria operated to select one option against others.

25. Recent sociological studies of business that have gotten beyond debates about whether managers or families or shareholders control corporations make several analytical points: (1) Firms cooperate as well as compete, to such an extent that networks of durable relations arise among firms in sectors, regions, and even within national economies; (2) interfirm networks are not regarded in purely strategic terms by firm managers; such networks provide "class-wide" referents with some degree of normative force. Within this literature, there are widely divergent views regarding such questions as how changes in business organization have affected the distribution of economic power. Michael Useem, for example, claims that an intercorporate management network is the engine behind the rise of the classwide principles associated with institutional capitalism. He shows that economic changes have facilitated the emergence of classwide social and political forms (Useem 1984; Burt 1983; Mintz and Schwartz 1985; Sabel et al. 1989; Zukin and DiMaggio 1990).

26. These claims about business political action refer both to results and aims; I am not claiming to have discerned purpose where none was manifest. The business press enthusiastically reviewed the failures of reform efforts in 1977–1978. A bulletin from the *Wall Street Journal* described the developments under the headline "Business Scores Unexpectedly High with the Democratic Congress": "Successes overshadow setbacks so far. The proposed consumer agency is sidetracked. Industry wins many exemptions, in committee voting, from the planned tax on oil and gas use. Unions shelve their plan for right-to-work repeal. Union-sought labor law revision will likely go over to next year. Employers hope to block an inflation escalator for the minimum wage" ("Washington Wire," June 24, 1977). And *Fortune* offered this advice: "Indeed, the Administration might do well to set the word 'reform' aside during the duration of the Carter presidency. That in itself would constitute a modest but far from insignificant reform" ("Furl That Reform Banner, Mr. President," December 1977).

27. For Marxists, this clarity provides a negative point of reference. Once the critique of class relations is made, explaining business action amounts to a political critique of that action as sustaining domination—x or y occurred because it was in capital's interests. For many neoclassical accounts, the view that articulated business preferences express the core logic of an entire social order gains a positive rather than a negative valence, anchoring broad notions of social and economic efficiency.

PART III

*Political Institutions and
Interest Groups*

9

Organized Interests and the Nation's Capitol

JOHN T. TIERNEY

Nowhere on the political landscape are the realities of contemporary interest group politics more evident—or, to some, more worrisome—than on Capitol Hill. Deliberately designed by the founders to be the national institution most open and accessible to the people, Congress is now inundated with a surfeit of lobbyists. Ranging from the American College of Nurse Midwives to the Casket Manufacturers Association of America, represented interests embrace the human experience from cradle to grave. The ways these tens of thousands of organizations approach national lawmakers reflect many of the important changes that have occurred both in the legal and procedural world of interest group politics (such as the emergence of political action committees) and in the larger political environment (such as the changing power structure in Congress, the widespread political application of computer technologies, and the general commercialization of politics). So if the changing realities of interest group politics are what we want to understand, there is probably no better place to focus our attention than on the nation's capitol.

Valuable though it may be to focus on change, such an emphasis entails at least two cognitive risks. First, it is easy (even for supposedly dispassionate analysts) to get carried away with noticing only the differences over time and to ignore the important continuities. After all, as one observer has wryly noted, one doesn't exactly acquire a reputation for great acumen in the academic world by stating that things today are pretty much as they were yesterday and as they likely will be tomorrow (Brown 1983a:4). As a result, in this chapter I am concerned with noting the continuities along with the changes in the nexus linking organized interests to Congress.

Second, it is too easy to view the developments we observe as dysfunctional, as contributing to institutional decline and to the perversion of democracy in the United States. Of course, that perception may be true. But fears along these lines are probably exaggerated when it comes to focusing on Congress because of the special expectations attached to this, the people's institution. This periodically elected representative assembly is the most profound institutional expression of American democracy. But it is an institution pervasively open to interest group importunings, rendered so both by the founders' design and by the forces of gradual institutional development. More than any other federal officials, members of Congress are exposed to the blandishments of private interests.

That openness is worrisome to many people. It is clear that lobbyists representing organized interests operate in the very thick of the legislative process, forging mutually beneficial relationships with legislators and their staffs and finding ways to make the structures and decisionmaking processes of Congress work for them. Each participant has resources of various kinds—information, strategically placed allies, political support, and the like—that the other needs. This mutuality of need binds legislators and lobbyists and draws representatives of organized interests into virtually every detail of the legislative process and into almost every facet of the pressurized world of congressional politics.

The nervousness all this causes on the part of many observers is nothing new. From the founders through the muckrakers to reform-minded observers today, a steady element of the American political ethos—and a constant refrain in American political commentary—has been distrust of organized private power in politics.

Nor is this concern felt only among some skeptical political elites. Popular concern is widespread and growing. In 1964, 64 percent of voters questioned by the University of Michigan's National Election Studies believed that government was "run for the benefit of all," whereas only 29 percent said it was "pretty much run by a few big interests looking out for themselves." In 1988, twenty-four years and innumerable Washington scandals later, the same survey group found the proportion reversed: 63 percent believed the country was run by a government of the few and for the few, whereas 31 percent thought it was run for the greater good (Yang 1989). When the focus is narrowed to Congress and special interests, the picture darkens still more. A *Washington Post*–ABC News poll of 1,513 randomly selected adults in May 1989 found continued and widespread mistrust of Congress as an institution and growing concern about the impact of special interest money on congressional elections and the legislative process. Seventy-five percent of those interviewed agreed with the statement that "most members of Congress care more about special interests than they care about people like you" (Morin 1989).

Some of this uneasiness may stem from the nature of contemporary press coverage of Capitol Hill. Investigative reporting puts a premium on illuminating the links connecting legislators and lobbyists. There is a greater journalistic payoff from such stories than from detailed analyses of policy issues. But popular distrust is also a reaction to ample evidence that when Congress acquiesces to special interests, the public pays. The constantly worsening savings and loan scandal is a case in point: For too long Congress heeded the wishes of the industry's powerful lobbying arm, gradually leading to a gross corruption of the public trust that will end up costing every American taxpayer thousands of dollars (Rosenbaum 1990).

It is no wonder that the central role of organized interests in the political life of the people's Congress raises so many concerns about, and carries such substantial implications for, democratic governance. Organized interest politics is the realm of our national political life that most readily accommodates the conversion of private or market resources into political ones, thus yielding tremendous inequalities among groups in terms of access and influence and producing political circumstances in which the public interest seems likely to be subjugated to special interests.

Thus it is important to consider whether the activities and influences of interest groups on Capitol Hill reflect far-reaching changes that pose grave threats to the roles and functions of time-tested institutions or reflect mere adaptations of a fundamentally healthy political system. Such judgments may ultimately be beyond the scope of this chapter—and beyond my threshold of wisdom. But these concerns should be kept in mind throughout the balance of this chapter, as I examine the techniques organized interests use to influence policymaking on Capitol Hill and consider whether and under what conditions organized interests are influential on the Hill.

THE PRINCIPAL TECHNIQUES OF INFLUENCE

Contemporary organized interests have many arrows in their quivers—many well-established political strategies and tactics, refined over the years for applying their resources in an effort to shape congressional decisions. Although more complete discussions of these techniques may be found elsewhere (Berry 1989a; Schlozman and Tierney 1986), it is worthwhile here to note the principal ways in which groups approach the task of shaping outcomes on Capitol Hill—in part to see what is new and what is not.

Influencing the Electoral Process

Nothing about the political activity of organized interests in recent years has generated more controversy or handwringing than their increasingly prominent role in financing congressional campaigns through political action committees. Of course, there is nothing particularly new about interest groups' giving money to political campaigns; this has been going on for decades. But congressional enactment in 1974 of changes in federal election campaign law altered the playing field by expanding the range of interests able to use PACs as instruments for contributing to campaigns. The explosion in the formation of PACs and their contributions has attracted tremendous attention from the daily press and from many observers who believe the 1974 "reforms" have unintentionally established a system of legal, institutionalized bribery that is producing "the best Congress money can buy" (Stern 1988).

Political scientists' efforts in recent years to examine the relationship between PAC contributions and congressional voting have failed to provide clear answers as to whether the quid pro quo of a campaign contribution is a policy favor. Reviewing the literature on this subject as part of a larger inquiry into campaign finance reform, David Magleby and Candice Nelson (1990:77–80) note that some studies find a relationship between campaign contributions and legislative behavior, others do not. Where a relationship has been detected, it appears that PAC influence is enhanced on issues of low visibility that generate no strong partisan conflict, constituency opinion, or ideological feeling on the part of the legislator. PAC influence seems to be less important on more visible issues and votes where partisan interests, constituency preferences, and ideological leanings are greater.

Most legislators and lobbyists insist—and some scholarly research (Langbein 1986) confirms—that if anything is being "purchased" with a PAC contribution, it is not influence over votes but access to legislators in order to be heard by them. Even if true, it is of little comfort to those who worry that interest group politics reflects many of the inequalities built into the larger political system. For example, it is clear that the business community accounts for the dominant share of PACs, whereas the interests of the disadvantaged (especially the poor and racial minorities) and diffuse publics (especially environmentalists and consumers) figure only marginally in the PAC picture (Schlozman and Tierney 1986). Thus it may be important in the abstract to distinguish access from influence. In practice, however, access begets influence, and unequal access begets unequal influence.

Widespread cynicism and concern about PAC financing of congressional campaigns is also exacerbated by some of the persistent and stark patterns in the flow of PAC money: the amount of PAC money collected by incumbents running without opposition; the tendency of PAC money to gravitate toward legislators in positions of power; and the custom of some PACs of contributing to both candidates in a race so as to be sure of being in the good graces of the winner (see Schlozman and Tierney 1986). For example, Common Cause calculates that in 1990, PACs contributed nearly $7 million to the 331 candidates challenging incumbents for House seats and more than $13 million to the 79 incumbents who ran for reelection unopposed (*Harper's* 1991).

But were it not for two facts—that the demon dollar is at the center of all this and that dollars are at least as unequally distributed in politics as they are in any other realm of life—these and similar patterns in PAC giving would raise few eyebrows because they are in fact reflections of perfectly reasonable political calculations. When organized interests get involved in electoral politics, they may be pursuing one or both of two goals. One objective is to influence the outcome of elections and, by affecting who wins or loses, to elect ideologically sympathetic officials and defeat hostile ones. This strategy dictates that contributions and campaign assistance be directed to ideologically congenial candidates who need help and who seem to have a reasonable chance of winning.

Another objective is to demonstrate enough political muscle or to create a sufficient sense of indebtedness on the part of winners so that they will be responsive to the organization's political needs. In pursuit of this objective, organizations will try to help incumbents who are on key committees (especially powerful ones with positions of institutional leadership in policy areas of concern) and to concentrate on races in geographically critical districts, such as where an association has many members or a corporation has a branch plant. Because the goal is to ensure that officeholders feel compelled to be responsive, organizations active in electoral politics frequently aid sure winners, even candidates running without opposition.

Shaping Opinions and Mobilizing Grassroots Pressure

Most of the activities of organized interests in Washington are conducted in relative obscurity—out of the glare of public attention, if not expressly behind closed doors. But sometimes an organization deliberately raises its profile and reaches out to the public, hoping either to shape public opinion in a way that will be helpful to the organization in its dealings with Congress or to mobilize the public to do something—usually to communicate its like-minded opinions to lawmakers. These indirect strategies of political influence based on public communications are nothing new; there is ample historical precedent for many of the techniques used today. However, in the contemporary period, political public relations has become a highly professionalized and complex business, applying to political position-taking the same techniques and skills that are used to market toothpaste and barbecue sauce.

One of the most conspicuous ways in which groups try to shape public opinion and the general political climate is by conducting large-scale advertising campaigns, not to promote a product or service but to make a statement about the organization itself, its work, and its views. In the past few years, for example, cigarette manufacturers and the tobacco industry's trade group, the Tobacco Institute, have taken their case to the public in a series of skillfully phrased advertisements. The ads, run primarily in newspapers and newsmagazines, convey several messages, among them: The tobacco industry generates jobs and tax revenues, thus rendering the multimillion-dollar tobacco price-support program a virtual bargain to taxpayers; like nonsmokers, smokers have rights, upon which zealous nonsmokers should not trample unreasonably; and the public should be skeptical of the scientific evidence that smoking causes disease.

Because individual advertising campaigns of this sort often seem quite novel—and because there are more and more of them these days from across the political spectrum—it is tempting to think that such campaigns constitute a new weapon in the arsenal of organized interests. But organizations have used them for many years. One of the first "modern" uses of such advertising was by the American Telephone and Telegraph Company, which in June 1908 launched a magazine advertising campaign designed primarily to defuse public uneasiness about the telephone monopoly (see Galli 1971). In the late 1940s and early 1950s, as part of its campaign against congressional enactment of national health insurance, the American Medical Association spent tens of millions of dollars on radio, magazine, and newspaper advertisements opposing this step toward "socialized medicine" (see Kelly 1956).

Although not a completely new means of "going public," the advertising that many organized interests now deploy has an attention-getting quality that makes it seem new or at least qualitatively different. Many of these ads use statistics in ways that are, at the least, misleading and self-serving. Moreover, these advertisements are frequently quite shrill and provocative, using an emotion-laden pitch to play on the public's anger and prejudice. Inflammatory rhetoric may be accompanied by gut-wrenching photographs—such as pictures of aborted fetuses or of hunters clubbing baby seals. Such ads contribute little to reasoned discussion of public policy, but they are often effective in casting opponents' views in the worst possible light and may even be effective in shaping public opinion—at least at the margins.

But when members of Congress are considering a policy issue before them, what often matters to them is not an amorphous perception of how the general public feels about the issue. Rather, they pay attention to whether there is a mobilized group of citizens out there who care intensely about the issue and are likely to act politically on their views. Understanding this, organized interests in recent years have honed their techniques for preying on legislators' heightened feelings of electoral insecurity and their sensitivity to the expressed preferences and particularistic needs of their constituents. To command legislators' attention, organized interests have refined various ways of mobilizing attentive constituents or mounting "grassroots" pressure.

One technique involves establishing a network of activists within the organization who can be relied on to contact lawmakers in response to an "action alert" issued by the organization. This is especially effective for (but is by no means limited to) organizations fortunate enough to have members in virtually every congressional district. The National Association of Letter Carriers' network is a good example. In each congressional district, a union activist is appointed by top union leaders in the state to serve as the local liaison responsible for forming special committees of letter carriers, retirees, and spouses who can be contacted by union headquarters in Washington and counted on to stimulate a flood of letters and phone calls to members of Congress. Union officials credit this system for the organization's successful political battles in the 1980s, such as the defeat of a Reagan administration plan to cap cost-of-living increases for retired postal workers (Starobin 1989).

Another way organizations stimulate grassroots pressure is by sending out a blizzard of direct-mail messages designed to agitate the recipients into contacting their legislators. With recent developments in data-processing and direct-mail technologies, such communications these days are highly individualized, informing recipients across the country—from International Falls to San Antonio and from Bangor to Olympia—how their individual legislators stand on an issue and why the need to contact them is so urgent.

The National Rifle Association is typical of the sort of organization—with a huge budget and a large, excitable membership—that finds this technique effective. In 1988 the NRA mounted an aggressive grassroots lobbying campaign, costing more than $1.7 million and involving an estimated 10 million mailings, in a successful effort to defeat an amendment pending in the House that would have imposed a seven-day waiting period on handgun purchases. Millions of NRA members around the country received "urgent" bulletins from Washington warning that legislators were preparing to impose "total, strict gun control on all America" and spend "billions of your tax dollars investigating you and other honest citizens" (Isikoff 1988). The widespread response from NRA members to this call for action was presumably instrumental in the organization's ability to overwhelm the coalition of police chiefs and gun-control advocates who backed the measure. Congress was finally able to overcome NRA opposition to the waiting period for handgun purchases in 1991 when it passed the Brady Amendment to the Omnibus Crime Act.

Because grassroots lobbying campaigns rely so heavily on recent tech-
nological developments, it is easy to forget that grassroots lobbying is not
a recent invention. This, too, is an ancient weapon in the pressure group
arsenal. At the start of the century, without so much as a microchip to aid
it, the Anti-Saloon League had a mailing list of over half a million people
(see Odegard 1928:76). This was not unique: Other organizations also
employed grassroots lobbying techniques similar to those of today (see
Herring 1929a:70).

What does seem new, however, is the extent to which these high-tech,
direct-mail campaigns excite national politics, lacing the public dialogue
about issues with the worst sort of cant. For example, the NRA's direct-
mail appeals for action attracted widespread criticism for casting the issue
(as well as the NRA's political enemies) in the starkest, most overblown
terms, playing on gun owners' fears, angers, and political prejudices. Of
course, the NRA by no means has a monopoly on sensationalism: Organizations across the political spectrum find it useful to make emotion-
laden appeals. Godwin shows in Chapter 14 that such appeals increase
current biases in political participation and radically change the lobbying
activities of elites who rely on direct marketing.

For anyone concerned with accuracy and honesty, as worrisome as the
sentimental hyperbole is the extent to which many of these campaigns
intentionally misrepresent the facts or the source of a message to the
public. For example, one of the hottest domestic policy issues in Washington in 1989 involved an elaborately orchestrated (and ultimately successful)
grassroots lobbying campaign to overturn a 1988 law that provided new
"catastrophic care" benefits to the elderly under the Medicare program.
The revolt was fueled by the National Committee to Preserve Social
Security and Medicare, a controversial direct-mail lobbying and advocacy
group that generated a flood of petitions, letters, and telephone calls to
congressional offices.

As Mark Hosenball (1989) reported in the *Washington Post*, Medicare
proponents widely assailed the committee for distorting the facts about
catastrophic health care financing in a way that unnecessarily scared senior
citizens about the likely tax burden they would have to bear. The headline
on one of the direct-mail appeals the committee sent to the elderly proclaimed "Your Federal Taxes for 1989 May Increase by Up to $1,600 ($800
for Singles)—Just Because You Are Over the Age of 65!" In fact, only 5.6
percent of the beneficiaries in 1989 (seniors in the highest tax brackets)
would actually have been required to pay the highest surtax rate.[1] Critics
also say the committee is little more than a direct-mail fund-raising operation that hyped this issue (as it did earlier in the 1980s with Social
Security) to raise money for itself and its direct-mail consultants and to

expand its valuable mailing lists, which it rents to other political organizations eager to tap the nation's senior citizens.

Members of Congress recognize that on many issues the seemingly spontaneous mail pouring into their offices has been inspired by some lobbying office in Washington. But just because they are not fooled by this contrivance does not mean they feel free to ignore it. In fact, electorally insecure legislators are increasingly responsive to these campaigns, going so far in some cases as to repeal legislative decisions before they have even taken effect. In 1983, for example, Congress repealed a law passed the previous year that would have required commercial banks and savings and loan associations to withhold for taxes 10 percent of the interest and dividends paid to depositors. In 1989 besieged legislators repealed not only the Medicare Catastrophic Coverage Act (as noted above) but also the so-called Section 89 of the 1986 tax law designed to curb discrimination in employee-benefit plans. In each of these cases, among many others, Congress reversed itself after having hit the pocketbook of some affluent constituency represented by lobbying organizations with a structure in place to stimulate a blitzkrieg grassroots repeal drive (Craney and Hook 1989).

Making the Case Directly

Advertising and grassroots lobbying campaigns can be effective in informing and mobilizing the public, but they also have an element of unpredictability about them. The message may get muddled, the expected response may never materialize, or the campaign may simply backfire, succeeding only in mobilizing the opposition without winning new converts. Thus organized interests find that to present their arguments in a more refined, focused, and controlled way, they must approach Congress and its members more directly.

Direct lobbying offers organized interests the clearest opportunity for presenting the substantive and political merits of their positions. By cultivating direct relationships with staff aides and lawmakers, especially those associated with key committees and subcommittees, lobbyists can position themselves to help draft legislation, plan legislative strategy, provide technical information, and demonstrate the consequences of assorted statutory alternatives—who will be affected, in what ways, to what extent, and with what likely political consequences.

Lobbying directly on the Hill is a very different enterprise today from what it was a quarter century ago, when Congress was still a rather oligarchical institution, with power concentrated in a handful of committee chairs who stood astride the policy process. In those days, the lobbying task was rather straightforward, for the number of legislators who had much of a say in how things progressed was relatively small.

Today the situation for those who want to make their case directly on the Hill is much more complicated. Since the late 1960s there have been a number of changes in Congress that have rendered the institution more accessible and open to organized interests while at the same time recasting the institutional character of Congress, making it more individualistic and unpredictable—and thus harder for organized interests to deal with—than in the past. These changes have altered the environment of legislative lobbying, opening up some new avenues for potential influence but also multiplying the number of persons on Capitol Hill who may have a say on policy matters and thus leaving groups intent on trying to influence legislative outcomes with little choice but to escalate the range and volume of their political activities (Schlozman and Tierney 1986).

In the aftermath of congressional reforms, especially in the House, that weakened committee chairs and decentralized power to subcommittee heads and to rank-and-file legislators, it is no longer possible for an interest group to make its case effectively by contacting only a few powerful legislators (Davidson 1981). Lobbyists now must cultivate a broader range of contacts, not only because there are more subcommittees whose jurisdictions touch each group's interests but also because single committees and subcommittees no longer exercise as much control over legislation as they once did. With the growing tendency to refer bills to multiple committees, and with the general relaxation of legislative norms that once inhibited floor challenges to committee decisions, threats to a group's legislative interests may come from anywhere in the chamber and at many more points during a bill's progress through the legislative labyrinth (see Bach and Smith 1988). This necessitates greatly increased attentiveness and effort on the part of organized interests.

A similar consequence stems from the adoption by both chambers of so-called sunshine rules, which liberalize public access to once secret markup sessions and conference committee meetings. Lobbyists serious about watching out for their organizations' interests can scarcely afford to be absent at such crucial stages of the legislative process.

The tremendous expansion and professionalization of congressional staff in the past two decades have also complicated the direct lobbying tasks of organized interests by multiplying still further the number of people with whom lobbyists need to establish contacts. Staffers often play the principal part in briefing legislators before votes on bills or amendments, so it is important for lobbyists to make their cases effectively to these aides. Moreover, when lobbyists are able to arrange one-on-one meetings with people on the Hill, they are more likely to be with congressional staff than with the legislators themselves. This is especially true on the Senate side, where the legislators are stretched thin and tend to be less conversant with the details of legislation and where the staff are given considerable authority by their bosses to negotiate and are thus a policy-making force in their own right (see Baker 1989:158–159; Malbin 1980).

To gain access to legislators or to command their direct attention, many organized interests find it useful to bring influential constituents to Washington to lobby their representatives. The notion underlying this approach is that in this era of congressional hypersensitivity to constituent concerns, an organized interest—say, for example, the American Hospital Association—has a better chance of making a persuasive case to a member of Congress on an issue it cares about if it brings in influential hospital trustees or administrators from the member's district than if it simply sends in one of the association's Washington lobbyists.

Playing the home-state card is not the only way of commanding a legislator's attention. Many groups try to increase their access by employing persons of high status as lobbyists. Washington is full of political notables who have hung out their shingles as lobbyists and earn huge incomes serving as hired guns for the various interests that retain them. Former members of Congress constitute a growing portion of this lobbying community. Until relatively recently, retired or defeated legislators tended to head back to their home states or districts after their years on Capitol Hill. But now many stay in Washington and use their contacts and access to buttonhole their former colleagues on behalf of clients (see Moore 1989).

Corporate chief executive officers constitute another category of elites who have taken on the task of directly lobbying Congress. Members of Congress tend to regard them as equals—and in some cases as celebrities. Legislators reluctant to make time in their busy schedules to meet privately with an obscure lobbyist for the automobile industry will *make* time when the head of General Motors requests an appointment. This is the main principle behind the Business Roundtable, an organization consisting of the CEOs from some 200 of the nation's largest industrial, financial, and commercial institutions. But whereas the Roundtable was distinctive in its approach fifteen years ago, the practice is now so widespread that, as Jeffrey H. Birnbaum (1990) points out, "lobbyist" would seem to have become an unwritten part of most corporate chief executives' job descriptions.

A New Wrinkle: Entrepreneurial Lobbying

One of the traits characteristic of contemporary national politics and policymaking is the increasingly prominent role of "policy entrepreneurs" who invest their political capital in pushing for policies that confer dispersed social benefits, with the costs to be borne by smaller segments of society.[2] Often these entrepreneurs are members of Congress or executive branch officials who serve as active, creative forces, advocating policies that serve the interests of the general public—for example, legislation intended to produce cleaner air and water, safer workplaces and consumer products, more rational transportation policies, or a fairer tax code. Public officials obviously are not alone in taking on such a role: There are also many lobbying organizations and public interest advocates pushing for such collective goods (see Berry 1977). (Ralph Nader is probably the quintessential example of a policy entrepreneur.)

In a sense, *all* organized interest groups are engaged in policy entrepreneurship to the extent that they invest their resources (money, staff, energy, information, and reputation for credibility) toward achieving policies they favor. That's what organized interests do, what they're expected to do. But as noted in previous chapters, the role of policy entrepreneurship in the lobbying business has taken on a new prominence in Washington in recent years with the proliferation of multiclient lobbying firms, law firms, and public relations firms that now litter the Washington landscape. They all do lobbying, and they all need a steady flow of clients to expand their profits. Jeffrey Berry (1989a:98) points out that this need "to drum up business and make their high hourly fees and retainers seem reasonable" leads them to "exaggerate their prowess with government." Of greater concern, and this is the new entrepreneurial twist, they sometimes find ways to tap into the public treasury to finance various kinds of projects. Having thus found some goods to supply, they look around for clients to "sell" them to.

A controversial case in point involved Cassidy and Associates, a large, multiclient Washington lobbying firm with a reputation for being able, among other things, to snare federal dollars for university research and construction projects (see Morgan 1989; Alston 1989). Forty of the firms' 100 clients in 1988 were colleges or universities. Using computerized compilations of appropriations bills to spot potential funding sources, lobbyists for the firm discovered a little-known entity called the National Defense Stockpile Transaction Fund. Gerald Cassidy, a former Senate staffer who heads the firm, persuaded members of the appropriations committees to pass millions of dollars through this fund to finance "strategic materials research centers" at universities in these legislators' own home states and districts—universities that already were, or later became, clients of Cassidy and Associates.

Here again, in its broad outlines this lobbying strategy represents nothing particularly new: Lobbyists are always on the lookout for new sources of federal dollars. But when seen as the sum of its individual parts, this picture is more disturbing, for it involves a "hired-gun" lobbying firm, staffed in part by former congressional aides who know the ins and outs of the spending process, finding ways to get funds earmarked for clients (and potential clients) through line items written directly into the appropriations process. As the competitiveness of the Washington lobbying industry grows, there may be increasing pressure on firms to find ways of drumming up business and satisfying clients eager for federal largesse.

The Darker Underside of Lobbying

In this age of policy complexity, the principal currency for lobbyists on Capitol Hill is information (Schlozman and Tierney 1986). But information is obviously not the only coin of the realm. Organized interests have various resources at their disposal that are used to induce cooperation or good will from members of Congress and their staffs. However legal most such exchanges might be, it is the offering of these inducements—and the eagerness with which people on the Hill accept them or, in many instances, solicit them—that gives rise to many of the grave concerns surrounding interest group activity.

The conventional wisdom among political scientists over the years has been that there are so many legitimate avenues of influence in Washington politics that bribery is unnecessary and corruption uncommon (see Turner 1958; Milbrath 1963; Fiorina 1989). But even if the illegal dealings that we associate with lobbying in the age of the robber barons are not widespread today, there are many subtler forms of "payment" (perhaps "favors" is a less loaded term) that seem to border on bribery inasmuch as they involve payments of cash or the provision of goods and services for which policy-makers would ordinarily have to expend personal funds.

Today, the best known of the regularized channels for funneling cash directly to legislators—as opposed to PAC contributions to their campaigns' war chests—is the honorarium, a payment (usually of $2,000) for giving a speech at a group's convention or making brief remarks at a breakfast meeting. The talk usually lasts less than a half hour; it is often a canned presentation prepared by a staffer. Until recently, congressional rules permitted members of the House to accept honoraria totaling up to 30 percent of their salaries; for senators, the ceiling was 40 percent. Thus, millions of dollars each year went directly into the pockets of legislators for their personal use.

Under pressure from reformers and from the glare of widespread media exposure of the honorarium racket, in late 1989 Congress passed the Ethics Reform Act, in which House members agreed to forgo honoraria after December 1990, in exchange for a hefty pay raise. Senators agreed to phase out honoraria more gradually, accepting a series of smaller raises. However, this new ethics law left plenty of loopholes that are sure to be exploited (Hook 1989).[3]

Even though House members are no longer permitted to pocket fees for speeches under the new law, organized interests wishing to "compensate" a legislator for giving a speech can make a contribution to the legislator's favorite charity instead. Previously, that practice had been common only among members who received more in honoraria than the maximum they were allowed to keep.[4] Because members tend to give their excess honoraria to organizations in their home districts or states, critics argue that these donations further tip the electoral scale in favor of the incumbents, who reap political benefits in the form of publicity and good will not available to challengers. Flush with interest group dollars, a legislator can, as Senator Alan Simpson put it to a reporter, "dribble it around the state looking like the great philanthropist of all time" (quoted in Hook 1989:3421).

Additionally, the new ethics law did relatively little to lessen the flow of gifts from organized interests to legislators and their staffs. The House abolished a long-standing rule restricting gifts from persons or groups with a "direct interest in legislation." Many members felt that the rule—which figured prominently in the House ethics investigation of former Speaker Jim Wright's relationship with Fort Worth businessman George Mallick—was hard to interpret. Instead, the new law now allows each House member to accept no more than $200 a year in gifts from any source except relatives; for senators the cap on gifts is $300. But even in Washington that kind of money can still buy a nice gift or a couple of tickets for the legislator and spouse to spend an evening at Wolf Trap or the Kennedy Center. Moreover, the new law actually liberalized rules governing meals in Washington paid for by lobbyists: It exempts such meals from the annual limit on gifts, so when a lobbyist takes a legislator out to a fancy Washington restaurant, it is no longer considered a gift under either House or Senate rules. Finally, the law still permits organized interests to pay all the travel expenses of legislators willing to give speeches at their conventions or meetings, thus doing nothing to stop the practice of legislators taking cushy vacations at lobbyists' expense.

In short, even under this newly enacted ethics law, billed as the most sweeping revision of the congressional code of conduct in twelve years, lobbyists can continue doing favors for members in the form of travel, wining and dining, and gifts. In one form or another, such social lobbying has long been a staple lobbying tactic (see Schriftgiesser 1951). Nor is there anything new about the concerns it provokes; the Progressives were as worried as current reform-minded observers about the potential for mischief that attends the exchange of possible inducements.

ARE ORGANIZED INTERESTS SOVEREIGN ON THE HILL?

If one were to pay attention these days only to what the national newsweeklies, the network news programs, and the other media have to say about the varied links connecting lobbyists and legislators, one could easily come to the view that organized interests have become sovereign on Capitol Hill. Members of Congress often seem to be portrayed as having capitulated in their responsibilities to protect the public interest, and Congress as an institution seems to have become a kind of political anemometer registering the force of prevailing interest group winds. The stories come in a steady stream, fostering the impression that the integrity of our most representative and democratic institution is gradually being compromised or undermined by the pernicious influence of special interests.

But it may be that the concerns here are vastly overstated—that the situation on Capitol Hill is not nearly as bad as it seems. Several considerations suggest that a more moderate interpretation is in order. First, the many genuine problems in the lobbyist-legislator nexus may be blown out of proportion or sensationalized by the media. News stories that describe hardworking public officials and interest group representatives collaborating in the pursuit of enlightened public policy are hard to make interesting and thus do not appear very often. By contrast, stories that link wealthy lobbyists to legislators in conflicts of interests, unsavory cash exchanges, or apparent sellouts of the public interest combine the two essential elements of popular journalism—celebrity and scandal—and are thus irresistible to many reporters, editors, and publishers. This helps explain, for example, the seemingly endless supply of articles in 1989 and 1990 about the "Keating Five"—the five U.S. senators who collected nearly $1.4 million in campaign donations from Charles Keating of the bankrupt Lincoln Savings and Loan.[5] Such considerations are important to keep in mind before we accept too readily the media-driven impression that "special interests" are the political scourge of our time.

Moreover, there is simply very little hard evidence, from either journalistic or scholarly inquiries, that the influence of organized interests enables them to routinely dictate congressional outcomes. This is not surprising in view of the large number of other participants in the legislative process who are in a position to bring formidable political resources to bear in pursuit of their policy preferences, providing counterweights to the expressed wishes of organized interests. Among them are the president and his advisers; generalist political executives, program administrators, and policy analysts in executive agencies; members of Congress, the legislative leadership, and congressional staffers; state and local officials; outside experts; and the general public. In other words, when it comes to voting on the issues before them, members of Congress are subject not merely to the claims and clamorings of attentive organized interests but to countervailing pressures as well—not least, the claims of party, the White House, constituency, and individual conscience.

Furthermore, one need only look at many of the big policy battles that have raged in Washington in the past quarter century—over consumer safety, environmental protection, occupational safety, transportation deregulation, and tax reform—to see that the "powerful interests" (in most of these cases, organized business interests) were unable to dictate outcomes completely to their liking. This was true even during the Reagan administration, as Paul Peterson suggests in Chapter 15 of this volume. Of course, business's relative losses in these battles were partly a consequence of the activities of other organized interests and of the efforts of policy entrepreneurs. But many analysts have suggested that such outcomes reflect something more profound—a gradual supplementing, if not a complete supplanting, of the "politics of interests" with a "politics of ideas," in which the power of a good idea or a symbolically appealing cause can be just as persuasive or forceful in the policymaking process as a vested interest (see Derthick and Quirk 1985; Quirk 1988; and Schulman 1988).

To the extent that there is such a new style of politics in Washington, it is no longer one in which organized interests, bureaucrats, and legislative leaders hold firm control over governmental action, but rather a much more open and fluid system in which power is extremely fragmented, policy entrepreneurialism abounds, and the ideas of experts, publicized and promoted through the media, may transcend self-interest or group interests in politics (Conlan et al. 1990).

Organized interests may not call all the shots on Capitol Hill these days, but they obviously have considerable influence. Exactly how much is difficult to specify. Casual observations and conclusions (such as those made above about the influence of business interests) are hazardous: Looking at which groups are involved in an issue and whether they seem to have won or lost tells us relatively little. After all, sometimes an apparent defeat masks the degree to which the outcome would have been worse for a group if it had not become involved at all. Similarly, a "victory" might offer false evidence of lobbying effectiveness, for the outcome might have been determined more by other factors (such as the unsolicited intervention of the president or of key legislators) than by interest group activity. In short, it is not always apparent who or what has made a difference in the outcome of a particular conflict and for what reason.

WHEN ORGANIZED INTERESTS
DO MAKE A DIFFERENCE

Still, it is possible to set forth some middle-level generalizations about the circumstances under which organized interests are most likely to have an impact on congressional politics and policymaking. First, an organized interest has a greater chance of influencing legislative outcomes when members of Congress feel pressured to publicly support the position of the interest group (even though privately they may disagree with the position) because they do not see how they might explain any public disagreement with the group. As Richard A. Smith (1989) has observed, such situations are likely to occur where the group is the "dominant constituency audience" for legislators on a particular issue (and legislators thus have reason to fear the electoral consequences of not supporting the group) or where the group's position is strongly supported by party leaders whom legislators do not wish to alienate or antagonize.

Following this line of argument, we see that the probability of success for an organized interest also depends upon the structure of conflict in a particular controversy. Organized pressure on members of Congress is less likely to bear results if it is met, as it often is, by opposing pressure.[6] Especially if this opposition is visible and involves a sizable threshold of attentive constituents, members will not feel as pressured to support the position of a more dominant group or of party leaders: They can point to a countervailing constituency interest. (Various sources of countervailing power are discussed by McFarland in Chapter 3.)

Lobbying success is also likely to vary with the nature of the demand. It is an old chestnut in American politics that organized interests in a defensive posture—that is, organized interests that are resisting some proposed change—are at an advantage over their opponents who seek political change (see Truman 1951; Dexter 1969). The complexities of the congressional policy process are such that any legislative policy measure must clear multiple hurdles, thus providing organized interests with many opportunities to delay or kill it. So an organization that is seeking to stymie a threatening measure is at a strategic advantage over one seeking to get a measure passed.

Moreover, organizations can ordinarily have greater influence on single, discrete amendments to bills than on entire pieces of legislation. Amendments are typically quite specific and sometimes technical (thus increasing the influence of the information provided by the group), and because they are generally narrower in impact, they do not typically attract broad opposition. For example, in spring 1990 various business and environmental groups found their efforts to reshape the broad outlines of a massive clean-air bill rebuffed by Senate leaders and the White House. But legislators quietly doled out scores of favors and concessions to a variety of special interests (including rocket and bus manufacturers, utilities, farmers, and universities), relaxing the bill's antipollution requirements for some and authorizing the funneling of federal dollars to others (see Kuntz 1990).

Obviously, to say that it is easier for an organized interest to affect the details than the broad outlines of a policy is not to trivialize this form of influence. On the contrary, the best case studies of policy formulation and implementation (see Brown 1983a; Melnick 1983; Katzmann 1986) demonstrate a central axiom of policy analysis: To know what a policy measure actually does, it is important to look beyond its broad purposes to the particulars; the details are what specify such critical matters as whom the measure covers, how much is to be spent, and who has the authority to implement it and under which constraints. How such participants are defined determines whether a measure will be a mere symbolic gesture or a potentially effective policy.

Finally, it is worth noting, at the risk of stating a truism, that the ability of organized interests to influence outcomes on Capitol Hill varies with their resources. Of course, the utility of resources varies under different conditions, depending on what it is the interest group is trying to accomplish: mobilize the public, secure a special tax break, block a damaging amendment, or defeat a political enemy at the polls. Money may be the most important of the resources that an organized interest can mobilize in its effort to affect congressional action. (Money, after all, is convertible: It can be used to buy other politically useful resources, such as staff, advertisements, access, and so on.) But it is clear that in dealing with Congress, other resources—for example, an appealing cause, a staff of skillful lobbyists, an attentive membership widely dispersed across most congressional districts—can often compensate for an absence of cash. Still, the total package of resources that an organization brings to the political fray in Congress has a significant bearing on the outcome.

What does all this add up to? Unfortunately, there is no ready answer to the question of how much influence organized interests now wield on Capitol Hill. On the one hand, the evidence presented here as well as in Chapters 15 and 16 does not support a conclusion that organized interests call all the shots at that end of Pennsylvania Avenue. So it is a mistake merely to accept wholesale the media's portrait of organized interests' determining congressional politics. On the other hand, it is equally oversimplistic to dismiss lobbying influence as negligible, as did many political scientists in the early 1960s. Much has changed. The empirical assertions that underpinned such a conclusion—for example, that organized interests in Washington lack resources needed to be effective (Bauer, Pool, and Dexter 1963) and also lack sufficient inducements to offer congressional officials in exchange for cooperation (Milbrath 1963)—simply no longer hold true (see Schlozman and Tierney 1986). Moreover, it seems clear from the preceding discussion that there are certain circumstances in which the involvement of an organized interest is likely to make a difference in political outcomes.

CONCLUSION

Perhaps the important question is not whether organized interests are influential on the Hill (surely they are) but whether the confluence of changes in these two realms of our political world—Congress and organized interests—pose serious threats to the integrity and effectiveness of our political system. Again there is no definitive answer, but after considering all the available evidence, we might see at least as much reason to be concerned as to be sanguine.

The problem, if there is one, is not that organized interests have developed insidious new ways of trying to affect outcomes on Capitol Hill. In fact, although there may be a new level of sophistication to their efforts, for the most part they are doing more of what they have been doing for years. But it does not take a Cassandra to see that in politics, as in oil spills or hazardous wastes, more of the same is not really the same: Where there was potential for Madisonian mischief before, there is now potential for long-term harm.

One consequence of the massive mobilization of organized interests in the political process is that our politics has become noticeably more shrill and unruly (see Huntington 1975); the political air is filled with static. In particular, many of the efforts of various groups to "go public" through issue advertising and grassroots lobbying campaigns reduce the clarity and debase the quality of our public discourse by misrepresenting the truth and using inflammatory rhetoric to appeal to public fears, prejudices, and ignorance. These campaigns of public mobilization also subject already skittish legislators to irreconcilable cross-pressures, thereby undermining the ability of our elected representatives to deliberate thoughtfully and exercise sound judgment.

The policy consequences of contemporary interest group activity may be even more disturbing than the consequences for political decorum. The lobbyists who swarm on Capitol Hill are crowding the public agenda with demands that tend to divert the attention of policymakers from the long run to the short run, from the substantively meritorious to the politically exigent. For the most part, when interests are well organized and politically involved, narrow interests prevail over broad ones in policymaking. The consequences of all this are far from benign, because interest groups are able to extract concessions from the government, such as a bailout of the savings and loan industry, that benefit their narrowly based constituencies in the short run but produce widely shared costs to be borne over a long time (see Thurow 1980; Olson 1982). Moreover, narrow interests are often able to stymie policies designed to confront problems having societywide implications, such as efforts to achieve hospital cost containment or reduction of the trade deficit, when those policies would impose disproportionate costs on their narrowly based but politically active constituencies. It is no wonder that so many Americans view with suspicion the connections between Congress and organized interests.

NOTES

I wish to acknowledge my intellectual debt to Kay L. Schlozman, with whom I coauthored *Organized Interests and American Democracy* and from whom I have learned much about interest group politics.

1. The committee later acknowledged the "misinformation," claiming it is difficult to discuss details accurately in a mere flier (Tolchin 1989).

2. There is a substantial, and growing, body of literature on policy entrepreneurship. See, for example, Wilson 1980b; Kingdon 1984; Polsby 1984a; Loomis 1988; and Conlan et al. 1990.

3. The following discussion of the 1989 ethics reform law draws heavily on Hook 1989.

4. For example, in 1988 Ways and Means Chairman Dan Rostenkowski (D–Ill.) collected over $220,000 in speaking fees, keeping $25,885 for himself and giving the balance to charity.

5. This is not to suggest that journalists are generally or routinely irresponsible in their coverage of Capitol Hill or organized interest politics. We would know far less about how this realm of politics works were it not for the careful reporting of many journalists. Still, the sensational stories are the ones that attract the attention of the press and thus of the public.

6. When a group faces organized opposition, it rarely emerges from a policy controversy with an unqualified victory. However, balanced competition is certainly not inevitable. The theories of Schattschneider (1960) and Olson (1965) predict that not all latent interests can be expected to organize in opposition to established groups. And the theories of Wilson (1973, 1980b) and Lowi (1969) on the patterns of interest group conflict suggest that most policy controversies do not involve head-on conflicts between organized interests.

10

Interest Mobilization and the Presidency

MARK A. PETERSON

At their inaugural ceremonies on the western terrace of the U.S. Capitol, incoming presidents are introduced to a vista that symbolically conveys much to them about the practical political situation they are about to experience. While delivering the inaugural address, the new president senses the presence of Congress, embodied both in the Capitol at whose steps he or she speaks and in the myriad legislative office buildings located to the north and south. Straight out from the west terrace, past the museums of the Smithsonian Institution and the imposing buildings of the federal establishment, at the end of the long Mall and near the White House, stands the Washington Monument, a remembrance of the man who launched the American presidency. When George Washington left office, he warned his fellow citizens about the evils of factions. Now, not far from his monument and just a few blocks from the president's own front door, lie the office complexes of "K Street Corridor," housing a significant proportion of the lobbyists, lawyers, consultants, and associations that press the business of thousands of interest groups on the executive and legislative officials of the government.

When Major Pierre C. L'Enfant created his grand plan for the capital city, he produced a "community plan . . . [that] no less than the Constitution, is a blueprint for the governing establishment" (Young 1966:2). Almost two centuries later, the geography of Washington seen by the new president from atop Capitol Hill retains its accuracy as a representation of the capital's political terrain. Institutions of governmental power are scattered throughout the community, sometimes scarcely visible to one another, and certainly separated by considerable distances. But where once marsh and bog prevented ready access, now these institutions may seem all too accessible, particularly to group advocates whose offices line the city's streets.

In this essay I examine the political geography of Washington, focusing on the interaction between the constitutional design of the American national government and the contemporary elaboration of the interest group system, and how that interaction has been managed by presidents in the modern era to secure influence, especially in Congress. I begin with a discussion of the institutional and group context of presidential leadership. Guided by recent empirical research, I then evaluate three group-directed strategies that presidents have pursued to advance their political and programmatic interests: using the instruments of government to intimidate their organized opponents, cultivating specific interests friendly to their administrations, and targeting their public liaison activities to mobilize their allies. I conclude by suggesting that the nature of the current group system and executive strategies designed to exploit it to the president's advantage are compatible with, not detrimental to, the reinvigoration of political parties.

COPING WITH SCATTERED INSTITUTIONS

The search for a viable way to link the presidency with Congress and other governmental institutions is not solely a phenomenon of the modern era. Almost as soon as the Constitution was ratified, establishing separate branches of government, national elected officials began to diverge into the coalescing factions of the nascent political parties that could potentially bring the president and Congress together. But even as a mature American party system emerged and became influential in electoral politics and policymaking, its deviation from the European model of parties with centralized organizations, control over recruitment, and ideological consistency meant that the institutional gap between the president and Congress could sometimes be bridged but not permanently narrowed. Chief executives have, therefore, sought additional means for invigorating their relationship with members of Congress and bringing cohesion to the Washington community. One approach has been the development of new institutional tools, such as the formalization of a congressional liaison office within the Executive Office of the President (EOP), as well as in agencies throughout the bureaucracy. Another more recent approach has been to place greater emphasis on the opportunity afforded by television technology for the president to forge direct alliances with the American public and to use the mobilization of the electorate as a way to prod Congress into action (see Kernell 1986; Lowi 1985).

Events since the early 1960s, however, have complicated the task of cultivating a workable bond between the president and Congress. Precisely when this relationship has become increasingly important, many observers have perceived a decline in the capacity of available institutions to tie the presidency to both the executive's political constituencies and other government institutions, such as Congress (Heclo 1981). The expanded role of the presidency in policymaking has raised the premium on successful presidential leadership throughout the government. Where once the executive departments served as the major sources of policy initiatives and the primary conduits of communication between the executive branch and other political institutions, now the White House as a "political communications command center" structures much of the policy agenda and bears "the burden of coalition building" (Kumar and Grossman 1984:285, 1986:93; see also Light 1982; Pika 1983:312–313). As the issues of domestic concern shifted in the 1960s and 1970s to include the more contentious arenas of redistributive and regulatory policies, as well as the nearly "no-win" demands of the late 1970s, the president became both more prominent and in greater need of effective links within the various policy communities (see Gais, Peterson, and Walker 1984:165; Light 1982:202–233).

Unfortunately for each resident of the White House, as the national focus on the presidency grew, the targets of presidential influence proliferated whereas the effectiveness of institutional go-betweens declined. Congress responded to the changing political world by fragmenting its power and structure (Ornstein 1983). The rest of the political system, according to Samuel Kernell (1986), was tranformed from a pluralistic system in which institutional leaders mediated the formation of broad-based and relatively enduring coalitions to one in which power and interests became so narrowly conceived that traditional patterns of coalition-building are no longer viable. The political parties, formerly the "major link to the centers and sources of power in a fragmented constitutional political system," arguably lost much of their ability to nurture close institutional relationships (Kumar and Grossman 1986:92).

Although the parties were perceived to be in decline, organized interests proliferated, and the interest group system changed in character. Beginning in earnest in the 1960s, the traditional occupationally based groups with fairly systematic access to the federal government were joined by an expanding range of cause-oriented "citizens'" groups. These new organizations by temperament and circumstance generally lacked close, insider relations with congressional committees and agencies within the executive branch and were quite willing to raise their often contentious concerns in more public political arenas, such as the House and Senate floors, the electoral domain, and the streets (Gais and Walker 1990; Walker 1983). The growth of these organizations, combined with the emergence of key social movements starting with the civil rights movement, has forced all political leaders, but none more than the president, to react to and try to manage a far more diffuse and unpredictable political world in the postwar era (Gais, Peterson, and Walker 1984; Heclo 1978; Miroff 1981; Peterson and Walker 1990).

The two institutions that are the generic topic of this essay—interest groups and the White House—have responded to this elaboration of the political and policymaking processes in mutually advantageous ways. As the White House has increased its influence over agenda-setting and other aspects of policymaking, many interest groups have sought to complement their existing strategies for influencing policy by obtaining direct access to the White House and even the president (Berry 1984; Kumar and Grossman 1986; Pika 1983). They join those groups for whom the previous system of interest representation failed to afford any meaningful access to government decisionmaking. For them, the White House has always been a target, and their efforts are only reinforced by the new prominence of the Executive Office of the President for interest group activity.

By the same token, presidents have increasingly cultivated relations with various interest groups to supplement the coalitional benefits derived from party organizations and affiliations. Because interest group organizations as a whole possess vast resources relevant to influencing the legislative process, and because members of Congress are perceived to offer access to groups enjoying active political action committees, presidents have been well advised to enlist favorable interest groups into their legislative coalitions. Where few such groups exist, presidents have been known to help stimulate their formation (Kumar and Grossman 1984:288–289; Page and Petracca 1983:158; Schlozman and Tierney 1986:325).

Cavorting with interest groups, however, poses some danger to the president as the one elected official the public expects to represent all of the people. Interactions with individual groups may lead to accusations that the administration is catering to special interests (Light 1982:94–95; Pika 1983:299). In addition, once some organizations are granted special access to the EOP, it is difficult both to constrain their demands on the presidency and maintain the quiescence of like-minded groups who have not yet gained the privilege of direct access (Copeland 1985:36; Gais, Peterson, and Walker 1984:181). And because interest groups are not bound to an administration by the common lineage and shared consequences of party, they may prove to be unstable and unreliable coalition partners as the issues of mutual concern change (Pika 1984:17).

Presidents, however, have the means to minimize the harm of involvement with groups. Unlike Capitol Hill, which despite the recent introduction of electronic security equipment remains a highly permeable institution, the White House complex is open to groups largely by presidential invitation only (Schlozman and Tierney 1986:327). In the words of an aide to President Ford, the White House "is not like Congress, where you always have a bunch of people wandering around and people putting bombs in toilet bowls. Inside the [White House] iron gate, they tend to develop, I hate to say it, a certain fortress mentality." More than physical barriers insulate the executive from special interest pleading. First, as Carol Greenwald (1977:215) argues, "the enormous range of presidential activity permits the President to solicit aid from groups when he needs them, and palm them off when the pressure lessens." Second, the very number and diversity of groups permit the White House to pick and choose which ones to favor with direct communication. Finally, with public financing of presidential campaigns, chief executives are not in need of electoral funds from interest groups, and few organizations can reliably mobilize large blocks of voters (Polsby 1983:154; Schattschneider 1975:50).

The institutional resources available within the White House to exploit strategically and interact with selected interest groups have become highly developed, as have most aspects of the Executive Office of the President since it was established in 1939 (Pika 1984:4). Beginning with Franklin Roosevelt, "liaison" functions were originally handled by a small number of White House assistants with informal responsibility, among their other duties, for maintaining contact with core groups in the Democratic coalition. By and large, that approach continued through several succeeding administrations, though the expanding number of presidential assistants permitted the evolution of greater staff specialization (Pika 1983:316, 1984:6–8). Ultimately, Charles Colson's efforts to mobilize support for some key legislative concerns of President Nixon "convinced Nixon of the value of an operation that generated support for the president and his programs on a routine basis" (Kumar and Grossman 1984:285). Watergate and Nixon's resignation, however, interfered with the inauguration of an office within the White House charged explicitly with liaison responsibilities.

Actually, the formal event was merely delayed. William Baroody, directing liaison activities following Colson's departure, persuaded President Ford of the benefits to be derived from an Office of Public Liaison (OPL) to "communicate, articulate, and support the President's programs, policies, and priorities in order to mobilize support for them."[1] Ford, an unelected president with little base of support, was willing to try almost anything to gain some leverage on the political system.[2] With the arrival of Anne Wexler as assistant to the president for public liaison in the middle of Jimmy Carter's administration, the Office of Public Liaison matured into a full-fledged arm of the coordinated effort to advocate the president's program in Congress. With some important amendments that will be discussed later, this process carried over into the Reagan White House and at least in rudimentary form retained a place in the Bush administration.

PRESIDENTIAL STRATEGIES
OF INTEREST MOBILIZATION

Having described the context of interest mobilization and the modern presidency, we are now left with the question, What have presidents in the contemporary era actually done to minimize the potential damage to their programmatic concerns generated by organized opponents and to turn the contemporary world of interest groups to their advantage? Three general strategies have been in evidence since the election of Franklin Roosevelt. First, some presidents, but none more so than Reagan, have used their influence over the budget and the design of federal programs to diminish the viability or effectiveness of organizations perceived to be at odds with the administration's objectives. Second, and more typically, chief executives have directed government benefits and actions toward interests whose political orientations are compatible with their own. Third, presidents have used both formal and informal methods of communication with interest organizations to help achieve their representational or programmatic goals.

Intimidating the Opposition

Especially since the current proliferation of interest groups began in the early 1960s, every president has complained about the threat to the national interest—usually defined as the administration's program—imposed by the parochial demands of "special interests." Although it is not uncommon for organizational opponents of the president to find their access to federal agencies restricted, presidential attacks on groups have usually been more rhetorical than instrumental, as when Jimmy Carter called the influence of PAC contributions to members of Congress "the single greatest threat to the proper functioning of our democratic system."[3] But one president, Reagan, did explicitly employ the powers of the Oval Office to threaten directly the livelihood or the political relevance of opposition groups by cutting their programs, ties to the pertinent decisionmakers, access, and operational grants and contracts.

The Reagan administration did not have to go out of its way to reduce or eliminate the government programs favored by liberal groups. Shrinking the federal establishment, or at least inhibiting its continued growth, was a core philosophical commitment of the president. But the magnitude of the budget and tax cuts Reagan proposed in 1981 and the mechanism by which budget reductions in particular were achieved unambiguously challenged the interests and influence of groups opposed to the administration (Ginsberg and Shefter 1988).

Congress, an open institution with a vast array of committees and subcommittees, is always permeable to lobbying organizations. The Reagan administration, strategically guided by Budget Director David Stock-man, a former member of Congress, fully understood that the success of its budget plan was in jeopardy if this accessibility to group interests was permitted to continue on budget decisionmaking. At Stockman's direction, the president's allies in Congress consolidated all desired changes in appropriations and authorizations into a single reconciliation bill. With Reagan's assistance, they went on to win a procedural battle in the Dem-ocrat-controlled House, requiring the budget cuts to be considered in a single up or down vote. The packaging issue decided, the funding reduc-tions and program consolidations were enacted with little opportunity for groups supporting the targeted programs to mobilize their resources and intervene in the legislative process. In addition, both the shift in congres-sional budgeting procedures toward the use of reconciliation and the large federal budget deficits that ensued from Reagan's success at cutting and indexing personal taxes and building up the defense expenditures resulted in a new kind of resource-scarce, conflictual, redistributive politics that pitted interest groups as much against one another as against the admin-istration (Wolman and Teitelbaum 1984).

President Reagan's assault on the budget and tax base of the federal establishment also had a subtler effect on group leaders antagonistic to the administration. According to Benjamin Ginsberg and Martin Shefter (1988:313–320), Reagan's economic program, in combination with his appeals to nationalistic and moralistic values, served to divorce ethnic workers, white southerners, and the middle class from the Democratic party. By extension, these voters were alienated from organizations and interest group leaders whose positions in support of labor, education, and consumer and environmental protection they otherwise may have found appealing. With President Reagan accenting their identities as patriots and taxpayers, rather than as beneficiaries of government programs and pro-tections, these citizens became less favorably disposed to the president's organizational opponents.

Eliminating or reducing the funding of certain federal activities is not the only means for thwarting the influence of groups with program-based interests. Along with the tremendous surge in the number of interest groups in evidence since about 1970 has come an accompanying increase in the number of groups with a direct presence in the nation's capital. As the federal government became involved in an expanding sphere of activ-ities, interest organizations representing everything from corporations to environmental activists either originated in the capital or moved their previously existing public affairs offices or even headquarters to Washing-ton (Schlozman and Tierney 1986:66–78). Myriad groups focusing on national political issues have little effective presence in state capitals. This concentration of organizational resources in Washington provided the

Reagan administration with a second method for challenging the power of the Left: Withdraw the locus of policy decisionmaking from Washington and scatter it among the fifty state capitals or even more widely throughout the nation.

Among the techniques the Reagan administration used to tame the federal establishment was what Peter Benda and Charles Levine (1988:123–126) term "debureaucratization," achieved through "devolution" and "privatization." Devolution sought to relinquish federal control of some programmatic issues by having state governments explicitly take charge of policy concerns currently borne by the national government, such as Aid to Families with Dependent Children, or by building on President Nixon's effort to consolidate federal categorical grant programs into block grants that yield state and local authorities greater discretion. Privatization was intended either to leave some federal activities to the marketplace, often achieved by selling government assets like the ConRail railroad freight system, or to require that some government services be contracted out to private businesses. Neither approach fulfilled the expectations of the administration, but in 1981 Reagan was able to persuade Congress to accept nine block grants that incorporated seventy-seven categorical programs.

In their study of twenty-five Washington-based organizations representing interests in the domain of human services, Wolman and Teitelbaum (1984:312–315) found that the administration's decentralization of federal programs had a pronounced effect on lobbying capacities of some interest groups. Though a few organizations, like the American Association of School Administrators, continued to see most of their concerns linked to the Washington policy agenda, some groups found it necessary to change their policy objectives or begin developing a stronger institutional base in the states, a finding confirmed by Thomas and Hrebenar in Chapter 7 of this book. Building up state bases would be no easy task, except for the groups already possessing an elaborate array of state-level affiliates.

Even if Reagan had enjoyed complete success in restructuring the activities of the federal government, not all programs could be eliminated, cut, or transferred to the states and private sector. Opposing interest groups would have plenty of opportunity to continue to press their demands upon federal officials. This potential for influence by the president's organized adversaries was tempered by a third facet of the administration's antigroup strategy: the limiting of group access by centralizing the selection of political appointees throughout the bureaucracy in the White House. Nixon, in an attempt foiled by the emergence of the Watergate scandal, laid the foundation of the "administrative presidency," thwarting the tendency of agency officials to become too cozy with clientele groups by ensuring that their first loyalty was to the president (Nathan 1975; Waterman 1989:8–10). The Reagan administration brought this approach to full fruition (Benda and Levine 1988:107–112; Lynn 1984). Minorities, civil rights activists, environmentalists, consumer advocates, and representatives of the poor found few friends among the ranks of Reagan's executive branch appointees and suffered restricted access to federal agencies as a result (Peterson and Walker 1986:169–172).

What makes the Reagan administration particularly unique, however, is that it not only sought to limit the influence of liberal and left-leaning groups in the Washington community, it also wanted to weaken the organizations themselves and effectively remove them from the collection of advocates able to lobby executive and legislative officials. President Reagan and his associates perceived that the world of interest groups included a vast array of liberal organizations who shared responsibility for the growth in government, and more perniciously, whose organizations and activities were actually financed by the government itself. To break the hold of these groups in Washington's policy communities, the administration launched a campaign to "defund the Left," intended to deprive these organizations of support and the capacity to influence the very government agencies that were thought to be effectively paying for these activities (Peterson and Walker 1986:163–164; Wolman and Teitelbaum 1984:304–305). General grants and service contracts to interest groups were curtailed and the Office of Management and Budget made a preliminary effort to prohibit any political activities by groups receiving federal funds. A photocopying machine purchased in part with federal dollars, for example, could not be used for any lobbying activities. The OMB's proposal was withdrawn, however, when it was recognized that the restriction would also affect administration's corporate allies.

Interest groups opposed to Reagan's policy objectives certainly experienced a dramatic change in their access and influence as a result of the administration's strategy of intimidation. But it would be erroneous to conclude that the actions of the administration were entirely successful, or that the same tactics are available to all presidents. First, despite Reagan's direct assault on the group system, the growth in the Washington-based interest group community kept pace during the 1980s (Peterson and Walker 1986:165–167). Indeed, the memberships of many organizations most vociferously opposed to the president actually grew dramatically, partially *because* of the administration's challenge. The Wilderness Society, for example, doubled in size from 1981 to 1983, leading the overall 13 percent increase in the memberships of the top eleven environmental groups (Waterman 1989:134).[4]

Second, the Reagan administration's plan to defund the Left was grounded in a misperception of the organizational bases of its adversaries. Most of the liberal activist groups of greatest concern to President Reagan were citizens' groups, but in 1980 they received, on average, only about

12 percent of their financial support from the federal government. By 1985 that had been trimmed to 8 percent, a reduction easily absorbed by increases in other resources. In contrast, government funding was more important to groups representing institutions and professionals in the nonprofit sector, the *least* partisan organizations in the interest group community (Peterson and Walker 1986:173–177). Some of these groups were devastated by the cuts in grants and contracts. In 1981, half the budget of the National League of Cities came from the federal government; by 1983 it received almost no federal support, forcing a reduction in staff from 120 to about 50 (Wolman and Teitelbaum 1984:315). Though the League of Cities endorsed many of the federal programs that the Reagan administration found suspect, as an organization representing nearly 1,000 municipalities and cities around the United States, it could hardly be classified as a fringe, leftist organization. To some extent, rather than limiting the influence of the most vocal liberal advocates, the administration's tactics made formerly "neutral" organizations in the nonprofit sector more partisan in opposition to the administration's programs.

Finally, Democratic presidents, or presidents without as great a commitment to reducing federal programs as Reagan demonstrated would have a more difficult time challenging opposing interests. For less conservative administrations, the targets of attack would have to include the business community, both corporations and their trade associations, as they are typically suspicious of government intervention on social welfare, civil rights, labor, consumer, and environmental issues. But as Charles Lindblom (1977) notes, the business sector enjoys a privileged political position, because even liberal presidents depend upon a well-functioning economy, which is largely determined by the decisions of business leaders. Democratic presidents cannot afford to challenge the legitimacy of business interests with the same enthusiasm the Reagan administration showed in its confrontations with "the Left."

Promoting and Winning Friends

Presidents are more inclined to employ rhetoric, make decisions, select personnel, and pursue programmatic initiatives that are appealing to potential allies among latent and organized interests than they are to threaten the effectiveness of opponents. It is in these terms that we often recognize presidents as leaders of coalitions composed of politically relevant interests. In the modern era, Franklin Roosevelt's name is synonymous with the New Deal coalition, a rather disparate but hardy amalgam of labor, blacks, Jews, Catholics, urban ethnics, southern whites, the economically underprivileged, and farmers brought together in the electoral arena during the 1930s and attracted by the administration's New Deal programs designed to combat the Great Depression. Once these groups became part of Roosevelt's electoral base, the president had members of his administration maintain informal ties with leaders and organizations representing these interests. Like other presidents, FDR appointed Cabinet officers and other officials partially with an eye to the interests associated with particular departments and agencies (Fenno 1959).

The respective Republican and Democratic coalitions maintained a considerable degree of stability through the Eisenhower and Kennedy administrations. Kennedy's administration contributed to the mobilization of women and the creation of groups such as the National Organization for Women (Walker 1990a: ch. 2; Freeman 1975). By the time of Johnson's presidency, the Democratic party coalition expanded to include both recently mobilized members of groups already favoring the party and new organizations composed of liberal activists. Johnson's Great Society initiatives, focusing on civil rights, social services, and the elderly, helped spawn new organizations supportive of these programs (Walker 1983:404). The community-action component of the war on poverty (Economic Opportunity Act of 1964) specifically contributed to the mobilization and political training of minority leaders who would go on to play a significant role in the organizational and political life of the country (Greenstone and Peterson 1976:xx).[5]

The actions of the Johnson administration ironically also sowed the seeds for the erosion of the New Deal coalition and presented Republicans with an opportunity to split the interests previously tied to the Democratic party. The popular issue of civil rights was extended into the much-resented realm of affirmative action and busing of school children to achieve racial integration. The prosecution of a Southeast Asian war stimulated an antiwar movement that challenged basic American middle-class values more widely.

Nixon launched the original effort to pull groups away from the Democratic fold. It came sequentially in two parts. First, the Nixon administration, guided by Attorney General John Mitchell, pursued a "southern strategy" in speechmaking, judicial appointments, and programmatic designs to entice white southerners, many of whom were antagonistic to black economic and political advancement, away from segregationist George Wallace and into the Nixon camp (see Evans and Novak 1972). Once that pursuit seemed secure, Nixon moved on to a "post-southern strategy" targeted at northern, blue-collar ethnics, often Catholics, uneasy about racial issues and despairing at the denigration of American values perceived to be embodied in the youth "rebellion," antiwar movement, and liberal permissiveness (Ehrlichman 1982:186–201). The electoral success of these strategies was evident in 1972, when President Nixon won reelection by a landslide, defeating Senator George McGovern, whose candidacy divided the Democratic party over the Vietnam War and the "social issues" of abortion, amnesty for draft dodgers, busing, and campus unrest (Miller et al. 1976).

Four years later, Carter, a southerner, successfully overcame these divisions by avoiding attention to the social issues and concentrating on the concerns likely to bridge the differences in the old New Deal coalition: the relatively poor performance of the economy and the political corruption of the Republicans as manifested by the Watergate scandal (Miller 1978). Once in office, Carter proposed legislation—such as national health insurance and labor law reform favored by organized labor, the Alaska lands bill supported by environmentalists, tax reform endorsed by liberal groups, and an urban program attractive to blacks and others—and made appointments—such as consumer activist Michael Pertschuk to the Federal Trade Commission and a record number of blacks and women to the federal bench—that reinforced ties between the administration and both old and new interest groups.

These groups did not always maintain harmonious relationships with the president, but they nevertheless enjoyed considerable access to the Carter administration and to the president himself. From his inauguration to the middle of 1979, Carter had thirty-five face-to-face meetings with union leaders, thirty with black organizations, twenty-one with public interest activists, and fifteen with Hispanic, Jewish, native American, Greek, elderly, and women's organizations (Orman 1987:59, 62).

While Carter was working with labor and other Democratically inclined groups, the Republican party was reinforcing its ties to business and the kinds of organizations articulating views consistent with Nixon's southern and post-southern strategies. Thomas Edsall (1984:73) characterizes the groups lining up with the GOP in the late 1970s as "the corporate lobbying community; ideological right-wing organizations committed to a conservative set of social and cultural values; Sunbelt entrepreneurial interests, particularly independent oil; a number of so-called neo-conservative or cold war intellectuals with hard-line views on defense and foreign policy issues . . . [and] economists advocating radical alteration of the tax system, with tax preferences skewed toward corporations and the affluent."

Reagan rode the support of these groups and voter rejection of Carter to the Oval Office in 1980. As president, Reagan worked to "reconstitute society," changing the nature of group alliances by assaulting his organized opponents, as discussed earlier, and bringing together the previously divergent groups that began to coalesce in the latter part of the 1970s. Evangelical Protestants were joined with Catholics by promoting a right-to-life position on abortion; upper-middle-class professionals were united with commercial interests; and business was nurtured as a more solid camp behind the administration (see Ginsberg and Shefter 1988). A decidedly conservative legislative and administrative program of lower taxes, less regulation, a disciplined money supply, and a reinvigorated defense establishment—implemented by an administration staffed with conservative and corporate operatives—buttressed group links to the administration. So did the president's interactions with group leaders. In his administration's first two and a half years, Reagan met personally with corporate leaders on forty-two occasions (the category enjoying the largest number of group encounters); with conservative and right-wing groups thirty times; with religious leaders in twenty-one meetings; and with Polish, Italian, and other ethnic group leaders eight times (Orman 1987:60, 63).

Mobilizing Allies

Crafting a strategy for vanquishing adversarial organizations and nurturing the emergence or reinforcing the presence of compatible interests is not always enough for a president to influence the interest group community. Presidents who wish to exploit their ties to the group system in order to propel their political or programmatic objectives must orchestrate their relations with group leaders by adopting a suitable "public liaison" strategy. No chief executive in the modern era has completely ignored the benefits to be derived from mobilizing organizational allies in the pursuit of administration goals.

Elsewhere (Peterson 1990b) I have argued that there are two dimensions to the interactions initiated by the White House with interest groups, which combine to identify four types of public liaison activities. The first dimension is the *breadth* of active relationships with the interest group community. "Inclusive" interactions involve the White House in communications with organizations located across the political and ideological spectrum. If the exchanges are "exclusive," then the president or presidential assistants limit their contacts to a relatively narrower range of groups, those indicating philosophical proximity to the administration. The *purpose* of the communications with interest groups constitutes the second dimension. Presidents may engage in public liaison activities either to enhance their "representational" functions as an elected tribune of the people or to fulfill their "programmatic" objectives in public-policy making.

The particular mix of these two dimensions that an administration practices at any given time or on any specific issue depends upon the orientation of the incumbent and the overall goals driving presidential decisions. A president who places a relatively low priority on the passage of legislation, for example, is less likely to engage in liaison strategies designed to achieve programmatic success. Personnel selection also plays a role. Presidents find it necessary to reward major campaign activists with government positions, and if one of those individuals lands in the Office of Public Liaison, he or she may pay most attention to representing the interests of the president's electoral coalition. The four types of public liaison activities can be identified according to these two dimensions of breadth and purpose:

1. *Liaison as consensus-building:* involving the White House in inclusive relationships with diverse groups in order to bring them together in coalitions supporting the president's programmatic objectives. The fundamentals of liaison as consensus-building were practiced most consistently by Johnson, especially during the 89th Congress. Johnson believed it was possible to add one interest to the next, however divergent their orientations, and gain their backing for legislation. Poor people, minorities, builders, developers, municipal officials, and construction supply companies, for example, often shared little politically but all had an interest in housing policy. They only had to be directed to recognize the benefits that each would obtain from the programs to construct affordable housing and urban parks. On this and many other issues LBJ instigated exchanges with groups and other political participants with legislative accomplishment explicitly in mind, and he saw little reason to exclude virtually any constituency from the process.

2. *Liaison as legitimization:* communicating with a broad array of organizations to bolster the president's position as a national representative, so as to regain or maintain acceptance of the incumbent and strengthen the president's political position. More than any other modern chief executive, Ford discovered immediately that his political legitimacy was in question. He had never stood before a national electorate, had assumed the presidency as an appointed vice-president, and suffered the residual tainting of the Watergate scandal, especially after granting Nixon a pardon in September 1974.

A first priority for Ford was not the presentation of a legislative agenda but rather restoring the public's confidence in the presidency and in him. He had to emphasize the president's role as representative of the nation, a task best fulfilled by communicating with leaders of groups embodying many political perspectives, from labor unions and the liberal National Education Association to business and foreign policy hard-liners. Though this task was not restricted to the newly established Office of Public Liaison, the OPL provided one of the means for Ford to communicate with the public, as represented by diverse groups, and to gain a legitimate hold on power.

3. *Liaison as outreach:* using the presidency as a place for groups outside of the political mainstream and with little previous access to government to gain a representational voice. The electoral coalitions of presidents are

often quite eclectic and include constituencies previously denied an opportunity to voice their concerns directly to sympathetic government officials. Jews and ethnics were outside interests until they developed ties with Democratic administrations like FDR's. Blacks have recently made inroads, gaining numerous political offices of their own, but direct communications with Kennedy and Johnson played an important role in bringing the message of civil rights to the Washington establishment.

By the time of the Carter administration, the composition of "outsider" groups had changed. Many gay rights activists and radical feminists, for example, supported Carter in the 1976 election. Carter's first public liaison assistant, Midge Costanza, therefore thought one of her responsibilities was to engage in outreach, giving these disenfranchised groups access to the Carter White House. The outsiders in Reagan's electoral base—right-wing ideological groups, evangelicals, and so on—came from the other end of the political spectrum. Some of his public liaison assistants, like Faith Whittlesey and Linda Chavez, provided these groups with the access that they could not receive elsewhere in the government. In both the Carter and Reagan administrations, part of the liaison effort was intended to reinforce the president's representational role, but for a limited set of constituencies.

4. *Liaison as governing party:* mobilizing groups philosophically attuned to the president's policy positions as part of a legislative coalition-building effort to support the administration's policy initiatives. Here the White House coordinates the use of interest groups to help build the majority coalitions needed in Congress to enact the president's legislative initiatives or to organize the forces required to block legislative actions the president opposes.

After Costanza left the Carter staff and was replaced by Anne Wexler, a consummate Washington insider, and in response to the difficulties the president was having with Congress, public liaison became an explicit arm of the White House campaigns to pass Carter's legislative programs. Wexler chaired many White House task forces created to orchestrate the legislative lobbying effort, and OPL brought scores of groups to the White House to be enlisted in behalf of programs like Carter's Alaska lands bill and his proposal for limiting increases in hospital costs. A few years later, Elizabeth Dole played a similar role as director of public liaison for President Reagan, helping to organize the lobbying by the business community and other supportive groups behind Reagan's 1981 program for economic recovery.

Although this typology of public liaison offers a useful conceptual basis for distinguishing among White House approaches to interactions with the interest group system, two clarifications are in order. First, although the four categories of public liaison are distinct from one another and an administration may emphasize one form of liaison over the others, all four have been utilized by all modern presidents, sometimes simultaneously. Second, the formal identification of public liaison assistants and the development of an Office of Public Liaison in the White House mean that increased resources are available to the president for working with interest groups, though individuals throughout the Executive Office of the President often participate in public liaison activities as well. In fact, most group interactions with the White House typically occur outside of the OPL, as Lucco (Chapter 11) shows in the area of consumer groups.

The Reagan administration provides an illustration of each of these points. The White House emphasized liaison as governing party, at least during the president's first term. This activity, however, was not to the exclusion of other kinds of interactions. Because of long-established traditions of White House access given to groups like the elderly and blacks, several liberal organizations maintained communications with Reagan's staff, ensuring a form of liaison as legitimization. In addition, once Dole became secretary of transportation and was replaced by more ideological public liaison directors, the OPL placed greater attention on outreach to right-wing organizations.

No matter what kinds of activities the OPL pursued, other officials in the Executive Office of the President also interacted with the interest group community. Indeed, in 1985 as many group leaders reported meeting with the Office of Management and Budget as with the OPL, but their orientations were quite different. Fewer than one-third of the groups communicating frequently with the OPL came from the profit sector; the figure for OMB was 60 percent. On the other hand, citizens' organizations were almost five times more prevalent among the OPL's most active constituency than was the case for the OMB. After 1981, group interactions with the OMB probably fit most closely the model of liaison as governing party, whereas the public liaison officials concentrated on outreach and legitimization.

In the middle of the Reagan administration and continuing into the presidency of George Bush, institutionalized public liaison began to experience a diminished presence in the White House. In Reagan's second term, the OPL was relocated under the overall direction of the White House Office of Communications, directed by conservative Patrick Buchanan. It remained there in the organizational design of the Bush White House. The diminution of the OPL's influence since the days of Wexler and Dole is readily apparent in its appeal to group leaders. The director of a key minority organization headquartered in Washington noted that his group's access to the White House had improved with the election of Bush, but his contacts were with Chief of Staff John Sununu. If his group had to rely on access through the OPL, he said, "we would be dead."[6]

Why would the role of the OPL in the White House be reduced? There are three possible explanations. First, after the major legislative victories in the early years of his administration, Reagan presented Congress with the smallest annual legislative agendas of any modern president (Peterson 1990b). As a continuity president, who some argue served the "third" term of the Reagan administration, Bush did not offer an expansive legislative program requiring the reinvigoration of the OPL. In both administrations, fewer resources had to be applied to liaison as governing party. Second, as Dole's immediate successors made the OPL a magnet for ideological concerns, the office itself became less central to the primary strategists in the White House. Outreach was left to the OPL while others in the EOP managed legislative coalitions. Finally, John Kessel (1984:251) has found that because of its formal ties with "special interests," the OPL is not looked upon favorably by other presidential aides. Only when independently influential individuals like Wexler have directed the OPL has it been elevated in the White House hierarchy.

Despite the decline in institutional prestige the Office of Public Liaison has suffered, the public liaison function itself retains its importance as a presidential strategy for influencing the interest group system. Bush and his aides continue to meet with group leaders in sessions organized by public liaison officials.[7] Officials throughout the Executive Office of the President still interact with group leaders for political and programmatic purposes. In formulating Bush's proposal for a clean air bill, for example, Roger Porter, the assistant to the president for economic and domestic policy, held sessions with both industry representatives and environmentalists (Duffy 1989:19). Interactions between the presidency and interest groups leaders formally orchestrated by the White House are now a permanent feature of American governance.

PRESIDENTS, INTEREST GROUPS, AND POLITICAL PARTIES

Modern presidents have the institutional means, and have demonstrated the willingness, to influence the interest group system to their advantage. Sometimes, presidents (like Reagan) have chosen to use their leadership of the government to thwart the political activities of their organized opponents, even to challenge the very existence of some groups. More often, administrations (such as Johnson's) focus on nurturing and aiding their allies in the interest group community. All recent presidents have in some way tried to get friendly interest groups to work on their behalf, either to reinforce the president's position as the people's representative or to facilitate the enactment of the president's legislative program.

But the extensive intercourse between interest representatives and the Executive Office of the President engendered by at least two of the three White House strategies for influencing the group system raises two fundamental and related concerns. First, for many observers, one of the most disconcerting modern political developments has been the proliferation of "special" interest organizations and the perception that American political institutions are consequently increasingly fragmented and ineffective. With so many groups projecting narrow interests into policymaking, and without centralized institutions able to cope with the resulting "demand overload" of government, it is feared that the polity has become ungovernable (Bell 1975b; Huntington 1975; King 1978; Olson 1982). According to this view, the ever expanding group system threatens the last bastion of the national interest: the presidency. The kind of intimate relations between the president and interest groups discussed in this essay only heightens the concern.

This argument, however, is overblown. On the one hand, the presidency has never been an unambiguous focal point of the national interest. The president's constituency may be national, but the victor's electoral coalition is as narrow as any other politician's. The ideological character of the interest groups generally given access to the Reagan White House only serves to dramatize the point. Further, it is clear that the president has considerable control over what forces are brought to bear on executive decisionmaking. On the other hand, to the extent that the presidency, like all institutions, is pressured by an expanding universe of interest groups, what are the alternatives? A return to times when large commercial interests could dominate much of American government and politics, often behind closed doors and to the disadvantage of latent interests (see Lindblom 1977; McConnell 1966)? The secret success of American politics in the modern era has been the capacity of the governmental system to bend and accommodate the restive forces of previously unorganized and unrepresented groups in our society, and thereby to maintain the legitimacy of the system (Etzioni 1977-1978; Walker 1990a).

The second related concern is that the invigoration of the group system is necessarily linked to the weakening of the political parties as institutions able to aggregate numerous and conflicting political demands and provide coherence to governance. As Walter Dean Burnham (1970:133) expresses it, "political parties . . . are the only devices thus far invented by the wit of Western man which with some effectiveness can generate countervailing collective power on behalf of the many individually powerless against the relatively few who are individually—or organizationally—powerful."

E. E. Schattschneider (1942:192) initiated the perspective—now ingrained in much scholarly thinking—that strong political parties and active interest groups are actually inimical to one another: "If the parties exercised the power to govern effectively, *they would shut out the pressure groups.* The fact that American parties govern only spasmodically and fitfully amid a multitude of lapses of control provides the opportunity for the cheap and easy use of pressure tactics. The role of pressure groups in American politics is directly and intimately related to the condition of the major parties." Robert Dahl (1982:190) followed Schattschneider's lead, repeating the notion that "the strength of parties in policy making tends to be inversely related to the strength of pressure groups." Indeed, one of the basic explanations offered for the growth of public liaison, not to mention the "public presidency," has been the decline of parties and the fragmentation of pluralism.

Political parties in the United States, though, have never had the overbearing strength to bring unity to a system that the Constitution intentionally cast apart at both the national and subnational levels. No matter what the condition of the parties, as the responsibilities of government increased in the twentieth century, new means had to be found to bind policymakers and other protagonists together. Yet this process does not require the abandonment of one institutional link in search of another. Without question the parties have suffered through hard times, but the effective management of the interest group system by political leaders may be the wellspring rather than the scourge of parties.

My argument has three facets. First, both parties and interest groups are in many senses forged by the same social forces. It is hard to imagine a system of politics in which they are not related (see Walker 1990a: especially ch. 2).[8] There are now signs—in the midst of a period of explosive growth in the interest group community—that the two major parties, especially the Republicans, are finding new institutional vigor. National and state party organizations have gained financial and technical resources, provided their candidates with more training and professional campaign assistance, and matured as programmatic rather than patronage-based entities. More citizens than ever are contacted by party representatives and, despite the decline in partisan affiliation among the public during the 1970s, a substantial majority of individuals continue to identify with either the Democratic or Republican parties (Edsall 1984:90–105; Eldersveld 1982:407–425; Price 1984:23–54; Schlesinger 1985).

Second, for all of the reasonable concerns about the splintering effects of political action committees—the campaign arms of voluntary associations, corporations, and unions—there is growing evidence that many PACs follow the cues of party campaign committees (Ehrenhalt 1985:2187; Edsall 1984:76–77). Such linkages are not surprising. Whether observed in the electoral or lobbying arenas, a significant proportion of the interest group community reflects ideological positions, takes stands on the issues of the day, or represents constituencies whose orientations are at least compatible with one of the two major parties. Sometimes the partisan ties are even explicitly stated by group leaders (Peterson and Walker 1986:177–179).

Third, the elaborate interest group system is becoming more of an instrument of political persuasion open to the influence of the president, the leader of the party in power. Presidents cannot command group leaders, and groups do have their own interests to pursue, but because the interest group community reflects the same broadly based philosophical cleavages that exist among government elites and the society at large, similarly oriented groups can be brought together (see Salisbury et al. 1987). Liaison is no substitute for an effective governing party, but it does provide an additional mechanism through which presidential leadership can be used to link the interest group system and the party system. The gap separating government institutions *can* be bridged.

Perhaps the real threat to the governability of the United States is not a battle between political parties and interest groups but rather the challenge posed against all institutions by the increasing role of presidentially led mass politics. Because even rejuvenated parties and willing coalition partners in the interest group community may not satisfy a president's desire for leadership of other government institutions, or because the new technologies of mass media are too tempting a means to bypass all mediated links to the electorate, presidents may too often choose to "go public." But governing a complex society requires accommodation, mediation, and deliberation, all of which, given able leadership, can still be accomplished on a broad range of issues in a highly elaborate system of interest groups (see Polsby 1978). These attributes are not easily found, however, in the electronic domain between the president's TelePrompTers and the public's television sets. This instrument of presidential influence is much more highly dependent upon personality and charisma and prone to be more divisive as the president's positions get chiseled into the stone of the evening news and major newspaper headlines. Further, to the extent that presidential candidates are selected based on the quality of their media skills in lieu of an understanding of group politics, an important asset for achieving governability is lost.

NOTES

This chapter derives in part from earlier work on which the following individuals offered much-appreciated comments: Stephen Ansolabehere, Jeffrey Berry, Christopher Bosso, Henry Brady, James Caesar, Jeffrey Cohen, James Davis, Joseph Pika, Robert Salisbury, Kay Schlozman, Jack Walker, Margaret Weir, and James Q. Wilson. I would also like to extend my deepest appreciation to scores of individuals in the Executive Office of the President, on Capitol Hill, and in the Washington press corps who granted me interviews, including former presidents Jimmy Carter and Gerald Ford.

1. The general story presented here is from an interview with an aide to presidents Nixon and Ford. The quote is taken from an August 23, 1974, memorandum from Baroody to Ford, reported in Copeland 1985:18.

2. Interview with Gerald Ford, Ann Arbor, Michigan, November 14, 1984.

3. For the effects of the Ford-Carter transition on group interactions with federal agencies, see Gais, Peterson, and Walker 1984:176–177. For the impact of the Carter-Reagan transition, see Peterson and Walker 1986:167–172. Quote is from the author's interview with Jimmy Carter, Plains, Georgia, June 20, 1984.

4. Peterson and Walker (1986) found, however, that in the aggregate the groups most critical of the Reagan administration, the most in support of expanded social services by the federal government, and reporting the sharpest decreases in cooperation with federal agencies as a result of the 1980 election lost about 10 percent of their members from 1980 to 1985.

5. Daniel P. Moynihan (1970:x) argues, however, that enhancing political participation was not the original purpose of the program, and that in fact because the ultimate emphasis on participation in the Community Action Agencies was "a direct threat to the Democratic coalition," Johnson opposed it.

6. Private conversation, Cambridge, Massachusetts, September 18, 1989.

7. Conversation with senior White House official, Washington, D.C., November 22, 1989.

8. Samuel J. Eldersveld (1982:66, 105–106) notes, for example, that the original party cleavages in the United States reflected interest group–type divisions between the Hamiltonians and Jeffersonians, and that today's national parties give considerable attention to the representation of their respective interests.

11

Representing the Public Interest: Consumer Groups and the Presidency

JOAN LUCCO

A reform movement concerned with the public interest has been taking place during the past forty years.[1] It initially surged in the late 1950s and 1960s with actions taken by advocates of numerous broad interests common to all citizens or very large groups of them.[2] Among these interests, usually referred to as public interests, were those of consumers, environmentalists, and peace seekers. The advocates believed that these widely held interests too seldom were taken into account in government policymaking processes.

Reformers were especially distressed by inattention to broad citizen interests in the executive branch arenas of policymaking. From the New Deal on, it was in this branch that a great deal of policy deeply affecting such interests was made, usually through largely private interaction between agency personnel and various producer interests. A principal remedy reformers sought was greatly increased representation of consumers and environmentalists in the executive agencies.

Consumer leaders of the 1950s were among the earliest proponents of compelling change in the agencies by inserting formal, distinct representation of broad nonproducer interests into their policy processes. They argued that the most successful approach to representation was through an executive branch entity with sufficient stature and independence to provide a knowledgeable, consistent, continuous, and effective presence in federal policymaking. This unit would represent the interests of consumers exclusively, allotting the largest proportion of its time to representing its consumer constituency in agency rulemaking and quasi-judicial proceedings. It would also put consumer interests on the record at congressional hearings and court proceedings as well as give consumers a voice in administration councils.

It was first thought that such goals could best be met in a "department of consumers" at the Cabinet level. When the prospects of a department dimmed, consumerists settled for a representative in the White House, becoming the first interest group to achieve such representation. In this chapter I focus on the case of consumer groups in order to examine and assess the value of formal White House representation to public interest groups in attaining their major goals.

Every instance of a unit devoted to formal consumer representation in the federal executive branch preceding the Bush administration has been lodged in the Executive Office of the President, sometimes in the White House Office section. President Kennedy established a Consumer Advisory Council (CAC) in 1962. In 1964 President Johnson added a Presidential Committee on Consumer Interests composed of the CAC and designated consumer liaisons in departments and agencies as well as a special assistant to the president for consumer affairs (SAPCA). Presidents Nixon, Ford, Carter, and Reagan retained a SAPCA. Esther Peterson was Johnson's first such assistant; she later served in the same role in the Carter administration. LBJ's second SAPCA was Betty Furness. Nixon, Ford, and Reagan all appointed Virginia Knauer. Nixon added an Office of Consumer Affairs and then moved it to the Department of Health, Education, and Welfare. Ford moved his assistant into the Office of Public Liaison. At the outset, Reagan placed his consumer aide in the OPL, where she had two portfolios in addition to that of consumers. Later, he moved her to the Department of Health and Human Services (HHS), giving her the new title of special adviser to the president for consumer affairs. To date, the Bush administration is following Reagan's later organizational pattern for the consumer unit.

I begin first by identifying the goals consumer advocates hoped to achieve through high-level representation in the executive branch and then by analyzing the advantages and disadvantages of White House representation for consumer groups. Next, I review the activities of consumer representatives in the administrations of six presidents, Kennedy through Reagan, in terms of their effectiveness in fulfilling the goals of consumer groups; I also offer brief comments on consumer representation in the Bush presidency. I place emphasis upon comparison across administrations regarding the operation of various representational processes and the factors bearing on their effectiveness. Finally, I draw conclusions with respect of consumer group goals.[3] That many characteristics of consumer groups are generic to numerous other groups represented in the White House enhances the possibility of generalizing the findings to other public interest groups with White House representation (for example, environmentalists) and to additional broad-based groups (such as women) represented there.

GOALS OF CONSUMER ADVOCATES

I define the goals of consumer advocates as those aims related to enhancing the strength of consumer representation in policymaking processes rather than to product-specific remedies. These were the top-priority goals of virtually all national-level consumer groups for more than two decades. Among the desired mechanisms for achieving enhanced representation were a Cabinet-level department, an independent agency, funded public participation in agency proceedings, greater ease in bringing class action suits, and enlarged standing to sue.[4]

For consumerists of the late 1950s and early 1960s, along with other reformers such as environmentalists and good-government advocates, lack of access for broad-based interests greatly detracted from the legitimacy of the government system. Like many critics of pluralism (Connolly 1969), consumerists believed that the system was biased toward the representation of interests organized around various producer concerns. If American government was to live up to its democratic promise, they believed, consumers should have representation in policymaking equal to that of other important actors in the society and the economy, especially business, labor, and agriculture. Consumer advocates called for a greater balance of interests in federal policymaking at hearings in almost every Congress from 1966 through 1978.

Consumer leaders did not desire to widen the scope of conflict simply by gaining entry to the circle of policy actors.[5] Mere access to the policy system would not satisfy them. They believed that a system based on logrolling, negotiation, and compromise was corrupt and immoral because it did not yield decisions according to the merits of issues as judged by general rules. Instead, the kind of decision produced in such a system was one that constituted a consensus based on what all parties could settle for. This critique was similar to the one advanced by Theodore Lowi in *The End of Liberalism* (1969) and other plural elitists. On the system's lack of legitimacy and its remedies, economist Persia Campbell, a principal early activist, has this to say in 1959:

> Laissez-faire is a myth. In the process of economic policymaking, administration and regulation by the Government, it is common knowledge that special interest groups play a dominant role, both directly through their lobbies and educational activities, and also through the great administrative departments oriented to their interests. . . . If the consumer interest, which approximates the public interest, and reflects our [national] economic goals,

could be effectively presented through an official responsible for giving it voice, and through expanding lay organizations, it could offset these special interest pressures. (U.S. Congress 1960:27)

Additionally, access was not enough because the resources (financial and otherwise) of consumer organizations were insufficient to allow them to be successful players in a system characterized by bargaining among producer interests and government personnel and by producers' bringing to bear considerable resources on behalf of their goals. Consumers' inability to sustain a strong membership organization precluded their possession of resources sufficient to provide significant incentives or sanctions to other political actors in the system, whether in the form of expertise, financial contributions, or reliable blocs of votes. Even public opinion, their strongest tool when they were able to muster it, was a volatile resource.

Consumer leaders of the late 1950s displayed a sophisticated awareness of consumer characteristics that would inevitably create difficulties in getting and keeping consumers organized, and consumerists cited these characteristics as a reason for insitutionalizing the representation of consumer interests in government.[6] Some advocates expressed the opinion that if the group's interests were looked after by a permanent institution in government, the inability to organize would no longer be an obstacle to achieving their goals in the marketplace (U.S. Congress 1960:29, 31, 86, 121).

Consumerists, like environmentalists, thought what was needed were new policymaking procedures. Procedural changes would force policymakers to accord consumers what was their right—to have their interests considered in decisions on issues relevant to their well-being. Decisions would be made on the merits after examination of a record of debate reflecting advocacy of all interests involved in an issue. As Albert Hirschman (1970:114) noted, the consumer advocates were using their voice for the purpose of making the country live up to its image "of providing the basic American values" of fair representation and equal opportunity. They had what Hirschman (1970:114) calls "the typically American conviction that institutions can be perfected, and that problems can be solved."

The goals of consumer leaders put them at the leading edge of what has been called "the new politics," which is characterized by a focus on new institutional arrangements and policy processes, distrust of big business and big government, and efforts toward participation of all interests, including the "public interest," even if such participation requires government mandates. Its features also include policymaking in arenas with more level playing fields and policy decisions based on what is "right," the decisions often made by a neutral judge on the merits of an issue instead of by compromises among interested parties. Proponents of "the new politics" hoped that the reforms would lead more often to policies reflecting the good of the public as a whole (Harris 1989a; Barber 1984; McCann 1986; Lowi 1986, 1988).

Consumerists' calls for reform went beyond the aim of bigger and better pluralism along the lines of formulations such as those of David Truman (1951) or Robert Dahl (1961). First, knowledge of all relevant policymaking proceedings would have to be available to anyone who wanted it. This goal was manifest in demands for freedom of information, openness in an increasing number of policymaking arenas, and timely advertisement in the Federal Register of proceedings in the executive branch. Second, the representational bodies proposed would have several unusual powers. They would have the authority to enter all relevant proceedings on behalf of consumers. They would also have the ability to subpoena witnesses, to submit direct interrogatories, and to appeal agency decisions regardless of whether they participated in the original action, and the assurance of independence through appointment of the administrator to a set term of office with removal for cause only. Third, new legislation would require the inclusion of citizens' points of view in the development of new regulations. Fourth, some procedures would provide funds for consumer witnesses with points of view that would otherwise go unheard.[7]

In the 1950s, consumer leaders thought that they could best achieve their goals through the creation of a department of consumers with Cabinet rank. However, when the advocates saw in 1960 that the hearings on a department would not lead to establishment of such a unit, they began to push for a consumer counsel at the White House.

Representation at the White House was a possibility because it was congruent with current presidential needs and desires (Lucco 1986). The combination of expanding presidential duties and declining support from a number of traditional sources of aid has led presidents to seek new providers of backing for their governance and electoral efforts. One way in which modern presidents have built the power base they need has been to reach out to interest groups. In some cases the reaching out included the appointment of a group's representative to the White House staff (Cronin 1975:ch. 5; Heclo 1981:166–182). Public interest groups and other groups organized around broad interests were a natural place for presidents to turn because they were growing in organization and strength and were themselves searching for sites of representation at the highest levels of policymaking. Among such interests that had representatives appointed to the White House were environmentalists, drug abuse opponents, women, the elderly, blacks, Hispanics, Jews, and ethnic Catholics.

WHITE HOUSE CHARACTERISTICS
AND ADVOCATE GOALS

Early consumer leaders viewed the presidency as an institution with certain characteristics that might be helpful for achieving the goals of an emerging group.[8] First, the presidency as the institution traditionally touted as the office where "all the people are represented" (McConnell 1966:chs. 4, 10; Smith 1987) seemed a natural site for helping a constituency that is basically coterminous with the population as a whole. Moreover, the era of the 1960s and early 1970s was one in which the institution of the presidency was in the ascendancy. During the early burst of new groups, the White House was increasingly the agenda-setter and was becoming more interested and skillful in manipulating the legislative process (Neustadt 1980; Wayne 1978:ch. 1; Dodd 1979:46–49). Agenda-setting is especially important for the fortunes of newly mobilized groups whose goals are only shakily on the national agenda, if at all (Cobb and Elder 1972). To cement a position on the national policymaking agenda is even more important to those diffuse groups with dim prospects for maintaining a degree of organization sufficient to exert significant pressure on the policymaking process. Perhaps not accidentally, it is such groups that have most often been represented on the White House staff in a formal mode. In addition to the general advantage of being attached to an institution with a premier position in the national policymaking scheme, representation in the White House offers several distinct advantages in the policymaking process, including access, visibility (with its accompanying publicity), and prestige.

Advantages of a White House Location

Access to the national agenda-setter was important and attractive to the groups. The advantage of access is the one upon which I focus in this chapter. Access could lead to influence over proposed legislation, executive orders, and highly publicized agenda-setting acts such as State of the Union addresses and special messages to Congress. A position in the White House affords its holder some degree of access, albeit minimal at times, to the president (Cronin 1975:123; Seidman 1977:14, 268).

In addition to acting favorably in response to a representative's advice or advocacy in matters of legislation, a president might also take advice from staff on appointments. For consumer groups, among others, the philosophy of those appointed to head agencies is considered very important indeed because of the degree of discretion these heads are able to exercise. Access also sometimes leads to information otherwise difficult to obtain about current policymaking affecting the interests of a group.

A great potential advantage of White House representation for any group, but especially for one fighting to become established, is the visibility of the White House (Grossman and Kumar 1981). The enormous publicity attendant upon presidents tends to throw the spotlight of public attention on White House staff (Anderson 1968:4). The president's special ability to attract publicity could offer a unique benefit to groups desiring to raise awareness of their needs in their previously unaroused members and in the public at large.

A White House location also enables an interest group to borrow some degree of prestige from the president. This prestige can benefit the group in several important ways. First, prestige associated with appointment of an interest group's representative to the White House confers upon the interest the stamp of legitimacy as a proper matter for governmental attention and action. This in turn bolsters the prospect of public support for government action favorable to the group. Second, prestige signals the group's legitimacy to government actors at all levels as well as to leaders of various organizations throughout society and enhances the probability of their responsiveness to group demands. Finally, the prestige of having been chosen for representation on the staff of the president may lend weight to a group's proposals for legislation and executive agency actions.

Consumer groups never viewed a White House presence as a sufficient voice in government. Rather, a representative at the White House was conceived as part of "covering all the bases" in a campaign to advance their interests, which included continued lobbying of Congress for other helpful measures.

Hazards and Liabilities of a White House Location

For all these advantages, a White House position is also characterized by dependency upon the president, which carries with it enormous potential for problems on the part of White House staff whose agenda might not closely fit with the goals and policies of the president. White House appointees are almost completely dependent upon the chief executive for the opportunity and ability to act for the interests of the external group they represent (Rourke 1969:24; Seligman 1956:422; Seidman 1977:79–80). Dependence is even more acute in the cases of staff whose appointment did not require confirmation by the Senate and who do not represent a department, agency, or other well-organized constituency.

A White House location also carries with it major hazards from the highly symbolic nature of the position. According to Murray Edelman (1964), the chief characteristic of symbolic solutions in politics is that they provide the image but not the reality of change. There is the appearance of action being taken, but nothing really happens. When a group accepts a symbolic solution to its problems, it ceases complaining even though its demands have not actually been met. Aides may find that the president exercises very little power on behalf of the interest they represent or even ignores what they are doing.

Because members of the White House staff are totally dependent upon the president for authority, deference from other political actors, administrative discretion, and budget and staff resources, the extent of a president's commitment to the causes that the White House staffer represents is crucial to a representative's ability to act on behalf of that group. Therefore, the potential worth of representation in the White House depends upon the factors conditioning presidential commitment to the advancement of the group's causes.

The factors likely to affect presidential commitment to the consumer group agenda include ideology, party, preferences for working in general policy areas, personal goals, general political context at a given time, policy priorities (including those on currently pending legislation), and perceived needs in a strategy for attaining reelection. These factors could also incline a president to be more responsive to the needs of groups other than consumers. With the following accounts of efforts by White House consumer representatives to reap the advantages of their White House position, I consider the effect of these factors on group success.

ACCESS, ADVISING, AND ADVOCACY

The major advantage of a White House position is access to top policymakers. However, despite considerable variation in the formal institutional position of consumer representatives, in no administration did representatives have the easy in and out of the Oval Office reserved for a particular small number of aides in each presidency. Interaction between the representatives and presidents was not frequent, although it was far more frequent in the Carter administration than in the others. It was primarily on ceremonial occasions that the representatives and the presidents were together. Thus very little advice or advocacy from the representative reached the president, either directly or indirectly. In all but one administration, wherever consumer advice or advocacy finally rested, it was rarely heeded.

Several factors of the advising process contributed to these outcomes. First, in only three administrations did the consumer representative even have formal direct access to the president. Second, in only one of these was this formal organization reflected in the actual reporting situation. Third, in most administrations, the top aides close to the president to whom the representatives reported were not sympathetic to the consumer group cause. Some of these aides did not feel it necessary to read the representative's memos or to convey any of their contents to the president. In several administrations, advocacy and even advising were not actually roles of the consumer representative, with access arrangements meaning little to the quest for consumer group goals. In all administrations but one, aides closer to the president, not the consumer adviser, made the important decisions on consumer affairs. In the following brief sections, I describe the arrangements for access of the consumer units in each administration, moving from those with the least to those with the most direct access. The sections include examples illustrating the ways in which consumer representatives' advice and advocacy were affected by the access arrangements. The examples selected relate to the representatives' advocacy of top consumer group priorities, primarily those emphasizing procedures that could force consideration of consumer interests in executive branch policymaking.

Kennedy

Kennedy was the first president to initiate authentic though minimal consumer representation at a high level of the executive branch. Political promises and potential constituency advantages notwithstanding, Kennedy decided not to create a consumer counsel. Rather, the Council of Economic Advisers (CEA) would have the principal consumer-related function, including supervision of the Consumer Advisory Council. The administration's delay in establishing representation and its weakened form were largely responses to business fears about consumer representation in the White House.[9]

In virtually all matters, the CAC would be dependent on the CEA.[10] Indeed, the president rarely received CAC advice directly. Kennedy met with the unit three times, twice on occasions that were largely ceremonial and once at a regular CAC meeting. The bulk of the members' access to the president was through the CEA, whose members received council advice and then conveyed it to top presidential assistants.[11] Because the CEA did not want the CAC attached to it, the host unit could not be expected to be very helpful in advancing the policy priorities of consumer groups. The principal objections to the CAC that Walter Heller, CEA director, raised were that the CAC was not related to the CEA's major missions and that it was difficult to finance. Anxiety over possible public dissent on the part of CAC members exacerbated the strain in relationships between CEA staff and CAC members.[12] A plaintive memo written by a CEA staff member captures the resentment the economic advisory unit felt toward the CAC. The memo was titled, "Who left this bastard on our doorstep?" and recommended that the CEA be relieved of its onerous responsibility (Seidman 1977:268). For their part, CAC members were deeply concerned that their messages might not be reaching the president through their organizational pipeline, namely, Heller.[13]

In the Kennedy administration, the major goal the consumer advisory unit advocated was the establishment of a counsel at the White House with direct access to the president and the ability both to represent consumers in agency procedings and before congressional committees and to advise the president. Although he ignored the CAC's wishes on most issues, Kennedy did follow the direction of his CAC's advice on the crucial matter of enhancing consumer representation at the White House. Yet he diluted its proposal so much that its intent was barely recognizable in his plan,[14] which featured an interagency President's Committee on Consumer Interests, with the representative as chair instead of as counsel who reported directly to the president and represented consumers in legislation and agency policy processes.

Ford

Ford made the office of his special assistant for consumer affairs part of the new Office of Public Liaison. Ford's SAPCA, Virginia Knauer, reported to the director of OPL, who reported to the president through one of Ford's top nine aides. The reorganization reflected the elimination of the SAPCA's role as advocate for consumer group goals and the superordinance of the assistant's new role as participant in the OPL's major program, promoting an image of the president's openness and candor.[15] Reinforcing the change in Knauer's role was Ford's nomination strategy. To placate the right wing of his party and business groups, he had to denounce the proposed consumer agency already condemned by Ford's chief rival, Ronald Reagan.[16]

Although consumer group leaders in the Ford era were making their most intense drive ever for an independent consumer agency with strong powers, the White House consumer representative had as her principal task the promulgation of the president's counterproposal to the agency through twelve public conferences held nationwide. Ford's plan called for weak consumer representatives in the agencies.[17]

Reagan and Bush

As Ford had done, Reagan placed his SAPCA in OPL, reporting to an assistant to the director of OPL who in turn reported to the president's chief of staff. This organization manifested the relative unimportance of consumer representation to Reagan compared to his predecessor. After a year and a half, the SAPCA was moved to HHS. Knauer's staffers reported that she saw the president once in a while but declined to mention the occasions for such meetings.

The SAPCA was unable to advocate group goals because there was no place in Reagan's agenda for any of them. In the 1980 campaign, Reagan strongly opposed strengthened consumer representation in government and disparaged the consumer movement. He stated that his basic goals for the economy, reduction of inflation and unnecessary government regulation, would be the best means of advancing the interests of consumers.[18]

Bush's placement of his special adviser to the president for consumer affairs replicated the organizational pattern of the Reagan era. Although the new SAPCA, Bonnie Guiton, had the title of presidential adviser, she was located in HHS. No striking changes from the preceding administration regarding access were evident, but Guiton did work with consumer groups on some projects acceptable to the groups. However, Bush gave no indication that he would be open to making top consumer group goals part of his agenda.

Johnson

Peterson and Furness under Johnson, Knauer under Nixon, and Peterson under Carter all formally had the privilege of reporting directly to the president. Formal access notwithstanding, in all but the Carter administration, the SAPCAs reported to top White House aides who were among the half dozen staffers closest to the president. The degree of actual access clearly turned on the consonance of the consumer groups' interests with those of the president. In no administration but Carter's was the consonance close enough to cut a clear path to the president for the consumer assistant.

Johnson's SAPCAs rarely saw the president on business. They saw him more often at social and ceremonial functions.[19] Peterson had more trouble in communicating with the "inner ring"[20] of advisers than did Furness. Neither saw the president often, but Furness believed she could see him if necessary, whereas Peterson felt she was barred from meetings with the president by certain aides, some more hostile than others. When Jack Valenti and Joseph Califano became important contacts, access to the president for Peterson and her written communications became more difficult than it had been when she reported to Walter Jenkins.

Furness reported to Califano, usually through Larry Levinson. Compared to that of her predecessor, the reporting system was relatively cordial and helpful for Furness, but she had considerable trouble getting through to the aides for help. Although her most important ideas did get to the president via the aides to whom she reported, she was sure that Califano also made decisions on behalf of the president.

Although the somewhat different visions of their roles certainly contributed to the communications difficulties Peterson and Furness encountered, the problems stemmed primarily from the various roles consumer affairs played in Johnson's program during the tenure of each SAPCA. One of the foremost roles Johnson desired his early consumer unit to play was that of contributor to the legitimation of his position as successor to the tragically fallen Kennedy. Thus Peterson, whom Kennedy had chosen[21] (but not announced) for the new post of SAPCA, was to continue Kennedy's legacy. Second, Johnson perceived that association with the popularity of the consumer issue would boost his own popularity. Reflecting this aim, Johnson said to Peterson, "Esther, I want every housewife in the country to know I'm on their side."[22] If Peterson's chief role seemed to be the development of a consumer constituency favorable to Johnson, Furness's was clearly to assist Johnson in his new efforts to achieve passage of particular consumer protection legislation. His changed attitude toward such legislation flowed partly from having already achieved success with his first set of legislative measures, budget problems, and the growing popularity of consumerism (Califano 1975:131–132).

Even though Furness became a strong advocate for consumer interests, she did not publicly dissent from administration positions, whereas Peterson occasionally expressed unauthorized, but not expressly prohibited, positions. These statements, intended to assist in fulfilling her task of raising consumer consciousness, often brought a flood of wrath upon the White House from the business community, making Peterson a political liability.

Access depends partially on the perception of what aides consider appropriate use of the channels to the president available. Both Peterson and her counterpart under Nixon often expressed a reluctance to bother the president for what could be seen as relatively minor matters. Peterson chose not to use numerous social contacts with the president to bring up problems associated with her representation of consumers.

Johnson's SAPCAs, like Kennedy's CAC, promoted a consumer counsel at the White House. They also worked for tough, enforceable features for the many consumer protection laws Johnson was trying to get on the books. In 1968, the administration did appoint a counsel with unclear responsibilities but put it in the Justice Department rather than in the White House.[23]

The SAPCAs were not able to greatly influence the administration's policies in regard to legislation considered high priorities of their offices, for example, credit practices and truth in packaging. First, Peterson found it difficult to persuade Johnson to include them on his legislative agenda (Peterson 1982:201). Nor did she play a central role in dealing with these issues when the administration bills were being drafted and promoted. Relegated to the sidelines, the consumer office was dismayed to see that the emphasis was on getting any kind of bill through the Congress, not necessarily one with the strong features it had advocated.[24] This high-lighted Johnson's tendency to be more concerned with his legislative batting average, as Larry O'Brien put it, than with the quality of the legislation (O'Brien 1974:196–197).

Nixon

Although he was personally not inclined to do so, Nixon felt forced by public opinion to appoint a consumer representative at the White House. Consumer issues were high on the public and congressional agendas during his tenure.

Virginia Knauer, Nixon's SAPCA, saw the president about once a month, most often in connection with speech writing, especially of the consumer messages Nixon felt compelled to send to Congress.[25] At first, her liaison was John Ehrlichman, counsellor to the president, then Peter Flanigan, known to business as "our man in the White House."[26] Though associated with Flanigan's office, Knauer usually had her work reviewed first by Flanigan's assistant. The staff to whom Knauer reported passed along to the president the ideas they approved or thought would interest him. Flanigan was the actual coordinator of consumer policies and programs for the administration and made substantial changes in Knauer's legislative and regulatory proposals, even in some cases after prior public statements about them had been approved.[27]

During the Nixon administration, two important types of proposals were made with the goal of strengthening consumer representation in the executive branch. Although Knauer was in general agreement with both, in the end Nixon's SAPCA was not able fully to support either. One plan Knauer advocated involved making the office of the SAPCA statutory and giving it the functions of a counsel that was to provide representation for consumers in agency and court proceedings. The other effort, number-one priority of the consumer movement, would have established a strong independent agency for consumer protection.

Knauer's work on a bill for her office was ignored in favor of recommendations from the Justice and Commerce departments working with Flanigan. The administration bill gave the counsel function to the Department of Justice (noted for its lack of sympathy for consumer interests) instead of to the White House Office. The Nixon proposal for an agency was a weak counterproposal to bills already under consideration on Capitol Hill. The SAPCA had to testify in 1971 and 1973 for the diluted administration proposals rather than those promoted by all others bearing credentials as consumer advocates. At the same time, other administration officials worked behind the scenes to gut the bills.[28]

Carter

Carter was the first president who viewed consumer groups as a significant constituency in his governing and electoral coalition. In addition, his populist leanings inclined him to identify with their program. As a result he gave the consumer representatives an authentic role at the White House. Esther Peterson accepted the position as Carter's SAPCA only after she received strong assurances from the president that she would report directly to him and that there would not be obstacles to her doing so (Peterson 1982:209–210). When the OPL was established at the Carter White House in 1978, adding the representatives of many groups to the staff, the consumer unit did not become part of it. Peterson remained the chief White House contact for consumers.[29]

Peterson's sole assignment for the first year was working for the passage of the top priority of consumer groups, the Agency for Consumer Protection (ACP) bill. She was given the authority to do everything in her power to secure the goal. During that year, Peterson met with Carter occasionally (four times) and more frequently with his top aides, Stuart Eizenstat and Simon Lazarus. Additionally, through telephone communications, Peterson prevailed upon the president to make appearances on behalf of the agency and to make last-minute calls to members of the congressional committee considering it.[30]

Even in the sympathetic Carter administration, the White House consumer representatives found staff to be an obstacle to the promotion of the top consumer proposal. What disturbed Peterson the most was the "pulling" of the bill from the congressional agenda without her approval. Although the tally by Peterson's office showed sufficient congressional votes for passage, other members of the administration thought that the bill couldn't pass in the current session. Consumer unit staff were also very disappointed in the lack of energy and precision with which the Office of Congressional Liaison approached their task as primary lobbyists for the bill.[31]

After the bill's defeat, Peterson's easy access to Carter continued and was enhanced by formal inclusion in the institutionalized system for domestic legislative development. The process centered on the so-called presidential review memorandum, which went to relevant members of the Executive Office and Cabinet who were asked for opinions on particular issues. Being a link in this paper loop was considered an important part of potential influence in the Carter White House (Wayne 1978:205). Peterson and her staff also participated in ad hoc and formal meetings of White House policymaking personnel, including the regular morning staff meetings.

Carter's SAPCA was given freedom to work on any consumer areas she considered significant. The first recommendation of her office was an outline of the administration's options in developing a consumer affairs policy.[32] Thus Carter's consumer unit basically planned its own access relationships with the rest of the EOP as well as its own policy directions.

Peterson's office continued to use its advising capacity to promote consumer group priorities and to assist in selections for appointments to consumer-sensitive agencies. The unit added the consumer group voice to executive branch policymaking by entering myriad comments into the records of agency rulemaking and even formally intervening in five agency adjudicatory proceedings. After the defeat of the ACP bill, groups generally viewed promotion of public participation in agency proceedings as the main priority, so Peterson requested that Carter include calls for institutionalized consumer representation on every feasible occasion. Heeding these requests, the president took several significant steps to expand opportunities for private citizens, public interest groups, and small businesses to participate in agency proceedings. These included support of bills already in congressional committees, requests in messages to Congress and heads of executive departments, and a bill.[33] Although Peterson had to fight to be included in some issues, the continual, systematic, and broad advising role of Carter's consumer office contrasted starkly with the episodic and extremely limited opportunities for advising available to its predecessors.

Evaluation of White House Access

Access turned out be a minor asset to consumer groups, for in no administration but one was the potential advantage of access fully realized. There were only small differences from administration to administration in the degree of actual access achieved. A position on the White House staff symbolized consumers' access to the president, but it did not provide access in significant measure. Consumer groups made themselves heard and exerted some influence on policymaking through their representatives at the White House. But the voice of the White House consumer representative was almost always a minor one and was unable to serve as an instrument of significant progress toward the enactment of consumer group policy priorities.

Of course, the value of access has to be judged partly by the extent to which a representative's advice is acted upon in a way favorable to the external constituency represented. Only in Carter's administration was the White House consumer representative a major architect of administration consumer affairs policy. There was a consistent preemption of the consumer advising function by aides closest to the presidents. Because the formal representatives of consumer groups, like those of all groups, have at least somewhat divided loyalties, it is not surprising that it was top aides with unimpeachable loyalty who made the decisions on consumer affairs. The ascendancy of the inner circle in policy advising seen here lends credence to the assertion by Stephen Hess that the people upon whom the president most depends always seem to belong to the inner White House staff rather than to other parts of the Executive Office (Hess 1976:161). When advice from the consumer advisers was acted upon favorably, it usually related to minor measures to assist some consumers in particular instances. For example, advice was taken that led to modest improvements in credit practices and the contents of hot dogs. No president but Carter acted upon a consumer representative's suggestions on matters central to consumer group priorities. And even Carter, who consistently worked for consumer causes, did not make them a major priority, except for the agency bill at the outset of his term. Of course, he lost the battle for the agency, thus underlining in one more way the fallacy of counting heavily on presidents for advancement of consumer goals. In the end, the value of a president as champion for group causes turns on a president's general effectiveness.

In sum, throughout six administrations, the consumer advocates' prime goal of compelling consideration of their interests in high-level executive policymaking to the same degree as those of other major interests in the economy was rarely realized through the potential advantage of White House access. The addition of a consumer representative to the presidency was an institutional alteration (some would call it a decoration), but it was not accompanied by changes in process within the institution sufficient to compel greatly increased consideration of consumer interests in policymaking. Neither was it instrumental in the enactment of changes in other policymaking institutions that would generate attention to those interests. This outcome is consistent with the general finding that presidents are free to do what they will with advisers on their staffs.

The utter dependence of White House aides upon the president means that group representatives will only be given the authority and other resources sufficient to significantly advance the interests of their external constituents if the president makes these interests a priority concern. For this to happen, the interests of the representative's external constituency would have to be almost completely consonant with those of the president in the relevant issue areas. The president's ideology, party concerns, policy and electoral priorities, and the general political context would all have to lend themselves to sympathy with consumer group goals.

The ideology and various party concerns of Republican presidents always operated in one way or another against making the consumer group agenda their own. On the other hand, for Democratic presidents, ideology and party tended to work in favor of the consumer groups' goals, even if not their major ones. Yet (except during the Carter years) the level of access and advice taken was only slightly higher in Democratic than in Republican administrations.

Neither was the political context (such as public opinion or the economic climate) a deciding factor in the value of access. At the height of pro-consumer public opinion, Nixon and Ford did everything in their power to stifle the consumer agenda. Ideology, reelection support from the conservative wing of their party, and higher regard for the agendas of other interest groups (such as business) and executive branch units (such as the Department of Commerce and the Department of Justice) contributed to Nixon and Ford's resolve to oppose the top consumer group proposals.

In contrast, at a time when the popularity of consumer issues had begun to wane, Carter nonetheless made consumer group priorities an important part of his campaign and governing program. For this president, philosophy, party, electoral, and governing incentives came together to make consumer group priorities consonant with what he saw as his own interests and thus a relatively significant concern for him. Carter had predelictions for policy directions close to those desired by consumer groups, especially those related to opening up the policymaking process to democratic participation. He also agreed with them that consideration of citizen group interests should be compelled by various mechanisms on the basis that it was morally right that they should be considered.[34] Moreover, he needed to overcome an image as a white southern conservative to win the favor of his party, many of whom doubted his progressive credentials. Finally, the consumer constituency itself was perceived as a helpful, although not major, part of a possible electoral and governing coalition (Fishel 1985:58–69; Pomper et al. 1977:145).

This investigation suggests that, given the conditions necessary for presidential support, institutionalized interest representation in the White House is not a guarantee for any significant policy changes or initiatives. It seems more likely that interests having continuous access to the president through channels based on real mutual needs will more frequently be able to turn that access into desired policy outcomes. As David Plotke shows in Chapter 8, representatives of business groups appear most often to have this type of access. Every administration apparently needs to placate business interests whether within or outside government. Presidents have to nourish relationships with the business community because of the important role business plays in determining economic prosperity. In order to fulfill the traditional role as custodian of the national interest and the modern role as guardian of prosperity, the president must work toward general economic success that benefits large portions of the citizenry (Lindblom 1977; McQuaid 1982). The related need to placate business necessarily diminishes the degree to which the president can be committed to advancing consumer and environmental interests (Lucco

1990), also an appropriate goal for the custodian of the national interest. This is the case because business groups are always the most intense and active opponents of measures that are consumer and environmental group priorities.

In view of these many obstacles to advising and advocacy, it may be that the greatest benefit to consumers that the White House representatives achieved through access was a heightened awareness of distinct consumer interests on the part of government officials who came in contact with this office. At the minimum, this may have led to a greater sensitivity by such officials to the interests of consumers.

It could be argued that the publicity and prestige captured by White House location was by itself sufficient to make the consumer representatives' tenures successful. Publicity is especially important for a diffuse aggregate such as consumers because it cuts information costs and is thereby a means of assuring that increased numbers of people will receive the information advocates of a cause wish to deliver and may consequently become mobilized (Downs 1957:ch. 13). In some administrations there is evidence of consumer mobilization resulting from White House publicity. However, it is impossible to distinguish between the effects of publicity emanating from the White House and of publicity generated by consumer advocates in Congress or the private sector. It is clear, though, that association with presidential prestige contributed to the legitimacy of consumer issues as concerns of the government.

Irrespective of advances facilitated by visibility and prestige, throughout the administrations studied, consumer group leaders believed that their White House position was insufficient to meet their representational needs in the policymaking process. Consequently, at least through the Carter administration, they continued their unrelenting campaign to establish executive branch structures and processes that could supplement White House actions on behalf of consumers. Their efforts make it clear that, despite the high degree to which formal White House offices of interest representation exhibit symbolism (as described in Edelman 1964), consumer groups have avoided the major hazards of symbolism, quiescence, or co-optation of those for whom the symbol was constructed.

IMPLICATIONS FOR THE FUTURE

Consumer interests as defined by consumer groups have been established as legitimate concerns for the governmental agenda despite strenuous efforts in the 1980s to delegitimize them (Harris and Milkis 1989:especially ch. 4). As a result, perhaps institutionalized representation in government is less important. The EPA, though not exclusively established to represent environmentalists in the way that the ACP was designed to represent consumers, has certainly often served as a vehicle for advancing the environmental agenda of organized groups. However, throughout the 1980s consumer groups themselves have provided a countervailing force in policymaking, albeit usually one with far fewer resources than opposing interests in any given policy battle. The question today is whether these private groups can sustain a sufficient counterbalance to other groups in the policymaking process that are smaller, better organized, and gifted with more material resources as well as the intensity of producer interests.

Citizen groups constitute only 4 percent of the total proportion of all groups represented by lobbyists in the nation's capital (Schlozman 1984:1012–1013). Can their ability to rouse public support compensate for their striking dearth of other resources? Many of them have found ways to frugally maintain themselves without depending upon government. In some cases they have also gone to work in grassroots arenas. Barring the attainment of an agency to act on their behalf, it may be that the only feasible representation in policymaking for most of these hard-to-organize interests is through independent private organizations of the type currently most effective. Such organizations generally have a small professional staff and broad support manifested by most members in continuing financial contributions but little other activity.

The Bush administration has made conciliatory moves toward consumer and environmental groups totally spurned by the Reagan administration. These actions most likely reflect not only Bush's desire to be kinder and gentler but also the administration's submission to the inevitability (notwithstanding efforts of the preceding administration) of the intrusion of public interest groups into the federal policymaking process. Consumer and environmental groups experience cycles of favor with government policymakers, but they have apparently institutionalized their concerns through a combination of publicity and legitimation based partially upon White House representation, some success in the 1970s at gaining legislative provisions for citizen representation in agency proceedings, and through their enduring, if tiny, presence in the universe of Washington lobbyists. Because of this institutionalization and the ability of consumer leaders to produce adverse publicity, the consumer groups also play some role in influencing electoral politics. This is the case as well for many of the other groups who attained formal representation at the White House in the 1960s and 1970s, for example, blacks and the elderly.

Strong public opinion is currently doing more to reinforce the efforts of environmental groups than those of consumer organizations to advance their agendas. Agency heads in the Bush administration have, however, initiated meetings with consumer group leaders and made amiable appearances at the first Consumer Assembly[35] of the 1990s. In these forums, they asked for consumer activists' support or at least participation in dialogue where support is out of the question. This reaching out may signal stoic acceptance of the consumer organizations as a force that must at least in some measure be taken into account in presidential and other executive branch policymaking of the 1990s, even if they are without an agency, department, or White House advocate of their own.

NOTES

1. Although there is continuing debate about what the public interest is or indeed if there is one, in the tradition of such scholars as E. E. Schattschneider (1975:26) and Grant McConnell (1966:364–368), I adhere to the idea that public interests are identifiable to the extent that something can be said about them. In common usage, public interests are collective interests belonging to all or very large groups of citizens.

2. The advocates were individuals and, increasingly, a type of organization known as a "public interest group," defined by Jeffrey Berry (1977:7) as "one that seeks a collective good, the achievement of which will not selectively and materially benefit the membership or activities of the organization."

3. The sources upon which the investigation reported here was based include documents from presidential libraries, other government documents, and numerous personal interviews with White House consumer representatives from each administration and their staffs as well as with consumer group leaders.

4. Evidence of consensus on priorities was obtained between 1978 and 1984 in personal interviews with consumer group leaders, including Esther Peterson, National Consumers League president and board member (as well as a member of the White House staffs of Johnson and Carter); Erma Angevine, executive director of the Consumer Federation of America from its founding in 1967 through 1973; Joan Claybrook, director of Public Citizen and previously of Congress Watch (groups founded by Ralph Nader), as well as director of the National Highway Traffic Safety Administration (NHTSA) under Carter; Sandra Willett, executive director of the National Consumers League; Mark Silbergeld, director of the Washington office of the Consumers Union; Lee Richardson, president and board member of the Consumer Federation of America as well as head of several state and local consumer groups (and White House staffer in the Nixon and Carter administrations); and Midge Shubow, officer of the Consumer Federation of America and press secretary to Carter's consumer assistant. Further evidence can be found in *Consumer Federation of America Policy Resolutions* (Washington, D.C.: Consumer Federation of America, annually) and James R. Wagner, "Consumer Agency: Is This Finally the Year?" *Congressional Quarterly Weekly Report*, February 5, 1977:205.

5. The concept of widening the scope of conflict to change the outcomes was discussed in Schattschneider 1960.

6. See Downs 1957 and Olson 1965 for academic theories concerning the difficulties of organizing broad, diffuse, nonproducer interests.

7. Other prominent consumer advocate priorities were mechanisms to force consideration of their interests in judicial policymaking processes that, it should be noted, increasingly related to judgments concerning the constitutionality of executive agency policymaking. Important among these were class action enhancement and enlarged standing to sue.

8. Interviews with Erma Angevine and Esther Peterson; minutes of the first meeting of the CAC, July 19, 1962, John F. Kennedy Library (hereafter, JFKL).

9. Memo on Meeting Dealing with Consumer Counsel, May 12, 1961, JFKL; Memo from John Lewis to Myer Feldman, August 15, 1963, JFKL.

10. The following activities and features of the CAC were under the jurisdiction of the CEA: plans for meetings, procedures, budget, staff, membership, and contact with other agencies and the public.

11. Minutes of the First Meeting of the CAC, July 19, 1962, JFKL.

12. Memos from Walter Heller to President Kennedy, October 8, 1962, and June 1, 1963, JFKL; Memos from Heller to Myer Feldman, July 29, 1963, and March 8, 1963, JFKL.

13. Minutes of the Third Meeting of the CAC, November 30, 1962, JFKL; Letter from Persia Campbell to Heller, March 13, 1963, JFKL.

14. CAC, Draft of First Report, June 25, 1962, JFKL; Caroline Ware, "Participant's Analysis of the Experience of Consumer Agencies in the Federal Government: 1933–1963," JFKL.

15. Don Bonafide, "White House Report/ Staff Is Organized to Ensure Accessibility to Ford," *National Journal*, December 28, 1974:1954–1957.

16. "Consumer Policy," *Congressional Quarterly Almanac* 1975:560.

17. See, for example, Memos from John Schlaes to John Byington, November 11, 1975, and November 12, 1975, Gerald R. Ford Library.

18. *New York Times*, August 21, 1982:23.

19. Except where otherwise noted, the following accounts of access to President Johnson are based primarily on oral histories of SAPCAs from the Lyndon B. Johnson Library (hereafter, LBJL) and personal interviews with White House staff.

20. This term is from Valenti 1984:13.

21. David Angevine (CAC member), Oral History, LBJL.

22. Peterson, Oral History, November 25, 1968, LBJL.

23. The appointee died soon after taking office and was not replaced.

24. In addition to Peterson's oral histories (LBJL), see Price 1972:28, 34, and Peterson 1982:206.

25. Interviews with Virginia Knauer. See also Andrea F. Schoenfeld, "CPR Report/Mrs. Knauer, Consumer Envoy Both for and to the White House," *National Journal*, January 10, 1970:90.

26. Walter Rugaber, "'Our Man' at White House," *New York Times*, January 7, 1973:35.

27. John D. Morris, "Lack of Authority Hampers Nixon Consumer Aide," *New York Times*, December 26, 1969:27; Nate Hasetine, "Information Drug Center Considered," *Washington Post*, March 26, 1963:A1; Schoenfeld, "CPR Report/ Mrs. Knauer," 90.

28. "Consumers," 29 *Congressional Quarterly Almanac* 1973:416–418; "Consumer Policy," 30 *Congressional Quarterly Almanac* 1974:309–314; Walterene Swanston, "Washington Pressures/ Consumer Federation of America Waging Spirited Battle for Survival," *National Journal*, July 8, 1972:1134–1135.

29. Interviews with Anne Wexler (head of OPL), Edward Cohen (Peterson's deputy), Lee Richardson, and Sandra Willett.

30. Interviews with Peterson, Cohen, and Shubow. See also "Speaker Calls Off Consumer Agency Vote," *Congressional Quarterly Almanac* 1977:437–438.

31. Interviews with Angevine, Cohen, Richardson, and Shubow. See also Larry Kramer, "Consumers' Voice Speaks Up," *Washington Post*, June 3, 1978:B8.

32. Interviews with Peterson and Cohen.

33. Interviews with Peterson and Cohen. See also "White House Consumer Post Given Decision-making Role," *Congressional Quarterly Weekly Report*, May 13, 1978:1182; "Carter Regulatory Reform Message," *Congressional Quarterly Weekly Report*, March 3, 1979:601–602.

34. Interview with Joan Claybrook. See also Hargrove 1988.

35. The Consumer Assembly, sponsored by the Consumer Federation of America (an umbrella organization of about 240 groups), is the largest annual meeting of consumer-related groups.

12

Conservative Interest Group Litigation in the Reagan Era and Beyond

KAREN O'CONNOR
BRYANT SCOTT McFALL

In 1980, conservatives widely heralded the election of Ronald Reagan as the dawn of a new era and a long-awaited opportunity to advance their considerable political agenda. This "blueprint for change" included not only a litany of new legislative proposals for Congress to consider but also the hope that the courts, too, could be used as a vehicle to reshape and reverse liberal judicial rulings that began in the Warren era (1953–1969). Moreover, there was a common understanding that the Reagan administration would not have to stand alone in its effort to reshape the judiciary and the direction of the law. By the mid-1970s, myriad conservative public interest law firms and special interest litigating groups were created. Moreover, many conservatives believed that these new voices would effectively pursue the conservative agenda through litigation.

In this article we examine conservative public interest litigation in the 1980s. Karen O'Connor and Lee Epstein (1983b) found that conservative interest group involvement in Supreme Court litigation grew steadily from 1969 to 1980. By 1980, conservative groups were participating in some fashion in one of every five cases decided by the Court. Later, in discussing the continued historical development of conservative litigators, Epstein (1986:156) concluded that "conservative interest group litigation will become an increasingly important phenomenon deserving of further study." Whether this expected growth and importance of conservatives as a presence in the Court has occurred, however, is unclear. Numerous researchers continue to document resort to the courts by interest groups (Epstein and Rowland 1991; Schlozman and Tierney 1986) and to assert that the courts, especially the Supreme Court, increasingly find themselves "in the position of having to mediate between group interests" (Epstein 1986:156). In light of scholarly expectations that conservatives would play an important role in the numerical increase and group conflict before the Supreme Court, an examination of conservative interest group participation before the Supreme Court is extremely timely.

Our examination is made even more important because by the late 1980s the print media were reporting conflicting accounts of the effectiveness and success of conservative forays into the judicial arena. Some journalists heralded the efforts of conservative public interest groups (Abramson 1988:18; Gest 1988:32), whereas others warned of their atrophy (Farney 1987:50). In this chapter we first discuss the role of interest groups in the judicial process. We then focus in detail on the development of conservative litigating interest groups. In the third section we provide quantitative data concerning rates of participation and discuss conservative public interest law in the Reagan era. To enrich the quantitative data presented here, we conducted a series of personal interviews with numerous key conservatives and conservative group litigators. Highlights from these interviews appear in the fourth section. In our concluding section we speculate on the future of the conservative public interest law movement.

INTEREST GROUPS IN THE JUDICIAL PROCESS

As early as 1908, Arthur Bentley noted that just as the legislature was open to lobbying efforts by organized outside interests, so, too, was the U.S. Supreme Court. Although Bentley focused largely on the role groups played in the selection process of Supreme Court justices, David Truman (1951) pointed out another type of interest group use of the courts: to maintain the status quo through litigation. According to Truman, these generally conservative groups often resorted to the courts after first achieving a voice in agency policymaking or access to legislators. Ironically, the first wave of scholars who examined the strategies and tactics of groups that lobbied the courts concentrated their efforts on liberal groups that sought change rather than the more politically powerful forces that chose litigation in the hope of reinforcing the status quo.

Clement E. Vose was one of the first to conduct a systematic study of one group's efforts to achieve change through the courts. In *Caucasians Only* (1959), Vose provided an exhaustive account of the NAACP's litigation activities that culminated in its successful effort to win judicial invalidation of racially restrictive covenants. Subsequently, other scholars "updated" accounts of the NAACP's efforts to improve the status of blacks in a variety of other areas: education (Kluger 1976; Wasby 1984), employment (Belton 1978; Greenberg 1977; Wasby 1986), and discriminatory imposition of the death penalty (Meltsner 1973), for example.

Given the liberal orientation of most academics writing well into the 1980s, it is not surprising to find that subsequent studies of the Vose genre usually also focused on liberal groups.[1] Most of these interest group scholars concluded that each of the groups studied preferred to sponsor cases to the High Court, although that was not always possible. Pure "test-case" litigation efforts are rare. One such effort began in 1939, NAACP officials decided to tackle segregated schools in the courts. Any efforts to obtain change in legislatures or school boards in the heart of the Jim Crow South would obviously have been futile, so the association's newly created Legal Defense Fund (LDF) launched a carefully conceived series of cases under the direction of Thurgood Marshall, its general counsel. This test-case strategy was designed to prime the Court to overrule *Plessey v. Ferguson*, 163 U.S. 537 (1896) and its shameful legacy. Even though the litigation campaign was carefully planned, plaintiffs well chosen, and a positive climate secured,[2] it still took the NAACP LDF fifteen years to achieve its initial goal in *Brown v. Board of Education*, 347 U.S. 483 (1954).

More recent research (Wasby 1984) reveals the problems faced by the NAACP in "controlling" cases, often considered a key factor in the success of a direct-sponsorship litigation strategy, whereby a single group controls the course of the litigation from the trial court to the U.S. Supreme Court (O'Connor 1980).

Although "control" has become increasingly difficult in a society of proliferating litigating groups (Bruer 1990)[3] some organizations continue to opt for that type of participation. In the 1970s, for example, the Women's Rights Project (WRP) of the ACLU, borrowing a page from the NAACP LDF tactic book, targeted the Supreme Court. At a time when Congress was debating the proposed Equal Rights Amendment, the WRP, under the expert direction of Ruth Bader Ginsburg, systematically brought a series of cases to the Supreme Court in an effort to convince the justices to find that gender was a suspect classification deserving strict scrutiny under the equal protection clause of the Fourteenth Amendment (S. Walker 1990:304–305). But, not surprisingly, as other groups began to litigate for women's rights, the WRP lost its ability to channel the "right" cases to the Court and in many instances was relegated to a more minor role as amicus curiae.

Amicus curiae is a Latin term meaning "friend of the court." The use of amicus curiae briefs dates back to the 1800s. In its original incarnation, the amicus brief was used to inform judges of relevant precedents that were applicable to a case before the court (Krislov 1963:695). As access to the U.S. Supreme Court as a party in interest became increasingly limited, the role of the amicus changed, eventually evolving into an important device by which interest groups were able to express their views. In fact, by the 1930s, the amicus curiae brief was viewed as "an active participant in the interest group struggle" (Krislov 1963:703). Today, members of the

Court appear to use the number of amicus briefs filed in a case as one indicator of the importance of the issues presented (Caldeira and Wright 1988). For example, in a dissenting opinion in a 1990 case noting the tedious nature of the Court's workload, Justice John Paul Stevens wrote, "This is not a decision that will be much celebrated or often cited. . . . Few cases are affected, and not a single brief amicus curiae was filed. . . . [This case] has no apparent importance" (quoted in Marcus 1990:A-12).

So by the 1970s, when the WRP of the ACLU launched its campaign to end gender bias through an expansive judicial interpretation of the equal protection clause, it is not surprising that it frequently filed an amicus curiae brief when a gender discrimination case *not* sponsored by the ACLU was docketed at the Supreme Court. As a group highly interested in the outcome of the case to be argued, it had a stake in the outcome of the litigation not all that different from that of the actual parties.

The WRP was not alone in its reliance on amicus curiae briefs. By 1980, interest groups were filing amicus curiae briefs in more than half of the noncommercial cases decided by the Court. In fact, "amicus curiae participation by private groups [became] the norm rather than the exception" in Supreme Court litigation (O'Connor and Epstein 1981–1982:318).

The inability to supervise a case from trial court to a guaranteed Supreme Court review is not the only reason groups opt for the amicus strategy. The cost of an amicus curiae brief, though it still presents the Court with a particular group's point of view, is considerably lower than the cost of direct sponsorship. The NAACP LDF is reported to have spent over $500,000 to litigate *Brown*. Today, the cost of direct sponsorship is far greater. And exclusive reliance on that strategy can be risky. If, for example, a group expends thousands of dollars to mold a case for appellate review and the U.S. Supreme Court declines to hear the case, a tremendous amount of money and effort may have been spent in vain. Thus many groups have opted to devote a considerable amount of their litigation resources to the filing of amicus curiae briefs (O'Connor and Epstein 1989). And they are a means by which relatively new organizations can have an immediate effect *and* visibility.

The utility of the amicus brief as a lobbying tool has been debated, but for some groups or in many situations, it may be the only way for a group to present its views to the Court. In the main, liberal groups generally have used a combination of direct sponsorship and amicus briefs before the U.S. Supreme Court. In contrast, most conservative groups, with the exception of socially conservative groups such as the Americans United For Life Legal Defense Foundation (a major mover in the abortion rights controversy), prefer the amicus curiae strategy. Most conservative groups are newer than their liberal counterparts, which accounts for part of that preference. From 1969 to 1980, for example, 254 of the 261 appearances by conservative groups before the U.S. Supreme Court were as amicus curiae. In contrast, "liberal groups sponsored 39 percent (N = 265) of the cases in which they [liberal groups] appeared" (O'Connor and Epstein 1983b:482).

THE REEMERGENCE OF
CONSERVATIVE INTEREST GROUP LITIGATION

Concerted conservative group involvement in litigation has a long albeit sporadic history. Vose (1972) and Epstein (1986) have examined in detail the litigation activities of several conservative interests, particularly in the development of cases challenging the constitutionality of federal aid to the states or for federal social or economic welfare programs. In the early 1920s, for example, several individuals and organizations that had been active in the movement to stop ratification of the Nineteenth Amendment, which gave women the right to vote, filed a series of test cases to invalidate the provisions of the Sheppard-Towner Maternity Act. This statute, the first federal grant-in-aid program, offered money to states to fund prenatal clinics. It was opposed by conservatives who viewed the act, like the Nineteenth Amendment, as yet another intrusion into family matters on the part of the government. Later, other conservatives organized to stop Franklin Roosevelt's New Deal legislation in the courts. Groups like the American Liberty League, the National Lawyers' Committee, and the Edison Electric Institute challenged a host of statutes as beyond the scope of congressional power to legislate. Their activities and a conservative Court stymied national recovery for several years until the "constitutional revolution" of 1937. At that time, the U.S. Supreme Court reversed earlier pro-business decisions and abandoned its laissez-faire stance.

Several conservative pro-business groups continued to thrive in the intervening years, but they accomplished little in the courts. It was not until the late 1960s, in fact, that conservatives again began to see the potential utility of a presence in the third branch of government. One of the first areas conservatives targeted was the liberal criminal rights decisions of the Warren Court. Although liberal groups, especially the ACLU, were routinely filing amicus curiae briefs in the Court urging it to afford expanded protections to criminal defendants, there was no voice from the Right defending the law-and-order position. It was to fill this void that the Americans for Effective Law Enforcement (AELE) was born. During the 1970s, the AELE, whose sole tactic is the filing of amicus curiae briefs, participated in almost every major criminal case decided by the Supreme Court.

Conservatives, however, were not solely concerned with issues of law and order. Other conservatives became concerned with issues of welfare reform and the environment, areas in which groups including the ACLU and environmentalists had made considerable inroads through litigation.

In the early 1970s, conservatives in the administration of California Governor Ronald Reagan became frustrated by the repeated victories of liberal public interest law firms that routinely challenged conservative governmental initiatives in court. Business interests also began to feel the pinch of these efforts as liberal groups won important victories in the areas of employment discrimination, the environment, and consumer product safety. One of the first conservatives to enunciate concern about the impact of liberal public interest law was Louis Powell. Just prior to his appointment to the U.S. Supreme Court, appearing before a meeting of the U.S. Chamber of Commerce, he noted:

> Other organizations and groups . . . have been far more astute in exploiting judicial action than American business. Perhaps the most active exploiters of the judicial system have been groups ranging in political orientation from "liberal" to far to the left. . . . It is time for American business—which has demonstrated the greatest capability in all history to produce and influence consumer decisions—to apply their great talents to the preservation of the system itself. (Powell n.d.)

These sentiments encouraged the California Chamber of Commerce to assist in the creation of the Pacific Legal Foundation (PLF), the first conservative public interest law firm in the country. Founded in 1973 in Sacramento, the state capital, the PLF immediately began to litigate in a variety of issue-areas, although it emphasized environmental litigation "generally opposing the claims of numerous environmental protection groups" (O'Connor and Epstein 1984:495).

The ability of the PLF to attract considerable corporate and foundation support allowed it to hit the ground running. These funds in turn helped the PLF to grow quickly and to make a considerable media splash. Conservatives around the nation were quick to take note. A study, in fact, was soon undertaken to determine if the California experience could work effectively in other parts of the country. This study led to the creation of the National Legal Center for the Public Interest (NLCPI), which was to act as a clearinghouse and national umbrella organization to facilitate the creation of other regional public interest law firms with a conservative agenda.

Aided by corporate support and funding from several major conservative foundations, the NLCPI moved quickly to tap conservative resources throughout the country. By 1977 the Southeastern, Mountain States, Gulf Coast and Great Plains, Mid-Atlantic, Mid-American, and Capital Legal foundations were created. Around the same time, the Washington Legal Foundation (WLF), a non-NLCPI firm, was founded by Dan Popeo, a young conservative attorney who had worked in the Nixon and Ford administrations. The WLF also fostered a conservative ideology but was always national in scope. All of these groups attempted to move quickly to make their conservative presence known in the courts.

And these regional firms were not the only groups established in order to bring their view of the public interest to court. For example, the Equal Employment Advisory Council (EEAC) and the National Chamber Litigation Center were created by pro-business interests in Washington, D.C., to litigate more exclusively in areas of concern to big business. The EEAC concentrates largely on issues of affirmative action and comparable worth and lobbies solely as an amicus curiae. In contrast, the National Chamber's litigation agenda includes a wider variety of issues of concern to members of the U.S. Chamber of Commerce.

Members of the religious Right also began to see the utility of litigation in the 1970s. In 1975 the Center for Law and Religious Freedom was created by the Christian Legal Society. It has participated in a variety of cases, especially those involving First Amendment issues, and generally urges the Court to adopt an accommodationist position toward the intermingling of church and state. Also founded in the 1970s was the Americans United for Life (AUL) Legal Defense Foundation. Caught off guard by the Court's liberalization of abortion laws in *Roe v. Wade*, 410 U.S. 113 (1973), pro-life activists quickly recognized that they would have to go to court as well as to the other branches of government to bring about an end to legalized abortion. Moreover, the Center for Law and Religious Freedom and the AUL Legal Defense Foundation frequently participate with another group founded in the 1970s, Concerned Women for America. Founded by Phyllis Schlafly and others who had opposed the Equal Rights Amendment, it was created to capitalize on that victory and to protect traditional family values. In many respects Schlafly's organization resembles the conservative groups that flourished after passage of the Nineteenth Amendment.

By the beginning of the Reagan era, numerous and varied conservative litigating groups were created to advance their version of the public interest in the courts. But did these groups, as scholars and conservatives predicted, resort to litigation in increasing numbers, making the courts a battleground of competing liberal and conservative group interests?

INTEREST GROUP PARTICIPATION BEFORE THE U.S. SUPREME COURT IN THE REAGAN ERA

Participation Rates

Either a liberal or conservative interest group participated in a Supreme Court case in 48.4 percent of the 577 cases decided by the Court in its odd

FIGURE 12.1
Overall Conservative and Liberal Participation in Supreme Court Cases, 1981–1987 Terms

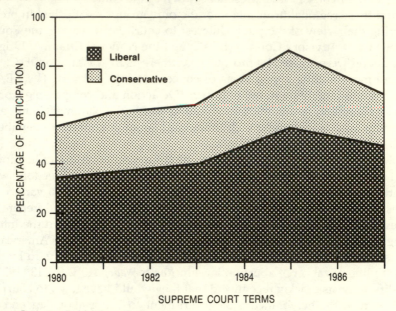

Source: Data compiled by the authors.

terms from 1981 to 1987. Liberal groups participated in 37 percent of the cases, whereas conservative groups were present in 26 percent.

As revealed in Figure 12.1 above, 1985 was an unusually high year for conservative participation. Otherwise, conservative group participation was relatively static during the 1980s and did not approach the increase predicted by O'Connor and Epstein (1983b) or Epstein (1986).

Reagan's election to the White House did not significantly alter conservative patterns of litigation. In the term prior to Reagan's inauguration, conservative groups participated as amicus curiae, as sponsors, or both in 21 percent of the cases (O'Connor and Epstein 1983b:481). With the exception of the 1985 term, this figure deviated only slightly over the course of the Reagan administration. It is clear that conservative interest groups did not step up their efforts to lobby the courts during the Reagan years.

Strategies

In their examination of the 1969–1980 terms of the Court, O'Connor and Epstein (1983b) found that the most common method of lobbying the Supreme Court by both liberal and conservative groups was via the amicus

FIGURE 12.2
Conservative and Liberal Strategies

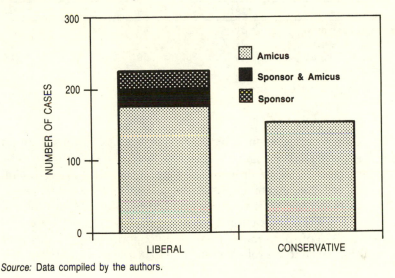

Source: Data compiled by the authors.

curiae brief. Liberal groups participated as direct sponsors of cases far more frequently than did conservative groups.

Our analysis of litigation in the 1981–1987 terms reveals little change in these patterns. As indicated in Figure 12.2, conservatives continued strongly to favor the amicus approach. Of the 154 cases in which conservative groups participated, all but 2 percent of their participation was as amicus curiae. According to Douglas McDowell (1989) of the EEAC, "Being a party in a case is tremendously expensive. You spend most of your money on pretrial maneuvering, and you could easily use up a whole year's budget on one case that never even gets to the point where the issue is presented. . . . It's a waste of time and money." For conservatives, filing an amicus brief was less resource-intensive and delivered more "bang for the buck" (Conrad 1989).

Filing amicus briefs also made it easier for some conservative groups to demonstrate to their members that they were "doing something." As McDowell (1989) said, "A group has to be able to show its members that their efforts are paying off, and filing amicus briefs is the easiest way to do that. If you are a party in a case and it gets resolved by summary judgment, you have nothing to show your membership. When we write an amicus brief, we send it to all our members." Thus the group can use the amicus brief to do more than influence the Court: It can also influence group members and encourage them to continue to support the group and its

TABLE 12.1
Trends in Conservative Litigation Strategies (in percent)

	1981	1983	1985	1987	TOTAL
Two or more conservative groups filed in one case	31	33	45	39	37
Conservatives and liberals filed in one case	38	35	50	36	40

Source: Data compiled by the authors.

goals. The amicus curiae, then, is another way for new groups to build their memberships and prestige.

In contrast to conservatives' preference for amicus curiae briefs, liberal groups sponsored 25 percent of the cases in which they participated. According to one conservative who preferred to remain unnamed, liberal groups had "ten times" the capital assets of conservatives and were able to assume the risks of sponsorship more easily. Sponsorship of test cases also forces the Court into the role of policymaker, a role most conservatives abhor.

Although liberals continued to sponsor cases at rates that dwarfed those of conservatives, their participation was 14 percent lower than the rate during the 1970s. This decline in liberal sponsorship could be due to several factors. Epstein (1986) and Gregory Caldeira and John Wright (1988) speculate that some of this decline could be attributed to the rising costs of litigation or the perceived limited benefits of amicus briefs. It could also be that as the Court has become increasingly conservative as new Republican appointees have taken their place on the bench, liberals are trying to keep cases out of the Court. During the 1988 term, for example, the ACLU agreed to settle an abortion clinic regulations case just before it was to be argued before the Court. In the wake of the restrictive *Webster v. Reproductive Health Services*, 109 S. Ct. 3040 (1989) case, pro-choice activists feared the Court would use the case to restrict women's access to abortions even further (Hardy 1989).

Conservative groups during the 1980s clearly did not step in to fill this void or to take full advantage of the dawn of the Rehnquist Court era (1986 to the present), but some more subtle changes in conservative strategy are evident from the 1980s data. Unlike their liberal counterparts, conservative interest groups generally eschew involvement in a case if another conservative group is already present. So in 1980, for example, more than one conservative group appeared in only 19 percent of the cases the Court heard that term. This was not so in the 1980s. As Table 12.1 indicates, two or more conservative groups filed briefs in over one-third of the cases. Most of this participation was in the form of individually filed briefs. In contrast, amicus briefs liberal groups file are frequently "love fests," that is, it is not uncommon to have thirty or more liberal groups coming together on one brief to apprise the Court of their collective view.

Whether they act in unison or not, it is clear that conservative interest groups tend to file if a liberal group participates. As also indicated in Table 12.1, conservative interest groups participated in 40 percent of the 211 cases in which liberal groups were present. And interviews with key players on both sides of the ideological fence make it apparent that it is conservatives who are filing when liberals are present. Liberal groups tend not to be fazed by conservatives in court (O'Connor and Ivers 1987); in contrast, conservatives routinely see themselves as reacting to liberal participation. They believe it is their collective responsibility to file to present "their view of the public interest" (Bolick 1989; Popeo 1989).

THE ROLE CONSERVATIVES NEVER PLAYED

These data reveal that the increase in conservative interest group litigation that researchers expected did not occur. In light of the proliferation of conservative groups in the late 1970s, the important question is, Why? Three closely related factors appear to be key to this static performance: (1) the election of Reagan, (2) the lack of coordination among conservative groups, and (3) the atrophy of several conservative groups.

The Election of Ronald Reagan

Reagan's election provided the first opportunity in many years for a large influx of conservatives into the ranks of the government, especially the Justice Department and legal offices of key agencies. A significant number of conservative lawyers left fledgling public interest law firms, initially depleting the legal and administrative talent of those organizations. These individuals frequently shared a common understanding that there was a conservative agenda to fulfill. Conservative public interest law firms were affected by this attitude on two levels. The first was membership. Some who were involved in conservative interest groups thought there was no longer "a tiger at the door" (Ayer 1989). Some perceived that membership in a conservative public interest law firm was superfluous now that conservatives controlled the White House. Clint Bolick, a former Mountain States Legal Foundation (MSLF) lawyer who held a string of government positions (including one at the Justice Department), typifies this sentiment. As the director of litigation for the conservative Landmark Legal Foundation Center for Civil Rights,[4] he suggested that the biggest impact of [conservatives in the Justice Department and the Office of Solicitor General] was in funding. For example, when Jim Watt left the Mountain States Legal Foundation to take over the Department of Interior, people erroneously assumed that all of their problems were taken care of. As a result, it was much more difficult for conservative groups to fund-raise in the 1980s than in the previous years.

Patrick McGuigan, director of the Institute for Government and Politics at the conservative Free Congress Research and Information Foundation, echoed these sentiments: "It's hard to raise money in an era where you are perceived as having a lot of clout with the administration in power."

That the Justice Department, including the influential Office of Solicitor General, rested firmly in the hands of conservatives also affected groups at the strategic level. Many conservative interest groups found that their goals overlapped those of the Justice Department or of other administrative agencies. Hence, they saw little need to spend scarce funds on litigation in some areas. According to Don Ayer (1989), principal deputy U.S. Solicitor General from 1986 to late 1988 and until May 1990 the second-ranking member of the Justice Department:

> Conservatives took over the Justice Department. The relationship was not one where conservatives had to sell anybody [in government] on the fundamental ideas that they had been promoting. . . . That battle was essentially won. Therefore, there wasn't any need for conservative interest groups to lobby us on the core issues, such as affirmative action.

Rex E. Lee, the first solicitor general in the Reagan administration, for example, was formerly on the Legal Advisory Board of the Mountain States Legal Foundation. According to Lee (1982), one of the major reasons he took the position was to advance the conservative agenda, particularly in the area of abortion. Because the Solicitor's Office promoted an agenda that conservative interest groups found "satisfactory," groups became complacent. Had there been a Democrat in the White House, conservative interest group litigation activity might have evolved differently. Robin Conrad (1989), director of litigation at the National Litigation Center of the U.S. Chamber of Commerce, surmised that "usually conservative interest group litigation will become more intense if there is a Democratic administration."

Although it is clear that a Justice Department sold on the fundamentals of conservativism affected conservative interest groups' decisions to litigate, it is less clear what sort of relationship the two shared. During his years with the Solicitor General's Office, Ayer (1989) found "no official or formal relationship between conservative interest groups and the Justice Department." He believed a formal relationship was absent because individuals including the solicitor general (Rex E. Lee), the Secretary of the Interior (James A. Watt), and other key players in the Department of Justice and the Department of Energy all had entered the government via their participation in conservative firms. Hence, there "was no need for conversation" between conservative interest groups and the government (Ayer 1989).

Leaders of several conservative groups indicated that in the absence of formal ties, many informal contacts were made (Popeo 1989). In an interview the leader of one group went so far as to note that his organization had "significant contacts in the Justice Department" and that they were in constant contact "in order to interchange and interface policy decisions." It would be inaccurate, however, to conclude that the Justice Department and conservative groups were in complete accord about the scope of the conservative agenda.

Although agreement on the conservative agenda was not always present during the Reagan administration, the president's numerous appointments to the federal bench created a climate ripe for the acceptance of a conservative agenda. Still, as Table 12.1 reveals, litigation by conservatives did not skyrocket. At least initially, Reagan's election ushered in a belief that the fostering of an activist judiciary was wrong. Conservative interest groups recognized that a conservative Court might improve their ability to combat liberal advances. Nevertheless, they perceived that the Court would eschew activism. Popeo of the WLF (1989) explained:

> Conservatives see that the Supreme Court is not going to make law from the bench; they are not going to rewrite the Constitution; they are not going to participate in any form of activism because they believe in judicial restraint. They will put the brakes on activism. The conservative public interest role is not significant enough to play the type of game where the Court is used as a political vehicle in order to achieve political goals that couldn't be accomplished at the ballot box.

Popeo posited that the best way to contrast liberals and conservatives was by comparing their respective litigation strategies. Liberal interest groups viewed the Supreme Court as a mechanism for accomplishing change unattainable through the duly elected legislatures; in contrast, conservatives saw the Court as a body that interpreted the law (Popeo 1989).

Whether or not his assessment of liberal and conservative activity is accurate, it does provide greater insight about why conservatives did not vigorously pursue an activist agenda with a receptive Supreme Court. It appears that they believed that even if they had pushed such an agenda, the Court would not have responded: "It may well be to the good that conservatives did not become more actively involved in the Reagan era. In the 1960s, we had a Court that was . . . shamelessly activist. They were willing to change and make up the law. This meant that they were less embarrassed and bothered . . . that the advocacy to which they were responding was shamelessly political" (Ayer 1989).

It is evident that conservatives set their agendas without regard for the increasingly conservative composition of the Supreme Court. Consequently, though Reagan's election was viewed as a step forward for the larger conservative movement, it did not generate heightened activity by conservatives. Nor did it appear to lead conservatives to band together formally.

Lack of Coordination Among Conservative Groups

As early as 1951, David Truman noted that the formation of alliances was an essential element of interest group prosperity. In the 1980s, however, conservatives rarely acted in concert. In many instances, they avoided cooperation altogether (Popeo 1989). Because most had not been formed until the mid-1970s, many of these groups believed that it was in their best interest to try to position themselves as *the* voice of conservatives in court. In addition, there was fairly intense competition among these groups for both funding and members. As Popeo (1989) observed, "Many groups worried that they were not perceived as the leader. . . . When conservatives tried to coordinate, they did so in the sense that, 'Hey, I'm the king of the mountain, and you guys fall somewhere in line behind me.' . . . The nature . . . of this movement has been that no one wants to be coordinated."

Bickering and petty jealousies also contributed to the lack of coordination among conservatives. Explained Bolick (1989):

> There is bitter and intense institutional jealousy among the conservative organizations. Whereas the Left has learned to work together, the Right has not. There is a perception that there is not enough support . . . so that there is constant competition for money. We are constantly battling among ourselves about what types of judicial action are legitimate. . . . It's also a function of the personalities involved. It's really pathetic how poorly we're able to work together.

Another reason for an absence of cooperation concerns the "diversity" of the conservative agenda. Many conservative pro-business groups refused to coordinate with other conservatives. For example, pro-business groups such as the Equal Employment Advisory Council and the National Litigation Center viewed such an association as counterproductive and not in the best interests or wishes of their members. McDowell (1989) of the EEAC explained, "We are not going to get on a brief with the Washington Legal Foundation. . . . Our members don't care about changing an abortion decision. We are not going to gain anything by pooling our resources with a hard-core conservative public interest law firm. *In fact, it hurts our credibility"* (emphasis added). The failure of conservative groups to coordinate litigation resulted in an increase in the number of conservative amicus briefs being filed in any given case. Unlike liberal groups that frequently file together on a single brief, these separate filings were the result of a conscious effort to abstain from coordination (Popeo 1989). In fact, this probably had a direct effect on the atrophy of several of these conservative groups, the third reason for the failure of conservatives to take advantage of the courts during the 1980s.

The Atrophy of Conservative Litigating Groups

The creation of so many conservative public interest law firms and special interest groups in such a short period in the 1970s led to intense competition for recognition, funds, members, and even personnel. The Capital Legal Foundation quickly broke away from its parent NLCPI and then went on to self-destruct when it invested all of its time and money in an unsuccessful defense of General William P. Westmoreland against CBS.[5] Although this case brought all kinds of media attention to Capital, it was not enough to counteract the impact of protracted litigation that also brought considerable negative publicity to the group. Its founders' attempt to set Capital apart from the pack was successful in one sense yet ultimately led to the group's demise. As Capital and the other new groups attempted to engage in "credit-taking" and to establish a niche for themselves, several failed, thus reducing the number of potential groups able to file amicus curiae briefs.

Popeo (1989), whose WLF survived the Reagan era intact, maintains that the demise of so many groups could be attributed to "poor management, poor leadership, and different priorities": Some groups "operated in a very stodgy, corporate way. They didn't make decisions flexibly enough, and they didn't have a broad enough base of support." Bolick (1989) stated it another way:

What is needed [to make successful leaders of these firms] is three things. First, he or she must be a good lawyer and be able to recognize a good lawsuit; second, he or she must be able to think as a public policy person; and, third, a leader must know how to raise money. For conservatives, finding a leader with these three qualities during the Reagan years was difficult.

The history of the Mountain States Legal Foundation illustrates Bolick's point. The MSLF was one of the last firms founded because of a lengthy search for a "westerner" to head it "who was politically savvy," attuned to the important issues facing the region, and able "to litigate federal laws west of the 100th meridian" (Mellor 1982). Under Watt's capable leadership, the firm grew and quickly established itself as a presence to be reckoned with in the western courts, especially in the areas of conservation and land use. It saw itself as a counterbalance to groups like the Sierra Club and was able to attract substantial financial support from foundations and businesses that were opposed to the claims of environmentalists. But Watt's successes in building the MSLF ultimately hurt the firm. When Reagan was elected in 1980, he turned to Watt to head the Department of the Interior. Watt took several key staff attorneys with him. Later other young staffers were to follow. According to Bolick, "the presence or absence of a single person in one of these law firms can make a huge difference." He cited Watt's departure from the MSLF as particularly crucial in accounting for the firm's demise. Solicitor General Lee (1982), also formerly of the MSLF, has noted that perhaps "the greatest measure" of the success of these firms was their placement of supporters and key personnel in the administration. Nevertheless, this depletion of talent had a profound negative impact on groups like the MSLF, which again had to find committed leaders with fund-raising talents.

These successes in placing individuals in the Reagan administration made for heady times. The MSLF and Pacific Legal Foundation, for example, quickly moved to take advantage of their Washington connections by creating Washington satellite offices. By the late 1980s, it became clear that there were simply not enough funds to keep such offices open, as the efforts expended to establish, fund, and maintain them sapped the firms' resources. All of this occurred at a time when it appeared that they were ready to expand their efforts tremendously.

These setbacks further exacerbated funding problems. Fund-raising was particularly problematic for many of these firms for several reasons, including the explosion of groups, similarity of interests, internal bickering, and the perception that there might not be a need for litigation outside that sponsored by the Reagan administration. To litigate required funds, all the more because, unlike liberal groups, most conservative groups initially refused to engage in litigation to recover attorneys' fees for their efforts. Many groups were forced to cut back tremendously or ceased to exist all together.

Thus the Reagan era did not bear the same fruit for conservative litigators as it did for some other segments of the New Right. From this analysis, we may draw several conclusions regarding the stagnation of conservative interest group litigation during this period. First, conservatives became satisfied with the president's judicial program, virtually took over the Justice Department, and often pushed conservative agendas mirroring those of their private organizations. Second, most groups were relatively new when Reagan came into office and often pursued high-visibility strategies, failing to cultivate their memberships or obtain adequate support from conservative foundations. They also viewed each other as rivals and did not develop close working relationships that might have made them stronger or stopped the duplication of efforts. Finally, their very "newness" and the internal voids left in several of the promising firms when staffers joined the Reagan administration resulted in the atrophy of many groups, especially those that were left leaderless. Thus a period of important settling out within the conservative public interest law community allowed only the most capable and politically savvy to survive.

The Future of the Public Interest Law Movement

During the Reagan administration, conservative interest groups foundered, wasting a "golden opportunity to make an impact on the laws of this country" (Bolick 1989). Many other conservatives have echoed these sentiments but have resolved to turn the tide. The chief justice of California's Supreme Court urged the Pacific Legal Foundation:

> You should not assume that the new court will so readily overturn or reexamine prior decisions. . . . These former decisions will remain comfortably in place until someone has the ambition . . . to raise the question of whether a reexamination of the underlying principles may be appropriate. I suggest [you] . . . play an even more useful and appreciated role than ever before in the development and reshaping of the civil and criminal law. (Quoted in Zumbrun 1989)

Ronald Zumbrun of the PLF and other conservatives believe they can meet this challenge. Although the Reagan administration clearly hurt the initial mobilization of conservative litigation efforts, in the long run the Reagan philosophy was a boon for the development of legal talent. The conservative Federalist Society, which was begun in 1982 at the law schools of the University of Chicago and Yale, has expanded to a network of more than thirty campus chapters. Its faculty advisers have included prominent conservative legal theorists, including Antonin Scalia before his appointment to the Supreme Court. Furthermore, the conservative University of Chicago now has a prominent East Coast counterpart, George Mason University, which serves as a beacon for conservatives. Its new faculty includes two recent albeit unsuccessful conservative nominees to the U.S. Supreme Court, Robert Bork and Douglas Ginsburg. These schools and members of the Federalist Society will undoubtedly provide a strong supply of legal talent and perhaps begin litigating for conservative causes, just as liberals have done for some years. Graduates of these law schools and the society have also recently become an important source of free legal services for the conservative public interest law movement. Many attorneys at high-priced firms now provide pro bono services for conservative causes, long an important resource of legal talent for liberal groups. Former Federalist Society members in private practice, for example, routinely assist in the filing of amicus curiae briefs in cases involving issues such as victims' rights and reverse discrimination (Freinwald 1988).

Groups like the Federalist Society and former members of the Reagan administration and conservative interest group litigators now seem ready to press the conservative agenda on the courts. Conservatives are beginning to see the Court as a potential ally. According to Zumbrun (1989), prior to 1987 it "was very difficult challenging the government in court." In 1987 the Court began to decide cases involving individual rights, land use, and affirmative action in the direction conservatives urged. These decisions began to whittle away at previous liberal precedents and gave renewed hope to conservatives. Finally, the legacy of the Reagan administration—the Rehnquist Court—was viewed as a potential long-term ally.

To capitalize on this friendly Court, conservatives are now engaged in a multifaceted program designed to further their agenda. Grants from the Lilly Endowment and other foundations have allowed the PLF to begin to computerize all pleas, research, tactics, and analysis for dissemination to all other conservative organizations. The PLF hopes that this service will also increase cooperation and contact among conservatives. Pooling resources in this manner is also expected to increase effectiveness.

CONCLUSION

Conservatives now view the 1990s as a tremendous opportunity to reverse many of the decisions of earlier, more liberal Courts. The addition of David Souter to the Court and the retirement of Thurgood Marshall are likely to further its conservatism. Thus more established groups like the Pacific and Washington Legal foundations are likely to continue to do more of the same, trying to target areas such as the environment, affirmative action, and property rights. Newer, and perhaps brasher, groups are trying to replicate the activities of the NAACP by searching out good test cases in order, ironically, to reverse many of the decisions won by the NAACP.

It is likely that the major impact of these groups will come through their sponsorship and not their participation as amicus curiae. Groups that are willing to seek out good test cases—whether the issue is abortion, the environment, affirmative action, or victims' rights—are much more likely to have an impact simply because they provide the money, expertise, and direction to get these cases to the Supreme Court. It seems fairly apparent that as the Court becomes increasingly conservative, these groups will enjoy a forum similar to that enjoyed by liberal groups during the Warren Court era. If they bring the cases, their chances of victory are high. Recent decisions from the Court, such as those dealing with the First Amendment, property rights, and criminal rights, clearly reveal its receptiveness to the arguments being offered by conservatives. Whether conservative firms will be the ones to capitalize on this is uncertain. It does appear, however, that the Reagan administration's fostering of a conservative ideology and the development of a conservative bar and judiciary will have a long-lasting impact on the public agenda as it continues to turn to the right.

NOTES

Karen O'Connor would like to thank Dean Howard O. Hunter and the Emory University Law School Research Fund for support for this project.

1. Other studies of liberal groups have focused on religious lobbies in establishment cases (Ivers forthcoming; Manwaring 1962; Sorauf 1976), women's organizations (O'Connor 1980; O'Connor and Epstein 1983a), and environmentalists (Wenner 1982).

2. The NAACP's efforts to cultivate a favorable climate included asking prominent law professors to place articles in prestigious law reviews urging the Court to overrule decisions that upheld the doctrine of separate but equal enunciated in *Plessey v. Ferguson,* 163 U.S. 537 (1896) relying on sociological data to buttress its legal arguments, and obtaining the support of the U.S. Department of Justice in the form of a supporting amicus curiae brief from the U.S. solicitor general, who is responsible for advancing the interests of the United States in court.

3. *Control* as used here means the ability of a group to initiate and retain direct sponsorship of a case through the appellate levels. Even if a group can control an individual case, it frequently has no say in other cases that may present similar issues to the Court. The kind of optimal litigation environment in which the NAACP operated, in which it was *the* representative of minority interests in court, seldom exists today.

4. The Landmark Legal Foundation Center for Civil Rights was founded by conservatives in the late 1980s. It is modeled after the NAACP LDF and focuses primarily on test-case litigation designed to bring about an end to policies promoting racial preferences such as affirmative action.

5. In 1982 General Westmoreland filed a $120 million libel suit against CBS for its documentary accusing Westmoreland of intentionally manipulating information about enemy strength during the Vietnam War. After a lengthy period in federal court, Westmoreland dropped the libel suit in 1985. CBS did not disavow the program or pay any money to Westmoreland, nor did the network demand the payment of court costs in settlement.

PART IV

Interest Group Activity and Influence

13

Social Movements as Interest Groups: The Case of the Women's Movement

ANNE N. COSTAIN

Traditional measures of interest group influence frequently fail to capture the impact social movements have on legislation. During the 1960s and 1970s, many of the legislative breakthroughs in Congress occurred in areas of intense concern to politically active social movements. With relatively little fanfare, Congress enacted sweeping new protection for the environment, including the Clean Air Act of 1970 and the National Environmental Policy Act of 1969. An unprecedented array of laws was passed safeguarding the rights of women, including the Civil Rights Act of 1964, with its amendment prohibiting sex discrimination in employment; the Education Amendments Act of 1972, barring discrimination in federally funded education programs; and the Equal Rights Amendment to the U.S. Constitution, which passed in Congress in 1972. At the same time, with much more publicity, Congress agreed to expand civil rights laws for racial minorities and created a new body of federal laws protecting consumers. The environmental, consumer, civil rights, and women's movements, as well as other movements of the period, publicized and pressed for major changes in existing public policies and succeeded in transforming the national political agenda as a result. In general Americans now have cleaner air and water, greater social equality, and more laws protecting consumers, but it remains unclear how these interests achieved such sweeping victories.

The apparent degree of influence exercised by social movements is particularly surprising in light of traditional interest group theory. Traditional measures of group influence include powerful constituents, interests that are strategically placed in a number of key congressional districts, and plentiful economic resources to invest in lobbying, yet social movements typically possess few of these characteristics. The features that identify and define social movements are efforts by "excluded groups to mobilize sufficient political leverage to advance collective interests through non-institutionalized means" (McAdam 1982:37). For black civil rights groups in the 1960s, that meant boycotts of segregated transportation systems, sit-ins at white lunch counters in the South, mass marches, and freedom rides to draw public attention and support for their cause. In addition to these noninstitutionalized actions, civil rights groups also engaged in political acts, including voter registration drives, court challenges, and legislative lobbying. The civil rights movement had to employ a mixture of confrontational and conventional tactics to open the political system to its issues because its chief constituents were outside the political process, often lacking even the right to vote. Other social movements, like the environmental movement, had advocates with votes and greater personal resources than most participants in the civil rights movement, but environmentalists still had to persuade these followers to mobilize. This was accomplished through a mixture of events like the first Earth Day in 1970 and protest demonstrations against the killing of whales for commercial purposes. These actions attracted the attention of the media and brought people together to achieve environmental goals. Use of the courts and legislative lobbying gave added focus to efforts to change public policy.

To use Roger Cobb and Charles Elder's (1983:88–93) term, interests such as civil rights and the environment, which have been excluded from the political process in the past, lack the clout necessary to "channel" legislation onto the political agenda. Because most of the legislative agenda is taken up either with routine items (such as annual appropriations), recurrent ones (such as tax reform, farm subsidies, or Social Security increases), or crisis items (such as responses to political change in Eastern Europe or African famines), intense competition exists to add new topics, especially of the kind most social movements champion. Social movements have to compete with groups controlling far more resources and access to policymakers in order to achieve a place on the agenda. That social movements seek collective goods, those which cannot be given selectively to individuals, weakens their case still further. As Olson's (1965) theory of collective action explains, interests pursuing collective goods have difficulty attracting and keeping members. Why should rational individuals pay dues and join an environmental group, for example, when a cleaner environment, new national parks, or improved animal habitat will be available to them, if achieved, whether or not they participated as individuals? Because one person's contribution is unlikely to make a difference in the political outcome, individuals tend to abstain from political activity.

Finally, social movements use noninstitutionalized means, frequently including mass marches, protests, and acts of civil disobedience to build support for their causes. These activities would traditionally put them outside the boundaries of accepted and therefore acceptable ways to promote change in a pluralist, democratic state (Cobb and Elder 1983; Gamson 1975; Lowi 1971). How can we explain the relative success of social movements in influencing Congress, given their representation of political outsiders, their quest for goods everyone can share, and their refusal to limit themselves to conventional politics? Perhaps traditional interest group theory is wrong, or at least incomplete.

SUCCESSFUL MOVEMENTS: TWO COMPETING VIEWS

Sociologists assume that successful social movements such as those mentioned above must have many of the characteristics that would give them clout in Congress. Like political scientists, they have focused on two major problems movements face: getting started and attracting and retaining members. The sociological theory of *resource mobilization* incorporates many of Robert Salisbury's (1969) ideas of exchange as a basis for interest group formation. As Salisbury notes, entrepreneurs/organizers of new groups invest capital in a set of benefits they then offer prospective members for the price of membership. Material benefits, such as cut-rate insurance, a glossy magazine, or travel discounts, are typically offered first. Solidary benefits of friendship and a sense of being part of a worthwhile group typically come later. These are often accompanied by purposive incentives that come from the feeling of having contributed to an important cause (Wilson 1973). Resource mobilization theory similarly suggests that entrepreneural individuals and external sponsors are necessary for the organization of excluded interests, such as the farmworkers in California and racial minorities (see Jenkins and Perrow 1977; McCarthy and Zald 1977).

If outside resources are needed to get the movement started, once the movement has begun, good organization is essential to retain members, who may otherwise stop contributing to the attainment of collective goods. Strong organization helps the interest deploy resources effectively, directing as much pressure as possible to achieve change. If these traditional interest group scholars and resource mobilization theorists are correct, we should be able to trace a flow of external resources into a successful movement—such as the women's, environmental, consumer, or civil rights movements—especially in its early years. We should also see either talented leadership, effective organization, or both guiding a new movement toward political power and legislative effectiveness.

Because resource mobilization theory and conventional measures of interest group effectiveness are largely complementary in identifying which variables are most important in determining the legislative access of social movements, it is possible to test them together. The influx of resources, frequently from outside sponsors, combined with entrepreneurial leadership and strategic access to Congress, would identify a social movement capable of influencing Congress.

However, there is also an alternative sociological explanation of social movement effectiveness that challenges many of these assumptions. *Political process theory* suggests that the presence of leadership and resources (particularly those provided by external groups) is less important in determining movement success than the structure of political opportunity faced by the movement (see McAdam 1982). Government reaction to the movement, not resources, is most important. When government is willing to tolerate, or even facilitate, a new movement, that movement is most likely to form and achieve political influence. According to this perspective, the relative balance of power between parts of the government and a new movement is likely to determine whether the movement is politically successful.

President Nixon's willingness to declare the 1970s "the decade of the environment" as well as his creation of the Environmental Protection Agency by executive order were more important to the success of the environmental movement, from this point of view, than the influx of new external resources. By contrast, government repression makes movement achievements very unlikely. Political process theory allocates a role to resources but finds internally generated resources as valuable as external sponsors. Similarly, process theory draws attention to the psychological readiness of potential group members, who begin to recognize their discontent as collective and to accept the possibility of a political solution (see Piven and Cloward 1979). Traditional interest group and resource mobilization theories suggest tracing the resources entering a movement, whereas political process theory leads us to examine the attitude of government officials with greater care.

THE STUDY

To test these alternative theories, I developed two data sets based on the contemporary women's movement. The first traces congressional action on legislation addressing women as a group.[1] The second consists of events data, showing the degree of agitation on behalf of women's rights in the United States based on *New York Times* coverage.[2] Through these two data sets, covering the period from 1950 to 1986, it is possible to test the relative explanatory power of a traditional interest group/resource mobilization theory versus political process theory in accounting for the legislative impact of social movements. I chose the women's movement primarily because it is one of the movements that achieved a surprising degree of legislative influence in the 1960s and 1970s but also because of its strong parallels, as a civil rights–based movement, to the black civil rights movement, which has been studied using a similar method (see Jenkins and Eckert 1986; McAdam 1982, 1983).

If process theory provides a better explanation of the influence movements exercise in Congress than does traditional interest group theory, this suggests the need to consider the state as a possible initiating actor rather than just a passive recipient of group pressure. It also means that the timing of movement emergence in the political process may be more critical in determining its political influence than either external sponsorship or new resources. By contrast, if leadership, outside groups, or the accumulation of resources is crucial, interest group theory is correct.

To examine congressional activity, a team of scholars using *U.S. Statutes at Large* and the *Congressional Record* as sources analyzed bills that addressed women as a group. The period selected, from 1950 to 1986, spans the time from the very early stirrings of a contemporary women's movement in the United States to its peak of activity and through its current decline. Bills were content-coded according to subject matter, then their percentage as part of the total congressional agenda for the year was calculated. This measure of legislative impact is a variant of that used by Benjamin Ginsberg (1976) to measure the impact of elections on Congress. Ginsberg employed a count of laws passed by Congress, justifying his measure as the most systematic way to gauge congressional policy output. Although numeric categorization of laws minimizes important questions about their significance and long-term impact, it is hard to conceive of another procedure capable of coding laws according to their importance over a long period of time. Laws build on one another. When an important law passes, there will usually be an appropriation and often substantive amendments in the years to follow. There are very few landmark "standalone" bills. By using the percentages of bills rather than absolute numbers, as Ginsberg did, fluctuations due to congressional rules changes or sessional variability are minimized.[3] A less biased measure of their importance relative to other subjects of legislation results from examining "women's" bills and laws as a *share* of the congressional agenda each year.

To examine the degree of agitation on behalf of women's rights during this time, a companion data set from the *New York Times Index* was compiled consisting of all events related to women's rights that were reported between 1950 and 1986. These data show the types of actions, subjects, initiators, and targets of women's rights and anti–women's rights activity in these years. They also indicate both the flow of resources into the movement as well as government support for and opposition to the movement. Although events data of this type have frequently been used to trace the onset and subsequent development of other social movements of this period, it is important to recognize what they can and cannot reveal. There is widespread agreement that, at the minimum, "The data are sufficient for gross comparisons; the more detailed the quantitative comparisons and conclusions based upon them . . . the greater the need for caution and independent verification" (see Gurr 1972:34).[4]

By comparing the timing of resource accumulation and other types of external aid with the pattern of government involvement on women's issues, including congressional action, we find that the source of movement success in influencing Congress becomes clearer. On the one hand, if resources flow into the movement close to its formative period and legislative victories follow, this is persuasive evidence that traditional interest group theory is correct. On the other hand, if government assistance precedes either an influx of resources or significant political impact, political process theory probably provides a more accurate explanation of social movement success.

RESOURCES AS AN EXPLANATION FOR THE SUCCESS
OF THE WOMEN'S MOVEMENT

Most current analyses of the legislative success of the women's movement employ a variant of traditional interest group/resource mobilization theory. It is clear, however, that neither theory in its pure form fits the case of the women's movement. The women's movement purposely, and often painfully, rejected the idea of entrepreneurial leadership (see Freeman 1973 and 1975). Early women's activists felt that this pattern was too close to a model of male hierarchical domination, with one leader and many followers. Although for the women's movement the national leader would most likely be a woman, this would still leave the majority of women without a voice to communicate their own interests. Also, aside from women's organizations, there were few outside patrons who contributed money to the women's movement (see Freeman 1975 and Harrison 1988).

The best-known accounts of the women's movement, including those by Joyce Gelb and Marian Palley (1987) and Jane J. Mansbridge (1986), stress the movement's ability to use issues to stretch tight resources. Both analyses argue how important it was for the women's movement to frame gender issues in terms of role equity (extending equal treatment to women) rather than role change (either opening new opportunities to women, such as a right to have an abortion, or threatening to change women's accepted role, such as allowing them to fill combat positions in the military). By this reasoning, Americans were ready to grant women equal pay for equal work but not to vote for a woman for president. An emphasis on role equity created a tactical environment in which the movement could coax change from government with existing resources by limiting the extent to which it challenged the status quo. Consequently, resources and support networks that were already available to women became sufficient to bring about political change. In *Why We Lost the ERA,* Mansbridge (1986) points out a problem created by this tactic: By arguing that the ERA would have such a limited impact, it was hard to energize supporters to work long enough to win its ratification.

The issue-based view of women's movement success is reflected in the timing of *congressional* activity on women's issues (Figure 13.1). By 1961, women's issues, for the first time since the end of World War II, composed more than 1 percent of the *bills introduced* in Congress. Most of these legislative introductions were versions of the Equal Rights Amendment, which began to emerge quite early in Congress, at least, as the premier women's issue. By contrast, the *passage of laws* addressing women as a group was slower. It was not until 1971 that the percentage of new laws with women as their subject jumped markedly. This legislative activity clearly preceded any large increase in movement resources. Figure 13.2 shows that fund-raising among women's groups started to pick up in 1971, but it was not until 1975 that there were regular reports of outside resources flowing into the women's movement. These data clearly confirm the suppositions of Gelb and Palley and Mansbridge that there were few external resources available to ease the start of a new women's movement.

However, problems remain in applying any version of traditional interest group theory to this particular case. First, the historical chronology is not consistent with the theory. Supportive governmental action preceded any appreciable increase in resources available to women, as well as the earliest efforts to organize a movement. It is not only the case that bill introductions in Congress rose in 1961 and 1962 (particularly for the ERA), but President Kennedy in late 1961 followed the advice of his party along with organized labor and appointed the first President's Commission on the Status of Women. Democratic party and labor union leaders opposed the ERA and were afraid that if the president did not seize the initiative on women's issues, Congress might go ahead and pass the ERA (see Harrison 1988). Although the presidential commission on women was established in large part to thwart the ERA, under the leadership of Esther Peterson it unearthed sufficient evidence of discontent among women, and of social, legal, and economic discrimination against women, to play an important role in shaping the early agenda of the women's movement (see Duerst-Lahti 1989). In 1963, at the mid-October ceremony where he accepted the commission's report, Kennedy remarked that civilization could be judged on its opportunities for women. He issued an executive order stating, "Enhancement of the quality of American life, as envisioned by the Commission's report, can be accomplished only through concerted action within the Federal Government, and through action by States, communities, educational institutions, voluntary organizations, employers, unions, and individual citizens" (quoted in Harrison 1988:164–165).

FIGURE 13.1
Congressional Agenda Space Taken by Women's Issues, 1958–1986

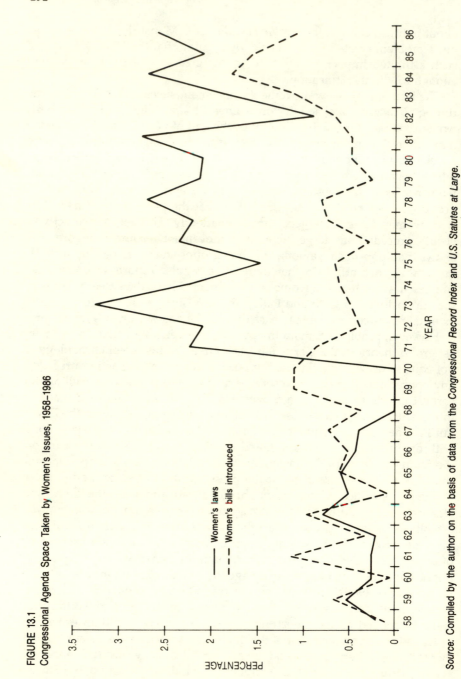

Women's laws
Women's bills introduced

PERCENTAGE

YEAR

Source: Compiled by the author on the basis of data from the *Congressional Record Index* and *U.S. Statutes at Large.*

FIGURE 13.2
Reports of New Resources Entering the Women's Movement, 1955–1986

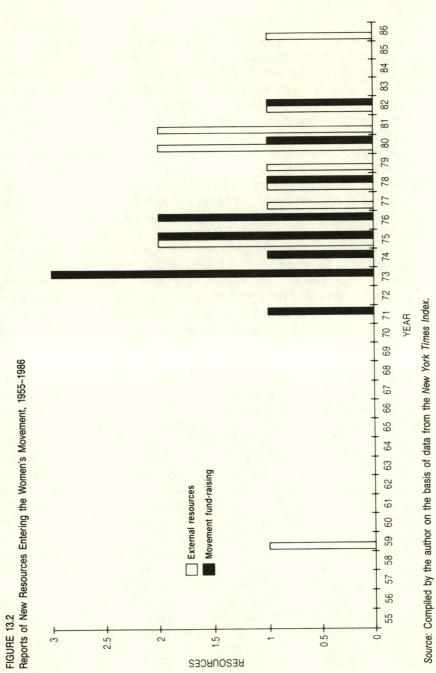

Source: Compiled by the author on the basis of data from the *New York Times Index*.

This language might well be considered a call to the next twenty years of agitation and progress on women's rights in the United States.

These early actions are notable in and of themselves, given the lack of new resources going to women's groups in this period. But they become still more surprising when considered in light of the fact that the first women's group in the contemporary women's movement, the National Organization for Women did not form until 1966. Most of the other second-wave feminist groups were organized in the late 1960s and early 1970s.

The applications of traditional group theory by Gelb and Palley and Mansbridge suggest that it is the tactical power of an idea—stressing role equity—that made the new movement conceivable. Thus it is possible that a vanguard of activists went to Washington early, or was given a forum by the mass media, and used it to persuade the political elite in Congress and the White House to act. Because ERA was the key women's issue from a very early point for both Congress and the president, Figure 13.3 shows the numbers of ERA and other women's issues covered in the *New York Times.* It is clear from this chart that coverage of the ERA in the *Times* came *after* congressional involvement with the issue, not before it. Stories on the Equal Rights Amendment began to rise in 1970, when Congress started to hold public hearings on the ERA and sex discrimination, and are scant before this.

Examining the overall coverage of women's rights and women's issues generally in the 1960s provides limited evidence that a new perspective on women's issues was being communicated to the public or to elites. Figure 13.4 breaks the stories down into categories: equality and discrimination, reports about the women's movement, politics, jobs and employment, and all others ("general"). During the 1960s, the "general" category is the largest, with reports on the overall plight of women dominating the category.[5] The early generality of concerns changes among women, as among all actors, in the 1970s, as issues involving legal equality increasingly come to dominate the agenda. Women's issues developed through government in a focused way, emphasizing equal rights very early and, in the media, through a slower, more diffuse process of sensitizing the public to existing conditions among American women. There is little evidence of a sea change in handling women's issues until the emergence of the ERA and issues of legal equality in the 1970s (Freeman 1975).

Another explanation that would still accord with a traditional interest group perspective is that *public opinion* pushed both the Congress and the president to act. In this view, the women's movement, even if it did not create this new opinion, at least interpreted it correctly and heightened its political influence. Paul Burstein (1985:40–56) has analyzed the repeated measures of attitudes toward women that extend back into this period. They consist of two questions that have been asked frequently from 1946

FIGURE 13.3
Women's Issues Covered in the *New York Times*, 1950–1986

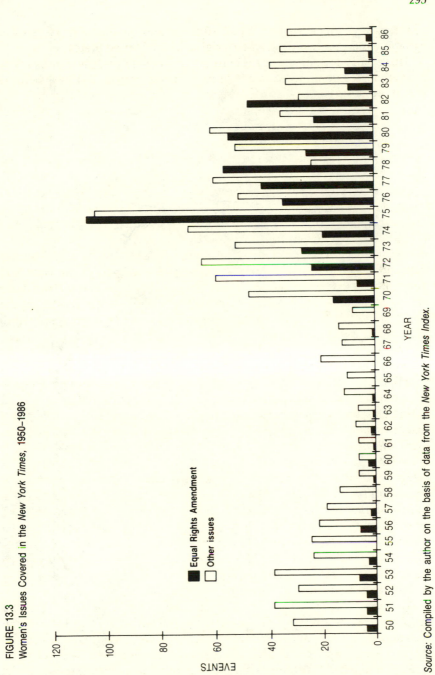

■ Equal Rights Amendment
□ Other issues

Source: Compiled by the author on the basis of data from the *New York Times Index*.

FIGURE 13.4
New York Times Coverage of Women's Issues, 1950–1986

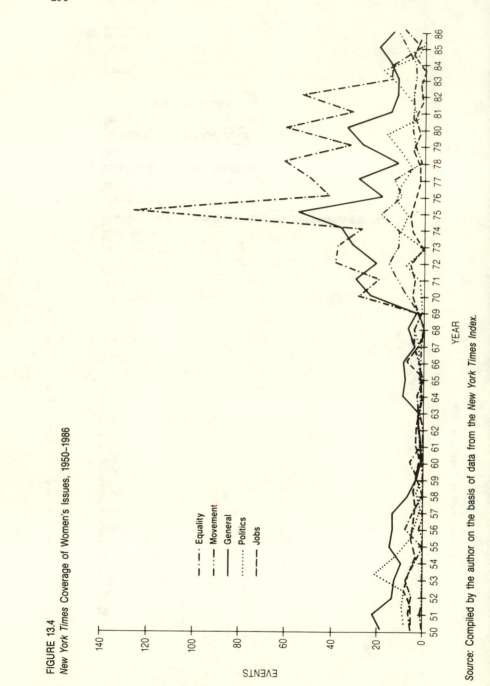

Source: Compiled by the author on the basis of data from the *New York Times Index.*

through the 1980s, with relatively minor variations in wording: "Do you approve of a married woman working in business or industry if she has a husband capable of supporting her?" and "Would you vote for a qualified woman for president?" From 1946 to 1969, there was an exceedingly slow rate of change in public responses to both issues. The labor force question became more favorable at the rate of seven-tenths of 1 percent per year. The willingness to vote for a qualified woman for president increased even more slowly, at a rate of three-tenths of 1 percent per year. By contrast, from 1969 to 1975, the pace of change on both issues quickened measurably. Support for married women in the labor force rose 1.9 percent per year, and willingness to vote for a woman president was up 2.8 percent per year. This suggests that Congress and the president, by their actions in support of women's rights, may have been at the forefront of change rather than responding to others who were the vanguard.

To summarize briefly, there is little evidence from these data that either traditional interest group theory or resource mobilization theory adequately explains the legislative impact of the women's movement. There was no influx of resources into the movement either prior to or coincident with the movement's emergence. Similarly, there is no evidence that the issues emphasized by women and women's groups changed in these early years. When a shift did finally occur, toward an emphasis on equal rights and the Equal Rights Amendment, it seemed to be more a result of governmental emphasis than an initiative from the movement.

POLITICAL OPPORTUNITIES
FOR THE WOMEN'S MOVEMENT

Political process theory emphasizes a change in *government behavior* toward women and women's issues as an important precursor to the appearance of a new movement. Government actions could shift from harassment or oppression of women as a group to neutrality. Or government neutrality could change to facilitation of the group's political aspirations. Figure 13.5 shows the number of favorable, unfavorable, and neutral events (as reported by the *New York Times*) that were initiated on women's issues by *all levels* of government. This figure suggests that increased support of women's issues is linked to the rise of the women's movement. Favorable governmental actions toward women increased in the early 1960s (Figure 13.5) during the period leading up to the founding of the National Organization for Women in 1966. It is also noteworthy how few negative governmentally sponsored acts there were in this same period. However, there is the confounding appearance of *more* supportive government acts relating to women in 1951 and 1953, when no movement was organized, than in the early 1960s, when it was. During the 1950s, the

FIGURE 13.5
Events Initiated by All Levels of Government

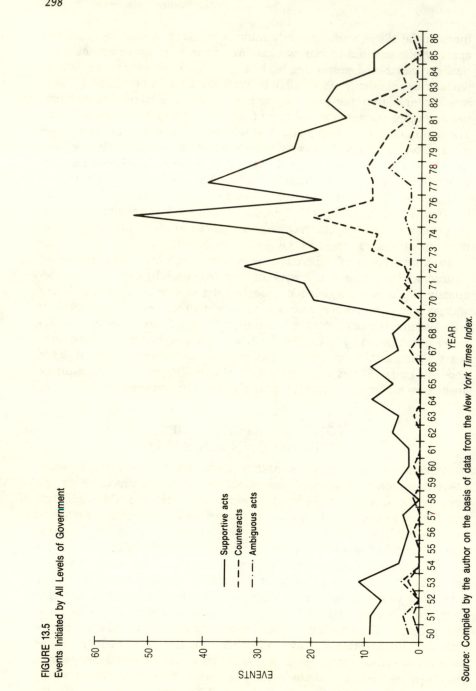

Source: Compiled by the author on the basis of data from the *New York Times Index.*

government also initiated more negative and ambiguous activities related to women than it did in the previous decade. Separating the actions of the *federal* government from state and local governments clarifies the picture. As we can tell from Figure 13.6, the federal government initiated as many positive acts as negative or ambiguous ones on women's issues in the 1950s. But by the early 1960s, the actions of the national government were almost uniformly supportive of women's rights. The shift from a friendly but somewhat ambiguous relationship between government and women in the 1950s to unalloyed support at the federal level in the 1960s seems promising as an explanation for the timing of the women's movement. Strong signals that government would help facilitate the movement's growth might have been all that was needed to spur formation of the movement.

At the same time, according to political process theory, the group itself should be better organized. A perceptible psychological shift should take place as group members begin to see their difficulties as amenable to political solutions. In the case of women, one should observe an increase in mutual cooperation, as diverse women's groups start to pool money, membership, and leadership, creating enough resources to apply pressure on government. Figure 13.7 shows some evidence that women's groups were initiating an increasing number of events supportive of women's rights in the 1960s, yet more such activity took place in the early 1950s. Figure 13.8, however, gives a somewhat different slant on women's activities. In the 1960s, individual feminists and groups of women met together, held conferences, and began to organize the underpinnings of a new women's movement. This did not happen to any notable extent in the decade before. Still, the overall number of reported events remains surprisingly small. There are two explanations for this. First, internal meetings at the start of a new social movement are rarely well covered in the press. Most journalists are probably unaware that a new movement is in the offing. The individuals and groups active in starting the new movement are unlikely to welcome press attention at this time, as they struggle to unite over goals, tactics, and issues. In the case of the women's movement, this natural reticence is intensified by the historical link to the bitter struggles among factions within women's groups, left over from the days of the suffrage movement. Efforts to reconcile these differences (which chiefly involved disagreement over the desirability of adding an equal rights amendment to the constitution) remained particularly problematic in the case of women's groups and were conducted as quietly as possible (see Cott 1987 and Harrison 1988).

Although there is more evidence supporting the view that government aided the emergence of the women's movement than the traditional perspective that new resources or tactics led to the movement's success, ambiguity remains about why parts of the government would *want* to

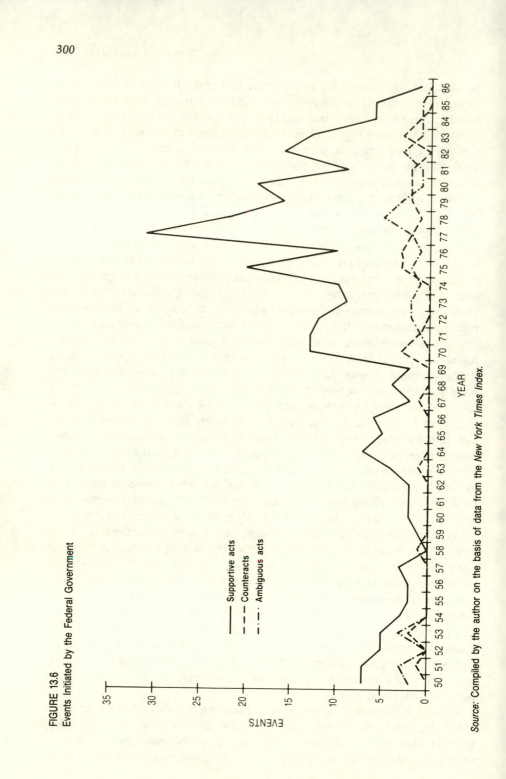

FIGURE 13.6
Events Initiated by the Federal Government

Supportive acts
Counteracts
Ambiguous acts

EVENTS

YEAR

Source: Compiled by the author on the basis of data from the *New York Times Index.*

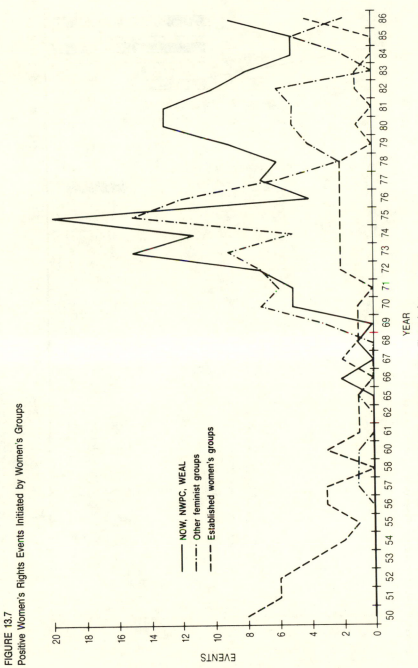

FIGURE 13.7
Positive Women's Rights Events Initiated by Women's Groups

NOW, NWPC, WEAL
Other feminist groups
Established women's groups

EVENTS

YEAR

Source: Compiled by the author on the basis of data from the *New York Times Index*.

302

FIGURE 13.8
Organizing and Resource Accumulation in the Women's Movement, 1955–1972

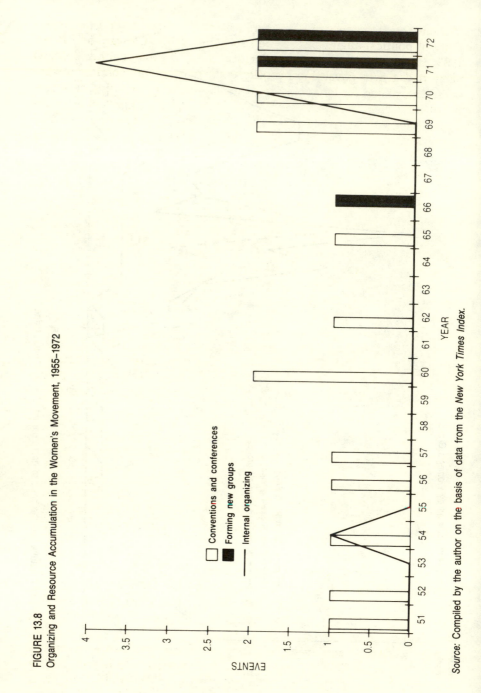

Source: Compiled by the author on the basis of data from the *New York Times Index.*

facilitate the emergence of a women's movement. One reason is the instability of political alignments in the 1960s and 1970s (Cloward and Piven 1983; Piven and Cloward 1979; Tarrow 1988). Because neither political party had a firm governing majority, both parties and politicians were openly searching for large blocs of votes to stabilize a winning coalition. A potential bloc of votes as large as women would be difficult to ignore even if there was not yet evidence that women were voting as a bloc. Social movements are recognized as having the potential to produce this kind of bloc voting. It is not unknown for political parties as well as candidates to position themselves so that they can profit from an electoral shift when it takes place. The public papers of presidents Dwight Eisenhower and John Kennedy, in particular, reveal an awareness of the significance of women as a potential voting bloc (see *Public Papers* 1956:1004; Harrison 1988:73–81).

Kennedy won the presidency by a razor-thin margin over Nixon in 1960. Kennedy (in contrast to Eisenhower) did not benefit from a gender gap in this election (Kenski 1988:50), and by many accounts, upon his taking office, his advisers urged him to take steps to gain more support from women and women's groups (see Harrison 1988:73–81). Although in his public remarks Kennedy did not talk specifically about a women's vote, there is evidence that he understood the women's issues that were emerging better than did his predecessors or successors. In an interview responding to a question from former first lady Eleanor Roosevelt about the contribution of educated women to American society, Kennedy answered,

> Well, I think when you look at Radcliffe College, that the curve of academic excellence at Radcliffe is higher than it is at Harvard. And therefore you assume that this is really the most highly developed student body. What happens to those girls 2 or 3 years later? They get married, many of them become housewives, and all that talent is used in this family life but is not used outside. . . . But I wonder whether they have the full opportunity to develop their talents. As the Greeks said, the definition of happiness is full use of your powers along lines of excellence, and I wonder whether they have that opportunity. (*Public Papers* 1963:342–343)

Beyond politicians searching for an electoral majority, it is increasingly being recognized that subgroups in government routinely act independently under certain conditions (for example, see Wilson 1980 and McFarland 1987). In the case of the women's movement in particular, it has long been understood that there are a number of "woodwork" feminists in elective and appointive offices of government and in the career civil service (Freeman 1975). These are people who, given external backing, would push a feminist position. Among the most visible in Washington in the 1960s and 1970s were representatives Martha Griffiths (D–Mich.),

Shirley Chisholm (D–N.Y.), Margaret Heckler (R–Mass.), Pat Schroeder (D–Colo.), and Charles Rose (D–N.C.) and senators Margaret Chase Smith (R–Maine) and Birch Bayh (D–Ind.). Members of the civil service who played important roles in advancing the cause of women's rights included Mary Eastwood, Catherine East, Marguerite Rawalt, and Richard Graham. In addition to these feminists, there were individuals within government agencies such as the Equal Employment Opportunity Commission whose ability to make independent decisions would increase by mobilizing a new group that would, to a degree, counter pressure from established groups (see Hole and Levine 1971:82). By introducing a new interest with somewhat different priorities from those of the black civil rights groups, which were applying a great deal of pressure on the EEOC, the commissioners had more room for independent judgment. Countervailing pressure from women's groups allowed the EEOC to pursue a sex discrimination case against the American Telephone and Telegraph Company (AT&T) that resulted in the largest single monetary settlement ever awarded in a discrimination case in the United States (Freeman 1975:188–190).

Government undoubtedly contained individuals with a variety of motives for facilitating the emergence of a women's movement. Some members of government could potentially benefit from an electoral gender gap. Others held principled beliefs that women should have more say politically. Finally, there were those who welcomed the extent to which women, as new participants in the political process, might dilute the power of existing groups in specific areas of policymaking, thereby increasing the autonomy of government decisionmakers. All these members of the government would have sufficient reasons to facilitate the formation of a new women's movement.

CONCLUSION

There is little evidence that the women's movement achieved the legislative impact that it did through amassing new resources, allies, or more effective political tactics. Instead, the data available suggest that government's position moved from positive neutrality on women's issues to facilitation. This was the result of a variety of factors ranging from the instability of electoral alignments and the recognition of the potential significance of a "woman's vote," to "woodwork" feminists already inside government. Added to these factors were the people within government agencies who looked forward to the time when women as a group would start to compete with other interests, such as promilitary groups, big business, and minorities. This added competition would result in some agencies' acquiring greater latitude to pursue their own policy agendas.

The case of the women's movement then raises questions about the usefulness of traditional emphases on resource accumulation and tactical strength as major determinants of legislative success for social movements. If this case is typical of movement politics, and there is evidence that it is (see Mueller 1987), shifting relationships between potential movements and government are a stronger signal of future movement influence than more traditional measures of outside patrons or early resource accumulation. The decline of hostile actions by government provides a special opportunity for movements to emerge and makes rapid gains in policy possible.

If this is the pattern followed by the contemporary women's movement, it has several important implications for women and the study of interest group politics. First, women's groups do not need to wait for external sponsors or feminist entrepreneurs to raise new resources. They have sufficient resources already if they can work toward common goals. Second, it is time to question the view that women made the gains they did by asking for small changes within the parameters of role equity rather than by emphasizing more sweeping political change under the banner of role change. We know statistically that women's lives were changing. More women were entering the work force, heading families, and having fewer children (see Klein 1984:32–93). Movement activists may have fared better arguing that the ERA would assist women in coping with these changes instead of emphasizing achievement of absolute equality with men. Along these lines, more of the lobbying by women's movement groups might productively have gone into examining the changes in women's roles that had already occurred and searching for legislative solutions to ease the period of transition. These might have included heightened emphasis on proposals for government-subsidized and -regulated daycare, maternal leave programs, reforms to Social Security, employment rights for women, and education. The assumption seems to have been made that the American public was more comfortable with fairness toward women, within traditional legal boundaries, than with changes in the condition of women. Although this is undoubtedly true to a degree, it is easy to overestimate. If we look at public attitudes toward voting for a woman for president, we see an abrupt shift in the late 1960s and early 1970s, when, in a relatively brief time, this willingness jumps from just over half to 80 percent of the public. This suggests that a less cautious women's movement may have achieved more than did the movement that ultimately developed. Finally, this type of analysis indicates that future women's movements are likely to be dependent on opportunities opened to them by government. If potential movements continue to reject entrepreneurial leadership as a way to "buy" their way into the political system, they will need to be very conscious of periods when politicians, government agencies, and the executive branch are receptive to changing the existing political balance by including women as a new interest.

The women's, environmental, civil rights, and consumer movements should be recognized as lingering presences within American politics. When political conditions are right, any and all of these movements have the potential to emerge and alter the established power balances within political institutions. Their indigenous resources, accumulated to a large extent during the peaks of their earlier mobilizations, give them the ability to successfully challenge more resource-laden conventional interests. It is government as an actor that helps determine when and in what form these recurrent movements will reappear.[6]

NOTES

I would particularly like to thank Douglas Costain, Evonne Okonski, Cynthia Pieropan, Oneida Mascarenas, and Steve Majstorovic, who assisted me in coding this data. I gratefully acknowledge the support of the Council on Teaching of the University of Colorado, which provided funding and a forum to try out some of these ideas.

1. To count bills, we searched the following headings in the *Congressional Record Index* and *U.S. Statutes at Large:* "Woman/women/women's," "Sex discrimination," and "Civil rights." We also looked at cross references to additional headings, including in our data set only legislation that explicitly mentioned gender. Although women as a majority of the population are affected by nearly all legislation, this data set is designed to single out bills that acknowledge women as a group rather than measuring the impact of specific laws on women.

2. These events data were gathered using the *New York Times Annual Index,* following a procedure similar to the one employed by Doug McAdams in his work on the civil rights movement (see McAdams 1982, 1983). The purpose of this code is to record all events contained in the synopses of the annual *Times* index that reflect agitation over women's rights in the period studied. All story synopses under the headings "Women: General" and "Women: United States" were read. All events that were selected were coded twice, once by me and once by either Evonne Okonski or Oneida Mascarenas, both graduate students. We resolved coding discrepancies through discussion and, in some cases, through reference to the complete story in the *Times.* For the years 1950 to 1986, intercoder reliability was above 90 percent. More complete information about coding categories and procedures is in the codebook available from the author.

3. There have been rules changes in this period in the number of legislators who are permitted to cosponsor a bill. There have also been sessional and cross-time fluctuations in the numbers of laws passed by Congress. Typically, more bills are introduced in the first session of Congress, and more laws are passed in the second session. During some periods, Congress has passed more bills than in others. In 1981, for example, Congress passed just 145 new laws, whereas in 1970 Congress passed 505 laws.

4. For example, it is valid to conclude that the amount of women's rights activity more than doubled in a two-year period when the number of events increases from twenty-five to sixty. If there are two protest events the first year and four the second, however, it is unwise to conclude that the frequency of protest doubled. The numbers are too small and the method both of coding and determining newspaper coverage too imprecise to permit this fine-grained analysis. The onset and the end of the movement alike are likely to be underreported, as, in

the first instance, reporters may not yet recognize that these events are newsworthy and, at the other end of the coverage, a waning "issue attention cycle" may lead newspapers to underreport continuing movement activities (Downs 1972; Jenkins and Eckert 1986).

A number of problems leading to possible inconsistencies in coding results have been identified, but empirical efforts to show *systematic* bias in *New York Times* coverage of social movement activity have generally failed (Burstein and Monaghan 1986; Johnson 1987). McAdams (1982) reports that 83 percent of all dated events between 1955 and 1962 on the black civil rights movement mentioned in nine qualitative accounts of the movement were covered in the *New York Times*. Jenkins and Perrow (1972) compared *New York Times* coverage of farmworkers' movement events with the coverage in the *Los Angeles Times* and the *Chicago Tribune*. There was no evidence that the *New York Times* emphasized different stories than the other papers, but the *Times* did pick up more stories than either of the other sources. *Times* reporting has also been shown to cover more "hard" news, including demonstrations, riots, and meetings of national organizations, than "soft" news, such as speeches and internal movement debates over tactics (Snyder and Kelly 1977).

5. If we consider only those *Times* stories initiated by women, we see a similar pattern. In the 1960s, women, like the other actors who raised women's issues, were unlikely to focus on specific complaints.

6. In the case of the women's movement, it appears that electoral instability and candidates' searching for a new majority coalition identified women as a potentially important voting bloc. By fashioning a political agenda that included equal rights for women (to win more support from women), the president and Congress helped mobilize a new feminist movement in the United States.

14

Money, Technology, and Political Interests: The Direct Marketing of Politics

R. KENNETH GODWIN

Political interests such as Right to Life, the National Organization of Women, the National Conservative Political Action Committee (NCPAC), the Sierra Club, the National Taxpayer's Union, and Common Cause play important roles in American politics today. Without direct marketing, most of these citizen action groups and political action committees could not exist, much less could they have an influence on American politics. Political interests use direct marketing to raise money, recruit new members, lobby public officials, and publicize issues, programs, and candidates. In this chapter I examine how political direct marketing works, how political interests use it, and its impacts on American politics.

I begin with a discussion of the advantages of the three marketing techniques—mail, phone, and television—and how interest groups use each for specific purposes. I then examine the changes direct marketing has effected in interest group membership, leadership, and tactics. I give special attention to whether direct marketing, because of its reliance on threat and fear to motivate persons to action, bears responsibility for the increasing political negativism and extremism in American politics. Finally, I discuss the extent to which direct marketing changes the types of issues that reach the American political agenda and the tactics used to influence the decisions concerning those issues.

THE IMPORTANCE OF DIRECT MARKETING

By far the most important direct-marketing tool is direct mail. During every electoral cycle, more than 200 million pieces of political direct mail reach millions of American citizens. These mailings induce over 14 million persons to give money to candidates and causes, raise over $1 billion in political contributions, and generate over 20 million letters to Congress (see Godwin 1988a:8).

The development of direct mail helps to explain the rapid growth of citizen action groups. Some, such as Common Cause, the National Taxpayer's Union, and the Environmental Defense Fund, were founded upon direct mail and depend almost completely upon it. Other groups, such as the Sierra Club and the American Association of Retired Persons, have used direct mail to increase substantially the size, power, and resources of their organizations.

Ideological political action committees, because they solicit contributions almost solely through direct mail, owe their entire existence to it as well. For these organizations, direct mail does double duty. Every fundraising letter is also a campaign letter. The ability of direct mail to simultaneously approach strangers, appeal for funds, and campaign for an issue or candidate raises new opportunities for political groups to organize and mobilize the mass public.

Television also markets politics. The U.S. Chamber of Commerce has its own closed-circuit television network as well as a weekly television program, "It's Your Business." The Reverend Jerry Falwell used his weekly religious broadcast, "The Old-Time Gospel Hour," to develop a list of potential donors to his right-wing Christian political group, the Moral Majority.

When it comes to mobilizing citizens for grassroots lobbying, the telephone becomes important. Using low-cost, long-distance services, interest groups can contact thousands of citizens to generate letters, telegrams, and phone calls to public officials. Groups can computerize membership lists, categorized by state or congressional district, using data-base programs. With such programs, the staff can generate the names and phone numbers of members who live in the districts of legislators who are undecided on a critical issue.

The emergence of these techniques has alarmed many political analysts. Columnist David Broder (1982:C7) writes that direct marketing and single-issue groups lead to political extremism and "gutless government." Sociologist Daniel Bell (1975a:194) and pollster Robert Teeter (quoted in *Newsweek* 1978:46) argue that direct marketing and the interest groups it spawns are further fragmenting the already dangerously fragmented political parties. Perhaps the strongest condemnation of direct-marketing technologies and their political outcomes is by political scientist Michael Hayes (1983), who believes that direct marketing creates a "mass society" in which intolerance triumphs and national elites not held accountable by elections manipulate the public and public policy.

Not all commentaries concerning direct marketing are negative. Some analysts believe these innovations will allow greater participation and more equitable access to political information. These observers see the direct links between elites and citizens as a major breakthrough toward a more democratic society. Using closed-circuit television, telephones, and home computers, citizens can participate directly in the decision process. For example, with two-way, closed-circuit television, citizens could vote directly in national referenda without leaving their homes.

HOW DIRECT MARKETING WORKS

The mailing process begins with a "prospect" list, the names of persons who have "purchased" a similar product. For example, a conservative PAC might obtain a list of persons from outside the state of North Carolina who contributed to Jesse Helms's 1990 campaign. Typically, only 1 or 2 percent of prospects reply, and prospecting often loses money. The sponsor incurs these costs to obtain a "house list"—the list of persons who actually responded. This list is a direct-mailer's most precious asset. The response rate for mailings to this list is often over 10 percent; equally important, the mailer can solicit the list again and again. When compared with traditional methods of soliciting, this constitutes a major breakthrough. Volunteers do not like to make repeated requests. It is particularly hard to go back two weeks after a person has made a donation. Yet previous givers are most likely to give again.

Direct mail can personalize communications and concentrate them on those persons who will most probably respond. The salutation can be to an individual, and the letter's form and substance can reflect that person's special attributes. For example, the Republican National Committee sends engraved invitations in mailings requesting donors to pledge $1,000, whereas Environmental Action, a left-wing environmental group, uses recycled paper and asks for $35.

Direct marketing concentrates on particular audiences. The Pro-Life Voter Identification Project supplies an impressive example of this. Recognizing that candidates taking public anti-abortion stands may lose a pro-choice vote for every pro-life vote they gain, volunteers call registered voters and ask them six questions concerning abortion. The volunteer then codes respondents who give strongly anti-abortion answers onto computerized lists by party identification and voting precinct. Pro-life candidates can purchase these lists and communicate their stance only to households containing pro-life registered voters.

Direct mail also stresses immediacy. It tells the reader that he or she must act before it's too late. An envelope from the Defenders of Wildlife shows a picture of a grizzly bear and a red slash stating, "NORTH

AMERICAN WILDLIFE EMERGENCY." Red letters call out, "IMMEDI-
ATE RESPONSE REQUESTED." Across the first page runs still another
red bar reading, "PRIORITY MESSAGE * PRIORITY MESSAGE * PRIOR-
ITY MESSAGE." Above the salutation are two paragraphs emphasizing
that if the recipient of the mailing does not take immediate action, "this
unique symbol of strength and courage may soon disappear from the
lower 48 states."

Critics charge that direct mail uses this fear of immediate harm as its
basic motivating force and that this increases political alienation, reduces
voter turnout, fosters "ersatz participation," "balkanizes" politics, and
encourages ideological bullies (Godwin 1988b). Does direct mail make
greater use of negative information and fear than other types of political
messages? Yes! A content analysis of a sample of direct mailings found
that between 35 and 40 percent of paragraphs in political mailings use
either fear or guilt to motivate recipients (Godwin 1988a:24). In a letter
for the NCPAC, Jesse Helms tells us: "Your tax dollars are being used for
grade school classes that teach our children that CANNIBALISM, WIFE-
SWAPPING, and the MURDER of infants and the elderly are acceptable
behavior" (Sabato 1984:57).

Fear dominates mailings because of an important psychological axiom:
Persons will do more to prevent the loss of something they already have
than to get something that they might obtain in the future (Tversky and
Kahneman 1981). Direct mail stresses the darker side of politics, portraying
the opposition with strong negative descriptors such as "bureaucrats,"
"left-wing hippies," "destroyers," and "so-called minorities." Mailings
unite these aspersions with names to form epithets such as "Ted Kennedy
liberals" and "Bush-league ideas." Perhaps most frequent is the use of the
word *enemies* rather than *opposition* or other, less provocative terms.

While they denigrate opponents, writers identify their organization and
the recipient with positive symbols such as "the majority," "Americans,"
and "decent." Jerry Falwell sent Moral Majority prospects a letter of
powerful descriptors with a membership card:

> Here is your official Moral Majority Membership Card. *I have issued this card
> to you because I believe that you are the kind of American who would like to see
> our nation returned to moral sanity. . . . So now, we are locked in a raging battle
> with the pro-abortionists, homosexuals, pornographers, atheists, secular human-
> ists, and others.* (italics in red in the original)

Conservatives are not alone in their use of such language. When I
matched mailings according to their use of fear, guilt, name-calling, and
the order in which these tactics were used, the letter most closely approximating the Moral Majority letter above was from Greenpeace, a radical
environmental group. Direct mail from Alan Cranston, perhaps the most

liberal member of the Senate, provided the closest match to a letter from arch-conservative Jesse Helms. Various wildlife groups use photographs of the killing of baby seals in much the same way pro-life groups use photographs of mangled fetuses.

Television Direct Marketing

Although direct mail is the most productive marketing technique, it is not the only option. Political direct marketing uses television and telephone services for fund-raising, recruiting, and mobilizing citizens. Cable television presents opportunities for achieving the immediacy of direct mail and adds the visual appeal that makes television such a special medium.

Currently, fundamentalist ministers including Jerry Falwell and Pat Robertson are the major users of cable television as a direct-marketing tool. These preaching politicians use religious broadcasts to prospect for new members, to raise funds for political purposes, and to mobilize their followers to political action. The political content of most broadcasts is limited, however, because politics must be interspersed with religion; by and large, religion gets first billing. Whereas direct mailings begin with the powerful combination of threat and appeal to personal efficacy, the religious television solicitations commence with a prayer and a hymn.

Although they are the most frequent political users of cable television, the Christian Right are not its only users. The U.S. Chamber of Commerce carries a syndicated television program to publicize the chamber's positions on political issues. The chamber also owns a subscription-based, two-way, closed-circuit television network, Biznet. This network makes it possible not only for people in the Washington, D.C., studio to talk to listeners in other cities, but for audiences at those locations to talk back.

Biznet carries personalization, concentration, and immediacy to their apex. Biznet also reaches the zenith in costs. When the network was originally developed, the chamber hoped that local chapters throughout the country would buy into it and purchase the necessary equipment to participate in the two-way broadcasts. This has not occurred. Despite being the most innovative use of television by a political interest group, the two-way, closed-circuit network remains limited largely to major metropolitan areas in the East and Midwest.

Direct Marketing by Phone

Like direct mail, contacting by telephone allows for substantial personalization, concentration, and immediacy. All of us are familiar with the call requesting support for a particular charity or the offer to clean our carpets. When it comes to political causes, the telephone works better for mobilizing persons already committed than for selling new prospects. Telephone contacts cannot prospect effectively because there is not enough time to make a sale. Mailings can include long letters, photographs, and multiple inserts; effective prospecting phone calls should last only about two minutes.[1] In addition, the cost of staff time in telephone prospecting is prohibitive. If the typical staff member makes fifteen calls per hour and the response rate is 2 percent, the average number of "sales" will be only three per day.

Although not a practical prospecting tool, long-distance telephone services are effective in mobilizing an organization's activists to political action. If a group has a list of enthusiasts on a particular issue, long-distance services such as WATS lines allow the national leadership to mobilize these persons in a matter of hours. Many organizations use "telephone tree" systems by which each member of the national staff calls one or two activists in each congressional district. These people, in turn, call three persons assigned to them and pass along the mobilization message. This progression continues in the mode of a chain letter until the entire network has been contacted.

The advantages of these telephone chains are that they are inexpensive, encourage member involvement, and can lobby effectively when time is short. In less than forty-eight hours, a group such as the Sierra Club or the National Right to Life can generate 10,000 letters, phone calls, and telegrams to members of Congress. The disadvantage is that members of the chain do not always follow directions. The greater the number of steps in the chain, the more likely it is that either the message becomes altered or that people fail to make the required calls.

DOES DIRECT MARKETING CHANGE WHO PARTICIPATES?

Having examined how direct marketing recruits and mobilizes, I now address the questions, Do these techniques lead to different types of political participants? And, if they do, how do they differ from those who have traditionally participated in interest group politics? Is it important whether a person joins a group in response to a direct-marketing solicitation or in response to social and occupational network ties? Supporters believe that direct marketing increases political equality by providing opportunities for individuals who previously were unlikely to participate. Opponents believe that direct marketing will increase participation by those who are more extreme and less tolerant.

Before direct marketing, greatest participation in voluntary associations came from persons who had high incomes and were college-educated, long-term residents of their communities, married, middle-aged, and male.[2]

These people were more likely to join social, civic, and political organizations because their social and business activities put them into contact with politically active citizens. This bias was still greater if religious or ethnic barriers were present. Supporters see direct marketing overcoming these biases because it does not rely on existing participants to recruit new ones. If individuals have telephones, televisions, or postal addresses, then direct marketing can reach them.

Although supporters argue that direct marketing will increase democracy, opponents suggest that direct marketing reduces tolerance and increases support for aggressive and illegal political activity. In past years, participants in interest group politics generally had crosscutting political memberships. For example, through social network ties a woman may belong to the League of Women Voters, the Association of Business and Professional Women, the Lady Jaycees, and the United Way. Her spouse may belong to the Jaycees, a trade association, and a local fishing club. The political persuasion in each of these associations differs, thus encouraging tolerance of other political views.[3]

Contrast the above crosscutting pattern with that encouraged by direct marketing. Instead of memberships in different types of voluntary associations, the direct-mail recruit belongs to several organizations with similar ideologies and goals. For example, an individual who joins the Environmental Defense Fund might also join the Sierra Club, Environmental Action, Earth First, and Nature Conservancy. The cause of this overlapping membership pattern is the mailing list. Once an individual responds to an appeal from one group, that association will trade or sell his name to other organizations with similar purposes. Each of these mailings shows the same persons and groups as the "good guys" and another set of individuals and organizations as "the enemy." For environmental group members, the enemies will be the developers, big oil, and industry. For persons who belong to the National Conservative Political Action Committee, Congressional Club, and organizations of the Christian Right, the enemy will be Ted Kennedy, homosexuals, secular humanists, and liberals. The expected result of this polarization is intolerance. In addition, because the portrayal of the threat to current values is so immense and imminent, persons who believe this portrayal may accept and encourage nondemocratic actions.

The expectations of supporters and critics of direct marketing yield two broad hypotheses: (1) Direct marketing encourages political equality by recruiting persons who have different demographic and socioeconomic characteristics compared to persons who became active through traditional channels, and (2) direct marketing encourages higher levels of political alienation, intolerance, extremism, and aggressive attitudes and behaviors.

Two studies directly tested these hypotheses. The first examined whether contributors to the Democratic party's national telethons differed from other party contributors (see Ellwood and Spitzer 1979). The second examined whether persons who joined environmental groups through direct mail differed from those who joined because of friendship ties (Godwin 1988a:53–66). Both studies found that, contrary to the hopes of supporters, direct marketing increases rather than decreases current socio-economic biases in participation. When compared to other party contributors, telethon contributors were 13 percent more likely to have attended college, 37 percent more likely to fall into higher income brackets, and 42 percent more likely to have professional or managerial jobs. The environmental group study discovered that direct-mail recruits were more likely to have graduated from college, had higher incomes, and were more likely to be from urban areas.

An examination of contributors to Christian Right political action committees, organizations that depend almost entirely on direct marketing for fund-raising, supports the above studies. Sixty-three percent of contributors had incomes over $50,000 per year and 75 percent were college graduates (Guth and Green 1984). These results show that direct marketing increases rather than decreases the difference in the rates of participation between the classes of Americans who have traditionally participated in American politics and those who have not.

Does direct marketing encourage political alienation, intolerance, extremism, and aggressive attitudes and behaviors? Because it makes participation easy, does it lead to participation by those less knowledgeable about politics and less active and experienced in democratic forms of political participation such as voting and campaigning? Because direct mail encourages overlapping rather than crosscutting group memberships, will its recruits be less tolerant of opposing ideas and more alienated from the political system?

The comparison of telethon contributors with other party contributors found that those who responded to the telethon were more ideologically extreme. Perhaps more importantly, these contributors were 74 percent more likely to support political protest activity. The comparisons among environmental group members showed more complex patterns. The study found that the relationships among direct-marketing recruitment and political knowledge, interest, and ideology were complex. As Figure 14.1 shows, when compared with social-network recruits, direct-marketing joiners tend either to participate less in politics and be less politically interested, knowledgeable, and active or they participate at very high levels and are highly interested and knowledgeable. In contrast, social-network recruits tended to have moderate levels of participation, interest, and knowledge.

FIGURE 14.1
Relationship Between Method of Recruitment and Political Interest and Knowledge

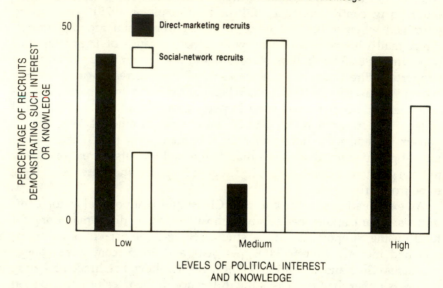

Source: Data from survey conducted by Resources for the Future and analyzed by author. Reported in Godwin 1988.

The above pattern shows that direct marketing attracts two kinds of people, and social networks reach still another. For one set of recruits, direct marketing lowers the costs of joining an organization and alerts them that a threat exists to their values. These new members need not seek out the organization nor worry about going to meetings or becoming active beyond making their contribution. The mail solicitation contains information about why the cause and the organization are worthwhile, and it includes the necessary reply card that makes it easy to become a member. Persons responding for these reasons are not as committed to the political cause as are other recruits. They have less political interest, knowledge, and experience, and, without a mail solicitation, they probably would not be involved in interest group politics. The other type of direct-marketing recruit feels strongly about the issue before receiving the marketing appeal. No special incentives are required to motivate these individuals. They have a strong commitment to the group's goals and have high scores on measures of political interest, participation, and ideology.

Falling between these two types of direct-marketing recruits are social-network joiners. They care more about the political goals and ideals of their group than the passive marketing recruits, but they are less extreme

FIGURE 14.2

Relationship Between Method of Recruitment and Political Alienation and Intolerance

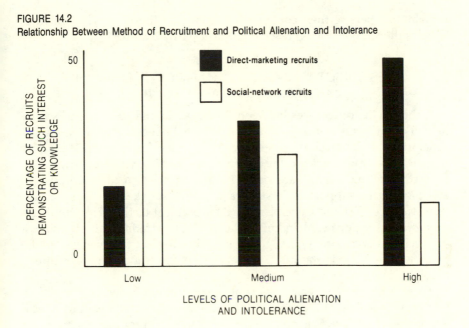

LEVELS OF POLITICAL ALIENATION
AND INTOLERANCE

and generally less active than the direct-marketing members who joined solely for political purposes.

Recruits' levels of political extremism, intolerance, and alienation exhibit a more straightforward pattern. Figure 14.2 shows that persons who joined in response to direct-marketing appeals were more likely to score high on all of these characteristics whereas social-network joiners tended to score much lower on these scales.

The strong positive association between direct-mail recruitment and aggressive participation and political alienation suggests that persons motivated by direct marketing are less committed to democratic norms and to the political system itself. This makes intuitive sense. The crosscutting memberships of social-network recruits moderate opinions. This encourages tolerance of opposing views and reduces alienation. In contrast, these influences do not temper the attitudes and opinions of direct-mail recruits.

Even in the areas of alienation and aggressive participation, direct marketing does not have the dire consequences that critics fear. Although direct-marketing recruits are more alienated and aggressive, examination of these recruits shows that the longer they stay with their group, the less alienated and aggressive they become (Godwin 1988a:64).[4] It would appear that even checkbook participation reduces political alienation, as contributors believe their contributions make a difference. This, in turn, reduces the support for aggressive political participation.

DOES DIRECT MARKETING CHANGE THE LOBBYING TACTICS OF INTEREST GROUPS?

Although the differences between direct-marketing recruits and social-network joiners are not as great as proponents hoped or critics feared, the generation of resources by direct marketing may force group leaders to pursue issues and tactics different from those of other interest groups. Direct-marketing recruits are not strongly attached to their groups. To avoid losing the support of these persons, direct-marketing-based groups may stress conflict and extremism in their political tactics. This emphasis may force the groups to abandon the tactic that has traditionally been most important in achieving policy goals: lobbying behind the scenes. To discover whether this is the case, I interviewed the leadership of eighteen citizen action groups.[5]

These interviews revealed a strong association between the degree to which an organization depends on direct mail and the probability that it will choose highly visible and emotional issues. In groups dependent on direct mail, issues were chosen to maximize media exposure, and the leadership tried to appear radical and innovative in its issue choices. The chief lobbyist for Friends of the Earth described this strategy: "We try to stay on the cutting edge of the movement in our selection of issues. That helps us show our members that we are aware of the changes that are occurring in the environment and that we're not standing still. We were the first to go into international issues, the first to have an antinuclear lobby, and the first to have a full-time disarmament lobbyist." Perhaps the most candid statement concerning the significance of media attention came from a consumer lobbyist who stated, "If the press isn't going to be interested, then neither are we. We have to show our members we're doing something."

With only one exception, if a group obtained at least 60 percent of its members or 40 percent of its income through direct mail, that group stressed emotional issues that received substantial press coverage. For example, a lobbyist from a group with 80 percent direct-mail members commented, "We have to emphasize emotional issues like toxic chemicals or nuclear waste. Court cases aren't places where the members can get involved, and so they have to feel strongly about the issues we choose. Superfund was a great issue for us, and EPA helped by keeping the issue hot. DDT and dioxin were good, too. James Watt, of course, was the best."

Groups that rely mainly on either social networks or material incentives for recruits contrast sharply with the above pattern.[6] Although issue

visibility and press coverage are important, they are not the key considerations. Instead, these groups choose issues that maximize their expertise
and have substantial impact. They are more likely to lobby on the implementation aspects of an old issue than to rush to be first with a new one.
For example, a lobbyist from the National Wildlife Federation stated: "We
try to research a piece of legislation and determine exactly which provisions will help to get effective action by the bureaucracy. We've learned
that just getting a bill isn't enough. We have to be sure that EPA or Interior
will implement it. . . . We don't just pick issues like [another environmental
group] because they're good press."

Those interviewed made it clear that the most important factor in the
choosing of highly visible issues was the group's dependence on direct
marketing for resources. For example, a staff member of the Women's
Equity Action League (WEAL) reported that her group stays away from
issues that are emotional or have high visibility. WEAL can do this and
concentrate on behind-the-scenes lobbying because it receives more than
90 percent of its income from foundations and government grants and
contracts. Alternatively, the National Organization for Women, because it
depends on direct mail for more than 70 percent of its membership, must
choose issues that mobilize its constituency and receive substantial media
attention. When the leadership of NOW didn't do this and chose instead
to lobby behind the scenes, many local chapters withheld membership
dues. Ultimately, the national leaders were fired and replaced with those
who chose more visible and emotional issues.[7]

Grassroots Lobbying

If direct-marketing-based groups must reduce their behind-the-scenes
lobbying, they may have an advantage in grassroots lobbying, that is,
lobbying by a congressperson's constituents rather than by lobbyists. Because direct-marketing-based groups choose visible and emotional issues,
they should be better able to mobilize grassroots efforts. In addition,
groups that obtain their membership and income largely through direct
marketing should be able to use these same tools to mobilize citizens to
pressure public officials. In addition, grassroots efforts increase loyalty to
the organization. By involving members in the lobbying process, the
groups make their members feel more efficacious. For all the above reasons, I hypothesized that the greater a group's dependence on direct
marketing, the higher the likelihood that it would use grassroots lobbying.

To test the hypothesis, I interviewed lobbyists and PAC directors of
eighteen citizen action groups and PACs. I asked them what percentage of
staff time and organizational resources the group devoted to grassroots
mobilizations and how many mobilizations they had attempted in the

previous year. My hypothesis was falsified. The major factor encouraging grassroots lobbying was not dependence upon direct marketing but whether the organization had a separate direct-mail department. This, in turn, depended upon the size of the organization. Because most direct-mail-based groups are smaller than their social-network-based counterparts, there is a negative relationship between a group's dependence on direct marketing for income and grassroots lobbying.

Separate mailing departments encourage grassroots lobbying because they reduce the costs of these projects to staff lobbyists. A lobbyist who wants to mobilize group activists on an issue calls the mailing department and indicates what material the letter should cover and which category of members should be contacted. Unless the lobbyist wants to become more intimately involved in the writing of the letter or the contacting effort, the mailing department takes care of the rest. In smaller groups, the lobbyist must handle most of the tasks involved in the mobilization, maintaining and updating lists of activists, writing the mobilization letter, and supervising many chores related to printing and mailing. If a telephone alert is used, the lobbyist handles this activity as well. A lobbyist from a pro-life group indicated how taxing these activities could be:

> When I have to organize a letter drive, I know that I am going to be working twelve hours a day for more than a week. You have to get the letter cleared upstairs, you have to get the printer moving, you have to update your files, and you have to find the money to do it. The worst part is that we rarely know if we are having an impact. When I go see a congressman, at least I have an idea what his reaction is.

Another lobbyist, from a women's organization, voiced similar complaints: "They're just not worth the effort most of the time. I don't know how many of the people on my list actually do what they're supposed to, but we have to do them [the mobilizations]. The members expect it. Otherwise we wouldn't do it—at least I wouldn't."

Citizen groups are not the only interest groups that use grassroots lobbying. Organizations that mail to customers as a part of their normal business activities often use direct-mail campaigns. When the government attempted to withhold taxes from savings accounts, the banks used their monthly statements to alert customers to this tax change and to encourage them to urge their elected officials to repeal this measure. Energy companies have used their billing notices to encourage customers to lobby for energy policies. The critical factor is not the type of interest group but whether that organization has a separate mailing department to handle the logistics.

In summary, when it comes to lobbying tactics, groups based on direct marketing are at a disadvantage in both direct and grassroots lobbying.

When personally contacting policymakers, direct-marketing-based groups are less able to lobby behind the scenes, concentrate on narrow issues, or pay close attention to implementation. Instead, they must select visible, extreme, and combative issues. In grassroots lobbying, the groups that depend most upon direct marketing rarely have the size or organizational structure necessary to maintain a separate direct-mail department. Yet this department is critical to organizing large grassroots efforts.

Ideological PACs and Political Negativism

A major criticism of direct marketing is that it encourages the growth of single-issue groups and ideological PACs, organizations that increase political negativism in American politics. This negativism, in turn, reduces confidence and trust in the political system. There is no doubt that direct-mail-based ideological PACs use fear and negativism.[8] The previously cited content analysis of direct mailings showed that ideological PACs use fear and extremism more than any other mailer. In his book *PAC Power* (1984:57), Larry Sabato characterizes mailings from ideological PACs as "pure emotion, lightning-rod issues, and 'hot' names." What are the consequences of ideological PACs for the American political system?

A comparison of ideological PACs with economic PACs—PACs that need not depend as heavily on direct mail—reveals three factors that distinguish the strategies and tactics of ideological PACs: (1) their willingness to lose a political struggle in order to fight the virtuous fight, (2) their readiness to spend money on challengers rather than incumbents, and (3) their use of independent spending in electoral contests.

The New Right spent millions to mobilize persons against the Panama Canal Treaty, despite knowing that the chance of defeating the treaty was small. Although they lost this fight, the leaders felt that this effort set the stage for future victories, especially the election of Reagan and a Republican majority in the Senate in 1980. Richard Viguerie (1981:90–93) stresses the importance of being willing to lose. He believes that this attribute is a major difference between the New Right and the Republican party:

> We're so irresponsible we don't even mind losing a fight. We fight anyway. Where the "responsible" Republican tries to appease and compromise, we try to win. Or if we lose, we want to come out of the fight with an issue to use against the liberals in the next election. . . . When you battle for a principle, you may lose the battle—but not the principle. The principle lives on, to shame and embarrass the winners.

This willingness to lose occurs because ideological PACs are not concerned with "access" (the ability to present one's case to officials after they are in office). Ideological PACs want to decide who gets into the office. This means they must defeat incumbents; to do this, ideological PACs make the ideological issues and principles clear. Sometimes this is done best with "lost causes."

The desire to change who is in office leads to the second major difference between ideological PACs and economic PACs. Ideological PACs devote a large proportion of their resources to help challengers, even though they know that incumbents win almost 90 percent of their races. The proportion of contributions from ideological PACs to challengers is three times that of corporate or trade association PACs (Federal Election Commission 1989). Obviously, if one wishes to change the makeup of Congress, one must either defeat incumbents or encourage them to resign.

The extensive use of independent spending constitutes the third factor that sets ideological PACs apart from other political action committees. This emphasis occurs for three reasons: (1) the limit on campaign contributions to $10,000 per election cycle, (2) the need to start early campaigning against an incumbent, and (3) the need to dissociate their messages from their candidates.

The $10,000 contribution limit makes independent expenditures necessary because ideological PACs typically focus their attention on only a few races. Part of their strategy for these races is to show that an incumbent is vulnerable and thus to encourage strong challengers to enter the contest. Ideological PACs often begin spending heavily against incumbents as much as a year before the general election. To maximize the damage done, ideological PACs emphasize the incumbent's negative characteristics. To ensure that they will not harm the reputation of their preferred candidate, ideological PACs dissociate their message from that person. The late Terry Dolan summarized this with his often-cited quote about the National Conservative Political Action Committee: "A group like ours can lie through its teeth, and the candidate it helps stays clean" (quoted by McPherson 1980:F1).

One impact of ideological PACs is the introduction of social or moral questions onto the political agenda and the increase in public awareness of such issues. Although elected officials, particularly those who have been the target of negative independent expenditures, may argue that abortion and prayer in public schools have no place in politics, democratic theory requires that the political system decide such issues. In a democracy the citizenry must decide which actions are left to individual choice and which fall within the purview of the state.

Ideological PACs also help to educate the public concerning how their elected officials have voted. Less than 15 percent of the voters knew how their congressperson voted on any issue during the most recent session of Congress and how his or her opponent would have voted on that same issue. Only 36 percent of adult citizens could identify their two home-state

U.S. senators (Roper 1984). Political action committees such as the Life Amendment PAC, the National Abortion Rights Action League PAC, NCPAC, and the League of Conservation Voters spend millions of dollars to change this situation.

CONCLUSION

In this chapter I examined how direct marketing works and how it has changed interest group politics in the United States. I found that direct marketing has made possible the development of numerous citizen action groups and political action committees. It is now possible for those who share similar political values to join together for political action even though they may live far apart, may not know one another, and may not share other economic, social, and demographic characteristics.

Direct marketing, whether through mail, television, or telephone, motivates people by showing them an immediate threat to their values. The potential of direct marketing to reach previously politically inactive persons and the emphasis on fear as the prime motivator led to hypotheses concerning who participates in response to these appeals and the tactics that direct-marketing-based groups will use in its lobbying and campaigning. Specifically, I investigated whether direct marketing broadened political participation by those previously unlikely to participate in interest group politics and whether direct marketing increased extremism and intolerance among the participating population.

The results of the analyses showed that direct marketing increases rather than decreases the current biases in participation. Direct-marketing recruits have more education and higher incomes than other interest group participants. The expectation that direct marketing would increase participation by less tolerant and more alienated individuals proved to be correct. This effect, however, appears to be moderated through time and through the effect of associational life itself.

Although direct marketing does not appear to change substantially who participates in politics, it radically changes the lobbying and electoral behavior of elites who depend on direct marketing for resources. These elites are less able to use the traditionally effective techniques of lobbying behind the scenes on narrow, less visible issues and of working out necessary compromises with opposition groups. Instead, to maintain the allegiance of their membership, direct-marketing elites must choose issues that receive press attention, are highly conflictual, and allow no compromise. In addition, direct-marketing groups can rarely afford to lobby on the implementation aspects of their issues. Even with respect to grassroots lobbying, direct-marketing groups are at a disadvantage because they lack the financial resources to effectively mobilize their membership. Thus although direct marketing has made it possible for numerous new groups to enter the interest group arena, these groups remain at a substantial disadvantage.

When comparing interest group electoral tactics, I found that ideological PACs, the type of political action committees most dependent upon direct marketing, do not spend their resources to gain access to current office-holders. Instead, they spend their resources to change who is in office. They back challengers and spend independently rather than contribute to incumbents. This orientation toward challengers has a long-term beneficial impact on American democracy by increasing the competitiveness of congressional elections (Magleby and Nelson 1990). That benefit, however, must be balanced against the harm created by the negative campaign tactics that these PACs stress.

In conclusion, direct marketing has brought more but not different participants into interest group politics, and it has increased public attention on social and moral issues such as the environment and abortion. Direct marketing has allowed citizens from Los Angeles to Boston and Seattle to Miami to pool their resources in support of cleaner air, abortion legislation, and school prayer. To successfully appeal to such dispersed constituencies, groups using direct marketing have used fear as a prime motivator and have stressed the more negative and conflictual aspects of politics in their lobbying and electoral activities. Although critics of direct marketing argue that the groups that it spawns have harmed American politics by increasing divisiveness and intolerance, the evidence presented in this chapter indicates that those groups most dependent upon direct marketing for their income and support remain at a disadvantage in lobbying and that the persons who respond to direct-marketing appeals become more tolerant the longer they remain involved with their group. With respect to the divisiveness that these groups introduce into the political arena, it is useful to quote Gilbert Steiner (1983:92), who wrote that "a divisive issue is not necessarily a destructive issue." In short, direct marketing has brought new issues onto the political agenda but has not yet changed the basic interest group pluralism in the United States, and, as yet, it does not appear to threaten that process.

NOTES

1. The two-minute limit is somewhat longer than most direct-marketing experts advocate. Interviews with political and private direct-market specialists found that most believe sixty seconds is the best message length. For a call to continue beyond that, the caller needs the permission of the person called. To receive this, the prospect must already have been convinced in the first minute that the product or idea being sold is important to them.

2. See, for example, Hyman and Wright 1971, Verba and Nie 1972, and Verba, Nie, and Kim 1978.

3. Crosscutting memberships and the tolerance they encourage are two of the most important assumptions of pluralist theory. These assumptions have been empirically tested, and in large part supported, by a number of studies. An excellent book on this subject is Sullivan, Pierson, and Marcus 1982.

4. Godwin 1988a:63. These results, however, may hold true only for groups, not PACs. Guth and Green (1984) found that contributors to multiple PACs were less tolerant than either party contributors or contributors to fewer PACs.

5. There were twenty-four total interviews with eighteen groups in Washington, D.C., in summer 1986. Nine of the groups were from the environmental movement and the other nine came from the women's, pro-life, pro-choice, and consumer movements.

6. The National Wildlife Federation (NWF), the Sierra Club, and the Audubon Society all rely heavily on direct mailings for membership renewals and to encourage new members, but the pattern of how members originally joined is quite different. For example, one-third of NWF members originally received their memberships as a gift.

7. See Costain 1981:104–105. A number of excellent accounts of the development and diversification within the women's movement have been written. These include Deckard 1977, Carden 1977, Freeman 1975, and Gelb and Palley 1982.

8. See Latus 1984:150. Also see Senator Dennis DeConcini's (D–Ariz.) statement against negative independent expenditures (*Congressional Record*, December 20, 1982). The senator's comment may have been prescient in that his role in the savings and loan scandals is sure to encourage negative independent expenditures in his next election campaign.

15

The Rise and Fall of Special Interest Politics

PAUL E. PETERSON

In his farewell address to administrative officials, President Reagan (1988:1615–1620) warned Americans against the power of special interests and iron triangles. "A triangle of institutions—parts of Congress, the media and special interest groups—is transforming and placing out of focus our constitutional balance," he cautioned, adding, "Some have used the term 'iron triangle' to describe what I'm talking about." Its power, said Reagan, "derives from its permanence" and "from its ability to focus debate and overwhelming resources—like campaign money and letter writing campaigns—on issues that don't command broad and intense national attention." An iron triangle of special interests, congressional subcommittees, and media hype has worked together to influence public policies in ways detrimental to the interests of the public at large and "has virtually shut off public debate. Special interest groups focus all their resources and members on this line or that in the budget. And Members of Congress . . . with the dependence on special interest campaign financing and their fear of bucking any group that is strongly committed to a spending program, take up the banner and join the charge." According to Reagan, we need to remember that "the strength of our nation has never been with the Washington colony but with the American people."

It is the burden of this essay that Reagan's warning was already dated at the time he gave his speech. The problem that he identified had been receding throughout his administration. Special interests may have been steadily gaining in influence throughout the 1960s and 1970s, but both during the Reagan years and during the initial years of the Bush administration, these groups lost much of the clout they had once acquired. Special interests were still an active part of the Washington scene, but the battles they were fighting were no longer taking place on favorable terrain. Defensive actions designed to protect advantages gained in the past were the best they could carry out. Often they settled for much less.

DEFINING SPECIAL INTERESTS

The declining influence of special interests was evident even in the way in which Reagan's farewell address was worded. As any undergraduate political science major knows, the third member of the fearsome iron triangle is the executive agency, not the news media. As Reagan himself pointed out, what gave special interests their power was their quiet, confidential, even clandestine mode of operations. Campaign contributions to key committee members, appointments to advisory boards within executive agencies, and the unnoticed movement of personnel between the public and private sectors have been the standard techniques by which special interests have shaped government policy. The special interest has traditionally seen the news media as an obstacle, not a fulcrum for action.[1]

This point depends, of course, on an objective definition of the concept of special interest. As used by politicians, the "specialness" of an interest lies in the eye of the beholder. For most participants in the political process, it is my policy proposals, your urgent needs, and his special interests. And in this world of practical politics, the term has acquired a twisted, almost perverse meaning. An interest is not "special" if it is particularly deserving but rather if it is particularly narrow, self-seeking, and disrespectful of the public good.

I attempt in this essay a less partisan, more analytically useful formulation of the concept of special interest, one that encompasses both groups to which I belong as well as those I abhor. My proposed definition is nonetheless consistent with the way in which the word has been used by those, including Reagan, who have spoken of the pervasive influence of special interests, lobbyists, and iron triangles in Washington politics. As I use the term in this essay, an interest is special if it consists of or is represented by a fairly small number of intense supporters who cannot expect that their cause will receive strong support from the general public except under unusual circumstances. Special interests have their greatest influence on public policy by identifying supporters within congressional committees and executive agencies who are most directly concerned with the cause. They may also try to influence presidential candidates, congressional party leaders, and the writers of party platforms, and they may try to promote their cause through the mass media. If they can get a favorable news story or win an influential politician to their side, it is a triumph they will exploit as best they can in the inside-bargaining game at which they excel. But these special interests do not ordinarily have the political clout to compel the attention of political leaders seeking a broad base of mass support. Their concerns are usually not key components of the overall political strategy of the two major political parties, their priorities are seldom main themes in major political campaigns, and they are readily sacrificed by major political figures when these have bigger fish to fry. Or to change the metaphor, when elephants begin to dance, many special interest ants are trampled.

Many of these insects are hardworking, meritorious, needy members of the body politic. But their size and shape force them to use the cracks, holes, and gullies of the political ground in which they find themselves; they can do little to mold the overall terrain. And one cannot ascertain their efficacy simply be looking at the vigor with which they are working. They try as hard as—or harder—to stave off mass destruction as to extend their political reach.

This understanding of special interest excludes from consideration those powerful groups that can command the attention of major political figures and help shape the main political strategies of the two political parties. No matter how self-interested or undeserving these powerful groups may be, they do not fit the definition of *special*. For example, the interests of retired citizens can no longer be regarded as special. The retired are so politically self-conscious, their associations so actively engaged, and their ability to shape the agendas of presidential candidates so massive that they must be regarded as major political players.

When special interests are distinguished in this way from the major political interests that shape the two-party struggle in American politics, then the changing role of the special interest in American politics becomes increasingly clear. At a time when resources were accessible and power was decentralized, the insects discovered many new cracks and holes in which they could prosper and multiply. In a later era of fiscal limits and concentrated power, the elephants trampled the ants.

GROUPS AND PARTIES

According to interest group theory, the influence of special groups will vary with the degree to which power is centralized and the extent to which strong, substantively committed political parties control policy alternatives. One way of testing this proposition in the American context is by finding a measure of special interest influence that allows one to make comparisons over a broad period. Then it may be possible to observe whether special interest influence is reduced as parties become stronger and the political system more centralized.

One way of estimating special interest influence is to measure the percentage of the gross national product (GNP) the federal government spent on activities *not* of paramount interest to one or both of the two major political parties. This category consists of all the federal money that is *not* spent on such items as financing the public debt, defense, programs for the elderly, and other programs central to the political strategies of either party, its presidential candidate, or its congressional leaders. It consists mainly of those items that are sometimes referred to as the domestic discretionary programs of the federal government. The word *discretionary* is at once misleading and quite to the point. It is misleading in the sense that all federal programs are discretionary; no legislation passed by Congress can prevent a future Congress from reversing or revising a policy. But the term is quite accurate in that the programs so labeled are those over which political leaders exercise *political* discretion—in the sense that they can spend more or less without sacrificing a high-priority concern of one or another of the two parties.

These discretionary programs are a residual category—all those items that are not specially set aside as being politically difficult to cut. They thus approximate those programs that are of concern to special interests but do not command the attention of the two parties. To determine what is important only to the special interests thus requires that we exclude from the analysis those programs that are so politically important that they cannot be dumped into an "etcetera" category.

The most obvious candidate for exclusion is the payment of the interest on the national debt. A default on the general obligation bonds and notes of the U.S. Treasury would have an immediate, far-reaching effect on the health of the national economy. No president, no party leader, and no responsible public official has advocated such an economically disastrous and politically suicidal policy.

Excluding expenditures for national defense as being of general, not special, interest is perhaps more controversial. The Democratic party has in recent years favored lower expenditures than those proposed by the Reagan and Bush administrations, and allegations of contractor influence, to say nothing of the influence of the military-industrial complex as a whole, abound. Yet defense policy remains a highly salient political issue of great importance to both parties. The Democratic party was careful to insist on a strong, if less wasteful, military capacity, and Republicans made a strong defense one of the key ways to differentiate themselves from the Democrats. Although special interests played a role in shaping the allocation of resources within the overall defense appropriation, the appropriation level was too central an issue during the cold war to be treated as politically peripheral.

Exlcuding Social Security from the special interest category may also raise eyebrows among some policy analysts. Although many experts feel benefits should be reduced in order to balance the budget or permit adequate funding of more critical programs for the needy, associations of the elderly have mobilized their constituents more successfully than almost any other Washington lobby. The elderly are also more likely to vote than many other age groups (Wolfinger and Rosenstone 1980:46–50). As a consequence, politicians seem more afraid of the Social Security issue than any other. These points, however, only testify to the general political significance of programs serving the elderly. If Republicans have tried to embarrass Democrats for their softness on defense issues, Democrats have countered by casting doubt on Republican support for Social Security, Medicare, and other programs that provide services and income support to retired members of the population. If Democrats vow their commitment to a strong defense, then Republicans, despite the partisan charges made against them, claim that they, too, are committed to a Social Security program. Thirty years ago, the elderly may have been considered just another special interest to which the parties could give half-hearted attention, but after the expansion of Social Security and the establishment of the Medicare program in the late 1960s and early 1970s, these interests became such an entrenched part of the political regime that the major polical parties ignored the opinions of senior citizens only at great political cost.[2]

Just as the interests of the elderly have become of general political concern, so have the interests of the truly needy who receive public assistance from broadly based support programs. These individuals receive cash assistance, food stamps, free medical care, and in many cases housing assistance. Both political parties regard the programs as part of the national safety net that has been constructed to help those in greatest financial need. If Republicans try to cut these programs, Democrats come quickly to their defense, charging Republicans with attempts to balance the federal budget on the backs of the poor.

But not all programs that are defended in the name of the poor and the needy have a sacrosanct political position. The poor who receive emergency energy assistance or obtain subsidized public-sector employment or benefits from community development corporations or any of a host of other federal programs that serve only a relatively small segment of the poor population are not beneficiaries of programs to which the parties attach high priority. These programs arbitrarily benefit some poor people and not others, often as the result of local administrative decisions. There is no nationally determined rationale that specifies who is to be included. Program survival thus depends upon the political efforts of special groups to defend the specific, narrow interests of those groups involved with and receiving benefits from these programs.

I have saved the most difficult classification problem—agricultural interests—until last. Withholding the label *special* from agricultural interests may strike urbanites as rather peculiar. Farmer demands for price supports and commodity restrictions would seem to be the quintessential example of the way in which an interest group, an executive department, and congressional subcommittees work together to win concessions for one sector of the American economy. All these elements are present in agricultural politics, to be sure, but there is another one as well: the key role that the farm states play in the competition between the two parties for control of the Senate. One person, one vote plays very little role in the processes of political representation in the one branch of the national government that is most open to partisan political change. Agricultural interests in southern, midwestern, and western states have great influence in statewide elections, and for either political party to ignore the power of agriculture very likely means sacrificing control of the Senate. As a result, broad bipartisan support for expensive agricultural policies has been a constituent part of American politics since the New Deal.[3]

The special interest programs include everything that remains in the federal budget after interest on the debt, defense, programs for the elderly, safety-net, and agricultural programs have been excluded. It includes programs for science, space, health, education, training and employment, transportation, commerce, housing, energy, veterans, environment, and aid to local governments. If the special interests are gaining in influence, these are the programs that should be growing in size, for these are the programs that only occasionally become subjects of great national debate and only episodically become a significant element in the broad political strategies of the two parties.

To estimate the influence of the special interests, we calculate the percentage of GNP the federal government spent on activities of concern to those interests. We use the percentage of GNP instead of the total cost in current or constant dollars as our measure of the size of a federal program because the percentage of GNP controls not only for inflation but also for the changing size of the national economy. In other words, by charting spending independent of changes in economic resources, we can measure fluctuations in the political influence of special interest groups.

THE GOOD OLD DAYS

By this measure, the power of special interests increased substantially between 1962 and 1980. During these years, the total cost of these federal programs expanded from 3.6 to 5.6 percent of GNP (Figure 15.1). This increment is over and above any increases that occurred as the result of inflation, population growth, or expansion in the economic capacity of the nation. Significantly, overall federal expenditures grew only from 20.1 to 22.8 of GNP during this same period (Figure 15.2). In other words, growth in special interest programs equals three-fourths of the entire increase in the total size of the federal budget during these two decades. It was a great time to be a special interest.

332

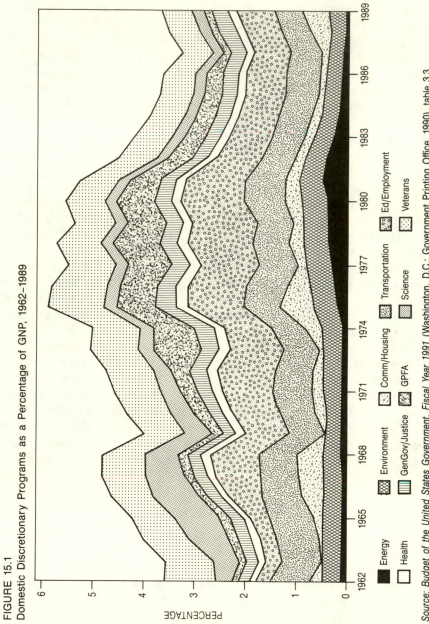

FIGURE 15.1
Domestic Discretionary Programs as a Percentage of GNP, 1962–1989

PERCENTAGE

Energy   Environment   Comm/Housing   Transportation   Ed/Employment
Health   GenGov/Justice GPFA   Science   Veterans

Source: Budget of the United States Government, Fiscal Year 1991 (Washington, D.C.: Government Printing Office, 1990), table 3.3.

FIGURE 15.2
Federal Government Expenditures as a Percentage of GNP, 1962–1989

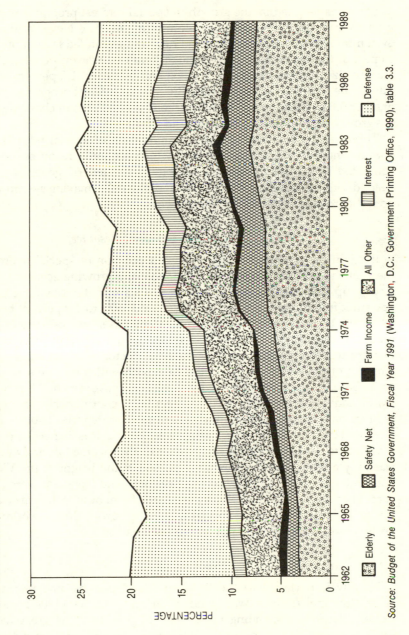

Source: *Budget of the United States Government, Fiscal Year 1991* (Washington, D.C.: Government Printing Office, 1990), table 3.3.

Some may argue that the growth in special interest programs was itself a function of party strategies and commitments. The New Frontier and, even more, the Great Society enacted new and expanded federal programs as part of the Democratic party's much-heralded war on poverty. And in fact the size of these programs does expand by nearly 1.2 percent of GNP during the Kennedy-Johnson years. But special interest programs grew by another 0.8 percent during the Nixon-Ford years. Partisan changes slowed the growth rate but hardly brought it to a halt.

Three factors contributed to the proliferation of special interest influence during this period: the ease with which economic resources could be converted into fiscal resources available to the federal government, the peace dividend, and the decentralization of the policymaking system within both the executive and legislative branches.

Politically Accessible Economic Resources

It might be thought that the enhanced position of special interests in the 1960s and 1970s was simply a function of a growing economy. But in fact group influence continued in the 1970s well after economic growth had sunk from 4.4 percent between 1960 and 1973 to 2.9 percent between 1973 and 1979 (Bosworth 1984). And in any case, our measure of group influence controls for changes in the size of the economy over time. In retrospect it seems that the key financial factor was not so much the strength of the U.S. economy as the ease with which economic resources could be translated into revenue by the federal government. During these two decades, tax increases occurred regularly, continuously, and silently as inflation shifted taxpayers into higher income categories liable to higher rates of taxation. Only once during this period was it necessary for a president to ask Congress for an increase in the income tax, and even that was only a temporary tax surcharge passed at the height of the Vietnam War (Peterson 1985). Otherwise, the president and Congress were able to enact tax cuts that did not seriously erode the fiscal base of the government. It was a politician's—and a special interest group's—dream world: silent tax increases; noisy, widely publicized tax cuts.

Peace Dividend

Equally important was the fiscal dividend that became increasingly hefty after the Vietnam War came to an end. As the 1960s began, the United States was spending more than 10 percent of its gross national product defending the country's interests in the cold war. After declining somewhat at the beginning of the decade, defense expenditures climbed back to 10 percent at the height of the Vietnam War. But expenditures shrank steadily as the war slowly wound down and the cold war gave way to détente. At the time the Soviets invaded Afghanistan, U.S. expenditures on defense had shrunk to 5 percent of GNP, releasing large sums of money for domestic programs (Figure 15.2). Much of the newly available money went for the politically popular retirement and safety-net programs; together, they expanded from 4.3 to 9.5 percent of GNP. But as we have seen, new moneys also became available for special interest programs.

Decentralization of Policymaking

The political engine that drove the growth in special interest programs through Democratic and Republican years alike seems to have been the decentralized policymaking system that evolved in the 1960s and 1970s. During these years Congress changed from a conservative, budget-sensitive, seniority-minded, southern-directed institution to an assembly of well-staffed, policy-energetic, electorally sophisticated politicians. Power shifted from committee chairs downward to subcommittee chairs and outward to the floor of Congress. The staff resources of individual members and subcommittee chairs doubled and tripled. Campaign finance contributions increased exponentially. Members of Congress traveled home more frequently, sent constituents more mail, and provided citizens more casework assistance than ever before. Membership on committees and subcommittees by congresspeople with a constituent interest in the programs they oversaw became a more pervasive practice. Even within the appropriations committees, it became accepted practice for subcommittee members to become advocates of the agencies they were supposed to be "watching."[4]

Centralizing institutions that could be expected to brake these expansionary forces were noticeably weakened. The presidency was distracted and weakened by Vietnam and Watergate. The House Rules Committee was enlarged and brought under the control of the Democratic Caucus. The chairs of the House Ways and Means and Senate Finance committees lost the commanding authority Wilbur Mills had enjoyed. The party leaders in the Senate and House were no longer towering titans whose displeasure was feared. Instead, they became adept at orchestrating the legislative process and being faithful servants to party members.

The advantages to special interests of these changes in Congress and the presidency are obvious. As Congress became more decentralized, fragmented, policy-minded, and sensitive to constituent concerns, special interests found numerous niches in which to place and promote their favorite programs. Centralizing institutions were unable to prevent these programs from wending their way through the labyrinthine legislative process (Fiorina 1977; Shepsle and Weingast 1984).

THE DECLINE OF SPECIAL INTEREST POLITICS

It was this world of special interest politics that Ronald Reagan attacked in 1980. Promises, promises, he said, were all that one could expect from the Democratic party. It was time for tax cuts, budget cuts, and the elimination of waste, fraud, and abuse in the federal budget. And in his first year in office he so changed the terms of the debate that the power of special interests was transformed overnight.

Decline of Special Interest Spending

It is little understood how dramatically the opportunities for special interests have changed since 1980. In 1980 special interest spending was peaking at 5.6 percent of GNP; by 1989 it had fallen to 3.7 percent, roughly the same level that it had been in 1962. In other words, by this measure, the world of special interests contracted back to the same level that existed before the New Frontier, the Great Society, Watergate, congressional reforms, the peace dividend, inflation-induced bracket creep, and all of the other forces that had seemingly transformed American national government.

The contraction of interest group power was obscured because it occurred at a time when the overall fiscal size of the federal government remained as high as it had been when Reagan took office. Federal expenditures in 1989 were 23 percent of GNP, approximately the same as they had been in 1981.

During the 1980s, programs that came under the protection of one or the other of the two major parties were treated relatively generously. Defense expenditures expanded from 5.7 to 6.1 percent of GNP as Reagan and his Republican followers made stronger defense a fundamental policy commitment, second only to a permanent reduction in the size of federal revenues. Retirement and health care programs for the elderly and safety-net programs for the poor remained at the combined level of 9.6 percent of GNP, only somewhat less than the 10 percent level they had reached at the end of the Carter administration. Agricultural programs expanded in order to counter the decline in the value of farm products on the world market and to compensate for the catastrophic drought experienced in the late 1980s. The cost of financing the greatly enlarged national debt expanded from 2 to 4 percent of GNP (see Figure 15.2).

All of these politically protected components of the federal budget survived Reagan tax cuts and antispending rhetoric basically intact. Those programs most favored by Republicans—deficit financing and national defense—grew. The one supported by a bipartisan coalition—agricultural assistance—also did well. The Democratic programs—Social Security,

Medicare, and safety-net programs—were not able to expand, but because the Democratic party gave them the highest priority, neither were they reduced in size.

Who lost? The special interests. And they lost quite uniformly. As can be seen in Figure 15.1, nearly all the special interest programs were reduced by roughly the same proportion. Although other components of the national budget were holding their own or expanding, these programs were being cut by 70 percent—from 5.3 to 3.7 percent of GNP—a reduction back down to the levels that had existed in 1962.

The factors that adversely affected the power of the special interests were, once again, threefold: the increased difficulty of translating economic resources into fiscal ones, the disappearance of the peace dividends, and the increased centralization of power in Washington.

Difficulty of Translating Economic Resources

The first year of the Reagan administration was its most decisive. In two dramatic pieces of legislation, the president obtained from Congress a major tax reduction, a sharp increase in the nation's defense budget, and deep cuts in discretionary domestic programs. Of these policy innovations, the tax cut, together with the indexation of income tax brackets, may have been the most far-reaching and permanent, for the tax cut made deficit politics central to the legislative process throughout the ensuing decade.

The size and significance of the tax cut was only partially understood at the time.[5] The impact was greatly enlarged by three factors that Reagan budget planners did not take into account when they initially proposed a 30 percent cut in the income tax. First, Democrats proposed very large alternative cuts—which Reagan enthusiastically accepted as cuts that could be made in addition to his own proposals. Second, Senate Republicans insisted on indexing tax rates, thereby eliminating bracket creep and making permanent the tax cuts that otherwise would have been slowly eroded by inflation-induced bracket creep. Third, the inflation rates between 1982 and 1984 were much lower than expected; when the indexation provision of the law became effective in 1984, much less bracket creep had occurred in the preceding three years than policymakers had predicted.

The size of the tax cuts were in fact so large that Congress, anticipating dramatic shortfalls in revenue, retracted in 1984 some of the cuts that had yet to come into effect. But even after this so-called tax increase of 1984, the revenue flow of the federal government was sharply reduced at a time when government expenditures were either remaining high or actually increasing. The size of the deficit was so large it seemed to threaten the long-term economic well-being of the country, and every policy issue was being debated in terms of its impact on the budget deficit. There was no way to reduce the deficit except through budget cuts or highly visible, politically unpopular tax hikes. With the president discovering that adamant opposition to a tax increase was a potent weapon against the "tax, tax, spend, spend," Democrats, politicians had to establish clear priorities. Important were policies that could affect the balance of power between the two parties. Less important—indeed, even unimportant—were special interest demands.

End of the Peace Dividend

Second only in importance to the tax cut of 1981 was the end of the peace dividend. With the Soviet invasion of Afghanistan, the era of détente had come to a close, and both Carter and Reagan pledged themselves to sharp increases in defense spending. The defense buildup began in the waning days of the Carter administration, the very time that support for special interest spending showed the first signs of softening. As the Reagan administration pushed for still larger defense increases, the pressures on the domestic side of the budget intensified, and the most vulnerable parts of the domestic budget—the special interest programs—took the biggest hit.

Centralization of Power

Finally, the structure of power in Washington became more and more centralized there. On the executive side, power shifted from the domestic departments and agencies to the Office of Management and Budget and the White House staff. As director of OMB, David Stockman curtailed the ease with which agencies could make a case for their own programs within the executive branch as well as their capacity to build alliances with congressional subcommittees. In addition, the Reagan administration changed the rules for appointment to cabinet and subcabinet positions. In prior administrations acceptability to the interests served by the department or agency ranked high among the qualifications for political appointment. Reagan's advisers were more concerned with making sure that these appointments were responsive to the president's agenda and would not develop close ties to career public servants, clientele organizations, or congressional subcommittee members and staff. One leg of the old iron triangle was amputated.[6]

Changes on Capitol Hill were just as dramatic. With the fiscalization of policy, budgetary decisions were postponed until the end of the legislative session, and virtually all items were considered in a single omnibus bill that covered almost the entire range of the federal budget. The president's supporters were the first to discover the effectiveness of this tactic when they combined new authorizing and appropriating legislation into one large Omnibus Budget and Reconciliation Act that promulgated the domestic budget cuts of 1981. But once the Democratic party recovered from the initial Reagan onslaught and gained more self-assurance, they discovered the same policy strategy. Bolstered by an increased majority in the House in 1982, the Democrats forestalled presidential vetoes by combining domestic and defense expenditures into one large budget. As a result, most budgetary decisions in the 1980s were the product of negotiations among congressional party leaders, top White House staff, and OMB officials. In 1982, 1983, 1985, 1986, and 1990, these negotiations were protracted disputes that were finally resolved only after the fiscal year had ended, veto threats had been made, government workers had been told that only essential employees should report to work, temporary continuing resolutions were passed, and a last-minute accord was finally reached. On other occasions (both before presidential election years and as Bush was enjoying his honeymoon years)—1984, 1987, 1988, and 1989—summit negotiations were held early enough so that the budget could be constructed in a somewhat less frantic atmosphere. But whether or not budgeting was highly confrontational, the main participants in the final negotiations were party leaders and top presidential advisers.[7]

In this centalized decisionmaking context, party interests took precedence. The highest priorities of the Democratic party were Social Security, Medicare, other retirement programs, and the safety net. The Republicans gave priority to keeping the tax cuts and committing more resources for defense. Within these constraints, both sides did their best to keep the budget deficit from escalating still higher.

The losers were the domestic agencies, the authorizing committees, and the appropriations committees. Budget resolutions drafted by the budget committees and backed by the party leaders took precedence over the fragmented, decentralized decisionmaking system that had facilitated programmatic expansion in earlier decades. The iron triangle's second leg was badly crippled. The results were steep cuts in programs affecting special interests.

The Gramm-Rudman-Hollings deficit reduction act formally recognized this new structure of power. This legislation required across-the-board budget cuts necessary to bring the budget into balance gradually over a five-year period. The legislation was designed to reduce budget deficits automatically: If Congress proved unable to keep appropriations from running in excess of predicted revenues by no more than the amount allowed by law, then budget cuts were to occur automatically through a process called sequestration.

In operation the law did not reduce deficits as quickly as called for in the original legislation. Congress postponed the effective date by which deep reductions in the size of the deficit were to occur, estimates of revenue by the OMB were overly optimistic so that actual deficits exceeded pro-jected ones, the costs of repaying savings and loan debts were shifted off the official budget, and Congress found enough other "smoke and mirrors" to promise more deficit reduction than actually happened (Wildavsky 1988).

Yet Gramm-Rudman-Hollings has had its effect both substantively and politically. It perpetuated a highly centralized budetary decisionmaking process by creating a crisis atmosphere in which fiscal policy was being made. And within the Gramm-Rudman-Hollings law itself, interest on the debt, certain defense programs, Social Security, and safety-net programs were exempted from automatic sequestration, giving them a privileged position that protected them during the high-level budget-cutting negoti-ations. After all these considerations were taken into account, programs dear to the hearts of the special interests simply had to be sacrificed.

In short, the special interests do not stand much of a chance when political decisions involve retrenchment rather than expansion. When tax increases are politically painful, when the peace dividend is no longer at hand, and when power is centralized into the hands of party leaders, party interests become paramount. Specific, narrow, parochial interests, no mat-ter how worthy, will suffer. Whether the elephants fought—as they did in 1981, 1983, or 1985—or danced—as they did in 1984, 1987, and 1989—the ants were trampled.

CONCLUSION

These signs of the decline of special interest influence must be inter-preted cautiously. The data presented here relate only to the fiscal policies of the federal government. There are no quantitative data on the extent to which special interests are benefiting from tax expenditures, regulatory policies, or trade restrictions. But impressionistic evidence in these policy areas is not inconsistent with the conclusions I have drawn from the fiscal data. The 1986 tax bill has been widely proclaimed as one of the most successful efforts to eliminate tax loopholes from the federal revenue-raising system, a defeat of the special interests that most political analysts thought was unimaginable (Birnbaum and Murray 1987). The process of government regulation was greatly centralized within the executive branch. Departments and agencies could no longer promulgate new regulations without first informing OMB of their intention to do so, then receiving OMB permission to hold hearings on the regulation, and finally winning OMB approval of the final regulations. The consequence of these new procedures was to greatly restrict the issuance of new requirements.[8] Finally, the politics of trade in the United States has yet to succumb to parochial interests to the extent that was generally expected in the early

1980s. Even after the U.S. balance of trade shifted decisively to the negative side, Congress was reluctant to require restrictions on trade, preferring instead to grant discretionary powers to the executive branch (Destler 1990). Indeed, Congress approved with relatively little controversy a common market agreement with Canada. And within the executive branch, restrictions on trade have been promulgated only episodically and inefficiently (Yoffee 1983). At a time when pressures from special interests have escalated, policy has hardly changed at all.

These findings thus support the thesis that strong parties and centralized decisionmaking leave interest groups in a relatively disadvantageous position. This was not the only factor that changed in the 1980s; in addition, fiscal deficits were high, the process of increasing taxes became more painful, and the peace dividend disappeared. Because these factors changed more or less simultaneously and there was a good deal of mutual interaction among them, we cannot be certain how much each contributed to the changed political position of the special interests. But at the very least there seems to be a correlation between the degree to which political processes are decentralized and the political influence of special interest groups.

Are these permanent changes in the American political system, or will special interests find a way to win renewed access to the policymaking system? Long-range prognostications are difficult to make, but I estimate that the world of the 1960s and 1970s will not soon be re-created. A new peace dividend may emerge in the 1990s. It is conceivable that defense expenditures could drop to 3 or 4 percent of GNP, well below the lows they reached in the early years of the Carter administration. Although this may give special interests some new opportunities, a complete turnaround is unlikely. The competition for the resources released for nondefense purposes will be intense. Deficit reduction will undoubtedly be a high priority, and this goal, by itself, could absorb the entire reduction in cost of national defense. Programs for the retired are becoming increasingly expensive, as the number of retirees grows and the cost of health care continues to rise at a rate faster than overall increases in the cost of living. The case for expanding the safety net to address the needs of the homeless, the underclass, and the permanently poor remains a powerful one, and, if resources become more plentiful, the paradox of poverty among wealth could become an increasingly salient political question. Unless tax indexation is eliminated or an alternative way of easily raising taxes is found, and unless power once again shifts from party leaders to congressional subcommittees, one must not expect the peace dividend by itself to bring back the good old days of interest group liberalism.

In his farewell address, George Washington warned against "entangling alliances." Reagan's cautionary words seem equally outdated.

NOTES

I wish to thank Mark C. Rom and Robert Lieberman for their research assistance. Some of the ideas expressed in this chapter appear in an earlier formulation (Peterson and Rom 1988).

1. See Polsby (1983:134), who writes of "new groups [that] are to an unprecedented degree the creatures of the media of mass communications."

2. These observations raise questions about the stability of our classification scheme. If the interests of the elderly may be categorized as "special" at one point in time (say, the 1920s) and as "general" at another point in time (say, at least since the 1960s), then one might argue that it is impossible to test any propositions based on the classification scheme.

My response to such concerns is twofold: (1) It is obvious that the interests central to the two-party struggle have changed over time; one therefore cannot permanently classify one set of interests as general, another as special. Shifts from one category to another cannot be avoided. (2) During the period under consideration in this chapter (1960–1990) no major shifts occurred, making it possible to compare the relative importance of special versus general interests at various points within the period.

3. To continue the discussion begun in the previous note, agriculture is a general interest that could conceivably become a special interest at some point in the future. However, once an interest has become a vested part of the political order, it can be difficult to dislodge it from its privileged place.

4. A good summary of the changes occurring in the 1960s and 1970s can be found in Shepsle 1989. On the way in which committees perform their "watchdog" role, see Aberbach 1990.

5. An insider's account of these events can be found in Stockman 1986.

6. The centralization of power within the executive branch is described in Moe 1985, Salamon and Lund 1984, and Kernell 1989.

7. Discussions of this more centralized decisionmaking process can be found in S. Smith 1989, Davidson 1988, and Shepsle 1989.

8. These activities were declared to be without the requisite legislative authority by the Supreme Court in *Dole v. United Steelworkers of America*, 110 U.S. 929 (1990). It is unclear whether OMB will change its procedures or find an alternative legal basis for justifying them.

PART V

Looking Ahead

16

The Future of
an Interest Group Society

MARK P. PETRACCA

Interest groups are an integral part of the American political landscape. They motivated the design of the republic and have continued to touch nearly every aspect of American political life since. Groups are one prominent way to explain politics in the United States, but, more importantly, they are deeply rooted in the country's political culture—a part of society that is at once cause for great pride as well as frequent apprehension.

Interest groups are neither peculiar to modernity nor an American institution. One need only read Cicero's *On the Commonwealth* or Machiavelli's *Prince* for a rich glimpse of the role that groups have played throughout history. Interest groups flourish in every democracy and even appear variously in totalitarian and authoritarian societies (see Ehrmann 1968).

Nevertheless, the United States is especially fertile ground for interest group politics. Madison understood that in a large nation a diversity of factions would be likely to flourish—to the ultimate benefit of the republic as a check on majority tyranny. In addition to the size of the country and its geographical diversity, there are also political and institutional reasons for the prominence of interest groups in the United States. "Federalism, the importance of geographical units of representation, nonprogrammatic political parties, fragmented realms of administrative bureaucracy, and the importance of Congress and its specialized committees within the national government's system of divided sovereignty" all, according to Theda Skocpol (1985:23–24), "encourage a proliferation of competing, narrowly specialized, and weakly disciplined interest groups."[1]

Ironically, perhaps, the relative weakness and fragmentation of the American state, when compared to other Western democracies, encourages the proliferation of interest groups. However, as Wilson argues in Chapter 4, more groups engaged in a wider variety of activities does not automatically translate into political influence, especially not for economic groups in the United States. Despite the advocacy explosion of the past two decades, Wilson's assessment is that economic interest groups in the United States have not made up the gap that exists between their standing and the standing of economic interest groups in other nations. Thus on the one hand, the structure of the American state (and its political system more generally) encourages and facilitates interest group politics; on the other hand, that same structure limits the influence that interest groups ultimately have on government policy.

The numbers, activities, and influence of interest groups may vary from one era to another, but their presence in the American political system is secure, barring the nation's abandonment of its experiment with democratic governance. My task in this chapter is briefly to highlight the role that interest groups will continue to play in American politics, refocus attention on some of the major themes elucidated in the previous chapters, identify some paradoxes stemming from that analysis, and ever so hesitantly offer a few educated speculations about the future of interest group politics in the United States. This chapter should be read neither as a grand summation nor as an encore in which every previous finding or insight is paraded out one more time for expected approval and recollection. Instead, it is a relaxed occasion for commentary, reflection, and speculation. Intended to ease the reader out of a rather intense and tightly written collection of chapters, this finale should precipitate only a pause in the continued investigation and discussion about the politics of interest.

THE ROLE OF INTEREST GROUPS
IN AMERICAN POLITICS

It is often too easy in the United States to get the impression that interest groups are an anathema to the democratic process. Conceding the inevitability of interest groups in a free society, most Americans still have very mixed feelings about them. Since the 1950s a vast number of political scientists have embraced interest group politics as an essential means of achieving the public good. But for the average American, interest groups are more likely to be associated with political corruption and influence peddling than they are with the public good. Let's face it: "The public good" is not the first phrase that comes to mind when someone mentions interest groups in a conversation.

People joining together to pursue their interests in the political arena— whether they're mothers outraged by the incidence of drunk driving or members of the National Cable Television Association outraged by the proposed reregulation of local cable television franchises—this is the essence of interest group politics. What is an interest to one group, however, may well be viewed as a "special interest" by another. And special interests are most always viewed as dangerous. Even Carter and Reagan could agree about that. Special interests are the "single greatest threat to the proper functioning of our democratic system," said Carter (quoted in Peterson 1990b:114); along with "parts of Congress and the media," they are "transforming and placing out of focus our constitutional balance," cautioned Reagan (1988:1615–1620). It's no surprise that, by and large, Americans know a lot more about the mischiefs of faction than we do about the indispensability of interests—even though both currents are very much alive and well in the American political ethos.

Interest groups are not external to political life in a free society; they are its bounty. The advocacy explosion of the past two decades signals that some important changes have taken and are taking place in American politics. This may be a symptom of what ails American politics, or it could be part of the cure. But in either case it is unlikely to be the ailment itself. We cannot banish interest groups from the playing field of American politics—at least not without paying a high price in the loss of liberty, as Madison well knew. Nor should we wish to do so, for they serve many necessary and important functions in the complex arena of American politics.

Interest groups perform important functions for their individual members and clients, the well-being of the political community, and the process of government policymaking.[2] At their most basic, these groups represent the interests of constituents and clients to the government and, in the process, aggregate interests for presentation to government officials. Interest groups create opportunities for political participation whereby individuals learn the skills necessary to be effective citizens. They also educate their individual members and the general public about policy issues through the various outreach, mobilization, publicity, and campaign activities they pursue. Indeed, if Salisbury's (1990) recent assessment is correct, interest groups now spend more time in Washington gathering information *from* government than they do trying to influence government policy.

To the benefit of the political community, interest groups provide an important outlet for the expression of concerns and frustrations by the individual, assist the individual in identifying with the political system, and link group members with broader community values. As Jane Mansbridge points out in Chapter 2, through deliberation, interest groups may also serve to transform the preferences of individual members—bringing people closer together in what they value and are determined to advocate.

Finally, interest groups also make significant contributions to the formal process of government policymaking. They help shape the agenda of issues that will receive serious attention by government officials; provide useful information and expertise to congressional committees and administrative agencies; designate members to serve on government advisory committees, task forces, and commissions to directly assist in the policymaking process; and serve as watchdogs during the implementation of public policy.

Few of these functions are performed exclusively by interest groups, though some may be performed more effectively by such groups than by other political organizations. In light of these functions, to paraphrase Harry Eckstein's (1960:163) conclusion about pressure groups, the case for interest groups in democratic systems may be even stronger than we had previously made it.[3]

ASSESSING THE POLITICS AND INFLUENCE OF INTERESTS

More than twenty years ago, Robert H. Salisbury set forth a rather modest agenda for interest group research in the introduction to a collection of previously published essays on interest group politics. Designed to move interest group scholarship beyond debates about the group approach to politics and the role that interest groups played in a democracy, Salisbury (1970:3) said that "since the early 1950s political scientists have been so preoccupied with one or another of these large questions that they have rather neglected some smaller ones: What are the various kinds of groups we see around us like? Who belongs and why? What do they do and to whom and with what effect?" These questions continue to motivate the study of interest groups, as they certainly have motivated Salisbury's prolific contribution to this field during the ensuing two decades.

One of the points frequently made and illustrated throughout this volume is that interest groups have been rediscovered for scholarly analysis by political scientists and other social scientists during the past decade, revitalizing this subfield of research and extending the boundaries of knowledge in a wide number of areas. What are some of the more interesting contributions this volume makes to the renaissance of research on interest groups? Rather than merely summarize the contributions of each individual chapter, I've attempted to synthesize some of these findings and arguments into a number of observations about the study of interest groups and the interest group system. Through this synthesis, I hope, a general picture of the interest group system will emerge.

Despite their common orientation to the dual themes of change and continuity in the interest group system, the preceding chapters demonstrate that there is no single question and most certainly no single approach that unites the study of interest groups. Neither is there a unifying theory nor even set of theories to guide interest group research.

Instead, a great many models and methods are employed in the contributions to this volume. These chapters illustrate, in various ways, that political scientists have changed how we explain what goes on in the interest group system. To begin with, we are looking in different places for interest group activity and influence. Mark Peterson analyzes the use of group strategies by presidents to fulfill their political and programmatic goals, Joan Lucco analyzes the struggle by consumer groups to gain access to the White House, and Clive Thomas and Ron Hrebenar study the changing pattern of interest group activity at the regional and state levels. And we are looking at what interest groups do that's different, as R. Kenneth Godwin does with a study of direct marketing. We test various models to explain why individuals join groups (Paul Sabatier in Chapter 5), why political mobilization occurs (David Plotke in Chapter 8), and under what conditions groups can be effective (Anne Costain in Chapter 13). We are using new analytical techniques to reveal the structure of interest group interaction with government officials (Salisbury, Heinz, Nelson, and Laumann's use of network analysis in Chapter 6) and to test propositions about group influence on government policy (Paul Peterson measures the impact of special interests on residual categories of the federal budget in Chapter 15). Finally, we are reconceptualizing the role that interest groups can play in the transformation of individual preferences and political deliberation, discussed with rigor and elegance by Mansbridge in Chapter 2.

In addition to changes in how we *study* interest group politics, these chapters also make substantive contributions to the identification of changes within the interest group system. Sabatier, Lucco, and Costain show in various ways that interest groups can and have overcome the problems of collective action that plagued a generation of political scientists. Environmental and consumer groups as well as the women's movement are groups that probably should not exist, given the collective goods they pursue and the large size of their organizations. They have managed to surmount difficulties attendant to group formation and maintenance by providing new constellations of selective benefits and appealing to motivations that lie beyond the realm of self-interest.

The state also plays an important role in shaping and facilitating the formation of interest groups, along with their activities and influence. Mark Peterson shows how the presidency directly intervenes to create groups sympathetic to his policies and to punish others opposed to them. Lucco shows the importance of formalized access to government officials in the White House for the attainment of consumer goals. Costain demonstrates that the success of the women's movement is in fact dependent upon the attitude of and opportunities provided by government officials. The growing dependence of interest groups on government officials for information, a point made in Chapter 6, also illustrates the potential for reciprocal influence between the state and the interest group system.

There are no monolithic powers in the interest group system today, if there ever were. Notwithstanding the privileged position of business (Lindblom 1977) and its potential for further political mobilization (Vogel 1989), Plotke shows the difficulties that business had to overcome to mobilize during the 1970s. Business is still powerful when it is united, but available evidence suggests that it has a difficult time remaining united, especially during periods of economic decline, when one sector is pitted against another for economic survival. Even were this not the case, Mc-Farland argues that new sources of countervailing power, such as the collapse of subgovernments and the rise of issue networks, the development of patrons for citizen groups, the success of social movements, and the ability of groups to overcome the liabilities of collective action, buttress the potential power of interest group monoliths in the process of policy-making.

We've started to understand the relationship between what interest groups do and the political behavior and attitudes of their members. Political scientists have traditionally emphasized the connection between what a group does for its members as a way of inducing people to join and keeping them members. Godwin's chapter on direct marketing, however, begins to unravel the political implications of this connection, showing that how an interest group solves its problems of organization and maintenance will "radically" change the lobbying and electoral behavior of its elites.

Finally, the chapters in this volume have a great deal to say about the influence of interest groups, probably the topic that elicits the greatest concern and fascination among scholars and the general public alike. Evaluations of interest group influence on government vary throughout the century. Conventional wisdom during the first third of the century was that "the lobby" wielded extensive power in government decisionmaking. The terms "controlling" (Goodnow 1900:150), "triumph" (Logan 1929:291), "effective," and "decisive" (Childs 1938:219) were used to define the degree of interest group influence on government policy. Many observers at the time concurred with Fred DeWitt Shelton (1926:17) that "interest group influence on Congress is greater today than ever before."

Within a decade or so, this wisdom was overturned. The impact of lobbying on the legislative process had apparently been overstated (see Finer 1949:459, 461). Lawrence Chamberlain's (1946) study of the origins of ninety major pieces of legislation from 1890 to 1945 showed that interest groups dominated the decisions in only seven cases, and four of these dealt with the tariff. None of the cases indicating the dominant influence of interest groups occurred after 1931. Thus despite an increase in the number of interest groups during the 1940s, as noted in Chapter 1, their influence was on the wane (see Penniman 1952). The rise of presidential power, the decline of tariff measures, the growth of labor as a countervailing force to business, and the transfer of legislative preparation from Congress to the bureaucracy accounted for the decline of interest group power in national legislation (Penniman 1952:98).

The rise of pluralism in the 1950s and early 1960s created a new view of interest groups and interest group influence. They were now a pervasive, powerful part of the political process (see Truman 1951; Latham 1952a; Dahl 1961), benign if functional elements in a democratic polity. However, their influence was never in doubt; indeed, their influence was the driving force behind the creation of the public good. The prominent critics of pluralism, such as Schattschneider (1960), McConnell (1966), and Lowi (1969), further documented the influence of interest groups on public policy but variously concluded that this influence subverted attainment of the public interest.[4]

Two main lines of argument challenged this popular view of interest group influence. First, case studies and empirical research showed that interest groups were far weaker in shaping legislation than the pluralists had supposed. A study of reciprocal trade policy by Bauer, Pool, and Dexter (1963:324) led to the conclusion that

> the lobbies were on the whole poorly financed, ill-managed, out of contact with Congress, and at best only marginally effective in supporting tendencies and measures which already had behind them considerable Congressional impetus from other sources. . . . When we look at the typical lobby, we find that its opportunities for maneuver are sharply limited, its staff mediocre, and its major problem not the influencing of Congressional votes but the finding of clients and contributors to enable it to survive at all.

Milbrath's (1970b:428) study of Washington lobbyists led to a similar conclusion: "The weight of evidence that this study brings to bear suggests that there is relatively little influence or power in lobbying *per se*." Second, a new theoretical framework developed by Olson (1965) explained why groups would have a difficult time convincing individuals to contribute to a group for the purpose of achieving a collective good. Contrary to pluralist assumptions, group formation would not occur automatically but only if membership was small or if selective inducements were used to get individuals to contribute to the common cause. Facing these challenges, groups would spend more time on maintaining membership than they possibly could on influencing government policy.

This conventional wisdom was in turn displaced by researchers drawn to the analysis of interest groups by the advocacy explosion of the late 1970s and 1980s. Changes in the structure of Congress and the decline of political parties—both discussed in Chapter 1—led students of congressional policy to discover the influential role that interest groups were playing in the formation of public policy.[5]

Many of the chapters in this volume point to a very different conclusion, bringing the assessment of interest group influence to the completion of its third cycle during this century. The conventional wisdom of the 1980s concerning the influence of interest groups on congressional and administrative policymaking may have been outmoded while it was being discovered. McFarland; Wilson; Salisbury, Heinz, Nelson, and Laumann; Tierney; Lucco; O'Connor and McFall; and Costain all identify new limits on the influence of interest groups. McFarland identifies four major sources of countervailing power—issue networks, patrons, social movements, and solutions to the problems of collective action—that save the system from collapse into the interest group stasis predicted by McConnell (1966), Lowi (1969), and other prominent plural elitists. Compared to Western European economic groups, Wilson argues, American interest groups are less well organized and as a result less influential in shaping government policy. Salisbury, Heinz, Nelson, and Laumann show that interest groups have shifted their functional emphasis from influence to information gathering.

Interest groups interacting with Congress are doing more of what they have been doing for years, according to Tierney. But Tierney finds that speculations about interest group influence are often overblown by journalists. And there is little evidence that organized interests dictate congressional outcomes, as Latham (1952a) once alleged. When it comes to promoting the public interest, Lucco argues that access to the presidency is no guarantee of group influence on government policy. The value of access to the presidency turns on a president's general effectiveness and willingness to act as a champion for consumer causes. Except during the Carter presidency, the goals of consumer groups were rarely realized. The great expectations of successful conservative "public interest" litigation did not become a reality, according to O'Connor and McFall. Personnel recruitment by the Reagan administration, which sapped the conservative movement of key participants; the lack of coordination among conservative groups; and the atrophy of several major conservative groups negated the triumphs forecast in conservative public interest litigation. By many accounts in this volume, the woman's movement is an example of a successful mass-based political movement. Costain, however, shows that the movement's success was not attributable to the traditional mobilization of interest group resources but to a shift in governmental emphases consistent with the goals of the movement.

Paul Peterson (Chapter 15) directly addresses the question of interest group influence, showing that the influence of special interests on residual categories of the federal budget has declined dramatically during the 1980s.

The mounting difficulty of translating economic resources into fiscal ones, the disappearance of the peace dividend, and the increased centralization of decisionmaking power in Washington changed the conditions under which interest groups had previously operated, to the demise of their impact on government expenditures.[6]

This is not to suggest that interest groups are without influence. Such a conclusion would be far removed from apparent reality. The weight of evidence in this volume suggests that there are limits to the influence of interest groups, that some particular venues of influence have declined, and that interest groups are certainly not as influential as we might expect from the advocacy explosion.

When are interest groups influential? Various conditions are identified in Chapter 1 and throughout the volume. Studies suggest that interest groups are more influential in the House than the Senate (see Baker 1989); when it comes to blocking the placement of issues on the government's agenda compared to creating them (see Kingdon 1984); the lower the level of partisanship, ideological, and campaign visibility on a particular issue (see Kingdon 1984); when the issue is linked to an identifiable constituency (see Kingdon 1981); when it comes to raising money and mobilizing campaign volunteers (see Herrnson 1988); and when it comes to the intensity by which legislators promote and advocate group positions (see Hall and Wayman 1990). Likewise, individual lobbies, such as the insurance (Kaplan 1988), farm (Scheuring 1982), hospitality (Pritchard 1982), and publishing lobbies (Gersh 1988), to name just a few, still laud their impact on government policy.[7]

Interest groups no doubt continue to influence government policy in a plethora of ways and in a great many arenas. Yet new empirical research on interest groups, of the sort represented in this collection, is beginning to refine our understanding of the changes in the influence interest groups wield under various political and institutional conditions.

THE PARADOXES OF INTEREST GROUP POLITICS

The contributions to this volume can also be viewed in terms of two paradoxes they suggest for interest group studies. Political paradoxes juxtapose commonsense wisdom about political life with new empirical findings. In short, a paradox contrasts the expected with the discovered—providing delight, chagrin, and even new insight. This is how conventional wisdom is overturned and new theories are fashioned.

The first and most obvious paradox concerns the relationship between the massive size of the interest group system and its apparent influence on government policy. We might expect that a larger number of interest groups, of enhanced capacity and with more diversified techniques of influence, would result in the greater impact of the interest group system as a whole. During the last decade at least, interest group politics is one example of where "more" turns out to be "less." We have a much larger interest group system than we did twenty years ago, and yet, as so many of the chapters illustrate, that system has less influence.

One possible outcome of this paradox is that, given the small governmental rewards to be had for such extensive mobilization, many groups will consolidate (as businesses might in a shrinking market) and others will simply go out of existence when they can no longer deliver to their members or clients. Ironically, as the size of the interest group community shrinks, the remaining groups may be empowered to reap larger rewards from their involvement in government policymaking.

By many accounts, the American interest group system has become more open and competitive (Wilson 1981; Knoke 1990; Heclo 1989; Berry 1989a; Moe 1989), resembling the vision of pluralism prevalent in the 1950s and 1960s—a vision not well grounded in reality at the time, as the critics of pluralism so forcefully maintained. The promise of pluralism was political responsiveness and stability, among many other attributes. However, the "new pluralism" of the 1980s may be conducive to political stalemate at best and ungovernability at worst. This new pluralism, then, has produced political conditions antithetical to effective governance and constitutes the second paradox. The reassertion of countervailing power may have stopped the political system from falling into a state of interest group stasis, as McFarland argues, but it has also prevented the system from responding very well to many of the most pressing problems on the national agenda (see Chubb and Peterson 1989). There might be a lesson out there for longtime advocates of pluralism: Sometimes wishes do come true, but you wish they hadn't!

This is most certainly not a new paradox but one that has been in the making for some time. It was probably first formally recognized in a report by the famous Trilateral Commission entitled *The Crisis of Democracy* (Crozier et al. 1975). The Trilateral Commission was formed by Zbigniew Brzezinski and David Rockefeller in 1973 to foster better relations among North America, Western Europe, and Japan. Although Reagan (and Thatcher) proved the Trilateral Commission wrong in many ways, the fundamental problem of governmental deadlock and incapacity remains with us. Reagan's momentous legislative victories early in his first term are the exceptions to the problems of governability forecast more than fifteen years ago. Some see the problem of deadlock linked to the separation of powers and the decline of parties (see Burns 1984, Sundquist 1986, and Robinson 1989), whereas others have diagnosed it as a function of what we now call the advocacy explosion (see Thurow 1980; Olson 1982).

One explanation for the paradox of ungovernability is that the new pluralism lacks one main ingredient clearly incorporated into the pluralist theories of Dahl (1961), namely, consensus. Pluralism of the 1950s and 1960s required consensus about the rules of the political game and about the issues most important for national attention. In our postelectoral era of shifting coalitions and sporadic policy change, consensus is nowhere to be found, or at the very least it's hard to locate.[8] It has to be built, issue by issue, sometimes vote by vote. That's tough going by any measure, especially with dozens of interest groups competing for attention and influence at the same time. As a result, policymakers have turned inward to find the seclusion they need to bargain, persuade, and eventually make decisions (see Light 1985; Birnbaum and Murray 1987). But as was the case with Social Security reform (see Light 1985), policymaking by "gangs" will be difficult to institutionalize in a system now accustomed to open competition. Likewise, policymaking in response to a crisis—feigned or authentic—is, if effective, a pretty unreliable and dangerous way to make important decisions.

The challenge this paradox presents for American politics is how to keep the system open but find a way to produce a consensus that enables action, without reducing the representational character of the entire process. This is a tall order for any polity but one that seems essential if we are to confront the current exigencies facing the union.

A RESEARCH AGENDA FOR THE FUTURE

New research produces new research questions. This volume is no exception. New questions have already been posed by a number of authors in the preceding chapters. Other questions or topics that merit further attention are identified below. Some are motivated by the need to know more about certain aspects of the contemporary interest group system; others seem intrinsically interesting to students of American politics. Readers will no doubt finish this volume with new questions of their own.

Although studies of political parties, the electorate, or more formal political institutions abound, there are no historical studies on the ebb and flow of interest group politics in the United States. No one has yet done for the study of interest groups what Walter Dean Burnham (1970) did for the study of parties in *Critical Elections*. That is to say, there are no broad historical treatments of the interest group system in the context of American political development. One of the biggest liabilities facing contemporary students of interest group politics is the absence of a reliable treatment of how and why the interest group system has changed since the founding of the republic. Although systematic research on the historical development of interest group politics is important in its own right, it is also essential for building theories about the evolution of the interest group system and its role in American politics. In addition, such work is necessary in order to make effective and meaningful comparisons about changes and continuities in the interest group system, as attempted in Chapter 1.[9]

At the risk of being accused of echoing a tired refrain (see Salisbury 1975), I must add that comparative research on interest groups also needs rejuvenation. The popularity of neocorporatism as a model for the analysis of interest groups and policymaking in Western Europe has tended to exclude the United States from relevant comparative analyses. Students of American politics are convinced that American exceptionalism explains not only why there is no socialism in the United States but also why there is no corporatism here either (see Salisbury 1979; Wilson 1982, 1990a). As a result, they are reluctant to look to neocorporatist nations for comparative data on the politics of interests. If we leave aside the very strong possibility that elements of corporatist policymaking exist in the United States,[10] there are many comparisons worth making, especially those involving the development, activities, and influence of noneconomic groups in Western democracies, as Wilson discusses in Chapter 4.

It is essential that, along with historical and comparative research, current large-scale empirical studies of interest groups, broadly defined, be given high priority among interest group scholars. If in another twenty years we are going to be in a better position to answer the questions we have posed here about change and continuity, then research of the sort undertaken by Schlozman and Tierney (1986); Berry (1977, 1989a); Salisbury et al. (1984, 1990); Laumann and Knoke (1987); Knoke (1990); Gais, Peterson, and Walker (1984); and Walker (1983) must be encouraged, refined, and enhanced.

It's time that the interest group subfield begin gathering systematic data about the Washington interest group community (as a start) in the same way that political scientists systematically gather data on elections, the electorate, and parties. Given the costs involved in such an enterprise, finding permanent institutional support is critical.[11] It might even be possible to develop a joint data-gathering project in conjunction with a few of the peak associations for lobbyists and consultants if appropriate inducements could be worked out for all parties. Perhaps we can do privately for the empirical study of interest groups what data from the Federal Election Commission has done for the study of political action committees.

The interest group system is no longer limited to the four or five categories of groups typically discussed in most texts prior to 1983, namely, agriculture, labor and unions, business, voluntary associations (e.g., the NRA), and public interest groups (e.g., Common Cause) (see Greenwald 1977; Wilson 1981; Hrebenar and Scott 1982). These categories and the groups they contained remain important focal points for interest group research, but the interest group system is now far more diverse. It includes in addition single-issue groups, social movements, and PACs, along with interest representatives, foreign agents, lawyers, and professional lobbyists and consultants. A great deal of scholarly attention has been invested in the analysis of membership groups and political action committees; much less is known about the 14,500 interest representatives who ply their trade in the nation's capital. Almost nothing is known about the thousands upon thousands of interest representatives operating at the state and local levels. The interest group system is increasingly dominated by institutions, professionals, and clients (see Salisbury 1984, 1986; Laumann et al. 1985)—a qualitatively and quantitatively different world from the one scholars are used to studying. We need to know what these institutions and individuals do if we are to understand the impact they may be having on the government as well as on the clients they represent.

Along with candidates, political parties, personal campaign managers, the media, and professional political consultants, interest groups have become a significant presence in what Sidney Blumenthal (1982) calls the "permanent campaign." Subgovernments and issue networks, the frameworks used to describe the connections among interest groups, legislators, and administrators, cannot help us explain the new networks of influence that are developing in the modern, candidate-centered campaigns among the aforementioned participants. We are just beginning to understand the role that political consultants are playing at all levels of electoral politics, challenging conventional wisdom about how campaigns are run, who runs them, and with what consequences (see Petracca 1989). We have yet to begin asking about the structure of reciprocity that may bind together interest groups, consultants, and candidates (for instance) in campaign triads that may evolve into decisionmaking networks or structures once the election is over and the process of political governance has begun.

Finally, to reiterate a point Mansbridge makes in Chapter 2, we must rethink the role that interest groups can play in the process of political deliberation and investigate appropriate mechanisms for enhanced deliberation among and between rank-and-file members and their designated representatives. As a vehicle for the representation of interests, interest groups may also be an effective way to transform the preferences of individual members and their leaders through various structures of deliberation. The transformation of self-regarding individuals into other-regarding citizens is an essential component of normative democratic theory and critical to the possibility of democratic practice. Through such a transformation, the consensus required for effective policymaking may be achieved and the public good fully addressed (see Petracca 1991).

PROGNOSTICATIONS

Political science is not well known for the breadth or the accuracy of its predictions. Many political scientists eager to test their skills at looking into the crystal ball get drawn into the horse-race fever of presidential elections every four years and try to predict a winner. Some winners, like Reagan in 1984, are easier to pick than others, like Carter in 1976. A few political scientists write books about the future of politics, which typically turn out to be long on discussions of the past and short on prediction. And occasionally someone makes a bold prediction that's both important and accurate.[12]

Usually, though, the vast majority of political scientists make incremental forecasts as a way to end a solid piece of empirical analysis. The predictions are not a prominent part of the research endeavor, nor is anyone held accountable for the predictions they might make—thank goodness![13] Few expected the demobilization of the American electorate during the last three decades, and we're just now beginning to explain it. For years a large cadre of political scientists was convinced of the eminent collapse of Eastern Europe and communism, yet no one even came close to foretelling the historic events of 1989–1990. None of this should come as a surprise, nor should it be cause for alarm, given the changeable nature of politics.

Nevertheless, there is little harm in speculating about the future based on extrapolations of contemporary trends and recognized propositions of political change—hence my use of the term *prognostications* instead of *predictions*. The following are visions of what might transpire over the next decade in the interest group system. They are not necessarily compatible but emerge from arguments made forcefully in this volume.

Probably the best (and safest) guess about the future is that it will look a lot like the status quo, or, to quote Schlozman and Tierney (1986) one last time, it will be "more of the same." At some point, however, "more of the same" is going to turn into something very different. How much of the same will still have the same effect on the political system and at what point more of the same will require new explanations and maybe even a new vocabulary are questions still pending. In Chapter 9 Tierney suggests that we may have already crossed the threshold beyond which the future is truly distinctive from the past. The qualities and quantities of that future interest group system may already be here, it's just that we have yet to recognize and fully define them.

A second speculation is that economic groups may eventually succeed in developing full-fledged forms of corporatist policymaking in conjunction with interested state actors. Neocorporatism in the United States would be justified on grounds that seemed very persuasive in the late

1970s and early 1980s—namely, the need for economic redevelopment, reindustrialization, and planning. This would precipitate a new, institutionalized role for interest groups, but one that has long been foreseen. Follett (1965), Herring (1929a), and others in the prewar period called for new forms of economic representation to supplant the more traditional ones based on territory and population. That call has been echoed in more recent times by advocates of industrial policy in the early 1980s. The "Reagan recovery" intervened and pushed industrial policy and the new forms of economic cooperation and planning that it entailed off the national agenda. However, if the American economy remains vulnerable to recession and continues to slide in international stature, it will take more than a Gipper of good tidings to keep this issue off the agenda during the 1990s.

A final speculation concerns what will happen to the interest group system in light of continued budgetary constraints. Interest groups lost influence during the Reagan years, according to Paul Peterson, because of the difficulty of translating economic resources into fiscal resources, the loss of the peace dividend, and the centralization of power in Washington. Although the fall of communism in Eastern Europe could have precipitated a new peace dividend, the crisis in the Persian Gulf and renewed calls for American military preparedness may already have "spent" the peace dividend for the immediate future. Because of an unprecedented deficit, the federal budget is likely to be tightly constrained for the remainder of the decade—even with the possibility of federal tax increases. As a result, the battle to influence budgets and appropriations will become even more intense and competitive. However, the armies of interest groups that have assembled in Washington during the past two decades are likely to look for new marching orders from their members and clients.

These new orders might take one or some combination of at least three different directions. Within Washington, interest groups will turn their attention back to administrative decisionmaking, regulatory policy, and policy implementation, seeking to use public law as an instrument to achieve what was once accomplished through government appropriations. Second, Washington-based interests will become even more involved in the electoral process as a way of bringing to Washington elected officials sensitive to their interests and indebted to them for ever growing campaign contributions. Despite the rejuvenation of party organizations, the party in the electorate will continue to decline in salience, and interest groups may take on a much larger role in the recruitment of candidates for public office, even as they have already gained considerable influence in the raising of funds, mass media advertising, and recruitment of campaign volunteers. The postelectoral era identified by Ginsberg and Shefter (1990) might increase institutional conflict in Washington, but it may also empower interest groups outside the capital to fully step into a vacuum created by the failure of the two-party system. A final possibility is that Washington-based interest groups will begin to pack their bags and set up shop around the country in state capitals. Professional lobbying firms remaining in Washington will begin to market their skills to the international community as business continues to dry up in the nation's capital.

In another two decades there will be fewer interest groups in Washington, and the ones that still exist will be more influential. Citizens will experience the growth of interest groups in their backyards and will have to cope with the unmediated and professionalized politics this will entail in state, county, and local elections and policymaking. America's cadre of professional lobbyists and consultants will export their craft to capitals throughout the world, including the emerging democracies in Eastern Europe, which will need professional lobbyists to peddle influence in Washington, London, Paris, and Bonn. In short, despite budgetary constraints in Washington, the interest group system will continue to expand into other markets and arenas of potential influence, creating them if necessary.

To these predictions I must add but one caveat: Do not be surprised if things turn out otherwise.

CONCLUDING COMMENT

Interest groups are going to continue to be an important part of the American political landscape as long as the Declaration of Independence, the Constitution, and the Bill of Rights define the American political regime. As long as the political needs of the American people are not being met by the institutions of political governance, there will be interest groups, and their numbers and variety will probably continue to increase.[14]

If there is a choice to be made about interest groups, it is how they should be brought into the political process to facilitate policymaking, governance, and ultimately the public good. The political system is much better off harnessing and channeling the energy of interest groups than it is trying to eradicate or marginalize them—were that even possible. Madison understood the grave danger in attempting the former, and it's doubtful that Americans would long tolerate an attempt to accomplish the latter. Reformers who would try either should rethink the consequences of a polity without associational life and its attendant psychological, sociological, and political benefits. The problems of policymaking without consensus, of government overload, and even of ungovernability are real, but the banishment or reduction of interest groups is surely not their cure. In fact, it may well be the case that interest groups are far more likely to be part of the remedy than they are part of the disease.

The American interest group system has not been transformed during the past two decades. There are too many continuities with the past to reach such a dramatic conclusion. However, we have seen reliable evidence in the previous chapters to conclude that the system and our understanding of it is in the process of being transformed. As citizens and scholars, we must give this process our vigilant attention and active participation. The politics of interests remains a prominent concern as long as Americans are at liberty to experience the challenge of self-government.

NOTES

1. For a similar explanation, see Friedrich 1946:510.

2. These comments are drawn primarily from Eckstein 1960, Ehrmann 1968, and Berry 1989a.

3. Eckstein's *Pressure Group Politics* (1960) is a now classic example of the case-study approach to political analysis and remains one of the most instructive works written about the politics of interests.

4. Bias in the pressure group system, the capture of administrative agencies by multiple elites, and policy without law make attainment of the public interest problematic.

5. See Fiorina 1977, Shepsle and Weingast 1984, and Moe 1989, among others.

6. The evidence compiled in this volume on the influence of interest groups is compatible with a number of other scholarly and journalistic studies and assessments (see Meier and Copeland 1983; Ginsberg 1986; Birnbaum and Murray 1987; Salisbury 1990; Peterson and Rom 1988; Nyhan 1991; Epstein and Rowland 1991).

7. There are, however, reasons to believe that this is an exercise in self-promotion rather than objective assessment.

8. See Ginsberg and Shefter 1990; King 1978, 1990.

9. McFarland's (1989) research on interest groups and political time is one obvious place to start.

10. See Brand 1988, Harris 1989b, and Petracca 1982.

11. Ideally, this could be a project undertaken by the American Political Science Association, at least as way of getting it up and running until other institutional sponsors can be located.

12. This might be said of James David Barber's famous prediction that Nixon's tragic flaw would lead to his demise as president. Within a short time, Watergate broke and Nixon was eventually forced to become the first president to resign from office.

13. As I tried to suggest in the Introduction, this limitation is to be expected given the inherent qualities of politics. We should not hesitate to make predictions, even if *fortuna* stands in the way of their accuracy. But one lesson we should learn from the experience of economists is that there's a big difference between the effects of making a prediction and the effects of translating that prediction into public policy. This is one of the key differences between political scientists and economists. Political scientists, on the one hand, study a subject that many recognize is impossible to predict. As a result, they make few predictions, of which only a very small number are ever taken into account in the formulation of public policy. Economists, on the other hand, think they study a subject amenable to prediction. As a result, they tend to make a great many predictions and often find themselves in positions of public authority to act upon them—with well-known and sometimes catastrophic results.

14. As with many other observations, V. O. Key, Jr., (1958:142) should be given credit for making this point as well.

Appendix

THE CHANGING STATE OF INTEREST GROUP RESEARCH: A REVIEW AND COMMENTARY

A Retrospective

Despite widespread concern about the impact of interest groups on American politics—be this impact beneficial or nefarious—the field of interest group studies has, as R. Douglas Arnold (1982:97–98) put it, been "theory rich and data poor," characterized by "relatively few empirical studies of interest groups as organizations or comprehensive study of how various groups operate politically." Arnold's identification of interest groups as an "under-tilled field" in political science has two important meanings. First, political science at the time lacked solid and systematic evidence upon which to found or test prevalent interest group theories. Second, Arnold correctly called attention to the fifteen- to twenty-year hiatus in the study of interest groups. Both problems are in the process of being overcome by a burst of new intellectual energy and research. During the 1980s, political scientists rediscovered the study of interest groups as an appropriate subject for scholarly attention and, as a result, added a wealth of new empirical data to our bank of knowledge on interest groups.

Arnold's 1982 pronouncement was neither novel nor a valedictory on the subject. Even during the heyday of the group approach to political science and the popularity of pluralism as empirical and normative theory, similar laments about the state of interest group research were being made. In the 1952 reissue of E. M. Sait's popular text, *American Political Parties and Elections*, first published in 1927, a lengthy chapter was devoted to the topic of pressure groups. Noting a marked increase in the number of pressure groups since the turn of the century, Howard R. Penniman, the editor of the volume (1952:100–101), nevertheless provided this rather bleak assessment of pressure group studies: "The truth is that we have very little notion of the struggle and role of pressure groups today. Few careful estimates have been made of the power of pressure groups. The major studies of lobbying either were made a considerable time ago or concern the internal politics of the pressure groups."[1] Of course, when Penniman made this comment, David Truman had just published *The Governmental Process* (1951) and Earl Latham's *Group Basis of Politics* (1952) had yet to appear. Penniman's assessment might not have differed very much even after the publication of these two, ultimately highly influential works. Truman had expressed his hope that the time would come when it would be possible to apply statistical methods to the study of interest groups and other forms of political behavior. Yet as the decade neared its end, that hope had not been realized.

Samuel Eldersveld's (1958:188) review of the American literature on interest groups produced this somber conclusion: "The role which interest groups perform in the political system and social system provide fascinating speculations, but as yet little real research." Eldersveld was aware that an "imposing descriptive research" on interest groups had "uncovered important facts about the origins, formal organization and operational techniques of pressure and interest groups." However, political scientists knew much less about "the intrinsic nature of the interest group, the reasons for the diversity in style and tactics, or the implications of organization for interest group effectiveness" (see also Garceau 1958:104).

Notwithstanding the important contributions made to interest group studies by Harry Eckstein (1960); E. E. Schattschneider (1960); Robert A. Dahl (1961); Raymond Bauer, Ithiel de Sola Pool, and Lewis A. Dexter (1963); Lester Milbrath (1963); and Mancur Olson (1965) during the early 1960s, for more than a decade the concerns of Eldersveld continued to be echoed in the discipline. "For all its descriptive wealth," wrote Henry Ehrmann (1968:491) in a contribution on "Interest Groups" for the *International Encyclopedia of the Social Sciences*, "American research has in the past provided little systematic reflection on the general role which interest groups play in political and social change." Despite demands for better empirical research, Ehrmann observed "no appreciable results." Even Milbrath (1968:444), whose landmark survey on Washington lobbyists was one of the first systematic treatments of this topic, observed in his contribution on "Lobbying" in the *International Encyclopedia* that the "paucity of empirical data makes it difficult to give an adequate evaluation of the role of lobbying in the political process." By the mid-1970s, Robert H. Salisbury (1975:176), one of the most persistent and prolific analysts of interest groups, observed a "nearly total absence of any kind of comprehensive compilation of interest group data of even the simplest kind."

Although the rediscovery of interest groups by political scientists during the 1980s has led to an outpouring of new empirical research, the calls for better data to answer new questions continue unabated. Allan J. Cigler (1989:6), for example, proposes that we study the vast number of individuals associated with organized interests. In this volume, Jane J. Mansbridge calls for empirical research describing the processes of mutual consultation and deliberation within interest groups, and Paul Sabatier suggests the need for empirical work on why people don't join interest groups when it appears otherwise feasible and in their interest to do so. These are but examples of the growing range of questions now being posed in response to new empirical knowledge about the interest group system. Of course, for intellectual and professional reasons, political scientists wouldn't have it any other way. There is an important difference, however, in the questions being posed today and the earlier laments of Penniman and others. Questions about interest groups in the 1990s will emerge from a state of relative knowledge rather than the "relative neglect" that characterized the late 1960s and 1970s (see Schlozman and Tierney 1986:ix) and, as a result, will advance and build knowledge in very specific directions.

Throughout the 1950s, 1960s, and 1970s, the demand for empirical data on the interest group system always seemed to outpace the supply. This disequilibrium was especially acute during the 1960s and 1970s. Graham K. Wilson (1981:ix) contributed to the rediscovery of interests in the 1980s by noting how ironic it was that as interest groups had become more important in American politics (i.e., during the 1970s), their importance to political scientists had declined. There is no definitive way to validate this observation, but some bits and pieces of evidence suggest the reasonability of this claim.

In the multivolume *Handbook of Political Science*, the extensive review essays on "Interest Groups" and "Group Theories" by Robert H. Salisbury (1975) and J. David Greenstone (1975), respectively, included only a few references to significant studies of interest group politics or interest groups published after the mid-1960s. Books by Lowi (1969) on interest group liberalism, Greenstone (1969) on the politics of labor, McFarland (1969) on pluralism, Dexter (1969) on Washington lobbyists, and Crenson (1971) on the second face of power, along with an important article by Salisbury (1969) on exchange theory, are the exceptions in an otherwise barren landscape of interest group research during this period.

Of course, these landmark review essays were published in 1975. It's possible that immediately prior to publication and well into the 1970s research on interest groups was proceeding at fever pace. However, the textbooks on interest groups published during the late 1970s and early 1980s confirm the paucity of new interest group research. For insights about interest group politics, Greenwald (1977), Ornstein and Elder (1978), Hrebenar and Scott (1982), and Wilson (1981) almost completely depend on research published in the late 1950s and 1960s and journalistic accounts published throughout the 1970s in places like *Congressional Quarterly Weekly Report*, the *National Journal, Washington Monthly*, and more popular magazines.

This is not to suggest that there was no new research on interest groups during this period. To the contrary, a number of significant studies on the new public interest movement (see McFarland 1976; Berry 1977), issue networks (Heclo 1978), and the politics of agriculture, labor, and business (see Wilson 1981:158) were published. However, new studies were in very short supply. Even textbooks on American government began to reflect the discipline's neglect of interest groups during the 1970s. For example, after consistently including a separate chapter on interest groups in eight editions of *Government by the People*, James MacGregor Burns, Jack Peltason, and Thomas Cronin eliminated this chapter in the ninth and tenth editions published in 1975 and 1978.[2] In 1981 a chapter on interest groups was back in this best-selling text, but the subject was not yet firmly rediscovered by the discipline. In fact, when the American Political Science Association put together a volume on the "state of the discipline" in 1982, a chapter on interest groups was nowhere to be found (see Finifter 1983). The "state" of interest group research could only be classified as "sorry."

As trying as it is to prove "relative neglect," it is even more difficult to explain why the neglect even happened when it did. As we've seen, interest groups took a great leap forward in number, variety, and activity during the 1970s and 1980s, and yet for at least a decade only journalists seemed to be paying attention. Perhaps political scientists simply had bigger fish to fry—such as the Vietnam War, the imperial presidency, Watergate, the resurgence of Congress, and Jimmy Carter. It's difficult to say for sure, but the press of these other compelling issues may simply have pushed interest groups to the back burner.

Other reasons also offer a more complete explanation. Cigler (1989:1) gives three additional and fairly persuasive explanations for the paucity of interest group research:

> Like the public at large, political scientists have often viewed interest groups with ambivalence, recognizing their inevitability, but uncomfortable with their impact, and have preferred to study political parties. The difficulty and expense of doing systematic empirical field research on interest groups has also discouraged scholarly inquiry. The "hard" data that do exist in the interest group area are often nominal or ordinal in scale, and hold little attraction to a generation of scholars looking to apply advanced statistical analysis.

To these I would add the political explanation that because pluralism suggested that interest group activity was quite normal and nothing to worry about and because early empirical work by Bauer, Pool, and Dexter (1963) along with Milbrath (1963) confirmed the weakness of interest groups, few scholars considered them to be worthy of extended research attention—especially given the scarce resources of time and funding for such "nonconsequential" activities. Ironically, the tragedy for the field of interest group studies may be attributable to the success that these early works had at persuading scholars to move on to more fruitful and consequential political terrain. Had pluralism not been as dominant a normative view of American politics and had early studies evidenced significant interest group influence in the halls of Congress (or elsewhere), then th 1970s might have been a different decade for interest group studies.

What changed in the early 1980s? This question is probably best answered directly by those scholars associated with pioneering the large-scale surveys and interviews of interest groups.[3] Short of surveying the surveyors, however, we can still offer a set of preliminary accounts. Perhaps a sufficient explanation rests with the political changes that took place in early 1980s: the election of Reagan in 1980, the new Republican majority in the Senate, the rise of very visible conservative interest groups, and Reagan's initial two-year success as president. The attack on economic and social regulation that began during the Carter years and was brought to full fruition by Reagan may also have contributed to a growing awareness that interest groups were having an impact on the political agenda as well as on the shape of public policy. With their near obsessive worries about the decline of political parties, political scientists turned to study interest groups for what they could learn about these recent changes and the impact they were having on the fragile party system. Thus both intellectual as well as political reasons may have inspired the scholarly rediscovery of interest groups.[4]

The New Interest Group Scholarship

The advocacy explosion of the 1970s and early 1980s was followed by a burst of scholarly research on the interest group system. This research was characterized by the analysis of data derived from large-scale surveys of various interest groups located in Washington, D.C., the testing of older theories and hypotheses in light of new large- and small-scale data bases, and efforts at reconceptualizing the role of interest groups in the political process. Although these studies differed in their design, the questions posed, and how the data was analyzed, when considered as a new body of information, they revolutionized what is known about the American interest group system and formed a solid foundation upon which further research, such as that presented in this volume, could be conducted.

Below, I review the questions posed and answers given by three of the major studies of interest groups during the 1980s. I conclude this section with a brief discussion of how the politics of interests is being reconceptualized by scholars studying the state, public policy, and political theory.

In 1980 and 1981, Jack L. Walker, late of the University of Michigan, began a large-scale survey of Washington-based voluntary associations open to membership and concerned with national policymaking. Three basic questions about interest groups initially defined Walker's inquiry: (1) Who joins national interest organizations? (2) How do groups come into existence in the first place? and (3) What tactics do groups follow in pursuit of their goals? This research agenda diverts attention from the question why individuals join interest groups—which dominates the collective action approach to the study of interest groups (see Olson 1965 and Sabatier in this volume)—to questions about the role played by institutions, governmental and nongovernmental, in the formation and maintenance of groups.

Walker (1983) discovered that most groups can be effectively classified by the occupational roles of their members, with the profit and nonprofit sectors constituting slightly more than two-thirds of the groups represented in the survey. After documenting the meteoric rise of interest groups, especially citizens' groups, during the late 1960s and 1970s, Walker showed that groups solve Olson's public goods dilemma by locating new sources of funding outside the groups, not by inducing large numbers of new members to join. The most important finding of this survey concerns the role that patrons play in the origin and maintenance of American interest groups: "The number of interest groups in operation, the mixture of group types, and the level and direction of political mobilization in the United States at any point in the country's history will largely be determined by the composition and accessibility of the system's major patrons of political action" (Walker 1983:404). In a different report on this research, Walker (1990b) took up the question of why certain groups were represented in Washington by political organization whereas others were not. Again, in addition to the need for political entrepreneurs to promote the formation of groups, Walker found that without institutions to serve as sponsors or patrons, no political organization representing a constituency would come into being. This helps to explain, says Walker, why the unemployed are not represented by a political organization in the nation's capital.

Walker and his research collaborators, Tom Gais and Mark A. Peterson, showed that the new tactics of interest groups were changing the structure of national policymaking. Specifically, by mobilizing supporters and expanding the scope of conflict, citizen groups "diminished the autonomy of subgovernments, made policy outcomes less predictable, and forced policy debate into forums open to the public" (see Gais et al. 1984:183). Thus Walker's study confirmed Heclo's (1978) observation that under the pressure of new groups and tactics, especially those of grassroots mobilization, powerful subgovernments in Washington—the iron triangles—were giving way to a proliferation of issue networks.

A follow-up study of an even larger number of Washington-based interest groups was conducted by Walker's research team in 1985 to understand the changes that might be occurring in the interest group system during the Reagan administration. Citizen groups continued to grow during the first term of the Reagan presidency. However, funding cutbacks were taking a toll on group maintenance for those groups dependent on support from sympathetic government agencies. As a result, Reagan had considerably more success in breaking the legs of the iron triangles than Carter had had, even though many of the triangles remained intact. The biggest impact of the Reagan administration on interest groups concerned access to government, confirming the importance of partisan ideology as a determinant of interest group access to the administrative agencies of government. According to Peterson and Walker (1986:172), there was a "virtual revolution" in the access Washington interest groups enjoyed because of the sharp partisan transition from the Carter to the Reagan presidencies.

Finally, Walker's studies also shed new light on the traditional question of how groups are able to attract and maintain members. King and Walker (1989) find that material and solidary incentives are not that significant as inducements for individuals to join a group. Instead, a mixture of professional and purposive benefits emerge as more important determinants of group membership. Precisely which benefits are provided turns out to be less a function of the desires and calculations of the individuals involved than a function of large institutions. Thus Walker comes full circle in widening our appreciation for the role that institutions, including government, play in creating, maintaining, and empowering organized interests. The need for a theory to account for this mixture of efficacious benefits is discussed and analyzed by Sabatier in Chapter 5.

A second major survey of organized interests based in Washington, D.C., was conducted by Kay Lehman Schlozman and John T. Tierney between 1981 and 1982. The results and their subsequent analysis are reported in *Organized Interests and American Democracy* (1986), arguably the most comprehensive treatment of the American interest group system published to date. Again, three main questions motivated their inquiry: (1) Who is represented? (2) What do organized interests do? and (3) When and under what conditions are organized interests most likely to prevail? In his contribution to this volume (Chapter 9), Tierney discusses the results of this study as they relate to interest group activity in Congress. However, a brief review of the answers given to the questions of the larger work is still merited.

Consistent with Schattschneider's (1960) observation about the bias of the pressure group system is Schlozman and Tierney's finding that the "pressure community" is heavily weighted in favor of business organization, whereas public interest groups and groups representing the less advantaged are underrepresented in Washington. Although there has been an increase in the mobilization of citizen groups consistent with Walker's findings, Schlozman and Tierney (1986:77) note that because of the rise of professional and trade associations and the decline of union representation, "business actually is a more dominating presence in Washington now than it was two decades ago."

Accompanying the sharp increase in the sheer number of interest groups in Washington has been an explosion of interest group activity, with Congress remaining the most important target for lobbying. Interest groups are now more active in more areas than ever before. New interest group activities and techniques of influence have tended to capture the analytical and journalistic spotlight, but Schlozman and Tierney discovered the enhanced use of older, more direct forms of lobbying in Congress as well. Instead of abandoning the old for the new techniques of influence, then, contemporary interest groups have added important new plays to their arsenals of influence in a much expanded field of competitors.

Unlike the many political scientists who believe congressional policymaking is not much influenced by the activity of organized intersts (see Bauer, Pool, and Dexter 1963; Milbrath 1963), Schlozman and Tierney (1986:314) conclude that in some circumstances "the activity of organized interests is especially likely to be effective." Influence will vary with the nature of the issue, the nature of the demand, the structure of conflict in a particular controversy, and the resources available to the group. Interest groups exercise the greatest influence on issues that are not very visible or highly charged with ideological controversy. Additionally, groups that are defending turf or preventing change will be more effective than those aiming for changes. Organized groups will also be more successful when they are unopposed than when they have a well-organized opposition. Finally, groups with access to a greater resource basis, including (but not limited to) money; an appealing cause; a widely dispersed membership; or expertise are more likely to be successful than those without.

In the final analysis, even though "there has been an explosion in both the number of organizations active in Washington politics and the volume of their activity, in terms of both the kinds of interests represented and the kinds of techniques of influence mobilized," Schlozman and Tierney (1986:388–389) decide that "what we have found is more of the same." This conclusion should not be interpreted as cause for complacency about the impact of organized interests on American democracy. To the contrary, "more of the same" may provide further evidence of the bias characterizing the American interest group system (see Schattschneider 1960) and may be "more" than the system can handle for effective governance (see Huntington 1981; Drucker 1989).

The third major study of interest representatives based in Washington is the result of an ongoing collaborative effort by Robert H. Salisbury, Edward O. Laumann, John P. Heinz, and Robert L. Nelson. What began as a study of Washington lawyers by Laumann and Heinz led to a sophisticated and extensive research program to get at the "core" of interest activity in the national policy domains of agriculture, energy, health, and labor.[5]

In a study of lawyers, this research team asked, What role do lawyers play in the representation of interests in Washington? They discovered (Laumann et al. 1985) that there had been "spectacular growth" in the presence of attorneys and law firms in Washington during the 1970s. However, most of the representational work was done by employees of interest organizations, sometimes with the collaboration of outside representation. Contrary to expectations about the role of lawyers in the Washington policymaking establishment, it turned out that "lawyers in private firms appear to play a much smaller role in Washington representation than do full-time employees of the organizations represented" (Laumann et al. 1985:481).

Extending their inquiry to other notables in the world of interest representation, the research team asked, Who has influence among private interest representatives located in Washington? Assumptions about the attributes that organizational clients find valuable have typically shaped models of national policymaking. For example, if substantive expertise is valued, then experts will be influential; if access to government agencies is valued, then policy specialists and former government officials turned guns for hire will be influential. Lawyers and other professionals are expected to wield considerable influence in this scheme of government. However, the research team (Nelson et al. 1987:191) showed that "lawyers and professionals in general are much less significant to national policy making than in another feature of the system—the organizational apparatus developed by interest groups to monitor and participate in the policy-making process." Thus lawyers are neither as essential to interest representation nor as influential as previously supposed. Of greater importance is the role of client organizations themselves and the representatives they hire to maximize their interests.

"Who works with whom?" was the next question posed. Specifically, what is the structure of the system defined by interaction among organized groups and between these groups and public officials? Analysis of the data from the four policy domains revealed that domain subsystems have relatively stable patterns of interaction, "quite sharply ideological and bipolar in the labor-policy domain but fragmented, primarily among sets of specialized producer organizations, in the other areas" (Salisbury et al. 1987:1228). Further analysis of the connections among members of the domain subsystem showed that there was no identifiable set of core actors, illustrating what the group called a "hollow" core. What sort of influence, then, do the "notables" active in the policy domain exercise? Notables exercise influence "as organizational spokesmen and mobilizers rather than as mediators whose contacts and connections facilitate the resolution of issues" (Heinz et al. 1990:381).

In Chapter 6 Salisbury and his colleagues continue to search for differences in the policy domains of labor, agriculture, energy, and health when it comes to the background of interest representatives and government officials that participate in the subsystem, the effects of partisanship in distinguishing interest representatives from government officials, the degree of specialization in or among the policy domains, and the specific tasks of interest activists. The data presented in Chapter 6 reveals that the overall pattern of American politics and public policy is characterized by linkages of groups and officials that resemble neither issue networks nor iron triangles.

I selected these three studies for review because of their size, likely impact on subsequent research, direct relevance to the politics of interests, and general familiarity to political scientists. However, they in no way represent the complete universe of new empirical research on interest groups pursued during the past decade.[6] There are, though, two other large-scale studies of voluntary associations worth mentioning because of the significance of their findings and because, as the research product of sociologists, they are less familiar to the political science community.

David Knoke's (1990) National Association Study was designed to construct a theory of collective action organizations to account for variations among them in internal and external political economies.[7] Fifteen years in the making, *Organizing for Collective Action* provides further evidence of the rapid increase in Washington-based advocacy groups and the proliferation of their influence tactics. Most prominent among these tactics are constituency lobbying and personal contact with federal officials and their staffs. When it comes to which tactics actually work to influence policymaking, Knoke shows that mobilizing resources from members is a more effective strategy than forming coalitions with other organizations—contrary to the recent tendency of interest groups to form such coalitions. Indeed, "relying on coalition partners is not only unhelpful, but might even reduce chances for policy success" (Knoke 1990:212). In addition and against the finding by Schlozman and Tierney that groups going it unopposed are likely to be more influential, Knoke (1990:212) finds that "having enemies [opponents] in the fight for policy objectives helps much more than it hurts."

The Organizational State (1987) by Edward O. Laumann and David Knoke is a second study that deserves enhanced attention by political scientists. Based on an extensive five-year study of policymaking in the fields of energy and health, Laumann and Knoke's work provides a plethora of insights relevant to the role of organized interests and their representatives in the structure of national policymaking. Possibly the most important finding from this study is that the core populations of national policy domains consist of large numbers of private as well as public organizations. Indeed, three-quarters of the hundreds of key actors in the policymaking process are nongovernmental collectivities. The national policy domains of

energy and health can be characterized by "the existence of large, exclusive, highly differentiated communities of policy-making organizations" (Laumann and Knoke 1989:49). This
constitutes a very different view of the policymaking process and the role of interest groups
within it. Policymaking is about the clash of governmental and nongovernmental organizations, who "within policy domains display the idiosyncratic nature of shifting organizational
interests" in contrast to the "rigid inflexible alignments structured along class, industry, or
party dimensions" (Laumann and Knoke 1989:50). "Overall," they conclude, "policies are
the product of decentralized contention among a plurality of organizations seeking to satisfy
their interests by influencing public authorities" (Laumann and Knoke 1989:49).

Significant contributions to the revitalization of research on interest groups have also
come from scholars who study the state and political institutions, public policy, and political
theory. The movement to bring the state back into the analysis of politics has meant the
rediscovery of the role the state plays in shaping public policy, the organization of interests,
and the definition of interests (Skocpol 1985; Wilson 1990b). State theory has two important
implications for interest group studies. At the conceptual level, it suggests that assumptions
about the bottom-up or society-centered explanations of interest formation and group mobilization are incomplete. Interest groups can no longer be viewed simply as reflections of
society. Rather, "the timing and characteristics of state intervention" affect "not only organizational tactics and strategies" but "the content and definition of interest itself" (Suzanne
Berger quoted in Skocpol 1985:23).[8] As a result, the structure and apparatus of the interest
group system are very much a function of the organization of the state at any given period in
its development. If we wish to study interest groups, we must also study the state—a point
confirmed by Costain's analysis of the women's movement (Chapter 13).

At the empirical level, state theory suggests that officials of the state—be they elected
representatives or administrators—are not agents of powerful groups or even necessarily vote
maximizers. Instead, "state officials are thought to have choices and these choices are crucial"
to the making of public policy (see Elkin 1985:6). Peter Katzenstein (1978:18) puts this in
slightly sharper language: "Interest groups are not autonomous agents exerting the pressure
which shapes policy but subsidiary agents of the state." In studies of social welfare (Weir et
al. 1988), disability (Mashaw 1988), energy (Chubb 1983), oil (Ikenberry 1988), and regulatory
policy (Wilson 1980b), scholars have concluded that the autonomy of administrative agents
and other state agents acts as an important determinant of public policy. And as McFarland
argues in Chapter 3, the autonomy of state agents also serves as a countervailing source of
power to the influence of special interests.

The rediscovery of the state by political science, sociology, and history has led to a
growing appreciation for the proposition that "political institutions define the framework
within which politics takes place" (March and Olsen 1989:18).[9] As a consequence, future
work on politics and interest groups in particular will have to cope with the reciprocal
influence that characterizes state-society relations.

Students of public policy and political theory have also made a significant contribution to
interest group studies by challenging the empirical assumption of self-interest upon which
political science has built explanations of political behavior by interest groups and politicians
as well as all others engaged in political life. Scholars have increasingly discovered that a
great deal of political behavior and political change cannot be explained by using models that
assume individuals are acting to maximize self-interest. Regarding political behavior, Gary
Orren (1988:24) observes:

> The single most compelling and counterintuitive discovery of research on political attitudes and
> behavior over the last thiry years is how weak an influence self-interest actually exerts. Evidence
> has steadily accumulated that ideas and values are autonomous and do not merely rationalize
> action in accordance with self-interest. Often values arise quite independently of an individual's
> life experiences and exert an independent influence on political behavior.

In explaining policymaking and political change, the self-interest model is also seriously constrained. For example, the pursuit of self-interest, whether by interest groups, elected officials, or bureaucrats, cannot account for the vast increases in spending for the poor in the 1960s and early 1970s; the growth of health, safety, and environmental regulation during the same period; the growth of government in the 1960s and 1970s; nor the rollbacks in government programs since the mid-1970s (see Kelman 1987, 1988). Likewise, the pattern and political success of industry deregulation in the late 1970s was exactly the opposite of that predicted by models based on the pursuit of self-interest (see Derthick and Quirk 1985).

There are two important consequences to the observation that ideas and values motivate political action and give rise to political change alongside the pursuit of self-interest. Explaining what interest groups do as a function of self-interest may be inaccurate. To explain why people join groups, why organizations mobilize for political action, or why political decisions are made will require a broader understanding of human nature than we have heretofore entertained. Even if they are accurate as an understanding of what motivates interest groups, we may want to revise assessments of their influence in light of the determinative effects of ideas and values. Explanations of legislative, presidential, administrative, or legal decisions (or nondecisions), previously accounted for by the pursuit of self-interest on the part of relevant political actors, may need revising. Future studies should certainly give due credence to the role of values and ideas as determinants of politics.[10]

Finally, political theorists like Jane J. Mansbridge are also making important contributions to change the study of interest groups by reemphasizing the role of interest groups in deliberative processes capable of enhancing the prospects for democratic governance.

NOTES

1. For an important assessment predating Penniman, see Childs 1938.

2. Interest groups were discussed elsewhere in the textbook. However, during this period they had lost their place in the organization of this best-selling classic.

3. Salisbury's (1989:5) explanation of how the Washington interest representatives project started suggests that it was just a matter of the right timing among a group of collaborators with similar and intersecting research agendas.

4. Additional reasons for the resurgence of interest group scholarship might include a growing journalistic literature on the impact of special interest money on elections and legislative behavior (see Drew 1983) and extensive research by comparativists on interest representation and intermediation in the corporatist polities of Western Europe (see Lehmbruch and Schmitter 1982; Berger 1981; Almond 1990; and other citations in Chapter 4 by Graham K. Wilson).

5. This project has led to the publication of numerous scholarly articles across the disciplines of political science, law, and sociology as well as to the completion of a book. See, among other works, Laumann et al. 1985; Nelson et al. 1987, 1988; Salisbury et al. 1987; Heinz et al. 1990; and Chapter 6 in this volume.

6. Other important studies include Browne 1985, 1990; Epstein and Rowland 1991; Evans 1989; Ginsberg and Green 1986; Goldfield 1987; Grenzke 1990; Hall and Wayman 1990; Kingdon 1984; Magleby and Nelson 1990; Rapoport, Stone, and Abramowitz 1991; Sabato 1984; Sorauf 1988; and Vogel 1989.

7. For a smaller study with equally important results on the link between incentives for mobilization and the influence of voluntary associations, see Knoke and Wood 1981.

8. Burgess (1933) came to a similar conclusion some time ago.

9. David Easton's (1990) new theory of political structure is also worth exploring in this regard.

10. On the limits and dangers of self-interest models of political explanation, see Petracca 1991.

References

Aberbach, Joel. 1990. *Keeping a Watchful Eye.* Washington, D.C.: Brookings Institution.

Abney, Glenn, and Thomas P. Lauth. 1985. "Interest Group Influence in City Policy-Making: The Views of Administrators." 38 *Western Political Quarterly* 148–161.

Abramson, Jeffrey B., F. Christopher Arterton, and Gary R. Orren. 1988. *The Electronic Commonwealth.* New York: Basic Books.

Abramson, Jill. 1988. "Conservative Legal Groups Plan Efforts to Keep Bush Administration on Reagan's Judicial Path." *Wall Street Journal,* November 21, A18.

Ackerman, Bruce, and William T. Hassler. 1981. *Clean Coal/Dirty Air.* New Haven: Yale University Press.

Adams, Gordon. 1982. *The Politics of Defense Contracting: The Iron Triangle.* New Brunswick, N.J.: Transaction Press.

Alderman, Geoffrey. 1984. *Pressure Groups and Government in Great Britain.* New York: Longman.

Alexander, Herbert E. 1990. "The PAC Phenomenon." In Edward Zuckerman, ed., *Almanac of Federal PACs: 1990.* Washington, D.C.: Amward Publications.

_____. 1984. *Financing Politics: Money, Elections, and Political Reform.* 3rd ed. Washington, D.C.: Congressional Quarterly Press.

Almond, Gabriel A. 1990. "Pluralism, Corporatism, and Professional Memory." In G. Almond, ed., *A Discipline Divided.* Beverly Hills, Calif.: Sage.

_____. 1988. "The Return to the State." 82 *American Political Science Review* 853–874.

Almond, Gabriel, and Sidney Verba. 1963. *The Civic Culture.* Princeton: Princeton University Press.

Alpin, John C., and W. Harvey Hegarty. 1980. "Political Influence: Strategies Employed by Organizations to Impact Legislation in Business and Economic Matters." 23 *Academy of Management Journal* 438–450.

Alston, Chuck. 1989. "Senator Byrd Launches Crusade Against Influence Peddling." *Congressional Quarterly Weekly Report,* August 5, 2009–2011.

Alt, James, and K. Alec Chrystal. 1983. *Political Economics.* Berkeley: University of California Press.

Anderson, Patrick. 1968. *The President's Men.* New York: Doubleday.

Arnold, R. Douglas. 1982. "Overtilled and Undertilled Fields in American Politics." 97 *Political Science Quarterly* 91–103.

Axelrod, Robert. 1984. *The Evolution of Cooperation.* New York: Basic Books.

Ayer, Donald. 1989. Personal interview in Washington, D.C., March 3.

Bach, Stanley, and Steven S. Smith. 1988. *Managing Uncertainty in the House of Representatives.* Washington, D.C.: Brookings Institution.

Bachrach, Peter, and Mortan Baratz. 1963. "Decisions and Non-Decisions: An Analytical Framework." 57 *American Political Science Review* 632–642.

Baker, Ross. 1989. *House and Senate.* New York: W. W. Norton.

Banfield, Edward. 1961. *Political Influence*. Glencoe, Ill.: Free Press.

Banfield, Edward, and James Q. Wilson. 1963. *City Politics*. Cambridge, Mass.: Harvard University Press.

Barber, Benjamin. 1984. *Strong Democracy*. Berkeley: University of California Press.

Barfield, Claude E., and William A. Schambra, eds. 1986. *The Politics of Industrial Policy*. Washington, D.C.: American Enterprise Institute.

Barry, Brian M. 1970. *Sociologists, Economists and Democracy*. London: Collier-Macmillan.

———. 1965. *Political Argument*. London: Routledge & Kegan Paul.

Bauer, Raymond A., Ithiel De Sola Pool, and Lewis Anthony Dexter. 1972. *American Business and Public Policy*. 2nd ed. Chicago: Aldine-Atherton Press.

———. 1963. *American Business and Public Policy*. New York: Atherton Press.

Baumgartner, Frank, and Jack Walker. 1988. "Survey Research and Membership in Voluntary Associations." 32 *American Journal of Political Science* 908–928.

Bavelas, Alex. 1960. "Leadership: Man and Function." 4 *Administrative Science Quarterly* 491–498.

Beard, Charles A. [1922] 1947. *The Economic Bases of Politics*. New York: Alfred A. Knopf.

Beer, Samuel H. 1976. "The Adoption of General Revenue Sharing: A Case Study in Public Sector Politics." 24 *Public Policy* 127–195.

———. 1969. *British Politics in the Collectivist Era*. Westminster, Md.: Random House.

Bell, Charles G. 1986. "Legislatures, Interest Groups and Lobbyists: The Link Beyond the District." 59 *Journal of State Government* (Spring) 12–18.

Bell, Daniel. 1975a. "The End of American Exceptionalism." 41 *Public Interest* 193–224.

———. 1975b. "The Revolution of Rising Entitlements." *Fortune*, April, 98–103.

Bellah, Robert N., et al. 1985. *Habits of the Heart*. New York: Harper and Row.

Belton, Robert. 1978. "A Comparative Review of Public and Private Enforcement of the Civil Rights Act of 1964." 31 *Vanderbilt Law Review* 905–961.

Benda, Peter M., and Charles H. Levine. 1988. "Reagan and the Bureaucracy: The Bequest, the Promise, and the Legacy." In Charles O. Jones, ed., *The Reagan Legacy*. Chatham, N.J.: Chatham House.

Bendor, Jonathan, and Dilip Mookherjee. 1987. "Institutional Structure and the Logic of Ongoing Collective Action." 81 *American Political Science Review* 129–154.

Bennett, James T., and Thomas J. DiLorenzo. 1987. "How (and Why) Congress Twists Its Own Arm: The Political Economy of Tax-Funded Politics." 55 *Public Choice* (October) 199–213.

Bentley, Arthur F. [1908] 1967. *The Process of Government*. Cambridge, Mass.: Belknap Press of Harvard University Press.

Berger, Suzanne, ed. 1981. *Organizing Interests in Western Europe: Pluralism, Corporatism and the Transformation of Politics*. Cambridge: Cambridge University Press.

Berman, Daniel M. 1964. *In Congress Assembled*. New York: Macmillan.

Berman, David R. 1979. *American Government, Politics and Policymaking*. Pacific Palisades, Calif.: Palisades Publishers.

Bernstein, Marver. 1955. *Regulating Business by Independent Commission*. Princeton: Princeton University Press.

Berry, Jeffrey M. 1989a. *The Interest Group Society*. 2nd ed. Glenview, Ill.: Scott, Foresman/ Little, Brown.

———. 1989b. "Subgovernments, Issue Networks, and Political Conflict." In Richard A. Harris and Sidney M. Milkis, eds., *Remaking American Politics*. Boulder, Colo.: Westview Press.

———. 1985. *Feeding Hungry People: Rulemaking in the Food Stamp Program*. New Brunswick, N.J.: Rutgers University Press.

———. 1984. *The Interest Group Society*. Boston: Little, Brown.

_____. 1978. "On the Origins of Public Interest Groups: A Test of Two Theories." 10 *Polity* 379–397.

_____. 1977. *Lobbying for the People*. Princeton: Princeton University Press.

Bessette, Joseph M. 1979. "Deliberation in Congress." Paper delivered at the annual meeting of the American Political Science Association, Washington, D.C.

Bhagwati, Jadish. 1982. "Directly Unproductive, Profit-seeking (DUP) Activities." 90 *Journal of Political Economy* 988–1002.

Binkley, Wilfred E., and Malcolm C. Moos. [1949] 1958. *A Grammar of American Politics*. 3rd ed. New York: Alfred A. Knopf.

Birnbaum, Jeffrey H. 1990. "Chief Executives Head to Washington to Ply the Lobbyist's Trade." *Wall Street Journal*, March 19, A-1, A-13.

Birnbaum, Jeffrey H., and Alan S. Murray. 1987. *Showdown at Gucci Gulch: Lawmakers, Lobbyists, and the Unlikely Triumph of Tax Reform*. New York: Basic Books.

Black, Cyril E., and John P. Burke. 1983. "Organizational Participation and Public Policy." 35 *World Politics* (April) 393–425.

Blaisdell, Donald C. 1957. *American Democracy Under Pressure*. New York: Ronald Press.

Blau, Joseph L., ed. 1954. *Social Theories of Jacksonian Democracy*. Indianapolis: Bobbs-Merrill.

Block, Fred. 1977. *Revising State Theory*. Philadelphia: Temple University Press.

_____. 1990. *Postindustrial Possibilities: A Critique of Economic Discourse*. Berkeley: University of California Press.

Blumenthal, Sidney. 1982. *The Permanent Campaign*. New York: Simon and Schuster.

Bolick, Clint. 1989. Personal interview in Washington, D.C., March 3.

Bosworth, Barry. 1984. *Tax Incentives and Economic Growth*. Washington, D.C.: Brookings Institution.

Bowles, Samuel, and Herbert Gintis. 1982. "The Crisis of Liberal Democratic Capitalism: The Case of the United States." 11 *Politics and Society* 51–93.

Bowles, Samuel, David Gordon, and Thomas Weisskopf. 1983. *Beyond the Wasteland*. Garden City, N.Y.: Doubleday.

Boyer, Robert, ed. 1988. *The Search for Labour Market Flexibility*. Oxford: Clarendon Press.

Bradshaw, Thorton, and David Vogel, eds. 1981. *Corporations and Their Critics: Issues and Answers to the Problems of Corporate Social Responsibility*. New York: McGraw-Hill.

Brand, Donald. 1988. *Corporatism and the Rule of Law*. Ithaca, N.Y.: Cornell University Press.

Braybrooke, David, and Charles E. Lindblom. 1963. *A Strategy of Decision*. New York: Free Press.

Broder, David. 1982. "When Campaigns Get Mean." *Washington Post*, October 31.

_____. 1979. "Let 100 Single-Issue Groups Bloom." *Washington Post*, January 7, C1, C2.

Brown, Lawrence D. 1983a. *New Policies, New Politics: Government's Response to Government's Growth*. Washington, D.C.: Brookings Institution.

_____. 1983b. *Politics and Health Care Organization*. Washington, D.C.: Brookings Institution.

Browne, William. 1990. "Organized Interests and Their Issue Niches: A Search for Pluralism in a Policy Domain." 52 *Journal of Politics* 477–509.

_____. 1988. *Private Interests, Public Policy, and American Agriculture*. Lawrence: University Press of Kansas.

_____. 1985. "Variations in the Behavior and Style of State Lobbyists and Interest Groups." 47 *Journal of Politics* 450–468.

_____. 1976. "Benefits and Membership: A Reappraisal of Interest Group Activity." 29 *Western Political Quarterly* 258–273.

Bruer, Patrick J. 1990. "The Motivations for Interest Group Litigation in a Changing Interest Group Environment." Paper presented at the annual meetings of the Midwest Political Science Association, Chicago.

Bryce, James. 1921. *Modern Democracies*, vol. 2. New York: Macmillan.

———— . 1910. *The American Commonwealth*, vol. 2. Rev. ed. New York: Macmillan.

———— . 1889. *The American Commonwealth*, vol. 1. London: Macmillan.

Buchanan, James M. 1986. "Then and Now, 1961–1986: From Delusion to Dystopia." Paper presented at the Institute for Humane Studies.

Budde, Bernadette A. 1980. "Business Political Action Committees." In Michael J. Malbin, ed., *Parties, Interest Groups, and Campaign Finance Laws*. Washington, D.C.: American Enterprise Institute.

Bureau of the Census. 1990. Table C-91. *Economic Report of the President*. Washington, D.C.: Government Printing Office.

Burgess, John W. 1933. *The Foundations of Political Science*. New York: Columbia University Press.

Burnham, Walter Dean. 1982. *The Current Crisis in American Politics*. New York: Oxford University Press.

———— . 1970. *Critical Elections and the Mainsprings of American Politics*. New York: W. W. Norton.

Burns, James MacGregor. 1984. *The Power to Lead*. New York: Simon and Schuster.

Burns, James MacGregor, J. W. Peltason, and Thomas E. Cronin. 1981. *Government by the People*. Englewood Cliffs, N.J.: Prentice-Hall.

Burstein, Paul. 1985. *Discrimination, Jobs, and Politics*. Chicago: University of Chicago Press.

Burstein, Paul, and Kathleen Monaghan. 1986. "Equal Employment Opportunity and the Mobilization of Law." 20 *Law and Society* 355–388.

Burt, Ronald S. 1983. *Corporate Profits and Cooptation: Networks of Market Constraints and Directorate Ties in the American Economy*. New York: Academic Press.

Business Roundtable. 1990. *Position Statements and Other Documents of the Business Round-table, 1973–1990*. New York: Business Roundtable.

Caldeira, Gregory A., and John Wright. 1988. "Organized Interests and Agenda-Setting in the U.S. Supreme Court." 82 *American Political Science Review* 1090–1127.

Calhoun, John C. [1853] 1953. *A Disquisition on Government and Selections from the Discourse*. Ed. C. Gordon Post. New York: Liberal Arts Press.

Califano, Joseph A., Jr. 1975. *A Presidential Nation*. New York: W. W. Norton.

Carden, Karen Lockwood. 1977. *Feminism in the Mid-1970's*. New York: Ford Foundation.

Cater, Douglas. 1964. *Power in Washington*. New York: Random House.

Chamberlain, Lawrence. 1946. *The President, Congress, and Legislation*. New York: Columbia University Press.

Chase, Stuart. 1945. *Democracy Under Pressure*. New York: Twentieth Century Fund.

Chester, Lewis, Godfrey Hodgson, and Bruce Page. 1969. *An American Melodrama: The Presidential Campaign of 1968*. New York: Viking.

Childs, Harwood L. 1938. "Pressure Groups and Propaganda." In Edward B. Logan, ed., *The American Political Scene*. Rev. ed. New York: Harper and Brothers.

Choate, Pat. 1990. *Agents of Influence*. New York: Alfred A. Knopf.

Chubb, John E. 1983. *Interest Groups and the Bureaucracy*. Stanford: Stanford University Press.

Chubb, John E., and Paul E. Peterson. 1989. "American Political Institutions and the Problem of Governance." In J. E. Chubb and P. E. Peterson, eds., *Can the Government Govern?* Washington, D.C.: Brookings Institution.

———— . 1985a. "Realignment and Institutionalization." In J. E. Chubb and P. E. Peterson, eds., *The New Direction in American Politics*. Washington, D.C.: Brookings Institution.

———— , eds. 1985b. *The New Direction in American Politics*. Washington, D.C.: Brookings Institution.

Cigler, Allan J. 1989. "Interest Groups: A Subfield in Search of an Identity." 8 *Vox Pop Newsletter*, 1, 3.

Cigler, Allan, and John Mark Hansen. 1983. "Group Formation Through Protest." In Allan J. Cigler and Burdett A. Loomis, eds., *Interest Group Politics*. Washington, D.C.: Congressional Quarterly Press.

Cigler, Allan J., and Burdett A. Loomis. 1986a. "Moving On: Interests, Power and Politics in the 1980s." In A. J. Cigler and B. A. Loomis, eds., *Interest Group Politics*. 2nd ed. Washington, D.C.: Congressional Quarterly Press.

―――, eds. 1986b. *Interest Group Politics*. 2nd ed. Washington, D.C.: Congressional Quarterly Press.

Cingranelli, David L. 1983. "State Government Lobbies in the National Political Process." 56 *State Government* 122–127.

Clark, Peter B., and James Q. Wilson. 1961. "Incentive Systems: A Theory of Organizations." 6 *Administrative Science Quarterly* 129–166.

Clarke, Jeanne Nienaber, and Daniel McCool. 1985. *Staking Out the Terrain*. Albany: SUNY Press.

Close, Arthur C. 1979–1991. *Washington Representatives*. 1st–14th annual eds. New York: Columbia Books.

Cloward, Richard, and Frances Piven. 1983. "Toward a Class-based Realignment of American Politics: A Movement Strategy." 13 *Strategy Policy* 2–14.

Cobb, Roger W., and Charles D. Elder. 1983. *Participation in American Politics*. 2nd ed. Baltimore: Johns Hopkins University Press.

―――. 1972. *Participation in American Politics*. Baltimore: Johns Hopkins University Press.

Cohen, David. 1988. "Forward: The 1990s and the Public Interest Movement." In Foundation for Public Affairs, ed., *Public Interest Profiles, 1988–1989*. Washington, D.C.: Congressional Quarterly Press.

Cohen, David, and Charles Lindblom. 1979. *Usable Knowledge: Social Science and Social Problem Solving*. New Haven: Yale University Press.

Cohen, Joshua, and Joel Rogers. 1989. "Secondary Associations in Democratic Governance." Paper prepared for the annual meetings of the American Political Science Association, Atlanta.

Coleman, William D. 1988. *Business and Politics: A Study of Collective Action*. Kingston, Ont.: McGill-Queens University Press.

Congressional Research Service. 1986. *Congress and Pressure Groups: Lobbying in a Modern Democracy*. Washington, D.C.: Government Printing Office.

Conlan, Timothy, Margaret Wrightson, and David Beam. 1990. *Taxing Choices: The Politics of Tax Reform*. Washington, D.C.: Congressional Quarterly Press.

Connolly, William E. 1969. *The Bias of Pluralism*. New York: Atherton Press.

Conrad, Robin. 1989. Personal interview in Washington, D.C., March 2.

Constantini, Edmond, and Kenneth Hanf. 1973. *The Environmental Impulse and Its Competitor*. Davis: University of California, Davis Institute of Governmental Affairs.

Constantini, Edmond, and Joel King. 1984. "The Motives of Political Party Activists." 6 *Political Behavior* 79–93.

Cook, Constance Ewing. 1984. "Participation in Public Interest Groups." 12 *American Politics Quarterly* 409–430.

Cook, Fay Lomax, and Wesley G. Skogan. 1990. "Agenda Setting and the Rise and Fall of Policy Issues: The Case of Criminal Victimization of the Elderly." 8 *Government and Policy* 395–415.

Cooper, Ann. 1986. "Third World Insurgent Groups Learning to Play the Washington Lobbying Game." 6 *National Journal* (8 February) 329–333.

―――. 1985. "Lobbying in the '80s: High Tech Takes Hold." 5 *National Journal* (September 14) 2036.

Copeland, Robert M. 1985. "Cultivating Interest Group Support: Public Liaison in the Ford Administration." Paper presented at the annual meetings of the Midwest Political Science Association, Chicago.

Costain, Anne N. 1981. "Representing Women: The Transition from Social Movement to Interest Group." 34 *Western Political Quarterly* 100–113.

Costain, Anne N., and W. Douglas Costain. 1983. "The Women's Lobby: Impact of a Movement on Congress." In Allan J. Cigler and Burdett A. Loomis, eds., *Interest Group Politics.* Washington, D.C.: Congressional Quarterly Press.

Costain, W. Douglas, and Anne N. Costain. 1981. "Interest Groups as Policy Aggregators in the Legislative Process." 14 *Polity* 249–272.

Cott, Nancy E. 1987. *The Grounding of Modern Feminism.* New Haven: Yale University Press.

Council on Governmental Ethics Law (COGEL). 1988. *Campaign Finance, Ethics & Lobby Law Blue Book, 1988–89: Special Report.* Lexington, Ky.: COGEL, through the Council of State Governments.

Craney, Glen, and Janet Hook. 1989. "Until 1980s, Congress Rarely Repealed Its New Laws." *Congressional Quarterly Weekly Report,* October 14, 2681.

Crawford, Kenneth G. 1939. *The Pressure Boys.* New York: Julian Messner.

Crenson, Matthew A. 1971. *The Un-Politics of Air Pollution.* Baltimore: Johns Hopkins University Press.

Croly, Herbert. 1915. *Progressive Democracy.* New York: Macmillan.

Cronin, Thomas E. 1989. *Direct Democracy.* Cambridge, Mass.: Harvard University Press.

———. 1975. *The State of the Presidency.* Boston: Little, Brown.

Crozier, Michel J., Samuel P. Huntington, and Joji Watanuki. 1975. *The Crisis of Democracy.* New York: Trilateral Commission and New York University Press.

Culhane, Paul J. 1981. *Public Lands Politics.* Baltimore: Johns Hopkins University Press.

Dahl, Robert A. 1989. *Democracy and Its Critics.* New Haven: Yale University Press.

———. 1985. *A Preface to Economic Democracy.* Berkeley: University of California Press.

———. 1982. *Dilemmas of Pluralist Democracy.* New Haven: Yale University Press.

———. 1970. *After the Revolution? Authority in a Good Society.* New Haven: Yale University Press.

———. 1961. *Who Governs?* New Haven: Yale University Press.

———. 1956. *A Preface to Democratic Theory.* Chicago: University of Chicago Press.

Davidson, Roger. 1988. "The New Centralization on Capitol Hill." *Review of Politics* (Summer) 345–364.

———. 1981. "Subcommittee Government—New Channels for Policymaking." In Thomas E. Mann and Norman J. Thomas, eds., *The New Congress.* Washington, D.C.: American Enterprise Institute.

Davis, Charles, and Sandra Davis. 1986. "Analyzing the Public Lands Subsystem." Paper presented at the annual meeting of the American Political Science Association, Washington, D.C.

Dawes, Robyn M., Alphons J. C. van de Kragt, and John M. Orbell. 1990. "Cooperation for the Benefit of Us—Not Me, or My Conscience." In Jane J. Mansbridge, ed., *Beyond Self-Interest.* Chicago: University of Chicago Press.

Deakins, James. 1966. *The Lobbyists.* Washington, D.C.: Public Affairs Press.

Deckard, Barbara. 1977. *The Women's Movement.* New York: Harper and Row.

DeGrazia, Alfred. 1958. "Nature and Prospects of Political Interest Groups." In Donald C. Blaisdell, ed., *Unofficial Government: Pressure Groups and Lobbies, The Annals* (of the American Academy of Political and Social Sciences) 113–122.

Derthick, Martha, and Paul J. Quirk. 1985. *The Politics of Deregulation.* Washington, D.C.: Brookings Institution.

Destler, I. M. 1990. "United States Trade Policymaking in the Eighties." Paper presented at the Conference on Politics and Economics in the Eighties, National Bureau of Economic Research, Cambridge, Mass.

Dexter, Lewis A. 1972. "Pros and Cons of Professional Lobbying in Washington." 1 *Capitol Studies* 3–10.

———. 1969. *How Organizations Are Represented in Washington.* Indianapolis: Bobbs-Merrill.

Dillion, Mary Earhart. 1942. "Pressure Groups." 36 *American Political Science Review* 471–481.

Dodd, Lawrence C. 1979. "Congress and the Cycles of Power." In William S. Livingston, Lawrence C. Dodd, and Richard L. Schott, eds., *The Presidency and the Congress: A Shifting Balance of Power.* Austin: Lyndon B. Johnson School of Public Affairs.

Dodd, Lawrence C., and Bruce I. Oppenheimer. 1981. "The House in Transition: Change and Consolidation." In Lawrence C. Dodd and Bruce I. Oppenheimer, eds., *Congress Reconsidered.* Washington, D.C.: Congressional Quarterly Press.

Dodd, Lawrence C., and Richard L. Schott. 1979. *Congress and the Administrative State.* New York: John Wiley.

Doig, Alan. 1986. "Influencing Westminster: Registering the Lobbyists." 39 *Parliamentary Affairs* (October) 517–535.

Downs, Anthony. 1989. "Social Values and Democracy." Paper presented at the annual meetings of the American Political Science Association, Atlanta.

———. 1972. "Up and Down with Ecology—The Issue Attention Cycle." 28 *Public Interest* 38–50.

———. 1957. *An Economic Theory of Democracy.* New York: Harper and Row.

Drew, Elizabeth. 1983. *Politics and Money.* New York: Macmillan.

Drucker, Peter. 1989. *The New Realities.* New York: Harper and Row.

———. 1971. "A Key to Calhoun's Pluralism." In P. Drucker, ed., *Men, Ideas, and Politics.* New York: Harper and Row.

Duchesne, Pierre, and Russell Ducasse. 1984-1985. "Must Lobbying Be Regulated?" *Canadian Parliamentary Affairs* (Winter) 2–7.

Duerst-Lahti, Georgia. 1989. "The Government's Role in Building the Women's Movement." 104 *Political Science Quarterly* 256.

Duffy, Michael. 1989. "Mr. Consensus." *Time,* August 21, 16–21.

Easton, David. 1990. *The Analysis of Political Structure.* New York: Routledge.

Eckstein, Harry. 1960. *Pressure Group Politics: The Case of the British Medical Association.* London: Allen & Unwin.

Edelman, Murray. 1964. *The Symbolic Uses of Politics.* Urbana: University of Illinois Press.

Edsall, Thomas Byrne. 1984. *The New Politics of Inequality.* New York: W. W. Norton.

Ehrbar, A. F. 1978. "The Backlash Against Business Advocacy." *Fortune,* August 28, 62–68.

Ehrenhalt, Alan. 1985. "Political Parties: A Renaissance of Power?" *Congressional Quarterly Weekly Report,* October 26, 2187.

Ehrlichman, John. 1982. *Witness to Power: The Nixon Years.* New York: Simon and Schuster.

Erhmann, Henry. 1968. "Interest Groups." In David L. Sills, ed., *International Encyclopedia of the Social Sciences,* vol. 7. New York: Macmillan.

———, ed. 1958. *Interest Groups on Four Continents.* Pittsburgh: University of Pittsburgh Press.

Eldersveld, Samuel J. 1982. *Political Parties in American Society.* New York: Basic Books.

———. 1958. "American Interest Groups: A Survey of Research and Some Implications for Theory and Method." In H. W. Ehrmann, ed., *Interest Groups on Four Continents.* Pittsburgh: University of Pittsburgh Press.

Elkin, Stephen L. 1985. "Between Liberalism and Capitalism: An Introduction to the Democratic State." In Roger Benjamin and Stephen L. Elkin, eds., *The Democratic State.* Lawrence: University Press of Kansas.

Ellwood, John W., and Robert J. Spitzer. 1979. "The Democratic National Telethons: Their Successes and Failures." 41 *Journal of Politics* 828–864.

Entman, Robert M. 1989. *Democracy Without Citizens.* New York: Oxford University Press.

Epstein, Edwin. 1980a. "Business and Labor Under the Federal Election Campaign Act of 1971." In Michael J. Malbin, ed., *Parties, Interest Groups, and Campaign Finance Laws.* Washington, D.C.: American Enterprise Institute.

———. 1980b. "The PAC Phenomenon: An Overview." 22 *Arizona Law Review* 355–372.

Epstein, Lee. 1986. *Conservatives in Court.* Knoxville: University of Tennessee Press.

Epstein, Lee, and C. K. Rowland. 1991. "Debunking the Myth of Interest Group Invincibility in the Courts." 85 *American Political Science Review* 205–217.

Etzioni, Amitai. 1984. *Capital Corruption: The New Attack on American Democracy.* San Diego: Harcourt Brace Jovanovich.

———. 1977-1978. "Societal Overload: Sources, Components and Connections." 92 *Political Science Quarterly* 607–631.

Evans, Diana. 1989. "Policy Making in the Concrete Triangle: Interest Group Demands and Committee Responses on Highway Legislation." Paper presented at the annual meetings of the American Political Science Association, Atlanta.

Evans, Rowland, Jr., and Robert D. Novak. 1972. *Nixon in the White House: The Frustration of Power.* New York: Random House.

Farber, Daniel A., and Philip P. Frickey. 1987. "The Jurisprudence of Public Choice." 65 *Texas Law Review* 873–927.

Farney, Dennis. 1987. "Mountain States' Conservative Legal Bite Loses Strength Due to Funding Woes, Ideological Rifts." *Wall Street Journal,* January 30, 50.

Federal Communications Commission (FCC). 1987. "Syracuse Peace Council v. Television Station WTVH, Memorandum Opinion and Order." 17 *Federal Communications Record,* FCC87-266: 5043–5058.

Federal Election Commission (FEC). 1989. "FEC Final Report Finds Slower Growth of PAC Activity During 1988 Election Cycle." Press release, October 31.

Feldstein, Martin, and Lawrence Summers. 1977. "Is the Rate of Profit Falling?" 1 *Brookings Papers on Economic Activity* 211–228.

Fenno, Richard F., Jr. 1959. *The President's Cabinet.* Cambridge, Mass.: Harvard University Press.

Ferejohn, John A. 1974. *Pork Barrel Politics.* Stanford: Stanford University Press.

Ferejohn, John A., and Morris P. Fiorina. 1975. "Closeness Counts Only in Horseshoes and Dancing." 69 *American Political Science Review* 920–925.

———. 1974. "The Paradox of Not Voting: A Decision Theoretic Analysis." 68 *American Political Science Review* 525–536.

Ferguson, Thomas, and Joel Rogers. 1986. *Right Turn: The Decline of the Democrats and the Future of American Politics.* New York: Hill and Wang.

Finer, Herman. 1949. *Theory and Practice of Modern Government.* New York: Holt, Rinehart and Winston.

Finifter, Ada W. 1983. *Political Science: The State of the Discipline.* Washington, D.C.: American Political Science Association.

Fiorina, Morris P. 1989. *Congress: Keystone of the Washington Establishment.* 2nd ed. New Haven: Yale University Press.

———. 1977. *Congress: Keystone of the Washington Establishment.* New Haven: Yale University Press.

Fishel, Jeff. 1985. *Presidents and Promises.* Washington, D.C.: Congressional Quarterly Press.

Flathman, Richard E. 1966. *The Public Interest.* New York: Wiley.

Follett, Mary P. [1918] 1965. *The New State.* Gloucester, Mass.: Peter Smith.

Foundation for Public Affairs. 1988. *Public Interest Profiles, 1988–1989.* Washington, D.C.: Congressional Quarterly Press.

Fox, Harrison W., and Susan Webb Hammond. 1977. *Congressional Staffs*. New York: Free Press.

Frankovic, Kathleen A. 1987. "The Democratic Nomination Campaign." In Kay Lehman Schlozman, ed., *Elections in America*. Boston: Allen and Unwin.

Freeman, J. Lieper. 1965. *The Political Process*. Rev. ed. New York: Random House.

Freeman, Jo. 1975. *The Politics of Women's Liberation*. New York: McKay.

———. 1973. "The Tyranny of Structurelessness." *Ms.*, July, 76–89.

Freeman, John R. 1989. *Democracy and Markets: The Politics of Mixed Economies*. Ithaca, N.Y.: Cornell University Press.

Freeman, Richard B., and James Medoff. 1984. *What Do Unions Do?* New York: Basic Books.

Freinwald, Aaron. 1988. "Conservatives Plot Post-Reagan Tactics." *Legal Times*, November 14.

Friedrich, Carl J. 1946. *Constitutional Government and Democracy*. Boston: Ginn.

Fritschler, A. Lee. 1983. *Smoking and Politics*. 3rd ed. Englewood Cliffs, N.J.: Prentice-Hall.

Frohlich, Norman, Joe Oppenheimer, and Oran Young. 1971. *Political Leadership and Collective Goods*. Princeton: Princeton University Press.

Gais, Thomas L., Mark A. Peterson, and Jack L. Walker. 1984. "Interest Groups, Iron Triangles, and Representative Institutions in American National Government." 14 *British Journal of Political Science* 161–185.

Gais, Thomas L., and Jack L. Walker. 1990. "Pathways to Influence in American Politics." *Mobilizing Interests in America*.

Galaskiewicz, Joseph. 1981. "Interest Group Politics from a Comparative Perspective." 16 *Urban Affairs Quarterly* (March) 259–280.

Galli, Anthony. 1971. "Corporate Advertising: More than Just a Nice Warm Feeling All Over." *Public Relations Journal*, November, 22.

The Gallup Report. 1981. "Participation in Interest Groups High." 191 (August): 45–55.

Galvin, Andrew. 1987. "Planting Seeds for Stronger Grass-roots Lobbying Efforts." *Beverage World*, May, 54–55.

Gamson, William A. 1975. *The Strategy of Social Protest*. Homewood, Ill.: Dorsey Press.

Garceau, Oliver. 1958. "Interest Group Theory in Political Research." In Donald C. Blaisdell, ed., *Unofficial Government: Pressure Groups and Lobbies, The Annals* (of the American Academy of Political and Social Sciences) 104–112.

Garson, G. David. 1978. *Group Theories of Politics*. Beverly Hills, Calif.: Sage.

Gelb, Joyce, and Marian Lief Palley. 1987. *Women and Public Policies*. 2nd ed. Princeton: Princeton University Press.

———. 1982. *Women and Public Policies*. Princeton: Princeton University Press.

Gersh, Debra. 1988. "Press Groups Lobby for Ad Business." *Editor and Publisher* (April 2) 18.

Gest, Ted. 1988. "The New Frontiers for Legal Warriors." *U.S. News and World Report*, December 5.

Gibb, Cecil A. 1954. "Leadership." In Gardner Lindzey, ed., *Handbook of Social Psychology*, vol. 2. Cambridge, Mass.: Addison-Wesley.

Ginsberg, Benjamin. 1986. *The Captive Public*. New York: Basic Books.

———. 1976. "Elections and Public Policy." 70 *American Political Science Review* 41.

Ginsberg, Benjamin, and John C. Green. 1986. "The Best Congress Money Can Buy." In B. Ginsberg and A. Stone, eds., *Do Elections Matter?* Armonk, N.Y.: M. E. Sharpe.

Ginsberg, Benjamin, and Martin Shefter. 1990. *Politics by Other Means*. New York: Basic Books.

———. 1988. "The Presidency and the Organization of Interests." In Michael Nelson, ed., *The Presidency and the Political System*. 2nd ed. Washington, D.C.: Congressional Quarterly Press.

Godkin, Edwin L. [1896] 1966. *Problems of Modern Democracy*. Ed. Morton Keller. Cambridge, Mass.: Belknap Press of Harvard University Press.

Godwin, R. Kenneth. 1988a. *One Billion Dollars of Influence.* Chatham, N.J.: Chatham House.
——— . 1988b. "The Structure, Content and Use of Political Direct Mail." 20 *Polity* 527–538.
Godwin, R. Kenneth, and Robert C. Mitchell. 1982. "Rational Models, Collective Goods, and Nonelectoral Political Behavior." 35 *Western Political Quarterly* 161–192.
Goldfield, Michael. 1987. *The Decline of Organized Labor in the United States.* Chicago: University of Chicago Press.
Goldman, Charles. 1981. "Two Decades of Change in a Nitrogen-Deficient Oligotrophic Lake." 21 *Verhandlungen der Internationalen Vereinigung für Theoretische und Angewandte Limnologie* 45–70.
Goodnow, Frank J. 1900. *Politics and Administration.* New York: Russell and Russell.
Gordon, David, Richard Edwards, and Michael Reich. 1982. *Segmented Work, Divided Workers: The Historical Transformation of Labor in the United States.* New York: Cambridge University Press.
Gormley, William, John Hoadley, and Charles Williams. 1983. "Potential Responsiveness in the Bureaucracy: Views of Public Utility Regulation." 77 *American Political Science Review* 704–717.
Grant, Wyn. 1983. "The Business Lobby: Political Attitudes and Strategies." 6 *West European Politics* (October) 163–182.
Grant, Wyn, with Jane Sargent. 1987. *Business and Politics in Britain.* London: Macmillan.
Gray, Robert T. 1978a. "Involved Business People: Powerful New Force for Change." *Nation's Business,* May, 23–30.
——— . 1978b. "Small Business Shows Big Clout." *Nation's Business,* September, 25–29.
Green, Mark. 1975. *The Other Government.* New York: Grossman.
Green, Mark, and Andrew Buchsbaum. 1983. "The Corporate Lobbies: The Two Styles of the Business Roundtable and Chamber of Commerce." In Mark Green, ed., *The Big Business Reader.* New York: Pilgrim Press.
——— . 1980. "How the Chamber's Computers Con the Congress." 12 *Washington Monthly* (May) 48–50.
Greenberg, Jack. 1977. *Judicial Process and Social Change: Constitutional Litigation.* St. Paul, Minn.: West.
Greenstone, J. David. 1975. "Group Theories." In F. I. Greenstein and N. W. Polsby, eds., *Handbook of Political Science.* Reading, Mass.: Addison-Wesley.
——— . 1969. *Labor in American Politics.* New York: Alfred A. Knopf.
Greenstone, J. David, and Paul E. Peterson. 1976. *Race and Authority in Urban Politics.* Chicago: University of Chicago Press.
Greenwald, Carol S. 1977. *Group Power: Lobbying and Public Policy.* New York: Praeger.
Grenzke, Janet. 1990. "Money and Congressional Behavior." In Margaret Latus Nugent and John R. Johannes, eds., *Money, Elections and Democracy.* Boulder, Colo.: Westview Press.
Griffith, Ernest S. 1939. *The Impasse of Democracy.* New York: Harrison-Wilton Books.
Grodzins, Morton. 1966. *The American System.* Chicago: Rand McNally.
Grossman, Michael, and Martha Joynt Kumar. 1981. *Portraying the President.* Baltimore: Johns Hopkins University Press.
Gurr, Ted. 1972. "The Calculus of Civil Conflict." 28 *Journal of Social Issues* 27–48.
Guth, James, and John C. Green. 1984. "Political Activists and Civil Liberties: The Case of Party and PAC Contributors." Paper presented at the annual meeting of the Mid-west Political Science Association, Chicago.
Guzzardi, Walter, Jr. 1980. "A New Public Face for Business." *Fortune,* June 30, 48–52.
——— . 1978. "Business Is Learning How to Win in Washington." *Fortune,* March 27, 52–58.
Habermas, Jürgen. [1974] 1979. *Communication and the Evolution of Society.* Trans. Thomas McCarthy. Boston: Beacon Press.
——— . [1973] 1975. *Legitimation Crisis.* Trans. Thomas McCarthy. Boston: Beacon Press.

Hadwiger, Donald F. 1982. *The Politics of Agricultural Research.* Lincoln: University of Nebraska Press.

Haider, Donald. 1974. *When Governments Come to Washington.* New York: Free Press.

Hale, Judith, and Ellen Levine. 1971. *Rebirth of Feminism.* New York: Quadrangle.

Hall, Richard L., and Frank W. Wayman. 1990. "Buying Time: Moneyed Interests and the Mobilization of Bias in Congressional Committees." 84 *American Political Science Review* 797–820.

Hamilton, Alexander, James Madison, and John Jay. 1961. *The Federalist Papers.* Ed. Clinton Rossiter. New York: New American Library.

Hamm, Keith E. 1983. "Patterns of Influence Among Committees, Agencies, and Interest Groups." 8 *Legislative Studies Quarterly* 379–426.

Hansen, John Mark. 1985. "The Political Economy of Group Membership." 79 *American Political Science Review* 79–96.

Hardin, Russell. 1982. *Collective Action.* Baltimore: Johns Hopkins University Press.

———. 1980. "Groups in the Regulation of Collective Bads." In Gordon Tullock, ed., *Public Choice in New Orleans.* Blacksburg, Va.: Public Choice Society.

Hardy, Thomas. 1989. "Simon Leading Martin, But It's Not Set in Stone." *Chicago Tribune,* December 2, C1.

Hargrove, Erwin C. 1988. *Jimmy Carter as President.* Baton Rouge: Louisiana State University Press.

Harper's. 1991. "Harper's Index," *Harper's,* August, p. 11.

Harris, Richard A. 1989a. "A Decade of Reform." In Richard A. Harris and Sidney M. Milkis, eds., *Remaking American Politics.* Boulder, Colo.: Westview Press.

———. 1989b. "Politicized Management: The Changing Face of Business in American Politics." In Richard A. Harris and Sidney M. Milkis, eds., *Remaking American Politics.* Boulder, Colo.: Westview Press.

Harris, Richard A., and Sidney M. Milkis. 1989. *The Politics of Regulatory Change.* New York: Oxford University Press.

———, eds. 1989. *Remaking American Politics.* Boulder, Colo.: Westview Press.

Harrison, Cynthia. 1988. *On Account of Sex: The Politics of Women's Issues, 1945–1968.* Berkeley: University of California Press.

Hayes, Michael T. 1986. "The New Group Universe." In Allan J. Cigler and Burdett Loomis, eds., *Interest Group Politics.* 2nd ed. Washington, D.C.: Congressional Quarterly Press.

———. 1983. "Interest Groups: Pluralism or Mass Society?" In Allan J. Cigler and Burdett A. Loomis, eds., *Interest Group Politics.* Washington, D.C.: Congressional Quarterly Press.

———. 1981. *Lobbyists and Legislators.* New Brunswick, N.J.: Rutgers University Press.

Heclo, Hugh. 1989. "The Emerging Regime." In Richard A. Harris and Sidney M. Milkis, eds., *Remaking American Politics.* Boulder, Colo.: Westview Press.

———. 1981. "The Changing Presidential Office." In Arnold J. Meltsner, ed., *Politics and the Oval Office.* San Francisco: Institute for Contemporary Studies.

———. 1978. "Issue Networks and the Executive Establishment." In Anthony King, ed., *The New American Political System.* Washington, D.C.: American Enterprise Institute.

Heinz, John P., Edward O. Laumann, Robert L. Nelson, and Robert H. Salisbury. Forthcoming. *Representing Interests: Structure and Uncertainty in National Policy Making.*

———. 1990. "Inner Circles or Hollow Cores? Elite Networks in National Policy Systems." 52 *Journal of Politics* 356–390.

Herring, E. Pendleton. 1940. *The Politics of Democracy.* New York: W. W. Norton.

———. 1936. *Public Administration and the Public Interest.* New York: McGraw-Hill.

———. 1930a. "Legalized Lobbying in Europe." 31 *Current History* 947–952.

———. 1930b. "What Makes a Lobbyist?" 159 *Outlook* (April) 572–573, 597.

———. 1929a. *Group Representation Before Congress.* Baltimore: Johns Hopkins University Press.

————. 1929b. "Why We Need Lobbies." *Outlook and Independent,* November 21, 492–493, 520.

Herrnson, Paul S. 1990. "Reemergent National Party Organizations." In L. Sandy Maisel, ed., *The Parties Respond.* Boulder, Colo.: Westview Press.

————. 1988. *Party Campaigning in the 1980s.* Cambridge, Mass.: Harvard University Press.

Hess, Stephen. 1976. *Organizing the Presidency.* Washington, D.C.: Brookings Institution.

Hibbs, Douglas. 1987. *The American Political Economy: Microeconomics and Electoral Politics.* Cambridge, Mass.: Harvard University Press.

Hirschhorn, Larry. 1984. *Beyond Mechanization: Work and Technology in a Postindustrial Age.* Cambridge, Mass.: MIT Press.

Hirschman, Albert O. 1970. *Exit, Voice, and Loyalty.* Cambridge, Mass.: Harvard University Press.

Holcomb, John M. 1988. "Introduction." In Foundation for Public Affairs, ed., *Public Interest Profiles, 1988–1989.* Washington, D.C.: Congressional Quarterly Press.

Hole, Judith, and Ellen Levine. 1971. *Rebirth of Feminism.* New York: Quadrangle.

Holtzman, Abraham. 1966. *Interest Groups and Lobbying.* New York: Macmillan.

Hook, Janet. 1989. "New Law Leaves Loopholes for Benefits to Members." *Congressional Quarterly Weekly Report,* December 16, 3420–3424.

Hosenball, Mark. 1989. "And Seal It with a Hiss." *Washington Post National Weekly Edition,* October 30-November 5, 24.

Hrebenar, Ronald, and Ruth K. Scott. 1990. *Interest Group Politics in America.* 2nd ed. Englewood Cliffs, N.J.: Prentice-Hall.

————. 1982. *Interest Group Politics in America.* Englewood Cliffs, N.J.: Prentice-Hall.

Hume, David. [1739–1740] 1978. *A Treatise on Human Nature.* Ed. L. A. Selby-Bigge; 2nd ed., ed. P. H. Nedditch. Oxford: Oxford University Press.

Huntington, Samuel P. 1988. "One Soul at a Time: Political Science and Political Reform." 82 *American Political Science Review* 3–10.

————. 1981. *American Politics: The Promise of Disharmony.* Cambridge, Mass.: Belknap Press of Harvard University Press.

————. 1975. "The Democratic Distemper." 41 *Public Interest* 9–38.

Hyman, Herbert H., and C. R. Wright. 1971. "Trends in Voluntary Association Memberships of American Adults: Replication Based on Secondary Analysis of National Sample Surveys." 36 *American Sociological Review* 191–206.

Ikenberry, John G. 1988. *Reasons of State: Oil Politics and the Capacities of the American Government.* Ithaca, N.Y.: Cornell University Press.

Ingram, Wesley, and Paul Sabatier. 1987. *Descriptive History of Land Use and Water Quality at Lake Tahoe, 1960–1985.* Davis, Calif.: Institute of Ecology.

Isikoff, Michael. 1988. "The NRA: Back in the Saddle." *Washington Post National Weekly Edition,* September 26-October 2, 15.

Ivers, Gregg. Forthcoming. "Organized Religion in the Supreme Court." *Journal of Church and State.*

Jacek, Henry J. 1986. "Pluralist and Corporatist Intermediation, Activities of Business Interest Associations and Corporate Profits." 18 *Comparative Politics* (July) 419–437.

Jackson, Brooks. 1988. *Honest Graft.* Washington, D.C.: Farragut Publishing.

Jackson, John, B. Brown, and D. Bositis. 1982. "Herbert McCloskey and Friends Revisited." 10 *American Politics Quarterly* 158–180.

Jacobson, Gary C. 1980. *Money in Congressional Elections.* New Haven: Yale University Press.

Jaffe, Louis. 1937. "Law-making by Private Groups." 51 *Harvard Law Review* 202–253.

Janda, Kenneth, Jeffrey M. Berry, and Jerry Goldman. 1989. *The Challenge of Democracy.* Boston: Houghton Mifflin.

Jenkins, Craig, and Craig Eckert. 1986. "Channeling Black Insurgency." 51 *American Sociological Review* 812–829.

Jenkins, Craig, and Charles Perrow. 1977. "Insurgency of the Powerless." 42 *American Sociological Review* 249–268.

Johnson, Chalmers. 1982. *MITI and the Japanese Economic Miracle: The Growth of Industrial Policy.* Stanford: Stanford University Press.

Johnson, Charles. 1987. "Content-Analytic Techniques and Judicial Research." 15 *American Politics Quarterly* 169–197.

Jones, Charles O. 1979. "American Politics and the Organization of Energy Decision Making." 4 *Annual Review of Energy* 99–121.

———. 1974. *Clean Air.* Pittsburgh: University of Pittsburgh Press.

———. 1961. "Representation in Congress: The Case of the House Agriculture Committee." 55 *American Political Science Review* 358–367.

Jordan, A. G., and J. J. Richardson. 1987. *Government and Pressure Groups in Britain.* Oxford: Clarendon Press.

Jordan, Grant. 1985. "Parliament Under Press." 56 *Political Quarterly* (April-June) 174–182.

———. 1981. "Iron Triangles, Woolly Corporatism, and Elastic Nets: Images of the Policy Process." 1 *Journal of Public Policy* (February) 95–125.

Kalt, Joseph, and Mark A. Zupan. 1984. "Capture and Ideology in the Economic Theory of Politics." 74 *American Economic Review* 279–300.

Kaplan, Sheila. 1988. "Hit and Run." *Common Cause Magazine,* July-August, 20–25.

Katzenstein, Peter J. 1985. *Small States in World Markets.* Ithaca, N.Y.: Cornell University Press.

———. 1978. "Introduction: Domestic and International Forces and Strategies of Foreign Economic Policy." In P. Katzenstein, ed., *Between Power and Plenty.* Madison: University of Wisconsin Press.

Katzmann, Robert A. 1986. *Institutional Disability: The Saga of Transportation Policy for the Disabled.* Washington, D.C.: Brookings Institution.

———. 1980. *Regulatory Bureaucracy: The Federal Trade Commission and Antitrust Policy.* Cambridge, Mass.: MIT Press.

Kaufman, Herbert. 1960. *The Forest Ranger.* Baltimore: Johns Hopkins University Press.

Kaus, Robert M. 1982. "There's No Shame Anymore." *Harper's,* August, 8–15.

Keeler, John. 1987. *The Politics of Neocorporatism in France.* New York: Oxford University Press.

Keeler, John T. S. 1985. "Situating France on the Pluralism-Corporatism Continuum—A Critique of and Alternative to the Wilson Perspective." 17 *Comparative Politics* (January) 229–249.

Keller, Bill. 1981. "Sometimes It Comes Up Astroturf: Special-Interest Lobbyists Cultivate the 'Grass Roots' to Influence Capitol Hill." 39 *Congressional Quarterly Weekly Report,* 12 September, 1739–1742.

Kelly, Stanley. 1956. *Professional Public Relations and Political Power.* Baltimore: Johns Hopkins University Press.

Kelman, Steven. 1988. "Why Public Ideas Matter." In Robert B. Reich, ed., *The Power of Public Ideas.* Cambridge, Mass.: Ballinger.

———. 1987. *Making Public Policy.* New York: Basic Books.

———. 1981. *Regulating America, Regulating Sweden.* Cambridge, Mass.: MIT Press.

Kenski, Henry C. 1988. "The Gender Factor in a Changing Electorate." In Carol M. Mueller, ed., *The Politics of the Gender Gap.* Newbury Park, Calif.: Sage.

Kent, Frank R. [1923] 1938. *The Great Game of Politics.* New York: Doubleday, Doran.

Kernell, Samuel. 1989. "The Evolution of the White House Staff." In John Chubb and Paul E. Peterson, eds., *Can the Government Govern?* Washington, D.C.: Brookings Institution.

———. 1986. *Going Public.* Washington, D.C.: Congressional Quarterly Press.

———. 1985. "Campaigning, Governing, and the Contemporary Presidency." In John Chubb and Paul E. Peterson, eds., *The New Direction in American Politics.* Washington, D.C.: Brookings Institution.

Kessel, John H. 1984. "The Structures of the Reagan White House." 28 *American Journal of Political Science* 231–258.

Kesselman, Mark. 1982. "The Conflictual Evolution of American Political Science: From Apologetic Pluralism to Trilateralism and Marxism." In J. David Greenstone, ed., *Public Values and Private Power in American Politics.* Chicago: University of Chicago Press.

Key, V. O., Jr. [1942] 1958 and 1964. 4th ed. *Politics, Parties, and Pressure Groups.* New York: T. J. Crowell.

———. 1949. *Southern Politics.* New York: Alfred A. Knopf.

King, Anthony. 1990. "The American Polity in the 1990s." In Anthony King, ed., *The New American Political System.* 2nd ed. Washington, D.C.: American Enterprise Institute.

———. 1978. "The American Polity in the Late 1970s: Building Coalitions in the Sand." In Anthony King, ed., *The New American Political System.* Washington, D.C.: American Enterprise Institute.

King, David C., and Jack L. Walker. 1989. "The Provision of Benefits by American Interest Groups." Presented at the annual meeting of the Midwest Political Science Association, Chicago.

Kingdon, John W. 1984. *Agendas, Alternatives, and Public Policies.* Boston: Little, Brown.

———. 1981. *Congressmen's Voting Decisions.* 2nd ed. New York: Harper and Row.

Klein, Ethel. 1984. *Gender Politics.* Cambridge, Mass.: Harvard University Press.

Klimoski, Richard J., and James A. Breaugh. 1977. "When Performance Doesn't Count: A Constituency Looks at Its Spokesman." 20 *Organizational Behavior and Human Performance* 301–311.

Kluger, Richard. 1976. *Simple Justice.* New York: Alfred A. Knopf.

Knoke, David. 1990. *Organizing for Collective Action.* New York: Aldine de Gruyter.

———. 1986. "Associations and Interest Groups." 12 *Annual Review of Sociology* 1–21.

Knoke, David, and James R. Wood. 1981. *Organized for Action: Commitment in Voluntary Associations.* New Brunswick, N.J.: Rutgers University Press.

Konrad, George, and Ivan Szelenyi. 1979. *The Intellectuals on the Road to Class Power.* New York: Harcourt Brace Jovanovich.

Kownslar, Allan O., and Terry L. Smet. 1980. *American Government.* New York: McGraw-Hill.

Krasner, Stephen. 1978. *Defending the National Interest.* Princeton: Princeton University Press.

Krieger, Joel. 1986. *Reagan, Thatcher, and the Politics of Decline.* New York: Oxford University Press.

———. 1984. "The Presidency and Interest Groups." In Michael Nelson, ed., *The Presidency and the Political System.* Washington, D.C.: Congressional Quarterly Press.

Kroger, William. 1978a. "Business PACs Are Coming of Age." *Nation's Business,* October, 39–41.

———. 1978b. "How Congressmen Respond to Mountains of Mail." *Nation's Business,* May, 36–38.

Kumar, Martha Joynt, and Michael Baruch Grossman. 1986. "Political Communications from the White House: The Interest Group Connection." 16 *Presidential Studies Quarterly* 92–101.

Krislov, Samuel. 1963. "The Amicus Curiae Brief: From Friendship to Advocacy." 7 *Yale Law Journal* 694–721.

Kuntz, Phil. 1990. "Clean-Air Bill: Dozens of Small Favors That Came Wrapped in a Big Package." *Congressional Quarterly Weekly Report,* April 7, 1060–1061.

Lane, Robert E. 1959. *Political Life.* New York: Free Press.

———. 1949. "Notes on the Theory of the Lobby." 2 *Western Political Quarterly* 154–162.

Langbein, Laura I. 1986. "Money and Access: Some Empirical Evidence." 48 *Journal of Politics* 1052–1062.

Laski, Harold J. 1921. *Studies in the Problem of Sovereignty*. New Haven: Yale University Press.

Latham, Earl. 1952a. *The Group Basis of Politics*. Ithaca, N.Y.: Cornell University Press.

————. 1952b. "The Group Basis of Politics: Notes for a Theory." 46 *American Political Science Review* 376–397.

Latus, Margaret. 1984. "Assessing Ideological PACs: From Outrage to Understanding." In Michael Malbin, ed., *Money and Politics in the United States*. Chatham, N.J.: Chatham House.

Lau, Richard, and David Sears, eds., 1986. *Political Cognition*. Hillsdale, N.J.: Lawrence Erlbaum.

Laumann, Edward O., and John P. Heinz, with Robert L. Nelson and Robert H. Salisbury. 1985. "Washington Lawyers—and Others: The Structure of Washington Representation." 37 *Stanford Law Review* 465–502.

Laumann, Edward, and David Knoke. 1989. "Policy Networks of the Organizational State: Collective Action in the National Energy and Health Domains." In Robert Perrucci and Henry R. Potter, eds., *Networks of Power*. New York: Aldine de Gruyter.

————. 1987. *The Organizational State: Social Choice in National Policy Domains*. Madison: University of Wisconsin Press.

Lee, Rex E. 1982. Personal interview in Washington, D.C., September 13.

Leggett, William. [1834] 1954. "Democratic Editorials." In Joseph L. Blau, ed., *Social Theories of Jacksonian Democracy*. Indianapolis: Bobbs-Merrill.

Lehmbruch, Gerhard, and Philippe C. Schmitter, eds. 1982. *Patterns of Corporatist Policy-Making*. Beverly Hills, Calif.: Sage.

Levine, Charles H., and James A. Thurber. 1986. "Reagan and the Intergovernmental Lobby: Iron Triangles, Cozy Subsystems and Political Conflict." In Allan J. Cigler and Burdett A. Loomis, eds., *Interest Group Politics*. 2nd ed. Washington, D.C.: Congressional Quarterly Press.

Levine, David. 1990. "The Transformation of Interests and the State." In Edward S. Greenberg and Thomas F. Mayer, eds., *Changes in the State*. Beverly Hills, Calif.: Sage.

Levitan, Sar A., and Martha R. Cooper. 1984. *Business Lobbies*. Baltimore: Johns Hopkins University Press.

Levitt, Arthur, Jr. 1980. "Small Business Discovers Its Strength." *Business Week*, 10 March, 23–24.

Levy, Deborah M. 1987. "Advice for Sale." 67 *Foreign Policy* (Summer) 64–86.

Lieber, Francis. 1859. *On Civil Liberty and Self Government*. Philadelphia: J. B. Lippincott.

Light, Paul C. 1985. *Artful Work: The Politics of Social Security Reform*. New York: Random House.

————. 1982. *The President's Agenda: Domestic Policy Choice from Kennedy to Carter*. Baltimore: Johns Hopkins University Press.

Lilley, William, and James C. Miller. 1977. "The New Social Regulation." *Public Interest* (Spring) 49–51.

Lindblom, Charles E. 1990. *Inquiry and Change: The Troubled Attempt to Understand and Shape Society*. New Haven: Yale University Press.

————. 1977. *Politics and Markets*. New York: Basic Books.

————. 1963. *The Intelligence of Democracy*. New York: Free Press.

Lipset, Seymour Martin, and William Schneider. 1987. *The Confidence Gap*. Rev. ed. Baltimore: Johns Hopkins University Press.

Lipset, Seymour Martin, Martin Trow, and James Coleman. 1956. *Union Democracy*. New York: Free Press.

Logan, Edward B. 1929. "Is Lobbying for Commercial Purposes Offensive?" 8 *Congressional Digest* (December) 289–291.

Longman, Phillip. 1983. "From Calhoun to Sister Boom-Boom: The Dubious Legacy of Interest Group Politics." *Washington Monthly,* June, 11–22.

Loomis, Burdett. 1988. *The New American Politician.* New York: Basic Books.

Loomis, Burdett A., and Allan J. Cigler. 1986. "Introduction: The Changing Nature of Interest Group Politics." In A. J. Cigler and B. A. Loomis, eds., *Interest Group Politics.* 2nd ed. Washington, D.C.: Congressional Quarterly Press.

Lowell, A. Lawrence. 1913. *Public Opinion and Popular Government.* New York: Longmans, Breen and Co.

Lowi, Theodore J. 1988. "Foreword: New Dimensions in Policy and Politics." In Raymond Tatalovich and Byron W. Daynes, eds., *Social Regulatory Policy.* Boulder, Colo.: Westview Press.

———. 1986. "The Welfare State, the New Regulation, and the Rule of Law." In Allan Schnaiberg et al., eds., *Distributional Conflicts in Environmental Resource Policy.* London: Gower.

———. 1985. *The Personal President.* Ithaca, N.Y.: Cornell University Press.

———. 1979. *The End of Liberalism.* Rev. ed. New York: W. W. Norton.

———. 1971. *The Politics of Disorder.* New York: Free Press.

———. 1969. *The End of Liberalism.* New York: W. W. Norton.

———. 1964a. "American Business, Public Policy, Case Studies and Political Theory." 16 *World Politics* 677–715.

———. 1964b. *At the Pleasure of the Mayor.* New York: Free Press.

Lucco, Joan. 1990. "Balancing Contending Interests at the White House." Paper presented at the annual meeting of the Midwest Political Science Association, Chicago.

———. 1986. "Roles of Interest Group Representatives at the White House: Consumer Units in the Modern Presidency from John F. Kennedy to Ronald Reagan." Paper presented at the annual meeting of the American Political Science Association, Washington, D.C.

Lukes, Steven. 1974. *Power: A Radical View.* London: Macmillan.

Lundquist, Lennart. 1980. *The Tortoise and the Hare: Clean Air Policies in the United States and Sweden.* Ann Arbor: University of Michigan Press.

Lynn, Laurence E., Jr. 1984. "The Reagan Administration and the Renitent Bureaucracy." In Lester M. Salamon and Michael S. Lund, eds., *The Reagan Presidency and the Governing of America.* Washington, D.C.: Urban Institute.

Maass, Arthur. 1983. *Congress and the Common Good.* New York: Basic Books.

McAdams, Doug. 1983. "Tactical Innovation and the Peace of Insurgency." 48 *American Sociological Review* 735–754.

———. 1982. *Political Process and the Development of Black Insurgency, 1930–1970.* Chicago: University of Chicago Press.

McCann, Michael W. 1986. *Taking Reform Seriously.* Ithaca, N.Y.: Cornell University Press.

McCarry, Charles. 1972. *Citizen Nader.* New York: New American Library.

McCarthy, John D., and Mayer N. Zald. 1977. "Resource Mobilization and Social Movements." 82 *American Journal of Sociology* (May) 1212–1241.

McCloskey, Herbert, Paul Hoffman, and Rosemary O'Hara. 1960. "Issue Conflict and Consensus Among Party Leaders and Followers." 54 *American Political Science Review* 406–427.

McConnell, Grant. [1953] 1969. *The Decline of Agrarian Democracy.* New York: Atheneum.

———. 1966. *Private Power and American Democracy.* New York: Alfred A. Knopf.

McCool, Daniel. 1989. "Subgovernments and the Impact of Policy Fragmentation and Accommodation." 8 *Policy Studies Review* 264–287.

McCubbins, Matthew, and Thomas Schwartz. 1984. "Congressional Oversight Overlooked: Police Patrols Versus Fire Alarms." 2 *American Journal of Political Science* 165–179.

McDowell, Douglas. 1989. Personal interview in Washington, D.C., March 2.

Macedo, Stephen. 1990. *Liberal Virtues*. Oxford: Clarendon Press.

Macey, Jonathan R. 1986. "Promoting Public-Regarding Legislation Through Statutory Interpretation: An Interest Group Model." 86 *Columbia Law Review* 223.

McFarland, Andrew S. 1991. "Interest Groups and Political Time: Cycles in America." 21 *British Journal of Political Science* 257–284.

_____ . 1987. "Interest Groups and Theories of Power in America." 17 *British Journal of Political Science* (April) 129–147.

_____ . 1984. *Common Cause*. Chatham, N.J.: Chatham House Press.

_____ . 1983. "Public Interest Lobbies Versus Minority Faction." In Allan J. Cigler and Burdett A. Loomis, eds., *Interest Group Politics*. Washington, D.C.: Congressional Quarterly Press.

_____ . 1976. *Public Interest Lobbies: Decision Making on Energy*. Washington, D.C.: American Enterprise Institute.

_____ . 1969. *Power and Leadership in Pluralist Systems*. Stanford: Stanford University Press.

McGrath, Phyllis S. 1979. *Redefining Corporate-Federal Relations*. New York: Conference Board.

MacIntyre, A. C. 1973. "Is a Science of Comparative Politics Possible?" In Paul G. Lewis and David C. Potter, eds., *The Practice of Comparative Politics*. London: Open University Press.

MacIver, R. M. 1937. "Interests." In Edwin R. A. Seligman, ed., *Encyclopaedia of the Social Sciences*, vol. 7. New York: Macmillan.

Mack, Charles S. 1989. *Lobbying and Government Relations*. New York: Quorum Books.

McKee, Oliver, Jr. 1930. "Lobbyists Extraordinary." 229 *North American Review* 82–88.

_____ . 1929. "Lobbying for Good or Evil." 227 *North American Review* 343–352.

Mackenzie, G. Calvin, ed. 1987. *The In-and-Outers: Presidential Appointees and Transient Government in Washington*. Baltimore: Johns Hopkins University Press.

McPherson, Myra. 1980. "The New Right Brigade." *Washington Post*, October 10, F1.

McQuaid, Kim. 1982. *Big Business and Presidential Power*. New York: William Morrow.

Magleby, David B., and Candice J. Nelson. 1990. *The Money Chase: Congressional Campaign Finance Reform*. Washington, D.C.: Brookings Institution.

Mahood, H. R. 1967. "Pressure Groups: A Threat to Democracy?" In H. R. Mahood, ed., *Pressure Groups in American Politics*. New York: Charles Scribner's Sons.

Maisel, L. Sandy, ed. 1990. *The Parties Respond*. Boulder, Colo.: Westview Press.

Malbin, Michael J. 1980. *Unelected Representatives*. New York: Basic Books.

Manes, Susan. 1990. "Up for Bid: A Common Cause View." In Margaret Latus Nugent and John R. Johannes, eds., *Money, Elections, and Democracy*. Boulder, Colo.: Westview Press.

Mansbridge, Jane J. Forthcoming. "Interest-group Rentseeking and Deliberative Benefits." In James Fishkin, Claus Offe, and Philippe Schmitter, eds., *Toward Post-Liberal Democracy: Political Theory and Institutional Reforms*.

_____ , ed. 1990. *Beyond Self-Interest*. Chicago: University of Chicago Press.

_____ . 1988. "Motivating Deliberation in Congress." In Sarah Baumgartner Thurow, ed., *Constitutionalism in America*, vol. 2. New York: University Press of America.

_____ . 1986. *Why We Lost the ERA*. Chicago: University of Chicago Press.

_____ . 1983. *Beyond Adversary Democracy*. Chicago: University of Chicago Press.

Manwaring, David. 1962. *Render Unto Caesar: The Flag Salute Controversy*. Chicago: University of Chicago Press.

March, James G., and Johan P. Olsen. 1989. *Rediscovering Institutions*. New York: Free Press.

Marcus, Ruth. 1990. "Few Fireworks Among the Tedium at the Supreme Court This Term: Most Cases on the Docket Fall Short of Landmark Status." *Washington Post*, March 25, A12.

Margolis, Howard. 1982. *Selfishness, Altruism, and Rationality*. Chicago: University of Chicago Press.

Marsh, David. 1976. "On Joining Interest Groups: An Empirical Consideration of the Work of Mancur Olson." 6 *British Journal of Political Science* 257–261.

Marwell, Gerald, and Ruth E. Ames. 1981. "Economists Free Ride, Does Anyone Else?" 15 *Journal of Public Economics* 295–310.

———. 1980. "Experiments in the Provision of Public Goods: Provision Points, Stakes, Experience, and the Free-Rider Problem." 85 *American Journal of Sociology* 926–936.

———. 1979. "Experiments in the Provision of Public Goods: Resources, Interest, Group Size, and the Free-Rider Problem." 84 *American Journal of Sociology* 1335–1360.

Marx, Gary T. 1969. *Protest and Prejudice.* New York: Harper and Row Torchbooks.

Mashaw, Jerry L. 1988. "Disability Insurance in an Age of Retrenchment: The Politics of Implementing Rights." In T. R. Marmor and J. L. Mashaw, eds., *Social Security: Beyond the Rhetoric of Crisis.* Princeton: Princeton University Press.

Masters, Marick F., and John T. Delaney. 1985. "The Causes of Union Political Involvement: A Longitudinal Analysis." 6 *Journal of Labor Research* (Fall) 341–362.

Matthews, Donald R. 1960. *U.S. Senators and Their Political World.* Chapel Hill: University of North Carolina Press.

Meidinger, Errol. 1987. "Regulatory Culture: A Theoretical Outline." 9 *Law and Policy* 355–386.

Meier, Kenneth J. 1987. *Politics and the Bureaucracy.* 2nd ed. Monterey, Calif.: Brooks/Cole.

Meier, Kenneth J., and Gary W. Copeland. 1983. "Interest Groups and Public Policy." 64 *Social Science Quarterly* (September) 641–646.

Mellor, William. 1982. Personal interview in Denver, Colo., September 2.

Melnick, R. Shep. 1983. *Regulation and the Courts.* Washington, D.C.: Brookings Institution.

Meltsner, Michael. 1973. *Cruel and Unusual: The Supreme Court and Capital Punishment.* New York: Random House.

Merriam, Charles E. [1934] 1964. *Political Power.* New York: Collier Books.

Michels, Robert. 1958. *Political Parties.* Glencoe, Ill.: Free Press.

Milbrath, Lester. 1970a. "The Impact of Lobbying on Government Decisions." In Robert H. Salisbury, ed., *Interest Group Politics in America.* New York: Harper and Row.

———. 1970b. "Lobbyists Approach Government." In Robert H. Salisbury, ed., *Interest Group Politics in America.* New York: Harper and Row.

———. 1968. "Lobbying." In David L. Sills, ed., *International Encyclopedia of the Social Sciences,* vol. 9. New York: Macmillan.

———. 1965. *Political Participation.* Chicago: Rand McNally.

———. 1963. *The Washington Lobbyists.* Chicago: Rand McNally.

Mill, John Stuart. [1859] 1974. *On Liberty.* New York: Pelican Books.

Miller, Arthur H. 1978. "A Majority Party Reunited? A Comparison of the 1972 and 1976 Elections." In Jeff Fishel, ed., *Parties and Elections in an Anti-Party Age: American Politics and the Crisis of Confidence.* Bloomington: Indiana University Press.

Miller, Arthur H., Warren E. Miller, Alden S. Raine, and Thad A. Brown. 1976. "A Majority Party in Disarray: Policy Polarization in the 1972 Election." 70 *American Political Science Review* 753–778.

Miller, Charles. 1987. *Lobbying Government: Understanding and Influencing the Corridors of Power.* New York: Basil Blackwell.

Miller, Tim R. 1985. "Changes in the Utility of the Subsystem Model for Public Policy Analysis: The Status of Water Policy Making in the U.S." Paper presented at the annual meeting of the American Political Science Association, New Orleans.

Miller, Warren, and M. Kent Jennings. 1987. *Parties in Transition: A Longitudinal Study of Party Elites and Party Supporters.* New York: Russell Sage.

Mills, C. Wright. 1956. *The Power Elite.* New York: Oxford University Press.

Mintz, Beth, and Michael Schwartz. 1985. *The Power Structure of American Business.* Chicago: University of Chicago Press.

Miroff, Bruce. 1981. "Presidential Leverage Over Social Movements: The Johnson White House and Civil Rights." 43 *Journal of Politics* 2–23.

Mitchell, Robert Cameron. 1984. "Public Opinion and Environmental Politics in the 1970s and 1980s." In Norman J. Vig and Michael E. Kraft, eds., *Environmental Policy in the 1980s: Reagan's New Agenda.* Washington, D.C.: Congressional Quarterly Press.

———. 1979. "National Environmental Lobbies and the Apparent Illogic of Collective Action." In Clifford Russell, ed., *Collective Decision-Making.* Baltimore: Johns Hopkins University Press.

Moe, Terry M. 1989. "The Politics of Bureaucratic Structure." In John Chubb and Paul E. Peterson, eds., *Can the Government Govern?* Washington, D.C.: Brookings Institution.

———. 1985. "The Politicized Presidency." In John Chubb and Paul E. Peterson, eds., *The New Direction in American Politics.* Washington, D.C.: Brookings Institution.

———. 1981. "Toward a Broader View of Interest Groups." 43 *Journal of Politics* 531–543.

———. 1980. *The Organization of Interests.* Chicago: University of Chicago Press.

Moon, Chung-in. 1988. "Complex Interdependence and Transnational Lobbying: South Korea in the United States." 32 *International Studies Quarterly* (March) 67–89.

Moore, W. John. 1989. "The Alumni Lobby." *National Journal*, October 9, 2188–2195.

Morehouse, Sarah McCally. 1981. *State Politics, Parties and Policy.* New York: Holt, Rinehart and Winston.

Morgan, Dan. 1989. "How One Lobby Discovered Budgetary Gold." *Washington Post National Weekly Edition*, June 26-July 2, 12.

Morgenthau, Hans J. 1960. *The Purpose of American Politics.* New York: Vintage.

Morin, Richard. 1989. "They're All Crooks—Whatever Their Names Are." *Washington Post National Weekly Edition*, May 29-June 4, 39.

Moynihan, Daniel P. 1970. *Maximum Feasible Misunderstanding.* New York: Free Press.

Mueller, Carol. 1987. "Collective Consciousness, Identity Transformation, and the Rise of Women in Public Office in the United States." In Mary Katzenstein and Carol Mueller, eds., *The Women's Movements of the United States and Western Europe.* Philadelphia: Temple University Press.

Mueller, Dennis. 1986. "Rational Egoism Versus Adaptive Egoism as a Fundamental Postulate for a Descriptive Theory of Human Behavior." 51 *Public Choice* 3–23.

Nadel, Mark V. 1971. *The Politics of Consumer Protection.* Indianapolis: Bobbs-Merrill.

Nadel, Mark V., and David Vogel. 1977. "Who Is a Consumer? An Analysis of the Politics of Consumer Conflict." 5 *American Politics Quarterly* (January) 27–56.

Nagel, Jack H. 1975. *The Descriptive Analysis of Power.* New Haven: Yale University Press.

Nathan, Richard P. 1975. *The Plot That Failed: Nixon and the Administrative Presidency.* New York: John Wiley.

Nelson, Robert L., John P. Heinz, Edward O. Laumann, and Robert H. Salisbury. 1987. "Private Representation in Washington: Surveying the Structure of Influence." 1987 *American Bar Foundation Research Journal* 141–200.

———. 1988. "Lawyers and the Structure of Influence in Washington." 22 *Law and Society Review* 2.

Neustadt, Richard E. [1960] 1980. *Presidential Power.* New York: John Wiley and Sons.

Newsweek. 1978. "Single-Issue Politics." November 6, 43–47.

Nie, Norman, Sidney Verba, and John Petrocik. 1976. *The Changing American Voter.* Cambridge, Mass.: Harvard University Press.

Niskanen, William A. 1971. *Bureaucracy and Representative Government.* Chicago: Aldine-Atherton.

Noble, Charles. 1986. *Liberalism at Work: The Rise and Fall of OSHA.* Philadelphia: Temple University Press.

Noll, Roger G. 1985. *Regulatory Policy and the Social Sciences.* Berkeley: University of California Press.

Noll, Roger G., and Bruce M. Owen. 1983. *The Political Economy of Deregulation.* Washington, D.C.: American Enterprise Institute.

Nordhaus, William O. 1975. "The Political Business Cycle." 42 *Review of Economic Studies* 169–190.

Nordlinger, Eric A. 1981. *On the Autonomy of the Democratic State.* Cambridge, Mass.: Harvard University Press.

Nugent, Margaret Latus, and John R. Johannes, eds. 1990. *Money, Elections, and Democracy.* Boulder, Colo.: Westview Press.

Nyhan, Paul. 1991. "Interest Groups Count Heads, Take Names in Survey." *Congressional Quarterly Weekly Report,* March 30, 787–789.

Oberschall, Anthony. 1973. *Social Conflict and Social Movements.* Englewood Cliffs, N.J.: Prentice-Hall.

O'Brien, Lawrence F. 1974. *No Final Victories.* New York: Doubleday.

O'Connor, Karen. 1980. *Women's Organizations' Use of the Courts.* Lexington, Mass.: Lexington Books.

O'Connor, Karen, and Lee Epstein. 1989. *Public Interest Law Groups.* New York: Greenwood Press.

———. 1984. "Rebalancing the Scales of Justice: Assessment of Public Interest Law." 7 *Harvard Journal of Law and Public Policy* 483–505.

———. 1983a. "Beyond Legislative Lobbying: Women's Rights Groups and the Supreme Court." 67 *Judicature* 134–143.

———. 1983b. "The Rise of Conservative Interest Group Litigation." 45 *Journal of Politics* 479–489.

———. 1981-1982. "Amicus Curiae Participation in U.S. Supreme Court Litigation: An Analysis of Hakman's 'Folklore.'" 16 *Law and Society Review* 312–320.

O'Connor, Karen, and Gregg Ivers. 1987. "Friends as Foes: The Amicus Curiae Participation and Effectiveness of the Americans for Effective Law Enforcement in Criminal Cases, 1969–1982." 9 *Law and Policy* 161–178.

Odegard, Peter. 1967. "Introduction." In Arthur F. Bentley, *The Process of Government.* Cambridge, Mass.: Belknap Press of Harvard University Press.

———. 1930. "Lobbies and American Legislation." 31 *Current History* 690–697.

———. 1928. *Pressure Politics: The Story of the Anti-Saloon League.* New York: Columbia University Press.

Offe, Claus, and Ulrich K. Preuss. 1991. "Democratic Institutions and Moral Resources." Paper presented at the Conference on Post-Liberal Democracy, Austin, February 8.

Offe, Claus, and H. Wiesenthal. 1985. "The Two Logics of Collective Action: Theoretical Notes on Social Class and Organizational Force." In Claus Offe, ed., *Disorganized Capitalism.* Cambridge, Mass.: MIT Press.

———. 1980. "The Two Logics of Collective Action: Theoretical Notes on Social Class and Organizational Force." In Maurice Zeitlin, ed., *Political Power and Social Theory,* vol. 1. Greenwich, Conn.: JAI Press.

Okin, Susan. 1990. *Justice, Gender, and the Family.* New York: Basic Books.

Olson, Mancur. 1982. *The Rise and Decline of Nations.* New Haven: Yale University Press.

———. 1979. "Epilogue: Letter to Denton Morrison." 2 *Research in Social Movements, Conflicts and Change* 149–150.

———. 1965. *The Logic of Collective Action.* Cambridge, Mass.: Harvard University Press.

Oppenheimer, Bruce I. 1974. *Oil and the Congressional Process.* Lexington, Mass.: Lexington Books.

Orman, John. 1987. *Comparing Presidential Behavior.* New York: Greenwood Press.

Ornstein, Norman J. 1983. "The Open Congress Meets the President." In Anthony King, ed., *Both Ends of the Avenue.* Washington, D.C.: American Enterprise Institute.

Ornstein, Norman J., and Shirley Elder. 1978. *Interest Groups, Lobbying and Policymaking.* Washington, D.C.: Congressional Quarterly Press.

Orren, Gary R. 1988. "Beyond Self-Interest." In Robert B. Reich, ed., *The Power of Public Ideas.* Cambridge, Mass.: Ballinger.

Orren, Gary R., and William G. Mayer. 1990. "The Press, Political Parties, and the Public-Private Balance in Elections." In L. Sandy Maisel, ed., *The Parties Respond.* Boulder, Colo.: Westview Press.

Osborne, David. 1984. "You Are *Not* Invited to the Permanent Party." 9 *Mother Jones* (August-September) 21–25, 42–47.

Page, Benjamin I., and Mark P. Petracca. 1983. *The American Presidency.* New York: McGraw-Hill.

Parton, J. 1870. "Pressure Upon Congress." 25 *Atlantic* (February) 145–159.

_____. 1869. "Log-rolling at Washington." 24 *Atlantic* (September) 361–378.

Patterson, Samuel C., and Gregory A. Caldeira. 1987. "Party Voting in Congress." Paper presented at the annual meeting of the Midwest Political Science Association, Chicago.

Pearson, James B. 1979. "Does Congress Listen? The Art of Communication." 45 *Vital Speeches of the Day* (June 1) 490–494.

Penniman, Howard R. 1952. *Sait's American Political Parties and Elections.* 5th ed. New York: Appleton-Century-Crofts.

Pertschuk, Michael. 1982. *Revolt Against Regulation: The Rise and Pause of the Consumer Movement.* Berkeley: University of California Press.

Peterson, Esther. 1982. "Consumer Representation in the White House." In Erma Angevine, ed., *Consumer Activists: They Made a Difference.* Mount Vernon, N.Y.: Consumer Foundation.

Peterson, Mark A. 1990a. "Interest Groups and the Presidency: Styles of White House Public Liaison." Revised version of paper presented at the annual meeting of the American Political Science Association, Washington, D.C., 1986.

_____. 1990b. *Legislating Together: The White House and Capitol Hill from Eisenhower to Reagan.* Cambridge, Mass.: Harvard University Press.

Peterson, Mark A., and Jack L. Walker. 1990. "The Presidency and the Nominating System." In Michael Nelson, ed., *The Presidency and the Political System.* Washington, D.C.: Congressional Quarterly Press.

_____. 1986. "Interest Group Responses to Partisan Change: The Impact of the Reagan Administration upon the National Interest Group System." In Allan J. Cigler and Burdett A. Loomis, eds., *Interest Group Politics.* 2nd ed. Washington, D.C.: Congressional Quarterly Press.

Peterson, Paul E. 1985. "The Politics of Deficits." In John Chubb and Paul E. Peterson, eds., *The New Direction in American Politics.* Washington, D.C.: Brookings Institution.

_____. 1971. "The Politics of Comprehensive Education in Three British Cities." 3 *Comparative Politics* 381–402.

Peterson, Paul E., Barry Rabe, and Kenneth Wong. 1986. *When Federalism Works.* Washington, D.C.: Brookings Institution.

Peterson, Paul E., and Mark C. Rom. 1988. "Lower Taxes, More Spending, and Budget Deficits." In Charles O. Jones, ed., *The Reagan Legacy.* Chatham, N.J.: Chatham House.

Petracca, Mark P. 1991. "The Rational Choice Approach to Politics: The Challenge to Normative Democratic Theory." *Review of Politics* (April) 289–319.

_____. 1989. "Political Consultants and Democratic Governance." 22 *PS: Political Science and Politics* (March) 11–14.

_____. 1988. "The Reagan Revolution and the Role of Federal Advisory Committees." Paper presented at the annual meetings of the Midwest Political Science Association, Chicago, April 14–16.

———. 1986. "Federal Advisory Committees, Interest Groups, and the Administrative State." 13 *Congress and the Presidency* 83–114.

———. 1985. "Federal Advisory Committees: Linking the Government to Interest Groups—How Tightly Is the Buckle Fastened?" Paper presented at the annual meetings of the American Political Science Association, New Orleans, August 29–September 1.

———. 1982. "The National Executive and Private Interests—Federal Advisory Committees: The 'Steel Bridge' to Corporatism." Paper presented at the annual meetings of the American Political Science Association, Chicago, September 1–4.

Phillips, Kevin. 1978. "The Balkanization of America." *Harper's*, May, 37–47.

———. 1969. *The Emerging Republican Majority.* New York: Russell Sage Foundation.

Philp, Mark. 1989. *Paine.* Oxford: Oxford University Press.

Pika, Joseph A. 1984. "White House Public Liaison: The Early Years." Paper presented at the annual meeting of the Midwest Political Science Association, Chicago.

———. 1983. "Interest Groups and the Executive: Presidential Intervention." In Allan J. Cigler and Burdett A. Loomis, eds., *Interest Group Politics.* Washington, D.C.: Congressional Quarterly Press.

Pinard, Maurice. 1975. *The Rise of a Third Party.* Rev. ed. Montreal: McGill-Queens University Press.

Piore, Michael J., and Charles F. Sabel. 1984. *The Second Industrial Divide.* New York: Basic Books.

Piven, Frances Fox, and Richard A. Cloward. 1979. *Poor People's Movements: Why They Succeed, How They Fail.* New York: Pantheon.

Pollock, James K. 1927. "The Regulation of Lobbying." *American Political Science Review* (May) 335–341.

Polsby, Nelson W. 1984a. *Political Innovation in America.* New Haven: Yale University Press.

———. 1984b. "The Prospects for Pluralism in the American Federal System: Trends in Unofficial Public Sector Intermediation." In Robert T. Golembiewski and Aaron Wildavsky, eds., *The Costs of Federalism.* New Brunswick, N.J.: Transaction Books.

———. 1983. *The Consequences of Party Reform.* New York: Oxford University Press.

———. 1981-1982. "Contemporary Transformations of American Politics: Thoughts on the Research Agendas of Political Scientists." 96 *Political Science Quarterly* (Winter) 551–570.

———. 1980. *Community Power and Political Theory.* 2nd ed. New Haven: Yale University Press.

———. 1978. "Interest Groups and the Presidency: Trends in Political Intermediation in America." In Walter Dean Burnham and Martha Wagner Weinberg, eds., *American Politics and Public Policy.* Cambridge, Mass.: MIT Press.

Pomper, Gerald M., et al. 1977. *The Elections of 1976.* New York: David McKay.

Popeo, Daniel. 1989. Personal interview in Washington, D.C., March 2.

Popper, Karl. 1959. *The Logic of Scientific Discovery.* London: Hutchison.

Powell, Louis. N.d. Untitled document. Philadelphia: Mid-Atlantic Legal Foundation.

Price, David E. 1984. *Bringing Back the Parties.* Washington, D.C.: Congressional Quarterly Press.

———. 1972. *Who Makes the Laws?* Cambridge, Mass.: Schenkman.

Price, Douglas. 1968. "Micro- and Macro-politics: Notes on Research Strategy." In Oliver Garceau, ed., *Political Research and Political Theory.* Cambridge, Mass.: Harvard University Press.

Pritchard, Garth. 1982. "The Hospitality Lobby: Who's Working for You in Washington?" *Cornell H.R.A. Quarterly* (November) 39–49.

Pruitt, Dean. 1982. *Negotiation Behavior.* New York: Academic Press.

Public Papers of the Presidents: Dwight D. Eisenhower, 1956. 1958. Washington, D.C.: Government Printing Office.

Public Papers of the Presidents: John F. Kennedy, 1962. 1963. Washington, D.C.: Government Printing Office.

Quirk, Paul J. 1989. "Toward a Theory of the Cooperative Resolution of Policy Conflict." 83 *American Political Science Review* 905–921.

———. 1988. "In Defense of the Politics of Ideas." 50 *Journal of Politics* 31–41.

Randall, Vicky. 1987. *Women and Politics: An International Perspective.* Houndsmills, Md.: Macmillan Educational.

Rapoport, Ronald B., Walter J. Stone, and Alan I. Abramowitz. 1991. "Do Endorsements Matter? Group Influence in the 1984 Democratic Caucuses." 85 *American Political Science Review* 193–203.

Reagan, Ronald. 1988. "Remarks to Administration Officials on Domestic Policy, December 13, 1988." 24 *Weekly Compilation of Presidential Documents.*

Redford, Emmette S. 1969. *Democracy in the Administrative State.* New York: Oxford University Press.

Reed, B. J. 1983. "The Changing Role of Local Advocacy." 5 *Journal of Urban Affairs* (Fall) 287–298.

Rhoads, Steven. 1985. *The Economist's View of the World.* Cambridge: Cambridge University Press.

Ricci, David M. 1984. *The Tragedy of Political Science.* New Haven: Yale University Press.

Richardson, James. 1990. "Special Interests Dominate Legislative Session." *California Journal* (November) 527–529.

Ripley, Randall B., and Grace A. Franklin. 1984. *Congress, the Bureaucracy, and Public Policy.* 3rd ed. Homewood, Ill.: Dorsey Press.

Robinson, Donald L. 1989. *Government for the Third American Century.* Boulder, Colo.: Westview Press.

Robyn, Dorothy. 1987. *Braking the Special Interests.* Chicago: University of Chicago Press.

Rockman, Bert A. 1988. "The Style and Organization of the Reagan Presidency." In Charles O. Jones, ed., *The Reagan Legacy.* Chatham, N.J.: Chatham House Press.

Rodgers, Daniel T. 1987. *Contested Truths.* New York: Basic Books.

Root, Elihu. 1907. *The Citizen's Part in Government.* New York: Charles Scribner's Sons.

Roper Organization. 1984. Poll released December 13.

Rosenbaum, David E. 1990. "S & L's: Big Money, Little Outcry." *New York Times,* March 18, sec. 4, 1 and 5.

Rothenberg, Lawrence. 1989. "Putting the Puzzle Together: Why People Join Interest Groups." 60 *Public Choice* 241–257.

———. 1988. "Organizational Maintenance and the Retention Decision in Groups." 82 *American Political Science Review* 1129–1152.

Rourke, Francis E. 1984. *Bureaucracy, Politics and Public Policy.* 3rd ed. Boston: Little, Brown.

———. 1969. *Bureaucracy, Politics and Public Policy.* 2nd ed. Boston: Little, Brown.

Sabatier, Paul. 1975. "Social Movements and Regulatory Agencies." 6 *Policy Sciences* 301–342.

Sabatier, Paul, and Susan McLaughlin. 1990. "Belief Congruence Between Interest Group Leaders and Members: An Empirical Analysis of Three Theories and a Suggested Synthesis." 52 *Journal of Politics* 914–935.

———. 1988. "Belief Congruence of Governmental and Interest Group Elites with Their Constituencies." 16 *American Politics Quarterly* 61–98.

Sabatier, Paul, and Donald McCubbin. 1990. "Membership in Interest Groups: An Empirical Analysis of Competing Theories." Unpublished paper, University of California, Davis.

Sabato, Larry J. 1988. *The Party's Just Begun.* Glenview, Ill.: Scott, Foresman/Little, Brown.

———. 1984. *PAC Power: Inside the World of Political Action Committees.* New York: W. W. Norton.

Sabel, Charles F., Garry B. Herrigel, Richard Deeg, and Richard Kazis. 1989. "Regional Prosperities Compared: Massachusetts and Baden-Württemberg in the 1980s." 18 *Economy and Society* 375–404.

Salamon, Lester M., and Michael S. Lund, eds. 1984. *The Reagan President and the Governing of America.* Washington, D.C.: Urban Institute Press.

Salisbury, Robert H. 1990. "The Paradox of Interest Groups in Washington, D.C.: More Groups and Less Clout." In Anthony King, ed., *The New American Political System.* Rev. ed. Washington, D.C.: American Enterprise Institute.

———. 1989. "The Washington Interest Representatives Project." 8 *Vox Pop Newsletter* 5.

———. 1986. "Washington Lobbyists: A Collective Portrait." In Allan J. Cigler and Burdett A. Loomis, eds., *Interest Group Politics.* 2nd ed. Washington, D.C.: Congressional Quarterly Press.

———. 1984. "Interest Representation: The Dominance of Interest Groups." 78 *American Political Science Review* 64–78.

———. 1983. "Interest Groups: Toward a New Understanding." In Allan J. Cigler and Burdett A. Loomis, eds., *Interest Group Politics.* Washington, D.C.: Congressional Quarterly Press.

———. 1979. "Why No Corporatism in the United States?" In Philippe Schmitter and Gerhard Lehmbruch, eds., *Trends Towards Corporatist Intermediation.* Beverly Hills, Calif.: Sage.

———. 1975. "Interest Groups." In F. I. Greenstein and N. W. Polsby, eds., *Handbook of Political Science,* vol. 4. Reading, Mass.: Addison-Wesley.

———, ed. 1970. *Interest Group Politics in America.* New York: Harper and Row.

———. 1969. "An Exchange Theory of Interest Groups." 13 *Midwest Journal of Political Science* 1–32.

Salisbury, Robert, John P. Heinz, Edward O. Laumann, and Robert L. Nelson. 1987. "Who Works with Whom? Interest Group Alliances and Opposition." 81 *American Political Science Review* 1217–1234.

Saloma, John S., III. 1984. *Ominous Politics: The New Conservative Labyrinth.* New York: Hill and Wang.

Satin, Mark. 1990. "You Don't Have to Be a Baby to Cry." 70 *New Options* 1–4.

Saye, Albert B., Merritt B. Pund, and John F. Allums. 1970. *Principles of American Government.* Englewood Cliffs, N.J.: Prentice-Hall.

Schattschneider, E. E. 1975. *The Semisovereign People.* Rev. ed. Hinsdale, Ill.: Dryden Press.

———. 1960. *The Semisovereign People.* New York: Holt, Rinehart and Winston.

———. 1942. *Party Government.* New York: Farrar and Rinehart.

———. 1935. *Politics, Pressures, and the Tariff.* New York: Prentice-Hall.

Schelling, Thomas C. 1960. *The Strategy of Conflict.* Cambridge, Mass.: Harvard University Press.

Scheuring, Ann Foley. 1982. "The Rising Power of the Farm Lobby." *California Journal* (November) 411–413.

Schick, Allen, Adrienne Pfister, and Howard R. Anderson. 1972. *American Government.* Englewood Cliffs, N.J.: Prentice-Hall.

Schlesinger, Joseph A. 1985. "The New American Political Party." 79 *American Political Science Review* 1152–1169.

Schlozman, Kay. 1984. "What Accent the Heavenly Chorus? Political Equality and the American Pressure System." 46 *Journal of Politics* 1006–1032.

Schlozman, Kay Lehman, and John T. Tierney. 1986. *Organized Interests and American Democracy.* New York: Harper and Row.

Schmitter, Philippe. 1988. "Corporative Democracy." Paper presented at the conference on Politische Institutionen und Interessenvermittlung, Constance, Germany.

———. 1974. "Still the Century of Corporatism?" 36 *Review of Politics* 85–131.

Scholten, Ilja, ed. 1987. *Political Stability and Neo-Corporatism*. Beverly Hills, Calif.: Sage.

Schriftgiesser, Karl. 1951. *The Lobbyists*. Boston: Little, Brown.

Schulman, Paul R. 1988. "The Politics of 'Ideational Policy.'" 50 *Journal of Politics* 263–291.

Schwartz, George. 1981. "Lobbying Effectively for Business Interests." 24 *Business Horizons* (September-October) 41–46.

Schwartz, John E. 1983. *America's Hidden Success: A Reassessment of Twenty Years of Public Policy*. New York: W. W. Norton.

Schwartz, Nancy. 1988. *The Blue Guitar: Political Representation and Community*. Chicago: University of Chicago Press.

Scott, Bruce R. 1985. "The U.S. Competitiveness." In B. Scott and George C. Lodge, eds., *U.S. Competitiveness in the World Economy*. Boston: Harvard Business School Press.

Scott, Bruce R., and George C. Lodge, eds. 1985. *U.S. Competitiveness in the World Economy*. Boston: Harvard Business School Press.

Sears, David, and Jack Citrin. 1985. *Tax Revolt: Something for Nothing in California*. Berkeley: University of California Press.

Sears, David, Richard Lau, Tom Tyler, and Harris Allen. 1980. "Self-Interest vs. Symbolic Politics in Policy Attitudes and Presidential Voting." 74 *American Political Science Review* 670–684.

Sedgwick, Arthur G. 1878. "The Lobby: Its Cause and Cure." 41 *Atlantic* (April) 512–522.

Seidman, Harold. 1977. *Politics, Position, and Power*. 2nd ed. New York: Oxford University Press.

Seligman, Daniel. 1980. "A Case for Adoption." *Fortune*, May 19, 74, 76.

———. 1979. "The Politics and Economics of 'Public Interest' Lobbying." *Fortune*, November 5, 74–75.

Seligman, Lester. 1956. "Presidential Leadership: The Inner Circle and Institutionalism." 18 *Journal of Politics* 410–426.

Selznick, Philip. 1957. *Leadership in Administration*. New York: Harper and Row.

———. 1953. *TVA and the Grass Roots*. Berkeley: University of California Press.

Shackleton, J. R. 1978. "Dr. Marsh on Olson: A Comment." 8 *British Journal of Political Science* 375–380.

Shafter, Byron. 1983. *Quiet Revolution: The Struggle for the Democratic Party and the Shaping of Post-Reform Politics*. New York: Russell Sage Foundation.

Shelton, Fred DeWitt. 1926. "Unofficial Representation at Washington." 116 *Independent* (January) 17–18, 26.

Sheppard, Burton D. 1985. *Rethinking Congressional Reform: The Reform Roots of the Special Interest Congress*. Cambridge, Mass.: Schenkman Books.

Shepsle, Kenneth. 1989. "The Changing Textbook Congress." In John Chubb and Paul E. Peterson, eds., *Can the Government Govern?* Washington, D.C.: Brookings Institution.

Shepsle, Kenneth A., and Barry R. Weingast. 1984. "Legislative Politics and Budget Outcomes." In Gregory B. Mills and John L. Palmer, eds., *Federal Budget Policy in the 1980s*. Washington, D.C.: Urban Institute.

Silbey, Joel H. 1990. "The Rise and Fall of Political Parties." In L. Sandy Maisel, ed., *The Parties Respond*. Boulder, Colo.: Westview Press.

Skinner, Quentin. 1989. "The State." In Terence Ball, James Farr, and Russell L. Hanson, eds., *Political Innovation and Conceptual Change*. Cambridge: Cambridge University Press.

Skocpol, Theda. 1985. "Bringing the State Back In: Strategies of Analysis in Current Research." In Peter B. Evans, Dietrich Rueschemeyer, and Theda Skocpol, eds., *Bringing the State Back In*. Cambridge: Cambridge University Press.

Skowronek, Stephen. 1982. *Building a New American State: The Expansion of Administrative Capacities, 1877–1920*. Cambridge: Cambridge University Press.

Smelser, Neil J. 1963. *Theory of Collective Behavior*. New York: Free Press.

Smith, Hedrick. 1989. *The Power Game*. New York: Ballantine Books.

Smith, Kathy B. 1981. "The Representative Role of the President." *Presidential Studies Quarterly* (Spring) 203–213.

Smith, Richard A. 1989. "Interpretation, Pressure, and the Stability of Interest Group Influence in the U.S. Congress." Paper presented at the annual meetings of the American Political Science Association, Atlanta.

Smith, Steven. 1989. *Call to Order: Floor Politics in the House and Senate*. Washington, D.C.: Brookings Institution.

Snyder, David, and William Kelly. 1977. "Conflict Intensity, Media Sensitivity, and the Validity of Newspaper Data." 42 *American Sociological Review* 105–123.

Sorauf, Frank J. 1988. *Money in American Politics*. Glenview, Ill.: Scott, Foresman/Little, Brown.

———. 1976. *The Wall of Separation: Constitutional Politics of Church and State*. Princeton: Princeton University Press.

———. 1964. *Political Parties in the American System*. Boston: Little, Brown.

Sorauf, Frank J., and Scott A. Wilson. 1990. "Campaigns and Money: A Changing Role for the Political Parties." In L. Sandy Maisel, ed., *The Parties Respond*. Boulder, Colo.: Westview Press.

Starobin, Paul. 1989. "Unions Turn to Grass Roots to Rebuild Hill Clout." *Congressional Quarterly Weekly Report*, September 2, 2253.

Steiner, Gilbert Y., ed. 1983. *The Abortion Dispute and the American System*. Washington, D.C.: Brookings Institution.

Steinfels, Peter. 1979. *The Neoconservatives*. New York: Simon and Schuster.

Stern, Philip M. 1988. *The Best Congress Money Can Buy*. New York: Pantheon.

Stewart, Richard B. 1975. "The Reformation of American Administrative Law." 83 *Harvard Law Review* 1667–1813.

Stigler, George J. 1975. *The Citizen and the State: Essays on Regulation*. Chicago: University of Chicago Press.

———. 1971. "The Theory of Economic Regulation." 2 *Bell Journal of Economics and Management Science* (Spring) 3–21.

Stockman, David. 1986. *The Triumph of Politics*. New York: Harper and Row.

Streck, Wolfgang. 1982. "Organizational Consequences of Corporatist Cooperation in West German Labor Unions." In Gerhard Lehmbruch and Philippe C. Schmitter, eds., *Patterns of Corporatist Policy-Making*. Beverly Hills, Calif.: Sage.

Streck, Wolfgang, and Philippe C. Schmitter, eds. 1985. *Private Interest Government*. Beverly Hills, Calif.: Sage.

Strong, Douglas. 1984. *Tahoe: An Environmental History*. Lincoln: University of Nebraska Press.

Sullivan, John L., James Pierson, and George E. Marcus. 1982. *Political Tolerance and American Democracy*. Chicago: University of Chicago Press.

Sundquist, James L. 1986. *Constitutional Reform and Effective Government*. Washington, D.C.: Brookings Institution.

Sunstein, Cass R. 1991. "Preferences and Politics." 20 *Philosophy and Public Affairs* 3–34.

———. 1990. *After the Rights Revolution: Reconceiving the Regulatory State*. Cambridge, Mass.: Harvard University Press.

———. 1989. "Interpreting Statutes in the Regulatory State." 103 *Harvard Law Review* 405–508.

———. 1985. "Interest Groups in American Public Law." 38 *Stanford Law Review* 29–87.

———. 1984. "Naked Preferences and the Constitution." 84 *Columbia Law Review* 1689.

———. 1983. "Deregulation and the Hard-Look Doctrine." *Supreme Court Review* 177.

_____. 1982. "Public Values, Private Interests, and the Equal Protection Clause." *Supreme Court Review* 127.

Syer, John C. 1987. "California: Political Giants in a Megastate." In Ronald J. Hrebenar and Clive S. Thomas, eds., *Interest Group Politics in the American West*. Salt Lake City: University of Utah Press.

Tarrow, Sidney. 1988. "National Politics and Collective Action: Recent Theory and Research in Western Europe and the United States." 14 *Annual Review of Sociology* 421–440.

Tesh, Sylvia. 1984. "In Support of 'Single-Issue' Politics." 99 *Political Science Quarterly* (Spring) 27–44.

Tesser, Abraham. 1978. "Self-Generated Attitude Change." 11 *Advances in Experimental Social Psychology* 289–338.

Thomas, Clive S., and Ronald J. Hrebenar. 1990. "Interest Groups in the States." In Virginia Gray, Herbert Jacob, and Robert Albritton, eds., *Politics in the American States: A Comparative Analysis*, 5th ed. Glenview, Ill.: Scott, Foresman/Little, Brown.

Thurow, Lester. 1980. *The Zero-Sum Society*. New York: Basic Books.

Tillock, Harriet, and Denton E. Morrison. 1979. "Group Size and Contributions to Collective Action: An Examination of Olson's Theory Using Data from Zero Population Growth." 2 *Research in Social Movements, Conflicts and Change* 131–158.

Tocqueville, Alexis de. 1969. *Democracy in America*. Ed. J. P. Mayer. Garden City, N.Y.: Doubleday.

Tolchin, Martin. 1989. "How the New Medicare Law Fell on Hard Times in a Hurry." *New York Times*, October 9, A1, A10.

Triebwasser, Marc A. 1978. "The Rise (and Perhaps the Fall) of an 'Apolitical' Conceptualization of Politics in Major College Level American Government Texts, 1900–1975." Ph.D. dissertation, New York University.

Truman, David B. 1971. *The Governmental Process*. 2nd ed. New York: Alfred A. Knopf.

_____. 1968. "Political Group Analysis." In David L. Sills, ed., *International Encyclopedia of the Social Sciences*, vol. 12. New York: Macmillan.

_____. [1951] 1953. *The Governmental Process*. New York: Alfred A. Knopf.

Tufte, Edward R. 1978. *Political Control of the Economy*. Princeton: Princeton University Press.

Turner, Henry A. 1958. "How Pressure Groups Operate." 319 *Annals of the American Academy of Political and Social Science* 67.

Tversky, Amos, and Daniel Kahneman. 1981. "The Framing of Decisions and the Psychology of Choice." 211 *Science* 453–458.

Twentieth Century Fund. 1984. *What Price PACs?* New York: Twentieth Century Fund.

Tyler, Tom. 1990. *Why People Obey the Law*. New Haven: Yale University Press.

Tyler, Tom, Kenneth Rasinski, and Eugene Griffin. 1986. "Alternative Images of the Citizen." 41 *American Psychologist* 970–978.

U.S. Congress. Senate. 1960. *Establish a Department of Consumers*. Hearings Before the Subcommittee on Reorganization and International Organizations of the Committee on Government Operations. 86th Cong., 2nd sess.

Useem, Michael. 1984. *The Inner Circle*. New York: Oxford University Press.

Valenti, Jack. 1984. "The White House Experience." *Washington Magazine*, March 4.

Vatter, Harold G., and John F. Walker. 1990. *The Inevitability of Government Growth*. New York: Columbia University Press.

Verba, Sidney. 1961. *Small Groups and Political Behavior: A Study of Leadership*. Princeton: Princeton University Press.

Verba, Sidney, and Norman H. Nie. 1972. *Participation in America*. New York: Harper and Row.

Verba, Sidney, Norman H. Nie, and Jae-on Kim. 1978. *Participation and Political Equality: A Seven Nation Comparison*. Cambridge: Cambridge University Press.

Viguerie, Richard. 1981. *The New Right: We're Ready to Lead.* Falls Church, Va.: Viguerie Company.

Vogel, David. 1989. *Fluctuating Fortunes.* New York: Basic Books.

———. 1986. *National Styles of Regulation.* Ithaca, N.Y.: Cornell University Press.

———. 1980-1981. "The Public Interest Movement and the American Reform Tradition." 95 *Political Science Quarterly* 607–627.

———. 1978. "Why Businessmen Distrust Their State: The Political Consciousness of American Corporate Executives." *British Journal of Political Science* 45–78.

Vose, Clement E. 1972. *Constitutional Change.* Lexington, Mass.: Lexington Books.

———. 1959. *Caucasians Only.* Berkeley: University of California Press.

Walker, Jack L. 1990a. *Mobilizing Political Interests in America: Interest Groups, Patrons, and Representation.* Unpublished manuscript.

———. 1990b. "Political Mobilization in America." In John E. Jackson, ed., *Institutions in American Society.* Ann Arbor: University of Michigan Press.

———. 1983. "The Origins and Maintenance of Interest Groups in America." 77 *American Political Science Review* 390–406.

Walker, Samuel. 1990. *In Defense of American Liberties: A History of the ACLU.* New York: Oxford University Press.

Wall, James A. 1975. "The Effects of Constituent Trust and Representative Bargaining Visibility on Intergroup Bargaining." 17 *Organizational Behavior and Human Performance* 244–256.

Wasby, Stephen L. 1986. "The Multi-Faceted Elephant: Litigator Perspectives on Planned Litigation for Social Change." 15 *Capital University Law Review* 145–189.

———. 1984. "How Planned Is 'Planned Litigation'?" 1984 *American Bar Foundation Research Journal* 83–138.

Waterman, Richard W. 1989. *Presidential Influence and the Administrative State.* Knoxville: University of Tennessee Press.

Watt, James. 1984. Personal interview in Washington, D.C., August 6.

Wattenberg, Martin P. 1990. "From a Partisan to a Candidate-Centered Electorate." In Anthony King, ed., *The New American Political System.* 2nd ed. Washington, D.C.: American Enterprise Institute.

Wayne, Stephen J. 1978. *The Legislative Presidency.* New York: Harper and Row.

Weidenbaum, Murray. 1988. *Rendezvous with Reality.* New York: Basic Books.

———. 1981. *Business, Government and the Public.* 2nd ed. Englewood Cliffs, N.J.: Prentice-Hall.

———. 1980. *The Future of Government Regulation.* New York: Acacom.

———. 1978. "The Costs of Government Regulation of Business." Report presented before the Joint Economic Committee, U.S. Congress, April 10.

Weingast, Barry, and Mark Moran. 1983. "Bureaucratic Discretion or Congressional Control? Regulatory Policymaking by the Federal Trade Commission." 91 *Journal of Political Economy* 765–800.

Weir, Margaret, Ann Shola Orloff, and Theda Skocpol. 1988. "Introduction." In M. Weir, A. S. Orloff, and T. Skocpol, eds., *The Politics of Social Policy in the United States.* Princeton: Princeton University Press.

Wenner, Lettie M. 1982. *The Environmental Decade in Court.* Bloomington: University of Indiana Press.

Western Federal Regional Council. 1979. *Lake Tahoe Environmental Assessment.* Washington, D.C.: Government Printing Office.

White, Louise G. 1976. "Rational Theories of Participation." 20 *Journal of Conflict Resolution* 255–278.

Wildavsky, Aaron. 1988. *The New Politics of the Budgetary Process.* Glenview, Ill.: Scott, Foresman.

_____. 1980. *How to Limit Government Spending*. Berkeley: University of California Press.

Wilkins, Robert. 1981. "Alexander McKenzie and the Politics of Bossism." In Thomas Howard, ed., *The North Dakota Political Tradition*. Ames: Iowa State University Press.

Will, George F. 1978. "Passionate Politics." *Newsweek*, May 1: 96.

Willets, Peter, ed. 1982. *Pressure Groups in the Global System*. London: Frances Pinter.

Wilson, Francis Graham. 1936. *The Elements of Modern Politics*. New York: McGraw-Hill.

Wilson, Frank L. 1987. *Interest Group Politics in France*. New York: Cambridge University Press.

Wilson, Graham K. 1990a. *Business and Politics*. 2nd ed. Chatham, N.J.: Chatham House Publishers.

_____. 1990b. *Interest Groups*. Oxford: Basil Blackwell.

_____. 1985a. *Business and Politics*. Chatham, N.J.: Chatham House Press.

_____. 1985b. *The Politics of Safety and Health*. New York: Oxford University Press.

_____. 1982. "Why Is There No Corporatism in the United States?" In Gerhard Lehmbruch and Philippe C. Schmitter, eds., *Patterns of Corporatist Policy-Making*. Beverly Hills, Calif.: Sage.

_____. 1981. *Interest Groups in the United States*. New York: Oxford University Press.

_____. 1977a. "Department Secretaries: Are They Really a President's 'Natural Enemies'?" 7 *British Journal of Political Science* 273–301.

_____. 1977b. *Special Interests and Policy-Making*. New York: John Wiley.

Wilson, James Q. 1986. "The Politics of Regulation: Toward a New Model of the Political Process." Paper presented at the annual meeting of the American Political Science Association, Washington, D.C.

_____. 1980a. "The Politics of Regulation." In James Q. Wilson, ed., *The Politics of Regulation*. New York: Basic Books.

_____, ed. 1980b. *The Politics of Regulation*. New York: Basic Books.

_____. 1973. *Political Organizations*. New York: Basic Books.

Wilson, Woodrow. 1908. *Constitutional Government in the United States*. New York: Columbia University Press.

_____. 1885. *Congressional Government*. Boston: Houghton, Mifflin.

Wolfinger, Raymond, and Steven Rosenstone. 1980. *Who Votes?* New Haven: Yale University Press.

Wolman, Harold, and Fred Teitelbaum. 1984. "Interest Groups and the Reagan Presidency." In Lester M. Salamon and Michael S. Lund, eds., *The Reagan Presidency*. Washington, D.C.: Urban Institute.

Yang, John. 1989. "Sudden Sanctimony: Congress Gets Ethical, Shuns Any Hint It Is in Debt to Big Givers." *Wall Street Journal*, August 4: A1.

Yoffee, David B. 1983. *Power and Protectionism: Strategies of the Newly Industrializing Countries*. New York: Columbia University Press.

Young, James Sterling. 1966. *The Washington Community, 1800–1828*. New York: Harcourt, Brace.

Zeiger, Richard. 1989. "The Persuaders." In Thomas R. Hoeber and Charles M. Price, eds., *California Government and Politics: Annual, 1989–90*. Sacramento: California Journal Press.

Zeigler, Harmon. 1988. *Pluralism, Corporatism, and Confucianism*. Philadelphia: Temple University Press.

_____. 1983. "Interest Groups in the States." In Virginia Gray, Herbert Jacob, and Kenneth N. Vines, eds. *Politics in the American States: A Comparative Analysis*. 4th ed. Boston: Little, Brown.

Zeigler, Harmon, and Michael Baer. 1969. *Lobbying: Interaction and Influence in American State Legislatures*. Belmont, Calif.: Wadsworth.

Zeigler, Harmon, and Hendrik van Dalen. 1976. "Interest Groups in State Politics." In Herbert Jacob and Kenneth N. Vines, eds., *Politics in the American States: A Comparative Analysis.* 3rd ed. Boston: Little, Brown.

Zeigler, L. Harmon, and G. Wayne Peak. [1964] 1972. *Interest Groups in American Society.* Englewood Cliffs, N.J.: Prentice-Hall.

Zeller, Belle. 1954. *American State Legislatures.* 2nd ed. New York: Thomas Y. Crowell.

——— . 1937. *Pressure Politics in New York.* New York: Russell and Russell.

Zukin, Sharon, and Paul DiMaggio, eds. 1990. *Structures of Capital: The Social Organization of the Economy.* New York: Cambridge University Press.

Zumbrun, Ronald A. 1989. "Public Interest Law in the 1990s: Strategies and Opportunities." Heritage Foundation Lectures, no. 223.

About the Book and Editor

Have special interests taken over the country, derailing the public agenda and threatening representative democracy? Or is it possible that the maturation of interest group politics will yield a more pluralistic and balanced society? Interest groups have changed over the past two decades, and so have the ways in which we study them. This volume charts the changes in interest group theory, organization, activity, and the influence of interest groups in the United States.

Leading scholars and practitioners trace notable shifts in interest group politics, including challenges to effective governance, new resources and techniques of influence, patterns of representation, and changing venues, targets, and characteristics of interest group activity. The mobilization of particular interests—including business, women, conservatives, and consumers—is given special attention. Institutional interactions and interest group evaluations round out the coverage.

Sixteen original essays written especially for this volume reflect the best and most current scholarship in the field. New empirical research, informed theoretical reflection, and experienced involvement are all rendered accessible in this thematically unified collection. Petracca has drawn together leading text authors, cutting-edge researchers, established scholars, and rising young stars to capture the attention and challenge the thinking of both novice and serious students of interest groups.

This compact yet diverse volume can provide the core of reading for a course on interest group politics, or it can supplement one of the leading texts in a wide range of courses in American politics. The distinguished lineup of contributors promises to make this book "must" reading for scholars, professionals, and practitioners, as well as for their students.

Mark P. Petracca is assistant professor of political science at the University of California–Irvine and has taught at the University of Chicago, Amherst College, and Beijing University. He is the author of numerous scholarly articles, coauthor of *The American Presidency*, a leading text in the field, and author of *Agenda-Building in American Democracy*. He is the recent recipient of the university's distinguished teaching award and combines his teaching and scholarship with media consultancy and frequent op-editorial contributions.

About the Contributors

ANNE N. COSTAIN is associate professor of political science at the University of Colorado in Boulder. The author or coauthor of numerous articles on interest groups, mass-based political movements, and women's issues, she is the author of a new book, *Inviting Women's Rebellion*, on the political impact of the women's movement.

R. KENNETH GODWIN is professor of political science at the University of North Texas. A student of comparative public policy, his most recent book is *One Billion Dollars of Influence: The Direct Marketing of Politics*. He is currently researching interest group activity and the public provision of private goods.

JOHN P. HEINZ is Owen L. Corn Professor of Law at Northwestern University and Distinguished Research Professor at the American Bar Foundation. Among other works, he is coauthor of *Chicago Lawyers* and *The Hollow Core, Private Interest in National Policy Making*, with Laumann, Nelson, and Salisbury, to be published in 1992.

RONALD J. HREBENAR is professor of political science at the University of Utah. He is author of several books and articles, including *Interest Group Politics in America* (1990) and "Interest Groups in the American States" in Virginia Gray et al., eds., *Politics in the American States* (1990). During 1982–83 he was a Fulbright Scholar in Japan.

EDWARD O. LAUMANN is George Herbert Mead Professor of Sociology and dean of the Division of Social Sciences at the University of Chicago. The author and coauthor of numerous books and articles including, *Bonds of Pluralism*, *Networks of Collective Action*, and *The Organizational State*, Laumann is also coauthor with Heinz, Nelson, and Salisbury of *The Hollow Core, Private Interest in National Policy Making*, to be published in 1992.

JOAN LUCCO, a graduate of the Johns Hopkins University, has most recently taught at George Washington University. She is the author of *Of the People: The Representation of Interests at the White House* (forthcoming). She has also served as a consultant on consumer protection, land use planning, and education.

JANE J. MANSBRIDGE is Jane W. Long Professor of the Arts and Sciences as well as professor in the Department of Political Science and faculty fellow at the Center for Urban Affairs and Policy Research at Northwestern University. She is the author of *Beyond Adversary Democracy* and *Why We Lost the ERA*, co-recipient of the American Political Science Association's Gladys M. Kammerer Award for the best publication in U.S. national policy and its Victoria Shuck Award for the best book on women and politics. Her recent edited volume, *Beyond Self-Interest*, collects work on the frontier of several social science disciplines on non–self-interested motivation in politics.

BRYANT SCOTT McFALL is a third year law student at the University of Texas Law School where he is the book review editor of the *Texas Law Journal*.

ANDREW S. McFARLAND is associate professor of political science at the University of Illinois at Chicago. Author of *Public Interest Lobbies* and *Common Cause*, among other books, his recent works include "Interest Groups and Political Times: Cycles in America" in the *British Journal of Political Science* (1991) and *Cooperative Pluralism: The Coal Policy Experiment* (forthcoming).

ROBERT L. NELSON is associate professor of sociology of Northwestern University. He is coauthor of *The Hollow Core, Private Interest in National Policy Making* with Heinz, Laumann, and Salisbury, to be published in 1992.

KAREN O'CONNOR is professor of political science at Emory University. A past chair of the Law, Courts, and Judicial Behavior Section of the American Political Science Association, she is the author of *Women's Organizations' Use of the Courts* and numerous articles on the role and impact of interest groups in the legal process.

MARK A. PETERSON is associate professor of government at Harvard University. Among his works on American governmental institutions is his recent book, *Legislating Together: The White House and Capitol Hill from Eisenhower to Reagan* (1990), which in an earlier incarnation won the 1986 E. E. Schattschneider Award for the best dissertation in American politics. He has also been an American Political Science Association Congressional Fellow, serving as a legislative assistant in the U.S. Senate.

PAUL E. PETERSON is Henry Lee Shattuck Professor of Government and director of the Center for American Political Studies at Harvard University. Author or editor of over a dozen books, he is most recently coauthor of *Welfare Magnets: A New Case for a National Standard*, coeditor of *The Urban Underclass*, and editor of a forthcoming volume on Congress, the president, and the making of foreign policy.

MARK P. PETRACCA is assistant professor of political science at the University of California, Irvine. Coauthor of *The American Presidency* and author of articles on many aspects of American politics, democratization, and political reform, he is also the author of a forthcoming book, *Agenda-Building in American Democracy*. He was a visiting professor at Beijing University in the People's Republic of China in 1987 and in 1988 received the UCI Alumni Association's Award for "Distinguished Teaching."

DAVID PLOTKE is assistant professor of political science at Yale University. He is the author of *The Democratic Political Order from the 1930s to the 1970s: Change and Order in Modern American Politics* and is working on a book tentatively titled, *Identities and Interests in Contemporary Collective Action*.

PAUL A. SABATIER is professor of environmental studies at the University of California, Davis. He is coauthor of *Implementation and Public Policy, Can Regulation Work?* and *Effective Policy Implementation* among other authored or coauthored books and articles on policy implementation, the role of interest groups and other actors in policy change, administrative policymaking, and theories of the policy process.

ROBERT H. SALISBURY is Souers Professor of American Government and chair of the Department of Political Science at Washington University. The author of numerous seminal articles in the field of interest group studies, he is also coauthor of *The Hollow Core, Private Interest in National Policy Making*, with Heinz, Laumann, and Nelson, to be published in 1992.

CLIVE S. THOMAS is professor of political science at the University of Alaska, Juneau. His publications include: editor of *Politics and Public Policy in the Contemporary American West* (1991) and several coedited books and coauthored articles and chapters with Ronald J.

Hrebenar on state interest groups. He has also served as a lobbyist and teaches seminars on the organization and techniques of lobbying.

JOHN T. TIERNEY is associate professor in the Department of Political Science at Boston College. His research interests and published works are varied, focusing on health policy, government corporations, and the linkages among lobbyists and legislators. Coauthor of *Organized Interests and American Democracy*, he is currently at work on a long-range project examining networks of power and influence in Washington policymaking.

GRAHAM K. WILSON is professor of political science at the University of Wisconsin, Madison. He has authored a number of books on interest groups, including *Interest Groups* (1990), *Business and Politics, a Comparative Introduction* (1990), and *The Politics of Health and Safety* (1985).

Index

Abortion, 232, 266, 269, 272, 274, 310, 324

Access. *See* Executive branch, access to

Accountability, 51

ACLU. *See* American Civil Liberties Union

ACP. *See* Executive branch, Agency for Consumer Protection

Activists, 207. *See also* Policy activists

Ad Hoc Committee of Educational Institutions and Organizations on Copyright Law Revision, 43

Advertising, 20, 36, 49, 177, 188, 219

AELE. *See* Americans for Effective Law Enforcement

AFBF. *See* American Farm Bureau Federation

Affirmative action, 231, 269, 280, 281(n4)

Affluence, 95

Afghanistan, 335, 338

AFL–CIO, 83, 87, 88, 91, 101, 142

Agriculture, 17, 18, 82, 83–84, 93–94, 132, 133, 137, 141, 143, 144, 152, 155, 166, 244, 330–331, 336

Aid to Families with Dependent Children, 228

A-K Associates of California, 17

Alaska, 232, 235

Alienation, 314, 317, 317(fig.)

Altruism, 36, 55(n5), 105

American Association of Retired Persons, 309

American Association of School Administrators, 228

American Bankers Association, 21

American Civil Liberties Union (ACLU), 265, 266, 267, 272

American Farm Bureau Federation (AFBF), 82, 83–84

American Liberty League, 267

American Medical Association, 206

American Political Parties and Elections (Sait), 363

American Political Science Association, 365

Americans for Effective Law Enforcement (AELE), 267

Americans United for Life (AUL), 266, 269

American Telephone and Telegraph Company (AT&T), 206, 304

Amicus curiae briefs, 265–267, 269, 270–272, 271(fig.), 272, 273, 277, 280, 281(n2)

Anti-Saloon League, 208

Antistatism. *See* Statism

Antiwar movement, 231

Appointments. *See under* Personnel issues

Aristotle, 101

Arizona, 156, 166

Arkansas, 166

Armory, Cleveland, 107

Arnold, R. Douglas, 363

Association of American Publishers, 43

AT&T. *See* American Telephone and Telegraph Company

Attorneys. *See* Lawyers/law firms

Audubon Society, 325(n6)

AUL. *See* Americans United for Life

Austria, 78, 85

Authors League of America, 43

Ayer, Don, 274–275

Baer, Michael, 157

Banking, 21

Baroody, William, 225

Bauer, Raymond, 19, 44–45, 56(n19), 83, 86, 351

Belgium, 78

Bell, Daniel, 309

Benda, Peter, 228

Benefits. *See under* Interest groups

Bentley, Arthur, 4, 72, 150, 264

Berman, Daniel, 13

Berry, Jeffrey, 10, 11, 13, 55(n9), 65, 107, 108, 132, 212, 261(n2)

Binkley, Wilfred, 13

Birnbaum, Jeffrey H., 211

Biznet, 312

Blacks, 231, 232, 235, 236, 246, 260, 264, 286

Blaisdell, Donald, 13

Block grants, 228

Blue-collar vote, 84

Blumenthal, Sidney, 357
Bolick, Clint, 273–274, 276, 277, 278
Bork, Robert, 279
Boycotts, 286
Brady Bill, 89, 207
Bribery, 213. *See also* Corruption
Broder, David, 309
Browne, William, 146
Brown v. Board of Education, 265, 266
Brzezinski, Zbigniew, 354
Buchanan, James, 50
Buchanan, Patrick, 236
Buckley v. Valeo, 51–52
Budgets, 24, 140, 226, 227, 253, 336–337, 338–339, 339–340, 359
Building a New American State (Skowronek), 66
Burnham, Walter Dean, 238, 355
Burns, James MacGregor, 365
Burstein, Paul, 294
Bush administration, 225, 236, 237, 243, 252, 260, 326, 329
Business, 15, 25, 27, 48, 69, 83, 86, 92, 135, 136, 138, 230, 233, 244, 254, 258–259, 268, 350, 367
    chief executive officers (CEOs), 211
    and cooperation, 180, 185, 189, 190
    critiques of, 187
    elites, 175, 177, 180, 185, 187, 188, 190, 193, 196(n15), 197(n21)
    and government, 85, 93, 180, 192. *See also* Business, and regulations
    organizations, 193(n2). *See also* Interest groups, and business mobilization; Political action committees, business
    political mobilization of, 175–193
    press, 196(n14), 198(n26)
    public views of, 175, 178, 245
    and regulations, 175, 179–180, 181, 182, 183–184, 187, 188, 190, 195(nn 8, 9). *See also* Regulatory issues
    shift to right, 186–187
    See also Corporations; Profits
Business Roundtable, 177, 180–181, 184, 185, 186–187, 188, 189, 190, 195(n12), 196(n14), 197(nn 20, 21), 211
Busing, 231, 232
By-product theory, 102, 104–106, 110, 115, 117, 119

CAC. *See* Executive branch, Consumer Advisory Council
Caldeira, Gregory, 272
Calhoun, John C., 3
Califano, Joseph, 252
California, 17, 26, 110, 152, 157, 166
    Chamber of Commerce, 268
    Supreme Court, 279

See also Lake Tahoe Basin
Campaign financing, 20, 49, 81, 84–85, 131, 152, 176, 191, 203–205, 322, 335. *See also* Political action committees, expenditures
Campbell, Persia, 244–245
Canada, 30(n30), 341
Candidate-centered campaigns, 27, 31(n52), 357
Capitalism, 79, 92, 198(n25)
Capital Legal Foundation, 277
Carolene Products. *See U.S. v. Carolene Products Co.*
Carter, Jimmy, 226, 232, 257, 258, 347, 367
    administration, 178, 181, 191, 198(n26), 225, 235, 243, 249, 252, 255–256, 259, 336, 338
Cassidy and Associates, 212
Catholics, 133, 135, 231, 232, 246
Caucasians Only (Vose), 264
CBI. *See* Confederation of British Industry
CBS, 277, 281(n5)
CEA. *See* Executive branch, Council of Economic Advisers
Center for Law and Religious Freedom, 269
CEOs. *See* Business, chief executive officers
Chamberlain, Lawrence, 350
Charity contributions, 214
Chavez, Linda, 235
Checks and balances, 49
Chicago, University of, 279
Christian Right. *See* Religious Right
Chrysler Corporation, 22, 189
Chubb, John E., 18
Cigler, Allan J., 364, 365
Citizens for Tax Justice, 39
Civic republican tradition, 49–50
Civil disobedience, 286
Civil rights, 73–74, 109, 223, 229, 231, 235, 285, 286, 306(n2), 307(n4)
Civil Rights Act (1964), 74
Clark, Peter B., 102
Class conflict, 92
Coalitions, 21–22, 40, 62, 67, 68, 69, 223, 230, 234–235, 237, 238, 255, 258, 303, 369
Cobb, Roger, 286
Coercion, 36, 104. *See also* Power issues
Cohen, Joshua, 49, 57(n26)
Cold war, 232, 329, 334
Collective action, 73, 74, 75–77, 89, 176, 179, 185, 189–190, 192, 286, 349
Collective goods. *See* Common good
Colson, Charles, 225
Commonality, 36, 37
Common Cause, 88, 89, 107, 204, 309
Common good, 33, 50, 61, 100, 104, 105, 107, 109, 124, 125, 261(n2), 286, 287, 327, 346, 351, 357, 366. *See also* Commonality
Commitment theory, 109–110, 114, 115, 117–118, 119, 125

Communications networks, 74, 75. *See also* Issue networks
Communications technology, 19, 23, 25–26, 94–95, 132, 222, 240. *See also* Media
Compromise, 36, 244
Computers, 25, 26, 94, 95, 165, 309, 310
Concerned Women for America, 269
Confederation of British Industry (CBI), 83, 84, 90
Conflict, 33, 36, 37, 42, 74, 141, 144, 217, 318
Congress. *See under* United States
Congressional Record, 289
Conrad, Robin, 274
Consensus, 355, 357
Conservatives, 263–281
Consociationalism, 55(n4)
Construction Users Anti-Inflation Roundtable, 196(n14)
Consultants, 22, 136, 357
Consumer Assembly, 260, 262(n35)
Consumers, 92, 94, 99, 101, 104, 109, 204, 227, 229, 285
  consumer groups, 242–261, 349
  consumer product safety, 268
  and future, 259–261
  goals of consumer advocates, 244–249, 254, 255, 257, 261(n7)
  White House representation, 246, 247–249, 256–257, 258. *See also* Presidency, special assistant to the president for consumer affairs
Contacts. *See* Personal contacts
Cooperation, 51, 299. *See also* Collective action; *under* Business
Co-optation, 64, 69, 259
Corporations, 14, 39, 80, 84, 85, 86, 87, 92, 136, 176, 179, 188, 194(n7), 198(n25), 232
Corporatism, 9, 38, 50–51, 54, 186, 197(n19)
  and deliberation, 41–47, 49
  democratic, 78–79
  European, 45–46, 57(n26), 78
  neocorporatism, 18, 85, 87, 356, 358–359
Corruption, 85, 203, 213, 232, 244, 346
Costain, Anne N. and W. Douglas, 43–44, 65
Costanza, Midge, 235
Countervailing power, 58–79, 94, 215, 217, 238, 260, 303, 350, 354
Courts, 91. *See also* United States, Supreme Court; *under* Federal government
Cranston, Alan, 311–312
Crawford, Kenneth G., 13
Crime, 38–39
Crisis of Democracy (Trilateral Commission), 354
Critical Elections (Burnham), 355
Culhane, Paul J., 69

Dahl, Robert, 5, 66, 239, 355

Data sources, 7, 113, 151, 153, 288–289, 365, 366. *See also* Methodology
Death penalty, 264
Debt. *See under* United States
Decentralization, 17, 18, 24, 25, 62, 85, 228, 334, 335. *See also* Power issues, centralization of power
DeConcini, Dennis, 325(n8)
Defenders of Wildlife, 310–311
Defending the National Interest (Krasner), 66
Defense, 17, 227, 233, 329, 334–335, 337, 339, 340
Deficits, 337–338, 339–340, 341, 359
Deliberation, 33, 51, 347, 357
  benefits, 32, 47
  collaborative, 38, 39–41
  competitive, 38–39, 53
  corporatist, 41–47. *See also* Corporatism
  meaning of, 35–37
  models, 37–47
  norms, 48. *See also* Democracy, normative theory
Democracy, 16, 20, 54(n2), 314, 322, 324
  adversary, 32–34, 36, 48
  centralized systems of, 94
  juridical, 78
  mixed, 33
  normative theory, 32–35, 46, 48, 357
  one-person/one-vote, 32, 33, 36, 53, 331
  pluralistic, 63. *See also* Pluralism
Democratic party, 84, 88, 93, 136, 137, 138, 139, 145–146, 175, 178, 183, 187, 191, 196(n13), 197(n21), 225, 227, 230, 231, 232, 235, 257, 291, 315, 329, 330, 334, 336–337, 339
Deregulation. *See* Regulatory issues
Dexter, Lewis Anthony, 19, 44–45, 56(n19), 83, 86, 351
Dillon, Mary E., 29(n14)
Direct marketing, 25–26, 308–324
Discretionary programs, 329, 332(fig.), 337
Discrimination, 285, 291. *See also under* Labor issues
District of Columbia Bar, 14
Disturbance theory, 101, 107
Dolan, Terry, 322
Dole, Elizabeth, 235, 236
Dole, Robert, 21
Domestic expenditures, 339. *See also* Discretionary programs
Downs, Anthony, 50
Drucker, Peter, 13
Drugs, 246

Earth Day, 286
Eckstein, Harry, 29(n4), 348

Economic issues, 33, 35, 63, 78–79, 155, 158, 167, 170, 172, 175, 197(n22), 230, 235, 252, 258, 334, 337–338, 359
  government's role in, 90–91, 94, 95. *See also* Business, and regulations; Regulatory issues
  growth models, 182, 182(table), 184–189, 190, 192, 193, 197(nn 18, 19)
  See also Business; Interest groups, economic; Interest groups, stasis
Edelman, Murray, 248
Edison Electric Institute, 267
Edsall, Thomas, 232
Education, 152, 177, 227, 264, 285, 313, 315, 323
EEAC. *See* Equal Employment Advisory Council
EEOC. *See* Equal Employment Opportunity Commission
Ehrlichman, John, 254
Ehrmann, Henry, 364
Eisenhower, Dwight, 84, 231, 303
Eizenstat, Stuart, 255
Elder, Charles, 286
Elderly, 24, 38–39, 166, 208, 209, 231, 236, 246, 260, 328, 329–330, 336, 341
Eldersveld, Samuel J., 241(n8), 363–364
Elections, 41, 52, 191. *See also* Campaign financing
Elites, 38, 40, 41, 45, 51, 53, 54, 61, 211, 310, 323
  elitist theory, 133
  See also Pluralism, plural elites theory; Power issues, power-elite theorists; *under* Business
Emotional issues, 318, 319, 321
Employment. *See* Labor issues
Energy policy, 18, 132, 133, 136, 137, 138, 143, 144, 369–370
Entrepreneurs. *See* Policy entrepreneurs; Political entrepreneurs; *under* Interest groups
Environmental Defense Fund, 309
Environmental groups/issues, 65, 73, 82, 84, 89, 92, 94, 95, 99, 101, 104, 109, 118, 143, 152, 166, 204, 217, 227, 229, 232, 237, 242, 246, 258–259, 267, 268, 278, 285, 286, 315, 324, 349, 371. *See also* Environmental Protection Agency; Lake Tahoe Basin; *individual groups*
Environmental Protection Agency (EPA), 259–260, 288, 318
EOP. *See* Presidency, Executive Office of the President
EPA. *See* Environmental Protection Agency
Epstein, Lee, 263, 267, 270, 272
Equal Employment Advisory Council (EEAC), 269, 276
Equal Employment Opportunity Commission (EEOC), 304

Equal Rights Amendment (ERA), 51, 265, 269, 285, 291, 294, 295(fig.), 297, 299, 305
ERA. *See* Equal Rights Amendment
Ethics Reform Act (1989), 213
Exchange theory, 100, 106–109, 114, 115, 118, 125–126
Executive branch, 91, 131, 133, 138, 141, 142, 144, 145, 242, 334, 341
  access to, 224–225, 228, 229, 236, 238, 247, 249, 253, 256–259
  Agency for Consumer Protection (ACP), 255, 256, 257
  Consumer Advisory Council (CAC), 243, 250–251, 262(n10)
  Council of Economic Advisers (CEA), 250, 262(n10)
  Office of Communications, 236
  Office of Consumer Affairs, 243
  See also Presidency
Extremism, 314, 317, 318, 321

Factions, 3, 8, 33, 35, 221, 299, 347
Fairness doctrine, 52
Falwell, Jerry, 309, 311, 312
Favors, 213–214, 217
FCC. *See* Federal Communications Commission
Fear, use of, 311, 321, 323, 324. *See also* Intimidation
Federal Communications Commission (FCC), 52
Federal government, 23–24, 49, 62, 64, 150, 299, 300(fig.)
  agencies, 42, 50, 67, 68, 71, 93, 146, 152, 164, 222, 242, 247, 251, 255, 256, 257, 260, 273, 304, 327, 335, 338
  courts, 42, 49, 50, 69, 275. *See also* United States, Supreme Court
  funds of, 212, 229, 230, 328–331. *See also* Government spending
  and governability, 354–355
  grants, 228, 267, 319
  See also Executive branch; Government officials; Regulatory issues; United States
Federalist Papers, 3, 5, 35, 50, 92
Federalist Society, 279
Federal Trade Commission (FTC), 67, 232
Feminism. *See* Women's movement; Women/women's issues
Finer, Herman, 13
First Amendment, 51–53, 164, 269, 281
Flanigan, Peter, 254
Florida, 152, 166
Fluctuating Fortunes (Vogel), 197(n22)
FNSEA. *See* France, Fédération Nationale des Syndicats d'Exploitants Agricoles
Follett, Mary, 9
Ford, Gerald, 225, 234, 243, 251, 258, 334
Forest Ranger, The (Kaufman), 66

Fourteenth Amendment, 265
France, 30(n30), 79, 85, 87, 91, 95
  Fédération Nationale des Syndicats
    d'Exploitants Agricoles (FNSEA), 90
  Patronat, 83
Freeman, Jo, 74
Freeman, Richard, 44, 65
Free-rider problem, 57(n24), 61, 82, 102, 104,
  105, 106, 110, 125, 126(n3), 180, 181
Friends of the Earth, 318
Fritschler, A. Lee, 69
FTC. *See* Federal Trade Commission
Fund for Animals, 107
Fund-raising, 20, 25, 138, 278, 291, 309, 312,
  315. *See also* Campaign financing
Furness, Betty, 243, 252, 253

Gais, Tom, 367
Gallup polls, 7, 27
Gardner, John, 107
Gays, 235
Gelb, Joyce, 290, 291, 294
Gender, 265, 266, 290, 304, 306(n1). *See also*
  Women/women's issues
George Mason University, 279
Germany, 78, 87. *See also* West Germany
Gifts, 214
Ginsberg, Benjamin, 13, 24, 227, 289, 359
Ginsburg, Douglas, 279
Ginsburg, Ruth Bader, 265
GNP. *See* Gross national product
Gormley, William, 118
Governmental Process, The (Truman), 101
Government by the People (Burns et al.), 365
Government officials, 132, 134(table), 135, 136,
  137, 137(table), 138, 139, 141, 145, 145–
  146(tables), 228, 349, 370
Government spending, 24, 64, 78, 183,
  197(n21), 328–331, 332–333(figs.), 336, 337,
  339, 371
Gramm-Rudman-Hollings Act of 1985, 78, 339–
  340
Grants, 228, 280. *See also under* Federal
  government
Grassroots mobilization, 26. *See also* Lobbies,
  grassroots lobbying
Great Britain, 30(n30), 83, 92, 99
  Labour party, 90, 93
  Ministry of Agriculture, Fisheries, and Food
    (MAFF), 93–94
  National Farmers' Union (NFU), 83, 84, 90,
    93
  noneconomic interest groups in, 88
  Parliament, 33
  Trade Union Congress (TUC), 84
Great Depression, 231
Great Society, 334

Greenstone, J. David, 364
Greenwald, Carol, 225
Gross national product (GNP), 331
Guiton, Bonnie, 252

Habermas, Jürgen, 45
Hardin, Russell, 57(n24)
Harris, Richard, 18
Hawley-Snoot Tariff Act, 77–78
Hayes, Michael, 309
Health and Human Services (HHS), Department
  of, 243, 251, 252
Health, Education, and Welfare, Department of,
  243
Health issues, 132, 133, 136, 137, 139, 143,
  146, 206, 336, 341, 369–370, 371
Heclo, Hugh, 39–40, 70–71, 94, 130, 131–132,
  367
Heinz, John P., 130, 368
Heller, Walter, 250, 251
Helms, Jesse, 311
Herring, E. Pendleton, 8, 13, 41
Herrnson, Paul, 20
Hess, Stephen, 257
HHS. *See* Health and Human Services,
  Department of
High politics, 68–69, 71
Hirschman, Albert, 245
Hispanics, 246
Honoraria, 213
Hosenball, Mark, 208
Housing, 234, 330
Human services, 228
Humphrey, Hubert, 196(n13)

Iacocca, Lee, 189
Ideas. *See* Politics of ideas
Incentives, 181. *See also* Interest groups,
  benefits; Interest groups, reasons for joining
Income, 313, 315, 323
Incumbents, 204, 214, 321, 322
Individualism, 79, 92, 172
Industrial policy, 90–91, 359
Inflation, 91, 252, 334, 337
Influence, 22, 42, 48, 228. *See also under*
  Interest groups
Information, 22, 32, 35, 38, 39, 40, 44, 47, 48,
  55(n9), 71, 108, 115, 119, 146, 147, 148,
  152, 213, 217, 246, 247, 259, 347, 352
  use of negative, 311. *See also* Negativism
Institutions, 14, 30(n31), 62, 92, 367
Interest formation, 193
Interest groups
  activities, 18–22, 116–117(tables), 147–148,
    148(table), 158, 161, 163–166, 185, 219–220,
    367–368
  assessment of, 81

attitudes toward, 7–11
benefits, 100, 102, 103(table), 104–106, 115, 116–117(tables), 117, 124, 367
and business mobilization, 184–185, 189–191. *See also* Business
changes concerning, 11–28, 86–87, 223, 349, 361
citizen groups, 16, 18, 23, 77, 108, 136, 142, 223, 229, 258, 260, 308, 318, 319, 320, 367
classifying, 80–81, 155, 156–157, 170
consequences of activities, 219–220
conservative, 263, 266, 267–269, 270, 270–271(figs.), 272, 273–279
consumer groups. *See under* Consumers
cycles of public/private action, 8–10, 27
definitions, 5–7, 29(n14), 80, 101, 126(n1), 153, 174(n4)
deliberative function. *See* Deliberation
economic, 81, 82–86, 89, 90–95, 102, 345–346
entrepreneurs, 100, 108. *See also* Exchange theory
externality groups, 140
foreign agents, 16–17
formation of, 74, 101–110, 111(table), 113–114, 302(fig.), 324, 366
fragmentation of, 85, 86–87, 92
funding for, 89, 108, 268, 274, 315
future of, 358–360
and governments, 72, 87, 101, 108, 130. *See also* Iron triangle; Triangle metaphor; Women's movement, government's role in
influence of, 22, 55(n3), 83, 106, 141, 147, 156, 165, 170, 203–214, 216–218, 224, 229, 285, 289, 328, 350–353, 354, 368. *See also* Interest groups, power of
intergovernmental, 16, 65, 152
internal negotiations, 43–47
justification for, 34–35
large, 101, 102, 126(n3)
leaders, 102, 106–107, 108, 110, 111(table), 118–119, 124, 125, 128(n14). *See also* Policy activists
liberal, 264–265, 266, 267, 268, 269–270, 270–271(figs.), 272, 273
maintenance, 107, 108, 118, 141
members, 7, 14, 80, 81, 83, 88, 89, 99–100, 102, 107, 108, 110, 111(table), 114, 115, 116–117(tables), 118–119, 120–123(tables), 124, 125, 229, 241(n4), 273, 313–314, 350, 366
monitoring function of, 147–148
monopolies of, 90
national–affiliate relationship, 152
numbers of, 10, 12, 13–18, 15(fig.), 18, 25, 27, 66, 75–76, 86, 94, 155, 157, 161, 163, 227, 238, 360
paradoxes concerning, 353–355

patrons, 23, 72–73, 74, 75, 77, 366
and policy details, 217–218
and policy implementation, 81–82, 92
political, 100, 102, 104
and political parties, 238–240, 328. *See also* Political parties
potential members, 117–119, 120–123(tables), 288. *See also* Free-rider problem; Interest groups, recruitment
power of, 158, 165–166, 170, 174(n8). *See also* Interest groups, influence of
and presidency. *See* Presidency, and public liaison
public, 94, 108, 176, 263, 268
reasons for joining, 115, 117, 128(nn 15, 16), 350, 367
recruitment, 314, 315–318, 316–317(figs.), 318, 323
in regions. *See* Regional issues
representatives of, 132, 137–138, 139, 141, 143, 156–157, 357. *See also* Personal contacts; Policy activists
resources available to, 81–82, 218, 224, 245, 302(fig.), 306, 368
role of, 346–348
single-issue groups, 16, 163, 309, 321
stasis, 59–60, 63, 64, 65, 77, 78
and state and local politics, 16, 17, 19, 24, 150–173, 159–160(figs.), 162(table), 168–169(table), 171(fig.), 357, 360
study of, 4–5, 28, 59, 76, 99, 130, 150, 151–152, 173, 173(n1), 264–265, 348, 351, 363–371, 371(n4). *See also* Data sources; Methodology
system of, 8–9, 11–28, 49, 159–160(figs.), 161, 162(table), 223, 238, 353–354, 356–357, 360–361, 364
tactics, 157–158, 165, 318–323, 369
theories, 101–110, 111(table), 328, 348, 363. *See also* Interest groups, traditional theories; *individual theories*
traditional theories, 285, 288, 289, 290, 291, 294, 297, 299, 305
weak economic vs. strong noneconomic, 90–95
welfare groups, 16
wildlife groups, 310–311, 312, 319, 325(n6)
See also Lobbies; Political action committees; Pressure groups; Special interests
International Encyclopedia of the Social Sciences, 364
International organizations, 17
Intimidation, 222, 226–230. *See also* Fear, use of
Intolerance. *See* Tolerance/intolerance
Iron triangles, 17, 18, 61, 64, 94, 142, 143, 147, 326, 327, 338, 339, 367. *See also* Subgovernments; Triangle metaphor

Issue networks, 17–18, 39–40, 70–72, 72–73, 74, 75, 77, 130, 357, 367
Italy, 83, 99

Jackson, Andrew, 85
Japan, 17, 79, 85, 87, 95
   Keidanren, 83, 90
Jenkins, Walter, 252
Jews, 133, 246
Johnson, Lyndon, 196(n13), 234, 241(n5), 243
   administration, 183, 231, 237, 252–254, 334
Journalists, 15, 220(n5). *See also* Press
Judiciary, 263. *See also* Federal government, courts; United States, Supreme Court

Katzenstein, Peter, 78
Kaufman, Herbert, 66, 79(n4)
Keating, Charles, 215
Kennedy, John F., 235, 243, 253, 291, 303
   administration, 183, 231, 250–251, 334
Kernell, Samuel, 223
Kessel, John, 237
Key, V. O., Jr., 4, 6, 13, 82
Keynesianism, 183, 186, 197(n21)
King, David C., 367
Knauer, Virginia, 243, 251, 254
Knoke, David, 11, 130, 369–370
Krasner, Stephen, 66

Labor issues, 44, 48, 90, 132, 133, 136, 141, 142, 143, 144, 146, 149, 155, 167, 178, 227, 244, 264, 291, 366
   discrimination, 268, 285, 304
   married women working, 297
   unions, 15, 44, 46, 56(n18), 82, 84, 86, 92, 99, 101, 126(n4), 135, 137, 141, 166, 179, 193(n1), 197(n21), 207, 291, 367
   See also Wages
Labor Law Study Committee, 196(n14)
Laissez-faire, 35, 244, 267
Lake Tahoe Basin, 110, 127(n10)
   League to Save Lake Tahoe, 112, 113–114, 116(table), 120–121(table), 124, 125, 128(n13)
   North Tahoe Chamber of Commerce, 112–113, 114, 117(table), 119, 122–123(table), 124, 125, 128(nn 12, 16)
   Tahoe Regional Planning Agency (TRPA), 112, 119
Landmark Legal Foundation Center for Civil Rights, 273, 281(n4)
Land use, 110, 280. *See also* Lake Tahoe Basin
Language, 311–312
Latham, Earl, 72, 363
Laumann, Edward, 130, 368, 369–370
Lawyers/law firms, 13, 14, 15, 136, 166, 212, 263, 268, 273, 281, 368–369

Layton, Betty, 128(nn 12, 16)
Lazarus, Simon, 255
Leadership, 76, 287–288, 290, 305. *See also* Interest groups, leaders
Lee, Rex E., 274, 275, 278
Lee, Richard, 72
Leggett, William, 3
Legi-Slate, 26
Legislation, 20–21, 24, 62, 253, 286, 306(n3), 350, 351
   categorization of, 289, 306(n1)
   legislative access, 288
Legislative branch, 133, 334. *See also* Legislation; United States, Congress
L'Enfant, Pierre C., 221
Leo Burnett Company (Chicago), 21
Levine, Charles, 228
Levinson, Larry, 252
Liberalism, 63. *See also* Interest groups, liberal
Liberty, 8, 35
Lieber, Francis, 3
Lilly Endowment, 280
Lincoln Savings and Loan, 215
Lindblom, Charles, 230
Litigation, 263–281
   control of cases, 265, 281(n3)
   test-case, 265, 267, 272
Living standards, 95
Lobbies, 3, 8, 14, 17, 43, 65–66, 115, 174(n4), 351, 364
   contract lobbyists, 156, 165, 167, 212
   direct lobbying, 209–211
   grassroots lobbying, 21, 205–209, 219, 309, 319–321, 323
   hidden, 153, 163
   laws concerning, 156–157, 161, 164, 166–167
   new outside, 19–20
   old-breed lobbyists, 19, 164
   professionalization of, 164, 167
   social lobbying, 214
   volunteer lobbyists, 167
   See also Interest groups; Pressure groups
Logic of Collective Action (Olson), 75, 82, 99–100
London, 88
Lowi, Theodore J., 58, 59, 60, 63, 68, 78, 220(n6), 244, 351

McAdams, Doug, 306(n2), 307(n4)
McCarthyism, 75
McConnell, Grant, 64, 351
McDowell, Douglas, 271, 276–277
Macey, Jonathan, 50
McFarland, Andrew S., 8–9
McGovern, George, 196(n13), 231–232
McGuigan, Patrick, 274
MacIver, R., M. 6

McKee, Oliver, Jr., 13
McKenzie, Alexander, 157
Madison, James, 3, 5, 7, 8, 35, 82
MAFF. *See* Great Britain, Ministry of
    Agriculture, Fisheries, and Food
Magleby, David, 204
Mailings, 26, 95, 207, 208, 209, 308–309, 310–
    312, 313, 314, 315, 318, 320
Majority rule, 33, 87
Mallick, Geroge, 214
Mansbridge, Jane J., 290, 291, 294
Manufacturing, 155
Marketing. *See* Direct marketing
Marshall, Thurgood, 265, 280
Marxists, 59, 192–193, 198(n27)
Meals, 214
Media, 294, 318, 326, 327. *See also*
    Communications technology; Press
Medicare, 24, 208, 209, 330, 337, 339
Medoff, James, 44
Merriam, Charles E., 4
Methodology, 128–129(nn 17, 18), 132, 349. *See*
    also Data sources
Mexico, 99
Middle class, 23, 73–74, 95, 161, 231
Milbrath, Lester, 13, 19, 351, 364
Mill, J. S., 38
Mills, C. Wright, 59
Mills, Wilbur, 335
Minorities, 204, 229, 235, 236, 285. *See also*
    Blacks; Hispanics
Mitchell, John, 231
Moe, Terry, 108, 119
Monopolies. *See under* Interest groups
Montana, 17, 156
Moos, Malcolm, 13
Moral Majority, 309, 311
Morehouse, Sarah McCally, 158, 160(fig.), 161
Morgenthau, Hans, 9
Mountain States Legal Foundation (MSLF), 273,
    274, 277–278
Moynihan, Daniel P., 241(n5)
MSLF. *See* Mountain States Legal Foundation

NAACP. *See* National Association for the
    Advancement of Colored People
Nader, Ralph, 107, 212
National Association for the Advancement of
    Colored People (NAACP), 264, 265, 266,
    280, 281(n2)
National Association of Letter Carriers, 207
National Association of Manufacturers, 142,
    196(n16)
National Chamber Litigation Center, 269
National Committee to Preserve Social Security
    and Medicare, 208–209

National Conservative Political Action
    Committee, 314, 322
National Defense Stockpile Transaction Fund,
    212
National Election Survey data, 7
National Institutes of Health (NIH), 143
National Lawyers' Committee, 267
National League of Cities, 230
National Legal Center for the Public Interest
    (NLCPI), 268, 277
National Organization for Women (NOW), 88–
    89, 231, 294, 319
National Recovery Administration (NRA), 9
National Rifle Association (NRA), 82, 89, 207,
    208
National Taxpayer's Union, 309
National Wildlife Federation, 319, 325(n6)
Negativism, 311, 321, 324
Negotiation, 42–47, 49, 55(n14), 244
Nelson, Candice, 204
Nelson, Robert L., 368
Neoclassical theories, 192–193, 198(n27)
Netherlands, 78, 85
Nevada, 110, 156. *See also* Lake Tahoe Basin
New Deal, 9, 13, 92, 197(n21), 230–231, 232,
    242, 267
New Frontier, 334
New Hampshire, 17
New Mexico, 156
New politics, 245–246
New Right, 321
New York (state), 17, 152
New York Times, 288, 289, 294, 295–296(figs.),
    297, 306(n2), 307(n4)
NFU. *See* Great Britain, National Farmers'
    Union
NIH. *See* National Institutes of Health
Nineteenth Amendment, 267, 269
Niskanen, William A., 64
Nixon, Richard, 84, 91, 196(n13), 225, 228, 231,
    243, 254, 258, 288, 334
NLCPI. *See* National Legal Center for the
    Public Interest
Noll, Roger G., 194(n10)
Nonprofit/not-for-profit organizations, 14, 66,
    73, 108, 135, 230, 366
Nordlinger, Eric, 66
North Dakota, 157
Norway, 85
NOW. *See* National Organization for Women
NRA. *See* National Recovery Administration;
    National Rifle Association

O'Brien, Larry, 254
Occupational Safety and Health Administration
    (OSHA), 93
O'Connor, Karen, 270

Offe, Claus, 38, 46, 51, 82
Office of Management and Budget (OMB), 138, 144, 146, 229, 236, 338, 340
Oil industry, 86
Older Americans Act (1965), 24
Olson, Mancur, 57(n24), 58, 59, 63, 73, 75, 78, 82, 99–100, 102, 104–106, 108, 110, 114, 117, 119, 124–125, 126(nn 3, 4), 127(n6), 195(n11), 220(n6), 286, 351, 366
OMB. *See* Office of Management and Budget
Omnibus Budget and Reconciliation Act, 339
Omnibus Crime Act, 207. *See also* Brady Bill
On Liberty (Mill), 38
OPL. *See* Presidency, Office of Public Liaison
Oregon, 156, 166
Organizational State, The (Laumann and Knoke), 369
Organized Interests and American Democracy (Schlozman and Tierney), 367
Organizing for Collective Action (Knoke), 369
Orren, Gary, 370
OSHA. *See* Occupational Safety and Health Administration
Owen, Bruce M., 194(n10)

Pacific Legal Foundation (PLF), 268, 278, 279, 280
PAC Power (Sabato), 321
PACs. *See* Political action committees
Paine, Thomas, 3, 29(n1)
Palley, Marian, 290, 291, 294
Panama Canal Treaty, 321
Partisanship, 136–139, 137(table), 141, 149(n1). *See also* Political parties
Parton, J., 13
Patrons. *See under* Interest groups
Peace dividend, 334–335, 337, 338, 340, 341, 359
Penniman, Howard R., 363
Persian Gulf crisis, 359
Personal contacts, 139, 144–146, 145–146(tables), 165, 190. *See also* Social networks
Personnel issues, 211, 279
  appointments, 233–234, 247, 248, 256, 275, 338
  revolving door, 131, 135, 327
Persuasion, 37, 38, 42
Pertschuk, Michael, 232
Peterson, Esther, 243, 252, 253, 255–256, 291
Peterson, Mark A., 11, 367
Photocopying, 43
Plessey v. Ferguson, 265, 281(n2)
PLF. *See* Pacific Legal Foundation
Plural elitism. *See* Pluralism, plural elites theory
Pluralism, 4, 5, 8, 34, 58, 63, 72, 151, 172, 239, 244, 325(n3), 351, 354, 355, 365

neopluralism, 65–70
plural elites theory, 59, 60–66, 68, 71, 75, 77, 78, 244
Policy activists, 133, 134(table), 135–136. *See also* Interest groups, representatives of; Policy entrepreneurs
Policy and research institutes, 177, 180, 188, 190, 195(n11)
Policy entrepreneurs, 211–212, 216. *See also* Policy activists
Policy implementation, 81–82
Policy specialization, 139–147
Political action committees (PACs), 14, 49, 138, 165, 167, 224, 239, 308, 309, 319
  business, 136, 175, 176, 177, 184, 189, 191, 194(n7)
  and congress, 204, 226
  economic, 321, 322
  expenditures, 81, 164, 193(n1), 204–205, 226, 321, 322
  fund-raising, 315
  ideological, 321–323, 324
  influence of, 20–21, 25, 204
  numbers of, 20, 191, 204
Political campaigns. *See* Campaign financing; Candidate-centered campaigns
Political culture, 92, 94, 150, 172
Political development, 150–151
Political entrepreneurs, 23, 67, 71, 73, 75, 76, 77, 89, 94
Political interest/knowledge, 315, 316, 316(fig.)
Political participation, 313–318, 347
Political parties, 6, 7, 23, 26–27, 31(n52), 33, 78, 93, 94, 109, 136–139, 146(table), 150, 151, 161, 172, 222, 223, 238–239, 241(m8), 303, 309, 328, 341, 354, 355, 359. *See also individual parties*
Political process theory, 288, 289, 290, 297
Political science, 37, 287, 347, 348, 358, 361(n13), 363, 370
Politics of ideas, 216, 370, 371
Politics of Regulation (J. Wilson), 67
Politics, Parties, and Pressure Groups (Key, Jr.), 4
Pool, Ithiel de Sola, 19, 44–45, 56(n19), 83, 86, 351
Poor people, 74, 95, 99, 101, 104, 204, 229, 330, 336, 341, 371
Popeo, Daniel, 275, 276, 277
Popper, Karl, 124
Porter, Roger, 237
Postal workers, 207
Powell, Louis, 268
Power issues, 5, 25, 32, 34, 37, 42, 48, 91, 158, 197(n22)
  balance of power, 58, 70, 288, 306, 338
  centralization of power, 337, 338–340 *See also* Decentralization

few defeat the many, 61, 62
power-elite theorists, 59
triadic power, 59, 67, 69, 71
See also Coercion; Countervailing power;
Interest groups, power of
Preferences, 32, 33, 42, 44, 49, 53, 192
changes in, 36, 37–38, 39, 41, 43, 45, 47, 347
Presidency, 68, 178, 221–240, 297, 305, 335
administrative, 228
aides/staff, 249–250, 255, 256–257, 258
Cabinet, 255
and Congress, 222–223, 225, 254, 255
Executive Office of the President (EOP), 222,
224, 225, 236, 237, 238, 243, 255, 256, 257
Office of Congressional Liaison, 255
Office of Public Liaison (OPL), 225, 234, 235,
236–237, 243, 251, 255
and public liaison, 225, 233–237, 239, 240.
See also Presidency, Office of Public Liaison
special assistant to the president for consumer
affairs (SAPCA), 243, 251–256
See also Executive branch
President's Commission on the Status of
Women, 74, 291
President's Committee on Consumer Interests,
243, 251
Press, 202–203, 215, 220(n5), 264, 299, 306(nn
2, 4), 318, 323. *See also* Journalists; Media;
under Business
Pressure groups, 4, 5, 29(nn 4, 12). *See also*
Interest groups
Prestige, 248, 259
Prices, 91
Prisoner's dilemma, 57(n24)
Privatization, 228
Privileges, 41
Process theory. *See* Political process theory
Profits, 176–181, 183, 184, 188, 189, 190, 192,
194(n4)
Progressive era, 8, 26, 92, 214
Pro-Life Voter Identification Project, 310
Protestants, 133, 232
Public assistance, 228, 330. *See also* Poor
people; Safety net programs
Public disclosure laws, 155–156, 164, 172
Public good. *See* Common good; Public interest
Public interest, 16, 27, 34, 39, 40, 48, 49, 53,
54, 57(n27), 62, 65, 242–261, 261(nn 1, 2),
279. *See also* Common good
Publicity, 259, 260
Public liaison. *See under* Presidency
Public opinion, 7–11, 53, 61, 175, 178,
182(table), 194(n3), 205–206, 245, 254, 258,
260, 294, 297, 305. *See also* Trust/distrust
Public relations, 15, 165, 205
Public works, 17

Rationality, 50, 105, 193
rationalistic theories, 178(table), 191, 192,
194(n4)
Rayburn, Sam, 140, 149(n2)
Reagan, Ronald, 16, 21, 24, 84, 181, 226, 227,
233, 237, 251–252, 268, 326, 327, 336, 347,
354
administrations, 17, 18, 24–25, 68, 71–72, 91,
135, 138, 178(table), 187, 207, 225, 226–
227, 232–233, 235, 236, 238, 243, 260,
269–273, 274–276, 278–280, 281, 321, 329,
337, 338, 352, 367
Reconciliation bills, 227
Reforms, 9, 26, 49, 73, 176, 191, 196(n15),
198(n26), 210, 246, 355
campaign finance, 84, 204
cycles, 62, 69, 71
Soviet, 78
welfare, 267
Regional issues, 166–167, 170, 172–173
economies, 167, 170
impact of state groups, 159–160(figs.),
162(table), 171(fig.)
previous group activity patterns, 153, 155–
158
ranking of effective interests in, 167, 168–
169(table)
regional legal foundations, 268
regional maps, 154(fig.), 159–160(figs.),
171(fig.)
Regulatory issues, 18, 24, 39, 64, 91, 92, 93,
99, 125, 152, 176, 177, 178, 195(n10),
196(n15), 197(n23), 233, 246, 252, 366,
371. *See also* Business, and regulations;
Lobbies, laws concerning
Religion, 33. *See also* Catholics; Protestants;
Religious Right
Religious Right, 269, 309, 312, 314, 315
Rent-seeking, 32, 37, 47, 49–51, 54, 55(n6)
Representation, 41, 53, 95
inequalities, 43, 47–49, 54
Republican party, 25, 78, 136, 137, 138, 139,
145, 157, 178, 191, 196(n13), 231, 232, 257,
321, 329, 330, 336
Reputations, 40, 322
Research. *See* Interest groups, study of; Policy
and research institutes
Resource extraction, 155
Resource mobilization, 65, 74, 75, 77
theory of, 287, 288, 297
Retired citizens. *See* Elderly
Revolving door. *See under* Personnel issues
Rights, 52–53, 280, 294, 297
Robertson, Pat, 312
Rockefeller, David, 354
Rodgers, Daniel T., 8
Roe v. Wade, 269

Rogers, Joel, 49, 57(n26)
Roosevelt, Franklin D., 225, 230, 231
Rourke, Francis, 66

Sabato, Larry, 321
Safety net programs, 337, 340, 341. *See also*
  Poor people
Sait, E. M., 363
Salisbury, Robert H., 6, 11, 22, 46–47, 56(n23),
  100, 106–107, 108, 114, 124, 287, 347, 348,
  364, 368
Samish, Arthur, 157
SAPCA. *See* Presidency, special assistant to the
  president for consumer affairs
Savings and loan scandal, 203, 325(n8)
Scalia, Antonin, 279
Scandinavia, 78
Schattschneider, E. E., 9, 77–78, 99, 220(n6),
  238–239, 351, 367
Schlafly, Phyllis, 269
Schlozman, Kay Lehman, 6, 45, 86, 87, 132,
  367–368
Schmitter, Philippe, 41, 45–46, 49, 56(n21),
  57(n30), 78
Scientific method, 105, 124
Sedgwick, Arthur G., 3
Self-interest, 34, 36, 40, 78, 80, 105, 106, 107,
  109, 370–371
Selznick, Philip, 64
Senior citizens. *See* Elderly
Sequestration, 339
Sex discrimination, 74
Shefter, Martin, 13, 24, 227, 359
Shelton, Fred DeWitt, 350
Sheppard-Towner Maternity Act, 267
Sierra Club, 309, 325(n6)
Simpson, Alan, 214
Skocpol, Theda, 345
Skowronek, Stephen, 66
Smith, Hedrick, 13, 19–20
Smith, Richard A., 217
Smith-Connally Act, 84
Socialism, 356
Social movements, 65, 73–75, 77, 223, 285–288
  McCarthy–Zaid interpretation of, 74
Social networks, 315–317, 316–317(figs.), 318.
  See also Personal contacts
Social psychology, 76
Social Security, 208, 329–330, 336–337, 339,
  340, 355
Social welfare, 109, 175. *See also* Common good
Sociology, 74, 287, 370
Souter, David, 280
Soviet Union, 78, 335, 338
Special interests, 62, 327–341, 346–347
  decline of, 336–340
  definition, 327–328

See also Interest groups
Specialization. *See* Policy specialization
Stability, 5
Stasis. *See under* Interest groups
State(s), 4, 289, 370
State and local politics, 20, 66, 86, 172, 184,
  228, 331. *See also under* Interest groups
Statism, 66, 183, 185–186, 187–188, 197(nn 19,
  21)
Status quo, 264, 358
Steiner, Gilbert, 324
Stevens, John Paul, 266
Stewart, Richard, 42
Stigler, George, 64
Stockman, David, 227, 338
Stone, Harlan Fiske, 52
Streck, Wolfgang, 45–46, 56(n21)
Subgovernments, 17, 18, 62, 64, 69, 70, 71, 73,
  133, 357, 367. *See also* Iron triangles
Subsidies, 63, 64–65, 73
Sunshine rules, 210
Sunstein, Cass, 49–50, 57(nn 27–29)
Sununu, John, 236
Sweden, 83, 85, 87, 92, 95
  Social Democratic party, 93
Switzerland, 78, 85
Symbols, 61, 248–249, 259

Taft-Hartley Act, 84
Tahoe Basin. *See* Lake Tahoe Basin
Taxation, 21, 39, 73, 85, 179, 180, 208, 209,
  226, 227, 232, 233, 320, 334, 337, 338,
  339, 340, 341
Teamsters union, 83, 87, 91
Technology, 94. *See also* Communications
  technology
Teeter, Robert, 309
Teitelbaum, Fred, 228
Telephones, 309, 310, 312–313, 324(n1). *See also*
  WATS lines
Telethons, 315
Television, 222, 240, 309, 310, 315
  cable, 312
Textbooks, 365
Third World, 16–17
Tierney, John T., 6, 45, 86, 87, 132, 367–368
Tillman Act of 1907, 84
Tobacco Institute, 206
Tocqueville, Alexis de, 3, 87
Tolerance/intolerance, 314, 315, 317(fig.), 324,
  325(nn 3, 4)
Trade associations, 80, 83, 86, 87, 104, 136,
  138, 176, 185, 189, 191, 195(n11), 367
Trade issues, 340–341
Triangle metaphor, 130, 131, 132, 139, 144, 149.
  See also Iron triangles
Trilateral Commission, 354

TRPA. *See* Lake Tahoe Basin, Tahoe Regional
  Planning Agency
Truman, David B., 4, 5, 72, 82, 99, 101–102,
  107, 108, 114, 115, 125, 126(nn 1, 2), 150,
  246, 264, 276, 363
Trust/distrust, 10, 51, 177, 202, 203, 245
Truth, 38, 55(n9)
TUC. *See* Great Britain, Trade Union Congress

Unemployed, 366
United States, 79, 80–95
  Commerce Department, 254, 259//Congress,
    10, 12, 18, 20, 25, 39, 42, 62, 68, 94, 131,
    140, 141, 142, 143, 144, 145, 145–
    146(tables), 177, 201–220, 223, 289, 297,
    331, 335, 337, 338–340, 341, 353, 367–368.
    See also Legislation; Legislative branch;
    Women/women's issues, and congressional
    activity; *under* Presidency
  Constitution, 49, 50, 90, 92. *See also*
    individual amendments
  debt, 329, 336, 340
  Energy Department, 275
  Forest Service, 79(n4), 127(n7)
  Interior Department, 278
  Justice Department, 253, 254, 258, 273, 274,
    275, 278
  noneconomic interest group mobilization in,
    88
  political participation in, 87–88
  Senate, 331. *See also* United States, Congress
  Solicitor General, 274, 275, 281(n2)
  State Department, 66
  Supreme Court, 51–53, 56(n15), 263–264,
    264–265, 265–266, 267, 269–273, 270(fig.),
    275, 280
  See also Federal government
Universities, 212
University of Michigan National Election
  Studies, 202
U.S. Chamber of Commerce, 142, 196(n16), 269,
  309, 312
Useem, Michael, 198(n25)
U.S. Statutes at Large, 289
U.S. v. Carolene Products Co., 52
Utah, 156
Utilitarianism, 34

Valenti, Jack, 252
Values, 42, 50, 139, 227, 231, 245, 314, 323,
  370, 371
Vetoes, 339
Vietnam War, 334, 335
Viguerie, Richard, 321
Vogel, David, 14–15, 197(n22)
Vose, Clement E., 264, 267
Voucher system, 41, 49, 56(n21)

Wages, 44, 90, 91, 95, 180, 183
Walker, Jack L., 23, 58, 60, 72, 73, 77, 89, 108,
  132, 366–367
Wallace, George, 231
Wall Street Journal, 196(n14), 198(n26)
War on poverty, 231, 334
Washington (state), 156, 166
Washington, George, 221
Washington Alert Service, 26
Washington, D.C., 11, 13–15, 15(fig.), 24, 151,
  191, 221, 227–228, 368
  residency in, 135
Washington Legal Foundation (WLF), 268–269,
  275, 277, 280
Washington Post, 208
  –ABC News poll, 202
Washington Representatives, 13–14
Watergate scandal, 164, 225, 228, 232, 335
WATS lines, 95, 313
Watt, James A., 274, 275, 277–278, 318
WEAL. *See* Women's Equity Action League
Webster v. Reproductive Health, 272
Weidenbaum, Murray, 27, 195(n8)
Welfare. *See* Public assistance
West Germany, 83, 99. *See also* Germany
Westmoreland, William P., 277, 281(n5)
Wexler, Anne, 225, 235, 237
Wexler, Reynolds, Harrison, and Schule (firm),
  21
White House. *See* Consumers, White House
  representation; Executive branch; Presidency
Whittlesey, Faith, 235
Who Governs? (Dahl), 72
Why We Lost the ERA (Mansbridge), 291
Wildavsky, Aaron, 64, 78
Wilderness Society, 229
Will, George, 16
Wilson, Graham, 6, 364
Wilson, James Q., 18, 26, 59, 60, 67, 68, 70,
  102, 106, 220(n6)
Wilson, Woodrow, 3
Wisenthal, H., 82
WLF. *See* Washington Legal Foundation
Wolman, Harold, 228
Women's Equity Action League (WEAL), 319
Women's movement, 285–306, 349, 352
  government's role in, 297, 298(fig.), 300–
    301(figs.), 304–305. *See also* Political
    process theory
  political opportunities for, 297, 299, 303–304
  resources, 290–291, 293(fig.), 294, 302(fig.),
    319
  See also Women/women's issues
Women/women's issues, 65, 73, 74–75, 88–89,
  93, 95, 133, 157, 166, 167, 231, 232, 235,
  246, 265, 269, 295–296(figs.)
  and congressional activity, 291, 292(fig.)

feminists in government, 303–304
role equity, 290, 294, 305
woman as president, 297, 305
women's vote, 267, 303, 307(n6)
See also Equal Rights Amendment; Women's
    movement
World wars, 9, 13

Wright, Jim, 214
Wright, John, 272
Wyoming, 17, 156

Zeigler, Harmon, 155
Zeller, Belle, 155, 156, 159(fig.)
Zero-sum situations, 37
Zumbrun, Ronald, 279, 280